SCHOOL
MATHEMATICS

SCHOOL MATHEMATICS

is issued in the following styles

PART I (two years' work); *with* and *without Answers.*
Also in two sections, A and B (each covering one
year's work); *without Answers only.*

PART II (3rd and 4th years); *with* and *without Answers.*
Also in two sections, A and B (each covering one
year's work); *without Answers only.*

PART III (for 5th year); *with* and *without Answers.*

By the same author

REVISION COURSE IN
SCHOOL MATHEMATICS

Provides a complete revision of the syllabus in mathematics for G.C.E. Ordinary Level.

By H. E. PARR and J. R. SHELLEY

MODERN MATHEMATICS

For use with *School Mathematics*, enabling topics of
'modern' mathematics to be introduced into each
year's work.

LONDON: G. BELL & SONS LTD
YORK HOUSE, PORTUGAL STREET, WC2A 2HL

SCHOOL MATHEMATICS

A UNIFIED COURSE

By

H. E. PARR, M.A.

Formerly Chief Mathematics Master and Second Master, Whitgift School
Late Scholar of Jesus College, Cambridge

PART II

LONDON
G. BELL AND SONS LTD
1974

First published 1950, *reprinted twelve times*

New Decimalized and Metricated Edition
Published February 1970
Reprinted September 1970, 1972, 1974

India
Orient Longman Ltd
Calcutta, Bombay, Madras, and New Delhi

Canada
Clarke, Irwin & Co. Ltd, Toronto

Australia
John Cochrane Pty Ltd, 373 Bay Street, Port Melbourne

New Zealand
Book Reps (New Zealand) Ltd, 46 Lake Road, Northcote,
Auckland 9

East Africa
J. E. Budds, P.O. Box 4536, Nairobi

West Africa
Thos. Nelson & Sons Ltd, P.O. Box 336, Apapa, Nigeria

South & Central Africa
Book Promotions Pty Ltd, 314 Sanlam Centre,
Main Road, Wynberg, Cape Province

PART TWO WITH ANSWERS ISBN 0 7135 1670 4
PART TWO WITHOUT ANSWERS ISBN 0 7135 1680 1
PART TWO, SECTION A. ISBN 0 7135 1702 6
PART TWO, SECTION B. ISBN 0 7135 1712 3

*Printed in Great Britain by Butler & Tanner Ltd
Frome and London*

PREFACE TO NEW EDITION

THE decimalization of the currency in 1971 would, in any case, necessitate a new edition of this book. In view of the probability that industry, and indeed the whole economy of the country, will be very largely metric by 1975, there would seem to be obvious advantages in making the changes caused by decimalization and metrication together. In this new edition, money sums have been decimalized in accordance with the recommendations of the Decimal Currency Board, and all the units of weights and measures have been made metric. A complete change to the metric system in everyday commercial life will doubtless take some years. In the meantime, the replacement of British Imperial units by metric ones will serve the purpose of familiarizing the pupil with the system he will increasingly encounter when he goes out into the world, tend to make him more metric-minded, and also save valuable teaching time which can be employed to better advantage in topics of modern mathematics.

In the case of sections of the book, chiefly mensuration, where the use of Imperial units makes the work fundamentally different, additional exercises in these units have been provided for the benefit of teachers who think that, during the change-over period, some practice in Imperial units is necessary.

The opportunity was taken to rearrange some of the subject matter, and also to introduce a few topics which have gained a place in the traditional course since this book was first published. Number systems have been included in Part I, and Part II contains sections on linear and quadratic inequalities and three-dimensional co-ordinates. A section on arithmetical and geometrical progressions has been added to Part III.

H. E. P.

August 1969

PREFACE TO FIRST EDITION

THE mathematics syllabus which was recommended for secondary schools by the Jeffery Report in 1944 has now been adopted, with only minor modifications, by all the examining bodies, and has met with the approval of an increasing number of schools. Whatever may be the future of the external examination system after 1950, the majority of secondary schools will base their work in mathematics upon this syllabus, even though the time which is devoted to the subject should prove inadequate for its completion.

This book is designed to cover the ground of that syllabus from the age of eleven plus to the standard of the present school certificate. Part I deals with the first two years' work, and Parts II and III complete the course. The book presupposes a knowledge of the ordinary processes of arithmetic, weights and measures, money sums, and long multiplication and division of whole numbers; revision exercises on these topics will be found in Part I, p. 158. Mathematics is treated as a unified subject, in the spirit of the Jeffery Report; and while certain topics would generally be described as chiefly geometrical, others as chiefly algebraic, and so on, it is hoped that no part of the subject is pursued to the temporary exclusion of the other parts.

Most teachers are of the opinion that it is unwise to keep a class on the same sort of topic for more than a week or so. In conformity with this view it will be found that subjects are broken into by other topics and subsequently resumed after an interval. Although it is intended that on the whole the order of the book shall be followed, it will often be possible for a teacher to pursue a particular topic further by omitting a few intermediate sections for the time being and coming back to them later.

The position of formal geometry has undoubtedly weakened a good deal during the last few years. It is hoped that most teachers will find that the amount of formal geometry in this book is sufficient for their requirements, and that those who consider there is too much will not find any difficulty in selecting which parts to omit.   Algebraic and (in Parts II and III) trigonometrical methods have been employed wherever these make the work easier or more instructive.

The author has followed closely the recommendations of the Mathematical Association's various reports on the teaching of Arithmetic, Algebra, and Geometry, and wishes to make his acknowledgements of the excellent hints and material contained in those reports.   He wishes also to thank Mr. A. H. G. Palmer, M.A., for his valuable suggestions and assistance.

H. E. P.

December 1948

NOTE

The Tables at the end of this volume are reproduced from Mr. C. V. Durell's *Mathematical Tables* by his kind permission.

CONTENTS

NOTE.   This Part is issued complete, with and without answers.   It is also issued in two separate sections, Section A and Section B, without answers. The following is the Table of Contents of the whole book.

SECTION A

CONTENTS

SECTION B

TABLES

LENGTH

10 millimetres (mm) = 1 centimetre (cm)
100 centimetres   = 1 metre (m)
1000 metres   = 1 kilometre (km)

CAPACITY

1000 millilitres (ml) = 1 litre (l) = 1000 cm^3

WEIGHT

1000 milligrammes (mg) = 1 gramme (g)
1000 grammes   = 1 kilogramme (kg)
1000 kilogrammes   = 1 tonne (t)

MONEY

British
100 new pence (p) = 1 pound (£)

American
100 cents = 1 dollar ($)

French
100 centimes (c) = 1 franc (fr)

TIME

60 seconds (s)   = 1 minute (min)
60 minutes   = 1 hour (h)
24 hours   = 1 day
7 days   = 1 week
365 days   = 1 ordinary year
366 days   = 1 leap year
100 years   = 1 century

ANGLE

60 seconds (60″) = 1 minute (1′)
60 minutes   = 1 degree (1°)
90 degrees   = 1 right angle

SECTION A

1. FURTHER PERCENTAGES (I)

PART I, § 35 (pages 220–230) should be revised before this section is commenced. Exercise I contains a short revision of the same work.

EXERCISE 1 (Oral)

1 Express the following fractions as percentages: $\frac{3}{8}$, $\frac{1}{3}$, $\frac{4}{5}$, $\frac{9}{5}$, $\frac{1}{500}$, 0·07, 0·35, 0·001.

2 Express the following percentages as fractions in their lowest terms: $12\frac{1}{2}\%$, $66\frac{2}{3}\%$, 125%, $16\frac{2}{3}\%$, $2\frac{1}{2}\%$, 175%.

Evaluate the following:

3 $33\frac{1}{3}\%$ of 24 cm   **4** 10% of £21   **5** 25% of 30p
6 110% of 30 g   **7** $102\frac{1}{2}\%$ of £40

In Nos. 8–13, express the first quantity as a percentage of the second:

8 4 m; 3 m   **9** 18p; 30p   **10** 6 g; 18 g

11 24 cm; 1 m   **12** 33 m; 22 m   **13** $7\frac{1}{2}$p; $2\frac{1}{2}$p

Percentage factors Suppose a number x is to be increased by 5%. We might calculate $\frac{5}{100}$ of x, and add the result to x. This is often the most convenient method. But in many problems on percentage a better way is to use a multiplying factor, especially when successive increases are considered. If the original number is 100, the increased number is 105, and the ratio of the new number to the original number is 105 : 100.

The new number is therefore $\frac{105}{100}$ of the original number.

Thus, to increase x by 5%, we multiply x by $\frac{105}{100}$, or 1·05.

Similarly, to decrease x by 5%, we multiply x by $\frac{95}{100}$, or 0·95.

The rule may be stated as follows:

To increase a number by $r\%$, multiply it by $\dfrac{100+r}{100}$.

Decreasing a number by a certain percentage is included in this rule by giving a negative value to r, for a decrease is really a *negative* increase.

When x has been increased by 5%, we say that the new number is 5% more than x. But it would not be correct to say that x is 5% less than the new number. Thus, an increase from 100 to 105 is an increase of 5%; but a decrease from 105 to 100 is a decrease of 5 in 105, not 5%.

EXERCISE 2 (Oral)

1 What multiplying factor increases a number by:
(i) 30%   (ii) 4%   (iii) 150%   (iv) $3\frac{1}{2}\%$ (v) $p\%$?

2 Express as decimals the multiplying factors which are equivalent to increases of: (i) $15\frac{1}{2}\%$ (ii) 250%   (iii) $4\frac{1}{4}\%$.

3 Express as decimals the multiplying factors which are equivalent to decreases of: (i) $2\frac{1}{2}\%$ (ii) 8%   (iii) 100%.

4 What percentage change will restore the price of an article to its original value after the following changes:

(i) an increase of 50%,   (ii) an increase of 20%,
(iii) a reduction of 50%,   (iv) a reduction of 20%?

Complete the following:

5 A is 65% of B; $\therefore A = \ldots\ldots \times B$, and $B = \ldots\ldots \times A$.

6 If $x = \frac{113}{100}y$, then $y = \ldots\ldots x$, and x exceeds y by $\ldots\ldots\%$.

7 If P exceeds Q by 7%, then $Q = \ldots\ldots \times P$.

8 If P is 7% less than Q, then $P = \ldots\ldots \times Q$.

9 If A exceeds B by 113%, then $\dfrac{A}{B} = \ldots\ldots$.

10 A shopkeeper who reckons his profit on his selling price says that he makes 20% gain. What would his profit be if reckoned on his cost price?

Example *The price of an article in a sale is reduced by* 30% *to 84p. What was the price before it was reduced?*

Method 1 Suppose the original price is 100p.

Then the new price $= 70$p.
Original price : new price $= 100 : 70 = 10 : 7$.
∴ the original price $= \frac{10}{7}$ of the new price
$= \frac{10}{7} \times 84$ p $= 120$p.

Method 2 Let the original price be x pence.

Then the new price $= \dfrac{70x}{100}$ pence.

$$\therefore \quad \frac{70x}{100} = 84.$$
$$\therefore \quad 7x = 840.$$
$$\therefore \quad x = 120.$$
∴ the original price $= 120$p.

EXERCISE 3 (Oral)

Say what is the ratio of the original number to the new number, when the following percentage changes take place:

1 An increase of 10%   **2** An increase of 250%
3 An increase of $33\frac{1}{3}$%   **4** A decrease of $12\frac{1}{2}$%

Increase the following numbers by the percentage given:

5 300 by 8%   **6** 40 by 75%
7 x by r%   **8** 25 by 100%

Decrease the following numbers by the percentage given:

9 60 by $66\frac{2}{3}$%   **10** 50 by x%
11 20 by 5%   **12** 24 by $37\frac{1}{2}$%

EXERCISE 4

Express the following percentages (i) as fractions in their lowest terms, (ii) as decimals:

1 40%, 92%, 106%, $37\frac{1}{2}$%   **2** 135%, $6\frac{1}{4}$%, $17\frac{1}{2}$%, $67\frac{3}{4}$%

Express the following as percentages:

3 $\frac{1}{12}$, $\frac{17}{15}$, $\frac{37}{40}$, 1·75   **4** 0·16, $\frac{3}{16}$, $\frac{11}{25}$, 0·085

5 Find what number, when increased by 4%, becomes 650.

6 A man's bank balance increased by 20% during the year. If at the end of the year it was £582, find what it was at the beginning of the year.

7 An increase of 12% in the price of an article is equivalent to an increase of 15p. Find the original price of the article.

8 The number of pupils in a school increased by 35% to 486 pupils. Find the number before the increase.

9 After 5% has been deducted from a bill, the amount to be paid is £5·70. Find the original amount of the bill.

10 What sum of money, when decreased by 15%, becomes £340?

11 The number of pupils in a school increases from 240 to 300. What percentage increase is this? What percentage decrease takes place if the number drops from 300 to 240 once more?

12 A shopkeeper sells an article at a profit of 25% above what it cost him. Find what he paid for an article which he sells at £2·90.

13 Find, to the nearest penny, 16% of £12·70.

14. If the cost price is £2·80 and the gain is $7\frac{1}{2}$%, find the selling price.

15. If the cost price is £3·60 and the selling price £5·22, find the gain per cent.

16 If the selling price is £396 and the loss is 28%, find the cost price.

17. There were 2700 boys and 2300 girls in an examination; 56% of the boys passed, and 46% of the girls. Find what percentage of the total number of candidates failed.

18. After being reduced by $16\frac{2}{3}$%, the price of an article is £2·10. Find the original price.

19 A rectangular field, 120 m long and 80 m wide, has its length and breadth both increased by 15%. Find the percentage increase in the area.

2. SIMULTANEOUS EQUATIONS

SUPPOSE that we are told that two numbers x and y are such that

$$3x + 2y = 36.$$

Obviously, we cannot *solve* this equation to find x and y. All that we can do is to find y if we know x, or to find x if we know y. Pairs of values of x and y which make $(3x + 2y)$ equal to 36 are said to **satisfy** the equation $3x + 2y = 36$.

We can make a table of values of x and y which satisfy this equation:

$x =$ 0	2	4	6	8	10	12
$y =$ 18	15	12	9	6	3	0

These are only a few of the values. There are many more besides these; for example, $x = 1\frac{1}{3}$, $y = 16$.

Now suppose, also, that x and y must satisfy another equation, namely $x + 2y = 20$.

Let us make a table of values of x and y which satisfy this equation:

$x =$ 0	2	4	6	8	10	12	14	16	18	20
$y =$ 10	9	8	7	6	5	4	3	2	1	0

The pair of values which occurs both in this table and also in the table for $3x + 2y = 36$ is $x = 8$, $y = 6$.

The equations are **simultaneously true,** i.e. true at one and the same time, if $x = 8$ and $y = 6$. They are not simultaneously true for any other pair of values of x and y.

Such a pair of equations as

$$\left.\begin{array}{r} 3x + 2y = 36 \\ x + 2y = 20 \end{array}\right\}$$

is called a pair of **simultaneous equations**, and $x = 8$, $y = 6$ is called their **solution.**

Method of elimination

In the equation $3x + 2y = 36$, the numerical factor 3 in the term $3x$ is called the **coefficient** of x. Similarly, the coefficient of y is 2.

The method of solving two simultaneous equations is to get rid of one letter, for example, y. The coefficients of y must be made numerically the same in both equations. Then, either by addition or subtraction, depending on whether the signs of the coefficients of y are opposite or alike, a new equation is produced which contains only one unknown letter x. This is called the **method of elimination**.

Example 1. *Solve the simultaneous equations*

$$3x - 2y = 8, \quad . \quad . \quad . \quad . \quad (1)$$
$$4x + 3y = 5. \quad . \quad . \quad . \quad . \quad (2)$$

We shall eliminate y, by making the coefficient -6 in one equation and $+6$ in the other. Multiply both sides of (1) by 3, and both sides of (2) by 2:

$$9x - 6y = 24,$$
$$8x + 6y = 10.$$

Now $-6y + (+6y) = -6y + 6y = 0$. We therefore *add* these two equations, and obtain

$$17x = 34.$$
$$\therefore x = 2.$$

Substitute 2 for x in equation (2),

$$8 + 3y = 5.$$
$$\therefore 3y = -3.$$
$$\therefore y = -1.$$

$$\therefore \text{ the solution is } x = 2, \; y = -1.$$

Check in (1): $3x - 2y = 6 + 2 = 8$.

Example 2. *Solve the simultaneous equations*

$$5x - 3y = 34, \quad . \quad . \quad . \quad . \quad (1)$$
$$3x - 4y = 16. \quad . \quad . \quad . \quad . \quad (2)$$

To eliminate y, multiply (1) by 4 and (2) by 3.

$$20x - 12y = 136, \quad . \quad . \quad . \quad . \quad (3)$$
$$9x - 12y = 48. \quad . \quad . \quad . \quad . \quad (4)$$

The coefficients of y are both -12, and

$$-12y - (-12y) = -12y + 12y = 0.$$

We therefore *subtract* equation (4) from equation (3):

$$11x = 88.$$
$$\therefore x = 8.$$

Substituting in (1),

$$40 - 3y = 34.$$
$$\therefore -3y = -6.$$
$$\therefore \quad y = 2.$$
$$\therefore \text{ the solution is } x = 8, \ y = 2.$$

Check in (2): $3x - 4y = 24 - 8 = 16$.

General hints

  (i) First decide which unknown letter to eliminate, and plan your work.

  (ii) Number your equations and explain your method.

  (iii) When one letter has been found, obtain the other by substituting in the easiest equation you have.

  (iv) Check the answer by substituting for both letters in the equation you have not used for finding the second letter.

EXERCISE 5

Solve the following simultaneous equations, and check your answers.

1 $x + y = 21,$ **2** $3x + y = 7,$ **3** $a + b = 10,$
    $x - y = 3$ $x + y = 3$ $a - b = -4$

4 $2x - y = 5,$
$3x + y = 5$

5 $3a + b = 1,$
$4a - b = 6$

6 $5x - 2y = 7,$
$3x - 2y = 1$

7 $2x - y = 10,$
$4x - y = 18$

8 $3a + 5b = 22,$
$3a - b = 10$

9 $4x - 3y = 23,$
$4x + 3y = 17$

10 $r - 3s = 1,$
$r - 5s = -1$

11 $x - 3y = 0,$
$2x - y = 15$

12 $r + 2s = 14,$
$2r + s = 13$

13 $3x - y = -2,$
$5x + 2y = -7$

14 $x - 2y = 8,$
$3x + y = 17$

15 $x - 2y = 3,$
$2y + x = 7$

16 $u - 2v = 7,$
$7u + v = 4$

17 $3x - y = 2,$
$x + 2y = 1$

18 $6x - 5y = 19,$
$9x - 4y = 21$

19 $3x + 4y + 9 = 0,$
$5x + 6y + 7 = 0$

20 $10x + 10y = 9,$
$4x - 5y = 0$

21 $3p + 4r = 3,$
$2p - 5r = -5$

22 $3x + 3y = 7,$
$6x - 6y = 7$

23 $5x - 4y = 6,$
$8x + 3y = 19$

24 $5a - 6b = 8\frac{1}{2},$
$a - 3b = 2$

25 $5x - 3y = 4,$
$3x + y = 1$

26 $5x + 2y = 8,$
$3x + 5y = 1$

27 $x - 2y = 19,$
$7x + y = 13$

28 $2r + 3s = 1,$
$2s - r = 10$

29 $a - b + 1 = 0,$
$3a = 2b$

30 $2a + 9b = 3,$
$a + 2b = 5$

31 $5x + 5y = 3,$
$3y - x = 0 \cdot 2$

32 $3a + 4b + 13 = 0,$
$5a + 6b + 11 = 0$

33 $7y - 2x = 0,$
$3y - 2x = 1$

34 $15x - 12y = 1,$
$5x + 3y = 5$

35 $2a + b = 3,$
$b - 4a = 1$

36 $8x - 3y = 7,$
$3x + 2y = 5\frac{1}{3}$

37 $6x + 5y = 3,$
$7x + 8y = 10$

38 $10a + 3b = 25,$
$15a - 2b = 5$

39 $x + 3y + 1 = 0,$
$9 - 2x - 2y = 0$

40 $2P - 3Q = 4,$
$3P + Q = 6$

41 $2x - 5y + 16 = 0,$
$3x - 2y + 13 = 0$

42 $21x - 6y = 7,$
$3y - 3x = 6\frac{1}{2}$

Problems leading to simultaneous equations

Example 3 *A certain number, formed of two digits, is three times the sum of its digits. It is also 45 less than the number formed by interchanging the digits. Find the number.*

Let the tens-digit be x and the unit-digit y.
Then the value of the number 'xy' is $10x + y$.

$$\therefore 10x + y = 3(x + y).$$
$$\therefore 10x + y = 3x + 3y.$$
$$\therefore 7x - 2y = 0. \quad . \quad . \quad . \quad . \quad . \quad (1)$$

The value of the number 'yx' is $10y + x$.

$$\therefore \quad 10x + y + 45 = 10y + x.$$
$$\therefore \qquad 9x - 9y = -45.$$
$$\therefore \qquad\quad x - y = -5. \quad . \quad . \quad . \quad (2)$$

To solve equations (1) and (2), first multiply (2) by 2:

$$2x - 2y = -10 \quad . \quad . \quad . \quad (3)$$

Subtract (3) from (1), since the coefficients of y are both -2:

$$5x = 10.$$
$$\therefore x = 2.$$

From (1) $\qquad\qquad 14 - 2y = 0.$
$$\therefore y = 7.$$

$\therefore$ the number is 27.

Check. The sum of the digits is $2 + 7 = 9$, and $3 \times 9 = 27$.
The number formed by interchanging the digits is 72, which exceeds 27 by 45.

EXERCISE 6

1 The sum of two numbers is 42, and their difference is 20. Find the numbers.

2 The sum of two numbers is 13. Twice the larger exceeds three times the smaller by 1. Find the numbers.

3 The greater of two numbers exceeds the smaller by 18. Twice the smaller number added to the greater number makes 42. Find the numbers.

4 A farmer finds that he can buy 2 cows and 5 sheep for £90, or 3 cows and 6 sheep for £123. Find the cost of a cow and of a sheep.

5 A certain number of two digits is equal to five times the sum of the digits. It is 9 less than the number formed by interchanging the digits. Find the number.

6 In the rectangle ABCD, AB $= (4x - y)$ cm, BC $= (x + 4)$ cm, CD $= (2x + y + 8)$ cm, DA $= 2y$ cm. Find x and y.

7 If 6 kg of apples and 5 kg of pears together cost 91p, while 3 kg of apples and 7 kg of pears together cost 95p, find the cost of 1 kg of pears.

8 The cost of 1 kg of tea and 3 kg of coffee is £1·50, and 6 kg of tea cost the same as 7 kg of coffee. Find the cost of each per kg.

9 Four years ago, a father was three times as old as his son then was. In 8 years' time he will be twice as old as his son will then be. Find their present ages.

10 The combined ages of a man and his son total 78 years. Eleven years ago, the father was three times as old as the son then was. Find their present ages.

11 When petrol costs 6p per litre and oil 30p per litre, a motor cyclist finds that the cost of petrol and oil for 1000 km is £3·78. When the price of petrol goes up to 7p and that of oil to 32p, the cost for 1000 km is £4·32. Find how many litres of petrol and of oil he uses for 1000 km.

12 Find two numbers such that 3 times the larger added to twice the smaller makes 84; and 4 times the larger exceeds 3 times the smaller by 27.

13 If A gives B 72p, B will have 3 times as much as A. If A gives B £1·08, B will have 6 times as much as A. Find how much they have at present.

14 Tickets at a concert were 20p and 15p, and programmes cost 2p each. Four-fifths of the 20p ticket-holders and three-quarters of the 15p ticket-holders bought programmes. The total money from the sale of tickets was £24·40, and from the sale of programmes £2·24. Find how many tickets were sold at each price.

15 A number between 300 and 400 has its tens-digit one more than its unit-digit. If the three digits are written in the reverse order, the number is increased by 198. Find the number.

3. BEGINNING FORMAL GEOMETRY

IN the course of Part I a knowledge of certain geometrical facts was acquired, chiefly by means of drawing and measurement. You are now going to learn how to prove the truth of geometrical statements, commencing with a few definitions and self-evident truths, then making certain assumptions which can easily be seen to be true, and using these to prove the truth of other geometrical statements. This study is called Formal Geometry, on account of the importance which is given to the form or style of the proofs. Geometry began in ancient Egypt, and consisted at first of various rules for finding areas of fields and for surveying the land afresh after the Nile floods had subsided. This gave rise to the name 'earth-measurement', which is the real meaning of the word 'geometry'. All these practical rules were used by the Egyptians without any formal proof. The Greeks learned them from the Egyptians, partly through Greek colonists in Asia Minor and partly through the travels of men like Pythagoras. The Egyptians were interested only in particular numerical problems, and were just as satisfied with an adequate approximation as with an exact answer. The Greeks, on the other hand, had a passion for accuracy and for general truths applicable in all cases and not merely in special cases. They founded the science of pure geometry, and soon acquired a knowledge of the subject far surpassing that possessed by their former teachers.

We shall begin formal geometry by a re-statement of certain obvious geometrical facts which we shall treat as assumptions. We shall then prove other geometrical facts, some of which you will have met before. These proofs are called **theorems,** and the facts which the theorems prove will later be used in other theorems. Exercises called **riders** follow each theorem or group of theorems; these differ from previous exercises because they are theoretical in character and are not to be done by calculation or accurate drawing.

Definition If a straight line OP meets another straight line AOB, as in Fig. 1, so as to make the adjacent angles POA, POB equal, each angle is called a **right angle.**

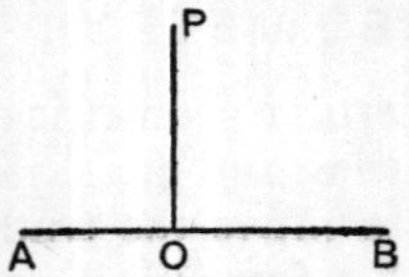

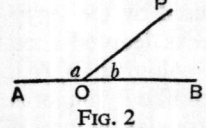

FIG. 1

An **acute** angle is an angle less than a right angle.

An **obtuse** angle is an angle greater than a right angle but less than two right angles.

A **reflex** angle is an angle between two and four right angles. Any two angles whose sum is two right angles are called **supplementary.** Two angles whose sum is one right angle are called **complementary.**

ASSUMPTION 1 **If a straight line stands on another straight line, the sum of the two adjacent angles so formed is equal to two right angles.**

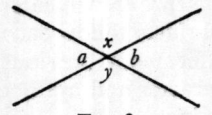

FIG. 2

In Fig. 2, if AOB is a staight line,

then $a + b = 2$ **rt.** $\angle$**s.**

Reference: adj., AOB *a str. line.*

ASSUMPTION 2 **If the sum of two adjacent angles is equal to two right angles, the exterior arms of the angles are in the same straight line.**

In Fig. 2, if $a + b = 2$ rt. $\angle$s,

then AOB **is a straight line.**

Reference: adj. $\angle$*s supp.*

ASSUMPTION 3 **If two straight lines intersect, the vertically opposite angles are equal.**

In Fig. 3, where two straight lines intersect,

$$a = b \quad \text{and} \quad x = y.$$

Reference: vert. opp. $\angle$*s.*

FIG. 3

Definition If two straight lines in the same plane do not meet, however far they may be produced in either direction, they are called **parallel** lines.

In Fig. 4, the line PQ is called a transversal;

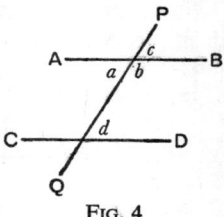

angles *a* and *d* are called **alternate** angles;

angles *c* and *d* are called **corresponding** angles;

angles *b* and *d* are called **interior** angles on the same side of the transversal (sometimes just 'interior angles').

FIG. 4

ASSUMPTION 4 (Properties of parallels)
If a transversal cuts two parallel lines,
  (i) **alternate angles are equal,**
 (ii) **corresponding angles are equal,**
(iii) **interior angles on the same side of the transversal are supplementary.**

In Fig. 4, if AB ∥ CD, (i) $a = d$,
                         (ii) $c = d$,
                        (iii) $b + d = 2$ rt. $\angle$s.

References:
        (i) $a = d$ (*alt.*, AB ∥ CD).
       (ii) $c = d$ (*corr.*, AB ∥ CD).
      (iii) $b + d = 2$ rt. $\angle s$ (*int. on same side of* PQ, AB ∥ CD).

ASSUMPTION 5 (Tests for parallels)
Two straight lines are parallel if a transversal makes
        (i) **two alternate angles equal,**
   or (ii) **two corresponding angles equal,**
  or (iii) **two interior angles on the same side of the transversal supplementary.**

In Fig. 4, if (i) $a = d$,
      or (ii) $c = d$,
     or (iii) $b + d = 2$ rt. $\angle$s,
        then AB ∥ CD.

How to mark figures   In many of the exercises which follow, the facts which you are given are marked in the figures in a manner now to be described.

Equal lines are shown by having the same mark, usually a dash or two dashes, placed on them, as in Fig. 5, where AB = CD.

Equal angles are shown by having the same small letter

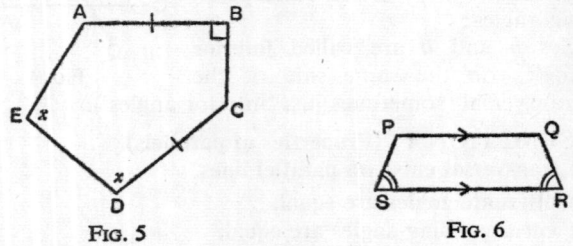

FIG. 5   FIG. 6

put inside them, as in Fig. 5, where ∠AED = ∠EDC; or the same mark, as in Fig. 6, where ∠PSR = ∠QRS.

A right angle is shown in Fig. 5, where ∠ABC = 90°.

Parallels are shown by arrows, as in Fig. 6, where PQ is parallel to SR (not to RS).

If a figure is not given, draw your own figure from the information contained in the question, and mark on it all the facts that you are given, in the way explained above.   Draw a separate figure for each question, accurate enough to be clear, and big enough for you to put small letters in the angles if necessary; but do not waste time by constructing bisectors of angles with compasses or drawing parallels correctly.   A freehand figure will usually be sufficient, though you will probably find it quicker at first to use a ruler for your straight lines.

When proving a rider, you must be careful not to make any assumptions beyond whatever facts are given in the problem, or the **data**, as they are called.   You must not assume lines or angles to be equal because they look equal in the figure. There must be a sound reason for every statement you make.

Example 1 *If a straight line stands on another straight line,* prove *that the bisectors of the two adjacent angles so formed are at right angles.*

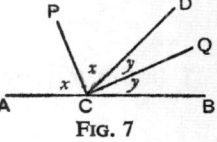

FIG. 7

Given CD meets AB at C; CP bisects ∠ACD, CQ bisects ∠BCD.

To prove that ∠PCQ is a right angle.

Proof. Since ∠s PCA, PCD are equal, call each angle x.
Since ∠s BCQ, DCQ are equal, call each angle y.
Then ∠ACD = $2x$ and ∠BCD = $2y$.
∴ $2x + 2y = 2$ rt. ∠s. (adj., ACB a str. line).
∴ $x + y = 1$ rt. ∠.
∴ ∠PCQ = 1 rt. ∠.

Example 2 *In Fig. 8, prove that*
$$∠BCD = ∠ABC + ∠CDE.$$

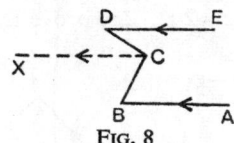

FIG. 8

Construction Draw a line CX parallel to AB and ED.

Proof ∠XCB = ∠ABC (alt., CX ∥ AB).
∠XCD = ∠CDE (alt., CX ∥ ED).
But ∠XCB + ∠XCD = ∠BCD.
∴ ∠BCD = ∠ABC + ∠CDE.

When the figure for a rider is given, and marked to show what facts are known, you need not copy out the question under the headings 'Given' and 'To prove'; state any construction necessary, and then go straight on to the proof. But when the problem is stated in general terms, as in Example 1, and you have to draw and letter your own figure, you must say what facts are given and what you are trying to prove, using your own lettering.

EXERCISE 7

(On Assumptions 1–3)

1 In Fig. 9, prove that $\angle ABD = \angle ACE$.

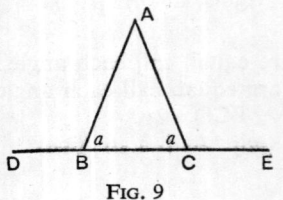

Fig. 9

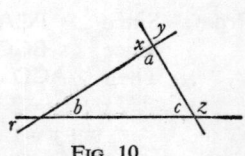

Fig. 10

2 In Fig. 10, if $r = y$, prove that $a = b$.

3 In Fig. 10, if $a = c$, prove that $x = z$.

4 In Fig. 10, if $y + z = 2$ rt. $\angle$s, prove that $a = c$.

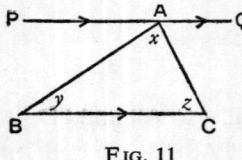

Fig. 11

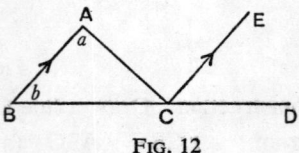

Fig. 12

(On Assumptions 4 and 5)

5 In Fig. 11, mark two pairs of equal angles, and hence use the figure to prove that $x + y + z = 2$ rt. $\angle$s.

6 In Fig. 11, if AC bisects $\angle$BAQ, prove that $x = z$.

7 In Fig. 12, prove that $\angle ACD = a + b$.

8 In the triangle ABC the angles B and C are equal. The side BA is produced to any point E, and AX is drawn through A parallel to BC and in the same sense (i.e. AX is *not* parallel to CB). Prove that AX is the bisector of $\angle$EAC.

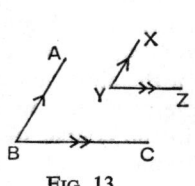

Fig. 13

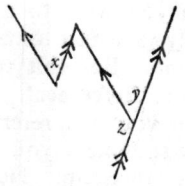

Fig. 14

9 In Fig. 13, prove that ∠ABC = ∠XYZ,

 (i) by joining BY and producing it,
 (ii) by producing XY to cut BC.

10 In Fig. 14, prove that $x = y$.

11 In Fig. 14, prove that $x + z = 2$ rt. ∠s.

Theorems We come now to the proof of the first theorem in Formal Geometry, and you should study carefully how the work is set out. It begins with a statement called the **general enunciation**. This announces in general terms what property or geometrical fact we are about to prove. Next comes the particular diagram and lettering which we are going to use, though the proof will apply, of course, to every figure that could be drawn. The stages of the argument which follow are:

(1) **Given**	Both these must be in terms of the letters of your own figure; they may be omitted if the enunciation of the theorem is given (as sometimes it is) in terms of the letters of a particular diagram.
(2) **To prove**	
(3) **Construction**	This says what lines have to be added to the figure in order to carry out the proof. These are usually shown as dotted lines in this book.
(4) **Proof**	This must contain a reason for every statement.

When you wish to use the theorem in a rider, it would obviously take too long to write out the general enunciation every time. For this reason you will find at the end of a theorem a **'Reference'**. This tells you the short, concise way in which you can refer to the theorem when you want to justify a statement you are making in the course of a rider or a later theorem. Never quote the number of a theorem, as the numbers are different in different text-books.

Sometimes you will find at the end of a theorem a further general statement which has been proved in the course of proving the theorem, or which may quickly be deduced from the theorem with little or no further proof. Such a statement is called a *corollary* to the theorem.

The proofs of the theorems need not be learnt at present, but they should be carefully studied, and used as models in your future work. You should try to imitate in your riders the setting-out of the theorems, and the clear, concise reasons given there for each step in the argument.

Before reading Theorems 1–3, you should revise Part I, § 16, page 89.

THEOREM 1

If one side of a triangle is produced, the exterior angle so formed is equal to the sum of the two interior opposite angles; and the sum of the three angles of the triangle is two right angles.

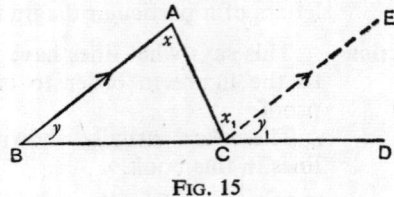

Fig. 15

Given a triangle ABC, with BC produced to D.

To prove that (i) $\angle ACD = \angle A + \angle B$,

(ii) $\angle A + \angle B + \angle ACB = 2$ rt. $\angle$s.

Construction Draw CE ∥ BA.

Proof With the lettering of the figure,

$$x_1 = x \quad \text{(alt., CE ∥ BA)},$$

and $\qquad y_1 = y \quad \text{(corr., CE ∥ BA)}.$

$$\therefore x_1 + y_1 = x + y,$$

i.e. $\angle ACD = \angle A + \angle B$.

Adding $\angle ACB$ to each side,

$$\angle ACD + \angle ACB = \angle A + \angle B + \angle ACB.$$

But $\quad \angle ACD + \angle ACB = 2$ rt. $\angle$s. (adj., BCD a str. line).

$\therefore \angle A + \angle B + \angle ACB = 2$ rt. $\angle$s.

References $\qquad \angle ACD = \angle A + \angle B \qquad$ (*ext. $\angle$ of $\triangle$*),

$\angle A + \angle B + \angle ACB = 180° \qquad$ (*angle-sum of $\triangle$*).

Note The exterior angle property of a triangle is more useful in riders than the angle-sum property, and should be employed whenever it is shorter to do so.

EXERCISE 8

1 In $\triangle ABC$, $\angle A = 90°$. Prove that $\angle B + \angle C = 90°$.

2 In Fig. 16, if $x = 2a$, prove that $a = b$.

3 In Fig. 16, if $a = 2b$, prove that $x = 3b$.

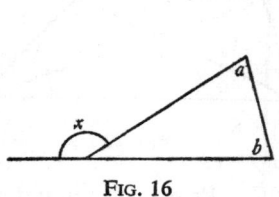

FIG. 16

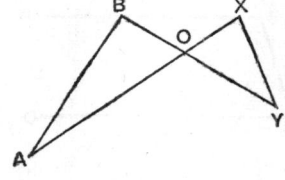

FIG. 17

4 In Fig. 17, if AOX and BOY are straight lines and $\angle OAB = \angle OYX$, prove that $\angle OBA = \angle OXY$.

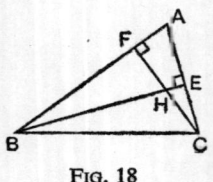

FIG. 18

5 In Fig. 18, prove that $\angle ECH = \angle FBH$.

6 In Fig. 18, prove that $\angle CHE = \angle A$.

7 In Fig. 19, if AD is perpendicular to BC, prove that $\angle B = \angle ACB$.

8 In Fig. 19, prove that
$\angle ACE - \angle ADC = \angle ADC - \angle ABD$.

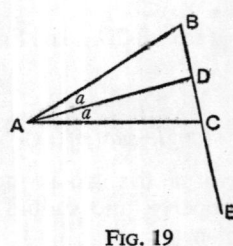

FIG. 19

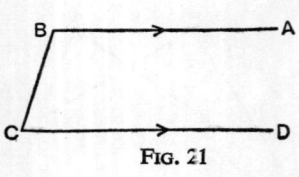

FIG. 20

9 In Fig. 20, if $x = y$, prove that $a = b$.

10 In Fig. 20, prove that $b + x = a + y$.

11 In Fig. 21, if the bisectors of the angles B and C meet at O, prove that $\angle BOC = 90°$.

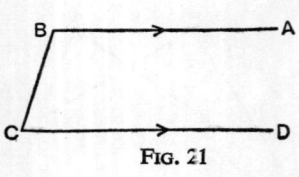

FIG. 21

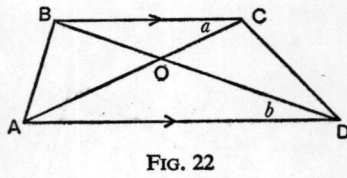

FIG. 22

12 O is any point inside △ABC. Prove, by joining AO and producing it, that $\angle BOC = \angle OBA + \angle BAC + \angle ACO$.

13 In Fig. 22, prove that $\angle COD = a + b$.

THEOREM 2

The sum of the interior angles of a convex polygon with *n* sides is (2*n* − 4) right angles.

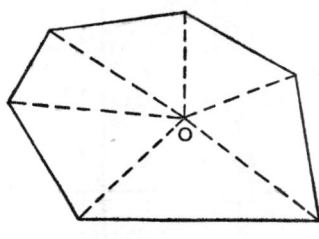

Fig. 23

Given a convex polygon with *n* sides.

To prove that the sum of the interior angles is (2*n* − 4) rt. ∠s.

Construction. Take any point O inside the polygon, and join it to each vertex.

Proof The polygon has *n* sides.

∴ there are *n* triangles in the figure.

The sum of the angles of each triangle is 2 rt. ∠s.

∴ the sum of the angles of all *n* triangles is 2*n* rt. ∠s.

These angles make up the interior angles of the polygon, together with the angles at O.

But the sum of the angles at O is 4 rt. ∠s.

∴ the sum of the interior angles of the polygon is (2*n* − 4) right angles.

Reference: angle-sum of polygon.

Corollary The sum of the interior angles of a quadrilateral is four right angles.

This is proved by giving *n* the value 4.

THEOREM 3

If all the sides of a convex polygon are produced in order, the sum of the exterior angles so formed is four right angles.

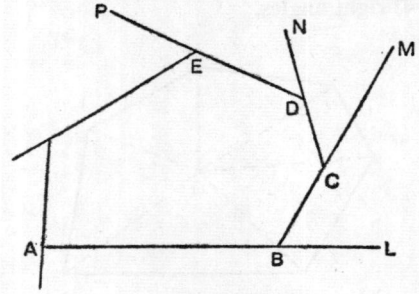

Fig. 24

Given a convex polygon ABCDE . . ., with the n sides AB, BC, CD, DE . . . produced to L, M, N, P. . . .

To prove that the sum of the exterior angles is 4 rt. ∠s.

Proof
  ∠ABC + ∠CBL = 2 rt. ∠s (adj., ABL a str. line),
  ∠BCD + ∠DCM = 2 rt. ∠s (adj., BCM a str. line),
  ∠CDE + ∠EDN = 2 rt. ∠s (adj., CDN a str. line),

and so on, n equations in all.

If we add together all the n equations, we have on the right-hand side ($n \times 2$) rt. ∠s, or $2n$ rt. ∠s.

On the left-hand side we have

(∠ABC + ∠BCD + ∠CDE + . . .) + (∠CBL + ∠DCM + ∠EDN + . . .).

Now ∠ABC + ∠BCD + ∠CDE + . . .
   = the sum of the interior ∠s of the n-sided polygon
   = $(2n - 4)$ rt. ∠s;

and ∠CBL + ∠DCM + ∠EDN + . . .
   = the sum of the exterior ∠s of the polygon.

∴ $(2n - 4)$ rt. ∠s + the sum of the exterior ∠s = $2n$ rt. ∠s.

∴ the sum of the exterior angles = $\{2n - (2n - 4)\}$ rt. ∠s
         = $(2n - 2n + 4)$ rt. ∠s = 4 rt. ∠s.

Reference: sum of ext. ∠s of polygon.

EXERCISE 9

1. Each exterior angle of a polygon is 40°. How many sides has the polygon?

2 If the sum of four angles of an octagon is 5 right angles, find the sum of the other four angles.

3 The sum of the interior angles of a polygon is 1440°. Calculate the number of sides.

4 ABCDE is a regular pentagon (or 5-sided figure); AB and DC are produced to meet at X. Calculate $\angle$BXC.

5 Which of the following angles can be the interior angle of a regular polygon: 120°, 130°, 140°, 156°, 168°? State the number of sides in each possible case.

4. CONGRUENCE: THE ISOSCELES TRIANGLE

FOUR tests for the congruence of two triangles were discussed in Part I (§ 27, p. 171). These are now repeated as Assumptions 6–9.

ASSUMPTION 6 (First Test for Congruence)

If two sides and the included angle of one triangle are respectively equal to two sides and the included angle of another triangle, then the two triangles are congruent.

In $\triangle$s ABC, PQR (Fig. 25),

if   AB = PQ, AC = PR,

and $\angle$A = $\angle$P,

then $\triangle$s $\dfrac{ABC}{PQR}$ are congruent.

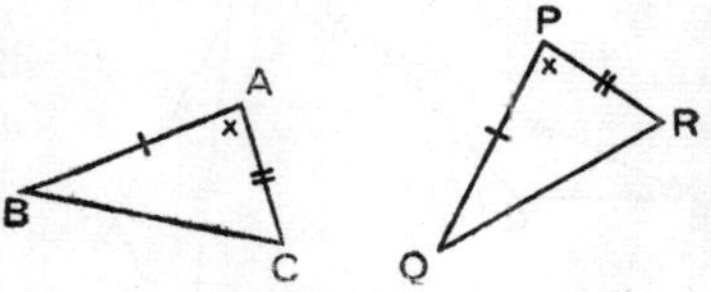

FIG. 25

Reference $\triangle$s $\dfrac{ABC}{PQR}$ are congruent (*SAS*).

Here S means 'side', A means 'angle', and the order of the letters indicates that the angle referred to is the angle *included* i.e. 'enclosed', by the two sides.

ASSUMPTION 7 (Second Test for Congruence)

If two angles and a side of one triangle are respectively equal to two angles and the corresponding side of another triangle, then the two triangles are congruent.

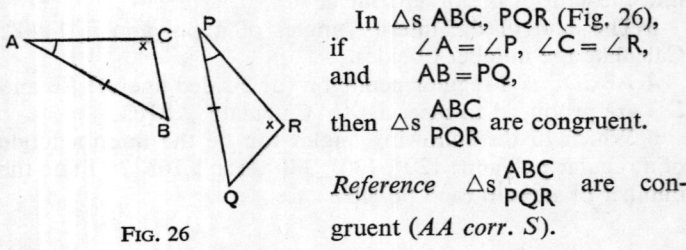

In △s ABC, PQR (Fig. 26),
if ∠A = ∠P, ∠C = ∠R,
and AB = PQ,

then △s $\begin{matrix} ABC \\ PQR \end{matrix}$ are congruent.

Reference △s $\begin{matrix} ABC \\ PQR \end{matrix}$ are congruent (*AA corr. S*).

FIG. 26

Note Instead of AB and PQ being equal, we could just as well have AC equal to PR, or BC equal to QR. But the two sides which are equal must *correspond*, i.e. they must be opposite to angles of the two triangles which are known to be equal.

ASSUMPTION 8 (Third Test for Congruence)

If the three sides of one triangle are equal to the three sides of another triangle, then the two triangles are congruent.

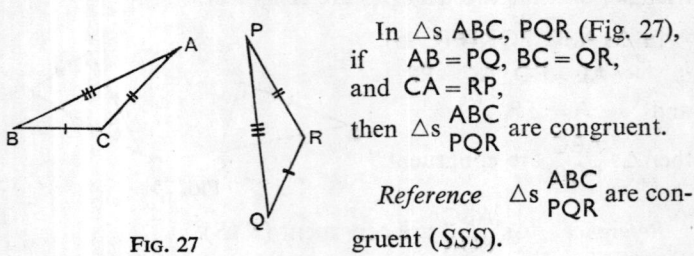

In △s ABC, PQR (Fig. 27),
if AB = PQ, BC = QR,
and CA = RP,

then △s $\begin{matrix} ABC \\ PQR \end{matrix}$ are congruent.

Reference △s $\begin{matrix} ABC \\ PQR \end{matrix}$ are congruent (*SSS*).

FIG. 27

Definition In a right-angled triangle, the side opposite the right angle is known as the **hypotenuse.**

ASSUMPTION 9 (Fourth Test for Congruence)

If two right-angled triangles have the hypotenuse and another side of the one triangle respectively equal to the hypotenuse and another side of the other triangle, then the two triangles are congruent.

In △s ABC, PQR (Fig. 28),

if the angles B and Q are right angles and AB = PQ, AC = PR,

then △s ABC / PQR are congruent.

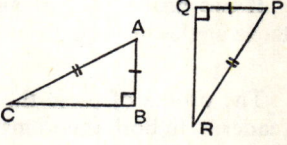

Fig. 28

Reference △s ABC / PQR are congruent (*RHS*).

The letters RHS stand for Right angle, Hypotenuse, and one other Side.

Note In Fig. 28, if the angles at B and Q were right angles, and we had AB = PQ and BC = QR, the triangles would be congruent, but the case of congruence would then be SAS instead of RHS.

If you compare Assumptions 6 and 9, you will see that two triangles are not necessarily congruent if they have two sides and a non-included angle of one equal respectively to two sides and a non-included angle of the other; but they are congruent if those non-included angles are right angles.

Assumptions 6–9 provide us with the following four tests for congruence:

SAS

AA corr. S

SSS

RHS

Notice that ASS (even if spelled backwards as SSA) is *not* a case of congruence. Nor is AAA.

The isosceles triangle

The properties of the isosceles triangle were stated in Part I, page 113. (See also Part I, p. 174, Example 1.) They are here repeated as Theorems 4 and 5.

THEOREM 4 (Isosceles Triangle Theorem)

The angles at the base of an isosceles triangle are equal.

THEOREM 5 (Converse of the Isosceles Triangle Theorem)

If two angles of a triangle are equal, then the sides opposite those angles are equal.

The proofs of these theorems are left as an exercise for the reader. In both theorems the bisector AD of the vertical angle BAC is drawn, and the triangles ABD, ACD are proved congruent.

Figure for Theorem 4   *Figure for Theorem* 5

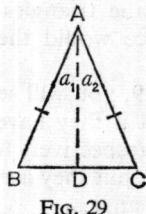   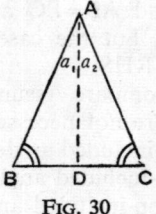

FIG. 29   FIG. 30

Converse theorems

If you examine Theorems 4 and 5, you will notice that what is given in Theorem 4 is the same as what has to be proved in Theorem 5; and what has to be proved in Theorem 4 is given in Theorem 5. For this reason Theorem 5 is called the **converse** of Theorem 4.

The converse of Theorem 4 can be proved to be true, but you must not assume that all converses are true. For instance, when two lines cross, the vertically opposite angles are equal, but equal angles are not necessarily vertically opposite.

EXERCISE 10

1 In Fig. 31, if AC bisects ∠BAD and ∠BCD, prove that AB = AD.

2 In Fig. 32, if AO = OD and OB = OC, prove that AB = CD. Which angle is equal to ∠ABO, and what conclusion do you draw from this fact?

3 In Fig. 32, if AB ∥ CD, and AO = OD, prove that OB = OC.

4 In Fig. 32, if AB ∥ CD, and AB = CD, prove that (i) AO = OD, BO = OC, (ii) △s AOC, DOB are congruent.

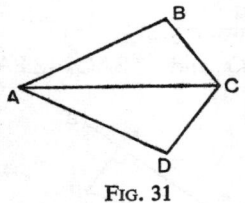

FIG. 31

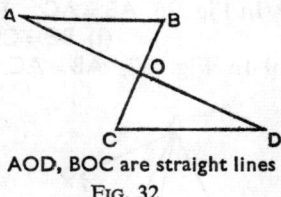

AOD, BOC are straight lines
FIG. 32

5 In Fig. 33, if AB = DC and ∠ABC = ∠DCB, prove that AC = DB.

6 In Fig. 33, if AX = DX and BX = CX, prove that ∠A = ∠D.

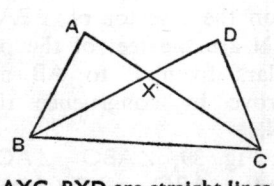

AXC, BXD are straight lines
FIG. 33

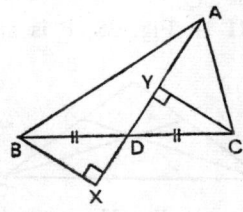

FIG. 34

7 In Fig. 34, X and Y are the feet of the perpendiculars from B and C to AD. Prove that BX = CY.

8 In Fig. 35, prove that △s AXY, XBZ are congruent, and deduce that XY = BZ.

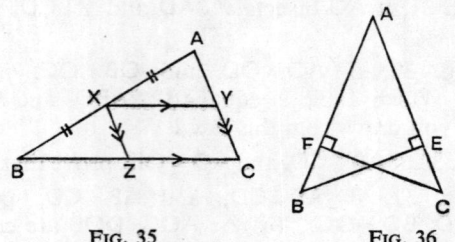

FIG. 35   FIG. 36

9 In Fig. 36, AB = AC. Prove that
(i) BE = CF, (ii) BF = CE.

10 In Fig. 37, AB = AC, AP = AQ and ∠BAC = ∠PAQ.

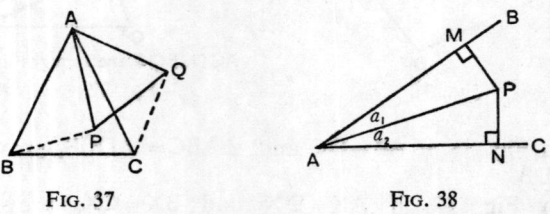

FIG. 37   FIG. 38

Prove that △s APB, AQC are congruent, and deduce that BP = CQ.

11 In Fig. 38, P is any point on the bisector of ∠BAC; M and N are the feet of the perpendiculars from P to AB and AC. Prove by congruence that PM = PN.

12 In Fig. 39, ∠ABC = ∠ACB; BX bisects ∠ABC, and CY bisects ∠ACB. Prove that BX = CY.

FIG. 39

13 In Fig. 31, if ∠B = ∠D = 90°, and BC = DC, prove that AC bisects ∠BCD.

14 AB and CD are two equal chords of a circle, centre O. Prove that ∠AOB = ∠COD.

15 In Fig. 31, if AB = AD and CB = CD, prove that ∠B = ∠D.

16 In Fig. 40, if ON is the perpendicular from the centre O of the circle to the chord AB, prove that AN = NB.

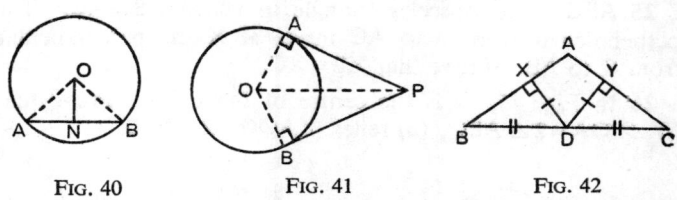

FIG. 40   FIG. 41   FIG. 42

17. In Fig. 41, PA and PB are the tangents from P to the circle whose centre is O. Assuming that the angles OAP, OBP are right angles, prove that PA = PB.

18 In Fig. 40, if AN = NB, prove that ∠ONA = ∠ONB, and deduce that ON is perpendicular to AB. (O is the centre.)

19. Two circles with centres A, B intersect at P and Q. Prove that AB bisects ∠PAQ.

20 In Fig. 42, prove that ∠B = ∠C.

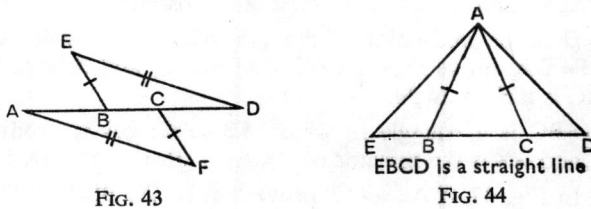

FIG. 43   EBCD is a straight line
                        FIG. 44

21 In Fig. 43, if AB = CD and ABCD is a straight line, prove that ED is parallel to AF.

(*Theorems 4 and 5*)

22 In Fig. 44, prove that ∠s ABC, ACD are supplementary.

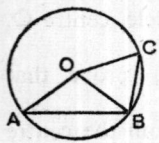

FIG. 45

23 In △ABC, AB = AC and the bisectors of ∠s ABC, ACB meet at I. Prove that IB = IC.

24 In Fig. 45, O is the centre of the circle. Prove that
∠OAB + ∠OCB = ∠ABC.

25 ABC is an isosceles triangle in which AB = AC. The perpendicular from B to AC meets at X the perpendicular from C to AB. Prove that XB = XC.

26 In Fig. 46, O is the centre of the circle. Prove that (i) ∠POA = 2∠ABO, (ii) reflex ∠AOC = 2∠ABC.

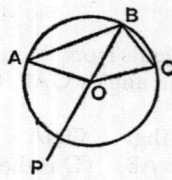

FIG. 46

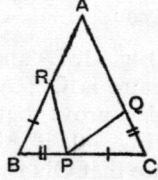

FIG. 47

27 In Fig. 44, if EB = CD, prove that △s ABE, ACD are congruent, and deduce that △AED is isosceles.

28 D is the mid-point of the side BC of a triangle ABC. If DB = DA, prove that ∠BAC = ∠B + ∠C, and deduce that ∠BAC is a right angle.

29 ABC is a triangle in which AB = AC; BA is produced to D, and AX is the bisector of ∠CAD. Prove that AX ∥ BC.

30 In Fig. 47, if AB = AC, prove that (i) △s BRP, CPQ are congruent, (ii) PR = PQ, (iii) ∠RPQ = ∠B.

5. ANGLE PROPERTIES OF THE CIRCLE

§ 38, Part I (pp. 236–244) should be revised before this section is done.

THEOREM 6

The angle which an arc of a circle subtends at the centre is double that which it subtends at any point on the remaining part of the circumference.

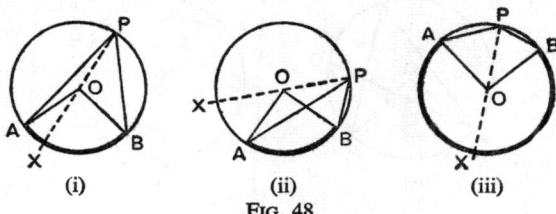

Fɪɢ. 48

Given a circle, centre O, an arc AB, and a point P on the remaining part of the circumference.

To prove that   ∠AOB = 2 ∠APB in Fig. 48 (i) and (ii),
          reflex   ∠AOB = 2 ∠APB in Fig. 48 (iii).

Construction   Join PO and produce it to any point X.

Proof   OA = OP (radii),

          ∴ ∠OAP = ∠OPA.

But   ∠AOX = ∠OAP + ∠OPA (ext. angle of △).

          ∴ ∠AOX = 2∠OPA.

Similarly,   ∠BOX = 2∠OPB.

Hence, in Fig. 48 (i),

      ∠AOX + ∠BOX = 2∠OPA + 2∠OPB

              = 2∠(OPA + ∠OPB).

          ∴ ∠AOB = 2∠APB.

In Fig. 48 (ii),

      ∠BOX − ∠AOX = 2∠OPB − 2∠OPA

              = 2∠(OPB − ∠OPA).

          ∴ ∠AOB = 2∠APB.

In Fig. 48 (iii), the arc AB is a major arc.   The proof is the same as for Fig. 48 (i), except that the word 'reflex' must be inserted before ∠AOB.

Reference   ∠AOB = 2 ∠APB (∠ *at centre*).

THEOREM 7

Angles in the same segment of a circle are equal.

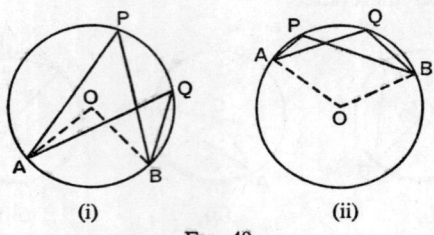

FIG. 49

Given a circle, centre O, and two ∠s APB, AQB in the same segment.

To prove that ∠APB = ∠AQB.

Construction Join OA, OB.

Proof   ∠AOB = 2∠APB (∠ at centre),
and   ∠AOB = 2∠AQB („   ).
∴ ∠APB = ∠AQB.

For Fig. 49 (ii), the word 'reflex' should be inserted before ∠AOB.

Reference   ∠APB = ∠AQB (*same seg.*).

THEOREM 8

The angle in a semicircle is a right angle.

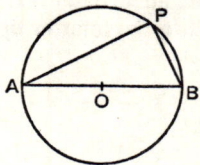

Fig. 50

Given a circle, centre O, a diameter AB and a point P on the circle.

To prove that ∠APB = 90°.

Proof ∠AOB = 2∠APB (∠ at centre).

But ∠AOB = 180° (AOB a str. line).

∴ ∠APB = 90°.

Reference ∠APB = 90° (∠ *in semicircle*).

THEOREM 9

(1) The opposite angles of a cyclic quadrilateral are supplementary.

(2) If a side of a cyclic quadrilateral is produced, the exterior angle so formed is equal to the interior opposite angle.

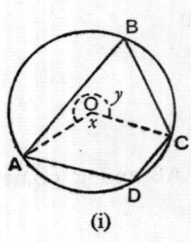
(i)

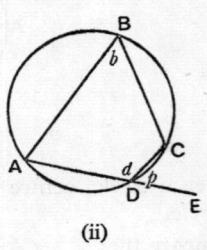
(ii)

Fig. 51

Given a quadrilateral ABCD whose vertices lie on a circle; AD is produced to E.

To prove that (1) ∠ABC + ∠ADC = 180°,
(2) ∠CDE = ∠ABC.

Construction　Let O be the centre of the circle. Join OA, OC.

Proof　(i) Denote the angles at O by x and y, as in Fig. 51 (i).

$$\angle ABC = \tfrac{1}{2}x \ (\angle \text{ at centre}),$$
and $\qquad \angle ADC = \tfrac{1}{2}y \ (\qquad ,, \qquad).$
$\therefore \ \angle ABC + \angle ADC = \tfrac{1}{2}x + \tfrac{1}{2}y$
$\qquad\qquad\qquad = \tfrac{1}{2}(x + y).$
But $\qquad\qquad x + y = 360°$ (angles at a point).
$\therefore \ \angle ABC + \angle ADC = 180°.$

Similarly, by joining OB and OD, it may be proved that ∠BAD + ∠BCD = 180°.

(2) Let $\angle ABC = b$, $\angle ADC = d$, and $\angle CDE = p$, as in Fig. 51 (ii).

Then $p + d = 180°$ (adj., ADE a str. line).
But $b + d = 180°$ (proved).
              $\therefore p = b$.

References $\angle ABC + \angle ADC = 180°$ (*opp. $\angle$s of cyclic quad.*)
              $\angle CDE = \angle ABC$ (*ext. $\angle$ of cyclic quad.*).

Note Theorem 9 (2) is more useful in calculations and riders than Theorem 9 (1).

EXERCISE 11

Easy problems on Theorems 6–9 will be found in Part I, Exercise 103, page 242.

1 ABCD is a cyclic quadrilateral. If $\angle BAD = 68°$ and $\angle BDA = 47°$, calculate $\angle ACD$.

2 In Fig. 52, if $\angle XAD = 35°$ and $\angle AXD = 48°$, calculate $\angle CBX$.

3 The circumcentre O of $\triangle ABC$ lies inside the triangle. If $\angle AOB = 130°$ and $\angle BOC = 88°$, calculate $\angle ABC$.

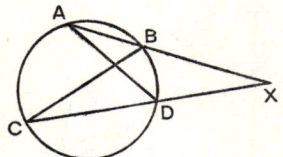

XBA, XDC are straight lines
FIG. 52

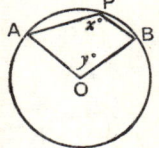

FIG. 53

4 The diagonals of the cyclic quadrilateral ABCD intersect at X. If $\angle AXB = 94°$, $\angle ACB = 51°$ and $\angle BDC = 30°$, calculate $\angle BAD$.

5 In Fig. 53, where O is the centre of the circle, find an equation connecting x and y.

6 In Fig. 54, if ∠PBA = 42°, calculate ∠QPA, ∠BPQ and ∠OQP.

7 In Fig. 54, if ∠PBA = x°, express in terms of x the number of degrees in ∠OQP.

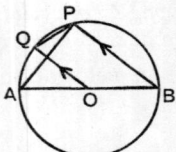

O is the centre of the circle
FIG. 54

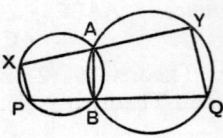

XAY, PBQ are straight lines
FIG. 55

8 D is any point in the side BC of an acute-angled triangle ABC; P is the circumcentre of △ADB, Q that of △ADC. If ∠APD = 106° and ∠AQD = 136°, calculate ∠BAC.

9 In Fig. 55, if ∠AXP = 82°, calculate ∠AYQ. What conclusion can you draw about the lines PX, QY?

10 In Fig. 56, if ∠BQC = 39° and ∠QBC = 54°, calculate ∠APB.

11 In Fig. 56, if ∠BQC = q° and ∠QBC = b°, find ∠APB in terms of q and b.

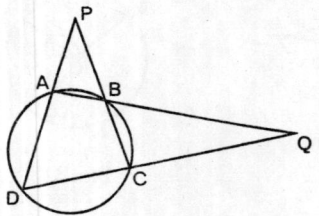

ABQ, DCQ, DAP, CBP are
straight lines
FIG. 56

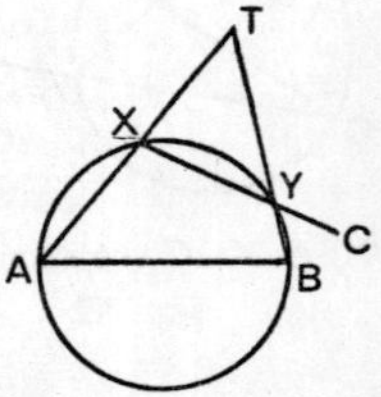

AB is a diameter; TXA, TYB,
XYC are straight lines
FIG. 57

12 In Fig. 57, if ∠AXY = 117°, calculate ∠BAY.

13 The diagonals of a cyclic quadrilateral ABCD intersect at O; $\angle AOB = 104°$, $\angle BCA = 46°$ and $\angle ABD = 33°$. Calculate $\angle ADC$.

14 In Fig. 52, if $\angle BXD = p°$ and $\angle XBD = q°$, express $\angle$s ACD, CDB, BAC in terms of p and q.

(*Theoretical*)

15 In Fig. 52, prove that $\angle XDA = \angle XBC$.

16 AB is a chord of a circle, centre O. The circle drawn on OA as diameter cuts AB at N. Prove that $AN = NB$. (Join ON and OB.)

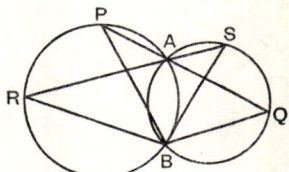

17 In Fig 58, prove that $\angle PBR = \angle QBS$.

18 In Fig. 55, prove that
   (i) $\angle PXA + \angle QYA = 180°$
      (Hint: use Theorem 9),
   (ii) XP is parallel to YQ.

PAQ, RAS are straight lines
FIG. 58

19 Two circles intersect at A and B; AP and AQ are diameters of the circles. Prove that PBQ is a straight line. (Join AB.)

20 In Fig. 57, prove that $\angle BYC + \angle ABX = 90°$.

21 ABCD is a cyclic quadrilateral. If AC bisects $\angle BAD$, prove that the triangle BCD is isosceles.

22 ABCDEF is a hexagon (not necessarily regular) inscribed in a circle. Prove that $\angle ABC + \angle CDE + \angle EFA = 360°$. (Join BE.)

23 ABC is an acute-angled triangle inscribed in a circle; O is the centre of the circle, N is the mid-point of BC. Prove that $\angle BON = \angle BAC$.

24 The side AB of a cyclic quadrilateral ABCD is produced to E, and CB is the bisector of $\angle EBD$. Prove that $CA = CD$.

25 In Fig. 52, if O is the centre of the circle, and $\angle ADC = x°$, $\angle BAD = y°$, express in terms of x and y the numbers of degrees in $\angle AOC$, $\angle BOD$, $\angle AXD$, and hence show that $\angle AOC - \angle BOD = 2\angle AXD$.

26 The bisector of the angle A of △ABC meets BC at D and the circumcircle of the triangle at E. Prove that the three angles of △ACD are equal to the three angles of △AEB. (Such triangles as these are called **equiangular.**)

27 In Fig. 59, AD and BE are two altitudes of △ABC; AD produced meets the circumcircle of the triangle at P. Prove that (i) ∠DBH = ∠EAH, (ii) ∠DBP = ∠DBH.

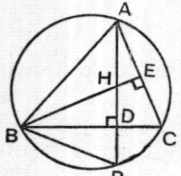

FIG. 59

Hence show that the △s DBP, DBH are congruent, and that HD = DP.

28 ABC is an acute-angled triangle inscribed in a circle, AK is the diameter drawn through A, and D is the foot of the perpendicular from A to BC. Prove that the triangles ABD, AKC are equiangular.

29 In Fig. 57, prove that ∠XBA + ∠YAB = ∠ATB. (Begin with ∠XBA = 90° − ∠XAB.)

30 In Fig. 58, prove that ∠RPB = ∠SQB. (Join AB.)

6. CO-ORDINATES: GRAPHS OF FUNCTIONS

Co-ordinates If we start from a certain point in a field, we could direct someone to go to a particular place by telling him to walk, say, 40 metres due east and then 30 metres due north.

The position of a point in a plane is described in a similar way. We draw two perpendicular lines Ox, Oy, as in Fig. 60. These are called the x-axis and the y-axis. An appropriate scale is chosen for each axis, suitable for the size and range of the numbers involved. The position of the point P is described by saying that we start from O, move 4 units x-wards (i.e. along Ox), and then 3 units y-wards (i.e. parallel to Oy). At the point P, we say that x is 4 and y is 3; or that

P has **co-ordinates** (4, 3); or merely P is (4, 3). **The *x* co-ordinate must always be named first in the bracket.**

Similarly, the position of Q is described by saying that we start from O, move (−2) units *x*-wards (i.e. 2 units to the left), followed by 4 units *y*-wards; Q is the point (−2, 4). Similarly, R is (−2, −3), and S is (2, −1).

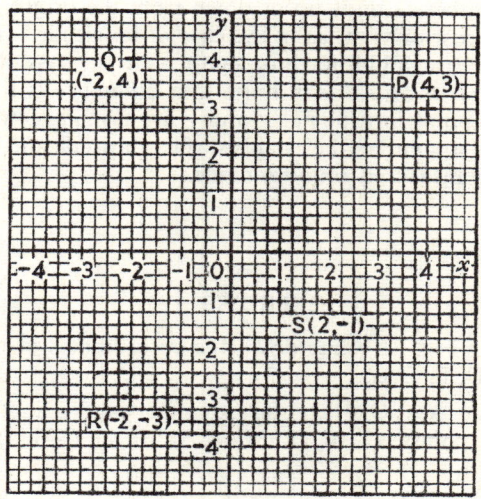

Fig. 60

O is called the **origin,** because it is the point from which we start counting. It is the point (0, 0). Points to the right of O have their *x* co-ordinates positive; those to the left of O have their *x* co-ordinates negative. Similarly, points above O have their *y* co-ordinates positive; those below O have their *y* co-ordinates negative.

When we have fixed the origin and the axes, a point is uniquely determined by its two co-ordinates; that is to say, a particular pair of co-ordinates belong to a particular point, and no other point has that pair of co-ordinates.

It will be seen that this method of fixing a point in a plane resembles the method of fixing a point on the earth's surface by latitude and longitude. The equator corresponds to the *x*-axis, the meridian of Greenwich to the *y*-axis. Longitude east or west of Greenwich corresponds to the *x* of a point, or the number of units to the right or left of the origin. Latitude north or south of the equator corresponds to the *y* of a point, or the number of units up or down from the origin. Instead of saying east or west, as in the case of longitude, we say *x* is + or −. Instead of north or south, as in the case of latitude, we say *y* is + or −. An important difference is that in the case of a point in a plane, *x* and *y* are *distances*, whereas in the case of a point on the earth's surface, latitude and longitude are *angles* measured round a circle.

EXERCISE 12

1 Using Fig. 61, write down the co-ordinates of the points A, B, C, D, E, F, G.

2 Draw axes O*x*, O*y* on squared paper, and plot the following points: (2, 0), (5, 3), (3, 5), (0, 1), (−3, 2), (−4, 0), (0, −4), (4, −1).

3 On squared paper, taking 1 cm as the unit on both axes, plot the points (−6, −1), (−4, 0), (−2, 0), (0, 0), (2½, 2), (3½, 0), (1½, −1). (This is the constellation known as the Great Bear.)

4 Taking 1 cm as the unit on the *x*-axis and 2 mm as the unit on the *y*-axis, plot the points P (2, 17), P′ (2, −17); Q (1, −10), Q′ (−1, −10); R (3, −5), R′ (−3, 5).

P and P′ are said to be **symmetrical** with respect to the *x*-axis. Q and Q′ are symmetrical with respect to the *y*-axis. R and R′ are symmetrical with respect to the origin, because they lie in a straight line with the origin and are equidistant from it, but on opposite sides.

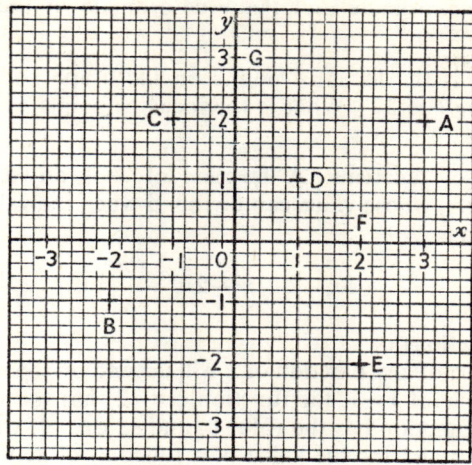

Fig. 61

5 Choose a scale on the x-axis so that x may have values from -4 to $+4$, and on the y-axis so that y may have values from 0 to 16.

Plot the points (0, 0), (1, 1), (2, 4), (3, 9), (4, 16). Mark also the points which are symmetrical with respect to the y-axis. Join all the points with a smooth curve, and verify that the co-ordinates of all the points fit the formula $y = x^2$.

6 The co-ordinates of a point on the graph paper are connected by the formula $y = 2x + 1$. Show that the co-ordinates of the points (0, 1), (1, 3), (2, 5) all fit the formula, and find the values of y if $x = -1$ and if $x = -2$.

Choosing a scale of 1 cm to a unit on both axes, mark all these points in a graph. Join them up by means of a ruler.

7 With a scale of 1 cm to a unit on the x-axis and $\frac{1}{2}$ cm to a unit on the y-axis, mark the points $(-3, -10)$ and $(3, 8)$. Join them up by means of a ruler, and find the co-ordinates of the points on this line whose x co-ordinates are $-2, -1, 0, 1, 2$.

Verify that, for each of these points on the line, the values of the x co-ordinate and the y co-ordinate fit the formula $y = 3x - 1$.

8 What is the locus of points on the graph paper whose x co-ordinate is 2? What is the locus of points whose y co-ordinate is 3?

Graphs of functions A **function** of x is any expression containing x, whose value can be found when the value of x is given. Thus

$$3x - 2, \quad x^2 - 2x, \quad \frac{120}{x}$$

are all functions of x.

The value of any function of x will depend on the value of x. For example, if $x = 1$, the function $(3x - 2)$ has the value 1; if $x = 2$, the function has the value 4, and so on. If we take the letter y to stand for the value of a function of x, y will have different values (in general) for different values of x. Our object is to show those different values of y in a graph.

When we drew statistical graphs in Part I, § 26, the values of what was there called the *independent variable* were measured along a line running *across* the page, and the values of some quantity which depended on that variable were measured along a line running *up* the page. This last quantity was usually the result of experiment, or observation and measurement, or based on information derived from published statistical tables. In order to draw the graph of a function, we have first to obtain the values of the function for different values of x, by substituting these values in the formula which expresses the function. The values of x are then measured across the page, and those of y up the page, x and y being treated as two co-ordinates in the manner described on page 38. The first step, therefore, must be to draw up a table of values of y for various values of x. These points are then plotted on graph paper, the x co-ordinate of any point being the value of x and the y co-ordinate being the value of y which corresponds in the table to that value of x. The scales on the x- and y-axes must be chosen so as to suit the size of your graph paper, bearing in mind what range of values of x and y are needed, whether any negative values are wanted, and so on.

Example 1 *Draw a graph to show the time in hours to travel a journey of* 120 *kilometres at various speeds.*

We first draw up a table of values showing the times in hours required to travel 120 km at 2, 3, 4, 5, . . . km/h. These are found by dividing 120 by 2, 3, 4, 5 . . . in turn. We omit speeds such as 7 km/h because they do not divide easily into 120, and we shall have plenty of points to plot without troubling about awkward values.

Speed in km/h .	2	3	4	5	6	8	10	12	15	20	30	40
Time in hours .	60	40	30	24	20	15	12	10	8	6	4	3

We draw the axes on the graph paper, the speed axis across the paper and the time axis up the paper, as in Fig. 62. The points are then plotted. Evidently, points between those plotted have a meaning: the speed might be, say, $4\frac{1}{2}$ km/h, in which case the time in hours would be $\frac{120}{4\frac{1}{2}}$ or $26\frac{2}{3}$ hours.

We therefore draw a smooth curve through the points, and from the graph so obtained we could read off the time to travel the distance of 120 kilometres at any given speed.

Suppose that the speed is x km/h.

The time to go 120 km at x km/h $= \frac{120}{x}$ hours.

In fact, we have really plotted the values of $\frac{120}{x}$ for values of x from 2 to 40. The curve in Fig. 62 on the next page is therefore said to be the **graph of the function** $\frac{120}{x}$ between $x=2$ and $x=40$.

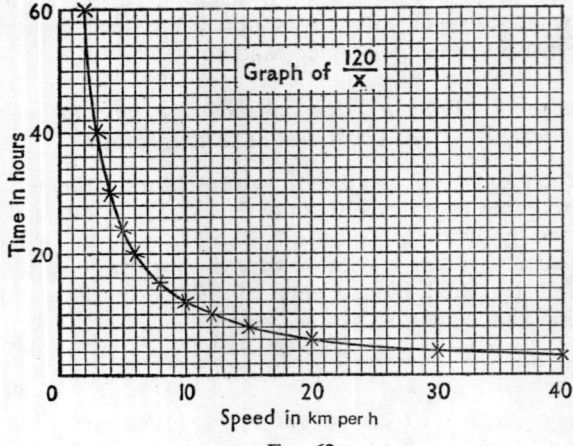

FIG. 62

If, now, we select any point on the speed axis, the height of the curve above the speed axis at that point is the value of $\frac{120}{x}$ for that value of x.

Notice that sometimes we speak of drawing the graph of a certain function of x; sometimes it is called the graph of 'y = a function of x'. The graph illustrates the behaviour of y for various values of x; it shows the different values of the function for different values of the variable x.

Example 2 *Draw the graph of the function* $(x+2)(4-x)$ *from* $x = -3$ *to* $x = 5$.

We must find the values of $(x+2)$ and $(4-x)$ for certain values of x, and multiply the two answers together. We therefore make four rows in the table of values, writing the values of x in the first row, the values of $(x+2)$ in the second, the values of $(4-x)$ in the third, and finally the values of the product $(x+2)(4-x)$ in the fourth row.

The table of values is:

$x =$	-3	-2	-1	0	1	2	3	4	5
$x + 2 =$	-1	0	1	2	3	4	5	6	7
$4 - x =$	7	6	5	4	3	2	1	0	-1
$y = (x+2)(4-x) =$	-7	0	5	8	9	8	5	0	-7

We choose a scale which gives a spread of 8 units (-3 to 5) on the x-axis, and 16 units (-7 to 9) on the y-axis. The points $(-3, -7)$, $(-2, 0)$, $(-1, 5)$, and so on, are plotted and joined up by a smooth curve, as in Fig. 63. Notice that the

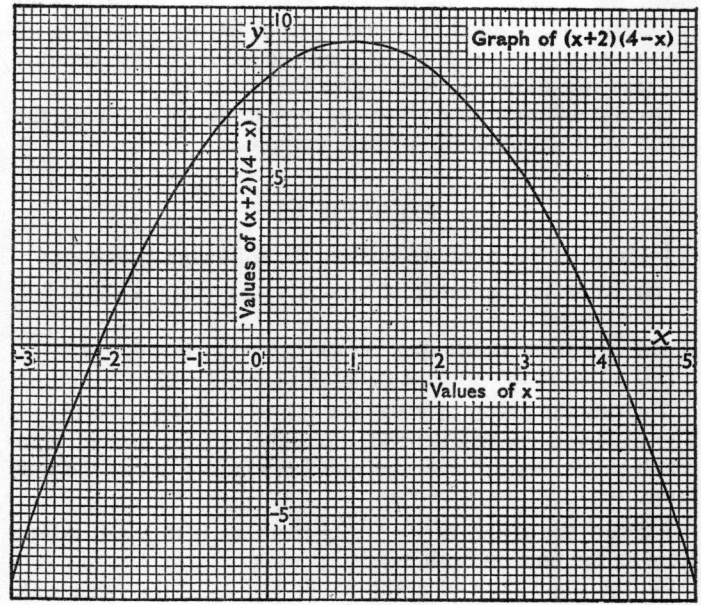

Fig. 63

curve is symmetrical about a certain line (the line $x=1$) and that the function reaches its greatest value at the point for which $x=1$. It is easy to see from the graph that the function $(x+2)(4-x)$ is positive between $x=-2$ and $x=4$, for the curve lies above the axis of x at all points inside this range. The function is negative in value if x is less than -2 or greater than 4.

It is essential, when drawing the graph of a function, to observe the rule that x must be measured along the axis running *across* the paper; for x is the independent variable, and we choose (within reason) what values it is to have. The values of the function, that is, the values of y, must be measured along the axis running *up* the paper.

When drawing up a table of values, work *horizontally*, not down the columns. In the last example, all the values of $(x+2)$ should be filled in, working from left to right; then all the values of $(4-x)$; and lastly all the values of the product of these two numbers, which give the values of y.

Do not attempt to choose the best scale for drawing the graph until the table of values is complete.

EXERCISE 13

1 Use Fig. 63, p. 45, to answer the following questions:

   (i) What is the value of $(x+2)(4-x)$ when $x=2\cdot8$, $1\cdot6$, $-2\cdot2$?

   (ii) For what values of x is $(x+2)(4-x)=6\cdot5$, 4, -1?

   (iii) What is the greatest value of $(x+2)(4-x)$?

2 Draw the graph of $y=x^2$ for values of x from -4 to $+4$ The scale you use will depend, of course, on the size of your graph paper; try 1 cm as the unit for x and $\frac{1}{2}$ cm as the unit for y.

3 Draw the graph of $y=5-2x$ from $x=0$ to $x=4$, taking 1 cm as the unit on both axes.

On the same sheet of graph paper and using the same scale and axes, draw the graph of $y=3x-6$.

Read off the value of x at the point where the two graphs cut.

4 Copy and complete the following table of values of the function $\frac{1}{10}x^3$ for values of x from -3 to 3:

$x=$	-3	-2	-1	0	1	2	3
$x^3=$	-27	-8					
$y=\frac{1}{10}x^3=$	$-2\cdot7$	$-0\cdot8$					

Draw the graph of the function, taking 2 cm as the unit on both axes.

5 Copy and complete the following table of values of the function $x(x-2)$:

$x=$	-1	$-\frac{1}{2}$	0	$\frac{1}{2}$	1	$1\frac{1}{2}$	2	$2\frac{1}{2}$	3
$x-2=$	-3	$-2\frac{1}{2}$	-2	$-1\frac{1}{2}$	-1				
$x(x-2)=$	3	$1\frac{1}{4}$	0	$-\frac{3}{4}$					

Plot the points and draw the graph of $y=x(x-2)$. Use it to answer the following questions:

(i) Is the graph symmetrical about any line?

(ii) Has y a greatest or a smallest value? If so, for what value of x does it occur?

(iii) Between what values of x is the function negative?

6 Draw the graph of the function $2x+1$ between $x=-1$ and $x=3$.

7 Draw the graph of the function $(x-2)(x-4)$ for values of x between 0 and 6.

8 Copy and complete the following table of values of the function $x(x+2)(x-4)$.

$x=$	-3	-2	-1	0	1	2	3	4	5
$x+2=$	-1	0	1	2					
$x-4=$	-7	-6							
$x(x+2)(x-4)=$	-21	0							

Plot the points and draw the graph of $y = x(x+2)(x-4)$, using a scale of 2 mm to the unit for the values of the function. Use your graph to answer the following questions:

(i) Is there a point where the value of the function is less, or greater, than the value at near points on each side of it? If so, what is the value of x there?

(ii) Between what negative values of x is the function positive? Between what positive values of x is the function negative?

9 A stone is thrown vertically upwards, from a point near the edge of a cliff, with a speed of 20 m/s. Assuming that, after t seconds, the stone has reached a height of $5t(4-t)$ metres above the level of the top of the cliff, copy and complete the following table of values for this function:

$t =$	0	$\frac{1}{2}$	1	$1\frac{1}{2}$	2	$2\frac{1}{2}$	3	$3\frac{1}{2}$	4	$4\frac{1}{2}$	5
$4-t =$	4	$3\frac{1}{2}$	3	$2\frac{1}{2}$		$1\frac{1}{2}$		$\frac{1}{2}$	0	$-\frac{1}{2}$	
$5t(4-t) =$	0	$8\frac{3}{4}$	15	$18\frac{3}{4}$		$18\frac{3}{4}$		$8\frac{3}{4}$	0	$-11\frac{1}{4}$	

Hence draw the graph of the function $5t(4-t)$ for values of t from 0 to 5, using a scale of 2 cm as the unit for t and 2 mm as the unit for the values of the function.

Use your graph to answer the following questions:

(i) How high is the stone above the top of the cliff after 0·8 s, after 2·8 s, after 3·8 s?

(ii) After how many seconds is the height of the stone above the top of the cliff 10 m? (There are two answers.)

(iii) What is the greatest height the stone reaches, and after how many seconds?

(iv) How long is it before the stone returns to the level of the top of the cliff?

(v) For how many seconds is the stone more than 5 m above the top of the cliff?

7. THE PARALLELOGRAM AND SPECIAL FORMS OF THE QUADRILATERAL

The parallelogram

Definition A **parallelogram** is a quadrilateral with both pairs of opposite sides parallel.

A parallelogram has also various properties, and these are proved in Theorems 10–12.

THEOREM 10

The opposite sides of a parallelogram are equal.

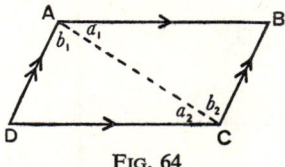

Fig. 64

Given a parallelogram ABCD (i.e. AB ∥ DC, BC ∥ AD).

To prove that AB = CD, BC = DA.

Construction Join AC.

Proof In the △s ABC, CDA,

$$a_1 = a_2 \text{ (alt., AB ∥ DC)},$$
$$b_2 = b_1 \text{ (alt., BC ∥ AD)},$$
$$AC = CA.$$

∴ △s $\begin{matrix} ABC \\ CDA \end{matrix}$ are congruent (AA corr. S).

∴ AB = CD, BC = DA.

Corollary. A diagonal of a parallelogram divides it into two congruent triangles.

Reference AB = CD (*opp. sides of parm.*).

THEOREM 11

The opposite angles of a parallelogram are equal.

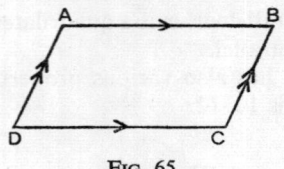

FIG. 65

Given a parallelogram ABCD (i.e. AB ∥ DC, BC ∥ AD).

To prove that

∠A = ∠C, ∠B = ∠D.

Proof

∠A + ∠B = 2 rt. ∠s (int. on same side of AB, BC ∥ AD);

∠C + ∠B = 2 rt. ∠s (int. on same side of BC, AB ∥ DC).

∴ ∠A + ∠B = ∠C + ∠B.

∴ ∠A = ∠C.

Similarly, ∠B = ∠D.

Reference ∠A = ∠C (*opp. ∠s of parm.*).

THEOREM 12

The diagonals of a parallelogram bisect each other.

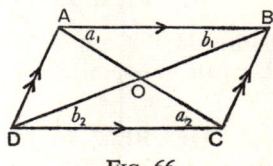

FIG. 66

Given a parallelogram ABCD whose diagonals AC, BD cut at O.

To prove that OA = OC, OB = OD.

Proof   In the △s AOB, COD,

$$a_1 = a_2 \text{ (alt., AB } \| \text{ DC)},$$
$$b_1 = b_2 \text{ (alt., AB } \| \text{ DC)},$$
$$AB = CD \text{ (opp. sides of parm.).}$$

∴   △s $\genfrac{}{}{0pt}{}{\text{AOB}}{\text{COD}}$ are congruent (AA corr. S).

∴ OA = OC, OB = OD.

Reference   OA = OC (*diags. of parm.*).

Theorems 13–16 contain certain tests by which we can recognize a quadrilateral to be a parallelogram. The proofs of these theorems are left to the reader. (See Exercise 14, Nos 1–4.

THEOREM 13

If one pair of opposite sides of a quadrilateral are equal and parallel, then the other pair of opposite sides are also equal and parallel.

THEOREM 14

A quadrilateral with both pairs of opposite angles equal is a parallelogram.

THEOREM 15

A quadrilateral with both pairs of opposite sides equal is a parallelogram.

THEOREM 16

A quadrilateral in which the diagonals bisect each other is a parallelogram.

SUMMARY

A parallelogram has the following properties:

  (a) opposite sides are parallel,
  (b) opposite sides are equal,
  (c) opposite angles are equal,
  (d) the diagonals bisect each other,
  (e) each diagonal bisects the figure.

A quadrilateral is a parallelogram if:

    (a) both pairs of opposite sides are parallel,
  or (b) both pairs of opposite sides are equal,
  or (c) one pair of opposite sides are equal and parallel,
  or (d) both pairs of opposite angles are equal,
  or (e) the diagonals bisect each other.

EXERCISE 14

1 Use Fig. 67 to prove Theorem 13.   (Prove △s ABC, CDA congruent; hence BC = DA and $x = y$, etc.)

2 Use Fig. 68 to prove Theorem 14.   (Prove that ∠A + ∠B = 180°.)

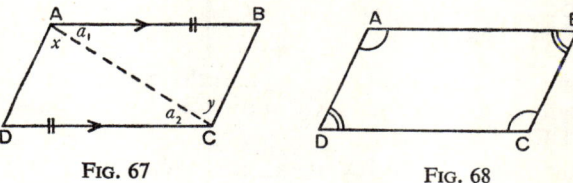

FIG. 67   FIG. 68

3 Use Fig. 69 to prove Theorem 15.   (Prove △s ABC, CDA congruent; hence $x = y$, etc.)

4 Use Fig. 70 to prove Theorem 16.   (Prove △s AOB, COD congruent; hence ∠OAB = ∠OCD, etc.)

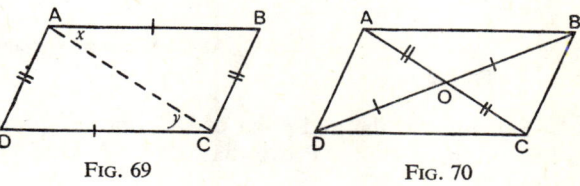

FIG. 69   FIG. 70

5 ABCD is a parallelogram whose diagonals intersect at O. (See Fig. 70.)   Any line through O meets AB at X and CD at Y.   Prove that △s AOX, COY are congruent, and deduce that OX = OY.

(This is the reason why the parallelogram is said to be *symmetrical* about O.)

6 In Fig. 71, if CQ = AB, prove that DP = 3AB.

7 In Fig. 71, prove that △s ADQ, BCP are congruent.

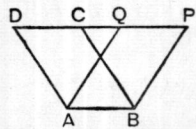

ABCD, ABPQ are parallelograms;
DCQP is a straight line
FIG. 71

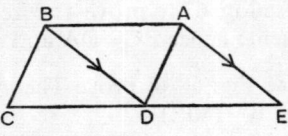

FIG. 72

8 In Fig. 72, ABCD is a parallelogram. The parallel through A to BD meets CD produced at E. Prove that ED = DC.

9 In Fig. 73, ABCD is a parallelogram. Prove that ∠PAB = ∠B.

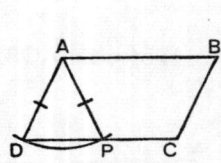

FIG. 73

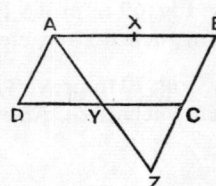

ABCD is a parallelogram
FIG. 74

10 In Fig. 74, Y is the mid-point of DC, and AY produced meets BC produced at Z. Prove that (i) △s AYD, ZYC are congruent, (ii) CZ = BC.

11 In Fig. 74, X and Y are the mid-points of AB and DC. Prove that AXCY is a parallelogram.

12 ABCD is a parallelogram; X is any point on AB, and Y is the point on CD such that CY = XA. Prove that AC and XY bisect each other.

13 In Fig. 70, let X be the mid-point of OB, Y that of OD. Prove that AXCY is a parallelogram.

14 Two parallelograms ABCD and ABXY are drawn with AB as a common side. Prove that DCXY is a parallelogram.

15 In Fig. 75, prove that △s AYD, CXB are congruent, and hence prove that BXDY is a parallelogram.

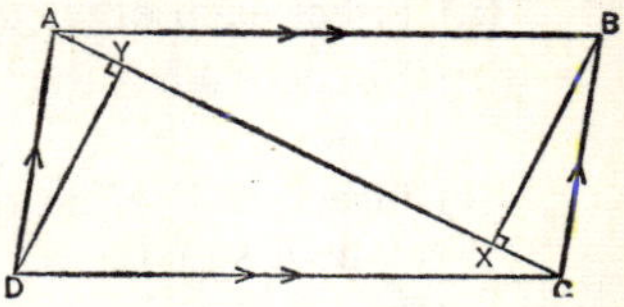

FIG. 75

Special forms of the quadrilateral

The rectangle, square and rhombus are special forms of the parallelogram. They therefore possess all the properties already proved for a parallelogram. In addition to these they have other properties, some of which have already been stated. For the sake of completeness the full list of properties is now given.

Properties of a rectangle

   (i) All the angles are right angles.

   (ii) The diagonals are equal.

Properties of a square

   (i) All the sides are equal and all the angles right angles.

   (ii) The diagonals are equal, and bisect each other at right angles.

   (iii) The diagonal makes an angle of 45° with the side.

Properties of a rhombus

   (i) All the sides are equal.

   (ii) The diagonals bisect each other at right angles.

   (iii) The diagonals bisect the angles of the figure.

It is always possible to decide when a quadrilateral is a parallelogram, rhombus, rectangle or square from the properties of its diagonals. A quadrilateral in which the diagonals

(i) bisect each other must be a parallelogram;

(ii) bisect each other at right angles must be a rhombus;

(iii) bisect each other and are equal must be a rectangle;

(iv) bisect each other at right angles and are equal must be a square.

Definitions A quadrilateral which has only one pair of opposite sides parallel is called a **trapezium**. A trapezium in which the non-parallel sides are equal is said to be **isosceles**.

EXERCISE 15

1 In Fig. 76, ABCD and APQR are squares. Prove that △s ABP, ADR are congruent, and deduce that BP = DR.

2 ABCD is a rhombus. The bisector of ∠BAC meets BC at P. Prove that ∠APB = 3∠PAB.

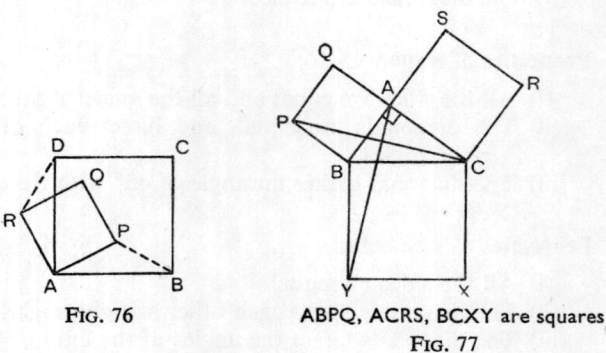

FIG. 76

ABPQ, ACRS, BCXY are squares
FIG. 77

3 In Fig. 77, prove that PAR is a straight line.

4 In Fig. 77, prove that △s ABY, PBC are congruent.

5 In Fig. 78, ABCD and APCQ are rectangles. Prove that PQ = BD.

Show further that the mid-point of AC is also the mid-point of BD and of PQ, and deduce that PBQD is a rectangle.

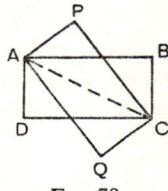
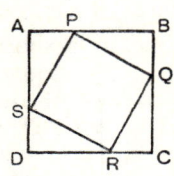

FIG. 78   FIG. 79

6 In Fig. 79, ABCD is a square; AP = BQ = CR = DS. Prove that

(i) △s APS, BQP are congruent,

(ii) PS = PQ,

(iii) ∠SPQ = 90°.

What kind of a quadrilateral is PQRS?

7 In Fig. 80, ABCD is an isosceles trapezium; BX is drawn parallel to AD. Prove that BXC is an isosceles triangle, and deduce that ∠D = ∠C.

8 In Fig. 80, use the result of No. 7 to prove by congruence that AC = BD.

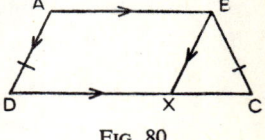

FIG. 80

9 Construct a rhombus with diagonals 5 cm and 4 cm long. Measure a side.

10 With ruler and compasses only, construct a rectangle with diagonals 5·6 cm long, the angle included by the diagonals being 60°. Measure the sides.

11 Construct a trapezium ABCD in which AB is parallel to DC, AB = 2·4 cm, BC = 3·0 cm, CD = 6·0 cm, DA = 2·2 cm. Measure AC. (Use the hint in Fig. 80, and begin by drawing △BXC.)

8. AREAS

SUPPOSE that the length AB of the rectangle ABCD in Fig. 81 is x units, and the breadth AD is y units. Then the area of the rectangle is xy units of area. We say that

area of rect. $ABCD = AB \times AD$ *or* $AB.AD$.

This is merely a short way of saying that the number of square units in the area is the product of the numbers of units of length in AB and AD.

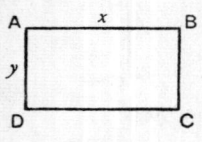

FIG. 81

If ABCD is a square, we call it *the square on* AB. Its area $= AB.AB$, which is written AB^2.

This notation is similar to that of algebra, where you will remember that we write a^2 instead of $a \times a$. Geometrical lengths can be treated just like single letters in algebra, and the rules for removing brackets are the same for both. These rules can be established algebraically, but it is useful to illustrate them geometrically. The figures given will be sufficient to indicate the proofs, which the reader should work out for himself.

Geometrical illustrations of algebraic identities

1          $k(a+b+c) = ka + kb + kc.$

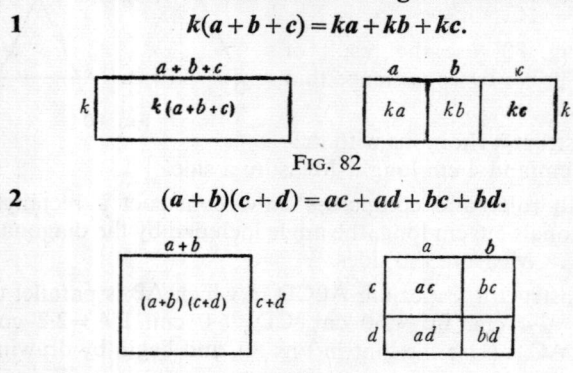

FIG. 82

2          $(a+b)(c+d) = ac + ad + bc + bd.$

FIG. 83

3 $$(a+b)^2 = a^2 + b^2 + 2ab.$$

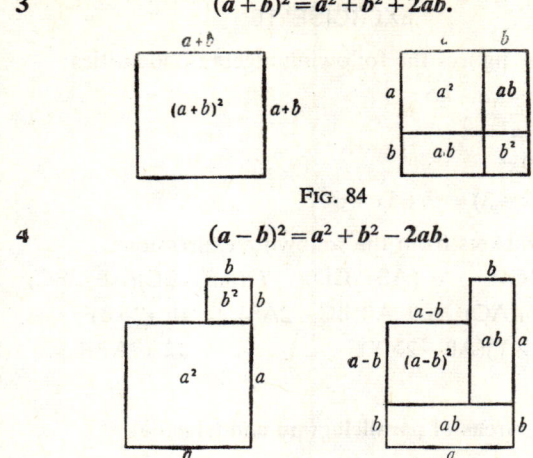

Fig. 84

4 $$(a-b)^2 = a^2 + b^2 - 2ab.$$

(i)   (ii)

Fig. 85

The area of Fig. 85 (i) is $a^2 + b^2$; when divided up as in Fig. 85 (ii), the area is $(a-b)^2 + 2ab$.

$$\therefore (a-b)^2 + 2ab = a^2 + b^2.$$
$$\therefore (a-b)^2 = a^2 + b^2 - 2ab.$$

5 $$a^2 - b^2 = (a+b)(a-b).$$

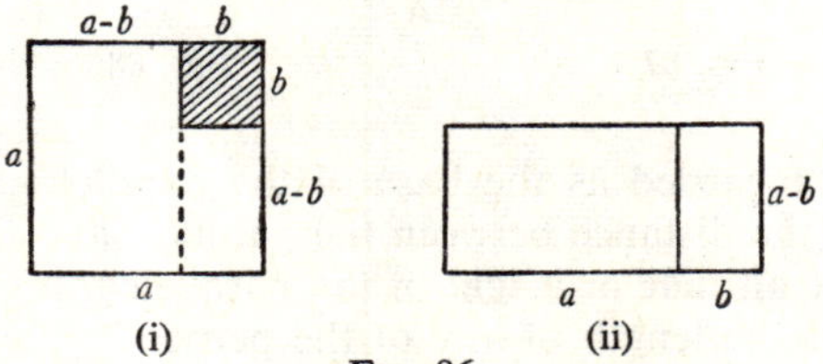

(i)   (ii)

Fig. 86

The area of the unshaded portion in Fig. 86 (i) is evidently $a^2 - b^2$. In Fig. 86 (ii), this unshaded portion is arranged as two rectangles, which together make up a rectangle of area $(a+b)(a-b)$.

EXERCISE 16

Illustrate by figures the following algebraic identities:

1 $k(a-b) = ka - kb$

2 $(2a)^2 = 4a^2$

3 $(3x)^2 = 9x^2$

4 $(x+2)(x+3) = x^2 + 5x + 6$

Remove brackets from the following expressions:

5 $(AB + BC)^2$ **6** $(AB - CD)^2$ **7** $(AB + BC)(AB - BC)$

8 $AB(AB + AC)$ **9** $AB(BC - 2AB)$ **10** $(2AB)^2$

11 $(AB + 2XY)(AB - 2XY)$ **12** $(3AB)^2$

Areas of parallelogram and triangle

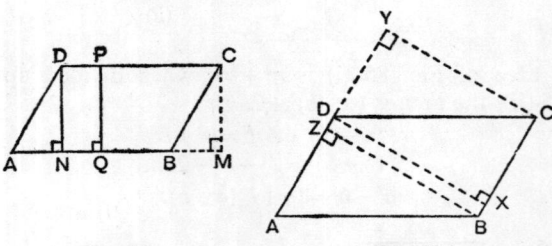

Fig. 87   Fig. 88

If AB is regarded as the base of the parallelogram ABCD in Fig. 87, the distance between the parallel sides DC and AB is called the **altitude** or **height** of the parallelogram. The altitude is thus the length of any of the perpendiculars DN, PQ, CM. It does not matter which point on DC we select in order to draw a perpendicular to AB; or we might select any point on AB and draw a perpendicular to DC. All these perpendiculars will be the same length, for the parallel lines DC and AB are everywhere the same distance apart.

In Fig. 88, BC is regarded as the base. In that case the altitude is the length of any of the equal perpendiculars DX, CY, or BZ.

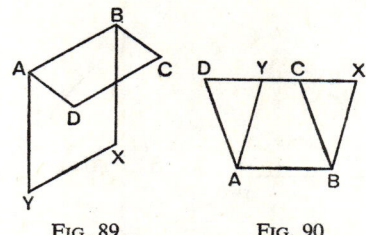

FIG. 89   FIG. 90

The two parallelograms ABCD, ABXY in Fig. 89 are said to be **on the same base** (AB).

The two parallelograms ABCD, ABXY in Fig. 90, where DYCX is a straight line, are said to be **on the same base (AB) and between the same parallels** (AB and DX). These two parallelograms may also be said to have **equal heights** or altitudes.

The same phrases are also used in connection with triangles. Thus, in Fig. 91, △s ABC, ABD are on the same base AB; in Fig. 92, they are on the same base AB and between the same parallels AB and CD.

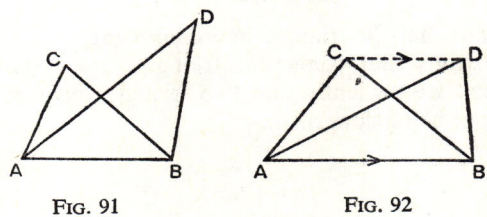

FIG. 91   FIG. 92

Any of the three sides of a triangle may be regarded as the **base**. When we have chosen one side as the base, the perpendicular to that side from the opposite vertex is called the

altitude or **height** of the triangle. Thus, in Fig. 93, if BC is
the base, then AD is the height; if AC is the base, then BE is
the height, and so on.

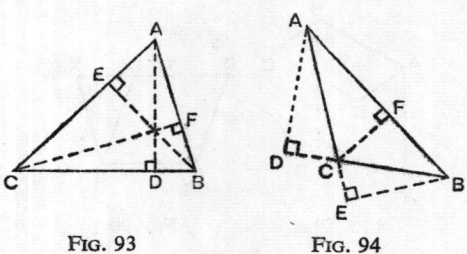

FIG. 93   FIG. 94

In Fig. 94, the triangle is obtuse-angled; and if we take BC
as the base it is necessary to produce it in order to draw a
perpendicular from A.   The three altitudes in this triangle are
AD, BE and CF.

Figures which are equal in area are called **equivalent**.

The symbol = is used for 'is equal in area to'. Thus

$$\triangle ABC = \triangle PQR$$

means that the triangles ABC, PQR are equal in area.   This
must not be confused with

$$\triangle ABC \equiv \triangle PQR,$$

which means that the triangles are congruent.

It is obvious that congruent triangles are equal in area,
but we shall see presently that two triangles may be equal in
area without being congruent.

THEOREM 17

Parallelograms on the same base and between the same parallels are equal in area.

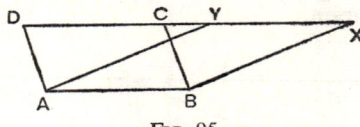

Fig. 95

Given two parallelograms ABCD and ABXY, on the same base AB and between the same parallels AB, DX.

To prove that ABCD = ABXY.

Proof   In the △s AYD, BXC,

$$\angle ADY = \angle BCX \quad \text{(corr., AD } \| \text{ BC),}$$
$$\angle AYD = \angle BXC \quad \text{(corr., AY } \| \text{ BX),}$$
$$AD = BC \qquad \text{(opp. sides of parm.).}$$

∴ △s $\begin{array}{c} \text{AYD} \\ \text{BXC} \end{array}$ are congruent (AA corr. S).

∴   they are equal in area.

Subtracting each in turn from the whole figure ABXD, we get

$$ABCD = ABXY.$$

Reference

Parm. ABCD = parm. ABXY (*same base* AB, *same* ∥*s* AB, DX).

Corollary 1   The area of a parallelogram is equal to the area of a rectangle on the same base and between the same parallels.

Corollary 2   Parallelograms on equal bases and between the same parallels are equal in area.

Thus, in Fig. 96, where ABCD, PQRS are two such parms.,

$$ABCD = ABRS$$
$$= PQRS.$$

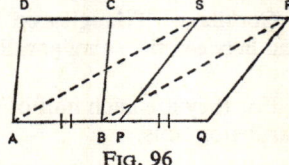

Fig. 96

THEOREM 18

If a triangle and a parallelogram are on the same base and between the same parallels, the area of the triangle is half that of the parallelogram.

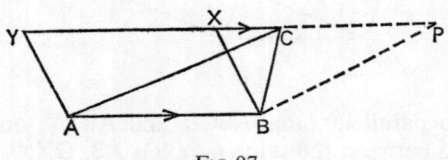

FIG 97

Given a triangle ABC and a parm. ABXY on the same base AB and between the same parallels AB, YXC.

To prove that $\triangle ABC = \frac{1}{2}$ parm. ABXY.

Construction Draw BP parallel to AC to meet YC produced at P.

Proof
$$BP \parallel AC \quad \text{(constr.)},$$
$$AB \parallel CP \quad \text{(given)},$$
$$\therefore ABPC \text{ is a parm.}$$

Now $\triangle ABC = \frac{1}{2}ABPC$ (diag. bisects parm.),
and parm. ABPC = parm. ABXY (same base AB, same $\parallel$s AB, YP).

$$\therefore \triangle ABC = \frac{1}{2} \text{ parm. ABXY.}$$

Reference $\triangle ABC = \frac{1}{2}$ parm. ABXY (*same base* AB, *same $\parallel$s* AB, YC).

Corollary Triangles on the same base (or on equal bases) and between the same parallels are equal in area.

For they are each half of the same parallelogram or of equal parallelograms.

The corollary to Theorem 18 is very useful in riders. It states that **if, in Fig. 98, CD is parallel to AB, then**

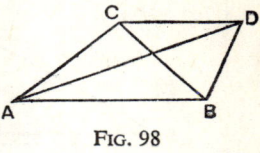

$\triangle ABC = \triangle ABD$ (*same base* AB,

same ‖s AB, CD).

Conversely, if $\triangle ABC = \triangle ABD$, **then**

CD ‖ AB.

FIG. 98

A particular case of this corollary is shown in Fig. 99, where, if D is the mid-point of BC,

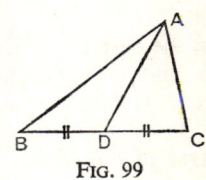

$\triangle ABD = \triangle ACD$ (*equal bases* BD, DC, *and same height*).

FIG. 99

Area formulae

Area of parallelogram The first corollary to Theorem 17 states that a parallelogram and a rectangle on the same base and between the same parallels are equal in area. But the area of the rectangle is base × height.

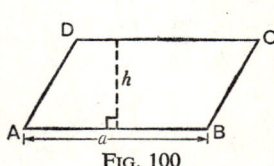

FIG. 100

Hence,
area of parallelogram = base × height.

In Fig. 100,
area of parm. ABCD $= ah$.

Area of triangle By Theorem 18, the area of a triangle is half that of a parallelogram on the same base and between the same parallels.

Hence,

area of triangle $= \frac{1}{2}$ base × height.

In Fig. 101,

$$\text{area of } \triangle ABC = \tfrac{1}{2}ah.$$

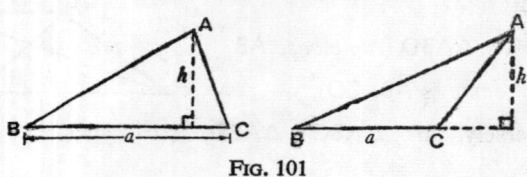

FIG. 101

In the case of a right-angled triangle, you should take as the base and the altitude the two sides which contain the right angle. If these are a, b units long, the area is $\tfrac{1}{2}ab$.

Area of trapezium

Let a cm and b cm be the lengths of the parallel sides and h cm the distance between them. The trapezium can be divided into two triangles of areas $\tfrac{1}{2}ah$ and $\tfrac{1}{2}bh$ cm², giving a total area of

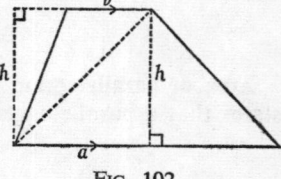

$$\tfrac{1}{2}ah + \tfrac{1}{2}bh, \quad \text{or } \tfrac{1}{2}(a+b)h \text{ cm}^2.$$

Hence,

area of trapezium = half the sum of the parallel sides multiplied by the distance between them.

FIG. 102

EXERCISE 17

(Constructions and calculations)

1 Draw a parallelogram ABCD in which AB = 3·6 cm, BC = 2·4 cm and ∠B = 63°.

Draw and measure the perpendiculars from A to BC and CD, and hence calculate the area of ABCD in two independent ways.

2 Draw a parallelogram ABCD in which AB = 5 cm, AD = 3 cm and the diagonal BD = 4·5 cm.

Draw and measure the perpendicular from A to CD produced, and hence calculate the area of ABCD.

3 Draw a triangle ABC in which AB = 3·2 cm, ∠A = 32° and AC = 6·0 cm.

Draw and measure the altitudes from B and C, and hence calculate the area of △ABC in two independent ways.

4 Draw a quadrilateral ABCD in which AB = 6·0 cm, BC = 7·0 cm, the diagonal AC = 8·0 cm, AD = 5·5 cm and DC = 4·0 cm.

Draw and measure the perpendiculars from B and D to AC, and hence calculate the area of ABCD.

5 Calculate the area of △ABC, if ∠A = 90°, AB = 3·6 cm and AC = 4·4 cm.

6 Calculate the area of a rhombus whose diagonals are 12 cm and 10 cm long.   (Use a property of the diagonals of a rhombus.)

7 In Fig. 103, if AP = 4 cm and CD = 6 cm, find the area of ABCD.

8 In Fig. 103, if the area of ABCD is 30 cm² and BC = 5 cm, calculate CQ.

9 In Fig. 103, if AB = 6 cm, AP = 3 cm, AD = 4 cm, calculate the area of ABCD.   Hence calculate the length of CQ.

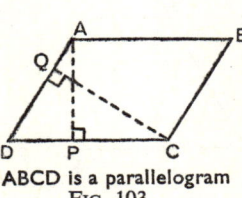

ABCD is a parallelogram
FIG. 103

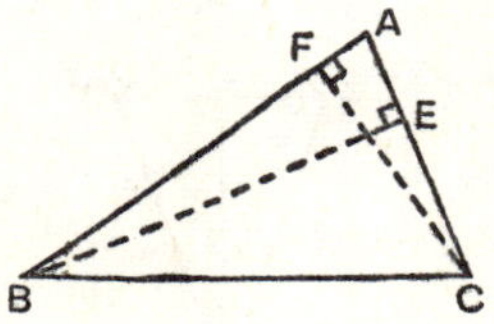

FIG. 104

10 In Fig. 104, if AB = 6 cm and CF = 3½ cm, calculate the area of △ABC.

11 In Fig. 104, if the area of △ABC is 27 cm² and BE = 9 cm, calculate AC.

12 In Fig. 104, if AC = 9 cm, BE = 5 cm and CF = 6 cm, calculate the area of △ABC, and hence find AB.

13 In Fig. 105, if AB = 4 cm and CN = 6 cm, calculate the area of △ABC, and find the length of the perpendicular from B to AC, given that AC = 7½ cm.

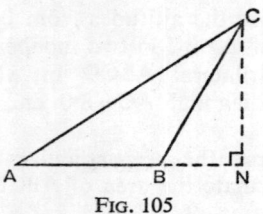

Fig. 105

14 In △ABC, ∠A = 90°, AB = 8 cm, AC = 6 cm. Calculate the area of the triangle and the length of the perpendicular from A to BC.

15 ABCD is a trapezium in which AB = 12 cm, DC = 8 cm, and the distance between the parallel sides AB and DC is 9 cm. Calculate the area of the trapezium.

16 In Fig. 106, ABCD is a kite, in which BD is the perpendicular bisector of AC. If AC = 2a cm and BD = 2b cm, find an expression for the area of ABCD.

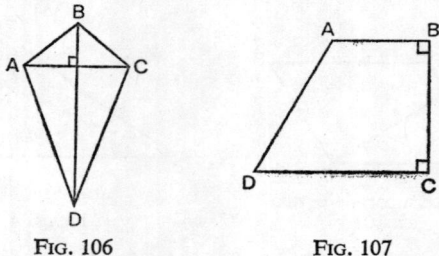

Fig. 106   Fig. 107

17 In Fig. 107, if AB = 4 cm, BC = 10 cm and CD = 6 cm, calculate the area of ABCD.

18 In Fig. 107, if AB = 5 cm, BC = 12 cm, CD = 8 cm, and X is the point in BC such that BX = 4 cm, calculate the area of △AXD.

19 Fig. 108 represents a field. A surveyor measures

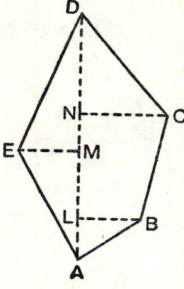

FIG. 108

distances along and perpendicular to AD, and makes the following record:

	Metres to D	
	380	
	200	130 to C
to E 90	160	
	60	110 to B
	from A	

This means that AL = 60 m, AM = 160 m, AN = 200 m, AD = 380 m, LB = 110 m, ME = 90 m, NC = 130 m.

Calculate the area of the field in square metres.

20 Calculate in square metres the area of the field whose dimensions are given in the following table:

	Metres to E	
	420	
	370	160 to D
	310	130 to C
to F 100	180	
	70	80 to B
	from A	

CONSTRUCTION 1

To construct a triangle equal in area to a given quadrilateral.

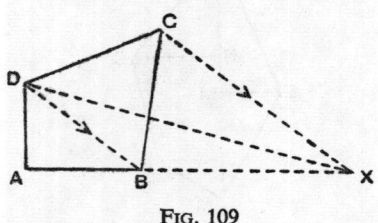

FIG. 109

Given a quadrilateral ABCD.

To construct a triangle equal in area to ABCD.

Construction　　Join DB.

Through C draw CX ∥ DB to meet AB produced at X.

Join DX.

Then ADX is the required triangle.

Proof　△XBD = △CBD (same base DB, same ∥s DB, CX).

∴ △XBD + △ABD = △CBD + △ABD.

∴ △ADX = quad. ABCD.

Note　A pentagon can be converted into a triangle of equal area by successive applications of the method given above. This is shown in Fig. 110, where we first construct the quadrilateral ABCX, equal in area to ABCDE. The quadrilateral ABCX is then converted into a triangle of equal area by means of Construction 1.

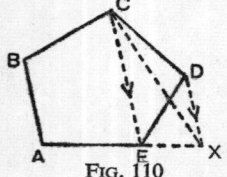

FIG. 110

EXERCISE 18

1 Draw a parallelogram ABCD in which AB = 5·0 cm, $\angle A = 62°$ and AD = 3·6 cm. Construct on base AB an equivalent parallelogram ABXY with the side AY 4·6 cm long. Measure the longer diagonal of ABXY.

2 Copy the parallelogram ABCD in No. 1 by pricking through the vertices, and construct an equivalent parallelogram ABXY on the same base AB and with the diagonal AX equal to AB. Measure the other diagonal.

3 Draw an equilateral triangle of side 5 cm, and construct an equivalent parallelogram with sides 5 cm and 3·6 cm. Measure the longer diagonal.

4 Draw a triangle with sides 3·8 cm, 3·4 cm and 5·8 cm. Construct an equivalent isosceles triangle with base 3·4 cm, and measure one of the two equal sides.

5 Draw a triangle ABC in which AB = 6·5 cm, BC = 4 cm and CA = 5·5 cm. Construct an acute-angled triangle PAB equal in area to △ABC and such that PB = 6 cm. Measure PA.

6 Draw a quadrilateral ABCD (with A and C on opposite sides of BD) in which AB = 2·5 cm, BC = 3 cm, CD = 5 cm, DA = 4 cm and BD = 5 cm.

Find a point X in AB produced which is such that △ADX = quad. ABCD. Draw and measure the perpendicular from X to AD, and hence calculate the area of the quadrilateral.

7 Draw a quadrilateral ABCD in which AB = 4·8 cm, BC = 2·0 cm, CD = 3·0 cm, AD = 4·0 cm and $\angle BAD = 50°$.

Construct a triangle equal in area to the quadrilateral and having D as one vertex, and hence find the area of ABCD.

8 Draw a parallelogram ABCD in which AB = 6 cm, $\angle ABC = 70°$ and the area is 27·6 cm². Measure BC.

9 Draw a parallelogram ABCD in which AB = 4·0 cm, BC = 6·0 cm and the diagonal AC = 5·0 cm. Construct a rhombus, equal in area to the parallelogram, each of whose sides is 6·0 cm. Measure the shorter diagonal.

10 Draw a regular pentagon (5 sides) with each side 3 cm long. Construct a triangle equal in area to it.

(Riders)

11 In Fig. 111, ABCD, ABXY, AYPQ are parallelograms, and QPBX is a straight line. Prove that ABCD = ABXY = AYPQ.

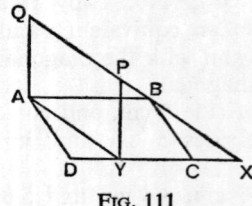
Fig. 111

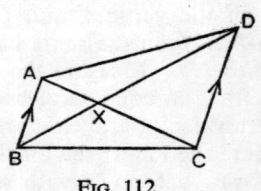
Fig. 112

12 In Fig. 112, state, with reasons, which triangle is equal in area to △ACD.
Deduce that △AXD = △BXC.

13 In Fig. 112, if AX = XC, state which triangle is equal in area to △DXC, and prove that △ABD = △CBD.

14 In Fig. 113, prove that △BPA = △BPC.

15 In Fig. 113, if BP = PE, prove that △BPC = △APE.

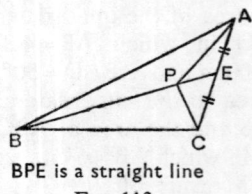
BPE is a straight line
Fig. 113

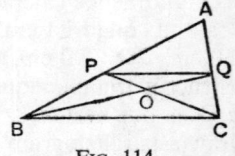
Fig. 114

16 In Fig. 114, if PQ is parallel to BC, prove that
      (i) △PBQ = △PCQ,
      (ii) △ABQ = △APC,
      (iii) △POB = △QOC.

17 In Fig. 114, if △ABQ = △ACP, prove that PQ is parallel to BC.

18 In Fig. 114, if AP = 2PB, explain why △APQ = 2△QPB. If also AQ = 2QC, prove that

> (i) △QPB = △QPC,
> (ii) PQ is parallel to BC.

19 In Fig. 115, prove that △DAC = △EBC.

20 The medians BE, CF of a triangle ABC intersect at G. By comparing each triangle with △ABC, prove that △AEB = △AFC. Prove also that △BGF = △CGE.

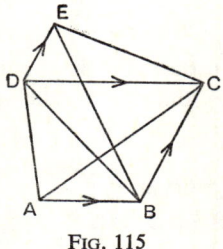

Fig. 115

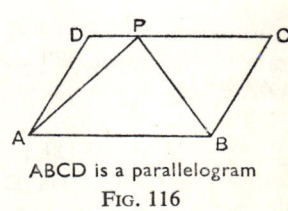

ABCD is a parallelogram

Fig. 116

21 In Fig. 116, state the relation between the areas of △PAB and the parallelogram ABCD.

Deduce that △PAB = △ADP + △BCP.

22 In Fig. 116, if BP is produced to meet AD produced at Q, prove that △QBC = △PAB. (Use Theorem 18.)

23 In Fig. 117, D is the mid-point of BC, and P is any

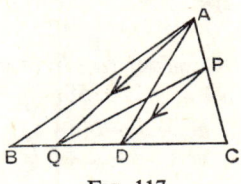

Fig. 117

point on AC. Prove that (i) quad. ABQP = △ADB, (ii) PQ bisects the area of △ABC.

24 In Fig. 118, ABCD is a parallelogram. Prove that

(i) △ABP = △DBP,
(ii) △ADQ = △BDQ,
(iii) △ABP = △ADQ.

25 In Fig. 119, X is any point on the diagonal BD of the

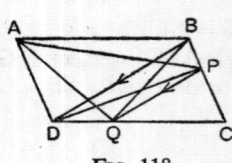

FIG. 118

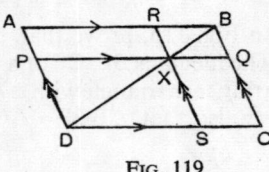

FIG. 119

parallelogram ABCD. Use the fact that the diagonal of a parallelogram bisects the area to show that the parallelograms ARXP, SXQC are equal in area.

9. MULTIPLICATION OF ALGEBRAIC EXPRESSIONS

Single-term multipliers We have already seen that

$$a(b+c) = ab+ac.$$

Each term inside the bracket must be multiplied by the factor outside. Thus,

$$2x(x+3) = 2x \times x + 2x \times 3$$
$$= 2x^2 + 6x.$$
$$3y(2y^2 - y - 4) = 3y \times 2y^2 + 3y \times (-y) + 3y \times (-4)$$
$$= 6y^3 - 3y^2 - 12y.$$

Binomial products Consider $(a+b)(c+d)$, which was illustrated geometrically in Fig. 83, p. 58.

This is the same as $a(c+d)+b(c+d)$,

or $ac+ad+bc+bd.$

Similarly,

$$(p-q)(x-y) = p(x-y) - q(x-y)$$
$$= px - py - qx + qy.$$

The middle step should be done in your head. The process of multiplying one bracket by another is called **expanding** the product, i.e. writing it out in full.

Example 1   *Expand* $(2x-3)(4x+5)$.
$$(2x-3)(4x+5) = 2x(4x+5) - 3(4x+5)$$
$$= 8x^2 + 10x - 12x - 15$$
$$= 8x^2 - 2x - 15.$$

After a little practice you will be able to do all the work mentally and write the answer straight down, by taking $2x$ times both the terms in the second bracket, and then -3 times both those terms.

Notice that $(2a+3)^2$ means $(2a+3)(2a+3)$.

EXERCISE 19

Expand:

1 $x(x+2)$ **2** $3(x-5)$ **3** $a(2+a)$ **4** $2b(b-3)$

5 $2t(t^2+t)$ **6** $ab(a+b)$ **7** $2y(3y+1)$ **8** $2a(4a-5)$

9 $bx(b-2x)$ **10** $7x(3+x)$ **11** $3x^2(1+4x+x^2)$

12 $3a(a+2b-1)$ **13** $2x(3x^2+x-4)$ **14** $3y^2(y^2-2y+3)$

15 $4ab(a^2+ab-b^2)$ **16** $(a+1)(a+2)$ **17** $(x+2)(x+4)$

18 $(2y+1)(y+1)$ **19** $(x+3)(2x-1)$ **20** $(x+3)(x-3)$

21 $(2-x)(3-x)$ **22** $(a+b)(x-y)$ **23** $(x+1)(x+1)$

24 $(a+3)^2$ **25** $(x-1)^2$ **26** $(3x+2)(x+4)$

27 $(a-5)^2$ **28** $(b-3)(b+4)$ **29** $(2x+a)(3x+a)$

30 $(y-2)(y+2)$ **31** $(2p+3q)^2$ **32** $(x-3y)(x+y)$

33 $(4+a)(3-2a)$ **34** $(a+b)^2$ **35** $(a-b)^2$

36 $(a+b)(a-b)$ **37** $(2x-1)(2x+1)$ **38** $(1-2x)(x+10)$

39 $(x+4)(3x-7)$ **40** $(a-x)(a+z)$ **41** $(y+1)(7y-5)$

42 $(4x-1)(3x+2)$ **43** $(2a-3)(a+4)$ **44** $(1-3x)(2-5x)$

45 $(2y-3)(y-5)$ **46** $(3-2x)(x+2)$ **47** $(b-6)(3b+16)$

48 $(2x-1)(4x+3)$ **49** $(4a+3b)(2a-3b)$

50 $(3x-5y)(2x+3y)$

The square of a bracket containing two terms   In Figs. 84, 85, p. 59, the expansions of $(a+b)^2$ and $(a-b)^2$ were illustrated geometrically.   We can verify that the same answers are obtained by multiplication.

Thus,
$$(a+b)^2 = (a+b)(a+b)$$
$$= a^2 + ab + ba + b^2$$
$$= a^2 + b^2 + 2ab.$$

Similarly,
$$(a-b)^2 = (a-b)(a-b)$$
$$= a^2 - ab - ba + b^2$$
$$= a^2 + b^2 - 2ab.$$

Learn by heart:
$$(a+b)^2 = a^2 + b^2 + 2ab;$$
$$(a-b)^2 = a^2 + b^2 - 2ab.$$

Now $(a+b)$ is the sum of the two terms a and b; $(a-b)$ is the difference of the same two terms.   The two formulae given above can thus be stated in words:

The square of the sum of two terms is equal to the sum of the squares of the two terms plus twice their product.

The square of the difference of two terms is equal to the sum of the squares of the two terms minus twice their product.

Notice particularly that the expansions of both $(a+b)^2$ and $(a-b)^2$ commence with $a^2 + b^2$.

Example 2   *Write down the squares of* (i) $2x + 3y$, (ii) $4x - 5y$.

(i) Comparing $(2x + 3y)^2$ with $(a+b)^2$, we change a into $2x$ and b into $3y$.   The result is
$$(2x+3y)^2 = (2x)^2 + (3y)^2 + 2.(2x).(3y)$$
$$= 4x^2 + 9y^2 + 12xy.$$

(ii) Comparing $(4x - 5y)^2$ with $(a-b)^2$, we change a into $4x$ and b into $5y$.   The result is
$$(4x-5y)^2 = (4x)^2 + (5y)^2 - 2.(4x).(5y)$$
$$= 16x^2 + 25y^2 - 40xy.$$

EXERCISE 20

Write down the squares of the following:

1 $x+5$ **2** $y+1$ **3** $a-1$ **4** $3x+y$

5 $3a+2$ **6** $a+2b$ **7** $b-a$ **8** $4x+y$

9 $5p-3q$ **10** $x+\frac{1}{2}$ **11** $\frac{x}{2}+y$ **12** $2b-a$

13 $3a-4b$ **14** $2x-3y$ **15** $2a+\frac{1}{3}$ **16** $2ab-\frac{1}{2}$

17 $3b-7$ **18** $2ac-1$ **19** $a+2bc$ **20** $2-5x$

21 Use the expansion of $(a+b)^2$ to find the value of 102^2, putting 100 for a and 2 for b.

22 Use the expansion of $(a-b)^2$ to find 999^2 and 998^2.

Simplify:

23 $(x-1)^2+(x+1)^2-2$ **24** $(2x-1)(x-4)-(x+2)^2$

25 $4(x-3)^2-3(x-1)^2+2(x+1)^2-3(x+3)^2$

26 $3(x-2)(x-1)-(x-3)^2-2(x-1)^2$

27 Express $3x^2-xy-y^2$ in terms of x, if $y=x-1$.

28 Show that $x^2+y^2+z^2-yz-zx-xy$ is unchanged if x is replaced by $(x+a)$, y by $(y+a)$, z by $(z+a)$.

29 If $x=2a-3b$, $y=a+2b$, $z=b-3a$, find the value of $x^2+y^2+z^2+2yz+2zx+2xy$.

30 Solve the equation
$$(x+1)^2+(x-3)(2x-1)=(2x-3)(x+2)+(x-2)^2$$

31 Solve $5(x+1)^2-2(x-1)(x-2)=3(x+3)^2+6$

32 Solve $(x+1)(x-5)-(x+2)^2=3$

10. SIMILAR FIGURES (I)

Part I § 31, (pp. 191–201) on Ratio should be revised before this section is commenced.

Shape When a boy makes a model of an aeroplane, it is obvious that everything must be 'to scale'. He might decide to have every length in the model one-fiftieth of the corresponding length in the aeroplane, in which case

$$\frac{\text{length of model}}{\text{length of aeroplane}} = \frac{1}{50},$$

and

$$\frac{\text{wing-span of model}}{\text{wing-span of aeroplane}} = \frac{1}{50}.$$

He would also consider it necessary to make any angles in the model (for example, those at which the wing-struts are set) the same as in the actual object.

It is worth noticing that the area of the wing-surface of the model would not be one-fiftieth of that of the aeroplane; nor would the weight of the model be one-fiftieth of that of the aeroplane, if they were made of the same material.

We say that the model and the aeroplane are *the same shape*. In the same way the picture thrown on the screen at a cinema and that on the photographic film are the same shape; that is, the angles of one are the same as those of the other, and the ratio of every length on the screen to the corresponding length on the film is the same. A map of a field and the actual field have the same relationship, and so have an architect's plan of a house and the actual house.

Suppose that we draw the plan of an irregular-shaped field to the scale of 1 cm to 200 metres. Each angle in the plan is the same as the corresponding angle on the ground. Also the ratio of any length in the plan to the corresponding length on the ground is always 1 cm : 200 m, or 1 : 20 000. (We have already called this the Representative Fraction of the map.) In order that the plan should be *the same shape* as the actual field, both these requirements must be met.

Similar polygons   Two polygons are said to be **equiangular** if the angles of the one are respectively equal to the angles of the other.

Thus, quadrilaterals ABCD and PQRS are equiangular if

$$\angle A = \angle P, \quad \angle B = \angle Q, \quad \angle C = \angle R, \quad \angle D = \angle S.$$

Two polygons are said to have their sides **proportional** if they have their corresponding sides in the same ratio.

Thus, quadrilaterals ABCD and PQRS have their sides proportional if

$$\frac{AB}{PQ} = \frac{BC}{QR} = \frac{CD}{RS} = \frac{DA}{SP}$$

Two polygons are said to be **similar** if they possess **both** these qualities, i.e. they are equiangular and have their sides proportional.

Similar figures should be named in such a way that the letters correspond.   Equal ratios can then be written down very easily.   Thus, if $\triangle s \; \frac{ABC}{PQR}$ are similar, we mean that

$$\angle A = \angle P, \quad \angle B = \angle Q, \quad \angle C = \angle R,$$

and that

$$\frac{AB}{PQ} = \frac{BC}{QR} = \frac{CA}{RP}.$$

Polygons can be equiangular without being similar.   For example, a rectangle 8 cm long and 3 cm wide and another rectangle 5 cm long and 4 cm wide have all their angles right angles, and they are therefore equiangular.   However, the ratio of their lengths is 8 : 5 and the ratio of their widths is 3 : 4, and these are not the same.   The sides are therefore not proportional, and the rectangles are not similar.

It is also obvious that polygons can have their sides proportional without being similar.   For example, a square with each side 2 cm and a rhombus with each side 3 cm have the ratio of their sides 2 : 3, but the angles of the square are not the same as those of the rhombus, so the figures are not similar.

EXERCISE 21

1 Draw △ABC in which BC = 8·0 cm, ∠B = 42°, ∠C = 55°. Measure AB and AC.

Draw also △PQR in which QR = 4·0 cm, ∠Q = 42°, ∠R = 55°. Measure PQ and PR, and compare your answers with AB and AC.

2 Draw △ABC in which BC = 9 cm, ∠B = 20°, ∠C = 49°. Measure AB and AC.

Draw also △PQR in which QR = 6 cm, ∠Q = 20°, ∠R = 49°. Measure PQ and PR; and test whether PQ and PR are the same fractions of AB and AC, respectively, as QR is of BC.

3 Draw △ABC in which AB = 4 cm, BC = 5 cm, CA = 6 cm. Measure the three angles of the triangle.

Draw also △PQR in which PQ is three-quarters of AB, QR is three-quarters of BC, and RP is three-quarters of CA. Measure the three angles of △PQR, and compare them with those of △ABC.

4 Draw △ABC in which AB = 4 cm, BC = 6 cm, CA = 8 cm. Measure the three angles of the triangle.

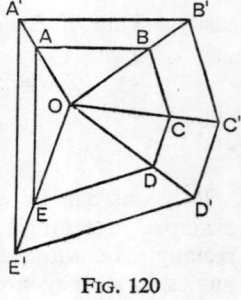

Draw also △PQR whose sides are four-fifths as long as those of △ABC. Measure the three angles of △PQR, and compare them with those of △ABC.

5 Draw a pentagon ABCDE in which ∠A = 90°, AB = 4 cm, ∠B = 110°, BC = 2·4 cm, ∠C = 142°, CD = 2 cm and ∠D = 130°.

Fig. 120

Construct a similar pentagon with each side one and a half times the corresponding side of ABCDE by the 'spider's web' method indicated in Fig. 120. O is taken anywhere inside or outside the pentagon; OA, OB, OC, OD, OE are produced to A', B', C', D', E', making OA' = 1½ OA, OB' = 1½ OB, and so on.

This is the principle of the magic lantern, where every part of the figure is magnified outwards from a point.

Similar triangles

The special importance of the triangle in map-making is due to the fact, brought out in Nos. 3 and 4 of the last Exercise, that the sides of a triangle can be increased or decreased in any given ratio without altering its angles. In fact, triangles which are equiangular necessarily have their corresponding sides proportional and are therefore similar; while triangles which have their corresponding sides proportional are necessarily equiangular, and are similar also. In No. 1 of the last Exercise the △s ABC, PQR were drawn so as to be equiangular, with QR one-half of BC. You should have found that PQ was one-half of AB, and PR one-half of AC. Similarly, in No. 2, QR was two-thirds of BC, and you should have found that PQ was two-thirds of AB, and PR two-thirds of AQ. Tests such as these show that:

If two triangles are equiangular, their corresponding sides are proportional.

In other words,

Equiangular triangles are similar.

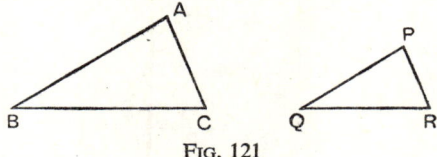

FIG. 121

Thus, in Fig. 121, if ∠A = ∠P, ∠B = ∠Q, ∠C = ∠R, then △s $\frac{ABC}{PQR}$ are similar, and

$$\frac{BC}{QR} = \frac{CA}{RP} = \frac{AB}{PQ}.$$

In No. 3 of the last Exercise, the triangles ABC, PQR have their corresponding sides proportional, each side of the latter being three-quarters of the corresponding side of the former.

You should have found that the triangles were equiangular. Similarly for No. 4, where each side of △PQR was four-fifths of the corresponding side of △ABC. The conclusion is that:

If the three sides of one triangle are proportional to the three sides of another triangle, then the triangles are equiangular, and therefore similar.

Thus, in Fig. 121, if

$$\frac{BC}{QR} = \frac{CA}{RP} = \frac{AB}{PQ},$$

then $\angle A = \angle P$, $\angle B = \angle Q$, $\angle C = \angle R$, and $\triangle s \, \frac{ABC}{PQR}$ are similar.

Two ways of comparing ratios of sides   Suppose that two triangles ABC, PQR have been proved to be equiangular. For shortness, let us denote the sides of △ABC by a, b, c, and those of △PQR by p, q, r, as in Fig. 122.

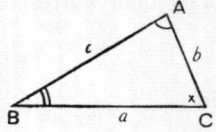
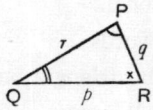

Fig. 122

Since $\triangle s \, \frac{ABC}{PQR}$ are equiangular, they are also similar.

$$\therefore \frac{BC}{QR} = \frac{CA}{RP} = \frac{AB}{PQ},$$

i.e.

$$\frac{a}{p} = \frac{b}{q} = \frac{c}{r}.$$

Consider the equation $\dfrac{a}{p} = \dfrac{b}{q}$.

Multiplying both sides by pq,

$$\frac{a}{\cancel{p}} \times \cancel{p}q = \frac{b}{\cancel{q}} \times p\cancel{q}.$$

$$\therefore \; aq = bp.$$

Now divide both sides by bq;

$$\frac{aq}{bq} = \frac{bp}{bq}.$$

$$\therefore \frac{a}{b} = \frac{p}{q}.$$

This shows that the two statements $\dfrac{a}{p} = \dfrac{b}{q}$ and $\dfrac{a}{b} = \dfrac{p}{q}$ are equivalent. Compare this with the statements $\frac{3}{4} = \frac{9}{12}$ and $\frac{3}{9} = \frac{4}{12}$ in arithmetic.

We see, then, that if two $\triangle$s $\begin{smallmatrix}ABC\\PQR\end{smallmatrix}$ have been proved to be equiangular and therefore similar, the equal ratios of sides can be written down in two ways:

$$(i)\quad \frac{BC}{QR} = \frac{CA}{RP} = \frac{AB}{PQ},$$

$$(ii)\quad \frac{BC}{CA} = \frac{QR}{RP} \quad \text{and} \quad \frac{CA}{AB} = \frac{RP}{PQ}.$$

EXERCISE 22

Give the reason why the pairs of triangles in Figs. 123–130 are similar. Express the fact in the form '$\triangle$s $\begin{smallmatrix}ABC\\PQR\end{smallmatrix}$ are similar,' and find the remaining sides and angles.

1

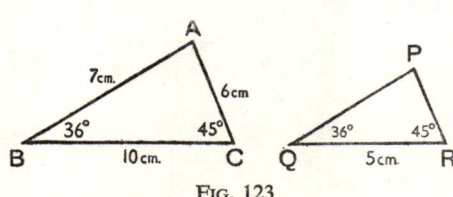

Fig. 123

2

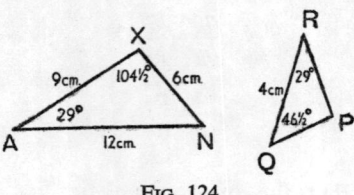

FIG. 124

3

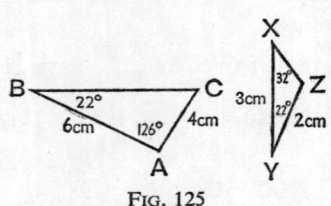

FIG. 125

4

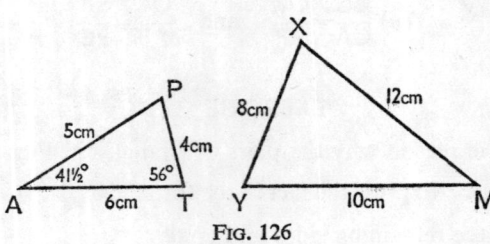

FIG. 126

5

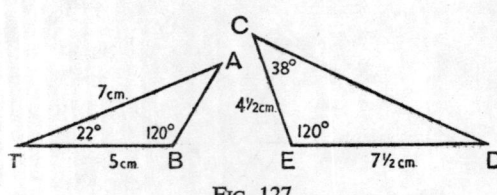

FIG. 127

6

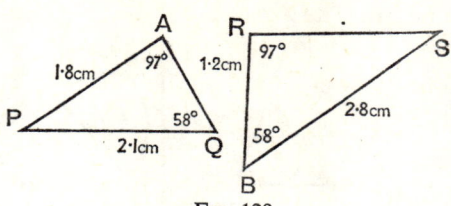

Fig. 128

7

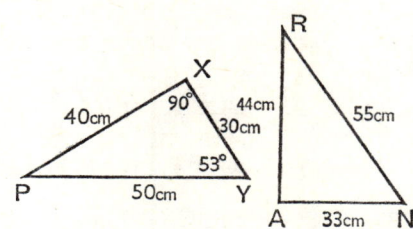

Fig. 129

8

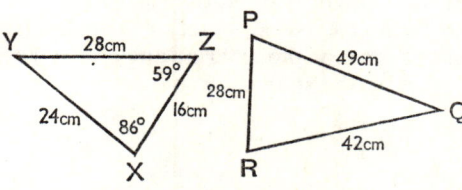

Fig. 130

9 In Fig. 131, on the next page, explain why △s $\begin{smallmatrix} AXY \\ ABC \end{smallmatrix}$ are similar, and complete the relations

(i) $\dfrac{AX}{AB} = \underline{} = \underline{}$,   (ii) $\dfrac{AX}{XY} = \quad$.

10 In Fig. 131, if $AX = 7$ cm, $AY = 6$ cm, $XY = 4$ cm and $BC = 7$ cm., calculate the lengths of AB and AC.

11 In Fig. 131, if $AB = 8$ cm, $BC = 6$ cm, $CA = 5\cdot2$ cm and $AX = 6$ cm, calculate XY and AY.

12 In Fig. 131, if AX = 3·5 cm, XY = 5 cm, AY = 2·5 cm and BC = 6 cm, calculate AB and YC.

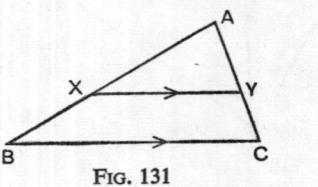

FIG. 131

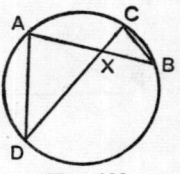

FIG. 132

13 In Fig. 132, where the two chords AB and CD of the circle intersect at X, point out two similar triangles, and complete the relations

(i) $\dfrac{AX}{CX} = \dfrac{XD}{\quad} = \dfrac{AD}{\quad}$; (ii) $\dfrac{AX}{AD} =$.

14 In Fig. 132, if AX = 6 cm, BX = 10 cm and DX = 12 cm, calculate CX.

15 In Fig. 132, if AX = 4 cm, CX = 3 cm, DX = 12 cm and AD = 10 cm., calculate BX and BC.

16 In Fig. 133, where two chords AB and CD of the circle are produced to intersect at X, point out two similar triangles. (*Hint:* use a property of the exterior angle of a cyclic quadrilateral.) Complete the statements

(i) $\dfrac{AC}{DB} = \dfrac{XA}{\quad} =$; (ii) $\dfrac{AC}{XC} =$.

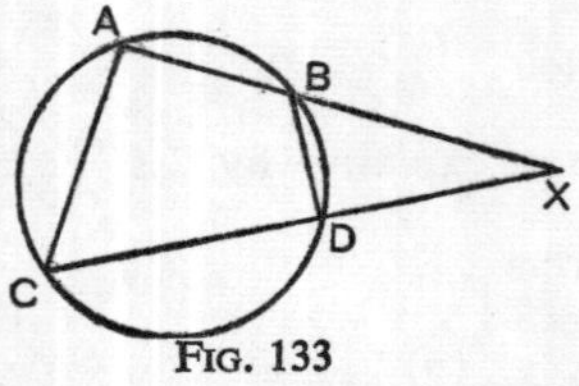

FIG. 133

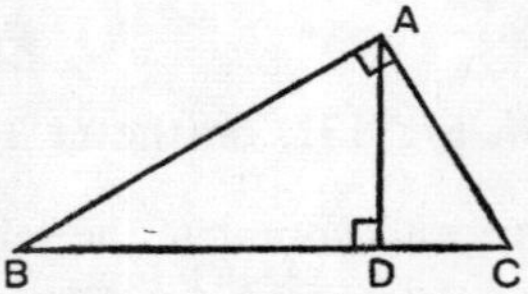

FIG. 134

17 In Fig. 134, explain why $\triangle$s $\begin{smallmatrix} ADB \\ CAB \end{smallmatrix}$ are similar, and complete the relations

(i) $\dfrac{AD}{BD} = \dfrac{CA}{\quad}$; (ii) $\dfrac{AD}{AB} =$.

18 A vertical pole 4 m high casts a shadow 1½ m long, and at the same moment a flagstaff casts a shadow 15 m long. Calculate the height of the flagstaff. (The triangle formed by the pole and its shadow is similar to that formed by the flagstaff and its shadow.)

11. TANGENT, SINE AND COSINE (I)

The tangent of an angle

IN Fig. 135, AOB is an angle of 35°; OP = 4 cm, OQ = 5 cm, OR = 8 cm, and PL, QM, RN are perpendicular to OB.

The triangles LPO, MQO, NRO are similar, for they each have an angle of 35° and a right angle.

$$\therefore \frac{LP}{OP} = \frac{MQ}{OQ} = \frac{NR}{OR}.$$

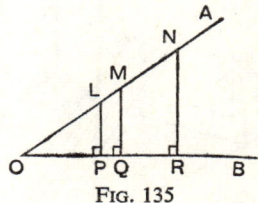

FIG. 135

You should make an accurate drawing of Fig. 135, and measure LP, MQ, NR, thus obtaining the values of the three ratios given above. The value of each ratio will be found to be approximately 0·7 in the case of an angle of 35°. It is evident that the value does not depend on the lengths of OP, OQ, OR, but only on the size of the angle AOB.

This constant ratio is called the **tangent of** ∠AOB, and is written **tan AOB**. Its value, when ∠AOB = 35°, has thus been found to be about 0·7, a fact which is written

$$\tan 35° = 0·7 \text{ (approx.).}$$

Definition If N is the foot of the perpendicular drawn from any point P in either arm of the angle AOB to the other arm, the ratio $\dfrac{PN}{ON}$ is called the **tangent of the angle** AOB.

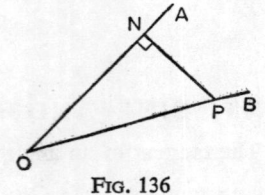

FIG. 136

Thus, in Fig. 136,

$$\textbf{tan AOB} = \frac{\textbf{opposite side (PN)}}{\textbf{adjacent side (ON)}}.$$

Fig. 137 shows how Thales, a Greek mathematician who

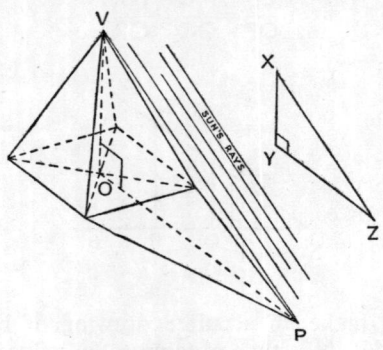

FIG. 137

lived about 600 B.C., found the height of a pyramid. O is the centre of the square base, VO is the height of the pyramid, and P is the tip of the shadow. At the same instant a vertical pole XY casts a shadow YZ.

The triangles VOP, XYZ are obviously similar.

$$\therefore \frac{VO}{OP} = \frac{XY}{YZ}.$$

By measuring OP (which is the length of the shadow of the pyramid + half the side of the base), XY and YZ, Thales was able to calculate VO, the height of the pyramid. He was in reality using the *tangent* of ∠VPO, but instead of saying that $\frac{VO}{OP}$ was equal to tan VPO, he calculated the tangent of the angle by dividing the height of a pole by the length of its shadow, i.e. $\frac{XY}{YZ}$.

Trigonometrical ratios The tangent is one of several ratios which are called trigonometrical ratios. The word 'trigonometry' is derived from two Greek words meaning 'a triangle' and 'measure', and the study of the science began in Greece in the second century B.C. The original object of the science was a practical one, namely, the calculation of the sides and angles of a triangle, and trigonometry was invented in order to meet the growing needs of astronomy. Just as 'earth-measuring' (geometry) grew beyond the needs of surveying, so 'triangle-measuring' (trigonometry) came in time to include a wider range of problems than those for which it was originally intended.

Tangents of angles found by drawing

Example 1 *Find by drawing and measurement* (i) *the value of tan* 42°, (ii) *the angle whose tangent is* 1·6.

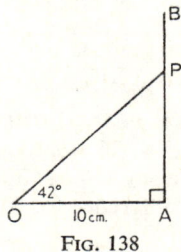

Fig. 138

(i) Draw a line OA 10 cm long, and draw a line AB perpendicular to OA. (It saves time to use graph paper.)

Make ∠AOP equal to 42°, P lying on AB.
By measurement, PA is found to be 9 cm.

$$\therefore \tan 42° = \frac{PA}{OA} = 0.9.$$

(ii) Draw OA and AB as before, and cut off from AB a length
AQ 16 cm long.   Join OQ, as in Fig. 139.

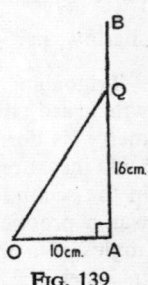

Then $\tan QOA = \dfrac{QA}{OA} = 1.6.$

∴ QOA is the required angle.
By measurement, ∠QOA = 58°.

Tangent tables   The method just described
for finding the tangents of angles by drawing
and measurement could not give the result to
more than two significant figures, and it is
not necessary to find them in this way as they
have all been calculated, and the results,

Fig. 139

correct to four significant figures, are given in the table of
Natural Tangents at the end of this book.   (They are called
natural tangents' to distinguish them from the logarithms of
tangents, otherwise known as 'logarithmic tangents'.)   The
table gives the tangents of angles from 0° to 90° at intervals of
6′, and by using the difference-columns at the side of the page
we can find the values of the tangent for intervals of 1′.   This
is an extract from the table of Natural Tangents:

	0′	6′	12′	18′	24′	30′	36′	42′	48′	54′	1′	2′	3′	4′	5′
64	2·0503	0594	0686	0778	0872	0965	1060	1155	1251	1348	16	31	47	63	78

From this we see that tan 64° = 2·0503,
                          tan 64° 36′ = 2·1060.
To find tan 64° 39′, we say tan 64° 36′ = 2·1060
                          add difference for 3′ = 0·0047

                          ∴ tan 64° 39′ = 2·1107.

You should check that the tangent of 64° 39′ lies between
tan 64° 36′ and tan 64° 42′.

As you will find later (§ 17) in the case of all other **four-figure** tables, such as squares, square roots and logarithms, the fourth decimal place is not absolutely reliable, and the results obtained by using tangent tables are not exact.   Always retain *four* figures throughout the working, and whenever a result is used in subsequent calculation, but give the final answer correct to *three* significant figures.

Example 2   *In* △ABC, ∠A = 90°, ∠B = 52° *and* AB = 5 *cm. Calculate* AC.

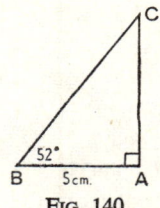

Fig. 140

$$\frac{AC}{5} = \tan 52°.$$

$$\therefore \ AC = 5 \tan 52°$$
$$= 5 \times 1·2799 = 6·3995.$$
$$\therefore \ AC = 6·40 \text{ cm (approx.)}.$$

Example 3   *In* △ABC, ∠A = 90°, AB = 8 *cm*, AC = 6 *cm. Calculate* ∠CBA.

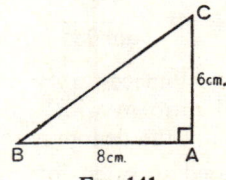

Fig. 141

$$\tan CBA = \frac{CA}{AB} = \frac{6}{8} = 0·75.$$

From the tables,   ∠CBA = 36° 52′.

Example 4 *A man on the top of a cliff 150 m high observes that the angle of depression of a boat at sea is 28°. Calculate the distance of the boat from the foot of the cliff.*

In Fig. 142, PQ represents the cliff, B the boat, and PA the horizontal through P. Suppose that QB = x metres.

$$\angle QPB = 90° - \angle APB$$
$$= 90° - 28° = 62°.$$

$$\therefore \frac{BQ}{PQ} = \tan 62°.$$

FIG. 142

$$\therefore \frac{x}{150} = \tan 62°.$$

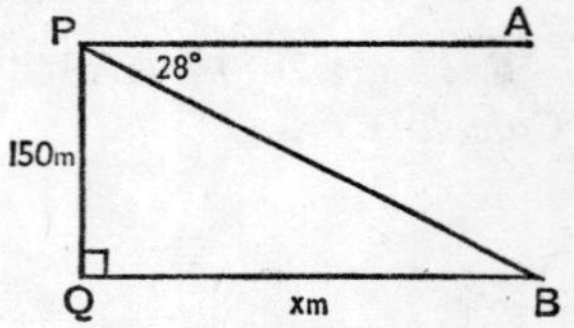

$$\therefore x = 150 \tan 62°$$
$$= 150 \times 1·8807$$
$$= 188·07 + 94·035 = 282·105.$$

∴ the distance of the boat from the foot of the cliff = 282 m (approx.).

Note This problem should not be solved as follows:

$$\tan PBQ = \frac{PQ}{QB}.$$

$$\therefore \quad \tan 28° = \frac{150}{x}.$$

$$\therefore \ x \tan 28° = 150.$$

$$\therefore \qquad x = \frac{150}{\tan 28°} = \frac{150}{0·5317}, \text{ etc.}$$

This method leads to unnecessary working. Always try to use a trigonometrical ratio in which the unknown quantity forms the *numerator*, not the denominator.

Greek letters are used so often for angles in trigonometry that you should learn the most frequent ones:

α	pronounced	alpha	θ	pronounced	theeta
β	„	beeta	φ	„	fie
γ	„	gamma			

EXERCISE 23

1 Find, by drawing and measurement (preferably on squared paper), the values of tan 20°, tan 30°, tan 45°, tan 50°, tan 60°. Compare your answers with those obtained from tables.

2 Find, by drawing and measurement, the angles whose tangents are 0·2, 0·8, 1·2, 2·1. Compare your answers with those obtained from tables.

3 Find from the tables the tangents of 18° 6′, 28° 27′, 41° 53′, 60° 35′, 75° 7′.

4 Find from the tables the angles whose tangents are: 0·4942, 0·9163, 2·0145, 1·1394, 0·7169, 2·7981.

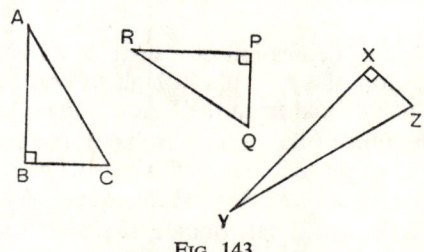

FIG. 143

Nos. 5–17 refer to Fig. 143, in which all the triangles are right-angled.

5 Write down expressions for (i) tan BAC, (ii) tan PQR, (iii) tan XYZ.

6 Write down expressions for (i) $\dfrac{AB}{BC}$, (ii) $\dfrac{XY}{XZ}$, (iii) $\dfrac{PQ}{PR}$.

7 BC = 5 cm, ∠ACB = 63°. Find AB.

8 PR = 8 cm, ∠PRQ = 32°. Find PQ.

9 XZ = 3 cm, ∠XZY = 58°. Find XY.

10 PR = 2·8 cm, PQ = 2 cm. Find ∠PQR.

11 AB = 5 cm, BC = 4 cm. Find ∠BAC.

12 PQ = 2·7 cm, PR = 3·6 cm. Find ∠PRQ.

13 XY = 8 cm, XZ = 3·17 cm. Find ∠XZY. (First find ∠XYZ.)

14 AB = 20 cm, BC = 9·46 cm. Find ∠ACB.

15 PR = 5 cm, ∠PQR = 65°. Find PQ. (First find ∠PRQ.)

16 AB = 4 cm, ∠ACB = 56°. Find BC.

17 XZ = 2 cm, ∠XYZ = 28°. Find XY.

18 The angle of elevation of the top of a tree from a point on the ground 30 m from its foot is 32°. Calculate the height of the tree.

19 Calculate the angle of elevation of the top of a tower 120 m high from a point on the ground 80 m from the foot of the tower.

20 P is 50 km N. and 41 km E. of Q. Calculate the bearing of P from Q.

21 The angle of depression of a boat at sea is observed by a man on the top of a cliff 100 m high to be 30°. Calculate the distance of the boat from the foot of the cliff.

22 N is the foot of the perpendicular from the centre O of a circle to a chord AB. If ∠OAB = 63° and AB = 4 cm, calculate ON. (First find AN, which equals ½AB.)

23 ABC is an equilateral triangle of side 10 cm; AD is an altitude. Find BD, AD and the area of the triangle.

24 A ladder leaning against a vertical wall makes an angle of 70° with the ground. Its foot is 2 m from the wall. Calculate the height above the ground of the top of the ladder.

25 Calculate the length of the shadow of a vertical flagstaff which is 10 m high, the sun's rays making an angle of 52° with the ground.

26 The sides of a rectangle are 3·5 cm and 4·2 cm. Calculate the angles which a diagonal makes with the sides.

27 A is 10 km N. of a point O, and B is 18 km E. of A. Calculate the bearing of B from O.

28 The steps of a staircase have a rise of 21 cm and a tread of 31·5 cm. Find the angle which the banister rail makes with the horizontal.

29 O is the centre of a circle of radius 2 cm and A is a point on the circumference. The tangent at A is drawn, and P is a point on the tangent such that ∠OPA = 20°. Calculate AP. (Assume that ∠OAP is a right angle.)

30 The diagonals of a rhombus are 10 cm and 12 cm long. Calculate the angles of the figure.

31 Use Thales' method (see Fig. 137) to find the height of a pyramid from the following information:

The pyramid is on a square base of side 252 m. It casts a shadow, measured from the base of the pyramid, 67 m long. At the same moment a pole 3 m high casts a shadow 3·6 m long. Find the height of the pyramid, and the sun's elevation at that moment. (These measurements are taken from the Great Pyramid of Gizeh, in Egypt.)

The sine and cosine of an angle

Suppose we draw any angle AOB, and mark a series of points P, Q, R . . . along OA, as in Fig. 144.

If we now draw perpendiculars PL, QM, RN . . . to OB, it is evident that the △s PLO, QMO, RNO . . . are equiangular and therefore similar.

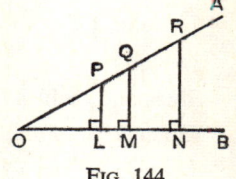

$$\therefore \frac{PL}{OP} = \frac{QM}{OQ} = \frac{RN}{OR} = \cdots$$

Thus the ratio $\dfrac{PL}{OP}$ does not depend on

FIG. 144

the length of OP, but only on the size of ∠AOB. This constant ratio is called the **sine of** ∠AOB, and is written **sin** AOB.

It is also true in the same figure that the ratios

$$\frac{OL}{OP}, \frac{OM}{OQ}, \frac{ON}{OR} \cdots$$

are equal, and that the value of the ratio $\dfrac{OL}{OP}$ depends only on the size of ∠AOB. This constant ratio is called the **cosine of** ∠AOB, and is written **cos** AOB.

Definition If N is the foot of the perpendicular from any point P in either arm of ∠AOB to the other arm, the ratio $\dfrac{PN}{OP}$ is called the **sine of** ∠AOB; and the ratio $\dfrac{ON}{OP}$ is called the **cosine of** ∠AOB.

Thus, in Fig. 145,

$$\sin AOB = \frac{\text{opposite side (PN)}}{\text{hypotenuse (OP)}},$$

and

$$\cos AOB = \frac{\text{adjacent side (ON)}}{\text{hypotenuse (OP)}}.$$

Notice that the first three letters of the words tangent, sine, and cosine are used to stand for these ratios.

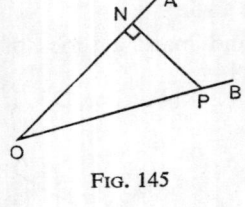

FIG. 145

Notice also that the sine and the cosine of an angle can never be greater than 1, since they are both fractions with the hypotenuse (the greatest side of a right-angled triangle) as denominator. The tangent, on the other hand, may have any value.

Sines and cosines found by drawing

Example 5 *Find, by drawing and measurement, the values of* sin 22°, cos 22°, sin 42°, cos 42°, sin 67°, cos 67°.

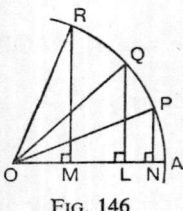

FIG. 146

Draw a portion of a circle with centre O and radius 10 cm. (Graph paper saves time.)

Mark a radius OA, and draw radii OP, OQ, OR such that ∠AOP = 22°, ∠AOQ = 42°, and ∠AOR = 67°. Draw PN, QL, RM perpendicular to OA, as in Fig. 146.

By measurement, we find that PN = 3·75 cm, QL = 6·70 cm, RM = 9·20 cm.

Also ON = 9·3 cm, OL = 7·4 cm, OM = 3·9 cm.

$\therefore$, approximately, $\sin 22° = \dfrac{PN}{OP} = \dfrac{3·7}{10} = 0·37.$

$\cos 22° = \dfrac{ON}{OP} = \dfrac{9·3}{10} = 0·93.$

$\sin 42° = \dfrac{QL}{OQ} = \dfrac{6·70}{10} = 0·67.$

$\cos 42° = \dfrac{OL}{OQ} = \dfrac{7·4}{10} = 0·74.$

$\sin 67° = \dfrac{RM}{OR} = \dfrac{9·20}{10} = 0·92.$

$\cos 67° = \dfrac{OM}{OR} = \dfrac{3·9}{10} = 0·39.$

Example 6 *Find by drawing and measurement the angle whose cosine is* 0·53.

Draw a line ON 5·3 cm long.   (See Fig. 147.)

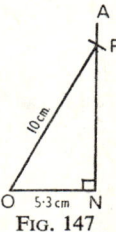

Fig. 147

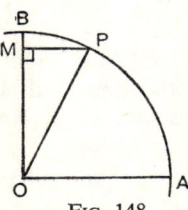

Fig. 148

Draw NA perpendicular to ON.

With centre O and radius 10 cm, draw an arc to cut AN at P.

Then PON is the required angle, since $\cos PON = \dfrac{ON}{OP} = 0·53.$

By measurement, $\angle PON$ is found to be about 58°.

Example 7 *Find by drawing and measurement the angle whose sine is* 0·89.

With centre O and radius 10 cm, draw a part of a circle, and mark two perpendicular radii OA, OB, as in Fig. 148.

Along OB, cut off OM equal to 8·9 cm.

Draw MP perpendicular to OB to meet the circle at P, and join OP.

Then POA is the required angle, for

$$\angle POA = \angle OPM \text{ (alt., MP } \| \text{ OA)},$$

and

$$\sin OPM = \frac{OM}{OP} = \frac{8·9}{10} = 0·89.$$

By measurement, $\angle POA$ is found to be about 63°.

Sine and cosine tables. It is clear from Fig. 146 that, if we compare the sines of the angles PON, QOL and ROM, we find that as the angle *increases*, the sine *increases*; for RM is greater than QL, and QL is greater than PN.

If, however, we compare the cosines of these angles, we find that as the angle *increases*, the cosine *decreases*; for OM is less than OL, and OL is less than ON.

If you look at the tables of sines and cosines at the end of the book, you will see that as the angle increases from 0° to 90°, the sine increases from 0 to 1, but the cosine decreases from 1 to 0. Tables of sines are used just like tables of tangents, the figures in the different columns being *added*: e.g. to find sin 38° 20', we say

$$\sin 39° \ 18' = 0·6334$$
$$\text{add difference for } 2' = 0·0004$$

$$\therefore \ \sin 39° \ 20' = 0·6338.$$

In the case of cosine tables, however, for the reason given above, figures in the difference columns are *subtracted*. There is a reminder of this fact at the top of the difference columns.

Thus, to find cos 39° 20', we say

$$\cos 39° \ 18' = 0·7738$$
$$\text{subtract difference for } 2' = 0·0004$$

$$\therefore \ \cos 39° \ 20' = 0·7734.$$

When reading off cos 39° 20', always check that your answer lies between cos 39° 18' and cos 39° 24'.

Complementary angles. In Fig. 149, ∠PON and ∠OPN are complementary angles, i.e. their sum is 90°.

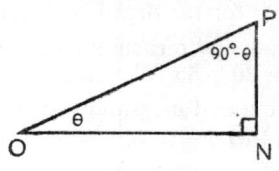

FIG. 149

$$\sin \theta = \frac{PN}{OP} = \cos(90° - \theta).$$

Thus, $\sin 60° = \cos 30°,$
         $\sin 10° = \cos 80°,$ and so on.

In other words, **the cosine of an angle is the sine of its complement, and the sine of an angle is the cosine of its complement.**

This is the reason for the prefix 'co' in the word cosine.

If cosine tables are not available, use the sine tables by looking up the sine of the complement of the given angle.

Example 8   *A ladder 7 m long rests on the ground at 52° to the horizontal, and leans against a vertical wall. Calculate how high up the wall the ladder reaches, and the distance of the foot of the ladder from the wall.*

In Fig. 150, AB is the ladder; △ANB is right-angled.

$$\therefore \ \frac{BN}{AB} = \sin 52°.$$

$$\therefore \ \frac{BN}{7} = 0.7880.$$

$$\therefore \ BN = 7 \times 0.7880 = 5.5160 \text{ m, or}$$
5·52 m (to 3 sig. figs.).

Also $\dfrac{AN}{AB} = \cos 52°.$

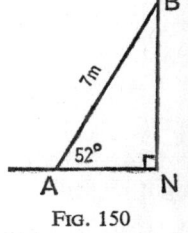

FIG. 150

$$\therefore \ \frac{AN}{7} = 0.6157.$$

$$\therefore \ AN = 7 \times 0.6157 = 4.3099 \text{ m, or } 4.31 \text{ m (to 3 sig. figs.).}$$

EXERCISE 24

Use squared paper for the drawing exercises.

1 Find, by drawing and measurement, the values of sin 18°, cos 18°, sin 30°, cos 30°, sin 70°, cos 70°.

2 Find, by drawing and measurement, the angle whose sine is: (i) ¾, (ii) 0·6, (iii) 0·47.

3 Find, by drawing and measurement, the angle whose cosine is: (i) ½, (ii) 0·65, (iii) 0·32.

4 Find from tables the sines of the following angles: (i) 15°, (ii) 27°, (iii) 18° 6′, (iv) 42° 22′, (v) 68° 51′, (vi) 29° 8′, (vii) 22° 27′, (viii) 42° 53′, (ix) 35° 35′, (x) 61° 11′.

5 Find from tables the cosines of the angles in No. 4.

6 Find from the tables the angles whose sines are: (i) 0·3453, (ii) 0·8599, (iii) 0·7828, (iv) 0·5712, (v) 0·5188, (vi) 0·9458, (vii) 0·7150, (viii) 0·1395, (ix) 0·7049, (x) 0·3512.

7 Find from the tables the angles whose cosines are: (i) 0·9128, (ii) 0·4289, (iii) 0·6667, (iv) 0·5340, (v) 0·2371, (vi) 0·8044, (vii) 0·9560, (viii) 0·1712, (ix) 0·6052, (x) 0·3181.

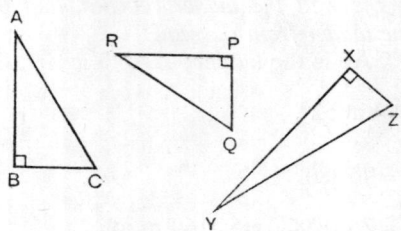

Fig. 151

Nos. 8–14 refer to Fig. 151 where all the triangles are right-angled.

8 Write down expressions for: (i) sin BAC, (ii) cos PRQ, (iii) sin XZY, (iv) sin PQR, (v) cos XZY, (vi) tan ACB, (vii) cos ACB, (viii) tan XYZ, (ix) cos XYZ, (x) sin ACB.

9 Write down expressions for the following, giving more than one answer in some cases:

(i) $\dfrac{AB}{AC}$ (ii) $\dfrac{PR}{PQ}$ (iii) $\dfrac{XZ}{YZ}$ (iv) $\dfrac{BC}{AB}$ (v) $\dfrac{PQ}{RQ}$

(vi) $\dfrac{XY}{YZ}$ (vii) $\dfrac{BC}{AC}$ (viii) $\dfrac{RP}{RQ}$ (ix) $\dfrac{XY}{XZ}$ (x) $\dfrac{AB}{BC}$

10 AC = 10 cm, $\angle ACB = 64°$; find AB and BC.

11 QR = 5 cm, $\angle PQR = 55°$; find PQ and PR.

12 YZ = 6 cm, $\angle XYZ = 25°$; find XY and XZ.

13 PQ = 2 cm, QR = 5 cm; find $\angle PRQ$.

14 AB = 6 cm, AC = 10 cm; find $\angle CAB$.

15 The diagonal of a rectangle is 16 cm long and makes an angle of 31° with one of the sides. Find the length and breadth of the rectangle.

16 A ladder 9 m long leans against a wall, and the foot is 2 m from the wall. Find the inclination of the ladder to the ground.

17 The string of a kite is straight, and 80 m long. It makes an angle of 54° with the horizontal. Find the height of the kite.

18 AB is a chord of a circle whose centre is O and radius 5 cm. If $\angle AOB = 80°$, calculate the length of AB. (Draw ON perpendicular to AB, and assume that $\triangle$s ONA, ONB are congruent.)

19 A circle has centre O and radius 5 cm. A is a point 15 cm from O, and T is the point of contact of the tangent from A. Calculate $\angle OAT$. (Assume that $\angle OTA = 90°$.)

20 A man walks 100 m up a slope of 12°. Through what vertical height has he risen?

21 ABCD is a rhombus in which AB = 5 cm and $\angle ABC = 70°$. Calculate the lengths of AC and BD.

EXERCISE 25

(Miscellaneous examples on sine, cosine and tangent)

1 A man, standing 100 m from the foot of a tower, observes that the angle of elevation of the top is 46°. Find the height of the tower.

2 A ladder 8 m long stands against a vertical wall, its foot being 2·2 m from the wall. Find the angle between the ladder and the wall.

3 A hill slopes upwards at an angle of 25° with the horizontal. Through what vertical height does a man rise when he walks 80 m up the slope?

4 A man on the top of a cliff 120 m high sees that the angle of depression of a boat at sea is 34°. How far is the boat from the foot of the cliff?

5 A man starts from O and walks 150 m on a bearing 025°. How far east of O is he then? How far north of O?

6 Calculate the angle of elevation of the top of a tower 42 m high from a point on the ground 25·2 m from the foot.

7 The pole of a bell-tent is 3 m long, and the length of the slant side of the tent is 4 m. Find the angle between the slant side and the ground.

8 The base of an isosceles triangle is 10 cm and the vertical angle is 74°. Calculate the length of the altitude drawn from the vertex to the base.

9 The string of a kite is 200 m long and makes an angle of 44° with the ground. Calculate the height of the kite.

10 A picture measures 150 cm from top to bottom, and rests with its lower edge against a wall, making an angle of 14° with it. Find the distance of the top of the picture from the wall.

11 A regular pentagon (five sides) is inscribed in a circle of radius 3 cm. Calculate the length of a side. (Draw a perpendicular from the centre of the circle to a side.)

12 Two men, standing on opposite sides of a tower 30 m high, measure the angles of elevation of the top as 33° and 26°. Calculate the distance apart of the men.

13 A pendulum 2 m long swings backwards and forwards through an angle of 15° each side of the vertical. Find to the nearest centimetre how high the tip of the pendulum rises above its lowest position.

14 Calculate the length of the base of an isosceles triangle in which the equal sides are each 4 cm long and the vertical angle is 110°.

15 The shadow of a telegraph pole is 4 m long when the sun's rays make an angle of 58° with the ground. Calculate the height of the pole.

16 A parallelogram has sides 4 cm, 6 cm and an angle of 65°. Calculate its area. (First draw the height of the parallelogram.)

17 The legs of a pair of compasses are 6 cm long. Find the distance between their tips if the legs contain an angle of 74°.

18 Calculate the height and the base of an isosceles triangle ABC with AB = AC = 4 cm and the vertical angle BAC = 26°.

19 ABC is a triangle right-angled at B, and AB = 10 cm; D is a point in BC such that the angle ADB = 67° 20′ and DC = 8 cm. Calculate BD and the angle ACB.

20 AB is a side of a regular pentagon (five-sided figure) inscribed in a circle of radius 5 cm, P is the mid-point of the arc AB. Calculate AB, PA and the distance of P from AB.

21 AB is a chord of a circle of radius 8 cm, O is the centre of the circle, and the angle AOB = 150°. Calculate the length of AB.
The tangents to the circle at A, B meet at T. Calculate AT. (The angles OAT, OBT are right angles.)

22 A regular ten-sided figure is inscribed in a circle of radius 2 cm. Calculate the length of a side and the perpendicular distance of a side from the centre of the circle.

23 ABCD is a trapezium in which AB is parallel to DC, the angle ADC = 64° 16′, N is the foot of the perpendicular from A to DC, AN = 12 cm, and BC = 18 cm. Calculate DN and the angle BCD.

24 The angle of depression of a boat at sea, from a point on a cliff top, is 8°. The boat is 800 m from the foot of the cliff. Find the height of the cliff.

If the boat comes 200 m nearer the cliff, what is then the angle of depression of the boat from the top of the cliff?

25 The triangle ABC is obtuse-angled at B, AB = 33 cm, BC = 25 cm; N is the foot of the perpendicular from C to AB produced, and CN = 24 cm. Calculate the angles BAC, ABC.

26 ABCD is a rhombus of side 5 cm. The diagonal AC is 5·6 cm long. Calculate the angle DAB and the other diagonal BD.

27 In the trapezium ABCD, the angles at B and C are right angles, the angle DAB = 122° 38′, AB = 6 cm, AD = 4 cm. Calculate BC and CD.

12. SIMPLE INTEREST

THE simple interest formula $I = \dfrac{P \times R \times T}{100}$ was proved in Part I (p. 260); £P is the principal, R the rate per cent per annum, T the number of years, £I the interest. Exercise 26 provides a short revision of the use of the formula.

EXERCISE 26

Find the simple interest and the amount in the following cases:

1 £600 for $3\frac{1}{2}$ years at 2% p.a.

2 £250 for 3 years at 3% p.a.

3 £60 for 1 year 3 months at 5% p.a.

4 £316 for $2\frac{1}{2}$ years at $3\frac{1}{2}\%$ p.a.

5 £79·50 for 2 years at 3% p.a.

6 £49·60 for 10 months at $2\frac{1}{4}\%$ p.a.

Find to the nearest penny the simple interest on:

7 £62·92 for 1 year 3 months at $2\frac{1}{2}\%$ p.a.

8 £516 for 2 years 9 months at $5\frac{1}{2}\%$ p.a.

9 £253 for 6 months at $3\frac{1}{4}\%$ p.a.

10 £401·19 for $1\frac{1}{2}$ years at 4% p.a.

Inverse problems The simple interest formula has hitherto been used in order to find I when the values of P, R and T are given. The same formula can be used in inverse problems; for example, if we know I, P and T, we can find R. This type of problem is illustrated in the worked examples which follow.

Example 1 *The simple interest on £750 for 2 years is £67·50. Find the rate per cent per annum.*

Let the rate $= R\%$ p.a.

Then the simple interest $= £\dfrac{750 \times R \times 2}{100} = £67\frac{1}{2}.$

$$\therefore \quad \dfrac{750 \times R \times 2}{100} = \dfrac{135}{2}.$$

$$15R = \dfrac{135}{2}.$$

$$\therefore \quad R = \dfrac{135}{2 \times 15} = 4\frac{1}{2}.$$

$$\therefore \qquad \text{the rate} = 4\frac{1}{2}\% \text{ p.a.}$$

Example 2 *Find the principal on which the simple interest for $1\frac{1}{4}$ years at $5\frac{1}{3}\%$ p.a. is £24.*

Let the principal be £P.   Then the interest $= £\dfrac{P \times 5\frac{1}{3} \times 1\frac{1}{4}}{100}$.

$$\therefore \quad \frac{P \times \overset{4}{\cancel{16}} \times \cancel{5}}{\underset{20}{3 \times \cancel{4}} \times \underset{5}{\cancel{100}}} = 24.$$

$$\therefore \qquad \frac{P}{15} = 24, \quad \text{and } P = 360.$$

$\therefore$ the principal $= £360$.

Example 3 *Find the time in which £960 amounts to £1059 at $2\frac{3}{4}\%$ p.a. simple interest.*

Let the time $= T$ years. Then the interest $= £\dfrac{960 \times 2\frac{3}{4} \times T}{100}$.

But the interest $= £1059 - £960 = £99$.

$$\therefore \quad \frac{960 \times 2\frac{3}{4} \times T}{100} = 99.$$

$$\therefore \quad \frac{\overset{12}{\cancel{960}} \times 11 \times T}{\underset{5}{4 \times \cancel{100}}} = 99.$$

$$\therefore \qquad T = \frac{\overset{3}{\cancel{9}}\cancel{9} \times 5}{\underset{4}{\cancel{12}} \times \cancel{11}} = 3\frac{3}{4}.$$

$\therefore$ the time is 3 years 9 months.

Example 4 *Find what principal amounts at simple interest to £400·50 in $2\frac{1}{2}$ years at $4\frac{1}{2}\%$ p.a.*

Let the principal $= £P$.

Then the interest $= £\dfrac{P \times 2\frac{1}{2} \times 4\frac{1}{2}}{100}$

$$= £\frac{P \times \cancel{5} \times 9}{2 \times 2 \times \cancel{100}} = £\frac{9P}{80}.$$
$$20$$

$\therefore$ the amount $= £P + £\dfrac{9P}{80} = £400\frac{1}{2}.$

$\therefore \qquad P + \dfrac{9P}{80} = \dfrac{801}{2}.$

$$40$$

$\therefore \qquad 80P + 9P = \dfrac{801 \times \cancel{80}}{\cancel{2}}.$

$\therefore \qquad 89P = 801 \times 40.$

$$9$$

$\therefore \qquad P = \dfrac{\cancel{801} \times 40}{\cancel{89}} = 360.$

$\therefore$ the principal $= £360.$

EXERCISE 27

Find the rate per cent per annum if:

1 The simple interest on £280 for 3 years is £29·40.

2 The simple interest on £350 for $1\frac{1}{2}$ years is £31·50.

3 The simple interest on £840 for $3\frac{1}{2}$ years is £132·30.

Find the principal on which:

4 The simple interest for $2\frac{1}{2}$ years at $4\frac{1}{2}\%$ p.a. is £81.

5 The simple interest for 3 years at $1\frac{1}{4}\%$ p.a. is £64·50.

6 The simple interest for 1 year 8 months at $1\frac{3}{4}\%$ p.a. is £35·70.

Find the time in which:

7 The simple interest on £320 at $1\frac{1}{2}\%$ p.a. is £18.

8 The simple interest on £560 at $5\frac{1}{4}\%$ p.a. is £7·35.

9 The simple interest on £240 at $4\frac{1}{2}\%$ p.a. is £36.

Find what sum of money at simple interest amounts to:

10 £486 in 2 years at 4% p.a.

11 £134·85 in $3\frac{1}{2}$ years at $2\frac{1}{2}\%$ p.a.

12 £90 in 10 months at 5% p.a.

13 In what time will £4 amount to £6·25 at 5% p.a. simple interest?

14 A boy who kept the same sum of money in a savings bank for a whole year found at the end of the year that the interest was £3·15. If the rate was 2½%, find how much he had in the bank.

15 A certain issue of National Savings Certificates cost £1 and amounted to £1·25 in 5 years. Find the rate per cent per annum simple interest to which this is equivalent.

16 In how many years will £100 amount to £200 at 15% p.a. simple interest?

17 A boy borrows 30p from another boy, and agrees to pay him one penny a month simple interest. Find the rate per cent per annum.

18 A man borrowed a sum of money, and the interest for 6 months at 3% p.a. was £3·15. Find how much he borrowed.

19 A man borrows a sum of money at 8% p.a. simple interest, and discharges the debt, principal and interest, at the end of 2 years by repaying £870. How much was the loan?

20 What sum of money will yield £81 simple interest in 2½ years at 2¼% p.a.?

21 The simple interest on a certain sum of money at 3% for 5 years exceeds the simple interest on the same sum at 4% for 3 years by £36. Find the sum.

22 At what rate per cent p.a. is the interest on £48 for 1 year the same as the interest on £72 for 1 year at 2½%?

23 After how many years is the simple interest on £240 at 4% p.a. equal to £33·60?

24 A man borrows £56 at 4½% p.a. At the end of 3 months he pays back £20. How much does he still owe, including interest?

25 A man borrowed £100 from the bank at 5½% simple interest, and when he repaid the loan the interest was £1·10. Find the number of days for which the money was borrowed.

36 Find in what time the simple interest on £96 at 2¾% p.a. is £4·40.

13. PLAN AND ELEVATION

THE principles underlying the methods of drawing plans and elevations were explained in sections 25 and 47 of Part I. The present section revises that work and contains some miscellaneous applications to various solids.

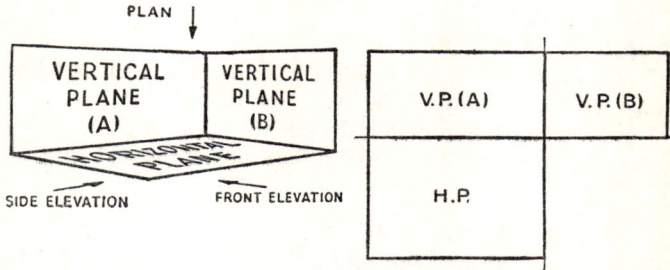

FIG. 152

Fig. 152 shows the arrangement of the planes on which the projections are made. In the exercises which follow, these planes will be referred to as the H.P., the V.P. (A) and the V.P. (B).

The plan is the projection on the H.P.; the front elevation is the projection on the V.P. (A); the side elevation is the projection on the V.P. (B).

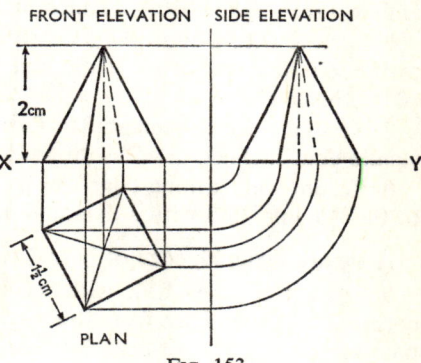

FIG. 153

Fig. 153 shows the plan, front elevation and side elevation of a square pyramid, height 2 cm and edge of base 1½ cm, standing on the H.P. with an edge of the base inclined at an angle of 30° with the XY line and a corner of the base ½ cm from that line.

EXERCISE 28

Draw the plan, front elevation and side elevation of the following solids:

A **cube** of edge 3 cm:

1 With one face on the H.P. and one vertical face making an angle of 30° with the V.P. (A).

2 Resting on an edge which is perpendicular to the XY line, a face making an angle of 30° with the H.P.

3 With a face horizontal and 1 cm above the H.P., a vertical edge touching the V.P. (A) and a face inclined at 20° with the V.P. (B).

A **square prism,** edge 3 cm and length of prism 4 cm:

4 Standing with one end on the H.P., the nearest long edge being 1 cm from the V.P. (A) and a long face inclined at 20° with that plane.

5 Resting on the H.P., with the end faces parallel to V.P. (A) and two rectangular faces inclined at 30° with the H.P.

6 Resting with a short edge on the H.P. and perpendicular to the XY line, with two of the rectangular faces inclined at 60° with the H.P.

7 Resting with a rectangular face on the H.P., and the square ends inclined at 45° with the V.P. (A).

8 Resting with a long edge on the H.P. and perpendicular to the XY line, and with a diagonal of each end vertical.

A **square pyramid,** edge of base 3 cm and height 4 cm:

9 Resting on the H.P., with its axis vertical, the nearest corner of the base 1 cm from the V.P. (A), and the edge of the base inclined at 30° with the XY line.

10 Having the base parallel to the V.P. (A), axis horizontal, and two edges of the base horizontal.

11 In an inverted position with the axis vertical, vertex on the H.P. and 4 cm from the XY line, two edges of the base being parallel to V.P. (A) and the other two to V.P. (B).

Hexagonal pyramid, edge of base 2 cm and height 5 cm:

12 Axis vertical, and base 1 cm above the H.P., two edges of the base being parallel to the XY line.

13 Axis horizontal, the base parallel to the V.P. (A), and two edges of the base horizontal.

14 Axis horizontal, the base parallel to the V.P. (B), and two edges of the base vertical.

15 Axis vertical and 4 cm from the V.P. (A), two edges of the base being inclined at 40° to the XY line.

Triangular prism, edge 3 cm, length of prism 6 cm:

16 Resting on the H.P., with the triangular ends parallel to V.P. (A).

17 Resting on a long edge which is perpendicular to the V.P. (A), with an end parallel to and $\frac{1}{2}$ cm from V.P. (A), and a rectangular face inclined at 20° with the H.P.

18 Resting with a triangular end on the H.P., one edge of this end inclined at 10° to the XY line and one of the long edges 2 cm from V.P. (A).

Hexagonal prism, edge 2 cm, length of prism 4 cm:

19 Resting with an end on the H.P., two faces being parallel to the V.P. (A).

20 Resting with a face on the H.P., two faces being parallel to the V.P. (A).

21 Resting with its axis vertical, an end on the H.P., two edges of the end inclined at 20° to the XY line.

Octagonal prism, edge 2 cm, length of prism 5 cm:

22 Resting with an end on the H.P., two faces being parallel to the V.P. (A).

23 Resting with a face on the H.P., two faces being parallel to the V.P. (A).

Circular cylinder, radius 2 cm, length 5 cm; **sphere,** radius $1\frac{1}{2}$ cm; **cone,** base-radius 2 cm, height 5 cm:

24 The cylinder, standing on the H.P., axis vertical, with the sphere resting on it at the centre of the top circular end.

25 The cylinder lying on the H.P., its axis perpendicular to V.P. (A).

26 The cone with its base on the H.P.

27 Describe the shape and position of the solids whose

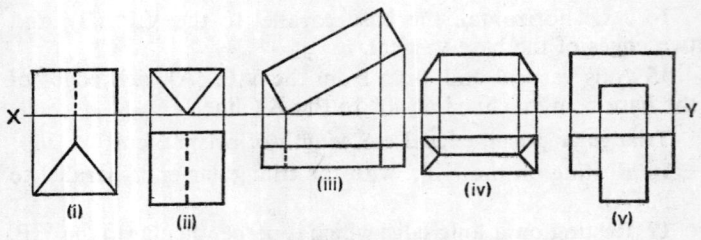

Fig. 154

plan and elevation are shown in Fig. 154. Illustrate by drawing sketches.

28 Describe the shape and position of the solids whose plan

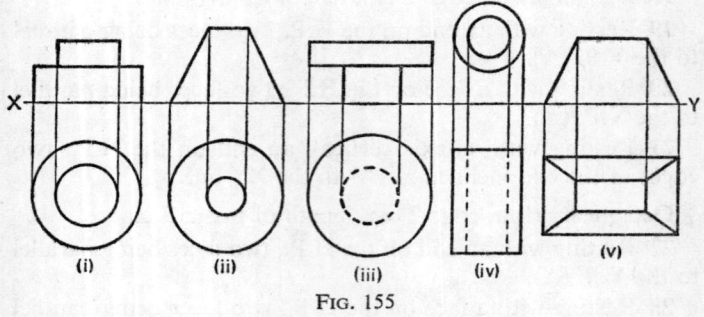

Fig. 155

and elevation are shown in Fig. 155. Illustrate by drawing sketches.

14. AVERAGES AND RATE OF WORKING

Averages The meaning of an average was explained in Part I (§ 48). If there are n quantities a, b, c, d . . ., then the **average** (or, more precisely, the **arithmetic mean**) is

$$\frac{a+b+c+d+ \ldots}{n}.$$

It follows that the sum of n quantities a, b, c, d . . . is n times their average.   This principle is used in the next example.

Example 1 *The average mark of* 20 *candidates in an examination was* 63. *The* 5 *weakest candidates had an average of* 36. *Find the average mark of the other* 15 *candidates.*

The total number of marks scored by all 20 candidates
$$= 20 \times 63 = 1260.$$
The total number of marks scored by the 5 weakest candidates $= 5 \times 36 = 180.$

∴ the total number of marks scored by the other 15 candidates $= 1260 - 180$
$$= 1080.$$

∴ the average mark for these 15 candidates $= \dfrac{\overset{360}{\cancel{1080}}}{\cancel{15}}$
$$ 5$$
$$= 72.$$

EXERCISE 29

Exercise 120, Part I, p. 294, should be revised first, especially the method of using an assumed mean.

1 The average age of a class of 20 boys was 15 years 6 months. When one boy left, the average of those remaining was 15 years 5 months. Find the age of the boy who left.

2 If 8 kg of tea at 41p per kg are mixed with x kg of tea at 31p per kg, write down the cost in pence of 1 kg of the mixture. If the average cost of the mixture is 35 p, find x.

3 The average height of 500 men is 178 cm. The average height of the 100 tallest is 184 cm. Find the average height of the rest.

4 A man walks a km at 6 km/h, and then returns a km at 4 km/h. Find and simplify to a single fraction his total time for the whole journey. Hence find his average speed for the journey.

5 A man walks for x hours at 6 km/h and then for y hours at 5 km/h. Write down the total distance he has walked, and find an expression for his average speed.

6 The average profit per year made by a company for its first 3 years was £470. In the first year the company made a loss of £226, and in the second year a profit of £760. Find the profit in the third year.

7 A shooting eight scored an average of 82 in a match. The highest individual score was 89. Find the average of the other seven members of the team.

8 A man buys x books at 96p each and $2x$ books at 60p each. Find the total cost of all the books, and the average cost per book.

9 For x completed innings a cricketer has an average score of 28 runs. In his next innings he scores 0. Find his new average.

10 The average age of x boys is b years, and the average age of y girls is g years. Find an expression for the average age of all the children together.

11 The average mark of 30 candidates in an examination was 43·6. Find the total marks scored by all the candidates. If the 12 weakest had an average of 31·5, find, correct to one decimal place, the average of the others.

12 The average reading of the barometer for Sunday, Monday and Tuesday was 753 mm. The average for Monday, Tuesday and Wednesday was 756 mm. The reading on Wednesday was 760 mm. Find the reading on Sunday.

Rate of working

Example 2   *A does a piece of work in 6 days, B does it in 4 days.   How many days should they take if they work together?*

In 1 day A does $\frac{1}{6}$ of the work, and B does $\frac{1}{4}$ of the work.

∴ in 1 day they do together $(\frac{1}{6} + \frac{1}{4})$, or $\frac{5}{12}$, of the work.

∴ A and B together do $\frac{5}{12}$ of the work in 1 day.

∴ they do $\frac{12}{12}$ of the work in $\frac{12}{5}$ days, or $2\frac{2}{5}$ days.

Compound units

In Example 2 above, A and B have different rates of doing work.   The method in that case is to add the fractions of the work that each does in 1 day.   If the rate of working is the same for all the men involved, it is simpler to work in some such compound unit as the man-hour or man-day, as in the next example.

Example 3   *A builder takes on* 100 *men to do a certain job. After they have worked for* 15 *days, he takes on an extra* 52 *men for* 3 *days, thus finishing the job.   How many men should he have taken on at the beginning in order to finish the job in* 12 *days?*

100 men in 15 days give 1500 man-days of work.

152 men in 3 days give 456 man-days of work.

∴ the total job requires 1956 man-days.

∴ the number of men to do the job in 12 days

$$= \frac{1956}{12}$$
$$= 163.$$

A compound unit in general use is the unit of electricity. This is the **kilowatt-hour**, which is 1000 watt-hours.   A 100-watt lamp, burning for 1 hour, uses 100 watt-hours; so does a 40-watt lamp burning for $2\frac{1}{2}$ hours.   A kilowatt radiator, burning for 1 hour, uses 1000 watt-hours or 1 kilowatt-hour, or one 'unit', as it is called. The dials on the electricity meter record how many kilowatt-hours, or units, are used.

EXERCISE 30

1 One man can do a piece of work in 4 hours, and another man can do it in 5 hours. How long would they take if they work together?

2 A can do a piece of work in 15 days, and B can do it in 3 days. How long will A and B take if they work together?

3 A man can do a piece of work in 12 days. When assisted by a boy, he can do the work in 9 days. How long would the boy take to do the work by himself?

4 One pipe can empty a cistern in 6 hours, another can empty it in 3 hours, and a third can empty it in 4 hours. How long will it take to empty the cistern if all three pipes are used?

5 A can do a piece of work in $4\frac{1}{2}$ days. A and B together can do the work in 3 days. Find how long B would take by himself.

6 A contractor undertakes to do a certain job in 32 days. He employs 12 men for 8 days, at the end of which time he finds that only one-fifth of the work is finished. How many additional men must he take on in order to complete the job in the 32 days?

7 A contractor engaged 15 men. After keeping them on a certain job for 4 days, he then took on 9 extra men, and the job was finished in a further 7 days. How many men, all working together, would he have needed in order to do the job in 6 days?

8 A farmer has 36 cows and enough food to feed them for 10 weeks. If he buys 9 more cows, for how many weeks will he be able to feed all his cows?

9 Find the number of units of electricity (i.e. kilowatt-hours) used in a week of 7 days (i) by a 60-watt lamp burning for 5 h every day, (ii) by a 2-kilowatt fire burning for $1\frac{1}{2}$ h every day.

10 Half of a piece of work is completed in 16 days by 21 men, each working 6 h a day. How many additional men must be employed in order that the work may be finished in 12 more days, all the men now working 7 h a day?

15. FACTORS

IN §9 we learned how to multiply algebraic expressions. It is very often useful to break up an expression into its separate factors. This is called **factorisation.**

Many arithmetical calculations are made less troublesome if we apply to them the principles of factorisation. Another use of the work of this section will be found later when we learn how to solve more difficult equations than we have had hitherto. Generally speaking, an algebraic expression is more useful in its factorised form than when it consists of several terms. Example 2, p. 44, is an illustration of this fact. In order to draw the graph of the function $(x+2)(4-x)$, a table of values is drawn up from $x = -3$ to $x = 5$. The calculation would be more tedious if the function were in the form $8 + 2x - x^2$.

It is important to remember that the expression $8 + 2x - x^2$ consists of three terms; but by factorising it as $(x+2)(4-x)$ we reduce it to a single term, with two factors.

You should always test whether your factors are correct by multiplying them out and seeing whether this gives the original expression. There is no excuse for having wrong factors.

There are various types of factorisation, and these will now be considered in turn.

Single-term factors   The easiest type of factor to find is the single-term factor, common to all the terms of an expression. Such a factor is sometimes called a 'shouting factor', because it is so obvious.

For example, $2x + 4y = 2(x + 2y)$.
∴ the factors of $2x + 4y$ are 2 and $(x + 2y)$.
Similarly, $3x + 12x^2 = 3x(1 + 4x)$,
$$4x^2y + 8xy^2 = 4xy(x + 2y).$$

Do not be content with one common factor if there are several.

Example 1 *Factorise $6x^2 - 9ax + 12x$.*

Factors common to all the terms in this expression are 3 and x.

Hence the expression $= 3x(2x - 3a + 4)$.

EXERCISE 31

Factorise the following expressions. If there are no factors, write 'none'.

1 $3x + 3y$
2 $a^2 + ab$
3 $6a + 3y$

4 $6x^2 + 4x$
5 $4a^2 - 6ab$
6 $2y - 8xy$

7 $8ab + 4ab^2$
8 $3x^2 + 2xy + x$
9 $a^3 - a^2b$

10 $6a^2b - 18ab^2$
11 $x^2 - 2y^2$
12 $ax + ay + az$

13 $6x^3 - 3ax^2$
14 $5x^2 + 15xy$
15 $a^2 + b^2$

16 $P + \dfrac{PRT}{100}$
17 $bW - aW$
18 $Mg + mg$

19 $\dfrac{Mv^2}{2} + \dfrac{mv^2}{2}$
20 $\pi r + 2r$
21 $\dfrac{Wu}{g} + \dfrac{wu}{g}$

22 $3xy - 6zx + 3x$
23 $xy^2 - 3x^2y$
24 $12a^2 - 16ax$

25 $a^2b + ab^2 + abc$
26 $4 + 2x^2$
27 $3a^2 - ab + ac$

28 $2x^3y - 6x^2y^2 + 10x^2y$
29 $2\pi r^2 + 2\pi rh$

30 $\pi r^2h + \frac{2}{3}\pi r^3$
31 $\frac{1}{2}m(v+1)^2 - \frac{1}{2}mv^2$

32 $8x^2yz + 4xy^2z + 12xyz^2$
33 $4x^3 + 6xy^2$

Use factors to simplify, and find the values of:

34 $79 \times 37 + 79 \times 63$
35 $98 \times 154 - 98 \times 54$

36 $219 \times 23 - 23 \times 19$
37 $\frac{1}{3}$ of $3472 - \frac{1}{3}$ of 2272

38 $361 \times 13 + 639 \times 13$
39 $2 \times \frac{22}{7} \times 59 - 2 \times \frac{22}{7} \times 52$

40 $68 \cdot 3 \times 29 + 31 \cdot 7 \times 29$
41 $83 \times 941 - 741 \times 83$

42 $(21 \cdot 73 \times 14 \cdot 6) + (21 \cdot 73 \times 5 \cdot 4)$

43 $287 \cdot 9^2 - (287 \cdot 9 \times 257 \cdot 9)$

44 $\frac{22}{7} \times 7 \cdot 84^2 - \frac{22}{7} \times 7 \cdot 84 \times 0 \cdot 84$

45 $(617 \times 793) + (786 \times 793) + (597 \times 793)$

46 3% of £145 − 3% of £45

47 $(3 \cdot 14 \times 4 \cdot 5^2) + (3 \cdot 14 \times 4 \cdot 5 \times 5 \cdot 5)$

48 $\dfrac{2240 \times 3 \cdot 76 \times 44}{32} - \dfrac{2240 \times 2 \cdot 76 \times 44}{32}$

49 Two circles have the same centre; the larger one has a radius of R cm and the smaller one a radius of r cm. Find an expression in terms of π, R and r for the difference between the circumferences of the two circles.

Factorise your expression and find its value when R = r + 1 and $\pi = 3 \cdot 14$.

Factors by grouping terms This is really an extension of the common factor method. Consider the expression

$$a(x+y) + b(x+y).$$

If the bracket $(x+y)$ is replaced by B, this becomes $aB + bB$. Now B is a common factor, so the expression may be written $B(a+b)$, and this is the same as $(x+y)(a+b)$. The factors of the expression are therefore $(x+y)(a+b)$.

Example 2 *Factorise* (i) $ab - ac + bd - cd$,
(ii) $x^2 + xy - 3x - 3y$.

(i) $ab - ac + bd - cd = a(b-c) + d(b-c)$
$= aB + dB$, if we write B for $(b-c)$,
$= B(a+d)$
$= (b-c)(a+d)$.

(ii) $x^2 + xy - 3x - 3y = x(x+y) - 3(x+y)$
$= xB - 3B$, if we write B for $(x+y)$,
$= B(x-3)$
$= (x+y)(x-3)$.

Notice especially in the last example that the first line of (ii) is *not* $x(x+y) - 3(x-y)$, because this would become $x^2 + xy - 3x + 3y$ if the brackets were removed. Remember that a minus sign before a bracket changes the signs inside the bracket when the bracket is removed. You should always check the first step by mentally removing the brackets you have inserted, so as to see if you get the same expression as you began with.

After a little practice you can leave out the step in which the bracket is replaced by B, and go straight to the answer. It is essential to make sure that the same bracket is repeated; for example, $x(x+y) - 3(x-y)$ has no factors.

Example 3 *Factorise* (i) $xa + xb - 2ya + 2yb$,
(ii) $x^2 + yz + xy + xz$.

(i) $xa + xb - 2ya + 2yb = x(a+b) - 2y(a-b)$.

This has no factors. It is the difference of two terms, one of which has $(a+b)$ as a factor and the other $(a-b)$ as a factor. Rearranged, the expression can be written as

$$xa - 2ya + xb + 2yb, \quad \text{or} \quad a(x-2y) + b(x+2y),$$

but again there are no factors.

(ii) $x^2 + yz + xy + xz = (x^2 + yz) + x(y+z)$.

This is not in factors, and there is no factor common to both terms. But if the terms of the expression are written in a different order, they can be grouped in such a way as to bring out a common factor. Thus,

$$\begin{aligned} x^2 + yz + xy + xz &= x^2 + xy + yz + xz \\ &= x(x+y) + z(y+x). \end{aligned}$$

Now $(x+y)$ is the same as $(y+x)$. If we denote it by B, the expression becomes $x\mathrm{B} + z\mathrm{B} = \mathrm{B}(x+z)$
$$= (x+y)(x+z).$$

EXERCISE 32

Factorise the following. If there are no factors, write 'none'.

1 $a(x+y) - b(x+y)$
2 $a(x+y) - b(x-y)$
3 $a(x+y) + b(y+x)$
4 $3x(y-z) - 2(y-z)$
5 $3a^2(x+y) - 6ab(x+y)$
6 $(a-b)^2 - 2(a-b)$
7 $p(x-1) + (x-1)$
8 $x - y - a(x-y)$
9 $a(x+2) - b(x-2)$
10 $2x(y+1) + d(y+1)$
11 $y(y-z) - 2(y+z)$
12 $4(1-x) + a(1-x)$
13 $a(a-b) - 3(a-b)$
14 $2a^2(a-x) + ax(a-x)$

15 $a(x + 2y) + b(2y + x)$ **16** $(x^2 - y)(3x + y) - (x^2 - y)(2x + 2y)$

17 $(4x + 2y)(a + b) + (2x + y)(a + 2b)$

18 $(x + y)(a - b) + (x + y)(b - c)$

19 $(a + b + c)(x + y) - (a + b + c)(y + z)$

20 $6(x - 2y)(2a + b) - 3(x - 2y)(a + b)$

21 $p(a - b) - q(b + a)$ **22** $a(c + d) - b(d + c)$

23 $pq(qr + st) + rs(st + qr)$ **24** $a(b + 2x) + 2c(b + 2x)$

25 $(x - 4y) + p(x - 4y)$ **26** $(4 - x) + y(4 + x)$

27 $p(x - y) - (x - y)$ **28** $a(a + 3) - x(a - 3)$

29 $6 - 2x + 3y - yx$ **30** $(a - b)^2 + 3(a - b)$

31 $(x - 1)^2 - yx + y$ **32** $(x + 2y)(x - y) + 3(x + 2y)$

33 $x^2 - x - yx + y$ **34** $1 + x^2 + xy(1 + x^2)$

35 $a^2(x + y) - bc(x + y)$ **36** $ax + ap - 2cx + 2cp$

37 $x^2 + 3x + 3a + ax$ **38** $x(p + q + r) + y(p + q + r)$

39 $x^3 + x - (x^2 + 1)$ **40** $2(x - 7)(x + 1) + x(x - 7)$

41 $5a + 5b + ax + bx$ **42** $3x + 3y - 8y(x - y)$

43 $2x^2(x^2 - 3x + 1) + 4(x^2 - 3x + 1)$ **44** $x + 2 - 3xy - 6y$

45 $x(a^2 + 2ab + b^2) - 3y(a + b)^2$ **46** $a^2 + b^2 + c(a + b)^2$

47 $3(x - y)^2 + 8a(x - y)$ **48** $(x + 2)(x - 1)^2 - 5(x + 2)$

49 $p(4x + 2y - z) - 2q(4x + 2y - z) - 5r(4x + 2y - z)$

50 $(p - 2q)^2 - (p - 2q)$ **51** $ax - 2a^2y + 2bx - 4aby$

52 $xy + y + (x - 1)(x + 1)$ **53** $2ax - 3bx - 4ay + 6by$

54 $(p - q)(p + q) - 2p + 2q$ **55** $ax - 3axt - by - 3byt$

56 $x^2 + 2xy + y^2 - 3x - 3y$ **57** $4ax - 12a - 9x + 27$

58 $xy - 12ab - 4bx + 3ay$ **59** $px + py - qx + qy$

60 $a^2b + a^2c - bc^2 - b^2c$ **61** $ax - bx - 4a + 4b$

62 $1 + x + x^2 + x^3$ **63** $x^2 - x + a - ax$

64 $7ap + bq - 7aq - bp$ **65** $3a - 3b - 2ab + 2a^2$

66 $x + 3 + 3ax^2 + ax^3$ **67** $x^2y + x - 4xy^2 - 4y$

68 $xt - 3xt^2 - y + 3yt$ **69** $6 - 10y + 3x^2 - 5x^2y$

Trinomials Any expression of the type

$$ax^2 + bx + c,$$

where a, b, c are numbers (positive or negative), is called a **trinomial** (three terms). On account of the fact that the highest power of x is x^2, or x squared, such an expression is also called a **quadratic function** of x (Latin *quadrum*, a square).

We found in Exercise 19 that the multiplication of two first-degree functions of x, such as $(2x-3)(4x+5)$, gives a quadratic function of x. To factorise a trinomial, therefore, we have to guess two brackets whose product would make the given trinomial.

Example 4 *Factorise* (i) $3x^2 + 17x + 10$,
(ii) $3x^2 - 17x + 10$.

(i) The term $3x^2$ shows that the brackets must be $(3x\quad)(x\quad)$.
The term 10 shows that the numbers at the ends of the brackets are 5 and 2, *or* 2 and 5, *or* 10 and 1, *or* 1 and 10.

The possibilities are thus:
$(3x+5)(x+2)$, $(3x+2)(x+5)$, $(3x+10)(x+1)$, $(3x+1)(x+10)$.
Any of these would, upon multiplication, produce a trinomial which began with $3x^2$ and ended with 10. Which would give the term $17x$ in the middle? Testing the above possibilities, we find that the only pair of factors which do this are $(3x+2)(x+5)$.

$$\therefore\ 3x^2 + 17x + 10 = (3x+2)(x+5).$$

(ii) Proceeding as before, we see that the only difference in the case of $3x^2 - 17x + 10$ is that the signs in the middle of both brackets must be minus, in order to give $-17x$ as the middle term when the brackets are multiplied out. Notice that the product of two negative numbers is a positive number; e.g. $-2 \times -5 = +10$.

$$\therefore\ 3x^2 - 17x + 10 = (3x-2)(x-5).$$

A useful hint when filling the second terms in the brackets is to try factors near together before you try those farther apart. Thus, in Example 4, try 5 and 2 before you try 10 and 1.

Example 5 *Factorise* $2x^2 + 7x + 6$ and $2x^2 - 7x + 6$.

The first step is $(2x\quad)(x\quad)$ in both cases.

The last term of each trinomial is $+6$, which suggests the factors 3 and 2, or 6 and 1, the signs in the brackets being both $+$ for $2x^2 + 7x + 6$, both $-$ for $2x^2 - 7x + 6$.

The possibilities are thus

$$(2x \pm 2)(x \pm 3),\ (2x \pm 3)(x \pm 2),\ (2x \pm 6)(x \pm 1),\ (2x \pm 1)(x \pm 6),$$

the $+$ signs being appropriate for the first trinomial and the $-$ signs for the second.

Notice that the first can be rejected at once, for $(2x + 2)$ has the common factor 2, and clearly 2 is not a factor of $2x^2 + 7x + 6$. A similar objection applies to the third of the above possibilities, where $(2x + 6)$ again has the common factor 2.

We are left only with the second and fourth, which we test by multiplication for the middle term $7x$. We find that $(2x + 3)(x + 2)$ is correct to give $+7x$, and $(2x - 3)(x - 2)$ to give $-7x$.

$$\therefore\ 2x^2 + 7x + 6 = (2x + 3)(x + 2),$$
and
$$2x^2 - 7x + 6 = (2x - 3)(x - 2).$$

Example 6 *Factorise* (i) $5x^2 + 13x - 6$, (ii) $5x^2 - 13x - 6$.

(i) The first step is $(5x\quad)(x\quad)$.

Since the product of the second terms in the brackets is to be -6, these two terms must be of unlike signs. The first possibilities to try are

$$(5x + 3)(x - 2),\ (5x - 3)(x + 2),\ (5x + 2)(x - 3),\ (5x - 2)(x + 3).$$

Multiplication shows that the last pair of factors are the only ones which give the correct middle term $+13x$.

If none of the above possibilities gave the correct middle term, we should have to try ± 6 and ∓ 1 at the ends of the brackets.

The factors of $5x^2 + 13x - 6$ are thus found to be

$$(5x - 2)(x + 3).$$

(ii) In the case of $5x^2 - 13x - 6$, the reasoning is as before, except that the middle term is to be $-13x$. The factors are

$$(5x + 2)(x - 3).$$

General rules for factorising $ax^2 + bx + c$

(i) Make two brackets and fill the first term in each bracket so as to give the product ax^2.

(ii) Find pairs of numbers, starting with those near together, whose product is c.

If c is $+$, the numbers in each pair are both $+$ if b is $+$, but both $-$ if b is $-$.

If c is $-$, these numbers are of opposite signs.

(iii) Choose that combination which makes the middle term correct when the brackets are multiplied together, rejecting any possibilities which would give either bracket a common factor which is not a factor of the trinomial.

(iv) Verify that the factors are correct by multiplying them together to see if they give the trinomial.

Success in factorising trinomials depends upon being able to multiply two brackets together easily and quickly. There are certain considerations which will save you trouble, but trial and error are generally necessary in the end.

Some trinomials are easily recognized as perfect squares; for example,

$$x^2 + 10x + 25 = (x + 5)^2.$$

Example 7 *Factorise* $6 + 5x - 4x^2$.

Notice that this trinomial is in *ascending* powers of x. *Do not turn it round.*

The first step is $(3 \quad)(2 \quad)$, although if this does not work we shall have to try $(6 \quad)(1 \quad)$.

Now fill the second terms in the brackets with factors of $-4x^2$. The possibilities are

$$\pm 2x \text{ and } \mp 2x \quad (\pm 2x \text{ is short for } +2x \text{ or } -2x),$$
$$\pm 4x \text{ and } \mp x, \qquad \pm x \text{ and } \mp 4x.$$

The factors which give $+5x$ as the middle term when they are multiplied together are found to be

$$(3+4x)(2-x).$$

Example 8 *Factorise $3x^2 - 14xy - 5y^2$.*

This trinomial is said to be 'homogeneous', each term being of the second degree, like the terms which are obtained when we expand $(x+y)^2$. Each factor will be homogeneous, and of the first degree, i.e. of the type $ax + by$.

The first step is $(3x \quad)(x \quad)$.

The possibilities for the second terms in the brackets are $+5y$ and $-y$, or $-5y$ and $+y$, or $+y$ and $-5y$, or $-y$ and $+5y$. By trial and error, the factors are found to be

$$(3x+y)(x-5y).$$

EXERCISE 33

Factorise the following. If there are no factors, write 'none'.

1 $x^2 + 7x + 10$	**2** $x^2 + 5x + 6$	**3** $x^2 + 5x + 4$
4 $2x^2 + 5x + 2$	**5** $2x^2 + 7x + 3$	**6** $y^2 + 7y + 12$
7 $3t^2 + 5t + 2$	**8** $2x^2 + 11x + 5$	**9** $3x^2 + 8x + 3$
10 $a^2 + 8a + 7$	**11** $18 + 9x + x^2$	**12** $4x^2 + 13x + 3$
13 $x^2 + 6x + 9$	**14** $2x^2 + 8x - 10$	**15** $2x^2 + x - 10$
16 $x^2 - x - 6$	**17** $2x^2 + 7x - 4$	**18** $3x^2 + x - 8$
19 $a^2 - 8a + 12$	**20** $3x^2 - 10x + 8$	**21** $x^2 - 3x - 10$
22 $x^2 - 7x - 10$	**23** $y^2 + 5y - 50$	**24** $6x^2 + 5x - 6$
25 $1 + 3x - 10x^2$	**26** $2a^2 - 7a - 15$	**27** $3x^2 + 12x + 4$
28 $1 - x - 20x^2$	**29** $6y^2 - 11y + 3$	**30** $2x^2 + 5x - 12$
31 $2x^2 + x - 6$	**32** $4x^2 - 7x + 10$	**33** $6x^2 - xy - 2y^2$
34 $3t^2 - 7t - 2$	**35** $3x^2 - 16xy + 5y^2$	**36** $4x^2 + 7x - 2$
37 $5 + 22x - 10x^2$	**38** $5x^2 - 7ax - 6a^2$	**39** $4t^2 - 11t + 6$
40 $8a^2 - 2a - 3$	**41** $1 + 8x + 16x^2$	**42** $4 - 13x + 10x^2$
43 $3x^2 - 7x - 20$	**44** $2x^2 - 11xy + 12y^2$	**45** $2 - x - 6x^2$
46 $6x^2 - x - 15$	**47** $3y^2 - 11y + 10$	**48** $7x^2 + 11xy - 6y^2$
49 $9x^2 - 12x + 4$	**50** $3x^2y^2 + 4xy + 1$	**51** $12 - 16a - 3a^2$

52 $9x^2 - 15x - 14$ **53** $7x^2 + 9xy - 10y^2$ **54** $3 - 4a - 4a^2$

55 $6x^2 + 5x - 6$ **56** $3t^2 - 13t - 10$ **57** $7x^2 - 2xy - 5y^2$

58 $72 - 14t - t^2$ **59** $5x^2 - 17x + 6$ **60** $4x^2 + 13x - 12$

61 $6b^2 + 17b - 14$ **62** $14x^2 + 41x - 28$ **63** $7x^2 + 25x - 12$

64 $3x^2y^2 + 2xy - 5$ **65** $2x^2 + 2x - 24$ **66** $6 - y^2 + 5y$

67 $3a^2 - 3a - 90$ **68** $11x - x^2 - 24$ **69** $x^2 - 2x + 8$

70 $10c^2 + 11c - 6$ **71** $12a^2 - a - 6$ **72** $4x^2 + 4x + 1$

The difference of two squares   On page 59 the identity

$$a^2 - b^2 = (a + b)(a - b)$$

was illustrated geometrically. It can also be verified by multiplying together the two brackets on the right; they make

$$a^2 - ab + ba - b^2, \text{ or } a^2 - b^2.$$

An expression of the form $a^2 - b^2$ is called the **difference of two squares,** and it can always be put into factors.

Consider, for example, $x^2 - 16$, or $x^2 - 4^2$.

We take the formula $a^2 - b^2 = (a + b)(a - b)$, and replace a by x and b by 4; the result is

$$x^2 - 4^2 = (x + 4)(x - 4).$$

Similarly, $25x^2 - 16y^2 = (5x)^2 - (4y)^2$
$$= (5x + 4y)(5x - 4y).$$

As a first step, put the given expression in the form

$$(\quad)^2 - (\quad)^2$$

Avoid the mistake of saying that the factors of $25x^2 - 16y^2$ are $(25x + 16y)(25x - 16y)$.

Example 9   *Factorise*   (i) $25x^2 - 1$
                            (ii) $9x^2y^4 - 16$,
                            (iii) $3x^2 - 48$.

(i) $25x^2 - 1 = (5x)^2 - (1)^2 = (5x + 1)(5x - 1)$.

(ii) $9x^2y^4 - 16 = (3xy^2)^2 - (4)^2 = (3xy^2 + 4)(3xy^2 - 4)$.

(iii) $3x^2 - 48 = 3(x^2 - 16)$
$$= 3(x^2 - 4^2) = 3(x + 4)(x - 4).$$

EXERCISE 34

Factorise the following.   If there are no factors, write 'none'.

1 $x^2 - 25$ **2** $4a^2 - b^2$ **3** $9 - 16x^2 y^2$ **4** $25x^2 - 49a^2$
5 $x^2 + y^2$ **6** $t^2 - 4$ **7** $9x^2 - 64$ **8** $a^2 - 9b^2$
9 $1 - 49t^2$ **10** $100x^2 - 1$ **11** $25 - 4x^2$ **12** $16x^2 + 9$
13 $x^2 y^2 - 16a^2$ **14** $49 - 9y^2$ **15** $y^2 - 169$
16 $121x^2 - 144y^2$ **17** $81p^2 - 36q^2$ **18** $k^2 + 25$
19 $8 - 2x^2$ **20** $3x^2 - 5y^2$ **21** $3x^2 - 192$
22 $36a^2 b^2 - 25x^2$ **23** $7a^2 - 63b^2$ **24** $x^2 + 4y^2$
25 $45 - 20a^2$ **26** $a^2 b^2 c^2 - 100$ **27** $25(x + y)^2 - 1$
28 $2x^2 - 3y^2$ **29** $a^4 - b^4$ **30** $3a^2 - 12$

Use factors to find the values of:

31 $100^2 - 99^2$ **32** $51^2 - 49^2$ **33** $\frac{22}{7}(28^2 - 21^2)$
34 $101^2 - 1$ **35** $98^2 - 4$ **36** $97^2 - 9$
37 $46^2 - 44^2$ **38** $5 \cdot 3^2 - 4 \cdot 7^2$ **39** $152^2 - 148^2$
40 $(1 \cdot 286)^2 - (0 \cdot 286)^2$ **41** $765^2 - 235^2$ **42** $158^2 - 58^2$
43 $\frac{1}{7}(53^2 - 46^2)$ **44** $999^2 - 1$ **45** $8 \cdot 7^2 - 1 \cdot 3^2$
46 $79^2 - 21^2$ **47** $312^2 - 308^2$ **48** $583^2 - 417^2$
49 $\frac{22}{7}(\{2\frac{1}{4}\}^2 - \{1\frac{1}{4}\}^2)$ **50** $\dfrac{269^2 - 137^2}{3 \times 7 \times 8}$ **51** $\dfrac{6 \cdot 51^2 - 2 \cdot 81^2}{0 \cdot 932 \times 74}$

52 Two circles have the same centre; the larger one has a radius R cm and the smaller one a radius r cm.   Find an expression in terms of π, R and r for the area between the two circles in square centimetres.

Factorise your expression and find its value when $\pi = \frac{22}{7}$, R = 2·4 and $r = 0·4$.

EXERCISE 35 (Miscellaneous Factors)

Factorise the following.   If there are no factors, write 'none'.

1 $x^2 + xy + 4x + 4y$ **2** $9a^2 - 225$ **3** $x^2 - 12x + 35$
4 $4a^2 - 11ab + 6b^2$ **5** $a^2 - ab + ac + bc$
6 $10 - 2x - x^2$ **7** $xy + 4y - 3x - 12$ **8** $25 - 16x^2$
9 $4x^2 + 4x + 1$ **10** $27x^2 - 75y^4$ **11** $3x^2 - 10x - 8$

12 $2 + 2x^2 + xy + x^3y$ **13** $12a^2b^2 - ab - 1$ **14** $a^2 - 2a - 35$

15 $8x^2 - 18$ **16** $5x^2 - 20a^2$ **17** $3x^2 + 7x - 20$

18 $x^2 + 3x - 18$ **19** $4x^2 + 5x - 9$ **20** $a^2 - 36x^2y^4$

21 $3x^2 - 7x - 4$ **22** $3pa + 3pb - 6qa - 6qb$

23 $1 + 2x - 15x^2$ **24** $x^4 - 25$ **25** $a^2 + 16$

26 $(x - y)^2 - 4$ **27** $3(x - 4)^2 - 12$ **28** $x^2 - 15x + 54$

29 $x^4 - 7x^2 + 12$ **30** $3ax - 3ay - 9x - 9y$ **31** $225x^2 - 1$

32 $x^3 + x^2 + x + 1$ **33** $x^2 - 2x - xy + 2y$

34 $2ab - 2ac + b - c$ **35** $6 + 11x - 10x^2$ **36** $3x^2 + 11x + 4$

37 $4x^2 + 7x - 2$ **38** $x^2 + 2x + 4$ **39** $(x + 2y)^2 - 9$

40 $2x^2 + 7x - 15$ **41** $ab - ac + cd - bd$ **42** $4t^2 + 13t + 3$

43 $n^2 + 4n$ **44** $x^2 - 8x + 16$ **45** $2a^2 + 5ab - 3b^2$

46 $a^2 - 7a - 30$ **47** $ax^2 - ay^2$ **48** $20 + t - t^2$

49 $3a^3 - 12ab^2$ **50** $p^2 - 2ap + 3bp - 6ab$

51 $x^2 + 2ax - b^2 - 2ab$ **52** $x^2 - (2a - 3b)x - 6ab$

53 $a^3 - a^2 - 9a + 9$ **54** $3x^3 - 3x^2 - 4(x^2 - 1)$

55 $2 - 72t^2$ **56** $a^2 + 2abx + b^2x^2 - c^2$

57 $9(x + 2)^2 - 12(x + 2) + 4$ **58** $12x^2 - 19x - 18$

59 $25x^2 - 4y^2 + 20x + 8y$ **60** $6t^2 - 11t - 10$

61 $(ax + by)^2 - (ay + bx)^2$ **62** $2p^2 - 3pq - 2q^2 + 2q - p$

63 $9(a + 2b)^2 - (2a + b)^2$ **64** $12a^2 + 8a - 15$

65 $a^2 - b^2 - a + b$ **66** $4a^3b - 12ab^2$

67 $15 - 6x + 8x^3 - 20x^2$ **68** $8y^2 + 29y - 12$

69 $\pi(r + t)^2h - \pi r^2h$ **70** $9 - x^2 - y^2 + 2xy$

71 $12p^2 - pq - 6q^2$ **72** $a^2 + 4ab + 4b^2 - 25c^2$

73 $8x^2 - 18y^2$ **74** $2\pi(R + r)^2h - \pi(R + r)h^2$

75 $x^2 + 2x(x + 1) + (x + 1)^2$ **76** $a^2 - 4b^2 + 3a + 6b$

77 $(x + 2y)^2 - 4(x + 2y) + 3$ **78** $3x^2 - 22xy + 7y^2 - 4x + 28y$

79 $a^2 - 3a(b + 2c) + 2(b + 2c)^2$ **80** $ax - 10 + 5a - 2x$

81 $p - q + (q - p)^2$ **82** $6y^2 - 3xy + 2yz - zx$

83 $1 + a - a^2 - a^3$ **84** $ac(b^2 + 1) - b(a^2 + c^2)$

16. QUADRATIC EQUATIONS (I)

IF we are told that $P \times Q = 3$, it is impossible to say what is the value of P or Q. For example, P might be 3, and Q would then be 1; or P might be 7, and Q would then be $\frac{3}{7}$.

But if $P \times Q = 0$, we can say that either $P = 0$ or $Q = 0$. The product of the two numbers P and Q is 0 if, and only if, one of them is 0.

The same principle is true when there are more than two factors. The product of a number of expressions is zero (i.e. 0) if, and only if, one of the expressions is zero. Stated in letters;

If $P \times Q \times R \times \ldots = 0$, then either $P = 0$ or $Q = 0$ or $R = 0 \ldots$

As an illustration of the principle, suppose we know that
$$(2x + 3)(x - 4) = 0.$$

Since the product of $(2x + 3)$ and $(x - 4)$ is 0, one of these expressions must be 0.

If $\qquad 2x + 3 = 0,$
then $\qquad 2x = -3.$
$$\therefore x = -\tfrac{3}{2}.$$
But if $\qquad x - 4 = 0,$
then $\qquad x = 4.$

We have thus solved the equation $(2x + 3)(x - 4) = 0$, for we have found the two values of x which satisfy the equation.

Observe particularly that we cannot say that x is necessarily $-\frac{3}{2}$, any more than we can say that x is necessarily 4. The correct conclusion to be drawn is not that $x = -\frac{3}{2}$ *and* 4, but that $x = -\frac{3}{2}$ *or* 4.

Example 1. *Find x if $(x - 5)(4x + 1) = 0$.*

Since $\qquad (x - 5)(4x + 1) = 0,$
then *either* $\qquad x - 5 = 0$ *or* $4x + 1 = 0.$
If $\qquad x - 5 = 0,$
then $\qquad x = 5.$
If $\qquad 4x + 1 = 0,$
then $\qquad 4x = -1.$
$$\therefore x = -\tfrac{1}{4}.$$
$$\therefore x = \text{either } 5 \text{ or } -\tfrac{1}{4}.$$

Example 2 *State in the form of an equation the fact that either $x=0$ or $x=3$.*

The equation is $x(x-3)=0$.

EXERCISE 36 (Oral)

1 If $xy=0$ and $x=1$, what is y?

2 If $xy=0$ and $x=0$, can you say what y is?

3 If $x=3$, what is the value of $(x-3)(x+4)$?

4 If $x=0$, what is the value of $x(2x+7)$?

5 If $(a-b)x=0$, can you say anything about x?

6 If $xy=3$, can you say anything about x?

7 If $(x+2)(y-3)=0$ and $x=-2$, can you say anything about y?

8 If $(x+2)(y-3)=0$ and $x=6$, can you say anything about y?

9 If $(y-7)(y+2)=0$, what conclusion can you draw?

10 If $t(2t-5)=0$, what conclusion can you draw?

In Nos. 11–15, combine the information given into a single equation.

11 Either $x=4$ or $x=5$ **12** Either $x=-4$ or $x=0$

13 Either $x=1$ or $x=2$ or $x=3$

14 Either $x=0$ or $x=1\frac{1}{2}$ **15** Either $x=\frac{1}{2}$ or $x=-\frac{1}{3}$

Solve the following equations:

16 $(x-1)(x-9)=0$ **17** $(z+5)(z-3)=0$

18 $t(t+1)(t+7)=0$ **19** $(y-2)^2=0$

20 $x^2=0$ **21** $x(x+4)=0$

22 $5(t+3)(t-8)=0$ **23** $(x-1)(x+2)(x-3)=0$

24 $(t-2)(t-5)(t-6)=0$ **25** $3y(y+6)=0$

26 $x^2(x-1)=0$ **27** $3x(x-1)^2=0$

28 $2t(2t-1)(3t-2)=0$ **29** $(4x+1)(x+4)=0$

30 $3(x-3)^2=0$ **31** $4x^2(3x-7)=0$

Quadratic equations We called $ax^2 + bx + c$ a **quadratic function** of x. A **quadratic equation** is an equation of the type

$$ax^2 + bx + c = 0.$$

From what has been said above, it is clear that, if we can break up the left-hand side of the equation into two factors, we can find two possible values of x which satisfy the equation.

Example 3 *Solve the equation* $2x^2 - 5x + 2 = 0$.

The factors of $2x^2 - 5x + 2$ are $(2x - 1)(x - 2)$.

$$\therefore (2x - 1)(x - 2) = 0.$$
$$\therefore \text{ either } 2x - 1 = 0 \text{ or } x - 2 = 0.$$

If $\qquad\qquad\qquad 2x - 1 = 0,$
then $\qquad\qquad\qquad 2x = 1.$
$\qquad\qquad \therefore \qquad\qquad x = \tfrac{1}{2}.$
But if $\qquad\qquad\quad x - 2 = 0,$
then $\qquad\qquad\qquad x = 2.$
$\qquad\qquad \therefore \qquad\qquad x = \tfrac{1}{2} \text{ or } 2.$

Do not leave out the argument 'either $2x - 1 = 0$ or $x - 2 = 0$'.

Example 4 *Solve the equation* $3x^2 = 10x + 8$.

The first step is to rearrange the equation with all the terms on the left and 0 on the right. This gives

$$3x^2 - 10x - 8 = 0.$$
$$\therefore (3x + 2)(x - 4) = 0.$$
$$\therefore \text{ either } 3x + 2 = 0 \text{ or } x - 4 = 0.$$

If $\qquad\qquad\qquad 3x + 2 = 0,$
then $\qquad\qquad\qquad 3x = -2.$
$\qquad\qquad \therefore \qquad\qquad x = -\tfrac{2}{3}.$
If $\qquad\qquad\qquad x - 4 = 0,$
then $\qquad\qquad\qquad x = 4.$
$\qquad\qquad \therefore \qquad\qquad x = 4 \text{ or } -\tfrac{2}{3}.$

The values of x which satisfy the equation are called its **roots**.

Example 5   *Solve the equation* $16x^2 = 8x - 1$.
$$16x^2 - 8x + 1 = 0.$$
$$\therefore (4x - 1)^2 = 0.$$

In this case the two factors of the left-hand side are both $(4x - 1)$. Instead of saying 'either ... or ...', we have only one conclusion:

$$4x - 1 = 0.$$
$$\therefore \qquad 4x = 1.$$
$$\therefore \qquad x = \tfrac{1}{4}.$$

Most quadratics have two roots, but the quadratic in this Example has only *one* root. We usually say that this equation has *two equal roots*, or that it has the root $x = \tfrac{1}{4}$ repeated.

EXERCISE 37

Solve the following equations:

1 $x^2 - 3x + 2 = 0$ **2** $x^2 + 3x + 2 = 0$ **3** $x^2 - 5x + 6 = 0$

4 $x^2 - 5x - 6 = 0$ **5** $x^2 - 3x = 0$ **6** $x^2 - 16 = 0$

7 $x^2 - 2x + 1 = 0$ **8** $x^2 = 1$ **9** $x^2 - x - 12 = 0$

10 $x^2 + 4x - 5 = 0$ **11** $2x^2 - 3x - 2 = 0$ **12** $6x^2 - 5x + 1 = 0$

13 $2x^2 - x - 10 = 0$ **14** $3x^2 + x - 2 = 0$ **15** $x^2 - 10x + 21 = 0$

16 $2x^2 - 7x + 6 = 0$ **17** $x^2 + x = 0$ **18** $4x^2 + 1 = 4x$

19 $2x^2 = 4x$ **20** $2x^2 + 12 = 11x$ **21** $3x^2 + 8x + 4 = 0$

22 $2x^2 + 5x = 3$ **23** $6x^2 + 5x = 6$ **24** $x^2 - 24 = 2x$

25 $(x + 2)(x + 3) = 20$ **26** $2x^2 - 18 = 0$ **27** $x^2 - 11x + 28 = 0$

28 $(2x - 1)^2 = 36$ **29** $x(x + 2) = 63$ **30** $x(x - 2) = 3(x - 2)$

31 $x^2 - 5x = 50$ **32** $3x^2 + x = 2$ **33** $4x^2 - 11x + 7 = 0$

34 $4x^2 + 12x + 9 = 0$ **35** $(2x - 1)(x - 1) = 6$

36 $x^2 + 6x + 9 = 0$ **37** $5x^2 - 17x + 6 = 0$ **38** $(2x + 3)^2 = 1$

39 $2x^2 = 50$ **40** $4x^2 + 16x + 15 = 0$

41 $(x - 4)^2 = (x - 4)(2x - 1)$ **42** $3x^2 + 5x - 2 = 0$

43 $2x = x^2 - 3$ **44** $x^2 - x(2 - x) = 0$ **45** $6x^2 + 17x = 14$

46 $(3x - 2)^2 - x^2 - 2x = 1$ **47** $(4 - 3x)^2 + 3x^2 = 16$

48 $(2 + x)^2 + (x - 1)^2 = 5$ **49** $3x^2 + 2x - 5 = 0$

50 $6x^2 + 6 = 20x$ **51** $3x^2 = 2x$

52 $(x - 1)(x + 2) = 4$ **53** $2x^2 + 7x - 4 = 0$

54 $(1 - 3x)^2 + 3x - 4x^2 = 9$ **55** $8x^2 - 6x - 2 = 0$

56 $(2x + 1)(x - 1) = 5$ **57** $14 - x^2 = \frac{1}{2}x$

58 $9x^2 = 64$ **59** $(2x - 7)^2 = 1$

60 $(3x + 2)^2 = 7(3x + 2)$ **61** $(x + 6)(x - 2) = 9$

62 $6x^2 = 4 + 23x$ **63** $3x^2 - 5 = 14x$

64 $6x^2 + 8x = 0$ **65** $4x^2 - 3x = 10$ **66** $10x^2 - 3x - 1 = 0$

67 $6x^2 + 7x + 1 = 0$ **68** $12x^2 + 7x - 12 = 0$

69 $6x^2 + 17x + 12 = 0$ **70** $x^3 - 9x = 0$ **71** $x^3 - x^2 - 2x = 0$

Express the following facts in the form of equations containing brackets but not fractions:

72 Either $x = -\frac{2}{5}$ or $x = 1\frac{1}{2}$ **73** Either $x = 0$ or $x = -\frac{4}{5}$

74 Either $x = \frac{1}{2}$ or $x = \frac{2}{3}$ **75** Either $x = \frac{4}{7}$ or $x = \frac{3}{4}$

76 Either $x = -1\frac{1}{2}$ or $x = -2\frac{1}{3}$ **77** $x = \pm 2$

78 $x = \pm \frac{3}{4}$ **79** $x = 0$ or 1 or 3

89 $x = 0$ or $\pm \frac{2}{3}$ **81** $x = 1$ or -1 or $-\frac{1}{3}$

Problems leading to quadratic equations

Example 6   *A marble is rolled up a smooth sloping groove, and it is known that the distance of the marble from the point of projection after t seconds have elapsed is $(60t - 12t^2)$ cm.   Find after what time the marble is 27 cm from the point of projection.*

We have to find what value of t makes $(60t - 12t^2)$ cm the same as 27 cm; i.e.

$$60t - 12t^2 = 27.$$
$$\therefore\ 60t - 12t^2 - 27 = 0.$$

Changing the signs throughout and rearranging the terms,
$$12t^2 - 60t + 27 = 0.$$

Dividing through by 3,

$$4t^2 - 20t + 9 = 0.$$
$$\therefore (2t - 1)(2t - 9) = 0.$$

Either $\qquad 2t - 1 = 0 \quad$ or $\quad 2t - 9 = 0.$
$$\therefore 2t = 1 \quad \text{or} \qquad 2t = 9.$$
$$\therefore \quad t = \tfrac{1}{2} \quad \text{or} \qquad t = \tfrac{9}{2}.$$

The marble is 27 cm from the point of projection after $\frac{1}{2}$ s (on the upward motion) and again after $4\frac{1}{2}$ s (on the downward motion).

Example 7 *The length of a room is 3 m more than the breadth, and the area is* 180 *square metres. Find the length and breadth of the room.*

Let the breadth be x metres; then the length is $(x + 3)$ metres.
$\therefore$ the area is $x(x + 3)$ square metres.

$$\therefore \qquad x(x + 3) = 180.$$
$$\therefore \quad x^2 + 3x - 180 = 0.$$
$$\therefore (x - 12)(x + 15) = 0.$$

Either $\qquad x - 12 = 0 \quad$ or $\quad x + 15 = 0.$
$$\therefore x \quad\;\; = 12 \quad \text{or} \quad x = -15.$$

But the breadth of the room could not be -15 m.
$\therefore$ the breadth is 12 m and the length 15 m.

It will be noticed from the above worked examples that the quadratic equation gives two solutions, but these are not both necessarily solutions of the problem. We must decide whether both solutions are admissible (as in Example 6) or one is inadmissible (as in Example 7).

EXERCISE 38

1 If I think of a number, square it, and add the number I first thought of, the result is 90. Find the number.

2 The length of a carpet is 5 m more than the width, and the area is 104 m². Find the dimensions of the carpet.

3 The height of a triangle is 4 cm more than the base, and the area is 48 cm². Find the length of the base.

4 The length of a carpet is $2\frac{1}{2}$ m more than the width, and its area is 26 m². Find its length and width.

5 A rectangular lawn is 12 m long and 8 m wide, and a path of uniform width runs all round it. If the area of the path is 156 m², find its width.

6 A room is 5 m long, and its height is the same as its width. If the area of the walls is 48 m², find the height of the room.

7 The sum of the n numbers 1, 2, 3, 4, 5, . . . up to n is known to be $\frac{n(n+1)}{2}$. If the sum of the first n numbers is 55, find n.

8 A picture measuring 8 cm by 6 cm is surrounded by a frame whose area is 51 cm². Find the width of the frame.

9 A polygon with n sides is known to have $\frac{n(n-3)}{2}$ diagonals. If a polygon has 54 diagonals, how many sides has it?

10 The hypotenuse of a right-angled triangle is 17 cm long, and one of the sides containing the right angle is 7 cm more than the other. Find the shortest side of the triangle.

11 The parallel sides of a trapezium are $(h+3)$ and $(h+5)$ cm long, and the distance between them is h cm. If the area is 32 cm², find h. (See p. 66 for the formula for the area of a trapezium.)

12 The sides of a right-angled triangle are $(2x-3)$, $(2x+1)$, $(2x+5)$ cm. Find the value of x.

13 Find three consecutive integers which are such that the square of their sum exceeds the sum of their squares by 724. (Take the integers as $x-1$, x and $x+1$.)

14 The length of a room exceeds the breadth by 4 m, and the area of the floor is 192 m². Find the breadth of the room.

15 ABCD is a square of side 10 cm; points X, Y are taken in AB, AD so that $AX = AY = x$ cm. Prove that the area of the triangle CXY is $(10x - \frac{1}{2}x^2)$ cm².
If the area of this triangle is 32 cm², find x.

16 Two numbers add up to 20. The sum of their squares is 20 less than 3 times their product. Find the numbers.

17 A room is 7 m long, 6 m wide, and a rectangular carpet is placed on the floor so as to leave a border of uniform width all round. If the area of this border is 22 m², find the length and breadth of the carpet. (Let the border be x metres wide.)

18 A piece of wire 40 cm long is cut into two parts, and each part is then bent into a square. If the sum of the areas of these squares is 68 cm², find the lengths of the two pieces of wire.

17. TABLES OF SQUARES, SQUARE ROOTS, RECIPROCALS

Four-figure tables Tables of squares, square roots, etc., are used to save time and trouble in arithmetical calculations, and four-figure tables are printed at the end of this book. It must always be remembered that the values obtained from them are correct only to three significant figures. If four-figure accuracy is required, it is necessary to use five-figure tables. The error in the fourth figure will generally be small, in fact not usually more than 1. This liability to error should be indicated by retaining all the four figures derived from the tables, but writing 'approx.' after a four-figure answer. Decimal points are omitted from the tables, and a rough estimate must be made to decide where the decimal point should be placed in the answer.

Table of squares Turn to the end of this book and find the table of squares of numbers. The 10 columns headed 0 to 9 are called the 'main columns'. Down the right-hand side of each page of squares there are 9 columns headed 1 to 9, which are called the 'difference columns'.

Example 1 *Use the tables to find the square of* 3·486.

Rough estimate is $3^2 = 9$.

Look for 34 (the first two figures of 3·486) in the left-hand column of the table.   The figures in this row, with the headings at the top of the page, are:

	0	1	2	3	4	5	6	7	8	9	1	2	3	4	5	6	7	8	9
34	1156	1163	1170	1176	1183	1190	1197	1204	1211	1218	1	1	2	3	3	4	5	6	6

Under the heading 8 in the main columns we find 1211; under the heading 6 in the difference columns, we find 4. Thus,

$$3·48^2 = 12·11$$
Add difference for   6   =   ·04
$$\therefore\ 3·486^2 = 12·15 \text{ approx.}$$

The decimal point is inserted in the answer so as to make it agree with the rough estimate.

The squares of all numbers such as 34·86, 348·6, 0·03486 will differ from the square of 3·486 only in the position of the decimal point.   They will all contain the same significant figures, 1215.   Thus,

$$(34·86)^2 = 1215,$$
$$(348·6)^2 = 121500,$$
$$(0·03486)^2 = 0·001215 \text{ (approx.).}$$

Notice that the square of a number greater than 1 is bigger than the number, but the square of a number less than 1 is smaller than the number.

If we require the square of a number with more than four significant figures in it, the number must be corrected to four significant figures when we are using four-figure tables.

Example 2 *Use the tables to find the square of* 438·67.

We correct this to 438·7.   Rough estimate, $400^2 = 160\,000$.

Look for 43 in the left-hand column.   In the same row as 43, and in the main column headed 8, we find 1918.   In the same row, in the difference column headed 7, we find 6, and add this to 1918.   The result is 1924.

$\therefore$ the square of 438·7 is 192 400 (approx.).

EXERCISE 39

Use the tables to find the squares of the following numbers:

1 165	**2** 4816	**3** 24·15	**4** 0·1629
5 1743	**6** 0·0317	**7** 1·385	**8** 71·46
9 0·001066	**10** 9999	**11** 0·2716	**12** 7843
13 0·8981	**14** 106·38	**15** 21·322	**16** 6·543
17 71·2	**18** 0·5396	**19** 23·496	**20** 384·9
21 0·0677	**22** 879	**23** 4·318	**24** 4208
25 1204	**26** 0·0202	**27** 4·5717	**28** 0·6487
29 10·09	**30** 0·3171	**31** 567·8	**32** 0·00987

Square root The method of finding square root by factors was explained in Part I;

e.g. $$15876 = 2^2 \times 3^4 \times 7^2,$$
∴ the square root of $15876 = 2 \times 3^2 \times 7 = 126$.

The symbol $\sqrt{}$ stands for 'the square root of.' Thus, $\sqrt{15876} = 126$.

Only a few numbers have exact square roots, but the tables give *approximately*, to four figures but with a possible uncertainty about the last figure, the square roots of *all* numbers.

There is a very important difference between squares and square roots which must not be forgotten when tables are being used. If two numbers have the same figures, but their decimal points are in different places, their squares will differ only in the position of the decimal point. But their square roots may differ in the actual figures, as well as in the position of the decimal point.

For example, $\sqrt{4} = 2$;
but $\sqrt{40} = 6\cdot325$ (approx.).

Consequently, we find that the square root tables are arranged on pairs of pages, with the numbers on the left running from 10 to 54 and from 55 to 99. We must decide what is the first significant figure in the square root and where the decimal point occurs. This is most important, and the method of procedure is as follows:

Before looking up the square root of a number, mark off the figures in pairs from the decimal point.   Write above the left-hand pair of figures (or figure, if there is an odd figure over when you have done the pairing) the largest number whose square is not greater than the number formed by this left-hand pair, and put a cross over each pair of figures.   The decimal point in the square root goes above that in the original number.

In order to find the figures of the square root from the tables, the method is the same as for reading off squares, but you must be careful to see that the answer commences with the same figure as your rough estimate. (Some square root tables use a double row of figures instead of separate pages for the two possible sets of figures.)

Notice that the square root of a number less than 1 is bigger than the number.

Example 3   *Use tables to find the square roots of:*
(i) 87640,   (ii) 876400,   (iii) 0·0008764,   (iv) 0·00008764.

(i)
$$\begin{array}{c|c|c} 2 & \times & \times . \\ \hline 8 & 76 & 40. \end{array}$$

Rough estimate 200.

Find the page on which the square root starts with 2.
$$\sqrt{87640} = 296 \cdot 1 \text{ (approx.).}$$

(ii)
$$\begin{array}{c|c|c} 9 & \times & \times . \\ \hline 87 & 64 & 00. \end{array}$$

Rough estimate 900.

Find the page on which the square root starts with 9.
$$\sqrt{876400} = 936 \cdot 1 \text{ (approx.).}$$

(iii)
$$\begin{array}{c|c|c|c} \cdot\,0 & 2 & \times & \\ \hline 0\cdot00 & 08 & 76 & 4 \end{array}$$

Rough estimate 0·02.

Find the page on which the square root starts with 2.
$$\sqrt{0\cdot0008764} = 0\cdot02961 \text{ (approx.).}$$

(iv) *Find the square root of* 0·00008764.

$$\begin{array}{c|c|c|c|}
\cdot\,0 & 0 & 9 & \\
0\cdot00 & 00 & 87 & 64 \\
\end{array}$$

Rough estimate 0·009.

Find the page on which the square root starts with 9.

$$\sqrt{0\cdot00008764} = 0\cdot009361 \text{ (approx.)}.$$

EXERCISE 40

Before the answers to this Exercise are written, make a rough estimate of the square root, giving the first significant figure and the position of the decimal point.

Find from the tables the square roots of:

1 4·7	**2** 47	**3** 473	**4** 0·473
5 84	**6** 8·5	**7** 850	**8** 8543
9 0·08543	**10** 8 543 000	**11** 17·98	**12** 0·4329
13 999·9	**14** 0·000556	**15** 23610	**16** 0·1
17 0·5	**18** 356·7	**19** 0·064	**20** 0·6531
21 0·0006	**22** 7·35	**23** 10·08	**24** 9317
25 93 000 000	**26** 0·03924	**27** 950	**28** 873·68
29 0·17348	**30** 365	**31** 0·0005	**32** 0·7

Square root of a fraction Since $\frac{4}{5} \times \frac{4}{5} = \frac{16}{25}$, the square root of $\frac{16}{25}$ is $\frac{4}{5}$. The square root of a fraction is thus found by taking the square root of the numerator and denominator.

The square root of a mixed number is found by reducing the mixed number to an improper fraction; e.g.

$$\sqrt{7\tfrac{9}{16}} = \sqrt{\frac{121}{16}} = \frac{\sqrt{121}}{\sqrt{16}} = \frac{11}{4} = 2\tfrac{3}{4}.$$

Notice that $\sqrt{4\tfrac{1}{9}}$ is not equal to $\sqrt{4} + \sqrt{\tfrac{1}{9}}$, or $2\tfrac{1}{3}$. This can be tested by squaring $2\tfrac{1}{3}$, which gives

$$2\tfrac{1}{3} \times 2\tfrac{1}{3} = \tfrac{7}{3} \times \tfrac{7}{3} = \tfrac{49}{9} = 5\tfrac{4}{9}.$$

The correct way to deal with $\sqrt{4\frac{1}{9}}$ is as follows:

$$\sqrt{4\tfrac{1}{9}} = \sqrt{\frac{37}{9}} = \frac{\sqrt{37}}{3} = \frac{6 \cdot 083}{3} = 2 \cdot 028 \text{ (approx.);}$$

or $\sqrt{4\frac{1}{9}} = \sqrt{4 \cdot 111} = 2 \cdot 027$ (approx.).

EXERCISE 41

Find the square roots of:

1 $\frac{9}{16}$	2 $\frac{289}{400}$	3 $\frac{49}{144}$	4 $\frac{196}{225}$	5 $\frac{81}{1600}$
6 $7\frac{1}{9}$	7 $20\frac{1}{4}$	8 $1\frac{9}{16}$	9 $4\frac{25}{36}$	10 $5\frac{1}{16}$
11 $12\frac{1}{4}$	12 $18\frac{7}{9}$	13 $44\frac{4}{9}$	14 $5\frac{41}{64}$	15 $4\frac{21}{25}$

Reciprocals The *reciprocal* of a number x is $\frac{1}{x}$. Thus the reciprocal of 2 is $\frac{1}{2}$; that of $\frac{1}{3}$ is 3; that of $2\frac{4}{5}$ is $\frac{5}{14}$. In using reciprocal tables you must insert the decimal point by first making a rough estimate of the answer.

The only difference between using square tables and reciprocal tables is that in the case of reciprocal tables the figure given in the difference columns must be *subtracted* from the number in the main column. This is on account of the fact that, as a number increases, its reciprocal decreases. For example, the reciprocal of 28·36 is *less* than the reciprocal of 28·3.

Example 4 *Find the reciprocal of* 0·4876.

$$\text{Rough estimate} = \frac{1}{0 \cdot 5} = 2.$$

From the table, the reciprocal of 0·487 = 2·053
Subtract difference for 6 = 0·003
———
2·050

∴ the reciprocal of 0·4876 = 2·050 (approx.).

EXERCISE 42

Find from the reciprocal tables the values of:

1 $\dfrac{1}{24\cdot36}$ **2** $\dfrac{1}{0\cdot7637}$ **3** $\dfrac{1}{8\cdot412}$ **4** $\dfrac{1}{0\cdot00526}$

5 $\dfrac{1}{2728}$ **6** $\dfrac{1}{29\cdot43}$ **7** $\dfrac{1}{67890}$ **8** $\dfrac{1}{0\cdot000235}$

9 $\dfrac{1}{0\cdot1534}$ **10** $\dfrac{1}{0\cdot1748}$ **11** $\dfrac{1}{3\cdot654}$ **12** $\dfrac{1}{36\cdot472}$

13 $\dfrac{1}{30\,070}$ **14** $\dfrac{1}{0\cdot05003}$ **15** $\dfrac{1}{2\cdot046}$ **16** $\dfrac{3}{10\cdot42}$

17 $\dfrac{2}{0\cdot572}$ **18** $\dfrac{5}{1\cdot732}$ **19** $\dfrac{2}{10\cdot94}$ **20** $\dfrac{3}{1\cdot414}$

Pythagoras' Theorem, which will be proved later in this book, states that the square on the hypotenuse of a right-angled triangle is equal to the sum of the squares on the other two sides; or, in Fig. 156,

$$a^2 = b^2 + c^2.$$

Tables of squares and square roots will be found very useful in calculations on this theorem, as the next worked examples show. It must be remembered that the results obtained are correct only to three significant figures.

If you draw a square ABCD, with side 1 cm, and draw the

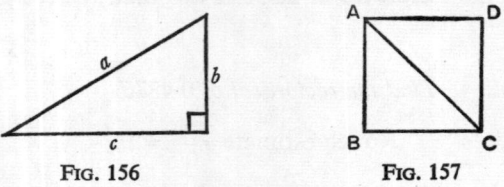

FIG. 156   FIG. 157

diagonal AC, as in Fig. 157, Pythagoras' Theorem applied to the right-angled triangle ABC shows that

$$AC^2 = AB^2 + BC^2 = 1^2 + 1^2 = 2.$$
$$\therefore AC = \sqrt{2} \text{ cm.}$$

The length $\sqrt{2}$ can therefore be drawn on paper, yet it cannot be measured exactly with a ruler. The square root tables give $\sqrt{2}$ as 1·414. This merely means that $\sqrt{2}$ lies between 1·4135 and 1·4145, and is nearer to 1·414 than to 1·413 or 1·415.

Example 5   *In Fig. 156, b = 5·8, c = 4·6.   Find a, correct to two decimal places.*

By Pythagoras' Theorem,

$$a^2 = b^2 + c^2 = 5\cdot8^2 + 4\cdot6^2$$
$$= 33\cdot64 + 21\cdot16 \text{ (using tables of squares)}$$
$$= 54\cdot80.$$
$$\therefore a = \sqrt{54\cdot8}$$
$$= 7\cdot403 \text{ (using square root tables).}$$
$$\therefore a = 7\cdot40 \text{ (to 2 decimal places).}$$

Example 6   *The cuboid shown in Fig. 158 has AB 6·3 cm, BC 4·2 cm and AE 2·7 cm.   Calculate the length of AG, to the nearest millimetre.*

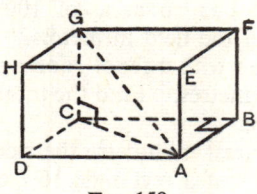

FIG. 158

Since $\angle ABC = 90°$, $AC^2 = AB^2 + BC^2$
$$= 6\cdot3^2 + 4\cdot2^2$$
$$= 39\cdot69 + 17\cdot64 = 57\cdot33.$$

Since $\angle ACG = 90°$, $AG^2 = AC^2 + CG^2$
$$= 57\cdot33 + 2\cdot7^2$$
$$= 57\cdot33 + 7\cdot29 = 64\cdot62.$$

$$\therefore AG = 8\cdot038 \text{ cm}$$
$$= 8\cdot0 \text{ cm (to the nearest millimetre).}$$

Example 7 *In Fig.* 156, $a = 6\cdot7$, $b = 4\cdot1$. *Find c, correct to three significant figures.*

By Pythagoras' Theorem,

$$b^2 + c^2 = a^2.$$

$$\therefore\ 4\cdot1^2 + c^2 = 6\cdot7^2.$$

$$\therefore\qquad c^2 = 6\cdot7^2 - 4\cdot1^2$$
$$= 44\cdot89 - 16\cdot81 \text{ (using tables of squares)}$$
$$= 28\cdot08.$$

$$\therefore\qquad c = \sqrt{28\cdot08}$$
$$= 5\cdot299 \text{ (using square root tables).}$$

$$\therefore\qquad c = 5\cdot30 \text{ (to 3 figures).}$$

EXERCISE 43

Nos. 1–5 refer to Fig. 156, p. 142.

1 If $b = 9\cdot84$, $c = 3\cdot62$, find a.   **2.** If $b = 17\cdot6$, $c = 8\cdot91$, find a.

3 If $a = 9\cdot07$, $b = 6\cdot72$, find c.   **4** If $a = 34\cdot6$, $c = 28\cdot5$, find b.

5 If $b = 14\cdot26$, $c = 11\cdot96$, find a.

6 The sides of a rectangle are 4·6 cm and 6·4 cm. Find the length of a diagonal.

7 A square field has an area of 100 000 m². Find the length of the side of the field in metres.

8 A square garden with a fence running all round it has an area of 1805 square metres. Find the total length of the fence, to the nearest metre.

9 Find to the nearest millimetre the side of a square whose area is equal to that of a rectangle 16·7 cm long and 9·4 cm wide.

10. Calculate to the nearest millimetre the length of the tangent from a point to a circle of radius 4 cm, if the point is 7 cm from the centre of the circle.

11 A chord of a circle is 10·6 cm long, and the radius of the circle is 6·5 cm. Calculate the distance of the chord from the centre of the circle.

12 ABC is an isosceles triangle in which AB = AC = 5·8 cm and BC = 3·7 cm. Find the length of the perpendicular from A to BC.

13 A rectangular field is x metres wide and $2x$ metres long. and its area is 42 000 square metres. Find x, to the nearest whole number.

14 A room is 5 m long, $4\frac{1}{2}$ m wide and $3\frac{1}{2}$ m high. Find in metres (i) the length of a diagonal of the floor, (ii) the distance from a corner of the floor to the opposite corner of the ceiling.

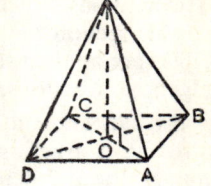

Fig. 159

15 Find the length of the diagonal of a cuboid 8·6 cm by 5·1 cm by 2·6 cm.

16 Find the diagonal of a cube whose edge is 4 cm.

17 Fig. 159 shows a pyramid on a rectangular base; ABCD is horizontal, and VO is vertical. AB = 6·3 cm, BC = 8·7 cm, VO = 10·8 cm. Calculate AC, AO and VA.

18 In Fig. 159, AB = 3·5 cm, BC = 4·2 cm and VA = 7·6 cm. Calculate AC, AO and VO.

19 If, in Fig. 159, ABCD is a square of side 4 cm and VO = 7 cm, calculate VA.

20 Copy Fig. 159 and mark the mid-point X of AB. If BC = 8 cm and VX = 6·5 cm, calculate VO.

In Nos. 21–23, use the formula $\dfrac{1}{f} = \dfrac{1}{u} + \dfrac{1}{v}$.

21 Find f if $u = 7 \cdot 62$ and $v = 5 \cdot 08$.

22 Find f if $u = 26 \cdot 3$ and $v = -38 \cdot 2$.

23 Find v if $u = 13 \cdot 7$ and $f = 24 \cdot 5$.

24 Two circular metal discs, of radii 1·7 cm and 2·5 cm, are both t cm thick. Find in terms of π and t an expression in its simplest form for the total volume of metal contained in the discs.

If the discs are melted down to form a single disc, also of the same thickness t cm, find the radius of this disc.

18. FRACTIONS

THE methods of dealing with fractions were explained in Part I. In this section the earlier work is revised, and the same principles are applied to some harder examples of arithmetical and algebraic fractions.

Simplification of fractions: cancelling As we have found already, a fraction can often be simplified by dividing its numerator and denominator by the same factor. Thus,

$$\frac{90}{210} = \frac{3}{7} \text{ (dividing numerator and denominator by 30),}$$

$$\frac{abc}{a^3c} = \frac{b}{a^2} \text{ (dividing numerator and denominator by } ac\text{).}$$

The process of dividing numerator and denominator of a fraction by the same factor (whether a numerical one or an algebraic one) is called **cancelling.** You should simplify a fraction in this way whenever you can, but always make quite certain that you are 'cancelling' something which is a genuine *factor* of the numerator and denominator, and not merely one term or part of these. The following worked example emphasises this point, and it is very important to be clear when it is correct to cancel and when it is not correct.

Example 1 *Simplify the fractions*

(i) $\dfrac{24+7}{21}$, (ii) $\dfrac{ab+c}{bc}$, (iii) $\dfrac{ab \times c}{bc}$, (iv) $\dfrac{x^2-y^2}{x^2-xy}$

(i) $\dfrac{24+7}{21} = \dfrac{31}{21}$, or $1\dfrac{10}{21}$.

It would be wrong to say $\dfrac{24+7}{21} = \dfrac{\overset{8}{\cancel{24}}+7}{\underset{7}{\cancel{21}}}$; for 3 is a factor, not

of the numerator, but only of one term of the numerator.

It would also be wrong to say $\dfrac{24+7}{21} = \dfrac{24+\overset{1}{7}}{\underset{3}{21}}$, for 7 is not a factor of the numerator.

(ii) $\dfrac{ab+c}{bc}$ cannot be simplified further.

It would be wrong to write $\dfrac{a\cancel{b}+c}{\cancel{b}c} = \dfrac{a+c}{c}$, or to write $\dfrac{ab+\overset{1}{\cancel{c}}}{b\cancel{c}} = \dfrac{ab+1}{b}$. Neither b nor c is a factor of the numerator.

(iii) In the case of $\dfrac{ab \times c}{bc}$, the numerator and denominator both have b and c as factors. We can therefore cancel these factors, and write

$$\frac{a\cancel{b} \times \cancel{c}}{\cancel{b}\cancel{c}} = \frac{a}{1} = a.$$

(iv) $\dfrac{x^2-y^2}{x^2-xy} = \dfrac{(x+y)(x-y)}{x(x-y)}$

$$= \frac{x+y}{x}, \text{ cancelling the factor } (x-y).$$

(Would it be correct to take this a stage further, and write

$$\frac{\cancel{x}+y}{\cancel{x}} = \frac{1+y}{1}, \quad \text{or} \quad 1+y?)$$

Sometimes a fraction is simplified by *multiplying* its numerator and denominator by the same quantity. Changing the sign of numerator and denominator is an example of this, for we are multiplying them by -1. Thus,

$$\frac{-2}{-5} = \frac{+2}{+5} = \frac{2}{5};$$

$$\frac{3}{-7} = \frac{-3}{+7} = -\frac{3}{7}.$$

Example 2 *Simplify*
$$\frac{\dfrac{1}{x}+\dfrac{1}{y}}{\dfrac{1}{x}-\dfrac{1}{y}}$$

Multiply each term of the numerator and denominator by xy. This gives

$$\frac{\dfrac{xy}{x}+\dfrac{xy}{y}}{\dfrac{xy}{x}-\dfrac{xy}{y}}=\frac{y+x}{y-x}.$$

This answer cannot be simplified further.

EXERCISE 44

Simplify the following fractions where possible:

1 $\dfrac{a^2}{ax}$ **2** $\dfrac{xy}{xz}$ **3** $\dfrac{abc}{bcd}$ **4** $\dfrac{-9xy}{6ay}$

5 $\dfrac{x+y}{y}$ **6** $\dfrac{12a^3b}{16a^2b^2}$ **7** $\dfrac{3x^3}{6x^6}$ **8** $\dfrac{1+3x}{6x^2}$

9 $\dfrac{-14ab}{-2a}$ **10** $\dfrac{15x^3}{-5x}$ **11** $\dfrac{1}{\frac{1}{2}+\frac{1}{3}}$ **12** $\dfrac{(7\times1\cdot6)+21}{14}$

13 $\dfrac{1}{x+\frac{1}{3}}$ **14** $\dfrac{\dfrac{a}{5}}{a+\frac{1}{5}}$ **15** $\dfrac{1+\dfrac{1}{x}}{y}$ **16** $\dfrac{\dfrac{x}{2}+\dfrac{x}{8}}{\frac{1}{4}}$

17 $\dfrac{3a}{a+\frac{c}{2}}$ **18** $\dfrac{\dfrac{1}{x}}{1-\dfrac{1}{x}}$ **19** $\dfrac{15a^3x^2y}{9axy^3}$ **20** $\dfrac{-14xy^4}{\dfrac{35y^2}{x}}$

21 $\dfrac{1+3a}{1+9a}$ **22** $\dfrac{\dfrac{a^2b}{4}}{\dfrac{ab^2}{6}}$ **23** $\dfrac{-\dfrac{x}{y}}{-\dfrac{b}{2y}}$ **24** $\dfrac{18a^2}{-27b^2}$

25 $\dfrac{a^2+2a}{a^2+4a}$ **26** $\dfrac{a^2}{a^2-b^2}$ **27** $\dfrac{6a^2x}{2b^2x^2}$ **28** $\dfrac{x^3+2x^2}{-4x}$

Example 3 *Simplify* (i) $\dfrac{x^2+x-12}{x^2-3x}$, (ii) $\dfrac{a^2-16b^2}{a^2+5ab+4b^2}$.

(i) $\dfrac{x^2+x-12}{x^2-3x} = \dfrac{(x-3)(x+4)}{x(x-3)}$

$\qquad\qquad = \dfrac{x+4}{x}$, cancelling the factor $(x-3)$.

This cannot be simplified further. Dividing numerator and

denominator by x gives $\dfrac{1+\dfrac{4}{x}}{1}$, or $1+\dfrac{4}{x}$, but this is no simpler

than $\dfrac{x+4}{x}$.

(ii) $\dfrac{a^2-16b^2}{a^2+5ab+4b^2} = \dfrac{(a)^2-(4b)^2}{a^2+5ab+4b^2}$

$\qquad\qquad = \dfrac{(a+4b)(a-4b)}{(a+4b)(a+b)} = \dfrac{a-4b}{a+b}$.

EXERCISE 45

Simplify the following fractions where possible. Write 'no simpler form' if the fraction cannot be simplified.

1 $\dfrac{x^2+x}{x^2+4x+3}$ **2** $\dfrac{ab-ac}{3b-3c}$ **3** $\dfrac{2x+2y}{x^2-y^2}$

4 $\dfrac{a^2-16}{a-4}$ **5** $\dfrac{x^2-3x+2}{x^2-7x+10}$ **6** $\dfrac{2x^2-18}{4x^2+12x}$

7 $\dfrac{x^2-5x+6}{2x-6}$ **8** $\dfrac{3x+3y}{3x-3y}$ **9** $\dfrac{x^2+3x-4}{2x^2+x-3}$

10 $\dfrac{x+x^2}{a+ax}$ **11** $\dfrac{x^2-y^2}{x^2-6xy+5y^2}$ **12** $\dfrac{4x^2-8x+3}{4x^2-2x}$

13 $\dfrac{2x^2-9x-5}{x^2-10x+25}$ **14** $\dfrac{9x^2-y^2}{6x+2y}$ **15** $\dfrac{a^2+ab}{4a^3b-4ab^3}$

16 $\dfrac{6a^2-a-2}{3a^2-5a+2}$ **17** $\dfrac{x^2+2x}{2x^2-3x-2}$ **18** $\dfrac{ax+by}{ay+bx}$

19 $\dfrac{x^2-2x-8}{2x^2-9x+4}$ **20** $\dfrac{3x-12}{2x^2-3x-20}$ **21** $\dfrac{1-5x+6x^2}{1-7x+12x^2}$

Addition and subtraction   Fractions are added and subtracted by converting them into equivalent fractions, all with the same denominator.

Example 4   *Simplify* $\dfrac{3}{4} - \dfrac{5}{7} + \dfrac{3}{14}$.

The expression
$$= \frac{21}{28} - \frac{20}{28} + \frac{6}{28}$$

$$= \frac{21 - 20 + 6}{28} = \frac{7}{28} = \frac{1}{4}.$$

Example 5   *Simplify* $\dfrac{a+b}{4} - \dfrac{a+2b}{12}$.

The expression
$$= \frac{3(a+b)}{12} - \frac{a+2b}{12}$$

$$= \frac{3(a+b) - (a+2b)}{12}$$

$$= \frac{3a + 3b - a - 2b}{12} = \frac{2a+b}{12}.$$

Notice that the line separating the numerator and denominator of the fraction $\dfrac{a+2b}{12}$ acts like a bracket round the numerator. For this reason a bracket must be put round $a+2b$ when the two fractions are combined into a single fraction.

Example 6   *Simplify* $\dfrac{2}{5x} + \dfrac{3}{2x} - \dfrac{1}{4x}$.

The L.C.M. of $5x$, $2x$, $4x$ is $20x$.

$\therefore$ the expression
$$= \frac{8}{20x} + \frac{30}{20x} - \frac{5}{20x}$$

$$= \frac{8 + 30 - 5}{20x}$$

$$= \frac{33}{20x}.$$

EXERCISE 46

Simplify:

1 $\dfrac{3}{4}+\dfrac{2}{5}$ **2** $\dfrac{x}{4}+\dfrac{2x}{5}$ **3** $\dfrac{1}{4x}+\dfrac{2}{5x}$

4 $\dfrac{a}{6}-\dfrac{a}{8}$ **5** $\dfrac{5a}{6}-\dfrac{3a}{8}$ **6** $\dfrac{2}{x}+\dfrac{3}{2x}$

7 $1+\dfrac{3}{x}+\dfrac{1}{2x}$ **8** $\dfrac{3}{5x}-\dfrac{1}{10x}$ **9** $\dfrac{1}{2x}+\dfrac{1}{3x}+\dfrac{1}{4x}$

10 $-\dfrac{4}{3a}+\dfrac{3}{2a}$ **11** $\dfrac{x}{6}-\dfrac{2x}{15}$ **12** $\dfrac{a}{2b}-\dfrac{a}{6b}$

13 $\dfrac{x}{4y}+\dfrac{x}{12y}$ **14** $\dfrac{8}{5a}-\dfrac{4}{15a}$ **15** $\dfrac{x}{y}+\dfrac{y}{x}+2$

16 $\dfrac{x-6}{3}+4$ **17** $x-\dfrac{3x}{7}$ **18** $\dfrac{1}{a}+\dfrac{a}{2}$

19 $\dfrac{x}{3xy}+\dfrac{z}{9yz}$ **20** $\dfrac{1}{xy}+\dfrac{1}{yz}+\dfrac{1}{zx}$ **21** $\dfrac{2}{x}+\dfrac{3}{x^2}+\dfrac{4}{x^3}$

22 $\dfrac{a+b}{2}+\dfrac{a-b}{3}$ **23** $\dfrac{5x^2}{8}-\dfrac{x^2}{2}$ **24** $\dfrac{x}{2}+\dfrac{2}{3}+\dfrac{1}{6x}$

25 $\dfrac{x}{y}+\dfrac{x^2}{y^2}$ **26** $\dfrac{5x}{3a}+\dfrac{17x}{6a}$ **27** $\dfrac{x}{2y}+\dfrac{x}{3y}-\dfrac{x}{4y}$

28 $\dfrac{2(x-y)}{5}+\dfrac{3(x+2y)}{2}$ **29** $\dfrac{2x-1}{3}-\dfrac{x}{2}$ **30** $1-\dfrac{4x-y}{3x}$

31 $2-\dfrac{x+y}{3x}+\dfrac{y}{6x}$ **32** $\dfrac{1-x}{x}-\dfrac{1-y}{y}$

33 $\dfrac{3x}{5}-\dfrac{x+2}{2}+\dfrac{x}{10}$ **34** $\dfrac{a+2b}{ab}-\dfrac{3a-b}{a^2}-\dfrac{1}{b}$

35 $\dfrac{3a-b}{2ab}-\dfrac{2b+c}{3bc}$ **36** $\dfrac{2x}{a}-\dfrac{3x}{b}+\dfrac{ax+bx}{ab}$

37 $\dfrac{3x}{5}+3-\dfrac{x-2}{3}+\dfrac{x}{15}$ **38** $\dfrac{2(x-2y)}{5}-\dfrac{x-3y}{4}$

39 $\dfrac{2x-3}{2}-\dfrac{x+4}{5}-\dfrac{x-5}{4}$ **40** $\dfrac{a+1}{3}+\dfrac{2a-3}{6}-\dfrac{4a}{9}$

When the denominators are more difficult, break them up into factors if they have any, find their L.C.M., and express each fraction with this as its denominator. Then combine the fractions into a single fraction, and remember to write down the denominator at every step of the working.

Example 7 *Find the L.C.M. of* $2x^2+4x-6$, x^2-9 *and* $5x^2+20+15$.

$$2x^2+4x-6=2(x^2+2x-3)=2(x-1)(x+3),$$
$$x^2-9 \qquad\qquad\qquad =(x-3)(x+3),$$
$$5x^2+20x+15=5(x^2+4x+3)=5(x+3)(x+1).$$
$$\therefore \text{ the L.C.M.} \qquad =10(x-1)(x+3)(x-3)(x+1).$$

Example 8 *Simplify* $\dfrac{2x+y}{x-3y}-\dfrac{x+y}{3x-y}$.

The L.C.M. of $(x-3y)$ and $(3x-y)$ is $(x-3y)(3x-y)$.

$$\therefore \text{ the expression} = \frac{(2x+y)(3x-y)}{(x-3y)(3x-y)} - \frac{(x+y)(x-3y)}{(x-3y)(3x-y)}$$

$$= \frac{(2x+y)(3x-y)-(x+y)(x-3y)}{(x-3y)(3x-y)}$$

$$= \frac{(6x^2+xy-y^2)-(x^2-2xy-3y^2)}{(x-3y)(3x-y)}$$

$$= \frac{6x^2+xy-y^2-x^2+2xy+3y^2}{(x-3y)(3x-y)}$$

$$= \frac{5x^2+3xy+2y^2}{(x-3y)(3x-y)}.$$

Example 9 *Simplify* $\dfrac{4}{a-b}+\dfrac{2}{b-a}$.

Notice that $b-a=-(a-b)$; for the rule for removing brackets gives $-(a-b)=-a+b=b-a$.

The L.C.M. is thus $(a-b)$, and we can change the denominator of the second fraction to $(a-b)$ by changing the sign in front of the fraction.

The expression $= \dfrac{4}{a-b} - \dfrac{2}{a-b} = \dfrac{2}{a-b}$.

EXERCISE 47

Find the L.C.M. of the following:

1 $2x+2y,\ 5x+5y$ **2** $3a+3b,\ 6a-6b$

3 $2x^2-2,\ 3x+3$ **4** $a^2-ab,\ a^2+ab,\ b^2+ab$

5 $a^2-b^2,\ a^2+2ab+b^2$ **6** $x^2-3x+2,\ x^2-5x+6$

7 $4x-4y,\ 8y-8x$ **8** $x-2y,\ 6y-3x$

9 $x^2-2x-3,\ x^2-9$ **10** $x^2-4xy+3y^2,\ -2x^2+7xy-3y^2$

Simplify:

11 $\dfrac{1}{x+1} + \dfrac{1}{x-1}$ **12** $\dfrac{1}{x+1} + \dfrac{1}{x+2}$ **13** $\dfrac{1}{a-2} - \dfrac{1}{a+2}$

14 $\dfrac{x}{x+y} + \dfrac{y}{x-y}$ **15** $\dfrac{1}{x+3} - \dfrac{2}{x-3}$ **16** $\dfrac{1}{x} + \dfrac{1}{x-y}$

17 $\dfrac{1}{2x-2y} - \dfrac{1}{3x-3y}$ **18** $\dfrac{1}{x} + \dfrac{1}{y} - \dfrac{2}{x+y}$ **19** $\dfrac{x+1}{x+2} - \dfrac{x+4}{3x+6}$

20 $\dfrac{b}{a(a+b)} + \dfrac{a-b}{(a+b)^2}$ **21** $\dfrac{b}{a-b} + \dfrac{a}{b-a}$ **22** $\dfrac{1}{2} + \dfrac{x}{2a-x}$

23 $\dfrac{1}{x} + \dfrac{y}{x^2-xy}$ **24** $\dfrac{2}{x+y} - \dfrac{x-2y}{x^2-y^2}$ **25** $\dfrac{1}{4x-4} + \dfrac{1}{x^2-1}$

26 $\dfrac{x}{x+2} + \dfrac{x}{x-2}$ **27** $\dfrac{1}{x-3} + \dfrac{1}{x^2-3x} + \dfrac{1}{x}$

28 $\dfrac{x+2}{x+3} - \dfrac{x-1}{x}$ **29** $\dfrac{x+1}{4x-8} + \dfrac{1}{(x-2)^2}$

30 $4 - \dfrac{a}{a-b}$ **31** $\dfrac{5}{2x-1} - \dfrac{7-x}{3x-1}$

32 $\dfrac{2}{x-1} - \dfrac{3}{x+2}$ **33** $\dfrac{a+2}{a-4} - \dfrac{a+3}{a-1}$

34 $\dfrac{y-1}{y-2} - \dfrac{y+2}{y+1}$ **35** $\dfrac{x}{1-x} - \dfrac{x}{1+x} + \dfrac{2x}{1-x^2}$

36 $\dfrac{1}{t-t^2} - \dfrac{1}{t+t^2}$ **37** $\dfrac{x+2}{2x-1} - \dfrac{x-2}{2x+1}$

Multiplication and division of fractions Factorise all the numerators and denominators, and then cancel. The answer should be left in factors.

To divide one fraction by another, change $\div$ into $\times$ and turn the divisor the other way up, as in the case of arithmetical fractions.

Example 10 *Simplify* $\dfrac{3a+9}{6a+6} \times \dfrac{a^2+3a+2}{a^2+2a-3}.$

The expression $= \dfrac{\overset{1}{\cancel{3}}(a+3)}{\underset{2}{\cancel{6}}(a+1)} \times \dfrac{(a+1)(a+2)}{(a+3)(a-1)}$

$$= \frac{a+2}{2(a-1)}, \text{ after cancelling } (a+3) \text{ and } (a+1).$$

Example 11 *Simplify*

$$\frac{x^2-xy}{4x^2-4xy-3y^2} \times \frac{2x^2+3xy+y^2}{x^2-y^2} \div \frac{x-2y}{2x-3y}.$$

The expression

$$= \frac{x(x-y)}{(2x-3y)(2x+y)} \times \frac{(2x+y)(x+y)}{(x+y)(x-y)} \times \frac{2x-3y}{x-2y}$$

$$= \frac{x}{x-2y}, \text{ after cancelling } (x-y), (2x+y), (x+y) \text{ and } (2x-3y).$$

EXERCISE 48

Simplify:

1 $\dfrac{x^2-x}{2} \times \dfrac{4}{x-1}$

2 $\dfrac{6x^2}{3x+3y} \times \dfrac{xy+y^2}{4x}$

3 $\dfrac{a}{b} \times \dfrac{b}{c} \times \dfrac{c}{a}$

4 $\dfrac{x-y}{x+y} \times \dfrac{y+x}{y-x}$

5 $\dfrac{x^2+2xy}{y} \div (x^2-4y^2)$

6 $\dfrac{3a}{b} \times \dfrac{b-b^2}{2-2b}$

7 $\dfrac{x-3}{x-1} \div \dfrac{x^2-9}{x+1}$

8 $\dfrac{x^2+x-2}{x} \times \dfrac{x^2}{x^2+5x+6}$

9 $\dfrac{x^2+3x-4}{x+2} \div \dfrac{x^2+5x+4}{x^2+4x+4}$

10 $\dfrac{x^2-5x-6}{x^2+x-2} \div \dfrac{x-6}{x-1}$

11 $\dfrac{4(x+1)}{x-3} \times \dfrac{2x-6}{3x+6} \div \dfrac{6x+6}{9x+18}$ **12** $\dfrac{4x+12}{x+3} \times \dfrac{x-2}{x+3} \div \dfrac{3x-6}{x}$

13 $\dfrac{x^2+2xy+y^2}{x^2-y^2} \div \dfrac{x-2y}{x-y}$ **14** $\dfrac{2}{a} \times \dfrac{a^2+3a}{4} \times \dfrac{a^2}{a^2-9}$

15 $\dfrac{x^2-xy}{y^2-yz} \times \dfrac{xy-xz}{xy-y^2}$ **16** $\dfrac{x^2-16}{x^2+4x+3} \times \dfrac{3x+9}{3x-12}$

Harder arithmetical fractions   Complex fractions should not be split up into parts, but should be dealt with as in the following worked example.

Example 12   *Simplify* $\dfrac{2\frac{1}{6} \times \frac{9}{28}}{6\frac{3}{7} - 3\frac{9}{14}}.$

$$\frac{2\frac{1}{6} \times \frac{9}{28}}{6\frac{3}{7} - 3\frac{9}{14}} = \frac{\frac{13}{6} \times \frac{9}{28}}{3\frac{6-9}{14}}$$

$$= \frac{\frac{13}{6} \times \frac{9}{28}}{2\frac{11}{14}}$$

$$= \frac{\cancel{13}}{\underset{2}{6}} \times \frac{9}{\underset{2}{28}} \times \frac{\cancel{14}}{\underset{3}{39}} = \frac{1}{4}.$$

EXERCISE 49

Find the value of:

1 $\dfrac{2\frac{2}{3}+1\frac{3}{5}}{2\frac{2}{3}-1\frac{3}{5}}$ **2** $\dfrac{1\frac{3}{4} \times 5\frac{1}{3}}{6\frac{11}{20}-5\frac{3}{10}}$ **3** $\dfrac{3\frac{1}{3}-1\frac{5}{6}}{2\frac{3}{4}+1\frac{1}{6}+\frac{1}{3}}$

4 $\dfrac{7\frac{1}{5} \times 5\frac{1}{7}}{7\frac{1}{5}-5\frac{1}{7}}$ **5** $\dfrac{1\frac{4}{5}+\frac{7}{13}}{1+(1\frac{4}{5} \times \frac{7}{13})}$ **6** $\dfrac{6\frac{1}{7}-3\frac{5}{14}}{3\frac{1}{2}+4\frac{3}{4}}$

7 $\dfrac{(\frac{3}{4}+\frac{5}{12}-\frac{2}{3})}{\frac{7}{15}+\frac{3}{20}-\frac{1}{30}}$ **8** $\dfrac{\frac{1}{2}+\frac{1}{3}-\frac{1}{4}}{(\frac{1}{2}+\frac{1}{3}) \times \frac{1}{4}}$ **9** $\dfrac{5\frac{7}{8}-1\frac{13}{40}}{\frac{3}{4}+1\frac{1}{5}} \div 4\frac{2}{3}$

10 $\dfrac{(\frac{2}{5} \times 10\frac{5}{12})+9\frac{3}{4}}{12\frac{11}{13} \times 2\frac{1}{2}}$ **11** $\dfrac{(3\frac{1}{7} \times 2\frac{1}{3})-2}{4\frac{1}{2}-3\frac{1}{9}}$ **12** $\dfrac{2\frac{3}{8}+6\frac{1}{4}-1\frac{1}{12}+\frac{1}{3}}{3\frac{3}{4} \times 1\frac{1}{6}}$

old books have t
giving $\frac{152}{217}$

In Nos. 13–16, simplify the fractions by cancelling before evaluating.

13 $\dfrac{0 \cdot 44 \times 0 \cdot 0583}{0 \cdot 0121}$ **14** $\dfrac{21 \times 51 \cdot 6 - 7 \times 22 \cdot 3}{14}$

15 $\dfrac{8 \cdot 19 \times (4 \cdot 56 + 2 \cdot 65)}{21 \cdot 84 \times 0 \cdot 7}$ **16** $\dfrac{4 \cdot 8\{(3 \cdot 5)^2 - (0 \cdot 5)^2\}}{0 \cdot 144}$

Equations containing fractions Multiply every term (on both sides of the equation) by the L.C.M. of the denominators of the fractions.

Example 13 *Solve the equation* $1 + \dfrac{3x-5}{20} - \dfrac{x+1}{5} = \dfrac{1}{2}(x+2).$

Multiply both sides by 20, which is the L.C.M. of 20, 5, 2.

$$20 + \frac{20(3x-5)}{20} - \frac{20(x+1)}{5} = \frac{20}{2}(x+2).$$

$$\therefore \ 20 + (3x-5) - 4(x+1) = 10(x+2).$$

$$\therefore \qquad 20 + 3x - 5 - 4x - 4 = 10x + 20.$$

$$\therefore \qquad\qquad\qquad\qquad -11x = 9.$$

$$\therefore \qquad 11x = -9, \qquad x = -\tfrac{9}{11}.$$

Example 14. *Solve the equation* $\dfrac{2y+5}{y-1} - \dfrac{y+4}{y+3} = 1.$

Multiply both sides by $(y-1)(y+3)$.

$$\frac{(2y+5)(\cancel{y-1})(y+3)}{\cancel{y-1}} - \frac{(y+4)(y-1)(\cancel{y+3})}{\cancel{y+3}} = (y-1)(y+3).$$

$$\therefore \ 2y^2 + 11y + 15 - (y^2 + 3y - 4) = y^2 + 2y - 3.$$

$$\therefore \qquad\qquad y^2 + 8y + 19 = y^2 + 2y - 3.$$

$$\therefore \qquad\qquad\qquad\qquad 6y = -22.$$

$$\therefore \qquad\qquad\qquad\qquad y = -\tfrac{22}{6}$$

$$= -\tfrac{11}{3} = -3\tfrac{2}{3}.$$

In the case of simultaneous equations, when the terms with x and y in them contain fractions or decimals, begin by clearing these terms of fractions.

EXERCISE 50

Solve the following equations:

1 $\dfrac{x-2}{3} - \dfrac{2x+1}{5} + 1 = 0$

2 $\dfrac{2x-1}{5} + \dfrac{3-2x}{4} = \dfrac{13}{20}$

3 $\dfrac{y-5}{2} + \dfrac{y+2}{3} = \dfrac{4y-1}{3}$

4 $\dfrac{4t-1}{2} + \dfrac{t+3}{3} + \dfrac{t+7}{6} = 0$

5 $\dfrac{2v-5}{5} + \dfrac{v-4}{3} = \dfrac{v+14}{30}$

6 $\dfrac{x-1}{3} + \dfrac{2-x}{4} + \dfrac{5x-4}{12} = 0$

7 $\dfrac{y+1}{3} - \dfrac{2y+3}{4} = \dfrac{5}{6}(y+1)$

8 $0 \cdot 7x + 56 = 0$

9 $2 \cdot 4x - 1 \cdot 3x + 4 \cdot 4 = 0$

10 $\dfrac{5x+2}{7} - \dfrac{x-3}{5} = \dfrac{1}{2}$

11 $\dfrac{3}{4x} - \dfrac{4}{3x} = 1\frac{1}{6}$

12 $\dfrac{x+5}{9} + \dfrac{x+2}{6} = \dfrac{2x+11}{12}$

13 $\dfrac{3y+4}{5} - \dfrac{2y+5}{3} = y+2$

14 $\dfrac{x+2}{3} - \dfrac{x+8}{4} + \dfrac{x-2}{2} = 0$

15 $\dfrac{3}{x+2} = \dfrac{5}{x}$

16 $\dfrac{1}{x} + \dfrac{3}{2x-7} = 0$

17 $\dfrac{2}{x+3} - \dfrac{1}{5x-2} = 0$

18 $\dfrac{1}{t-1} = \dfrac{3}{7t}$

19 $\dfrac{y-4}{y+8} - 2\frac{1}{2} = 0$

20 $\dfrac{2}{2x+5} - \dfrac{4}{x-3} = 0$

21 $0 \cdot 14x + 0 \cdot 16x = 4 \cdot 5$

22 $\dfrac{1}{x} - \dfrac{10}{3x} = \dfrac{2}{15}$

23 $\dfrac{4}{3x} - 4 + \dfrac{2}{x} = \dfrac{4}{5}$

24 $\dfrac{x+3}{2\frac{1}{2}} + \dfrac{x-2}{3\frac{1}{3}} = \dfrac{3}{5}$

25 $\dfrac{4}{5}(x+1) - \dfrac{x}{3} = 2\frac{2}{3}$

26 $\dfrac{2x+1}{2\frac{1}{2}} + \dfrac{x-1}{4} - \dfrac{3x+4}{3} = 0$

27 $\dfrac{y+1}{7} + \dfrac{4y+10}{11} + 3 = 0$

28 $\frac{1}{6}(t+2) - \frac{1}{9}(2t-3) = \frac{1}{12}(1-3t)$

29 $\frac{3}{4}(2x-5) + \frac{1}{6}(x+7) = \frac{2}{3}(x-2)$

30 $\dfrac{3t+12}{4} - \dfrac{2t-5}{5} + \dfrac{3-7t}{10} = \dfrac{t}{20}$

Solve the simultaneous equations:

31 $\dfrac{x-6}{3} + \dfrac{3-y}{2} = 0,$

$\dfrac{x+2}{5} = \dfrac{2y+1}{3}$

32 $\dfrac{p}{4} + \dfrac{3q}{2} = 15,$

$\dfrac{3p}{20} - \dfrac{q}{10} = 1$

33 $\dfrac{3x}{2} + \dfrac{4y}{3} = 4,$

$\dfrac{x}{4} + \dfrac{y}{2} + 1 = 0$

34 $2{\cdot}1x - 3{\cdot}6y = 9{\cdot}3,$

$1{\cdot}1x + 1{\cdot}2y = 4{\cdot}1$

35 $\dfrac{1}{3}(3x-y) = 2,$

$\dfrac{x+y}{4} + \dfrac{1}{2} = 0$

36 $\dfrac{y}{2} - \dfrac{x}{9} = 6,$

$\dfrac{2x}{3} + \dfrac{3y}{5} = 0$

37 $\dfrac{3x}{2} + y = \dfrac{y+2}{4},$

$\dfrac{x-3y}{2} = \dfrac{6x+1-y}{3}$

38 $\dfrac{x+2}{6} - \dfrac{y+1}{2} = x+y+1,$

$\dfrac{x-4}{6} - \dfrac{y+3}{2} = 0$

39 $\dfrac{x+y}{x-y} = 1\tfrac{1}{2},$

$\dfrac{x+y}{15} - \dfrac{x-y}{20} + \dfrac{2}{5} = 0$

40 $\dfrac{x+2}{6} = \dfrac{x+y+3}{2},$

$\dfrac{x+y-2}{3} = \dfrac{y+1}{4}$

Problems leading to fractional equations

Example 15   *A man takes* 1 *hour longer to row* 8 *km upstream against a current flowing at* 2 *km/h than to row the same distance downstream with the same current.   Find his speed in still water.*

Suppose his speed in still water is x km/h.

Then his speed upstream $= (x-2)$ km/h, and his speed downstream $= (x+2)$ km/h.

The time to row 8 km upstream $\quad = \dfrac{8}{x-2}$ h.

The time to row 8 km downstream $= \dfrac{8}{x+2}$ h.

$$\therefore \quad \frac{8}{x-2} - \frac{8}{x+2} = 1.$$

$$\therefore \quad \frac{8(x+2) - 8(x-2)}{(x-2)(x+2)} = 1.$$

$$\therefore \quad \frac{8x + 16 - 8x + 16}{x^2 - 4} = 1.$$

$$\therefore \quad \frac{32}{x^2 - 4} = 1.$$

Multiply both sides by $(x^2 - 4)$,

$$32 = x^2 - 4.$$

$$\therefore \quad x^2 - 4 = 32.$$

$$\therefore \quad x^2 = 36.$$

$$\therefore \quad x = 6 \quad \text{or} \quad -6.$$

The answer -6 is obviously inadmissible.

$\therefore$ the man's speed in still water $= 6$ km/h.

EXERCISE 51

1 A sum of £100 is divided equally among a number of people. If there had been five more people, the share of each would have been £1 less. Find the number of people.

2 In Fig. 160, if XT is the tangent at T to the circle, it can be shown that $\dfrac{XB}{XT} = \dfrac{XT}{XA}$. If AB = 9 cm and XT = 6 cm, find the length of XB.

3 The price of an egg went up by $\frac{1}{2}$p, and as a result the number of eggs which could be bought for 35p was two less than the number which could previously be bought for 36p. Find the original cost of an egg.

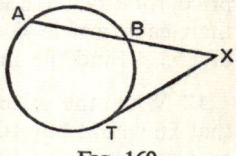

FIG. 160

4 A boy calculates that his time to cycle 30 km would have been half an hour less if he had cycled 2 km/h faster all the way. Find the speed at which he cycled.

5 A motorist drove on a certain road at 64 km/h when the surface was good, and at 16 km/h when it was bad. Over a total distance of 56 km his average speed was 44·8 km/h. How much of the road was good?

6 An aeroplane can travel at 160 km/h in still air. It flies from P to Q, a distance of 400 km, and back to P, the wind blowing throughout the journey from Q to P. If the total journey takes 5 h 20 min, find the velocity of the wind.

7 I cycled to a neighbouring town at 15 km/h, spent 25 min there, and, leaving my bicycle, walked back at 6 km/h. The whole journey occupied 1 h 35 min. Find the distance to the town.

8 A man walks at 6 km/h and runs at 10 km/h. He wishes to get to the station, 3 km away, in 26 minutes. How far must he run?

9 An estate of £8550 is to be divided equally among a certain number of people. If there were four less people, the share of the rest would be increased by £120. Find the number of people.

10 Two men walk a distance of $17\frac{1}{2}$ km. The speed of one of the men is $\frac{1}{2}$ km/h faster than the other, and he takes 10 min less for the journey. Find their rates of walking.

11 A man bought a certain number of articles, all the same price, for £54. He sold all except 2 of them at a price £1 more than each article cost him, and the sale produced the total of £55. Find the number of articles he originally bought.

12 When the price of apples fell by 2p per kg, a man found that £6 would buy 10 kg more than before. Find the original cost per kg.

13 A regular polygon has n sides. Write down the number of degrees in each interior angle and also in each exterior angle.
If the interior angle exceeds the exterior angle by 108°, find n.

14 A boy cycled to a place 40 km from his home and then returned. On the return journey he was delayed by fog, which reduced his average speed by 4 km/h. As a result the return journey took 30 minutes longer than the outward one. Find his speed on the outward journey.

19. LOCI (I)

THE idea of a **locus** was introduced in Part I, § 34, p. 212, where the word was used to describe the path or pattern traced out by a point which moves according to a given law. Four loci of particular importance were stated, and these will now be repeated and discussed in a more formal manner.

(i) **The locus of points at a given distance from a given point O is a circle with O as centre and the given distance as radius.** See Fig. 161.

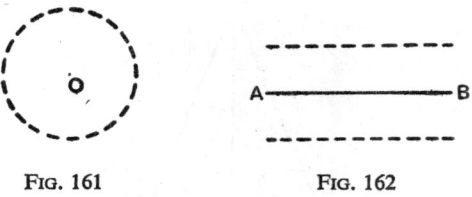

FIG. 161   FIG. 162

(ii) **The locus of points at a given distance from a given straight line AB is the pair of straight lines, both parallel to AB and at the given distance from AB.** See Fig. 162.

(iii) **The locus of points equidistant from two given points
A and B is the perpendicular bisector of AB.** See Fig. 163.

(iv) **The locus of points equidistant from two given intersecting straight lines AOB, COD is the pair of straight lines
bisecting the angles between AB, CD.** See Fig. 164.

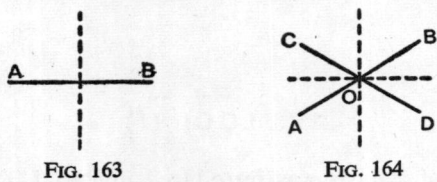

FIG. 163   FIG. 164

Statements (iii) and (iv) are contained in Theorems 19 and
20. Both these theorems are in two parts. The first part
proves that every point on the specified locus obeys the given
law, and the second part proves that every point which obeys
the given law lies on the specified locus.

THEOREM 19

(i) **A point on the perpendicular bisector of the straight line
joining two given points is equidistant from them.**

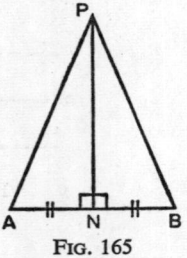

FIG. 165

Given two points A and B, N the mid-point of AB, and P
is any point on the perpendicular bisector PN of AB.

To prove that PA = PB.

Proof In the △s PNA, PNB,

$$AN = BN \quad \text{(given)},$$
$$\angle ANP = \angle BNP \quad (90°, \text{ given}),$$
$$PN = PN.$$

∴ △s $\substack{\text{PNA} \\ \text{PNB}}$ are congruent   (SAS).

$$∴ \quad PA = PB.$$

(ii) **A point equidistant from two given points lies on the perpendicular bisector of the straight line joining them.**

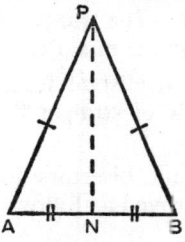

FIG. 166

Given two points A and B; P is a point such that PA = PB.
Construction Let N be the mid-point of AB. Join PN.
To prove that PN is perpendicular to AB.
Proof In the △s PNA, PNB,

$$NA = NB \quad \text{(constr.)},$$
$$PA = PB \quad \text{(given)},$$
$$PN = PN.$$

∴ △s $\substack{\text{PNA} \\ \text{PNB}}$ are congruent   (SSS).

$$∴ \quad \angle PNA = \angle PNB.$$

But $\angle PNA + \angle PNB = 180°$ (adj., ANB a st. line).
$$∴ \quad \angle PNA = \angle PNB = 90°.$$

Summary The locus of points equidistant from two given points is the perpendicular bisector of the straight line joining them.

Reference   *Perp. bisector locus.*

THEOREM 20

(i) **A point on the bisector of a given angle is equidistant from the arms of the angle.**

(ii) **A point which is equidistant from two given intersecting straight lines lies on one of the bisectors of the angles formed by them.**

Reference   Angle bisector locus.

The proof of this theorem is left as an exercise for the reader (see Exercise 52, No. 1). The two parts of the theorem enable us to make the following summary:

The locus of points equidistant from two given intersecting straight lines is the pair of straight lines bisecting the angles between the given lines.

The fact that the four bisectors form two perpendicular straight lines may be proved as follows:

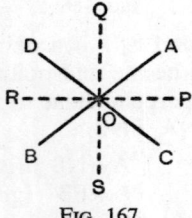

Fig. 167

Let the bisectors be OP, OQ, OR, OS, as in Fig. 167.

$\angle AOC + \angle AOD = 180°$ (adj., COD a st. line).

But $\angle POQ = \angle POA + \angle AOQ$

                 $= \tfrac{1}{2}\angle AOC + \tfrac{1}{2}\angle AOD = 90°$.

Similarly, angles QOR, ROS, SOP are right angles.

Some of the locus questions in Exercise 92, p. 218, of **Part I** should be done again before the following exercise.

EXERCISE 52

1 (i) P is a point on the bisector of an angle AOB; M, N are the feet of the perpendiculars from P to OA, OB. Prove that the triangles POM, PON are congruent, and deduce that PM = PN.

(ii) OA, OB are two straight lines, and a point P is such that its perpendicular distances PM, PN from OA, OB are equal. Prove that the triangles POM, PON are congruent, and deduce that P lies on the bisector of ∠AOB.

2 Draw a triangle ABC in which AC = 3·6 cm, ∠A = 41°, ∠C = 109°. Find by construction the points which are equidistant from B and C, and also equidistant from AB, AC. Measure their distances from B.

3 Copy the triangle ABC of No. 2, and construct (i) the locus of points equidistant from A and B, (ii) the locus of points equidistant from B and C. Hence find the point O which is equidistant from A, B and C. Measure OA, and draw the circle with centre O and radius OA. It is called the **circumcircle** of △ABC. (See p. 188.)

4 Draw a triangle ABC in which AB = 5·8 cm, BC = 4·8 cm and CA = 3·8 cm. Construct (i) the locus of points equidistant from AB, AC, (ii) the locus of points equidistant from BC, BA. Hence find the point I, inside the triangle, equidistant from AB, AC, BC. Measure the length of the perpendicular from I to AB, and draw the circle with this length as radius and I as centre. It is called the **incircle** or inscribed circle of △ABC. (See p. 197.)

5 Draw a triangle ABC in which AB = 3·8 cm, BC = 4·8 cm and CA = 4·3 cm. Using ruler and compasses only, construct (i) the locus of points which are equidistant from CA and CB, (ii) the point X on this locus which is outside the triangle and is 2·8 cm from B. Measure CX.

6 Using ruler and compasses only, draw a triangle ABC in which AB = 6·0 cm, BC = 4·0 cm and ∠ABC = 60°. Find the point D, on the opposite side of AC from B, such that ∠DAB = 60° and AD = DC. Measure the length of DB.

7 Draw an angle ABC of 35°. Find by construction a point P in the arm BA such that the length of the perpendicular from P to BC is 4·0 cm. Measure PB.

8 Draw a triangle ABC in which AB = 6·0 cm, ∠ABC = 50° and BC = 4·6 cm. Find by construction all the points which are 2·0 cm from the side AB and 6·0 cm from the point C. Measure their distances from A.

20. INDICES AND LOGARITHMS

Positive integral indices

If n is any positive integer (i.e. whole number), a^n is a short way of writing

$$a \times a \times a \times a \times \ldots \text{ to } n \text{ factors.}$$

The rules for multiplying or dividing two powers of a have been given in Part I: if m and n are positive integers,

$$a^m \times a^n = a^{m+n};$$

$$a^m \div a^n = a^{m-n} \text{ (provided } m \text{ is greater than } n).$$

EXERCISE 53 (Oral)

Simplify:

1 $a^3 \times a^2$	**2** $b^2 \times b^5$	**3** $c \times c^3$	**4** $x^3 \times x^3$
5 $x^8 \div x^2$	**6** $x^3 \div x$	**7** $a^{12} \div a^3$	**8** $b^2 \div b^2$
9 $x^2 \times x^6$	**10** $y^{10} \div y^5$	**11** $(a^3)^2$	**12** $(x^5)^2$
13 $a^7 \times a^3$	**14** $d \times d^4$	**15** $a^8 \div a$	**16** $x^{20} \div x^5$
17 $x^6 \times x^6$	**18** $a^2 \times a^3 \times a^4$	**19** $\dfrac{a^3 \times a^7}{a^4}$	**20** $a^2 \times b^3$

Fractional and negative indices   If n is not a positive integer, e.g. if $n = 2\frac{1}{2}$ or $-\frac{3}{4}$ or 0, the definition of a^n given above has no meaning. If we want to use symbols such as $a^{\frac{1}{2}}$, a^{-3} we must first say what they mean. Now it would obviously be convenient to have the same rules whether the indices were positive integers or fractions or negative numbers. Since, therefore, we can define these new powers of a in whatever manner we like, we will define them as obeying the law

$$a^m \times a^n = a^{m+n}$$

for *all* values of m and n, and see what meaning of such symbols as $a^{\frac{1}{2}}$, a^{-2}, a^0 this definition gives us.

Example 1 *Find the meanings of* $16^{\frac{1}{2}}$, $9^{\frac{1}{2}}$ *and* $a^{\frac{1}{2}}$.

By the law of indices, $16^{\frac{1}{2}} \times 16^{\frac{1}{2}} = 16^{\frac{1}{2}+\frac{1}{2}} = 16^1 = 16$.

$\therefore$ $16^{\frac{1}{2}}$ is the number whose square is 16.

$$\therefore\ 16^{\frac{1}{2}} = \sqrt{16} = 4.$$

Similarly, $\qquad\qquad 9^{\frac{1}{2}} = \sqrt{9} = 3,$

and $\qquad\qquad\quad a^{\frac{1}{2}} = \sqrt{a}.$

Example 2 *Find the meaning of* $8^{\frac{1}{3}}$.

By the law of indices, $8^{\frac{1}{3}} \times 8^{\frac{1}{3}} = 8^{\frac{1}{3}-\frac{1}{3}} = 8^{\frac{2}{3}}$.

$$\therefore\ 8^{\frac{1}{3}} \times 8^{\frac{1}{3}} \times 8^{\frac{1}{3}} = 8^{\frac{2}{3}} \times 8^{\frac{1}{3}}$$
$$= 8^{\frac{2}{3}+\frac{1}{3}} = 8^1 = 8.$$

$\therefore$ $8^{\frac{1}{3}}$ is the number whose cube is 8.

$\therefore$ $8^{\frac{1}{3}} =$ the cube root of $8 = 2$.

The symbol for 'cube root' is $\sqrt[3]{\ }$.   Hence we see that
$$a^{\frac{1}{3}} = \sqrt[3]{a}.$$

Example 3 *Find the meaning of* a^0.

By the law of indices, $a^2 \times a^0 = a^{2+0} = a^2$.
Divide both sides by a^2,

$$a^0 = \frac{a^2}{a^2} = 1.$$

The same answer could be obtained from the law $a^m \div a^n = a^{m-n}$ by making m equal to n, thus giving $a^n \div a^n = a^0$. But obviously $a^n \div a^n$ is 1.

Example 4 *If a is not 0, find the meaning of a^{-3}.*

$$a^{-3} \times a^3 = a^{-3+3} = a^0 = 1.$$

Divide both sides by a^3, $\quad a^{-3} = \dfrac{1}{a^3}$.

Similarly, $a^{-1} = \dfrac{1}{a}$, $a^{-2} = \dfrac{1}{a^2}$, and so on.

The laws of indices The symbol a^m, when m is not a positive integer, has been defined as obeying the law

$$a^m \times a^n = a^{m+n},$$

which was found to be true when m and n were positive integers. With this definition, we have obtained the following meanings for negative and fractional indices:

$$a^0 = 1,$$

$$a^{-n} = \frac{1}{a^n} \text{ (provided that } a \text{ is not 0)},$$

and $a^{\frac{1}{2}} = \sqrt{a}$, $\quad a^{\frac{1}{3}} = \sqrt[3]{a}$, $\quad a^{\frac{1}{4}} = \sqrt[4]{a}$, etc.

We shall assume that the division law of indices,

$$a^m \div a^n = a^{m-n},$$

holds good if the above definition is adopted.

A third useful law of indices is $(a^m)^n = a^{mn}$. This can easily be seen to be true when m and n are positive integers, e.g. $(a^4)^3 = a^4 \times a^4 \times a^4 = a^{4+4+4} = a^{12}$.

We shall assume that the law is still true when m and n are negative or fractional, e.g. $(a^{\frac{4}{3}})^3 = a^{\frac{4}{3} \times 3} = a^4$.

We thus have the following laws of indices which are true for all values of m and n, whether positive integral, negative, or fractional:

$$a^m \times a^n = a^{m+n}$$
$$a^m \div a^n = a^{m-n}$$
$$(a^m)^n = a^{mn}$$

EXERCISE 54

Express as powers of a:

1 The squares of a^2, a^3, a^4, $a^{\frac{1}{2}}$, $a^{1\frac{1}{2}}$.

2 The square roots of a^4, a^8, a, a^6.

3 The cubes of a^2, a^3, a^4, $a^{\frac{2}{3}}$.

4 The cube roots of a^3, a^6, a, a^2.

5 $(a^4)^3$ **6** $(a^3)^2$ **7** $a \times a^{\frac{1}{2}}$ **8** $a^2 \times a^2 \times a^2$

9 $(a^3)^4$ **10** $(a^{\frac{1}{2}})^3$ **11** $(a^{\frac{1}{3}})^2$ **12** $(a^9)^{\frac{1}{3}}$

Give the numerical values of:

13 $25^{\frac{1}{2}}$ **14** $10^3 \div 10^5$ **15** 10^{-1} **16** $27^{\frac{1}{3}}$

17 $36^{\frac{1}{2}}$ **18** $1000^{\frac{1}{3}}$ **19** 10^0 **20** 2^{-3}

21 5^{-1} **22** $(\frac{1}{2})^0$ **23** $(\frac{1}{9})^{\frac{1}{2}}$ **24** $(\frac{1}{2})^{-1}$

25 10^{-3} **26** $(0\cdot1)^3$ **27** $64^{\frac{1}{2}}$ **28** $(\frac{1}{16})^{-\frac{1}{4}}$

29 Use the square root tables to find, correct to 3 places of decimals, the numerical values of (i) $2^{\frac{1}{2}}$, (ii) $20^{\frac{1}{2}}$, (iii) $3^{\frac{1}{2}}$, (iv) $10^{\frac{1}{4}}$.

30 Use the fact that $10^{\frac{1}{4}} \times 10^{\frac{1}{4}} = 10^{\frac{1}{2}}$ to find the value of $10^{\frac{1}{4}}$, correct to 3 places of decimals.

Powers of 10 From the square root tables we find that $\sqrt{10} = 3\cdot162 \ldots$

$$\therefore \ 10^{\frac{1}{2}} = 3\cdot162 \ldots$$

Again, $10^{\frac{1}{4}} \times 10^{\frac{1}{4}} = 10^{\frac{1}{2}} = 3\cdot162 \ldots$

$$\therefore \ 10^{\frac{1}{4}} = \sqrt{3\cdot162} = 1\cdot779 \ldots$$

Similarly, $10^{\frac{1}{8}} = \sqrt{1\cdot779} = 1\cdot333 \ldots$

Also $10^{\frac{2}{3}} = (10^3)^{\frac{1}{6}} = \sqrt[6]{10^3} = \sqrt[6]{1000} = \sqrt{31\cdot62}$
$$= 5\cdot623 \ldots$$
$$10^{\frac{3}{8}} = (10^3)^{\frac{1}{8}} = \sqrt[8]{1000} = \sqrt[4]{31\cdot62} = \sqrt{5\cdot623}$$
$$= 2\cdot372 \ldots$$

In a similar way we can find $10^{\frac{5}{8}}$ and $10^{\frac{7}{8}}$. Also we know that $10^0 = 1$.

We are now able to draw up a table of values of 10^x for

$x = 0, \frac{1}{8}, \frac{1}{4}, \ldots, \frac{7}{8}, 1$, the values being correct to two places of decimals.

Values of x	0	0·125	0·25	0·375	0·5	0·625	0·75	0·875	1
Values of 10^x	1	1·33	1·78	2·37	3·16	4·22	5·62	7·50	10

The graph of 10^x is shown in Fig. 168. The pupil should draw his own graph on as large a scale as possible, and use it for Exercise 55 on the next page.

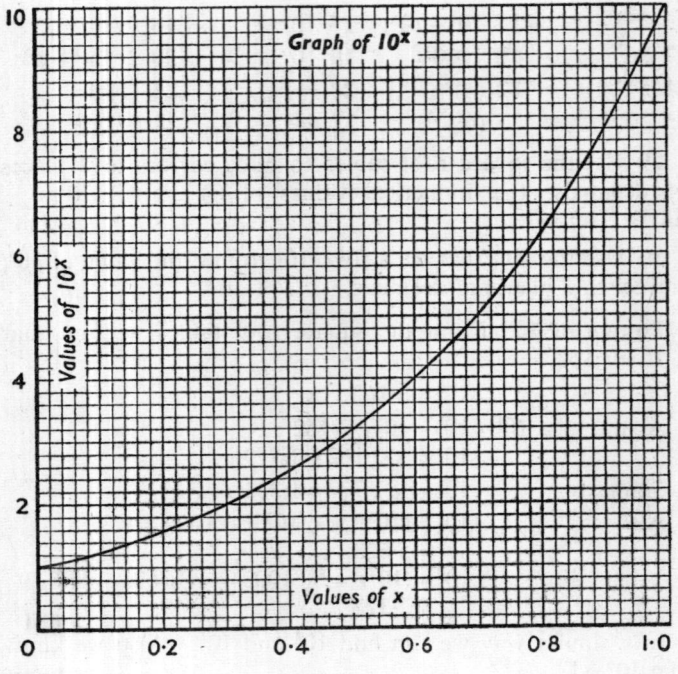

FIG. 168

EXERCISE 55

Use the graph of 10^x (Fig. 168) for the following exercise:

1 Find the values of: (i) $10^{0·6}$, (ii) $10^{0·2}$, (iii) $10^{0·55}$, (iv) $10^{0·9}$, (v) $10^{0·46}$.

2 Express as powers of 10: (i) 1·5, (ii) 2·5, (iii) 8, (iv) 5, (v) 6·5.

3 Find the values of $10^{0·3}$ and $10^{0·5}$. Multiply these answers together, and compare the result with the value of $10^{0·8}$ as read from the graph.

4 Find a and b if $2·2 = 10^a$, $3 = 10^b$. Find also the value of 10^{a+b} from the graph. Is the answer right?

5 Copy the following piece of calculation, filling up the blank spaces:

$$4 \times 1·6 = 10^{····} \times 10^{····}$$
$$= 10^{····+····}$$
$$= 10^{···}$$
$$=$$

Is the answer correct?

6 Use the graph to find the value of $3 \times 2·75$.

7 Use the graph to evaluate $(2·5)^2$.

8 Use the graph to evaluate $1·9 \times 4·7$.

9 Find a and b if $8 = 10^a$, $2 = 10^b$. Find also the value of 10^{a-b} from the graph. Is the answer right?

10 Copy the following piece of calculation, filling up the blank spaces:

$$4 \div 1·6 = 10^{····} \div 10^{···}$$
$$= 10^{····-····}$$
$$= 10^{····}$$
$$=$$

Is the answer correct?

11 Use the graph to evaluate $7·6 \div 4$.

12 Use the graph to evaluate $6·3 \div 3·5$.

Logarithms If a number is expressed as 10^x, the index x is called the **logarithm** of the number.

For example, the graph in Fig. 168 shows that, as nearly as can be read, $2 = 10^{0.30}$.

∴ the logarithm of 2 is 0·30 (approximately).

A few numbers, such as 100 and 1000, are exact powers of 10, and these numbers therefore have exact logarithms. Thus, $100 = 10^2$, and so the logarithm of 100 is 2. The logarithms of other numbers could be read off from the graph of 10^x, and this is what was done in Exercise 55. By drawing much larger graphs you could find the index, and therefore the logarithm, more accurately. But it is not necessary to do this, because tables have been compiled from which the logarithm can be read off quickly and easily. Even these, however, are not exact. At the end of this book are four-figure tables, and the logarithms there are given to four decimal places, with the same unreliability in the fourth figure as in the case of the other tables. Other logarithm tables are published which are correct to 5 decimal places, and others again correct to 7 decimal places.

Logarithm of a number between 1 and 10 Since $10^0 = 1$ and $10^1 = 10$, a number between 1 and 10 must lie between 10^0 and 10^1, and the corresponding index of 10 lies between 0 and 1.

∴ the logarithm of a number between 1 and 10 is a decimal quantity lying between 0 and 1.

We shall now explain how to find this decimal.

Example 5 *Find the logarithm of* 6·238.

Turn to the tables of logarithms at the end of the book, and find the row beginning with 62 (the first two figures of 6·238). The following extract from the tables shows this row, with the numbers printed at the tops of the columns:

	0	1	2	3	4	5	6	7	8	9	1	2	3	4	5	6	7	8	9
62	7924	7931	7938	7945	7952	7959	7966	7973	7980	7987	1	1	2	3	3	4	5	6	8

The first two figures, 62, of the number 6·238 are found in the left-hand column. The main column headed 3 (the third figure) gives ·7945. The difference column headed 8 (the fourth figure) gives a figure 6, which is added to the last figure of ·7945, making ·7951. Set out in full:

The logarithm of 6·23   = ·7945
Difference for 8   =   6

∴ the logarithm of 6·238 = ·7951 (approx.)

The above working is done mentally. Do not forget to insert a decimal point in front of the four figures obtained.

To find the logarithm of a number such as 3, find the row beginning with 30.

EXERCISE 56

Use the tables of logarithms to express the following numbers as powers of 10:

1 3·6	**2** 6·3	**3** 8·2	**4** 8	**5** 3
6 2·76	**7** 3·65	**8** 5·7	**9** 3·02	**10** 1·08
11 5·10	**12** 6·731	**13** 8·174	**14** 3·333	**15** 4·09
16 9·981	**17** 3·008	**18** 8·709	**19** 2·005	**20** 5·991
21 9·207	**22** 5·464	**23** 1·007	**24** 2·803	**25** 4·448
26 4·230	**27** 7·181	**28** 3·049	**29** 2·110	**30** 6·663

In order to find the value of any given power of 10, the process of looking up the logarithm is reversed. Anti-logarithm tables give the answer directly, but their use is not recommended at first.

Example 6 *Find the values of* (i) $10^{0·5798}$, (ii) $10^{0·6684}$, (iii) $10^{0·7294}$, (iv) $10^{0·3149}$.

(i) In the tables of logarithms, ·5798 occurs in the 38 row in the column headed 0.

∴ the significant figures in the value of $10^{·5798}$ are 380.

But the answer must be between 10^0 and 10^1, i.e. between 1 and 10.

∴ $10^{·5798} = 3·80$ (approx.).

(ii) ·6684 gives the significant figures 466.
$$\therefore 10^{·6684} = 4·66 \text{ (approx.).}$$

(iii) ·7292 gives the significant figures 536.

We need a further 2, added to the last figure of ·7292, to make ·7294. This 2 is found in the difference columns headed 2 and 3, and we take whichever we like as the fourth figure of the answer.
$$\therefore 10^{·7294} = 5·362 \text{ (approx.).}$$

(iv) ·3139 gives the significant figures 206.

A further 10 added to the last figure is needed to make ·3149. No difference column contains 10; the column headed 4 contains 8, and the column headed 5 contains 11. We therefore take 5 as the fourth figure.
$$\therefore 10^{·3149} = 2·065 \text{ (approx.).}$$

EXERCISE 57

Use the logarithm tables to find the values of:

1 $10^{·4771}$	**2** $10^{·9345}$	**3** $10^{·8062}$	**4** $10^{·9647}$
5 $10^{·4857}$	**6** $10^{·6646}$	**7** $10^{·8831}$	**8** $10^{·9390}$
9 $10^{·5109}$	**10** $10^{·6704}$	**11** $10^{·9062}$	**12** $10^{·8005}$
13 $10^{·2682}$	**14** $10^{·5089}$	**15** $10^{·1723}$	**16** $10^{·0030}$

Find the numbers whose logarithms are:

17 ·5320	**18** ·0473	**19** ·2451	**20** ·7476
21 ·8598	**22** ·9191	**23** ·3118	**24** ·9913
25 ·5922	**26** ·1528	**27** ·0814	**28** ·8627
29 ·9174	**30** ·0784	**31** ·8349	**32** ·6500

Multiplication and division

Example 7 *Evaluate* 2·241 × 3·042.
Rough check: 2 × 3 = 6.

$$2·241 \times 3·042 = 10^{·3504} \times 10^{·4832}$$
$$= 10^{·3504 + ·4832}$$
$$= 10^{·8336}$$
$$= 6·818$$

$$\begin{array}{r} ·3504 \\ ·4832 \\ \hline ·8336 \\ \hline \end{array}$$

or 6·82 (correct to 3 sig. figs.).

Example 15 *Evaluate* $736 \cdot 2 \times 21 \cdot 83$.

No.	Log.
736·2	2·8670
21·83	1·3391
16080	4·2061

Ans. 16 100 (to 3 sig. figs.).

Example 16 *Evaluate* $487 \cdot 2 \div 39 \cdot 01$.

No.	Log.
487·2	2·6877
39·01	1·5912
12·49	1·0965

Ans. 12·5 (to 3 sig. figs.).

Example 17 *Evaluate* $(18 \cdot 63)^5$.

No.	Log.
18·63	1·2702
	5
2 244 000	6·3510

Ans. 2 240 000 (to 3 sig. figs.).

Example 18 *Evaluate* $\sqrt[3]{654 \cdot 3}$.

No.	Log.
654·3	2·8158
	÷ 3
8·681	·9386

Ans. 8·68 (to 3 sig. figs.).

EXERCISE 60

Evaluate the following, first giving the four figures of the answer as obtained from the tables and then correcting the answer to three significant figures:

1 $69 \cdot 6 \times 18 \cdot 73$ **2** $127 \cdot 5 \times 3 \cdot 58$ **3** $339 \cdot 4 \times 73 \cdot 45$
4 $286\,700 \div 351 \cdot 2$ **5** $6040 \div 28 \cdot 61$ **6** $536 \cdot 6 \div 4 \cdot 77$
7 $36\,807 \div 43 \cdot 02$ **8** $234 \cdot 5 \times 67 \cdot 8$ **9** $3006 \div 86 \cdot 2$

10 $4365 \times 3 \cdot 298$ **11** $6496 \cdot 8 \div 753 \cdot 4$ **12** $78 \cdot 34 \times 7 \cdot 693$

13 $1000 \div 46 \cdot 82$ **14** $39\ 074 \times 22 \cdot 78$ **15** $5267 \div 63 \cdot 7$

16 $(27 \cdot 55)^2$ **17** $(876 \cdot 4)^2$ **18** $(10 \cdot 84)^3$

19 $\sqrt{876 \cdot 8}$ **20** $\sqrt[3]{7695}$ **21** $(6 \cdot 085)^4$

22 $(7 \cdot 603)^5$ **23** $\sqrt{9694}$ **24** $\sqrt[4]{87 \cdot 43}$

25 $(78 \cdot 52)^3$ **26** $\sqrt[3]{284 \cdot 3}$ **27** $\sqrt[4]{48\ 932}$

Numbers less than 1 Suppose we want the logarithm of 0·3685. From the logarithm tables we find that the logarithm of 3·685 is ·5664. In other words, $3 \cdot 685 = 10^{\cdot 5664}$.

Now
$$0 \cdot 3685 = 3 \cdot 685 \div 10$$
$$= 10^{\cdot 5664} \div 10^1$$
$$= 10^{\cdot 5664 - 1} = 10^{-1 + \cdot 5664}.$$

Similarly,
$$0 \cdot 03685 = 3 \cdot 685 \div 100$$
$$= 10^{\cdot 5664} \div 10^2$$
$$= 10^{\cdot 5664 - 2} = 10^{-2 + \cdot 5664}.$$

Now $-1 + \cdot 5664 = - \cdot 4336$, and $-2 + \cdot 5664 = -1 \cdot 4336$. But we do not write them in this way, because the logarithms of numbers between 0 and 1, though negative, are always written with the decimal part positive.

For shortness, $-1 + \cdot 5664$ is written with the minus sign above the figure 1, to show that it does not refer to the part ·5664, thus:

$$\bar{1} \cdot 5664.$$

This is read 'minus 1 plus point 5664'. Later this can be shortened still further to 'bar 1 point 5664'.

Similarly, $-2 + \cdot 5664 = \bar{2} \cdot 5664$, and so on.

We can now make a table of the logarithms of various numbers less than 1, all of which have the same significant figures:

No.	Log.
·3685	$-1 + \cdot 5664$
·03685	$-2 + \cdot 5664$
·003685	$-3 + \cdot 5664$
·0003685	$-4 + \cdot 5664$

The decimal part of the logarithm is always ·5664. There is also a negative integer or whole number in front of ·5664, and the rule for this whole number is:

Count the number of figures between the decimal point and where the decimal point would be in the standard form.

This is the same rule as that given on page 176 for numbers greater than 10; but for numbers less than 1 we have to put a minus sign in front of the number obtained by the rule.

Example 19   *Find the logarithm of* 0·00007143.
Starting with 7·143 (the standard form), we have to move the decimal point five places to the left in order to obtain 0·00007143.   ∴ the whole number of the logarithm is − 5.
Also the decimal part of the logarithm, from the tables, is ·8539.
∴ the logarithm of 0·00007143 = − 5 + ·8539, or $\bar{5}$·8539.

Example 20   *Find the number whose logarithm is* − 4 + ·6133, or $\bar{4}$·6133.
Deal first with the decimal part of the logarithm. This gives the significant figures 4105.
Now deal with the negative whole number part of the logarithm. To do this, put the significant figures in the standard form 4·105, and then move the decimal point four places to the left, thus making 0·0004105.
∴ the number whose logarithm is $\bar{4}$·6133 = 0·0004105.

EXERCISE 61

Use the tables to write down the four-figure logarithms of:

1 0·6739	**2** 0·00348	**3** 0·05682	**4** 0·985
5 0·0308	**6** 0·0007	**7** 0·101	**8** 0·0006
9 0·005073	**10** 0·3177	**11** 7·65	**12** 0·0104
13 10·66	**14** 0·000453	**15** 0·80906	**16** 0·0025

17 0·0001 **18** 19·48 **19** 0·15882 **20** 208·4
21 $3·08 \times 10^{-3}$ **22** 46×10^{-2} **23** $65·72 \times 10^{-6}$
24 $5·4 \times 10^4$ **25** 225×10^{-7}

Use the tables to write down to four figures the numbers whose logarithms are:

26 $-1 + ·6332$ **27** $-4 + ·7648$ **28** $-2 + 0·0703$
29 $-5 + 0·0759$ **30** $-1 + ·3805$ **31** $-3 + ·8720$
32 $\bar{1}·4771$ **33** $\bar{4}·9980$ **34** $-3 + ·4972$
35 4·6541 **36** $\bar{2}·5732$ **37** $\bar{5}·7678$
38 $\bar{1}·7042$ **39** 2·6000 **40** $\bar{3}·664$

When dealing with logarithms some of which have the whole number part positive and some negative, you will find it simplest at first to write the whole number part in full with the proper sign in front of it. The following worked examples show how this is done, but after a little practice you will probably be able to do the working mentally.

Example 21 *Simplify* (i) $3·67 + \bar{2}·75$, (ii) $\bar{4}·56 + \bar{2}·83$.

   (i) $+3 + ·67$ (ii) $-4 + ·56$
       $-2 + ·75$ $-2 + ·83$

   $+1 + 1·42 = 2·42.$ $-6 + 1·39 = -5 + ·39$
                                    $= \bar{5}·39.$

Example 22 *Simplify* (i) $\bar{3}·2689 - 1·5727$,
                     (ii) $\bar{3}·2863 - \bar{5}·7204$.

  (i) $-3 + ·2689$ We cannot take ·5727 from ·2689, so
      $+1 + ·5727$ we borrow 1 from -3, thus making it
                    -4, and proceed to take ·5727 from
                    1·2689, and $+1$ from -4.

  $-4 + 1·2689$
  $+1 + ·5727$

  $-5 + ·6962 = \bar{5}·6962.$

(ii) $-3+\cdot2863$
    $-5+\cdot7204$
———————

$-4+1\cdot2863$
$-5+\ \ \cdot7204$
———————
$1+\ \ \cdot5659=1\cdot5659.$

We cannot take ·7204 from ·2863, so we borrow 1 from −3, thus making it −4, and proceed to take ·7204 from 1·2863, and −5 from −4. Notice that $-4-(-5)$
              $=-4+5=1.$

Example 23 *Simplify* (i) $\bar{2}\cdot57\times3$, (ii) $\bar{6}\cdot4726\div3$, (iii) $\bar{4}\cdot7642\div3$.

(i) $-2+\ \cdot57$
        3
———————
$-6+1\cdot71=-5+\cdot71=\bar{5}\cdot71.$

(ii) $3)-6+\cdot4726$
    ———————
    $-2+\cdot1575=\bar{2}\cdot1575.$

(iii) 4 is not exactly divisible by 3, and the first number above 4 which is a multiple of 3 is 6. We therefore express −4 as −6+2;

$$3)-6+2\cdot7642$$
$$-2+\ \ \cdot9214=\bar{2}\cdot9214.$$

EXERCISE 62

Simplify the following:

1 $\bar{2}\cdot3+\bar{3}\cdot4$	**2** $\bar{4}\cdot6+\bar{1}\cdot8$	**3** $\bar{2}\cdot8+\bar{1}\cdot4$	**4** $\bar{3}\cdot5+2\cdot7$
5 $2\cdot4+\bar{1}\cdot6$	**6** $5\cdot8+\bar{2}\cdot3$	**7** $\bar{4}\cdot8-3\cdot5$	**8** $\bar{3}\cdot4-1\cdot7$
9 $\bar{2}\cdot4-\bar{3}\cdot6$	**10** $0\cdot8-2\cdot3$	**11** $0\cdot4-2\cdot8$	**12** $3\cdot1-\bar{2}\cdot6$
13 $1\cdot3-\bar{4}\cdot8$	**14** $\bar{2}\cdot3-4\cdot6$	**15** $\bar{2}\cdot2-\bar{3}\cdot6$	**16** $0\cdot0-\bar{3}\cdot2$
17 $\bar{2}\cdot4\times2$	**18** $\bar{1}\cdot6\times3$	**19** $\bar{3}\cdot8\times4$	**20** $\bar{2}\cdot7\times5$
21 $\bar{2}\cdot4\div2$	**22** $\bar{3}\cdot4\div2$	**23** $\bar{4}\cdot7\div3$	**24** $\bar{1}\cdot2\div4$
25 $\bar{9}\cdot3\div3$	**26** $\bar{7}\cdot1\div3$	**27** $\bar{5}\cdot7\div2$	**28** $\bar{3}\cdot4\div10$
29 $\bar{4}\div5$	**30** $\bar{2}\cdot3404\div4$	**31** $\bar{3}\cdot65\div2$	**32** $\bar{1}\cdot88\div3$

Example 24　*Evaluate* 47·87 ÷ 0·04632.

No.	Log.
47·87	1·6800
0·04632	$\bar{2}$·6658
1033	3·0142

Ans. 1030 (to 3 sig. figs.).

Example 25　*Evaluate* (0·03067)³.

No.	Log.
0·03067	$\bar{2}$·4867
	3
0·00002884	$\bar{5}$·4601

Ans. 0·0000288 (to 3 sig. figs.).

Example 26　*Evaluate* $\sqrt[3]{0·04731}$.

No.	Log.	
0·04731	$\bar{2}$·6750	3) −3 + 1·6750
	÷ 3	$\overline{-1 + 0·5583}$
0·3617	$\bar{1}$·5583	

Ans. 0·362 (to 3 sig. figs.).

EXERCISE 63

Evaluate the following, first giving the four figures of the answer as obtained from the tables and then correcting the answer to three significant figures:

1　0·3478 × 5·861

2　0·009276 × 21·07

3　0·6412 × 0·03801

4　0·7412 ÷ 126·8

5　0·00437 ÷ 0·0388

6　0·1789 × 847·6

7　36·72 ÷ 0·09209

8　1·1 ÷ 8·634

9　24·721 ÷ 0·3075

10　2·749 × 0·000862

11　0·4716 ÷ 0·07118

12　100 ÷ 0·04292

13　287 ÷ 0·6114

14　10 ÷ 0·07654

15　7658 × 0·0345

16　0·4972 × 43·76

17 $0.00286 \div 0.000717$ **18** 0.01624×18.61

19 $(0.638)^2$ **20** $(0.05412)^3$ **21** $(0.719)^3$

22 $(0.0429)^4$ **23** $\sqrt{0.6623}$ **24** $\sqrt[3]{0.05713}$

25 $\sqrt[4]{0.915}$ **26** $(0.3913)^3$ **27** $\sqrt[3]{0.007}$

28 $\sqrt[5]{0.0806}$ **29** $(0.002263)^2$ **30** $(0.8827)^5$

21. CHORD PROPERTIES OF THE CIRCLE

PART I, § 36, p. 231, should be revised before this section is done.

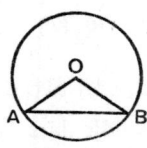

FIG. 169

If AB is any chord of a circle whose centre is O, then OA = OB (radii).

∴ O lies on the perpendicular bisector of AB. It follows, therefore, that

The centre of a circle lies on the perpendicular bisector of any chord.

This is equivalent to the two following statements:

The perpendicular from the centre of a circle to a chord bisects the chord.

Reference   Perp. from centre to chord.

The line joining the centre of a circle to the mid-point of a chord is perpendicular to the chord.

Reference   Line joining centre to mid-point of chord.

The proofs of these two statements by the method of congruent triangles are left as an exercise for the pupil. See p. 29, Ex. 10, Nos. 16, 18.

THEOREM 21

Equal chords of a circle are equidistant from the centre.

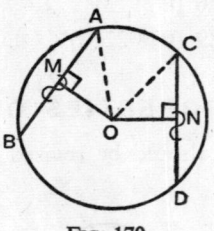

Fig. 170

Given a circle, centre O, and two equal chords AB, CD.

To prove that the perpendiculars OM, ON from O to AB, CD are equal.

Construction   Join OA, OC.

Proof   AM $=\frac{1}{2}$AB   (perp. from centre to chord),

and   CN $=\frac{1}{2}$CD   („   „   „   „   „).

But   AB = CD   (given),

∴ AM = CN.

In the right-angled △s AMO, CNO,

AMO, CNO are the right angles   (given),
    AO = CO   (radii),
    AM = CN   (proved).

∴ △s $\begin{matrix}\text{AMO}\\\text{CNO}\end{matrix}$ are congruent   (RHS).

∴ OM = ON.

Reference   OM = ON (*equal chords equidistant from centre*).

Corollary   Equal chords of two equal circles are equidistant from the centres of those circles.

THEOREM 22

Chords of a circle which are equidistant from the centre are equal.

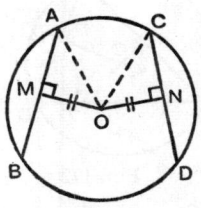

Fig. 171

Given a circle, centre O, and two chords AB, CD; the perpendiculars OM, ON to these chords are equal.

To prove that AB = CD.

Construction   Join OA, OC.

Proof   In the right-angled △s AMO, CNO,

> AMO, CNO are the right angles   (given),
> $$AO = CO \qquad \text{(radii)},$$
> $$OM = ON \qquad \text{(given)}.$$

∴ △s $\begin{matrix} AMO \\ CNO \end{matrix}$ are congruent   (RHS).

∴   AM = CN.

But   AB = 2 AM   (perp. from centre to chord),

and   CD = 2 CN   (,,   ,,   ,,   ,,   ,,).

∴   AB = CD.

Reference   AB = CD (*chords equidistant from centre*).

Corollary Chords of two equal circles which are equidistant from the centres of those circles are equal.

CONSTRUCTION 2

To construct the circumcircle of a triangle.

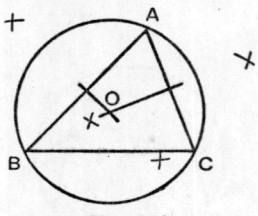

FIG. 172

Given a triangle ABC.

To construct a circle to pass through A, B, C.

Construction   Draw the perpendicular bisectors of AB, AC to meet at O.
With centre O, radius OA, draw a circle.
This is the required circle.

Proof   Since O lies on the perpendicular bisector of AB,

$$OA = OB.$$

Since O lies on the perpendicular bisector of AC,

$$OA = OC.$$

Hence $$OA = OB = OC.$$

∴ the circle, with centre O and radius OA, passes through A, B, C.

This is the same problem as that of constructing a circle to pass through three given points which do not lie in a straight line.   A circle cannot be drawn through three points A, B, C which lie in a straight line, for the perpendicular bisectors of AB and AC in Construction 2 would in that case not meet.

Three or more straight lines are said to be **concurrent** when they meet at the same point (Latin, *con* together, *curro* I run).

The proof of Construction 2 shows that

The perpendicular bisectors of the three sides of a triangle are concurrent.

For the point O, where the perpendicular bisectors of AB and AC meet, has been proved to be equidistant from B and C.

∴ O lies on the perpendicular bisector of BC.

Example   *Calculate the angle which a chord of length 7·2 cm subtends at the centre of a circle of radius 5 cm.*

Let O be the centre of the circle, AB the chord (see Fig. 173). Draw ON perpendicular to AB.

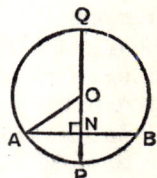

O is the centre

Fig. 173

Then

$$AN = \tfrac{1}{2}AB$$

(perp. from centre to chord)
$$= 3\cdot6 \text{ cm.}$$

$$\sin AON = \frac{AN}{AO} = \frac{3\cdot6}{5}$$

$$= 0\cdot72.$$

∴ $\angle AON = 46° \ 3'.$

∴ $\angle AOB = 2\angle AON$

$$= 92° \ 6' \text{ (approx.).}$$

EXERCISE 64

Some of Exercise 100, p. 233, Part I should be done again before this exercise is begun.

Answers which are approximate should be calculated to three significant figures. Measurements should be made to the nearest millimetre.

(Calculations and constructions)

1 In Fig. 173, if OA = 6 cm and AB = 8 cm, calculate ON.

2 In Fig. 173, if OA = 7 cm and ON = 4 cm, calculate AB.

3 Draw a straight line AB 4 cm long, and construct a circle of radius 3 cm to pass through A and B.

4 Construct the locus of the mid-points of chords 6 cm long in a circle of radius 5 cm.

5 Draw △ABC in which BC=7 cm, ∠ABC=47°, ∠ACB =62°. Construct the circumcircle and measure its radius.

6 Draw a triangle with sides 5, 6, 7 cm. Construct its circumcircle and measure the radius.

7 Draw a triangle ABC in which AB=4·0 cm, BC=6·0 cm and ∠BAC=120°. Construct its circumcircle and measure the radius.

8 A chord of a circle is 10 cm long and is 12 cm from the centre. Find the distance of a chord 20 cm long from the centre of the circle.

9 In Fig. 173, if PN=2 cm and NQ=8 cm, calculate the length of AB.

10 In Fig. 173, AB=8 cm and ∠AOB=76°. Calculate the length of ON.

11 Construct two circles of radii 3·0 cm and 2·0 cm such that their common chord is of length 2·5 cm. (Begin with the common chord.)

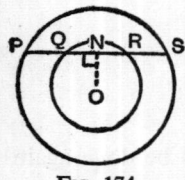

FIG. 174

12 In Fig. 174, both circles have the same centre O. If QR=4 cm, OQ=3 cm and OP=7 cm, calculate ON², PN² and PS.

13 Draw a quadrilateral ABCD in which AB=4·2 cm, BC=2·4 cm, AC=4·4 cm, CD=3·2 cm and AD=4·8 cm. Construct two concentric circles, one passing through A, B, and the other through C, D. Measure their radii.

14 In Fig. 174, if OP=12 cm, OQ=6 cm and PS=22 cm, calculate the length of QR.

15 In a circle of radius 6 cm there are two parallel chords of lengths 10 cm and 8 cm. Calculate the distance between them when they are (i) on opposite sides of the centre, (ii) on the same side of the centre.

16 In Fig. 173, if AB=6 cm and NP=1 cm, calculate OA. (Let OA=r cm, and use the right-angled triangle ONA.)

(*Theoretical*)

17 State the locus of the mid-points of parallel chords of a circle, and illustrate by a sketch.

18 In Fig. 175, A and B are the centres of the circles, and PQRS is perpendicular to AB.   Prove that PQ = RS.

19 Two circles, centres X and Y, intersect at A and B; M is the mid-point of AB, and MX, MY are joined.   Prove that XMY is a straight line.

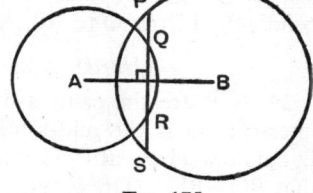

20 In Fig. 174, where the circles have the same centre O, prove that PQ = RS.

21 Given a point P inside a given circle, show how to draw a chord AB passing through P and such that AP = PB.

Fig. 175

22 In Fig. 173, if AB = *l* cm, ON = *p* cm and OA = *r* cm, prove that $l^2 + 4p^2 = 4r^2$.

23 AB, CD are two equal chords of a circle which cut at right angles at X; O is the centre of the circle; P, Q are the mid-points of AB, CD.   Prove that OPXQ is a square.

24 In Fig. 176, prove that PQ = RS. (Draw perpendiculars from the centres of the circles to PQ and RS.)

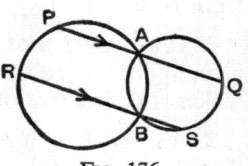

25 The circles, centres A and B, intersect at X and Y; PXQ is a line parallel to AB through X, cutting the circles at P and Q; R and S are the feet of the perpendiculars from A, B respectively to the line PQ.   Prove that (i) RS = AB, (ii) PQ = 2AB.

Fig. 176

26 ABCD is a quadrilateral whose diagonals intersect at O. Prove that the quadrilateral formed by the circumcentres of the triangles AOB, BOC, COD, DOA is a parallelogram. (Notice that the circumcentre of △AOB lies at the intersection of the perpendicular bisectors of OA and OB.)

27 PQ is a variable chord of given length drawn in a given circle. State the locus of the mid-point of PQ.

28 O is the centre of the circumcircle of △ABC, and OA bisects the angle BAC. Prove that AB = AC. (Draw perpendiculars from O to AB, AC.)

(Harder miscellaneous exercises)

29 A, B are the centres of two equal circles which do not intersect; O is the mid-point of AB; a straight line through O cuts one circle at P, Q and the other circle at R, S. Prove that PQ = RS. (Draw perpendiculars from A, B to PQRS.)

30 A thin rectangular plate 6 cm long and 4 cm wide rests horizontally in a hemispherical bowl of radius 5 cm. Calculate the height of the centre of the plate above the lowest point of the bowl.

(*Hint*: let AB, in Fig. 173, represent the diagonal of the rectangle.)

31 A, B are the centres of two equal circles. A straight line drawn parallel to AB cuts one circle at P, Q and the other circle at R, S. Prove that PQ = RS. (Draw perpendiculars from A, B to PS.)

32 Two spheres of radii 5 cm and 4 cm have their centres 6 cm apart. Find by accurate drawing the radius of the circle which is their curve of intersection.

33 In Fig. 173, if AB = l cm, OA = r cm, NP = d cm, prove that $l^2 + 4d^2 = 8rd$.

34 A hemispherical bowl whose diameter is 12 cm is partly filled with water. The greatest depth of the water is 2 cm. Find the diameter of the circular water-surface.

35 Two circles, both of radii 7 cm, cut at A and B. If AB = 6 cm, calculate the distance between the centres of the circles.

36 A sphere passes through all the vertices of a cuboid which is 6 cm by 3 cm by 2 cm. Calculate its radius.

22. TANGENT PROPERTIES OF THE CIRCLE

A **tangent** to a circle was defined in § 42, p. 263, Part I, and some of the easy tangent properties of the circle were discussed. The section should be revised before the more formal treatment of the present section is begun. The fundamental property is:

ASSUMPTION 10 **A tangent to a circle is perpendicular to the radius drawn through the point of contact.**

Reference (See Fig. 177, where O is the centre of the circle, and PT the tangent at P.)

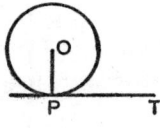

FIG. 177

$\angle$ OPT $= 90°$ (*tan. perp. radius*).

Another way of expressing the same fact is:

The perpendicular to a tangent at its point of contact passes through the centre of the circle.

CONSTRUCTION 3

To construct the tangent to a given circle at a given point on the circumference.

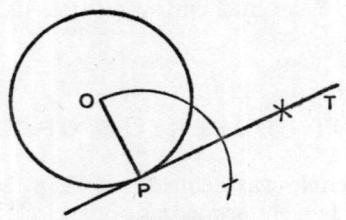

FIG. 178

Given a circle, centre O, and a point P on its circumference.

To construct the tangent at P to the circle.

Construction Join OP.
Through P draw the line PT perpendicular to OP.
Then PT is the required tangent.

Proof OP is a radius and $\angle OPT = 90°$.
∴ PT is the tangent at P.

Note The right angle OPT may be constructed with compasses (as in Fig. 178) or by means of a set square.

If any point T on the tangent is joined to O (see Fig. 178), then

$$\tan TOP = \frac{TP}{OP}.$$

Hence the tangent of $\angle TOP$ is the ratio

$$\frac{\text{length cut off on the tangent}}{\text{radius of circle}},$$

and this explains how the trigonometrical ratio known as the 'tangent' obtained its name.

CONSTRUCTION 4

To construct the tangents to a given circle from a given point outside the circle.

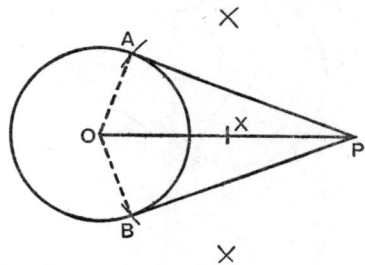

Fig. 179

Given a circle, centre O, and a point P outside it.

To construct the tangents from P to the circle.

Construction Join OP, and bisect it at X.

With centre X, radius XO, draw a circle, and let it cut the given circle at A and B.
Join PA, PB.
Then PA, PB are the required tangents.

Proof Join OA, OB.

$$XO = XP \text{ (constr.)},$$

∴ the circle, centre X, radius XO, passes through P, and OP is a diameter.

∴ $\angle OAP = 90°$ (∠ in semicircle).

But OA is a radius of the given circle.

∴ PA is a tangent (tan. perp. radius).

Similarly, it may be proved that PB is also a tangent.

THEOREM 23

The two tangents from an external point to a circle are equal.

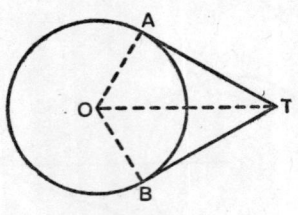

FIG. 180

Given two tangents TA, TB to a circle, centre O, from an external point T.

To prove that TA = TB.

Construction   Join OA, OB, OT.

Proof   In the right-angled △s OAT, OBT,

OAT and OBT are the right angles (tan. perp. radius),

$$OA = OB \quad (radii),$$
$$OT = OT.$$

∴ △s $^{OAT}_{OBT}$ are congruent   (RHS).

$$∴ TA = TB.$$

Reference   TA = TB (*equal tangents*).

Corollary   The centre of a circle lies on the bisector of the angle between the two tangents from an external point.

For △OAT ≡ △OBT (proved),
∴ ∠ATO = ∠BTO.

CONSTRUCTION 5

To construct the inscribed circle of a triangle.

Given a triangle ABC.

To construct the inscribed circle of △ABC.

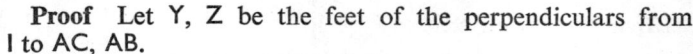

FIG. 181

Construction   Draw the bisectors of ∠s ABC, ACB to meet at I.

Draw IX perpendicular to BC, meeting it at X.

With centre I, radius IX, draw a circle.

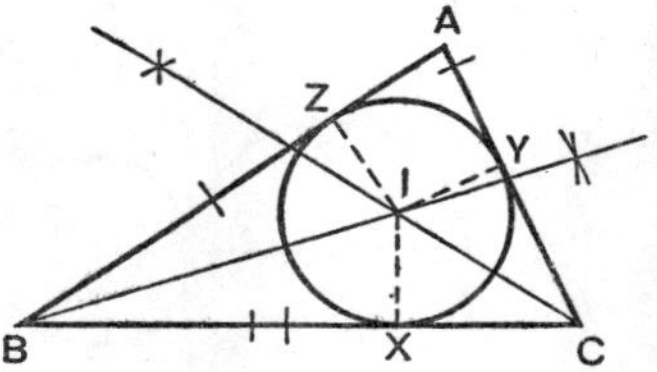

This is the inscribed circle of △ABC.

Proof   Let Y, Z be the feet of the perpendiculars from I to AC, AB.

I lies on the bisector of ∠ABC.

$$\therefore \ IZ = IX.$$

Again, I lies on the bisector of ∠ACB.

$$\therefore \ IY = IX.$$

Hence $IX = IY = IZ.$

∴ the circle, centre I and radius IX, passes through X, Y, Z.

Also IX is a radius and ∠IXB = 90° (constr.).

∴ BC is a tangent to the circle (tan. perp. radius).

Similarly, CA and AB are tangents to the circle.

Contact of circles   Two circles are said to **touch each other** at a point when they have the same tangent at that point; the point is called the **point of contact** of the circles. The circles are said to touch **externally** when they are on opposite sides of their common tangent, and **internally** when they are on the same side of their common tangent.

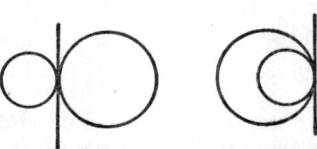

External contact   Internal contact

FIG. 182

THEOREM 24

If two circles touch, the line joining their centres passes through the point of contact.

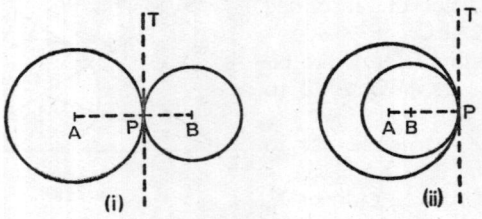

Fig. 183

Given two circles, centres A and B, touching at P.

To prove that A, P, B are in the same straight line.

Construction Draw the common tangent PT to the two circles. Join AP, BP.

Proof Since AP is a radius and PT a tangent,
$$\therefore \ \angle APT = 90° \ (\text{tan. perp. radius}).$$

Since BP is a radius and PT a tangent,
$$\therefore \ \angle BPT = 90° \ (\text{tan. perp. radius}).$$

∴ in both figures A and B each lie on the straight line through P perpendicular to PT.

∴ A, P, B are in the same straight line.

Reference APB is a straight line (*pt. of contact on line of centres*).

Corollary If two circles touch EXTERNALLY, the distance between their centres is equal to the SUM of their radii; if they touch INTERNALLY, the distance between their centres is equal to the DIFFERENCE of their radii.

In Fig. 183 (i), $\qquad$ AB = AP + PB.
In Fig. 183 (ii), $\qquad$ AB = AP − BP.

EXERCISE 65

(For easy questions on tangent properties of the circle, see Exercise 112, page 266, Part I.)

1 A point P is 8 cm from the centre of a circle of radius 3 cm. Calculate to the nearest millimetre the length of the tangent from P to the circle.

2 Two circles of radii 7 cm and 4 cm have the same centre. Calculate to the nearest millimetre the length of a chord of the outer circle which is a tangent to the inner one.

3 Two circles of radii 2 cm and 5 cm touch (i) externally, (ii) internally. Find the distance between their centres in each case.

4 In Fig. 184, if AY = 3 cm, BZ = 5 cm and CX = 2 cm, calculate the lengths of BC, CA, AB.

5 In Fig. 184, if ∠ABC = 42° and ∠ACB = 66°, calculate ∠BIC.

6 Draw a circle with radius 3·5 cm and mark a point P 6 cm from the centre. Construct the two tangents from P to the circle, and measure their lengths.

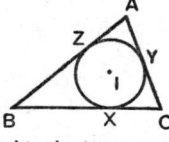

I is the incentre;
X, Y, Z are the
points of contact

FIG. 184

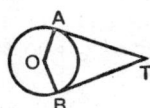

O is the centre of
the circle: TA, TB
are tangents

FIG. 185

7 Draw a triangle ABC in which AB = 3·4 cm, BC = 4·8 cm and CA = 4·2 cm. Construct the inscribed circle of the triangle, and measure its radius.

8 In Fig. 185, if ∠ATB = 38°, calculate ∠AOB.

9 Two circles of radii 3·6 cm and 7·4 cm have the same

centre.   Find the length of the tangent from any point on the outer circle to the inner circle.

10 In Fig. 184, if $\angle ABC = 58°$ and $\angle ACB = 70°$, calculate $\angle CXY$, $\angle BXZ$ and $\angle YXZ$.

11 In Fig. 184, if $\angle ABC = 62°$ and $\angle BAC = 34°$, calculate the angles of $\triangle XYZ$.

12 In Fig. 186, if $\angle A = 76°$, $\angle B = 106°$, $\angle C = 96°$, calculate the angles of the quadrilateral PQRS.

13 In Fig. 184, if $\angle ACB = 90°$, prove that $\angle AIB = 135°$.

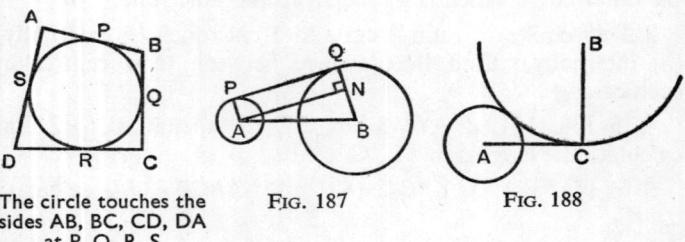

The circle touches the sides AB, BC, CD, DA at P, Q, R, S

Fig. 186

Fig. 187

Fig. 188

14 In Fig. 187, A and B are the centres of circles of radii 2 cm and 7 cm, and $AB = 13$ cm; PQ touches the circles at P and Q, and AN is perpendicular to BQ.   Show that PQNA is a rectangle, and calculate the length of PQ.

15 In Fig. 188, A and B are the centres of two circles which touch; AC touches the circle with centre B.   If $BC = x$ cm, $AC = 5$ cm, and the radius of the small circle is 2 cm, use Pythagoras' Theorem to form an equation containing x, and hence find the radius of the larger circle.

(*Theoretical*)

16 State the locus of the centres of circles which touch a given straight line at a given point.

17 State the locus of the centres of circles of radius 2 cm which touch a fixed circle of radius 5 cm (i) externally, (ii) internally.

18 State the locus of the centres of circles of radius 3 cm which touch a fixed circle of radius 1 cm internally.

19 State the locus of the centres of circles which touch a fixed circle at a given point on its circumference. (The contact may be either external or internal.)

20 In Fig. 189, prove that PX = PY.

21 In Fig. 185, prove that OATB is a cyclic quadrilateral, and that, if AO is produced to X, ∠BOX = ∠ATB.

22 In Fig. 185, prove that
∠ATB = 2 ∠OAB.

23 O is the centre of a circle and AB is any chord; AN is drawn perpendicular to the tangent at B to the circle. Prove that
∠OBA = ∠BAN.

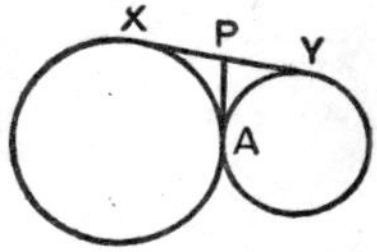

PA touches both circles at A; XPY touches the circles at X, Y

Fig. 189

24 AB is a diameter of a circle, and AP is any chord through A. The tangent to the circle at B cuts AP produced at T. Prove that ∠ATB = ∠PBA.

25 In Fig. 186, if AP = a cm, BQ = b cm, CR = c cm and DS = d cm, express AB + CD in terms of these letters, and deduce that AB + CD = BC + AD.

26 In Fig. 185, if A moves round the circle, but AT is a fixed length, what can you say about the length of OT? State the locus of points from which the tangents to a given circle are of fixed length.

27 State the locus of points the tangents from which to a given circle include a given angle.

28 In Fig. 185, prove that OT bisects AB at right angles.

29 In Fig. 184, if BC = a cm, CA = b cm, AB = c cm and IX = r cm, write down expressions for the areas of △s BIC, CIA, AIB. Hence show that the area of △ABC is $\frac{1}{2}r(a+b+c)$ cm².

30 In Fig. 184, if AY = x cm, BZ = y cm and CX = z cm, prove that the perimeter of △ABC = 2($x+y+z$) cm.

31 In Fig. 189, prove that P is the circumcentre of △XAY. Hence prove that ∠XAY = 90°.

32 In Fig. 190, prove that ∠BAY = ∠BCA.

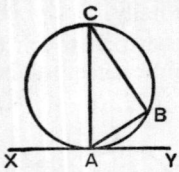

XAY is the tangent at A; AC is a diameter

FIG. 190

Deduce that, if P is any point on the *major* arc AB of the circle, then ∠BAY = ∠BPA.

(The angle BPA is said to be in the **alternate segment** to ∠BAY, and the property here proved is called the alternate segment theorem. See later, p. 379.)

33 In Fig. 190, mark any point Q on the *minor* arc AB of the circle, and join it to A, B, C. Prove that

(i) ∠CAX = ∠CQA,
(ii) ∠CAB = ∠CQB,
(iii) ∠BAX = ∠BQA.

(This proves that the obtuse angle BAX, between the chord AB and the tangent AX, equals the angle which the chord subtends in the segment alternate to ∠BAX.)

23. ARC PROPERTIES OF THE CIRCLE

Equal arcs In Fig. 191, we have two arcs AB, CD of a circle whose centre is O. It is obvious that, if

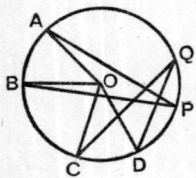

FIG. 191

∠AOB = ∠COD, then arc AB = arc CD, and conversely, if arc AB = arc CD, then ∠AOB = ∠COD.

Suppose APB is the angle subtended by the arc AB at any point on the circumference, and CQD that subtended by the arc CD.

∠APB = ½∠AOB (angle at centre),
and ∠CQD = ½∠COD („ „ „).

It follows that, if the angles AOB, COD, subtended at the centre of the circle, are equal, so are the angles APB, CQD, subtended at the circumference.

Instead of being arcs of the *same* circle, AB and CD might

have been taken as arcs of two *equal* circles, when the same argument as that used above would have applied. We can sum up what has been said in the following statement:

ASSUMPTION 11 **In equal circles (or in the same circle), equal angles at the centres or at the circumferences are subtended by equal arcs.**

References (See Fig. 192, where O and P are the centres of the circles.)

$$\text{Arc } AB = \text{arc } CD \ (\because \ \angle AOB = \angle CPD);$$
$$\angle AOB = \angle CPD, \text{ or } \angle AXB = \angle CYD$$
$$(\because \ arc \ AB = arc \ CD).$$

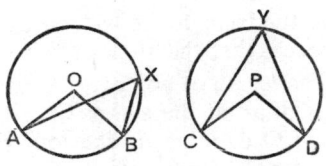

FIG. 192

Suppose, in Fig. 192, that arc $AB = $ arc CD, and that the chords AB, CD are drawn.

In the $\triangle$s OAB, PCD,

$$OA = PC \qquad \text{(radii of equal circles)},$$
$$OB = PD \qquad (\quad ,, \quad ,, \quad ,, \quad ,, \quad),$$

and $\qquad \angle AOB = \angle CPD \ (\because \ \text{arc } AB = \text{arc } CD).$

$\therefore \triangle$s $\begin{smallmatrix} OAB \\ PCD \end{smallmatrix}$ are congruent (SAS).

$$\therefore \ AB = CD.$$

Hence, if arc $AB = $ arc CD, we have shown that
chord $AB = $ chord CD.

In equal circles (or in the same circle), the chords of equal arcs are equal.

Example *Calculate the angles of the triangle formed by joining the points XII, III and VII on a clock-face.*

FIG. 193

See Fig. 193. The arc which represents a five-minute space is one-twelfth of the circumference.

∴ it subtends an angle of one-twelfth of 360°, or 30°, at the centre of the clock-face.

∴ it subtends an angle of 15° at one of the hour-divisions at the circumference.

∴ $\angle ACB = 3 \times 15° = 45°$,
$\angle BAC = 4 \times 15° = 60°$,
$\angle ABC = 5 \times 15° = 75°$.

∴ the angles of the triangle are 45°, 60°, and 75°.

(Notice, as a check, that the angle-sum is 180°.)

Calculation of the length of an arc The arc AB in Fig. 194 subtends an angle of $x°$ at the centre O of the circle. If we draw radii through O dividing up the four right angles there into 360 degrees, these radii cut off equal arcs on the circumference of the circle. The arc AB contains x of these equal arcs, while the whole circumference contains 360 of the same arcs.

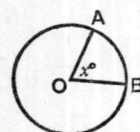

FIG. 194

If follows that the arc AB is $\dfrac{x}{360}$ of the circumference of the circle.

If r cm is the radius of the circle, the length of the circumference is $2\pi r$ cm, where π is approximately 3·142. (See § 46, p. 280, Part I.)

Hence, if an arc subtends an angle $x°$ at the centre of a circle of radius r cm,

$$\text{the length of the arc} = \frac{x}{360} \times 2\pi r \text{ cm.}$$

Calculation of the area of a sector Just as the arc AB in Fig. 194 is $\dfrac{x}{360}$ of the circumference, so the area of the sector

OAB is $\dfrac{x}{360}$ of the area of the circle.   Hence, if a sector of a circle of radius r cm contains an angle of $x°$,

$$\text{the area of the sector} = \frac{x}{360} \times \pi r^2 \text{ cm}^2.$$

EXERCISE 66

(*Numerical*)

Take π as $3\frac{1}{7}$ unless otherwise stated.

1 In Fig. 195, calculate $\angle$s ABD, BAD, BCD, and say what fractions of the circumference are the minor arcs BC, AD, BD and CD.

2 In Fig. 195, show that the minor arc CD equals the arc ABC.

3 In Fig. 195, if the radius of the circle is 3·5 cm, calculate the length of the minor arc AB, to the nearest millimetre.

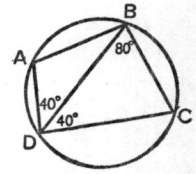

FIG. 195

4 AB is a diameter of a circle, and P is a point on the circle such that $\angle PAB = 30°$. Show that the arc AP is twice the arc PB.

5 AB is an arc of a circle, centre O and radius 6 cm.   If $\angle AOB = 70°$, calculate (i) the length of the arc AB, (ii) the area of the sector AOB.

6 ABC is an equilateral triangle inscribed in a circle of radius 5 cm.   Calculate to the nearest millimetre the length of the minor arc AB.   (Take π as 3·142.)

7 ABCDE is a regular pentagon inscribed in a circle, centre O and radius 5 cm.   Calculate (i) the length of the minor arc AB, (ii) the area of the sector AOB.   (Take π as 3·142.)

8 The angle of a sector of a circle of radius 10 cm is 144°. Calculate the area of the sector and the length of its arc.

9 ABCDE is a regular pentagon inscribed in a circle. Calculate the angles of $\triangle$ABD.

10 Calculate: (i) the angle subtended at I on a clock-face by the arc joining VI and VIII, (ii) the angle subtended at VIII by the arc joining I and V. Deduce that the chord joining I and VI is perpendicular to that joining V and VIII.

11 AB is a side of a regular hexagon inscribed in a circle, centre O, and AC is a side of a regular octagon inscribed in the same circle. C lies on the minor arc AB. Calculate ∠BOC and the angles of △ABC.

12 AB is a side of a square, and AP a side of a regular hexagon, both inscribed in the same circle, and A lies on the minor arc BP. Calculate the angles of △ABP.

13 An isosceles triangle ABC is inscribed in a circle; AB = AC, and ∠A = 36°. The bisectors of angles B and C meet the circle at P and Q. Show that the pentagon APCBQ has all its sides equal.

14 ABCDEFGH is a regular octagon inscribed in a circle. Calculate the numbers of degrees in the angles of △ABD and in those of △ADG.

15 A, B, C are three points on a circle; ∠ABC = 36°, ∠ACB = 84°. P is the mid-point of the minor arc AB, Q that of the minor arc AC. Calculate ∠s BCQ, CQP.

(*Theoretical*)

16 AB, CD are two parallel chords of a circle. Prove that arc AC = arc BD. (Join AD.)

17 Two equal circles cut at A and B; PAQ is a straight line through A, cutting one circle at P and the other at Q. Prove that ∠BPA = ∠BQA.

18 ABCD is a quadrilateral inscribed in a circle, and AB = CD. Prove that AD and BC are parallel. (Join AC.)

19 AB, AC are two equal chords of a circle; P is the mid-point of the minor arc AB, Q that of the minor arc AC. Prove that the chords AQ, PB are equal, and that PQ = AB.

20 A and B are two points on the circumference of a circle; X is the mid-point of the minor arc AB, and P is any point on the major arc AB. Prove that, for all positions of P, the line PX is the bisector of ∠APB.

REVISION PAPERS

PAPERS 1–5 (§ 1–8)

Paper 1

1 A shop increases all its prices by 16%. Find, to the nearest penny, the new prices of articles previously marked: (i) 150p, (ii) 70p, (iii) £13·50.

2 Solve the equations: $2(x-2y+2)-3(y-x)=9+3y$,
$$3x-2y=5.$$

3 In $\triangle ABC$, $AB=AC$; E is the mid-point of AC, F that of AB. Prove that the $\triangle s$ FBC, ECB are congruent, and deduce that $\angle FCB = \angle EBC$.

4 ABCDE is a pentagon in which AB is parallel to ED and BC is parallel to AE. If $\angle A = 73°$ and $\angle D = 150°$, calculate $\angle C$.

5 Draw the graph of the function $\frac{1}{2}(x-1)(x-3)$ from $x = -1$ to $x = 5$. For what values of x is $\frac{1}{2}(x-1)(x-3)$ equal to 2?

6 ABCD is a trapezium in which AB is parallel to DC and $\angle ADC = 90°$. If $AD = 6$ cm, $AB = 7$ cm and $DC = 4$ cm, calculate the areas of $\triangle BDC$ and $\triangle ABD$.

Paper 2

1 A man receives an increase of salary of 12%, thus bringing his salary up to £1960. Find his salary before the increase.

2 Solve the equations:

$$\frac{2x-y}{4} = 2x - 1,$$

$$4x - y = 2.$$

3 ABC is a triangle in which $AB = AC$ and $\angle B = 72°$. The bisector of $\angle B$ meets AC at D, and the line drawn through A parallel to BC at E. Prove that $AD = BD$ and that $AE = DE$.

4 The diagonals of a cyclic quadrilateral ABCD intersect at X; $\angle ADX = 46°$, $\angle ACD = 37°$, $\angle AXB = 109°$. Calculate $\angle ABC$.

5 ABCD is a parallelogram whose diagonals cut at O; P is the mid-point of OA, Q the mid-point of OC. Prove that BPDQ is a parallelogram, and that its area is half that of ABCD.

6 Draw a quadrilateral ABCD in which AB = 2 cm, BC = 3 cm, CD = 5 cm, AD = 4 cm and BD = 5 cm.

Find by construction a point P in AB produced such that $\triangle ADP$ is equal in area to the quadrilateral ABCD. Draw and measure the perpendicular from P to AD, and hence calculate the area of ABCD.

Paper 3

1 If the value of a car depreciates each year by 15% of its value at the beginning of the year, and the present value of a car is £510, find (i) the value in a year's time, (ii) the value a year ago.

2 Solve the equations:
$$2(x - y + 4) - 3(2x + y + 2) = 0,$$
$$3x + 2y = 5.$$

3 Four angles of a hexagon are 140°, 80°, 130°, 100°, and the other two angles are equal. Find the remaining angles.

4 ABC is a triangle in which $\angle A = 38°$; AD is drawn parallel to BC, meeting the bisector of $\angle ABC$ at D. If $\angle CAD = 84°$, calculate $\angle BDA$.

5 Draw the graph of the function $x + \dfrac{4}{x}$, plotting the points for which $x = 1, 1\frac{1}{2}, 2, 2\frac{1}{2}, 3, 3\frac{1}{2}, 4$. For what values of x does $x + \dfrac{4}{x}$ equal $4\frac{1}{2}$?

6 ABCD is a parallelogram; P is the mid-point of AB, Q that of CD; PQ, AQ, PC are joined. Prove that (i) APQD, PBCQ, APCQ are parallelograms, (ii) the area of APCQ is half that of ABCD.

Paper 4

1 The cost of an article in a shop is reduced by $4\frac{1}{2}\%$, i.e. by 63p. Find the new price.

2 Solve the equations:
$$3q - p = 6,$$
$$5p - 6q + 18 = 0.$$

3 In Fig. 196, O is the centre of both circles; AB, CD are diameters. Prove by congruence that BD = AC.

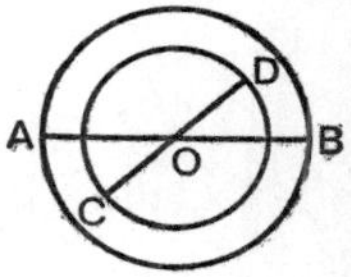

4 AB is a diameter of a circle and P is a point on the circumference. If AP = 8 cm and the radius of the circle is 5 cm, calculate the length of BP.

5 Prove that the area of a rhombus whose diagonals are of lengths $2a$, $2b$ cm is $2ab$ cm².

Fig. 196

6 A regular polygon is such that each interior angle is four times each exterior angle. How many sides has the polygon?

Paper 5

1 A tradesman buys goods at £89 per tonne. At what price per kg, to the nearest penny, must he sell them in order to gain $37\frac{1}{2}\%$ on his outlay?

2 Solve the equations: $\dfrac{y}{9} = \dfrac{x}{2}$,
$$4y - 5x = 6\tfrac{1}{2}.$$

3 With ruler and compasses only, draw a square ABCD with side 3 cm. On AB as base, construct an equilateral triangle ABP, with P inside the square. Without measurement, prove that △s APD, BPC are congruent.

4 Find the interior angle of a regular polygon with 20 sides.

5 ABCD is a parallelogram; squares ABXY, BCPQ are drawn outside the parallelogram on the sides AB and BC. Prove that (i) ∠XBQ = ∠BAD, (ii) △s XBQ, BAD are congruent, (iii) DB, QX are equal and perpendicular.

6 ABCD is a trapezium in which the parallel sides AB and DC are 4·6 cm, 2·8 cm long respectively; $\angle A = 112°$, $\angle B = 41°$. If E is the point in AB such that AE = 2·8 cm, explain why EC is parallel to AD.

Use this fact to construct the trapezium ABCD, and measure BC. By making any necessary measurement, find also the area of ABCD.

PAPERS 6–10 (§ 9–16)

Paper 6

1 Expand: (i) $(5x + 2y)(2x - 3y)$, (ii) $(1 - 2a)^2$, (iii) $\left(x + \dfrac{1}{x}\right)^2$.

2 In Fig. 197, explain why $\triangle$s $\begin{smallmatrix} ABC \\ PQC \end{smallmatrix}$ are similar, and calculate the lengths of PQ, PC.

3 The angle of elevation of the sun at a certain moment was 48°. Calculate to the nearest centimetre the length of the shadow of a man 180 cm high.

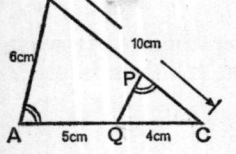

FIG. 197

4 Calculate the rate % p.a. if the simple interest on £550 for 3 years is £74·25.

5 Draw a plan, front elevation and side elevation of a hexagonal pyramid, each edge of the base of which is 2 cm and the height $4\frac{1}{2}$ cm, if the pyramid stands on the H.P. with two edges of the base parallel to the XY line.

6 A cricketer's average was 26 for 6 completed innings. In the first 5 innings he obtained 18, 51, 6, 17, 0 runs. Find his score in the sixth innings.

Paper 7

1 (i) Expand $(3 + x)(4 - x)$ and $(a + 2b)(a + 5b)$.
   (ii) Factorise $2x^2 - 7x - 4$ and $3y^2 - 75$.

2 ABC is a triangle in which $\angle BAC = 90°$; D is the foot of the perpendicular from A to BC. Prove that △s $\begin{smallmatrix}ADC\\BAC\end{smallmatrix}$ are similar, and calculate BC if CD = 2 cm, CA = 6 cm.

3 In △ABC, AB = AC = 10 cm, BC = 7 cm. Calculate ∠B. (Draw the altitude from A.)

4 Find the rate % if the simple interest on £5680 for 5 years is £1704.

5 Draw the plan and front elevation of a cone, base-radius 2 cm and height 6 cm, standing on the H.P.

6 ABCD is a rectangle in which AB = 11 cm, BC = 6 cm, and X is the point in the side BC which is 2 cm from B; P is a point in the side CD such that the angle APX is a right angle. If CP = x cm, prove that △s ADP, PCX are similar, and find x.

Paper 8

1 In Fig. 198, explain why △s $\begin{smallmatrix}APQ\\ABC\end{smallmatrix}$ are similar. Calculate the lengths of AC and PB.

2 In △ABC, ∠B = 90°, ∠A = 58° and AC = 4 cm. Calculate the lengths of BC and AB.

3 Find what sum of money will amount to £1323 in 2 years at 4% p.a. simple interest.

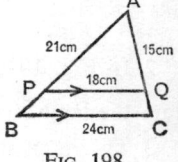

Fig. 198

4 Draw the plan, front elevation and side elevation of a triangular prism of edge 3 cm and length 5 cm, if the prism stands with a triangular end on the H.P., one edge of this end making an angle of 20° with the XY line and the nearest long edge 2 cm from V.P. (A).

5 A class of 15 boys took an examination in which 7 boys obtained an average mark of 40 and 7 others obtained an average mark of 50. The average of the whole class was 46. How many marks did the other boy obtain?

6 Factorise: (i) $ab + 2ac - 3b - 6c$, (ii) $6x^2 - 5x + 1$, (iii) $x^2 - 16t^2$, and solve the equation $3x^2 + 5x - 2 = 0$.

Paper 9

1 Expand (i) $(a - b)(b - a)$, (ii) $(5x + \frac{1}{2}a)(5x - \frac{1}{2}a)$.

2 A vertical pole 5 m high throws a shadow 2 m long on level ground. At the same moment the length of the shadow of a tower is 15 m. Calculate the height of the tower.

3 The side of an equilateral triangle is 6 cm. Calculate its height and area.

4 In what time will the simple interest on £520 be £81·90, if the rate % p.a. is $3\frac{1}{2}$?

5 A piece of work can be done by 30 men in 9 days. After they have been working for 3 days, 12 of the men are taken off the work. Find how many days it will take the remaining 18 men to finish the work.

6 Factorise: (i) $1 + 3x - 4x^2$, (ii) $6a^2 - 18a^3$, and solve the equation $2x^2 + 5x + 3 = 0$.

Paper 10

1 Simplify: (i) $(x+1)(x+2) + (x-3)(x-4) - (x-2)(x+3)$,

(ii) $(a+b)^2 - (a-b)^2$; (iii) $(1+t)\left(1 - \dfrac{1}{t}\right)$.

2 In Fig. 199, explain why $\triangle$s $\begin{smallmatrix} ABD \\ AEC \end{smallmatrix}$ are similar, and calculate the lengths of CE, DE.

3 Two men stand on opposite sides of a tower 100 m high and in line with it. They measure the angles of elevation of the top to be 28° and 34°. Calculate the distance apart of the men.

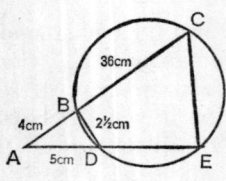

FIG. 199

4 What principal will give £67·20 simple interest in 3 years at $3\frac{1}{2}$% p.a.?

5 Draw the plan, front elevation and side elevation of a cube of edge 4 cm, standing on the H.P. with one vertical face making an angle of 35° with the V.P.(A).

6 Factorise: (i) $(x+2)^2 - 9$, (ii) $\pi R^2 + 2\pi Rh$, (iii) $18a^2 - 8b^2$; and solve the equation $8x^2 + 6x + 1 = 0$.

PAPERS 11–15 (§ 17–23)

Paper 11

1 Use tables to find x, if $x^2 = 27 \cdot 8^2 + 31 \cdot 4^2$.

2 Simplify: (i) $\dfrac{x-3}{3(x-2)(x-1)} + \dfrac{3}{7(x-2)}$, (ii) $\dfrac{\dfrac{1}{2x} - \dfrac{1}{3y}}{\dfrac{1}{3x} + \dfrac{1}{2y}}$.

3 Use logarithm tables to evaluate, to three significant figures: (i) $3 \cdot 487 \times 7 \cdot 864$, (ii) $3 \cdot 487 \div 7 \cdot 864$.

4 Draw $\triangle ABC$ in which $AB = 4$ cm, $\angle A = 109°$, $\angle B = 42°$. Find by construction the points which are equidistant from A and C, and also equidistant from BA and BC. Measure their distances from C.

5 Draw $\triangle ABC$ in which $BC = 8$ cm, $CA = 7$ cm, $AB = 5$ cm. Construct: (i) the circumcircle of the triangle, (ii) the tangent at the point A to this circle. Measure the acute angle between this tangent and the side CA.

6 Find the angles of the triangle formed by joining the points III, VII and X on a clock-face.

Paper 12

1 Use tables to evaluate: (i) $\sqrt{8 \cdot 765^2 + 3 \cdot 456^2}$,

(ii) $\dfrac{1}{19 \cdot 71} + \dfrac{1}{41 \cdot 23}$.

2 Simplify: (i) $x - \dfrac{3}{2x+1}$, (ii) $\dfrac{6}{2x+3} - \dfrac{3}{x-1}$; and find in its simplest form the product of these two expressions.

3 Evaluate, correct to three significant figures:

(i) $0 \cdot 4722 \div 3 \cdot 164$, (ii) $2 \cdot 187 \times 0 \cdot 0866$.

4 Construct $\triangle ABC$ in which $\angle A = 90°$, $BC = 8 \cdot 0$ cm and $AB = 6 \cdot 6$ cm. Construct the inscribed circle of the triangle, and measure its radius.

5 The arc AB of a circle is one-third of the whole circumference; C, D are points on the major arc AB such that

$\angle$BAD$=82°$, and arc BC$=$arc CD. Calculate $\angle$ABD and $\angle$BDC.

6 ABCD is a parallelogram; P is the mid-point of AB, Q that of CD. If the circle with centre P, radius PA, touches the circle with centre Q, radius QC, prove that PQ$=$AB.

Deduce that the parallelogram ABCD must be a rhombus.

Paper 13

1 Use tables to evaluate: (i) $(\sqrt{0 \cdot 641} + \sqrt{2 \cdot 718})^2$,

$$\text{(ii)} \quad \frac{1}{(0 \cdot 4652)^2}.$$

2 Simplify: (i) $2\frac{2}{3} \times \left(\frac{1}{6} - \frac{0 \cdot 7}{5 \cdot 6}\right)$, (ii) $\dfrac{\frac{1}{2\frac{1}{2}} + \frac{1}{3\frac{1}{2}} + \frac{1}{4\frac{1}{2}}}{3\frac{2}{3} \div \frac{7}{12}}$.

3 Evaluate by means of logarithm tables, correct to three significant figures, (i) $\sqrt[3]{62 \cdot 86}$, (ii) $(4 \cdot 371)^4$.

4 A and B are two fixed points 4 cm apart. State precisely what is the locus of a variable point P which moves so that: (i) $\angle$APB$=90°$; (ii) the area of $\triangle$APB$=6$ cm^2.

5 ABCD is a quadrilateral in which $\angle$A$=100°$, $\angle$B$=96°$, $\angle$C$=80°$. A circle is inscribed in the quadrilateral touching AB, BC, CD, DA at P, Q, R, S respectively. Find the angles of the quadrilateral PQRS.

6 Two circles, of radii $5\frac{1}{2}$ cm and $10\frac{1}{2}$ cm, touch a straight line at points 12 cm apart. Calculate the distance between their centres, (i) if the circles lie on the same side of the line, (ii) if they lie on opposite sides of the line. (See Fig. 187, p. 200, for a hint.)

Paper 14

1 Use tables to evaluate, to three significant figures:

(i) $\sqrt{4623}$, (ii) $(46 \cdot 23)^2$, (iii) $\dfrac{1}{46 \cdot 23}$.

2 Simplify: (i) $\dfrac{6\frac{2}{7} - 4\frac{5}{14}}{3\frac{1}{6} + 1\frac{1}{3}} \times \dfrac{3\frac{3}{4}}{5\frac{1}{7}}$, (ii) $\dfrac{6 \cdot 5 \times 10^8}{1 \cdot 3 \times 10^4}$.

3 Evaluate, correct to three significant figures:

(i) $526 \div 0 \cdot 04736$, (ii) $(0 \cdot 0657)^3$.

4 Draw $\triangle ABC$ in which $AB = AC = 5 \cdot 6$ cm, $BC = 5 \cdot 0$ cm. Construct (i) the locus of the centre of a circle which touches BC at B, (ii) the locus of the centre of a circle which passes through A and B. Hence construct a circle which touches BC at B and passes through A. Measure its radius.

5 Two circles having the same centre are of radii 4 cm, 7 cm. Calculate the radius of a circle (i) which touches the larger circle internally and the smaller circle externally, (ii) which touches both circles internally.

6 AB, CD are two chords of a circle, centre O, which intersect at X, and OX bisects $\angle AXC$; L, M are the feet of the perpendiculars from O to AB, CD. Prove that (i) $\triangle$s OXL, OXM are congruent, (ii) the chords AB, CD are equal.

Paper 15

1 Use tables to evaluate, correct to three significant figures:

(i) $\sqrt{0 \cdot 8637 + \sqrt{0 \cdot 8637}}$, (ii) $\sqrt{\dfrac{1}{23 \cdot 45}}$.

2 Evaluate $\dfrac{(5\frac{1}{4})^2 - (4\frac{1}{5})^2}{(4\frac{1}{2})^2} \div 1\frac{2}{5}$.

3 By means of logarithm tables, evaluate, to three significant figures: (i) $0 \cdot 0005834 \times 67 \cdot 7$, (ii) $\sqrt[4]{0 \cdot 4113}$.

4 A hollow right circular cone with a plane base is of height 36 cm and base-radius 15 cm. Make an accurate scale-drawing to find the radius of the largest sphere which can be placed inside it.

5 Draw a straight line AB, 6 cm long. Construct through B a straight line such that the length of the perpendicular to it from A is 4 cm. (Commence with a circle, centre A, radius 4 cm.)

6 Draw a triangle ABC in which $AB = 6 \cdot 0$ cm, $BC = 8 \cdot 0$ cm, $CA = 7 \cdot 0$ cm. Construct the circumcircle of the triangle, and measure its radius.

PAPERS 16–23 (§ 1–23)

Paper 16

1 A man bought an article for £79·80 and sold it so as to gain 15% on his cost price. Find for how much he sold it.

2 In Fig. 200, ABCD and CPQR are parallelograms of equal area, and DCP, BCR are straight lines. Prove that

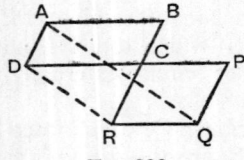

FIG. 200

$$\triangle DAR = \triangle DQR.$$

Deduce that DR and AQ are parallel.

3 In $\triangle ABC$, $AB = AC = 9$ cm, $BC = 3$ cm. D is a point in AB such that $CD = 3$ cm. Prove that $\triangle s \begin{smallmatrix} CBD \\ ABC \end{smallmatrix}$ are similar, and calculate the length of BD.

4 Draw the plan, front elevation and side elevation of a pyramid on a square base of edge 3 cm and height 5 cm, if the axis is horizontal and parallel to the XY line, and two edges of the base are horizontal.

5 Simplify: (i) $\dfrac{1}{3x-1} + \dfrac{4}{2x-1}$, (ii) $\dfrac{x^2+x-2}{x} \times \dfrac{3x^2}{x^2-4}$.

6 The radii of two concentric circles are 12 cm and 7 cm. Find, to the nearest millimetre, the length of a chord of the larger circle which touches the smaller circle.

Paper 17

1 Solve the equations: $3(x-y) - 4(x+y) = 10$,
$3(x+y) + 4(x-y) = 5$.

2 AB is a diameter of a circle; A, P, Q, R, B are points in order on a semicircle, and AR is joined. Prove that $\angle APQ + \angle QRB = 270°$.

3 Factorise: (i) $ax - ay - bx + by$, (ii) $x^2 - \frac{1}{4}y^2$, (iii) $6x^2 - 13x + 2$.

4 Evaluate to three significant figures:

$$\text{(i) } \frac{26\cdot42}{102\cdot8}, \quad \text{(ii) } \sqrt[3]{627000}.$$

5 Draw a triangle with sides 4 cm, 6 cm, 8 cm. Construct its inscribed circle, and measure the radius.

6 A hemispherical bowl has an internal radius of 8 cm. It contains some water, and the greatest depth of this water is 3 cm. Calculate the diameter of the circular water-surface.

Paper 18

1 A farmer finds that he can buy 3 cows and 4 sheep for £108. The cost of 2 cows exceeds that of 5 sheep by £3. Find the cost of a cow and of a sheep.

2 AB is a diameter of a circle whose centre is O; P is a point on the circle, and OQ is the radius parallel to BP and drawn in the same sense; PQ is joined. If $\angle ABP = x°$, express in terms of x the number of degrees in $\angle BPQ$.

3 E and F are the feet of the perpendiculars from B and C respectively to the opposite sides of $\triangle ABC$. Prove that $\triangle$s AEB, AFC are similar. Calculate AB if BE = 12 cm, CF = 9 cm and AC = 15 cm, and verify your answer by finding the area of the triangle in two ways.

4 The ends of a hexagonal prism have each edge 1·5 cm long, and the length of the prism is 5 cm. Draw a plan, front elevation and side elevation of the prism as it rests with a long face on the H.P. and the long edges parallel to the XY line.

5 Solve the equations: (i) $2x^3 + 7x^2 + 3x = 0$, (ii) $t + 2 = \dfrac{8}{t}$.

6 ABC is a triangle inscribed in a circle, and AB = AC; P is a point on the minor arc AB of the circle, AP produced meets CB produced at Q, and PB is joined. Prove that (i) $\angle QPB = \angle ABC$, (ii) $\angle PBA = \angle AQB$.

Deduce that $\triangle$s $\dfrac{ABQ}{APB}$ are similar, and that $\dfrac{AB}{AP} = \dfrac{AQ}{AB}$.

Paper 19

1 ABCD is a parallelogram. The circumcircle of $\triangle ABC$ cuts CD (produced if necessary) at E. Prove that AE = AD.

2 Draw the graph of the function $4 - x^2$ from $x = -3$ to $+3$, plotting every half-unit value of x.   Read off from your graph the value of the function if $x = 2 \cdot 3$.

3 PQRS is a parallelogram in which PQ $= 5$ cm, QR $= 4$ cm and $\angle$PQR $= 65°$.   Calculate the area of the parallelogram. (Draw RN perpendicular to PQ.)

4 Use tables to evaluate, correct to three significant figures, $\sqrt{a^2 + b^2 + c^2}$ when $a = 17 \cdot 54$, $b = 13 \cdot 22$, $c = 19 \cdot 49$.

5 ABCD is a quadrilateral inscribed in a circle; CD is produced to F, and the bisector of $\angle$ABC meets the circle at E. Prove that DE (produced if necessary) bisects $\angle$ADF.

6 A square ABCD is inscribed in a circle of radius 4 cm. Find the area of the minor segment cut off by the chord AB. (Take π as $3 \cdot 142$.)

Paper 20

1 Draw the graph of the function $\dfrac{4}{x + 2}$ from $x = -1\frac{1}{2}$ to $x = 3$.   Find for what value of x the function is equal to $1 \cdot 1$.

2 A can do a piece of work in 9 days, B can do it in 6 days. How many days should they take if they work together?

3 Factorise: (i) $a(x^2 - y^2) + b(x - y)$, (ii) $a^4 - a^8$,
   (iii) $2a^2b - 6ab^2 - 8abc$.

4 Solve the equations: (i) $\dfrac{x - 1}{4} - \dfrac{x - 2}{3} = 1$;
   (ii) $1 - y - 12y^2 = 0$.

5 Simplify: (i) $\dfrac{1\frac{1}{2} + 2\frac{1}{3} + 3\frac{1}{4}}{1\frac{1}{2} + 2\frac{1}{3} - 3\frac{1}{4}}$,
   (ii) $\dfrac{1}{1 + x} - \dfrac{1}{x(2 - x)} - \dfrac{3}{(1 + x)(2 - x)}$.

6 Draw a circle, centre O, of radius $3 \cdot 0$ cm, and mark a point A on its circumference.   Find a point B which is $4 \cdot 6$ cm from O and $2 \cdot 4$ cm from A.   Construct (i) the locus of the centre of a circle which passes through A and B, (ii) the locus of the centre of a circle which touches the first circle at A.

Hence construct a circle to pass through B and to touch the first circle at A.   Measure its radius.

Paper 21

1 Factorise: $12a^2 + 7a - 49$,
$$5x^2 - 20y^2,$$
$$2a - 6b + a^2 - 3ab.$$

2 Evaluate pq, when
$$p = 4 \cdot 7 \times 10^2, \quad q = 2 \cdot 3 \times 10^{-3}.$$

3 Solve the simultaneous equations
$$\tfrac{1}{4}x + y = 2\tfrac{1}{2},$$
$$4x - \tfrac{2}{7}y = -17.$$

4 Simplify (i) $\dfrac{5\frac{3}{7} - 2\frac{9}{14}}{2\frac{1}{6} \div 3\frac{1}{9}}$, (ii) $\dfrac{8}{x} \div \dfrac{2 - 2x}{x - x^3}$.

5 A man bought x golf balls for £3. Write down the cost in pence of each. If the cost of a golf ball had been 5p less, he would have obtained five more balls for £3. Find the value of x.

6 On the sides AB, AC of a triangle ABC, equilateral triangles ABP, ACQ are drawn outside the triangle. Prove that the triangles PAC, BAQ are congruent.

Paper 22

1 A householder's electricity bill consists of a fixed payment, together with a charge of a certain amount for each unit used. When the number of units used was 428, the total bill was £11·69. When the number of units was 740, the bill was £17·15. Find the fixed payment and the charge per unit.

2 Simplify $\dfrac{x+6}{x-1} - \dfrac{3x+13}{x+5} + 2$.

3 Factorise: $4x^3y - 12xy^2$,
$$a^2 - 4b^2 + 3(a + 2b),$$
$$2x^2 + 5x - 12.$$

4 Evaluate by logarithms, to three significant figures:
  (i) $0 \cdot 487 \times 23 \cdot 96$,
  (ii) the cube root of $0 \cdot 5913$.

5 A regular pentagon (five sides) is inscribed in a circle of radius 5 cm. Calculate the perpendicular distance of a side from the centre of the circle and also the length of a side of the pentagon.

6 Draw a parallelogram ABCD in which AB = 6 cm, AD = 3·5 cm and the diagonal BD = 5·5 cm. Construct and measure the perpendicular from A to CD produced, and hence calculate the area of the parallelogram.

Paper 23

1 At the first 15 home matches of a football club, the average number of tickets sold per match was 273·4. Find the total number of tickets sold.

If there were four more home matches, find how many more tickets must be sold to bring the average up to 300 tickets per match for the whole season.

2 Write down the number of kilogrammes of apples which can be bought for 48p when apples are x pence per kilogramme.

If the price goes up by 1p per kilogramme, a woman finds that she can buy one kilogramme less for 49p than she formerly bought for 48p. Find the value of x.

3 Solve the equation
$$\tfrac{1}{3}(x-5) - \tfrac{1}{4}(6-x) = \tfrac{1}{6}(7-4x).$$

4 Simplify (i) $\dfrac{3\frac{2}{3} + 1\frac{5}{6}}{3\frac{2}{3} - 1\frac{5}{6}}$, (ii) $\left(\dfrac{1}{9}\right)^{\frac{1}{2}}$, (iii) $10^{1\cdot415}$.

5 Draw the graph of the function $x^2 - 4x - 3$ from $x = -2$ to $x = 6$. From your graph, estimate (i) the value of $x^2 - 4x - 3$ when $x = -1\cdot5$ and when $x = 3\cdot2$, (ii) for what values of x the function is equal to 1·4.

6 ABCD is a quadrilateral whose vertices lie on a circle. AB and DC meet at P, DA and CB meet at Q. If $\angle BPC = 37°$ and $\angle PBC = 56°$, calculate $\angle AQB$.

SECTION B

24. FURTHER LOGARITHMIC CALCULATION: FORMULAE

THE rules for logarithmic calculation were given on p. 178. In a more complicated expression, the sum of the logarithms of the numbers in the denominator is subtracted from the sum of the logarithms of the numbers in the numerator. The work is best set out as in the examples which follow. Two logarithm columns are used, the first one containing logarithms which are to be multiplied or divided by some number.

Example 1 *Evaluate* $\sqrt{\dfrac{8\cdot69}{(21\cdot72)^3 \times 0\cdot786}}$

No.	Log.	
8·69		0·9390
$(21\cdot72)^3$ 0·786	1·3369 × 3	4·0107 $\bar{1}$·8954
		3·9061
		$\bar{3}$·0329 ÷ 2
0·03284		$\bar{2}$·5164

Here 3 log 21·72 is added to log 0·786, their sum subtracted from log 8·69 to give the log of the fraction, and the result halved in order to find the log of the square root of the fraction.

Ans. 0·0328 (to 3 sig. figs.).

Example 2 *Evaluate* $\dfrac{34 \cdot 86 \times \sqrt[3]{(0 \cdot 4215)}}{(0 \cdot 0291)^2 \times \sqrt{(0 \cdot 8864)} \times 169}$

No.	Log.	
34·86		1·5424
$\sqrt[3]{0 \cdot 4215}$	$\bar{1} \cdot 6248 \div 3$	$\bar{1} \cdot 8749$
Num.		1·4173
$(0 \cdot 0291)^2$	$\bar{2} \cdot 4639 \times 2$	$\bar{4} \cdot 9278$
$\sqrt{0 \cdot 8864}$	$\bar{1} \cdot 9476 \div 2$	$\bar{1} \cdot 9738$
169		2·2279
Den.		$\bar{1} \cdot 1295$
194·0		2·2878

Ans. 194 (to 3 sig. figs.).

The use of logarithm tables replaces multiplication and division by addition and subtraction, which are much simpler processes. Numbers cannot be added by adding their logarithms. If there are any + or − signs in the expression which is to be evaluated, these operations must be done by ordinary calculations, not by logarithms.

EXERCISE 67

In the following calculations, the number at the foot of the 'number column' should show the answer to four figures as given by the tables. This answer should then be corrected to three significant figures.

Find the values of:

1 $\dfrac{1760 \times 7 \cdot 718 \times 43 \cdot 8}{19 \cdot 5}$

2 $\dfrac{72 \cdot 01}{101 \cdot 3 \times 5 \cdot 387}$

3 $\dfrac{0 \cdot 4045 \times 283}{94 \cdot 37 \times 3 \cdot 283}$

4 $\dfrac{(19 \cdot 49)^2}{3 \cdot 664 \times 5 \cdot 127}$

5 $\dfrac{3 \cdot 142 \times 0 \cdot 7821}{22 \cdot 47 \times 1 \cdot 081}$

6 $\dfrac{(0 \cdot 8417)^2}{2 \cdot 31 \times 0 \cdot 0471}$

7 $\dfrac{\sqrt{0.03118}}{14.12 \times 23.5}$

8 $\sqrt{\dfrac{5.317 \times 18.05}{0.8377}}$

9 $\dfrac{1.283 \times 53.7 \times 167}{42.71 \times (14.97)^2}$

10 $\dfrac{(0.3176)^3 \times 18.09}{47.8}$

11 $\dfrac{270.6 \times (7.12)^2}{87.62 \times 94.3}$

12 $\dfrac{836.1}{24.7 \times \sqrt{284.9}}$

13 $\dfrac{7.018 \times (0.6821)^2}{0.06187}$

14 $\dfrac{0.0041 \times 538.6}{0.00728}$

15 $\dfrac{2.176 \times (0.583)^3}{86.41 \times 0.1}$

16 $\dfrac{6.894 \times 32 \times 0.05}{(2.566)^3 \times 100}$

17 $\dfrac{\sqrt{476.1}}{\sqrt[3]{88.27}}$

18 $\dfrac{14.18 \times \sqrt[3]{121.2}}{(22.35)^2 \times 90.6}$

19 $\dfrac{3.142 \times (0.8412)^2}{\sqrt[3]{377.4}}$

20 $\dfrac{68.3 \times 0.094 \times 1.055}{(37.2)^2 \times \sqrt{147}}$

21 $\dfrac{72.08 \times 0.1166 \times 3.14}{(8.447)^2}$

22 $\dfrac{695 \times \sqrt{0.8989}}{(12.7)^2 \times 172.8}$

23 $\dfrac{\sqrt[3]{0.5486}}{6.81 \times \sqrt{0.7291}}$

24 $\dfrac{46.179 \times \sqrt[3]{84.81}}{\sqrt{174}}$

25 $\dfrac{37.62 \times 0.0548}{8.762}$

26 $\dfrac{4.735 \times (0.2875)^2}{\sqrt{279.6}}$

27 $\sqrt{\dfrac{8.571 \times 3.262}{4.138}}$

28 $\dfrac{1}{3}\sqrt{\dfrac{25^3}{8 \times 3.142}}$

29 $\dfrac{0.4162 \times 3.219 \times 6.83}{21.64 \times 0.358}$

30 $\dfrac{37.2}{3.86}\sqrt{\dfrac{0.5312}{(0.3651)^3}}$

31 $\dfrac{(0.4017)^2 \times 15.62}{(0.2871)^3 \times 39.61}$

32 $\dfrac{19.36 \times \sqrt{0.8433}}{256.2 \times (1.468)^4}$

33 $\sqrt[4]{\dfrac{83.71 \times 14.22}{9307}}$

34 $\dfrac{\sqrt{0.0364} \times (0.4677)^3}{0.6171 \times 0.7153}$

35 $(0.09735)^{\frac{2}{3}}$

36 $(0.8172)^{2.4}$

37 $(0.0714)^{-\frac{2}{5}}$

38 $\dfrac{\sqrt[3]{0.7251}}{6.87 \times \sqrt{0.8242}}$

39 $\dfrac{31.72 \times 0.07412}{28.61 \times 5.934}$

40 $\sqrt[5]{\dfrac{0.4673}{49.51 \times 3.784}}$

41 $\sqrt[4]{\dfrac{64 \times 1650 \times 144}{56 \cdot 3 \times 1 \cdot 523}}$

42 $\sqrt{\dfrac{2 \times 0 \cdot 1413 \times 0 \cdot 3257}{0 \cdot 1413 + 0 \cdot 3257}}$

43 $\dfrac{0 \cdot 0537 \times 6 \cdot 184}{\sqrt{0 \cdot 4321}}$

44 $\dfrac{4 \cdot 712 \times \sqrt[3]{0 \cdot 168}}{0 \cdot 07341}$

45 $\sqrt{\dfrac{0 \cdot 0785 \times 0 \cdot 02541}{0 \cdot 004218}}$

46 $8 \cdot 624 \times \sqrt{\dfrac{18 \cdot 42}{32 \cdot 16}}$

47 $\sqrt[3]{\dfrac{3 \times (1 \cdot 467)^2 \times 0 \cdot 234}{4}}$

48 $\dfrac{2135 \times 0 \cdot 03781}{(11 \cdot 6 \times 7 \cdot 5) + (3 \cdot 6 \times 4 \cdot 5)}$

49 $(0 \cdot 5721)^3 + (0 \cdot 474)^3$

50 $\dfrac{\sqrt{(0 \cdot 8174 \times 53 \cdot 56)}}{(2 \cdot 56)^2}$

EXERCISE 68 (Formulae)

Take log π as $0 \cdot 4971$.

1 Find V from the formula $V = \pi r^2 h$, when $r = 3 \cdot 241$, $h = 0 \cdot 768$.

2 Find the value of $\dfrac{Wv^2}{2g}$ when $W = 439$, $v = 0 \cdot 362$ and $g = 980$.

3 Find t from the formula $t = 2\pi \sqrt{\dfrac{l}{g}}$, when $g = 981$, $l = 864$.

4 Find I from the formula $I = \dfrac{nE}{R + nr}$, when $E = 2 \cdot 25$, $R = 11 \cdot 56$, $r = 1 \cdot 35$ and $n = 6$.

5 If $A = P\left(1 + \dfrac{r}{100}\right)^n$, find A when $P = 5867$, $r = 3\frac{1}{2}$ and $n = 5$.

6 Calculate W from the formula $W = \dfrac{kbd^2}{l}$, if $k = 68$, $b = 0 \cdot 167$, $d = 0 \cdot 36$ and $l = 12 \cdot 7$.

7 If $T = \dfrac{PD^2 l}{w}$, find the value of T if $P = 53 \cdot 8$, $D = 1 \cdot 96$, $l = 3 \cdot 7$ and $w = 5 \cdot 8$.

8 From the formula $h = \dfrac{wv^2}{1 \cdot 25r}$, find h when $w = 4 \cdot 709$, $v = 60$ and $r = 2341$.

9 Find V from the formula $V = \dfrac{(t + 461) \times v}{T + 461}$, when $t = 720$, $v = 1072$ and $T = 1108$.

10 If $a = \dfrac{(w + 10) \times V^2}{4480 WS}$, calculate the value of a when $w = 124$, $W = 7 \cdot 92$, $V = 2650$, $S = 17 \cdot 6$.

11 Evaluate $49000 \left(\dfrac{R - r}{R + r} \right) \left(\dfrac{900 + T + t}{900} \right)$ when $R = 29 \cdot 73$, $r = 25 \cdot 46$, $T = 69$ and $t = 33$.

12 The area of a triangle, A m², is found from the formula $A = \sqrt{s(s - a)(s - b)(s - c)}$ where a, b, c are the lengths of the sides in metres and $s = \frac{1}{2}(a + b + c)$. Find in square metres the area of a triangle whose sides are 0·84, 1·34 and 0·72 metres.

13 If $d = k \sqrt[3]{\dfrac{H}{N}}$, calculate d when $k = 176$, $H = 59$ and $N = 3$.

14 If $W = \dfrac{mH}{D^2 N^3}$, find W when $m = 1 \cdot 43 \times 10^7$, $H = 18$, $D = 5 \cdot 5$ and $N = 164$.

15 Find x from the formula $x = \dfrac{4\pi^2 kl}{T^2 - t^2}$, if $k = 0 \cdot 0787$, $l = 0 \cdot 206$, $T = 12 \cdot 83$ and $t = 6 \cdot 046$.

Evaluate the following, giving the result in the form $A \times 10^n$, where A is in standard form and n is an integer:

16 $\dfrac{2\pi^2 e^4 m}{h^3}$, where $\pi = 3 \cdot 142$, $e = 4 \cdot 77 \times 10^{-10}$, $m = 2 \cdot 73 \times 10^{-17}$ and $h = 6 \cdot 57 \times 10^{-27}$.

17 $\dfrac{P^2 g}{a}$, where $P = 1 \cdot 78 \times 10^3$, $g = 9 \cdot 81 \times 10^2$, $a = 3 \cdot 27 \times 10^{-1}$.

25. MENSURATION

IN this section, various formulae for areas and volumes will
be collected together. Some of these have been given before,
and are repeated here for revision; some will be new, and will
be given without proof. When a formula is quoted, such as
$\pi r^2 h$ for the volume of a cylinder, it is usual to omit the units.
If r and h are given in centimetres, the volume is in cubic
centimetres; if in metres, the volume is in cubic metres, and so
on. Of course, it would be wrong to work with r measured in
centimetres and h in metres; both must be in the same units.

In mensuration exercises, be careful to state the units of
your answer at every stage of the work. Use logarithm
tables whenever they simplify the working; and if you are
going to use logarithms, do not waste time cancelling unless
you get rid of a number altogether by so doing.

Rectangle   **Area = length × breadth**

$$\text{Length} = \frac{\text{area}}{\text{breadth}}$$

$$\text{Breadth} = \frac{\text{area}}{\text{length}}$$

Parallelogram   **Area = base × height** (see § 8, p. 65).

Triangle   **Area = ½ base × height**

If the lengths of the sides are a, b, c, and if $s = \frac{1}{2}(a+b+c)$,
i.e. the semi-perimeter, it can be proved that

$$\textbf{Area} = \sqrt{\{s(s-a)(s-b)(s-c)\}}.$$

Example 1 *Find in square metres the area of a triangular field
whose sides are 423 m, 476 m, 509 m.*

If the sides are a, b, c,

$$
\begin{array}{ll}
a = 423 & s-a = 281 \\
b = 476 & s-b = 228 \\
c = 509 & s-c = 195
\end{array}
$$

$$\therefore\ 2s = a+b+c = 1408.$$
$$\therefore\ \qquad s = 704.$$

Notice, as a check before going further, that the right-hand column adds up to 704, or s. This is because

$(s-a)+(s-b)+(s-c)=3s-a-b-c=3s-2s=s.$

Area of field $= \sqrt{\{s(s-a)(s-b)(s-c)\}}$ m^2
$= \sqrt{(704 \times 281 \times 228 \times 195)}$ m^2.

No.	Log.
704	2·8476
281	2·4487
228	2·3579
195	2·2900
	9·9442 ÷ 2
93780	4·9721

∴ the area = 93800 m^2 (to 3 sig. figs.).

Trapezium, with parallel sides a, b, at a distance h apart:

$$\text{area} = \frac{h(a+b)}{2}$$

EXERCISE 69

Use logarithms where suitable.

1 Find in cm^2 the area of a rectangle 41·6 cm by 0·94 m.

2 Find in centimetres the length of a rectangle whose area is 4172 cm^2 and breadth 0·48 m.

3 Find the area of ABCD in Fig. 201 if AD = 6·4 cm and CK = 8·2 cm.

4 If the area of ABCD in Fig. 201 is 71·64 cm^2 and AH = 8·6 cm, calculate AB.

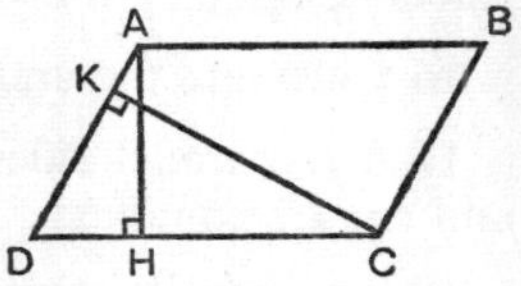

FIG. 201
ABCD is a parallelogram

5 In Fig. 201, if AD = 3 cm, ∠ADC = 68° and AB = 4 cm, calculate the area of ABCD.

6 Calculate the area of a rhombus whose diagonals are of lengths 2·8 cm, 3·7 cm.

In Nos. 7–10, AH and BK are altitudes of △ABC. (See Fig. 202.)

7 If AC = 2·7 cm and BK = 5·4 cm, calculate the area of △ABC.

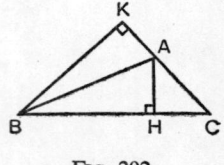

8 If the area of △ABC is 9·86 cm², and BC = 5·6 cm, calculate AH.

9 If AB = 3 cm, BC = 4 cm and ∠ABC = 40°, calculate AH and the area of △ABC.

FIG. 202

10 If AC = 2 cm, AB = 3 cm and ∠BAC = 130°, calculate the area of △ABC.

Calculate the areas of the triangles in Nos. 11–14.

11 Sides 5 cm, 5 cm, 8 cm.

12 Sides 5 cm, 6 cm, 7 cm.

13 Sides 9·6 cm, 8·8 cm, 8·3 cm.

14 An equilateral triangle, side 12 cm.

15 ABC is a triangle in which ∠A = 90°, AB = 3 cm, AC = 4 cm; D is the foot of the perpendicular from A to BC. By finding two different expressions for the area of the triangle, calculate the length of AD.

16 Calculate the area of a regular hexagon of side 10 cm.

17 The parallel sides of a trapezium are 2·4 cm, 2·8 cm, and are 1·7 cm apart. Calculate the area of the trapezium.

18 The parallel sides AB, DC of a trapezium ABCD are 4·2 cm, 7·8 cm, AD = 4 cm and ∠ADC = 65°. Calculate the length of the perpendicular from A to DC, and the area of the trapezium ABCD.

Prism   Volume = area of cross-section × length

$$\text{Length} = \frac{\text{volume}}{\text{area of section}}; \text{ area of section} = \frac{\text{volume}}{\text{length}}$$

Circle of radius r: **circumference $= 2\pi r$**

$$\text{area} = \pi r^2$$

Circular cylinder of radius r, height h:

area of curved surface $= 2\pi rh$

volume $= \pi r^2 h$

The *total* surface area (including the two ends) $= 2\pi rh + 2\pi r^2$

$$= 2\pi r(h + r).$$

The formula for the volume of a cylinder can be deduced from that of a prism.

These formula for circles and cylinders were given in § 46, Part I, pages 280–284. Easy exercises on them are on pages 281–5 of that book.

Example 2   *Find in cubic centimetres the volume of metal in a pipe 4 m long, external diameter 50 cm, if the metal is 1 cm thick. (Take π as $3\frac{1}{7}$.)*

The external radius of the pipe $= 25$ cm.

The internal radius $= 24$ cm.

$\therefore$ the area of the cross-section $= \pi(25^2 - 24^2)$ cm²

$$= \pi(25 + 24)(25 - 24) \text{ cm}^2$$

$$= 49\pi \text{ cm}^2.$$

$\therefore$ volume of metal $= 49\pi \times 400 \text{ cm}^3$

$$= \overset{7}{\cancel{49}} \times \frac{22}{\cancel{7}} \times 400 \text{ cm}^3$$

$$= 61600 \text{ cm}^3 \text{ (to 3 sig. figs.).}$$

In exercises on circles and cylinders, do not substitute a numerical value for π until absolutely necessary. Take the value as 3·142, unless $3\frac{1}{7}$ simplifies the working, and take log π as 0·4971. Give results to three significant figures.

EXERCISE 70

1 A prism 12 cm long has triangular ends with sides 3, 4, 5 cm. Calculate the volume of the prism.

2 A shed with a sloping roof is 3 m high at the back, 1·65 m high in front, and 2·4 m wide from front to back. The shed is 4·35 m long. Calculate its volume in cubic metres.

3 The cross-section of a prism, 18 cm long, is an isosceles triangle with sides 5, 5, 6 cm. Calculate its volume.

Find the circumferences and areas of the following circles:

4 Radius 35·4 cm.   **5** Diameter 42·9 m.

6 Find the area of the ring between two concentric circles of radii 9·5 cm and 6·4 cm.

Find the volumes and the areas of the curved surfaces of the circular cylinders in Nos. 7–9:

7 Diameter 11 cm, height 24 mm.

8 Diameter 3·5 cm, height 2 m.

9 Diameter $4\frac{1}{2}$ cm, height $5\frac{1}{2}$ cm.

10 Find the total surface area (including ends) of a solid circular cylinder of diameter 9 cm and length 72 cm.

11 A cable consists of a copper core of diameter 1 cm encased in rubber 1 cm thick, the diameter of the cable being 3 cm. Calculate in cubic centimetres, to the nearest whole number, (i) the volume of copper in 1 metre of cable, (ii) the volume of rubber in the same length of cable.

Pyramid   Volume $= \frac{1}{3} \times$ **area of base** $\times$ **height**

A **right** pyramid is one in which the slant edges joining the vertex to the corners of the base are all equal. The faces are thus isosceles triangles; and the surface area of the pyramid is found by calculating the areas of these triangles and of the base. The formula given above for the volume of a pyramid is true whether the pyramid is right or not; but the proof is too difficult to be given at this stage.

Example 3   *Find* (i) *the volume of a right pyramid standing on a square base of side 4 cm, the slant edges being all 6 cm long,* (ii) *the area of one of the sloping faces.*

(i) Fig. 203 shows the pyramid. Let the height VO be h cm.

Since $\angle AOB = 90°$,

$$OA^2 + OB^2 = AB^2 \quad \text{(Pythagoras' Theorem)}.$$

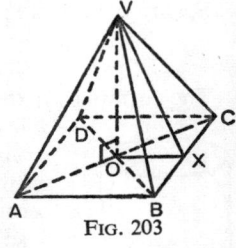

Fig. 203

But $OA = OB.$

$\therefore 2OA^2 = AB^2 = 16.$

$\therefore \quad OA^2 = 8.$

Since $\angle VOA = 90°$,

$VO^2 + OA^2 = VA^2.$

$\therefore h^2 + 8 = 36.$

$\therefore h^2 \quad = 28.$

$\therefore h \quad = \sqrt{28}.$

$\therefore$ the volume of the pyramid $= \frac{1}{3} \times$ base area $\times$ height

$= \frac{1}{3} \times 16 \times \sqrt{28} \text{ cm}^3$

$= 28 \cdot 22 \text{ cm}^3$ by logs.

$\therefore$ the volume of the pyramid $= 28 \cdot 2 \text{ cm}^3$ (to 3 sig. figs.).

(ii) Let X be the mid-point of BC.

Since $\angle VOX = 90°$,

$VO^2 + OX^2 = VX^2 \quad$ (Pythagoras' Theorem).

But $VO^2 = 28$ and $OX = 2.$

$\therefore \quad\quad\quad\quad VX^2 = 28 + 4 = 32.$

$\therefore \quad\quad\quad\quad VX = \sqrt{32}.$

$\therefore$ the area of $\triangle VBC = \frac{1}{2} . BC . VX$

$= \frac{1}{2} . 4 \sqrt{32} \text{ cm}^2$

$= 2 \times 5 \cdot 657 \text{ cm}^2 = 11 \cdot 314 \text{ cm}^2.$

$\therefore$ the area of each sloping face $= 11 \cdot 3 \text{ cm}^2$ (to 3 sig. figs.).

Right circular cone, with base-radius r, height h, and slant height l. (See Fig. 204.)

The cone may be considered as a right pyramid on a circular base.

By Pythagoras' Theorem, $r^2 + h^2 = l^2$.

Area of curved surface $= \pi r l$

$$\text{Volume} = \tfrac{1}{3}\pi r^2 h$$

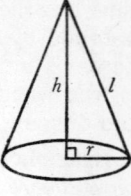

FIG. 204

The formula for the curved surface is not proved at this stage. The formula for the volume is deduced from that for the volume of a pyramid.

Sphere of radius r: **area of surface $= 4\pi r^2$**

$$\text{volume} = \tfrac{4}{3}\pi r^3$$

The formula for the volume cannot be proved at this stage.

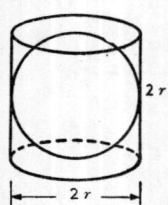

FIG. 205

The formula for the surface area is obtained from a theorem of Archimedes, a Greek mathematician who lived in the third century B.C. He proved that the surface of a sphere is equal to the area of the curved surface of the cylinder which has the same diameter and height as the sphere (see Fig. 205).

Example 4 Calculate the number of spherical shot, each of radius $2\frac{1}{2}$ mm, which can be cast from 1000 cubic centimetres of metal.

Volume of each shot $= \tfrac{4}{3}\pi . (\tfrac{1}{4})^3$ cm³.

$\therefore$ number of shot in 1000 cm³ $= \dfrac{1000}{\tfrac{4}{3}\pi . (\tfrac{1}{4})^3}$

$$= \dfrac{1000 \times \overset{16}{\cancel{64}} \times 3 \times 7}{\cancel{4} \times 22} = \dfrac{168000}{11}$$

$$= 15\ 300 \text{ (to 3 sig. figs.).}$$

EXERCISE 71

Use logarithms where suitable and take log π as 0·4971.

Pyramid

Find the volumes of the following right pyramids:

1 Square base, side 4 cm, height 6 cm.

2 Rectangular base 6 cm by 4 cm, height 9 cm.

3 Triangular base, sides 3 cm, 4 cm, 5 cm, height 8 cm.

4 Triangular base, each side 4 cm, height 6 cm.

5 Triangular base, sides 4 cm, 5 cm, 6 cm, height 12 cm.

6 Find the volume and the total surface area (including the base) of a right pyramid whose height is 12 cm and whose square base is of side 10 cm.

Cone

Find the volumes of the following right circular cones:

7 Height 9 cm, base-radius 4 cm.

8 Height 4 cm, slant height 5 cm.

9 Height 8·5 cm, base-radius 2·4 cm.

Find the areas of the curved surfaces of the following right circular cones:

10 Slant height 10 cm, base-radius 8 cm.

11 Slant height 9 cm, height 7 cm.

Sphere

Find the volumes and surfaces of the following spheres:

12 Radius 3·5 cm.   **13** Diameter 16·8 cm.

14 A cylindrical tank, radius 20 cm, contains water to a depth of 20 cm. A solid metal sphere of radius 9 cm is placed in it. Find how many centimetres the water level rises. (Do not substitute for π.)

15 A right circular cone, of base-radius 6 cm and height 12 cm, and a hemisphere of radius 6 cm are joined together with their circular faces in contact, so as to form a solid. Find the volume and total surface area of this solid.

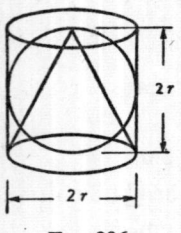

16 A spherical shell has an inner radius of 16 cm and an outer radius of 18 cm. Find the volume of material in the shell.

17 Write down, in terms of r, the volumes of the cone, sphere, and cylinder shown in Fig. 206. Hence show that these volumes are in the ratios $1 : 2 : 3$.

FIG. 206

Degree and dimensions The **degree** of an algebraical term is the sum of the powers of the different letters which occur.

Thus, a, b, $a+b$, x are of the 1st degree;
            a^2, b^2, ab, xy, y^2 are of the 2nd degree;
            a^3, a^2b, abc, xy^2 are of the 3rd degree.

Looking back over the various formulae which have occurred in this section on Mensuration, the student will notice that all lengths are of the first degree, all areas are of the second degree, and all volumes are of the third degree. A line is said to be one-dimensional, a surface two-dimensional and a solid three-dimensional. It follows that the degree of any mensuration formula must be the same as the dimensions of whatever is denoted by that formula.

Consider, for example, the formula $\pi r^2 h$ for the volume of a circular cylinder of radius r and height h. This is of the third degree (remember that π is a number, and does not affect the degree). The total surface area is $2\pi r^2 + 2\pi rh$, which is of the second degree.

Consideration of the degree of a formula will help you to avoid mistakes. For example, $4\pi r^3$ could not be the correct formula for the surface of a sphere, as it is not of the second degree.

Exercise: State the degree and dimensions of each of the formulae given in thick type in this section.

Notation for area and volume units   The fact that an area is two-dimensional and a volume three-dimensional enters into the notation for the symbols used. A square metre is written as m², a cubic centimetre as cm³, and so on.   Thus the units of length are

mm, cm, m, km;

those of area   mm², cm², m², km²;

and those of volume mm³, cm³, m³, km³.

EXERCISE 72

(Miscellaneous problems on Mensuration)

Use logarithms wherever suitable, and take log π as 0·4971.

1 Find the weight of a brass cylinder 7·4 cm long, 6·2 mm in diameter, if 1 cubic centimetre of brass weighs 8·4 grammes.

2 Calculate the area of a triangle with sides 8·6 m, 7·4 m and 6·2 m.

3 Find the area of a regular 10-sided polygon inscribed in a circle of radius 2 cm.

4 If 1 cm³ of brass weighs 8·4 g, calculate the side of a square brass plate, 1 mm in thickness, which weighs 4725 g.

5 A circular lead disc has radius 24 cm and thickness 12 cm. It is melted down and converted into 200 000 spherical balls all of equal radius.   Find this radius.

6 A thread of mercury 15·7 cm long is run out from a straight tube of uniform cross-section, and the mercury weighs 0·108 g.   If 1 cubic centimetre of mercury weighs 13·6 g, calculate the diameter of the tube.

7 A metal pipe has an internal diameter of 5 cm, and the metal is 2 mm thick.   If 1 cm³ of metal weighs 7·7 g, find the weight of a metre length of the pipe.   (Take $\pi = \frac{22}{7}$.)

8 A solid metal cone, of base-radius 3 cm and height 12 cm, is placed on the bottom of a cylindrical vessel whose base-radius is 6 cm.   Water is poured into the vessel until the top of the cone is just covered, and the cone is then removed. Calculate the final depth of water in the vessel.

9 An isosceles triangle with its base angles 70° is inscribed in a circle of radius 10 cm. Calculate the length of each side and the area.

10 A solid metal sphere of radius 6 cm is melted down and recast in the form of a solid circular cylinder of length 20 cm. Find the radius of the cylinder.

11 A rectangular block of metal 47·50 cm by 31·75 cm by 9·50 cm is drawn into wire of radius 0·175 cm. Find in kilometres, to 3 significant figures, the length of the wire.

12 A hollow metal sphere has internal and external radii 10 cm and 11 cm. If it weighs 11·65 kg, find the weight of 1 cubic centimetre of the metal.

The rest of the Exercise involves the use of British Imperial units.

13 A railway cutting is of uniform cross-section in the form of a trapezium whose parallel sides are 90 ft and 40 ft. The cutting is 36 ft deep. Calculate how many cubic yards of earth must be excavated in making 100 yards of the cutting.

14 A swimming bath, 100 ft long and 20 ft wide, has vertical sides. The water is 8 ft deep at one end and 3 ft 6 in deep at the other, the depth increasing uniformly. Calculate (i) the number of ft^3 of water in the bath, (ii) the number of gallons of water, if 1 ft$^3 = 6\frac{1}{4}$ gallons.

15 Find to the nearest ton the weight of water which falls on a 20-acre field during a rainfall of $\frac{1}{2}$ in, if 1 ft^3 of water weighs 62$\frac{1}{2}$ lb.

16 A cylindrical pipe has a diameter of 10 in. Water flows through it at the rate of 15 ft/s, the cross-section of the stream in the pipe being half that of the pipe. Find how many gallons of water, to the nearest gallon, flow out of the pipe in 1 min. (Take $\pi = \frac{22}{7}$; 1 ft$^3 = 6\frac{1}{4}$ gallons.)

17 A spherical shell is made of copper, which weighs 550 lb per ft^3. The outside diameter is 12 in, and the copper is $\frac{1}{4}$ in thick. Calculate the weight of the shell in pounds.

18 A rectangular tank, on a square base, holds 38 gallons of water when filled to a depth of 17 in.   Find the length of a side of the base.   (1 gallon = 277·3 in³.)

19 A garden roller is 18 in in diameter and 16 in wide. Find to the nearest square yard the area rolled during 200 revolutions.

20 Find in cubic feet the volume of a mile of wire whose circular cross-section has a radius 0·042 in.

21 A cylindrical hole of diameter $5\frac{1}{4}$ in is bored centrally through a cube of metal, each edge of which is 9 in long. Calculate the volume of the remaining part of the metal, correct to the nearest cubic inch.

22 The base of a right pyramid is a rectangle 6 in by 8 in, and the slant edges are each 9 in long.   Find (i) the volume of the pyramid, (ii) the total area of the sloping faces.

23 A cable consists of a copper core of radius $\frac{7}{8}$ in surrounded by rubber $\frac{1}{2}$ in thick, so that the radius of the cable is $1\frac{3}{8}$ in.   Calculate in cubic inches, to the nearest whole number, the volume of rubber in a yard of cable.

If copper weighs 554 lb per ft³, find in pounds, to 3 significant figures, the weight of copper in a yard of cable.

24 A piece of paper 2 miles long and 9 ft wide is wound on to a roller 9 ft long and 6 in diameter, the complete roller forming a cylinder 9 ft long and 2 ft in diameter.   Calculate (i) the area of the paper in acres, (ii) the thickness of the paper in inches, correct to 2 significant figures.

26. MID-POINT AND INTERCEPT THEOREMS

THE following section contains a formal treatment of some geometrical facts which were discussed in a more elementary manner in Part I; and a revision of pages 179–182 of that book would be useful before the proofs of the theorems are studied. ·

THEOREM 25 (Mid-point Theorem)

The straight line joining the mid-points of two sides of a triangle is parallel to the third side and equal to one-half of it.

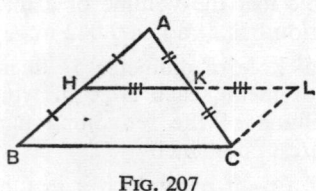

Fig. 207

Given that H, K are the mid-points of the sides AB, AC of △ABC.

To prove that HK ∥ BC, HK = ½BC.

Construction   Produce HK to L, so that HK = KL. Join CL.

Proof   Since AK = KC and HK = KL (given and constr.), AHCL is a parallelogram (diags. bisect each other).

∴ AH, LC are equal and parallel (opp. sides).

But   AH = HB (given).

∴ HB, LC are equal and parallel.

∴ HBCL is a parallelogram.

∴ HL ∥ BC and HL = BC (opp. sides).

But   HK = ½HL (constr.).

∴ HK ∥ BC, HK = ½BC.

Reference   *AH = HB and AK = KC,*

∴ HK ∥ BC and HK = ½BC (*mid-point theorem*).

THEOREM 26 (The Intercept Theorem)

If three or more parallel straight lines make equal intercepts on one transversal, they will make equal intercepts on any other transversal.

Given the parallel lines AP, BQ, CR, DS, cutting a transversal at A, B, C, D, so that AB = BC = CD, and cutting another transversal at P, Q, R, S.

To prove that PQ = QR = RS.

Construction Through A, B draw AX, BY parallel to PQRS to meet BQ, CR at X, Y respectively.

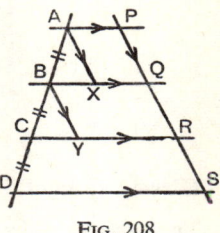

FIG. 208

Proof In the △s ABX, BCY,

$$AB = BC \qquad \text{(given)},$$
$$\angle ABX = \angle BCY \qquad \text{(corr., } BQ \parallel CR),$$
$$\angle BAX = \angle CBY \qquad \text{(corr., } AX \parallel BY).$$

∴ △s $\begin{matrix} ABX \\ BCY \end{matrix}$ are congruent   (AA corr. S).

∴   AX = BY.

Now APQX, BQRY are parallelograms (both pairs of opp. sides ∥).

∴   AX = PQ, BY = QR   (opp. sides of ∥ gram.).

∴   PQ = QR.

Similarly,   QR = RS.

Reference   *AB = BC = CD and AP ∥ BQ ∥ CR ∥ DS,*

∴   PQ = QR = RS (*Intercept theorem*).

Corollary **The straight line drawn through the mid-point of one side of a triangle, and parallel to another side, bisects the third side.**

This is a special case of Theorem 26 in which the points A and P (Fig. 208) are the same point. It is the converse of the Mid-point Theorem.

CONSTRUCTION 6

To divide a given straight line into _n_ equal parts

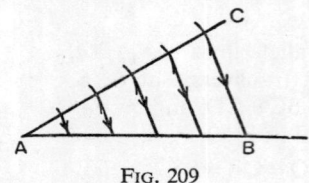

FIG. 209

Given a straight line AB.

To construct points dividing AB into _n_ equal parts.

Construction Through A draw a line AC making any convenient angle with AB.

With any suitable radius, and starting with A as centre, draw arcs so as to mark off _n_ equal lengths along AC.

Join the last point of intersection to B.

Through the other points of intersection, draw parallels to this straight line to meet AB.

Then these parallels divide AB into _n_ equal parts.

Proof The intercepts made by the parallels on AC are equal;

∴ the intercepts made by them on AB are equal.

EXERCISE 73

1 In Fig. 210, prove that BFED is a parallelogram.

2 In Fig. 210, prove that ∠EDF = ∠A.

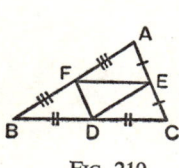

Fig. 210

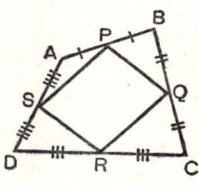

Fig. 211

3 In Fig. 211, by applying the mid-point theorem to △s ABC, ADC in turn, prove that PQ is equal and parallel to SR.

Hence prove that PR, QS bisect each other.

4 AB is a chord of a circle, centre O; AC is the diameter through A; N is the foot of the perpendicular from O to AB. Prove that ON = ½CB.

5 In Fig. 210, prove that four triangles are congruent.

6 In Fig. 211, if AC = BD, prove that PQRS is a rhombus.

7 In Fig. 211, if AC is perpendicular to BD, prove that PQRS is a rectangle.

8 ABCD is a parallelogram; P is the mid-point of AB, Q that of DC; DP and QB cut AC at X, Y respectively. Prove that DP, QB are parallel (first prove that PBQD is a parallelogram), and hence prove that AX = XY = YC.

9 D is the mid-point of the side BC of △ABC; P is the mid-point of AD, and BP produced meets AC at X; the parallel through D to BX meets AC at Y. Prove that AX = XY = YC.

10 H, K are the mid-points of the sides AB, AC of △ABC; BC is produced to D so that CD = ½BC. Prove that HKDC is a parallelogram, and that DH passes through the mid-point of KC.

11 X is the mid-point of the side AB of a parallelogram ABCD. The straight line through B parallel to XD meets AD produced at Y. Prove that AY=2BC.

12 ABCD is a trapezium, with AB parallel to DC; X, Y are the mid-points of AD, BD respectively, and XY produced meets BC at Z. Prove that Z is the mid-point of BC.

13 V is the vertex and ABC the triangular base of a pyramid. D, E, F are the mid-points of VA, VB, VC respectively. If AB=BC=CA, prove that DEF is an equilateral triangle.

14 H, K are the mid-points of the sides AB, AC of △ABC; P is any point in BC, and L, M are the mid-points of PB, PC respectively. Prove that HKML is a parallelogram.

15 In Fig. 212, prove that
(i) EX = ½ DA,   (ii) EB = ½ (DA + FC).

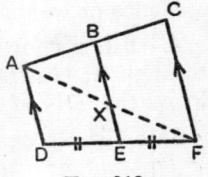

Fig. 212

16 AB is a diameter of a circle, centre O. P and Q are two points on one of the semicircular arcs AB. X, Y are the feet of the perpendiculars from A, B respectively to the chord PQ produced. Prove that XP=QY. (Draw ON perpendicular to PQ, and use Theorem 26.)

17 X is one of the points of intersection of two circles, centres A and B; M is the mid-point of AB. A straight line through X, perpendicular to MX, meets one circle at P and the other circle at Q. Prove that PX=XQ. (Draw perpendiculars from A, B to PXQ.)

18 AB is a diameter of a circle, centre O; P and Q are two points on one of the semicircular arcs AB. Straight lines through P, Q perpendicular to PQ meet AB at M, N respectively. Prove that OM=ON. (Draw the perpendicular from O to PQ.)

19 In △ABC, D is the mid-point of BC, E is the mid-point of AC; AC is produced to F so that CF=½AC; FD produced meets AB at G; and the parallel through C to AB meets FD at H.   Prove that GD = DH = HF.

20 ABC is the triangular base and V the vertex of a pyramid; D is the mid-point of VB, E that of VC, F that of AB, and G that of AC.   Prove that (i) DEGF is a parallelogram, (ii) DG, EF bisect each other.

What fact could you state about the line joining the mid-points of VA and CB?

21 E, F are the mid-points of the sides AC, AB respectively of △ABC; BE cuts CF at G, and AG is produced to H so that GH = AG.   Apply the mid-point theorem to △s ABH, ACH, in order to prove that (i) BGCH is a parallelogram, (ii) GH passes through the mid-point of BC, (iii) EG = ½BG.

(This rider proves that **the three medians of a triangle are concurrent**; G, their point of intersection, is called the **centroid** of the triangle, and it lies one-third of the way up each median, measured towards the vertex.)

27. QUADRATIC EQUATIONS (II)

Fractional equations

Equations containing fractions frequently lead after simplification to quadratic equations.

Example 1   *Solve the equation* $\dfrac{5}{y-4} - \dfrac{4}{y-5} + \dfrac{3}{y-2} = 0.$

Multiply each side of the equation by $(y-4)(y-5)(y-2)$.
$$5(y-5)(y-2) - 4(y-4)(y-2) + 3(y-4)(y-5) = 0.$$
$$\therefore\ 5(y^2-7y+10) - 4(y^2-6y+8) + 3(y^2-9y+20) = 0.$$
$$\therefore\ 5y^2-35y+50 - 4y^2+24y-32 + 3y^2-27y+60 = 0.$$
$$\therefore\qquad\qquad 4y^2 - 38y + 78 = 0.$$
$$\therefore\qquad\qquad 2y^2 - 19y + 39 = 0.$$
$$\therefore\qquad\qquad (2y-13)(y-3) = 0.$$
Either $\qquad 2y-13 = 0$ or $y-3 = 0.$
$$\therefore\qquad\qquad 2y = 13\quad\text{or}\quad y = 3.$$
$$\therefore\qquad\qquad y = 6\tfrac{1}{2}\quad\text{or}\quad 3.$$

EXERCISE 74

Solve the following equations:

1 $x - 4 = \dfrac{9}{x+4}$ **2** $x - 5 + \dfrac{6}{x} = 0$ **3** $x + 1 = \dfrac{6}{x}$

4 $x = \dfrac{1}{x}$ **5** $x + 2 = \dfrac{25}{x+2}$ **6** $\dfrac{x+5}{x-3} = x$

7 $\dfrac{2x+1}{3} = \dfrac{1}{x-2}$ **8** $\dfrac{3x+1}{5} - \dfrac{2}{x-2} = 0$ **9** $\dfrac{3}{2x-1} - \dfrac{x}{x+10} = 0$

10 $\dfrac{1}{x-5} - \dfrac{2}{3} = \dfrac{2}{x}$ **11** $\dfrac{2y+5}{y-1} - \dfrac{y+4}{y+3} = 1$

12 $\dfrac{1}{y-3} + \dfrac{2}{y-1} = 1$ **13** $\dfrac{5}{x+1} - \dfrac{1}{x} = \dfrac{6}{x+4}$

14 $\dfrac{1}{v+1} - \dfrac{1}{v+4} = \dfrac{1}{6}$ **15** $\dfrac{3}{t+3} - \dfrac{2}{2t+1} = -1$

Suppose the terms of a quadratic equation have all been brought to the left-hand side, with 0 on the right. If the left-hand side has factors which are readily found, that method is the quickest and should always be used. If, however, the quadratic has no factors, or if you are unable to find the factors, you must solve the equation either by 'completing the square' or by using a formula. Both these ways will now be explained, and you can choose which method you prefer.

Solution by completing the square This method consists in arranging the terms containing x^2 and x on the left-hand side, and the term without x on the right. A suitable number is then added to both sides so as to make the left-hand side an exact square.

A few examples will make it clear what numbers must be added.

Thus, $x^2 + 6x$ becomes an exact square if we add 9, for it then becomes $x^2 + 6x + 9$, which is $(x+3)^2$.

Similarly, by adding 25, $x^2 - 10x$ becomes $x^2 - 10x + 25$, or $(x-5)^2$.

If we add 1 to $x^2 - 2x$, it becomes $x^2 - 2x + 1$, or $(x-1)^2$.

Now consider $(x+a)^2$, which is, when expanded,

$$x^2 + 2ax + a^2.$$

This shows that $x^2 + 2ax$ becomes an exact square if we add a^2; and a^2 is (half of $2a$)^2, i.e. the square of half the coefficient of x. The rule for completing the square is thus:

To make $x^2 + bx$ an exact square, add the square of half the coefficient of x, i.e. $\left(\dfrac{b}{2}\right)^2$.

Then

$$x^2 + bx + \left(\frac{b}{2}\right)^2 = \left(x + \frac{b}{2}\right)^2.$$

Similarly,

$$x^2 - bx + \left(\frac{b}{2}\right)^2 = \left(x - \frac{b}{2}\right)^2.$$

Example 2 *Add a term to the expressions:* (i) $x^2 - \frac{8}{9}x$, (ii) $x^2 + x$ *so as to make them exact squares, and write the result in each case as the square of a bracket.*

(i) The square of $\frac{4}{9}$ is $\frac{16}{81}$.

$$x^2 - \frac{8}{9}x + \frac{16}{81} = (x - \frac{4}{9})^2.$$

(ii) The square of $\frac{1}{2}$ is $\frac{1}{4}$.

$$x^2 + x + \frac{1}{4} = (x + \frac{1}{2})^2.$$

EXERCISE 75

Add a number to each of the following expressions so as to make it an exact square, and then write it in the form $(x+a)^2$.

1 $x^2 + 4x$ **2** $x^2 + 12x$ **3** $x^2 - \frac{10}{3}x$

4 $x^2 + 5x$ **5** $x^2 - \frac{2}{5}x$ **6** $x^2 + \frac{2}{7}x$

7 $x^2 + \frac{7}{9}x$ **8** $x^2 - \frac{7}{3}x$ **9** $x^2 - x$

Example 3 *Solve* $x^2 - 6x - 16 = 0.$

The equation is $\qquad x^2 - 6x = 16.$

To complete the square on the left-hand side, add 3^2 to both sides,

$$x^2 - 6x + 3^2 = 16 + 9.$$
$$\therefore \qquad (x-3)^2 = 25.$$

Taking the square root of both sides, and remembering that the square root of 25 is either $+5$ or -5,

$$x-3=+5 \quad \text{or} \quad x-3=-5.$$
$$\therefore \ x=8 \quad \text{or} \quad x=-2.$$
$$\therefore \text{ the roots are } 8, \ -2.$$

This quadratic has been solved by completing the square, in order to illustrate the method, but the quickest way to solve it is to say $(x+2)(x-8)=0$. In the next example we consider a quadratic which does not factorise.

Example 4 *Solve $x^2+8x-4=0$, giving the roots correct to two decimal places.*

The equation is $\qquad x^2+8x=4.$

To complete the square, add 4^2 to both sides.

$$x^2+8x+4^2=4+16.$$
$$\therefore \qquad (x+4)^2=20.$$

Taking the square root of both sides,

$$x+4=\pm\sqrt{20}.$$

[The right-hand side is read as 'plus or minus root 20', and means either $+\sqrt{20}$ or $-\sqrt{20}$. There is no need to consider $\pm(x+4)$ on the left-hand side, since $-(x+4)=+\sqrt{20}$ is the same equation as $+(x+4)=-\sqrt{20}$, and $-(x+4)=-\sqrt{20}$ is the same as $+(x+4)=+\sqrt{20}$.]

$$\therefore x=-4+\sqrt{20} \quad \text{or} \quad -4-\sqrt{20}.$$

Using the square root tables for $\sqrt{20}$,

$$x=-4+4\cdot472 \quad \text{or} \quad -4-4\cdot472.$$
$$\therefore x=0\cdot472 \quad \text{or} \quad -8\cdot472.$$

$\therefore$ the roots, correct to two decimal places, are
$$0\cdot47, \ -8\cdot47.$$

Example 5 *Solve* $3x^2 - 7x - 2 = 0$, *giving the roots correct to two decimal places.*

The equation is $3x^2 - 7x = 2$.

Divide both sides by 3, so as to change the coefficient of x^2 to 1.

$$x^2 - \frac{7}{3}x = \frac{2}{3}.$$

Add $\left(\frac{7}{6}\right)^2$ to both sides.

$$x^2 - \frac{7}{3}x + \left(\frac{7}{6}\right)^2 = \frac{2}{3} + \frac{49}{36}.$$

$$\therefore \left(x - \frac{7}{6}\right)^2 = \frac{24 + 49}{36} = \frac{73}{36}.$$

Take the square root of both sides.

$$x - \frac{7}{6} = \pm \frac{\sqrt{73}}{6}$$

$$= \pm \frac{8 \cdot 544}{6}.$$

$$\therefore \quad x = \frac{7}{6} \pm \frac{8 \cdot 544}{6}$$

$$= \frac{7 \pm 8 \cdot 544}{6}$$

$$= \frac{15 \cdot 544}{6} \quad \text{or} \quad \frac{1 \cdot 544}{6}.$$

$$\therefore \quad x = 2 \cdot 591 \quad \text{or} \quad -0 \cdot 257.$$

$\therefore$ the roots, correct to two decimal places, are $2 \cdot 59$, $-0 \cdot 26$.

EXERCISE 76

Solve the equations:

1 $(x+3)^2 = 16$ **2** $(x-2)^2 = 25$ **3** $(x-1)^2 = 1$
4 $(x+1)^2 = \frac{1}{9}$ **5** $(x+2)^2 = \frac{9}{4}$ **6** $(x-4)^2 = \frac{36}{25}$

Simplify the following:

7 $3 \pm 5 \cdot 681$ **8** $-2 \pm 4 \cdot 117$ **9** $-4 \pm 1 \cdot 768$
10 $6 \pm 2 \cdot 74$ **11** $4 \pm 5 \cdot 472$ **12** $-5 \pm 1 \cdot 234$

Solve the following equations by completing the square, giving the roots correct to two decimal places:

13 $x^2 + 6x + 7 = 0$ **14** $x^2 - 4x - 7 = 0$

15 $x^2 + 8x - 4 = 0$ **16** $x^2 - 2x - 5 = 0$

17 $x^2 + 10x - 3 = 0$ **18** $x^2 - 8x + 14 = 0$

19 $x^2 - 7x + 9 = 0$ **20** $x^2 - 5x + 2 = 0$

[If additional exercises on completing the square are required, Exercise 77 may be used.]

Solution by formula When the coefficient of x^2 in a quadratic equation is a number other than 1, and especially when the coefficient of x is an odd number, the process of completing the square becomes rather troublesome, and most people prefer to use a formula for the roots. We shall now consider the general equation $ax^2 + bx + c = 0$, and work out the formula by the process of completing the square. Once this has been done, the formula can be used in any particular case by substituting the appropriate values for a, b, c.

Example 6 *Find a formula for the values of* x, *if* $ax^2 + bx + c = 0$.

The equation is $ax^2 + bx = -c$.

Divide both sides by a, so as to change the coefficient of x^2 to 1.

$$x^2 + \frac{b}{a}x = -\frac{c}{a}.$$

Add to both sides $\left(\dfrac{b}{2a}\right)^2$.

$$x^2 + \frac{b}{a}x + \left(\frac{b}{2a}\right)^2 = -\frac{c}{a} + \frac{b^2}{4a^2}$$

$$= \frac{-4ac + b^2}{4a^2} = \frac{b^2 - 4ac}{4a^2}.$$

$$\therefore \left(x + \frac{b}{2a}\right)^2 = \frac{b^2 - 4ac}{4a^2}.$$

Take the square root of both sides.

$$x + \frac{b}{2a} = \pm \sqrt{\frac{b^2 - 4ac}{4a^2}}$$

$$= \pm \frac{\sqrt{b^2 - 4ac}}{2a}.$$

Subtract $\frac{b}{2a}$ from both sides.

$$x = -\frac{b}{2a} \pm \frac{\sqrt{b^2 - 4ac}}{2a},$$

or

$$x = \frac{-b \pm \sqrt{b^2 - 4ac}}{2a}.$$

We have thus proved that:

If $ax^2 + bx + c = 0$, then $x = \dfrac{-b \pm \sqrt{b^2 - 4ac}}{2a}$.

Example 7   *Solve by formula the equation $3x^2 - 7x - 2 = 0$.*
This equation is the same as $ax^2 + bx + c = 0$ if $a = 3$, $b = -7$, $c = -2$.

By the formula, $x = \dfrac{-b \pm \sqrt{b^2 - 4ac}}{2a}$

$$= \frac{-(-7) \pm \sqrt{(-7)^2 - 4 \times 3 \times (-2)}}{2 \times 3}$$

$$= \frac{7 \pm \sqrt{49 + 24}}{6}$$

$$= \frac{7 \pm \sqrt{73}}{6}$$

$$= \frac{7 \pm 8 \cdot 544}{6}$$

$$= \frac{15 \cdot 544}{6} \quad \text{or} \quad -\frac{1 \cdot 544}{6}.$$

$\therefore\ x = 2 \cdot 591 \quad \text{or} \quad -0 \cdot 257.$

$\therefore\ x = 2 \cdot 59 \quad \text{or} \quad -0 \cdot 26$ (to 2 decimal places).

When solving a quadratic by means of the formula, arrange the equation in the form $ax^2 + bx + c = 0$, free from fractions and with the coefficient a positive; state the values of the letters a, b, c; substitute these values in the formula, and then simplify the result. Do not try to substitute and simplify in one step.

General hints for quadratic equations

Use the factor method whenever possible.

If there are no factors, or if you are unable to find them, you must choose between completing the square and using the formula. The actual arithmetic is the same in both cases, as you will see by comparing Examples 5 and 7. Unless the equation lends itself to the completion of the square, e.g.

$$x^2 + 2x = 4, \ x^2 - 4x = 3,$$

you are recommended to use the formula, especially if the coefficient of x is an odd number and the coefficient of x^2 is a number other than 1. If you propose to solve quadratics by the formula, it is essential that you should know it by heart.

Nature of the roots If, having completed the square or used the formula, you arrive at a point where you have to take the square root of a number, such as 49, which has an exact square root, the quadratic must have had factors. The condition for this is that $(b^2 - 4ac)$ should be an exact square.

If $b^2 - 4ac = 0$, the formula shows that both roots are the same; for the quantity following the sign $\pm$ is 0.

If $(b^2 - 4ac)$ is a negative number, the quadratic has no roots, for you cannot take the square root of a negative number. In such a case, do not go any further with the work, but write 'No roots.'

EXERCISE 77

Solve the following equations, giving the roots (if they involve decimals) correct to two places of decimals.

1 $x^2 + 3x + 1 = 0$ **2** $x^2 + x - 1 = 0$
3 $x^2 - 2x - 4 = 0$ **4** $2x^2 - 4x + 1 = 0$
5 $3x^2 - 6x - 2 = 0$ **6** $x^2 + 4x - 11 = 0$
7 $2x^2 + 3x - 2 = 0$ **8** $x^2 + 5x - 3 = 0$

9 $3x^2+8x-5=0$ **10** $2x^2-5x-4=0$

11 $3x^2-2x-3=0$ **12** $x^2-10x+21=0$

13 $x^2+x=3\frac{3}{4}$ **14** $2x^2-7x+4=0$

15 $5x^2+8x+2=0$ **16** $3x^2-2x+4=0$

17 $x^2-8x=12$ **18** $2x^2-3x+1=0$

19 $(x-1)^2=7$ **20** $3x^2-12x-4=0$

21 $2x^2+5x+2=0$ **22** $x^2+5x=15$

23 $x^2=x+5$ **24** $4x^2+7x-2=0$

25 $2x^2-4x+5=0$ **26** $x^2-4x=5\frac{1}{2}$

27 $(x+3)^2=10$ **28** $6x^2-11x+3=0$

29 $9x-x^2-15=0$ **30** $\frac{2}{5}x^2+2x+1=0$

31 $7x^2+2-10x=0$ **32** $x^2-x+6=0$

33 $x^2+1=2\frac{1}{3}x$ **34** $3x(x-1)=4$

35 $5-x=6x^2$ **36** $x(x+3)=(x-1)(2x-1)$

37 $\dfrac{1}{x}-\dfrac{1}{x+3}=\dfrac{3}{4}$ **38** $\dfrac{2}{x}+\dfrac{1}{x-1}=\dfrac{2}{x-2}$

39 $\dfrac{1}{x}-\dfrac{1}{x+1}=\dfrac{1}{3}$ **40** $\dfrac{x+1}{x}=\dfrac{x+4}{5}$

41 $(x+2)(x+3)+(x+4)(x+5)=x^2+3x+52$

42 $\dfrac{1-x}{2-x}+\dfrac{1}{2}=\dfrac{2-x}{3-x}$ **43** $\dfrac{2}{x}=\dfrac{1}{x+4}-\dfrac{3}{x-2}$

44 $\dfrac{5}{x-5}-\dfrac{4}{x-3}=\dfrac{3}{x+3}$ **45** $\dfrac{1}{2x}+\dfrac{1}{2x-4}=\dfrac{2}{5}$

Problems   Exercise 78 contains problems whose solutions lead to quadratic equations.   As in the case of the problems in Exercise 38, the roots of the quadratic equation must be tested in the problem in order to see whether both are admissible.

EXERCISE 78

1 When a certain number is added to its own square, the result is 72.   Find the number.

2 The length of a room is 4 m more than the breadth, and the area of the floor is 96 m².   Find the breadth of the room.

3 A rectangle measures 5 m by 8 m. When the length and breadth are both increased by the same amount, the area becomes 88 m². Find the increase in the length and breadth.

4 The sides of a right-angled triangle are x cm, $(x+1)$ cm and $(x+2)$ cm. Prove that x must have the value 3.

5 The height of a triangle is 5 cm less than the base. If the area is 33 cm², find the height.

6 A rectangular lawn is 10 m long and 6 m wide. A path of uniform width runs all round it, and the total area of this path is 80 m². Find its width.

7 The formula $S = \frac{1}{2}n(n+1)$ gives the sum S of the numbers 1, 2, 3, 4, . . . up to n. Find n if $S = 66$.

8 A farmer wants to use 60 m of fencing to form a rectangular sheep-pen. One of the long sides of the rectangle is to be the hedge of the field, and the fencing is to run along the other long side and the two short sides. If the area of the pen is to be 400 m², find the short sides of the rectangle.

9 The sides of a right-angled triangle are $(x-1)$, $(x+1)$, and $(x+4)$ cm. Find the value of x correct to the nearest tenth.

10 A photograph 6 cm by 4 cm has a border of uniform width all round it. The area of the border is 39 cm². Find its width.

11 Two concentric circles are drawn, the radius of one being 2 cm greater than that of the other. The area of the ring enclosed between the two circles is one-quarter of the area of the smaller circle. Calculate the radii of the circles, correct to three significant figures. (Do not substitute for π.)

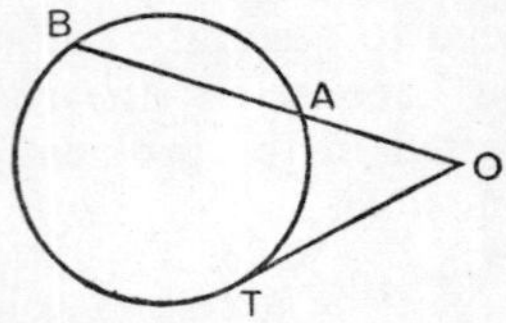

12 In Fig 213, it can be proved (see § 43) that $OT^2 = OA \cdot OB$. If AB = 6 cm and OT = 4 cm, calculate the length of OA.

Fig. 213

13 Find three consecutive numbers such that the square of their sum exceeds the sum of their squares by 484.

14 In the triangle ABC, the angle A = 90°, AB = x cm, AC = $(\frac{1}{3}x - 1)$ cm and BC = $(x + 1)$ cm.   Find x.

15 A circular cylinder of height 6 cm has a total surface area (including the two ends) of 572 cm².   Find its base-radius.   (Take π as $\frac{22}{7}$.)

16 The distance between the parallel sides of a trapezium is h cm, and the parallel sides are $(2h + 3)$ and $(4h - 1)$ cm long. The area of the trapezium is 52 cm².   Find h.

17 In Fig. 214, the circle whose centre is P, radius r cm, touches the two perpendicular radii OA, OB of a circle of radius 5 cm and also touches the circumference of that circle.   Calculate r, correct to three significant figures.

(Apply Pythagoras' Theorem to △PNO.)

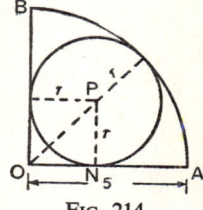

Fig. 214

18 A shopkeeper bought a certain number of articles for £9, and sold all except 4 of them at a price 10p more than each article had cost him.   He received from the sale £14.   Find the number of articles he bought.

19 A fruiterer bought a certain number of pineapples for £4·20.   Three of them became unsaleable, but he sold all the rest at a price which was 3p more than each pineapple had cost him.   His profit on the deal was 39p.   Find how many pineapples he bought.

28. RATIO PROPERTIES OF THE TRIANGLE

THE idea of the ratio of two lengths was introduced in § 31, Part I (page 194), and it would be useful to revise that section before going on to the formal proof of the geometrical properties which are there discussed.

THEOREM 27

If a straight line is drawn parallel to one side of a triangle, it divides the other two sides in the same ratio.

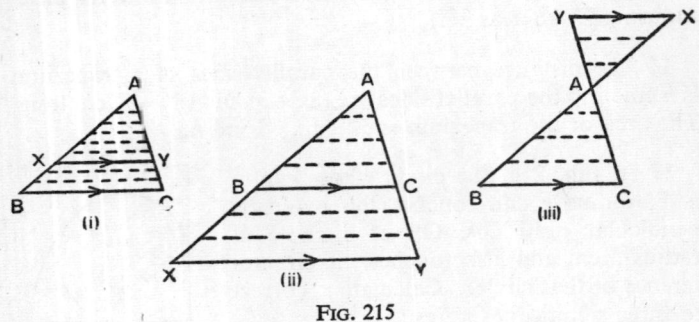

Fig. 215

Given a triangle ABC and a line parallel to BC meeting AB at X, AC at Y (produced in either direction if necessary).

To prove that   AX : XB = AY : YC.

Proof Let   AX : XB = p : q,

where p and q are whole numbers.

Divide AX into p equal parts, and XB into q equal parts, all these parts being equal.

Through the points of division draw parallels to BC.

These parallels divide AC into equal parts (intercept theorem).

Also AY contains p of these equal parts, and YC contains q of them.

$$\therefore \ AY : YC = p : q.$$
$$\therefore \ AX : XB = AY : YC.$$

Corollary   AX : AB = AY : AC

and   XB : AB = YC : AC

Reference In $\triangle ABC$, $XY \parallel BC$;
$$\therefore AX : XB = AY : YC.$$

Converse of Theorem 27   If a straight line divides two sides of a triangle in the same ratio, it is parallel to the third side.

We shall assume the truth of the converse without proving it.

Note on Theorem 27   In Fig. 215 (i), X divides AB internally in the ratio 7 : 3; in Fig. 215 (ii), X divides AB externally in the ratio 7 : 3; in Fig. 215 (iii), X divides BA externally in the ratio 7 : 3.

It is not always possible to express AX : XB in the form $p : q$, where p and q are whole numbers.   For example, if AX is equal to the diagonal of a square and XB is equal to the side of the square, AX : XB = $\sqrt{2} : 1$, a ratio which cannot be expressed by means of whole numbers.   The proof of the theorem in such a case is too difficult for a school course.

Alternative method for Theorem 27

Construction   Join BY, CX.

Proof   Since △s AXY, BXY have bases AX, XB and the same vertex Y,

$$\triangle AXY : \triangle BXY = AX : XB.$$

Similarly,   △AXY : △CXY = AY : YC.

But △BXY = △CXY (same base XY, same ‖s XY, BC).

$$\therefore AX : XB = AY : YC.$$

CONSTRUCTION 7

To divide a given straight line in a given ratio, (i) internally, (ii) externally.

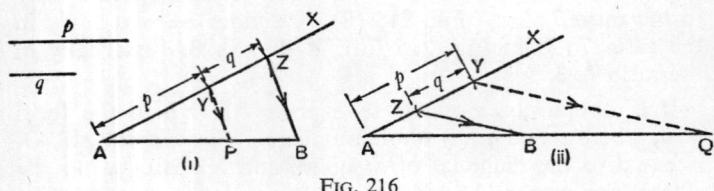

FIG. 216

Given a straight line AB, and two straight lines of lengths p, q units.

To construct (i) a point P in AB such that AP : PB = p : q,

                  (ii) a point Q in AB produced such that AQ : QB = p : q.

(i) Construction Draw any line AX, and cut off from it AY equal to p units and (in the *same* direction) YZ equal to q units. Join ZB.

Through Y draw the parallel to ZB to meet AB at P.

Then P is the required point.

Proof In △AZB, YP ∥ ZB (constr.).

      ∴ AP : PB = AY : YZ = p : q.

(ii) Construction If p is greater than q, draw any line AX, and cut off from it AY equal to p units and (in the *opposite* direction) YZ equal to q units. Join ZB.

Through Y draw the parallel to ZB to meet AB produced at Q.

Then Q is the required point.

Proof In △AZB, YQ ∥ ZB (constr.).

      ∴ AQ : QB = AY : YZ = p : q.

Note If p is less than q, start by drawing through B a straight line BX.

EXERCISE 79

(Exercise 83, Part I, should be revised first)

(*Numerical and constructions*)

1 In Fig. 217, if XM = 4½ cm, LY = 20 cm, YN = 15 cm, NZ = 9 cm, calculate XL and MZ.

2 In Fig. 217, if XL = 12 cm, LY = 21 cm, NZ = 16 cm, XM = 8 cm, calculate YN and MZ.

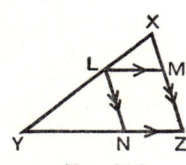

Fig. 217

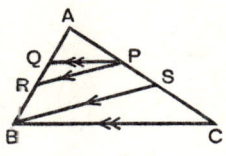

Fig. 218

3 In Fig. 218, if AQ = 3 cm, QR = 2 cm, RB = 4 cm, AP = 3½ cm, calculate PS and SC.

4 In Fig. 218, if AP = 10 cm, PS = 8 cm, AQ = 4 cm, RB = 6 cm, calculate QR and SC.

5 In Fig. 218, if AQ = 2 cm, QR = 6 cm, AP = 6 cm, PS = 3 cm, calculate RB and SC.

6 Draw a line AB 3 cm long, and find by construction (i) the point P which divides AB internally in the ratio 3 : 2, (ii) the point Q which divides AB externally in the ratio 3 : 2. Measure PQ.

7 Repeat No. 6, making the ratio in both cases 5 : 3.

8 Find by accurate drawing and measurement, but without any calculation, the value of $\dfrac{2\cdot6 \times 5\cdot3}{4\cdot7}$. (Suppose the value of the expression is x; then $4\cdot7 : 2\cdot6 = 5\cdot3 : x$.)

9 Solve by a geometrical construction the equation $\dfrac{4\cdot25}{3} = \dfrac{5\cdot5}{x}$.

(Riders)

10 In Fig. 217, prove that $\dfrac{XM}{MZ} = \dfrac{ZN}{NY}$.

11 In Fig. 219, prove that $\dfrac{AP}{AB} = \dfrac{AB}{AS}$.

12 In Fig. 220, prove that PR is parallel to AC.

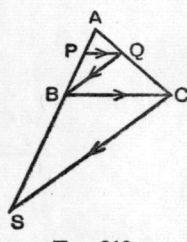

FIG. 219

13 In Fig. 221, prove that YZ is parallel to BC.

14 P is any point on the diagonal AC of a quadrilateral ABCD; PX is drawn parallel to AB to meet BC at X; XQ is

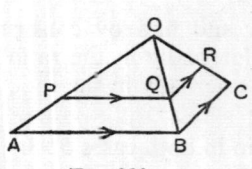

FIG. 220

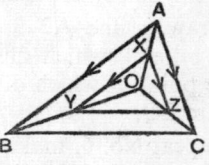

FIG. 221

drawn parallel to BD to meet CD at Q. Prove that PQ is parallel to AD.

15 P is any point in the side AB of a quadrilateral ABCD; PQ, PR are drawn parallel to AC, AD respectively, meeting BC, BD at Q, R. Prove that QR is parallel to CD.

THEOREM 28

The bisector (internal or external) of the vertical angle of a triangle divides the base (internally or externally) in the ratio of the other two sides.

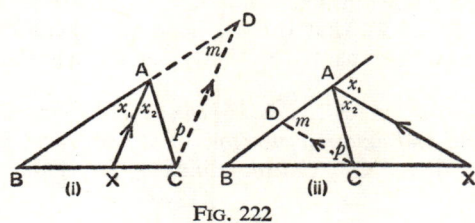

FIG. 222

Given a triangle ABC, and the line AX bisecting $\angle$ BAC internally in Fig. 222 (i), externally in Fig. 222 (ii); AX meets BC or BC produced at X.

To prove that $BX : XC = BA : AC$.

Construction   Through C draw a parallel to XA to meet BA (produced if necessary) at D.

Proof   Using the notation marked in the figure,

$$x_1 = m \quad \text{(corr. } \angle s, \text{ AX} \parallel \text{DC)},$$

and

$$x_2 = p \quad \text{(alt. } \angle s, \text{ AX} \parallel \text{DC)}.$$

But

$$x_1 = x_2 \quad \text{(given)}.$$

$$\therefore m = p.$$

$$\therefore AC = AD.$$

But in $\triangle BCD$, $XA \parallel CD$.

$$\therefore BX : XC = BA : AD.$$

$$\therefore BX : XC = BA : AC.$$

Reference   *AX bisects* $\angle BAC$,

$$\therefore BX : XC = BA : AC.$$

Converse of Theorem 28 **If a straight line through the vertex of a triangle divides the base (internally or externally) in the ratio of the other two sides, it bisects the vertical angle (internally or externally).**

For there is only one point which divides the base of a triangle internally in the ratio of the other two sides; and Theorem 28 shows that this is the point where the internal bisector meets the base. Similarly for the external bisector.

Example   *In △ABC, AB = 6 cm, BC = 5 cm, CA = 4 cm. The internal and external bisectors of ∠BAC meet BC and BC produced at P and Q.   Calculate the length of PQ.*

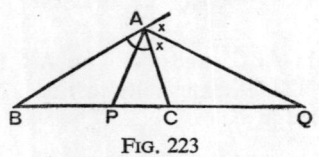

FIG. 223

$$BA : AC = 6 : 4 = 3 : 2.$$

$$\therefore BP : PC = 3 : 2.$$

$$\therefore \quad BP = \tfrac{3}{5} \text{ of } 5 \text{ cm } = 3 \text{ cm}.$$

Also $$BQ : QC = 3 : 2.$$

Let $$BQ = x \text{ cm, then } QC = (x - 5) \text{ cm}.$$

$$\therefore \quad \frac{x}{x-5} = \frac{3}{2}.$$

$$\therefore 3(x - 5) = 2x.$$

$$\therefore 3x - 15 = 2x.$$

$$\therefore \qquad x = 15.$$

$$\therefore \quad PQ = BQ - BP = (15 - 3) \text{ cm} = 12 \text{ cm}.$$

EXERCISE 80

(*Numerical*)

1 In △ABC, AB = 5 cm, BC = 6 cm, CA = 3 cm. The internal and external bisectors of ∠BAC meet BC and BC produced at P and Q respectively. Calculate the lengths of BP and BQ.

2 In △ABC, AB = 6 cm, BC = 9 cm, CA = 7·5 cm. The internal and external bisectors of ∠BAC meet BC and CB produced at D and E respectively. Calculate the length of DE.

3 The internal bisector of the angle A of △ABC meets BC at P. If the perimeter of the triangle is 45 cm, BP = 9 cm and CP = 6 cm, find the lengths of AB and AC.

4 In △ABC, ∠B = 90°, AB = 4 cm, BC = 3 cm. The internal bisector of ∠BAC meets BC at X. Calculate the length of BX: (i) by means of Theorem 28, (ii) by using trigonometrical tables for ∠BAC, and thus finding ∠BAX and BX.

5 In △ABC, BC = *a*, CA = *b*, AB = *c*. The internal bisector of ∠A meets BC at P. Find in terms of *a*, *b*, *c* the lengths of BP and CP.

(*Theoretical*)

6 The internal bisector of the angle A of △ABC meets BC at D; DE is drawn parallel to BA to meet AC at E. Prove that BA : AC = AE : EC.

7 The external bisector of the angle A of △ABC (in which AB is greater than AC) meets BC produced at X. The straight line drawn through X parallel to CA meets BA produced at Y. Prove that AB : AC = YB : YA.

8 D is the mid-point of the side BC of △ABC. The bisectors of ∠s ADB, ADC meet AB, AC at X, Y respectively. Prove that (i) AX : XB = AY : YC, (ii) XY is parallel to BC.

9 P is any point inside △ABC; the bisectors of ∠s BPC, CPA, APB meet BC, CA, AB at X, Y, Z respectively. Prove that

$$\frac{BX}{XC} \times \frac{CY}{YA} \times \frac{AZ}{ZB} = 1.$$

10 In the quadrilateral ABCD the sides AB and AD are equal; the bisectors of angles BAC, CAD meet BC, CD at X, Y respectively. Prove that XY is parallel to BD.

11 Prove the validity of the following method for dividing a line AB, 4 cm long, internally and externally in the ratio 3 : 2.

With centre A, radius 6 cm, draw an arc; with centre B, radius 4 cm, draw an arc to cut the first arc at C; join CA, CB; draw the internal and external bisectors of ∠ACB, to meet AB and AB produced at P and Q; then P and Q are the required points.

Draw an accurate figure, and measure PQ.

12 **Apollonius' Circle** A and B are fixed points 3 cm apart, and P is a point such that PA : PB = 3 : 2. Find by construction the points X, Y where the internal and external bisectors of ∠APB meet AB and AB produced.

What is the size of ∠XPY?

Deduce that, if P is a variable point such that PA : PB = 3 : 2, then the locus of P is a circle on XY as diameter.

Draw an accurate figure.

29. DENSITY

The **density** of a substance is the weight of unit volume. The units must always be named. The standard method of stating density is in terms of kilogrammes per cubic metre, written as kg m⁻³, but other units sometimes used are kilogrammes per litre and grammes per litre. Thus, the density of lead is 11400 kg m⁻³, or 11·4 kg per litre, or 11400 g per litre.

If we know the weight of a certain volume of a substance, then

$$\text{density} = \frac{\text{weight}}{\text{volume}},$$

the units being those in which the weight and volume are measured.

Example *A rectangular block of metal 15 cm by 10 cm by 5 mm weighs 667·5 g. Find the density of the metal.*

The volume $= 15 \times 10 \times \frac{1}{2}$ cm³ $= 75$ cm³.

$$\therefore \text{ the density} = \frac{667·5}{75} \text{ g per cm}^3 = \frac{667·5 \times 10^6}{75 \times 10^3} \text{ kg m}^{-3}$$

$$= \frac{\overset{133500}{\cancel{667500}}}{\underset{15}{\cancel{75}}} \text{ kg m}^{-3} = 8900 \text{ kg m}^{-3}.$$

EXERCISE 81

Use logarithms where they are suitable, and give answers to three significant figures.   Take π to be 3·142, and log π to be 0·4971.

1 Find in kilogrammes the weight of a rectangular block of stone 50 cm by 38 cm by 4 cm, the density being 2700 kg m⁻³.

2 A rectangular block of metal, 5·2 cm by 4·1 cm by 2 cm, weighs 298 g.   Find the density of the metal.

3 A flask weighs 20 g when empty, 60 g when full of water, and 94 g when full of sulphuric acid.   Find the density of sulphuric acid.

4 Find the weight in kilogrammes of a wooden beam 4·8 m long, with uniform rectangular cross-section 42 cm by 30 cm, if the wood has a density 680 kg m⁻³.

5 A cylindrical cork has a cross-section of 1·8 cm² and length 5·4 cm. Find its weight, if the density of cork is 240 kg m⁻³.

6 Find the weight in kilogrammes of a rectangular block of lead measuring 21·6 cm by 12·8 cm by 4·6 cm, if the density of lead is 11400 kg m⁻³.

7 A metal sheet is 21 cm long, 14 cm wide and 1·4 mm thick. If it weighs 432 g, find the density of the metal.

8 The internal and external radii of a flat ring made of iron are 4 cm and 4·9 cm, and the thickness is 1·38 cm. Find the weight of the ring, if the density of iron is 7600 kg m⁻³.

9 A solid right circular cone, made of lead, has base-radius 6 cm and height 16 cm. Find its weight, the density of lead being 11400 kg m⁻³.

30. THE LINEAR FUNCTION

Direct proportion We have already had examples of one quantity being directly proportional to another; e.g. the number of kilometres travelled by a train running at constant speed, and the number of minutes which have elapsed; or the circumference of a circle and its radius. The test which should be applied to see whether y is directly proportional to x is: if you double x, do you double y; if you treble x, do you treble y; or if you halve x, do you halve y? If the answer to these questions is 'yes', we say that y is directly proportional to x, or y varies directly as x. (The word 'directly' is sometimes omitted.) If that is the case, the ratio $y : x$ is constant, and does not change its value for different values of x and y.

As an example, consider $y = 3x$.

If $x = 4$, $y = 12$.
If $x = 2 \times 4$, or 8, $y = 24$, which is 2×12.
If $x = 3 \times 4$, or 12, $y = 36$, which is 3×12.

Thus y is directly proportional to x, and $\dfrac{y}{x}$ is always 3.

Now let us draw the graph of $y = 3x$.   The table of values is:

$x =$	-2	-1	0	1	2	3
$y =$	-6	-3	0	3	6	9

The graph is the line PQ in Fig. 224.

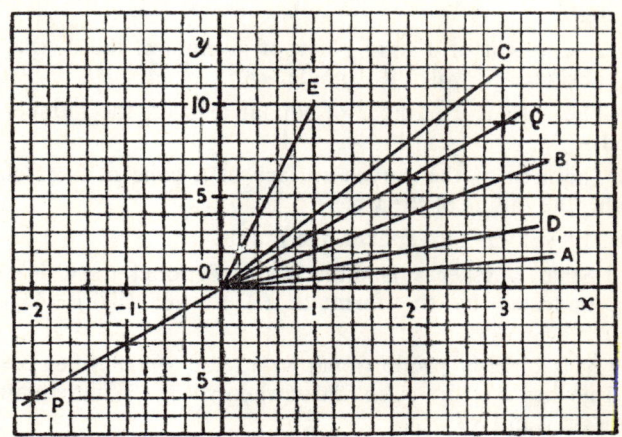

Fig. 224

Exercise: Find the equations of the lines OA, OB, OC, OD, OE in Fig. 224.   What is the constant ratio of y to x in each case?

We now see that the formula for direct proportion between y and x is $y = ax$, where a is some constant (i.e. unchanging) number; and that the graph, when corresponding values of x and y are plotted, is a **straight line through the origin.**

EXERCISE 82

In Nos. 1–9 state whether the first quantity is directly proportional to the second:

1 The circumference of a circle, the radius.

2 The simple interest on a given principal at a fixed rate per cent p.a., the number of years.

3 The length of an arc of a given circle, the angle subtended at the centre of the circle.

4 The area of a circle, the radius.

5 The length of the diagonal of a square, the side of the square.

6 The weight of a solid block of given size, the density of the substance of which it is made.

7 The cost of a number of similar articles, the number of articles.

8 The area of the curved surface of a cone of fixed slant height, the radius of the base.

9 The volume of a sphere, the radius.

10 State whether y is directly proportional to x, if they are connected by the formula: (i) $y = 4x$; (ii) $y = 4x + 5$; (iii) $y = 4x^2$.

11 y is directly proportional to x, and $y = 18$ when $x = 3$. Find y when $x = 15$. Also find x when $y = 3$. What equation connects y and x?

12 If y is directly proportional to x, and $y = 8$ when $x = 3$, what equation connects x and y? Find y when $x = 4\frac{1}{2}$, and find x when $y = 2$.

The law $y = ax + b$.

Let us consider the graph of the equation $y = 3x - 5$, from $x = -2$ to $x = 4$. The table of values is:

$x =$	-2	-1	0	1	2	3	4
$y =$	-11	-8	-5	-2	1	4	7

The graph is shown in Fig. 225.

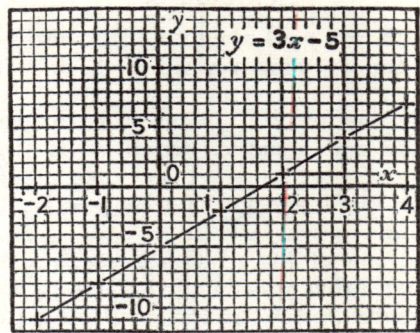

$$y = 3x - 5$$

FIG. 225

Observe, in the table of values, that the values of x increase by 1 each time as we go along the table, while those of y increase by 3. Although y is not directly proportional to x, the *changes* in y are directly proportional to the *changes* in x. This fact causes the slope to be the same throughout, and the graph is a straight line. We say that the line is the graph of the equation $y = 3x - 5$, or that it is the graph of the function $3x - 5$.

The same argument can be used for any function of x which is of the first degree, i.e. contains no higher powers of x than the first power. Thus:

The graph of $y = ax + b$ is a straight line, not passing through the origin unless $b = 0$. **Equal increases of x lead to equal increases of y.**

For the reason given above, $ax + b$ is called a **linear function** of x, and its graph, being a straight line, can be drawn by plotting three points only (the third one as a check to the first two) and joining them with a ruler. The three points should not be taken too near together.

If a is negative, the graph has a downward slope, and equal increases in the value of x lead to equal decreases in the value of y.

EXERCISE 83

1 If $y = ax + b$, and $y = 4$ when $x = 2$, and also $y = -2$ when $x = 0$, find a and b. Find y when $x = 3$, and find x when $y = -5$.

2 A temperature of $x°$ C is the same as one of $y°$ F. Explain why x and y are related by a law of the type $y = ax + b$.

If $x = 0$ when $y = 32$, and $x = 100$ when $y = 212$, find a and b, and the value of x when $y = 0$.

Draw the graph of the relation between x and y from $x = -30$ to 100. From your graph, express (i) 40° C, 55° C, 78° C in Fahrenheit, (ii) 98° F, 150° F, 10° F in Celsius.

3 The effort P kg wt necessary to raise a load W kg by means of a certain machine is given by the following table:

W =	5	15	20	25	40
P =	3·4	5·8	7·0	8·2	11·8

By plotting a graph, show that these results fit a formula of the type $P = aW + b$, and find values for a and b. Find the effort necessary to raise a load of 32 kg, and also what load can be raised by an effort of 4·8 kg wt.

4 Various weights are hung on the end of a spring, and the stretched length of the spring is measured in each case. The following is the table of values:

Weight in grammes, x .	6	8	12	18
Length in cm, y . . .	4·6	5·3	6·7	8·8

Plot these readings, and show that x and y obey the law $y = ax + b$, where a and b are constants, and find their values.

Find also the natural length of the spring (i.e. the length when $x = 0$), and also the load which will stretch the spring to a length of 7·9 cm.

5 Water runs out of a cistern so that after x minutes there are y litres left in the cistern, where $y = 70 - 6x$. Make a table of the values of y when $x = 0, 1, 2, 3, 4, 5$, and verify that the decreases in y are proportional to the time that has elapsed. Illustrate by drawing the graph.

6 The quarterly charge for electricity in a certain house is £1·50 'standing charge' (however much current is consumed) together with a charge of $1\frac{1}{2}$p for each unit consumed above 80. If the total charge is y pence and the number of units consumed altogether is x, find a formula for y in terms of x, and illustrate by means of a graph.

7 Which of the following are linear functions?

$$\text{(i) } 5 - 3x, \quad \text{(ii) } 5 + \frac{3}{x}, \quad \text{(iii) } x^2 + 5, \quad \text{(iv) } 5x.$$

Which of these give straight line graphs? Which functions are directly proportional to x? In which functions are their increases or decreases proportional to those of x?

8 If $y = 3x - 2$, prove that $x = \frac{1}{3}y + \frac{2}{3}$.
(This verifies that if y is a linear function of x, then x is a linear function of y.)

9 If $2y + 3x = 8$, prove that $y = -1\frac{1}{2}x + 4$, and thus show that y is a linear function of x.

10 Using the same axes and scales for both, draw the graphs of $y = 2x + 1$ and $y = 10 - x$, from $x = 0$ to $x = 5$. Read off the co-ordinates of the point where they intersect.

11 Draw on the same axes, from $x = -3$ to $+3$, the graphs of:

$$\text{(i) } y = 3x + 2, \quad \text{(ii) } y = \frac{1}{2}x + 2, \quad \text{(iii) } y = -2x + 2.$$

Verify that these lines all cut the y-axis at the same point. What are the co-ordinates of the point where the line $y = ax + b$ cuts the y-axis?

12 Draw on the same axes, from $x = -1$ to $x = 4$, the graphs of:

$$\text{(i) } y = 8 - 2x, \quad \text{(ii) } y = 6 - 2x, \quad \text{(iii) } y = -2x,$$

What do you notice about the lines?

13 Draw the graphs of the equations $x = 2$, $x = 6$, $y = 3$, $y = 7$. (The graph of $x = 2$ is the locus of all points whose x co-ordinate is 2; i.e. a line parallel to the y-axis, 2 units away.)

Gradient Fig. 226 shows the graphs of: (i) $y = 4x + 3$, (ii) $y = x + 3$,   (iii) $y = \frac{1}{2}x + 3$,   (iv) $y = 3 - \frac{1}{2}x$,   (v) $y = 3 - 4x$.

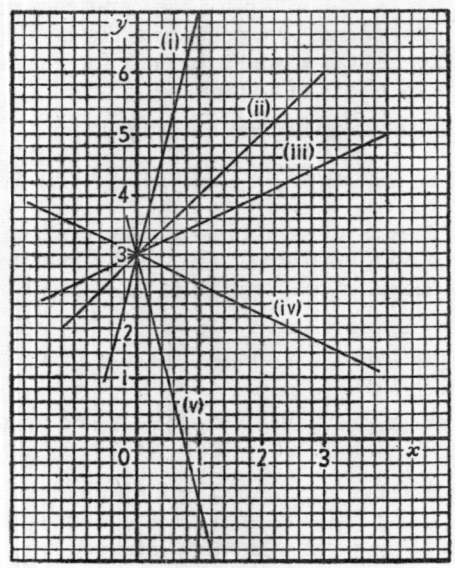

FIG. 226

In (i), y increases four times as fast as x.   In (ii), y increases at the same rate as x.   In (iii), y increases half as fast as x. In (iv), y decreases half as fast as x increases.   In (v), y decreases four times as fast as x increases.

The rate at which y increases compared with the rate at which x increases is called the **gradient** of the line, and we can read the gradient at a glance by looking at the coefficient of x. The gradient of (i) is 4, that of (ii) is 1, that of (iii) is $\frac{1}{2}$, that of (iv) is $-\frac{1}{2}$, and that of (v) is -4.   If lines slope upwards to the right, like the first three, their gradients are positive. If they slope downwards to the right, like (iv) and (v), their gradients are negative.   Parallel lines all have the same gradient.

We often speak of the 'gradient of a function', by which we mean the gradient of the graph of the function.   Thus

The gradient of the function $ax + b$ is a.

The word 'gradient' is sometimes used differently in ordinary speech, when the gradient of a road is said to be 1 in 150. This usually means that the road rises 1 m vertically in a distance of 150 m measured along the road.

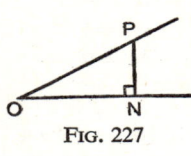

Fig. 227

In mathematics we should take the phrase to mean that the road rises 1 m vertically in a distance of 150 m measured horizontally.   In Fig. 227, the gradient of a road often means $\dfrac{PN}{OP}$, which is the *sine* of the angle PON, whereas in mathematics the gradient is $\dfrac{PN}{ON}$, which is the *tangent* of the angle PON.

Provided that the scales on the two axes are the same, the gradient a of the line $y=ax+b$ is the tangent of the angle which this line makes with the x-axis.

Gradient with different scales   If different scales are used on the two axes, this fact must be taken into account when reading off the gradient from a graph. Thus, in Fig. 228 the gradient is the ratio of the change in y to that of x, i.e. $\dfrac{BC}{AC}$.   But this is not $\frac{1}{2}$, as the scale on which BC is measured is different from that on which AC is measured. The true value of the gradient $\dfrac{BC}{AC}$ is $\dfrac{5}{1}$, or 5.

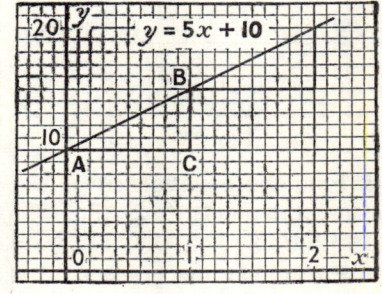

Fig. 228

Similarly, in Fig. 225, the gradient is actually 3, but the tangent of the angle of slope is $\frac{3}{5}$.

EXERCISE 84

1 What are the gradients of the graphs of: (i) $y = 6x + 7$, (ii) $y = 6 + x$, (iii) $y = 4 - 3x$, (iv) $y = \frac{1}{3}x + 4$, (v) $y = 3 - \frac{1}{4}x$?

Give the equations of the lines through the origin parallel to these lines.

2 Show that $(0, 4)$ and $(3, 5)$ satisfy the equation $y = \frac{1}{3}x + 4$, and hence prove that this is the equation of the line joining these two points. What is its gradient?

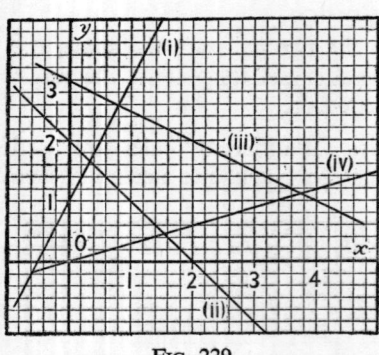

FIG. 229

3 In Fig. 229, find the equations of the lines marked (i), (ii), (iii), (iv).

(For (i), notice that $y = 1$ when $x = 0$, and the gradient is 2; $\therefore$ the equation is $y = 2x + 1$.)

4 Find the equation of the straight line which passes through the point $(1, 2)$ and has a gradient 3. (Let the line be $y = 3x + b$. Now put $x = 1$ when $y = 2$.)

5 Find the equation (i) of the straight line which passes through the points $(0, 2)$, $(3, 1)$; (ii) of the straight line which passes through the points $(2, 7)$, $(4, 13)$.

6 Prove that **the gradient of the line joining** (x_1, y_1) **and** (x_2, y_2) **is** $\dfrac{y_1 - y_2}{x_1 - x_2}$.

Gradient of a travel graph Often the scales on the two axes are not only different, they measure essentially different quantities. The gradient of a travel graph is obtained by dividing the increase in the number of kilometres travelled by the increase in the number of hours. This is a speed in kilometres per hour. Fig. 230 shows the travel graphs of a walker (OA), a cyclist (OB) and a motorist (OC). Their speeds are, respectively, 6 km per hour, 16 km per hour and 40 km per hour.

The gradient of a travel graph represents the speed.

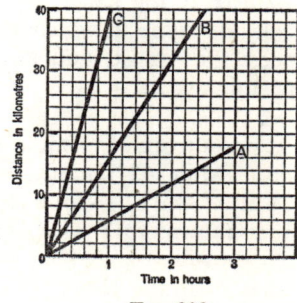

FIG. 230

EXERCISE 85

1 A boy sets out at noon to cycle along a certain road at a steady speed of 16 km/h. At the same instant a man starts from the same place along the same road, walking at 6 km/h. After 1 hour the man boards a bus which is travelling along the same road at a steady speed of 32 km/h. Draw travel graphs for the boy and the man, and hence find at what time the bus overtakes the boy, and what is the distance from the starting-point of the boy at that time.

2 A cyclist starts from a town A at 12 noon and cycles at a steady speed of 20 km/h towards a town B which is 48 km away.   At 1.30 p.m. a motorist leaves B and travels towards A at a steady speed of 52 km/h.   Draw graphs showing the distances of both men from A from noon to 2 p.m., and hence find when the cyclist and the motorist meet, and how far they are from A at that moment.

3 A cyclist leaves his house at noon and cycles at a steady speed of 14 km/h.   Half an hour later a motorist sets out from the house along the same road at a steady speed of 42 km/h.   He travels to a town 56 km away, stays there half an hour, and then returns at the same speed by the same route.   Find graphically the time at which the motorist, on his return journey, meets the cyclist, and the distance from home at which the meeting occurs.

4 A man sets out at noon from X to walk at 7 km/h to Y, which is 20 km away.   After 45 minutes he meets a bus travelling from Y to X at 32 km/h.   When the bus reaches X it waits 10 min and then returns to Y with the same speed as before.   Draw a graph showing the distances of the man and the bus from X at different times, and find when and where the man is overtaken by the bus on its return journey to Y.   Find also at what time the bus reaches Y.

5 P, Q, R, S are four stations in order on a railway line. PQ = 30 km, QR = 20 km, RS = 46 km.   A train leaves P at 12 noon and travels to S, stopping for 5 min at Q and again for 5 min at R, the speed between stops being uniform.   The train reaches S at 1.30 p.m.   Draw a graph to show its distance from P at any time.

A second train starts from S at 1 p.m. and travels non-stop to P at 80 km/h.   Find graphically when the trains meet, and at what distance from P this occurs.

Half planes Any line in a plane divides the plane into two regions, one on each side of the line.   These regions are called **half planes.** Consider, for example, the line $x = 2$, which is the locus of all points whose x co-ordinate is 2.   All points to the left of this line have their x co-ordinate less than 2, while all points to the right of it have their x co-ordinate greater than 2.

In order to discuss the half planes into which a line divides a plane, we shall need symbols, which you may have met already, for 'is greater than' and 'is less than'. These are $>$ and $<$.

The statement '4 is greater than 3' is written

$$4 > 3.$$

The statement '4 is less than 5' is written

$$4 < 5.$$

Notice that the narrower end of the sign $>$ or $<$ is nearer to the smaller quantity.

The statement 'x is either greater than 2 or equal to 2' is written

$$x > 2,$$

which is read as

'x is greater than or equal to 2'.

If we think of the number scale in Fig. 231, where both positive and negative numbers are arranged in a line in such a way that the numbers get bigger as we go up (somewhat in the manner of the numbers on a thermometer), it is obvious that any number on this scale is greater than a number below it.   Particular care must be taken when negative numbers are involved.   Thus,

$$-3 < -2 \text{ (although } 3 > 2),$$
$$1 > -3,$$
$$-\tfrac{1}{2} < -\tfrac{1}{4}.$$

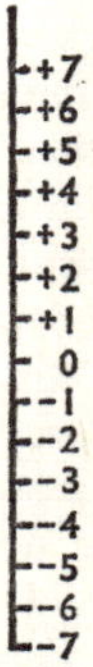

Fig. 231

Using these inequality symbols, we can say that the half plane to the left of the line $x=2$ is denoted by $x<2$; that to the right of the same line is $x>2$.

Similarly, $y>-4$ denotes the half plane above the line $y=-4$ (a line parallel to the x-axis and 4 units below it); $y<-4$ denotes the half plane below the same line.

Fig. 232 shows the graph of $y=3x-5$. The region above the line is denoted by $y>3x-5$; that below the line is $y<3x-5$. All the points for which y is equal to $3x-5$ lie on the line. Thus the region denoted by $y \leqslant 3x-5$ includes all points on or below the line.

The usual method of indicating a half plane in a diagram is to leave *unshaded* the region named, and to shade instead a part of the *other* half plane. Thus, in Fig. 232, the half plane indicated is $y \leqslant 3x-5$, the region below the line.

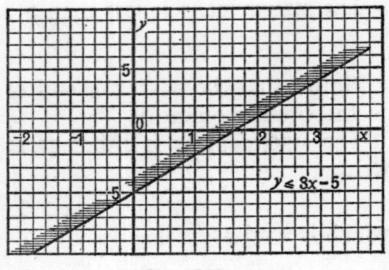

FIG. 232

Example 1 *Show in a diagram the region of the plane which is denoted by $x \geqslant -1$, $y \geqslant 1$, $2x+3y \leqslant 6$.*

The region $x \geqslant -1$ lies to the right of or on the line $x=-1$, so we shade to the left of this line. (See Fig. 233.)

The region $y \geqslant 1$ lies above or on the line $y=1$, so we shade below this line.

The region $2x+3y \leqslant 6$ lies below the line $2x+3y=6$, convenient points on which might be $(0,2)$ and $(3,0)$. The quickest way to determine which side of the line is required is to try, say, $x=0$ and $y=0$, which makes $2x+3y$ equal to 0. Now $0<6$, therefore the origin belongs to the region $2x+3y \leqslant 6$.

The required region is the triangle ABC in Fig. 233.

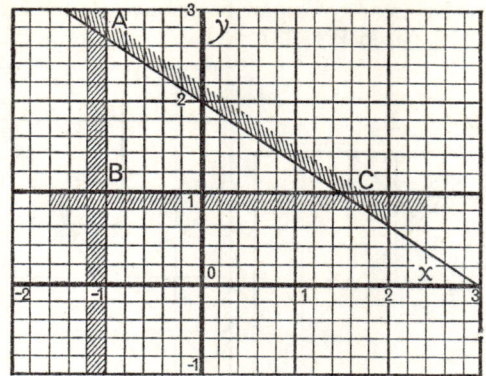

FIG. 233

EXERCISE 86

Indicate in a sketch each of the half planes named in Nos. 1–8.

1 $x > -2$ **2** $x < 4$ **3** $y > 3$ **4** $y < -1$

5 $y > x$ **6** $y > -x$ **7** $x + 2y > 1$ **8** $x - 2y < 1$

9 Name by means of a pair of inequalities the area shaded (i) in Fig. 234, (ii) in Fig. 235.

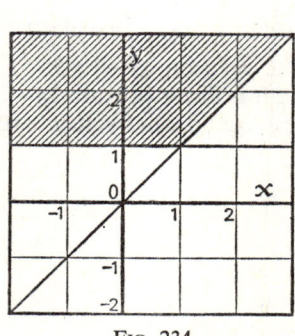

FIG. 234

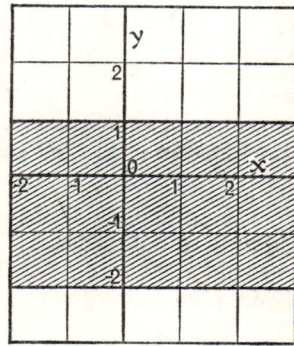

FIG. 235

10 Name by means of a pair of inequalities the area shaded (i) in Fig. 236, (ii) in Fig. 237.

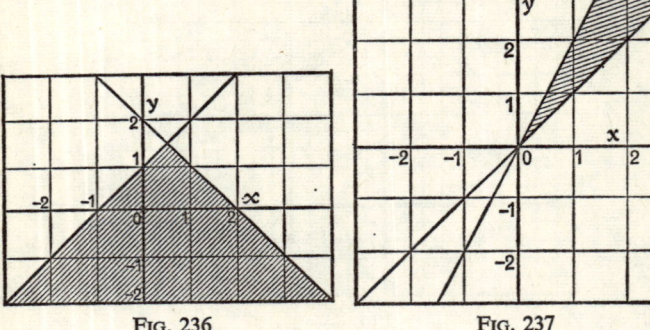

FIG. 236   FIG. 237

Show by shading, as in Fig. 236, the regions indicated in Nos. 11–15.

11 $x > 1$, $y < 2$ **12** $-2 < x < 2$ **13** $y < x$, $x > 1$

14 $x < 0$, $y > 0$ **15** $x - y > 2$, $x < 1$

Draw sketches and indicate by shading as in Fig. 233 the regions represented in Nos. 16–19.   (Leave the region named *unshaded*.)

16 $x > 0$, $y > 0$, $x + y < 1$ **17** $x < 2$, $y < 2$, $y < x + 1$

18 $y < x + 4$, $x < 3$, $y > 1$ **19** $y < x$, $y > \frac{1}{2}x$, $2x + y > 2$

Linear inequations   Consider the relation $3x - 1 > 5$.   This is an example of an **inequation,** and it is **linear** because $3x - 1$ is a linear function of x.   We require to find what values x may have if

$$3x - 1 > 5.$$

Adding 1 to both sides,

$$3x > 6.$$

Dividing both sides by 3,

$$x > 2.$$

∴ x can have any value greater than 2.

This result can also be seen from a sketch graph of the line $y = 3x - 1$. At all points of the line to the right of the point (2, 5), y is greater than 5, and therefore $3x - 1 > 5$.

This example shows that the method of solving an inequation (adding the same thing to both sides, subtracting the same thing from both sides, multiplying or dividing both sides by the same number) is the same as the method of solving an equation, with the important exception that **both sides of an inequation must not be multiplied or divided by a negative number without reversing the direction of the inequality sign.**

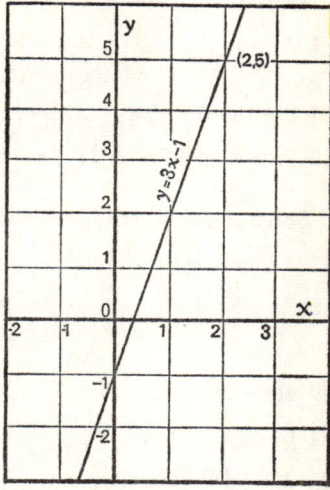

Fig. 238

For example, $6 > 5$, but when both sides are multiplied by -1 it is not true that $-6 > -5$, because in fact $-6 < -5$.

Similarly, if $\qquad x > 2,$

then $\qquad\qquad -x < -2.$

Example 2 *Solve the inequation* $3 - 4x \leqslant 6 + x$.
$\qquad 3 - 4x \leqslant 6 + x.$

$\therefore \quad -4x - x \leqslant 6 - 3$ (subtracting x from both sides and also 3).

$\therefore \qquad -5x \leqslant 3.$

$\therefore \qquad 5x \geqslant -3$ (multiplying both sides by -1 and reversing the inequality sign).

$\therefore \qquad x \geqslant -\frac{3}{5}$ (dividing both sides by 5).

EXERCISE 87

State the solutions of the following inequations:

1 $3x > 1$ **2** $2x < 1$ **3** $3x \geqslant -1$

4 $-3x > 3$ **5** $-2x \leqslant 10$ **6** $x + 2 < 0$

7 $2y - 5 \geqslant 0$ **8** $3 - x > 5$ **9** $3x > 1 + 2x$

10 $2x + 4 \geqslant 4 + 2x$ **11** $3x - 5 > 4$ **12** $4 > 2x - 6$

Solve the following inequations:

13 $3x < x + 4$ **14** $\frac{1}{2}x + 4 \leqslant 1 + x$

15 $7x - 6 > 8$ **16** $3(x + 1) > 5(x + 2)$

17 $\frac{3}{5}x - 1 < x$ **18** $3 - 4x > 2x - 1$

19 $6(x - 2) \geqslant 3(2 - x)$ **20** $4(y + 2) > 3(y + 3)$

21 $6 - 2(x - 1) < 12$ **22** $2(3y - 4) \leqslant 3(4y - 3)$

23 $3(1 - 4x) < 9 + 6x$ **24** $5 - 3x < 6 - 3x$

31. INDICES AND SURDS

Indices   On p. 168 the following laws of indices were stated:

$$a^m \times a^n = a^{m+n},$$
$$a^m \div a^n = a^{m-n},$$
$$(a^m)^n = a^{mn}.$$

It was emphasised in § 20 that these rules can be proved only when m and n are positive integers (and, in the case of (ii), when m is greater than n). Fractional and negative powers were defined by assuming these laws to be true also when m and n were not positive integers, and seeing what meaning this gave for such expressions as 2^0, 2^{-3}, $2^{\frac{1}{2}}$ and $2^{\frac{2}{3}}$.

The results were as follows:

$$2^0 = 1;$$

$$2^{-3} = \frac{1}{2^3} = \frac{1}{8};$$

$$2^{\frac{1}{2}} = \sqrt{2};$$

$2^{\frac{5}{2}}$ can be considered either as $(2^{\frac{1}{2}})^5 = (\sqrt{2})^5$, or as $(2^5)^{\frac{1}{2}} = \sqrt{32}$.

Example 1 *Evaluate* $64^{-\frac{2}{3}}$.

$$64^{-\frac{2}{3}} = \frac{1}{64^{\frac{2}{3}}} = \frac{1}{(64^{\frac{1}{3}})^2} = \frac{1}{4^2} = \frac{1}{16}.$$

Note that $64^{\frac{2}{3}}$ may be regarded either as $(64^{\frac{1}{3}})^2$ or as $(64^2)^{\frac{1}{3}}$. The former method has been chosen because it is easier to guess the cube root of 64 and then square the answer than to find the cube root of 4096.

EXERCISE 88

Simplify:

1 3^{-2} **2** 1000^0 **3** $27^{\frac{1}{3}}$ **4** $(\frac{1}{3})^{-2}$

5 $32^{\frac{2}{5}}$ **6** $(0 \cdot 04)^{\frac{1}{2}}$ **7** $(10^{\frac{2}{3}})^{-\frac{3}{2}}$ **8** $289^{-\frac{1}{2}}$

9 $(\frac{2}{3})^{-4}$ **10** $(\frac{1}{10})^{-1}$ **11** $(0 \cdot 027)^{\frac{2}{3}}$ **12** $2^a \times 2^{-a}$

13 $125^{-\frac{1}{3}}$ **14** $(625x^2)^{-\frac{1}{2}}$ **15** $(8x^6)^{\frac{2}{3}}$ **16** $(1\frac{7}{9})^{\frac{1}{2}}$

Negative indices are useful in the symbolic expression of units.

Thus, a speed in km per hour is the result of dividing a distance in kilometres by a number of hours, and we therefore write it either as km/h or (better) as km h^{-1}.

A density is a number of kilogrammes divided by a number of cubic metres, and is written kg m^{-3}.

Numbers expressed in standard form   Indices are useful for expressing numbers in the form

$$A \times 10^n,$$

where A is in standard form (i.e. between 1 and 10) and n is an integer, positive or negative. This method is especially common in the case of very large or very small numbers.

When a number is expressed as $A \times 10^n$, the index n tells us how many places (to the right if n is positive, to the left if n is negative) the decimal point in A must be moved to give the required number. The number n also tells us the characteristic of the logarithm; e.g. the logarithm of 2×10^{12} is 12·3010.

As an example of this method of expressing numbers, the coefficient of expansion of copper is 0·0000167, or $1·67 \times 10^{-5}$. The distance of the sun from the earth is 150 000 000 km, or $1·5 \times 10^8$ km.

This method of expressing numbers makes it easier to compare one with another, for example, 0·0000000461 and 0·0000000097. These are:

$$4·61 \times 10^{-8} \quad \text{and} \quad 9·7 \times 10^{-9},$$

and the second is obviously the smaller.

EXERCISE 89

Give all answers in the form $A \times 10^n$, where A is in standard form.

1 Simplify $2 \times 10^5 \times 3 \times 10^9 \times 5 \times 10^{-11}$.

2 Evaluate pq when $p = 3 \times 10^8$, $q = 4 \times 10^{-7}$,

3 If the volume of a molecule of water is $1·5 \times 10^{-23}$ cm^3, find the number of molecules in a litre.

4 If the area of the ocean is 367 000 000 000 000 m^2 and the average depth is 3850 m, find the volume in m^3.

5 Write down the squares of 4 100 000 and 0·0000041.

6 Evaluate $\frac{3}{80} \times 10^{-13} \times (6 \times 10^{-5})^2$.

Surds $\sqrt{4}=2$, $\sqrt{9}=3$, $\sqrt[3]{8}=2$; these are called **rational numbers,** because they can be written down exactly.

But $\sqrt{2}=1\cdot414\ldots$, $\sqrt{3}=1\cdot732\ldots$, $\sqrt[3]{9}=2\cdot08\ldots$; these cannot be obtained exactly, but only to whatever degree of accuracy is required. The roots are said to be **irrational numbers,** or **surds.**

The number π, whose value is $3\cdot14159265\ldots$, is irrational. We use $3\cdot14$ or $3\cdot142$ or $3\frac{1}{7}$, whichever approximation seems appropriate or convenient; but it must always be remembered that these are only approximations.

Sometimes a surd can be expressed in terms of a simpler surd, as is shown in the next example.

Example 2 *Simplify* $\sqrt{12}$, $\sqrt{20}$, $\sqrt{27}$, $\sqrt{1008}$.

$$\sqrt{12} = \sqrt{2^2 \times 3} \qquad = 2\sqrt{3},$$
$$\sqrt{20} = \sqrt{2^2 \times 5} \qquad = 2\sqrt{5},$$
$$\sqrt{27} = \sqrt{3^2 \times 3} \qquad = 3\sqrt{3},$$
$$\sqrt{1008} = \sqrt{2^4 \times 3^2 \times 7} = 2^2 \times 3\sqrt{7} = 12\sqrt{7}.$$

Example 3 *Express* $5\sqrt{2}$, $3\sqrt{5}$, $6\sqrt{10}$ *as the square roots of single integers.*

$$5\sqrt{2} \ = \sqrt{25} \times \sqrt{2} \ = \sqrt{25 \times 2} = \sqrt{50}.$$
$$3\sqrt{5} \ = \sqrt{9} \times \sqrt{5} \ = \sqrt{9 \times 5} \ = \sqrt{45}.$$
$$6\sqrt{10} = \sqrt{36} \times \sqrt{10} = \sqrt{360}.$$

Multiplication of surds

Example 4 *Simplify* (i) $\sqrt{12} \times \sqrt{18}$, (ii) $\sqrt{6} \times 4\sqrt{2} \times \sqrt{15}$.

(i) $\sqrt{12} \times \sqrt{18}$

$$= \sqrt{12 \times 18}$$
$$= \sqrt{2^2 \times 3 \times 3^2 \times 2} = 2 \times 3 \times \sqrt{6} = 6\sqrt{6}.$$

(ii) $\sqrt{6} \times 4\sqrt{2} \times \sqrt{15} = 4 \times \sqrt{6 \times 2 \times 15}$
$$= 4 \times \sqrt{3 \times 2 \times 2 \times 3 \times 5}$$
$$= 4\sqrt{3^2 \times 2^2 \times 5}$$
$$= 4 \times 3 \times 2\sqrt{5} = 24\sqrt{5}.$$

The foregoing examples will have brought out the following rules for the treatment of square roots:

$$\sqrt{a} \times \sqrt{b} = \sqrt{ab},$$

$$\frac{\sqrt{a}}{\sqrt{b}} = \sqrt{\frac{a}{b}}.$$

Note It is easy to verify, by putting $a = 25$ and $b = 16$, that $\sqrt{a+b}$ is not equal to $\sqrt{a} + \sqrt{b}$; also $\sqrt{a-b}$ is not equal to $\sqrt{a} - \sqrt{b}$.

Notice that $\sqrt{7} \times \sqrt{7} = 7$, this being the definition of $\sqrt{7}$. Do not say $\sqrt{7} \times \sqrt{7} = \sqrt{49} = 7$.

Division of surds

Example 5 *Evaluate to three decimal places:* (i) $\dfrac{1}{\sqrt{2}}$, (ii) $\dfrac{9}{\sqrt{75}}$, *given that* $\sqrt{2} = 1 \cdot 414$ *and* $\sqrt{3} = 1 \cdot 732$.

(i) $\dfrac{1}{\sqrt{2}} = \dfrac{1 \times \sqrt{2}}{\sqrt{2} \times \sqrt{2}} = \dfrac{\sqrt{2}}{2} = \dfrac{1 \cdot 414}{2} = 0 \cdot 707$ (to 3 dec. places).

(ii) $\dfrac{9}{\sqrt{75}} = \dfrac{9}{\sqrt{25 \times 3}}$

$$= \frac{9}{5\sqrt{3}} = \frac{9 \times \sqrt{3}}{5\sqrt{3} \times \sqrt{3}} = \frac{9\sqrt{3}}{5 \times 3}$$

$$= \frac{3\sqrt{3}}{5}$$

$$= \frac{3 \times 1 \cdot 732}{5}$$

$$= \frac{5 \cdot 196}{5}$$

$$= 1 \cdot 039 \text{ (to 3 dec. places)}.$$

Example 5 shows how to avoid the labour of dividing by a decimal when a surd occurs in the denominator. It is much quicker to divide $1 \cdot 414$ by 2, in (i) above, than to divide 1 by $1 \cdot 414$. Similarly, in (ii), the method given above is less trouble than to say $\dfrac{9}{\sqrt{75}} = \dfrac{9}{8 \cdot 660}$, etc.

EXERCISE 90

Express each of the following in terms of as small a surd as possible:

1 $\sqrt{48}$	2 $\sqrt{60}$	3 $\sqrt{8}$	4 $\sqrt{27}$
5 $\sqrt{18}$	6 $\sqrt{24}$	7 $\sqrt{1728}$	8 $\sqrt{108}$
9 $\sqrt{288}$	10 $\sqrt{125}$	11 $\sqrt{720}$	12 $\sqrt{90}$

Express the following as the square roots of single integers:

13 $3\sqrt{5}$	14 $8\sqrt{3}$	15 $4\sqrt{5}$	16 $5\sqrt{8}$
17 $6\sqrt{2}$	18 $3\sqrt{6}$	19 $7\sqrt{3}$	20 $\frac{1}{2}\sqrt{24}$

Simplify the following:

21 $\sqrt{5} \times \sqrt{50}$	22 $2\sqrt{3} \times 3\sqrt{2}$	23 $\sqrt{3} \times \sqrt{2} \times \sqrt{6}$
24 $\sqrt{12} \times \sqrt{18}$	25 $\sqrt{2} \times \sqrt{8}$	26 $\sqrt{12} \div \sqrt{6}$
27 $\sqrt{2} \times \sqrt{\frac{1}{2}}$	28 $\sqrt{30} \times \sqrt{2} \times \sqrt{3}$	29 $\sqrt{2} \times \sqrt{6} \times 8$
30 $(\sqrt{2}+1)^2$	31 $(\sqrt{2}-1)^2$	32 $(\sqrt{3}+1)(\sqrt{3}-1)$
33 $\sqrt{14} \times \sqrt{\frac{1}{7}}$	34 $(\sqrt{3}-\sqrt{2})^2$	35 $(\sqrt{5}-2)(\sqrt{5}+2)$

Express the following in a form not containing surds in the denominator, and then evaluate, correct to three decimal places, given that $\sqrt{2}=1\cdot414$, $\sqrt{3}=1\cdot732$, $\sqrt{5}=2\cdot236$:

36 $\dfrac{1}{\sqrt{3}}$	37 $\dfrac{3}{\sqrt{2}}$	38 $\dfrac{10}{\sqrt{5}}$
39 $\dfrac{1}{\sqrt{50}}$	40 $2\sqrt{\dfrac{4}{3}}$	41 $\dfrac{5}{\sqrt{8}}$

32. TANGENT, SINE AND COSINE (II)

Use of logarithmic sines, etc.

From the table of Natural Sines, we find sin 62° 30′ = 0·8870.
From the table of Logarithms, log 0·8870 = $\bar{1}$·9479.

This number, which we call the 'logarithmic sine' of 62° 30′, can be obtained directly from the table of Logarithmic Sines, and we say that log sin 62° 30′ = $\bar{1}$·9479. In the same way we have tables of logarithmic cosines and logarithmic tangents.

As the sine of an angle is always less than 1, the log sine contains $\bar{1}$ or $\bar{2}$, which is printed only at the beginning of each row.

Example 1   *Evaluate* 3·86 *sin* 62° 30′.

No.	Log.
3·86	0·5866
sin 62° 30′	$\bar{1}$·9479
3·424	0·5345

Ans. 3·42 (to 3 sig. figs.).

Example 2   *Evaluate* $\dfrac{47\cdot2}{tan\ 24°\ 11'}$

No.	Log.
47·2	1·6739
tan 24° 11′	$\bar{1}$·6523
105·1	2·0216

Ans. 105 (to 3 sig. figs.).

In the case of log cos tables, we must remember that the cosine of an angle, and therefore the logarithm of the cosine, decrease as the angle increases. For this reason the numbers in the difference columns have to be *subtracted*. For example, to find log cos 36° 10′:

$$\log \cos 36°\ 6' = \bar{1}\cdot9074$$
$$\text{Difference for } 4' = 0\cdot0004$$
$$\therefore \log \cos 36°\ 10' = \bar{1}\cdot9070$$

Example 3   *In* $\triangle ABC$, $b = 3.42$, $A = 41° 20'$, $C = 90°$.   *Find a and c.*   (*See Fig.* 239.)

$\dfrac{a}{b} = \tan A.$

$\therefore a = b \tan A = 3.42 \tan 41° 20'.$

$\therefore a = 3.01$ (to 3 sig. figs.).

No.	Log.
3.42	0.5340
tan 41° 20'	$\bar{1}$.9443
3.008	0.4783

Also $\dfrac{b}{c} = \cos A.$

$\therefore c \cos A = b.$

$\therefore \qquad c = \dfrac{b}{\cos A} = \dfrac{3.42}{\cos 41° 20'}.$

$\therefore \qquad c = 4.55$ (to 3 sig. figs.).

No.	Log.
3.42	0.5340
cos 41° 20'	$\bar{1}$.8756
4.554	0.6584

Note: When a had been found, c could have been obtained as follows:

$c^2 = a^2 + b^2$ (Pythagoras' Theorem)

$\qquad = 3.008^2 + 3.42^2 = \ldots$

But this method is usually more trouble than the method above, unless the numbers involved are very simple.

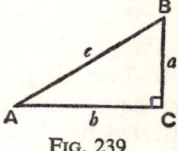

Fig. 239

EXERCISE 91

This exercise refers to Fig. 239; solving $\triangle ABC$ means finding such sides and angles of the triangle as are not given.

Solve $\triangle ABC$, given that:

1 $A = 51°$, $c = 8.93$ **2** $b = 11.6$, $c = 13.2$

3 $b = 2.48$, $a = 3.19$ **4** $a = 4.68$, $c = 9.82$

5 $A = 23°$, $b = 4.24$ **6** $A = 36°$, $a = 5.71$

7 $B = 66° 10'$, $b = 3.61$ **8** $B = 58° 25'$, $a = 2.27$

The right-angled triangle In all our examples hitherto, it will be noticed that the angle whose sine, cosine or tangent is used is one angle of a right-angled triangle; and without a right angle we cannot read off any of the trigonometrical ratios from the figure. The following list of geometrical properties, already known to the pupil, in which right angles occur, will be useful in Exercise 92.

1. Isosceles or equilateral triangle: the bisector of the vertical angle is perpendicular to the base and bisects it.

2. Rhombus: the diagonals bisect each other at right angles, and they also bisect the angles of the rhombus.

3. Rectangle: the diagonals are equal.

4. Parallelogram: area = base × height. Triangle: area = ½ base × height. In either case draw an altitude from a vertex.

5. Chord of a circle: the perpendicular from the centre of the circle bisects the chord.

6. Semicircle: the angle in a semicircle is a right angle.

7. Tangent to a circle: perpendicular to the radius drawn to the point of contact.

8. Two tangents from an external point to a circle: they are equal, and the angle between them is bisected by the line joining the point to the centre of the circle.

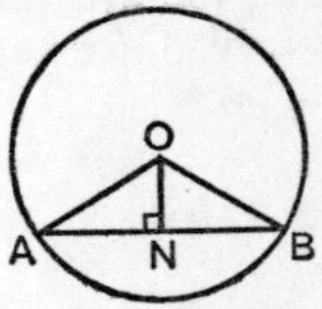

FIG. 240

Example 4 *A chord of a circle is 7·6 cm long and subtends an angle of 82° at the centre. Calculate the radius of the circle.*

In Fig. 240, O is the centre of the circle, AB the chord; ON is perpendicular to AB.

∴ AN = NB = 3·8 cm, and ∠AON = 41°.

Now
$$\frac{AN}{AO} = \sin AON.$$

∴
$$\frac{3·8}{AO} = \sin 41°.$$

∴ AO sin 41° = 3·8.

$$\therefore \qquad AO = \frac{3 \cdot 8}{\sin 41°}.$$

No.	Log.
3·8	0·5798
sin 41°	$\bar{1}$·8169
5·793	0·7629

$\therefore$ AO = 5·79 cm (to 3 sig. figs.).

EXERCISE 92

1 In $\triangle ABC$, BC = 3·6 cm, $\angle ABC = \angle ACB = 78°$. Calculate the length of AB and the area of the triangle.

2 An isosceles triangle has base 8·4 cm and height 10·6 cm. Calculate the base angles and the equal sides.

3 In $\triangle ABC$, AB = AC = 7·6 cm, BC = 3·4 cm. Calculate the base angles and the area of the triangle.

4 In $\triangle ABC$, AB = AC = 3·9 cm, and the altitude from A is 2·8 cm. Find (i) the vertical angle, (ii) the area of the triangle.

5 The sides of an equilateral triangle are each 4·7 cm long. Find (i) the height, (ii) the area of the triangle.

6 The height of an equilateral triangle is 4·2 cm. Find the length of a side and the area of the triangle.

7 The diagonals of a rhombus are 4·6 cm and 6·2 cm. Find (i) the acute angle of the rhombus, (ii) the length of a side, (iii) the area.

8 The sides of a rectangle are 9·6 cm and 7·3 cm. Find the acute angle between the diagonals.

9 In $\triangle ABC$, AD is the altitude from A. If BC = 3·1 cm, AB = 2·4 cm and $\angle B = 57°$, obtain an expression for the length of AD, and calculate the area of the triangle.

10 In the parallelogram ABCD, AB = 6·4 cm, AD = 2·9 cm and $\angle A = 62°$. Calculate the area of ABCD.

11 A chord of a circle 8 cm long subtends an angle of 112° at the centre.   Find the radius of the circle.

12 A chord of a circle is 7·6 cm from the centre and subtends an angle of 123° at the centre.   Find the length of the chord and the radius of the circle.

13 AB is a diameter of a circle; P is a point on the circumference such that AP = 6·7 cm and ∠PAB = 39°.   Calculate PB and AB.

14 The tangents from an external point to a circle are 5·8 cm long, and include an angle of 44°.   Find the distance of the point from the centre of the circle, and the radius of the circle.

15 O is the centre of a circle of radius 7·6 cm; P is a point such that OP = 13·2 cm.   Find the lengths of the tangents from P to the circle, and the angle between them.

16 Find the area of a regular pentagon (five sides), if each side is 10 cm long.

17 Find the area of a regular hexagon inscribed in a circle of radius 10 cm.

18 In △ABC, A = 42°, C = 90°, AC = 11·2 cm; D is the foot of the perpendicular from C to AB.   Calculate the length of CD and the area of △BCD.

19 In △ABC, ∠A = 90°, AB = 12·7 cm, AC = 5·3 cm; AD is an altitude.   Calculate BD, CD, AD, and verify that $AD^2 = BD.CD$.

20 A ladder leans against a wall, with its foot on the ground and its top 7 m above the ground.   If the inclination of the ladder to the ground is 68°, find its length.   If the bottom of the ladder is pulled ½ m farther from the wall, find the new inclination of the ladder to the ground.

21 The top of a cliff is 77 m above sea-level at low tide. The angle of depression of a buoy is 12° 20′ at low tide and 11° 40′ at high tide.   Find the rise of the tide to the nearest tenth of a metre.

22 In the parallelogram ABCD, AB = 14 cm, BC = 9 cm and ∠A = 67°. Calculate the lengths of the sides of the rectangle formed by the bisectors of the angles of the parallelogram.

23 AB is a diameter of a circle, C is a point on the circumference; AC produced meets the tangent at B in the point D. If AB = 16 cm and ∠CAB = 24°, find CD.

24 A chord of a circle is 6 cm long, and subtends an angle of 36° at the circumference. Find the radius of the circle.

25 A and B are the points of contact of the tangents from P to a circle of radius 20 cm. If ∠APB = 57°, calculate the lengths of PA and AB.

26 ABCDE is a regular pentagon of side 4·8 cm. Calculate the length of BD, and the perpendicular distance of A from CD.

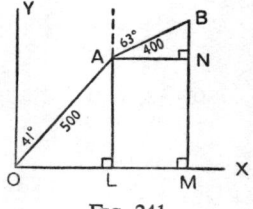

Example 5 *A man starts from a point O, walks 500 m on a bearing 041°, and then walks 400 m on a bearing 063°. Find how far he then is east and north of O.*

Fig. 241

In Fig. 241, OX is drawn in the direction east; AL, BM are perpendicular to OX, and AN is perpendicular to BM.

The distance of B east of O = OM = OL + LM = OL + AN

$$= 500 \sin 41° + 400 \sin 63°$$
$$= 500 \times 0·6561 + 400 \times 0·8910$$
$$= 328·05 + 356·40$$
$$= 684·45 \text{ m } or \text{ 684 m (to 3 sig. figs.).}$$

The distance of B north of O = BM = MN + NB = LA + NB

$$= 500 \cos 41° + 400 \cos 63°$$
$$= 500 \times 0·7547 + 400 \times 0·4540$$
$$= 377·35 + 181·60$$
$$= 558·95 \text{ m } or \text{ 559 m (to 3 sig. figs.).}$$

Example 6 *A path over a hill goes from* A *to* B *for* 300 *m up a slope of* 15°, *then from* B *to* C *for* 200 *m up a slope of* 5°, and then descends from C *to* D *at an angle of* 10° *with the horizontal. If* D *is* 70 *m higher than* A, *calculate the distance* CD.

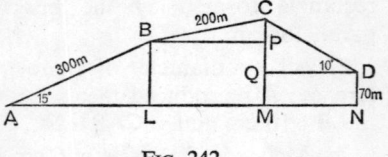

FIG. 242

In Fig. 242, ALMN is horizontal; BL, CM, DN are vertical. Draw BP and DQ perpendicular to CM.

$$CM = CP + PM = CP + BL$$
$$= 200 \sin 5° + 300 \sin 15°$$
$$= 200 \times \cdot 0872 + 300 \times \cdot 2588$$
$$= 17 \cdot 44 + 77 \cdot 64 = 95 \cdot 08.$$

$$\therefore CQ = CM - QM = CM - DN$$
$$= 95 \cdot 08 - 70 = 25 \cdot 08.$$

Now in the right-angled $\triangle CQD$,

$$\frac{CQ}{CD} = \sin CDQ.$$

$$\therefore CD \sin 10° = 25 \cdot 08.$$

$$\therefore \qquad CD = \frac{25 \cdot 08}{\sin 10°}.$$

No.	Log.
25·08	1·3993
sin 10°	$\bar{1}$·2397
144·4	2·1596

$$\therefore CD = 144 \text{ m (to 3 sig. figs.).}$$

Projections Examples 5 and 6 illustrate the method of 'projections'. In Fig. 241 OL is the **projection** of OA on the line OX, LM is the projection of AB on OX. The distance OM is the sum of the projections of OA and AB on the line OX, and the distance BM is the sum of the projections of OA and AB on the line OY.

Similarly, in Fig. 242, the lengths AL, LM, MN are the projections of AB, BC, CD on a horizontal; the lengths BL, CP, CQ are the projections of AB, BC, CD on a vertical.

A map always shows the horizontal projection, or the projection on a horizontal plane, of the actual distance. On a map of the hill in Example 6, the distances shown are AL, LM and MN, and these differ, if only slightly, from the true distances AB, BC and CD. The distance AL in Fig. 242 is called the **horizontal equivalent**, often abbreviated to H.E., of the distance AB. The gradient of the path AB is $\dfrac{BL}{AL}$, and not $\dfrac{BL}{AB}$. This is the same meaning of the word gradient as that given on p. 271.

Most gradients in this country are not steep enough to make any appreciable difference between the actual distance and the horizontal equivalent, but in a mountainous part, such as the Lake District, the difference is noticeable.

EXERCISE 93

1 A man walks 600 m N. 37° E. from a point O; he then walks 500 m N. 70° E. Find his distance north of O and east of O.

2 A ship steams 8 km on a bearing 026° from A to B, then 10 km on a bearing 074° from B to C. Find the bearing of C from A, and the distance AC.

3 A man walks 150 m from A to B; he then turns through an angle of 40°, and walks 120 m to C. Find the distance AC and ∠CAB. (Draw CN perpendicular to AB produced.)

4 ABCD is a trapezium in which the parallel sides AB, DC are 5 cm apart; AB = 8 cm, ∠D = 63°, ∠C = 36°. Calculate AD, BC and CD. (Draw perpendiculars from A, B to CD.)

5 An airman flies 60 km on a bearing 167°, then 110 km on a bearing 252°. Find how far and in what direction he must fly in order to return to his starting-point.

6 A shaft descends 220 m at an angle of 32° with the horizontal, and then 186 m at an angle of 24° with the horizontal. Find what vertical distance below the starting-point has been reached.

7 From the top of a cliff 400 m high, the angles of depression of two boats at sea in line with the foot of the cliff are 12° and 21°. Find the distance between the boats.

8 A tower is 100 m high; from the top of it the angle of depression of a distant point is 11° 30', and from the bottom of it the angle of elevation of the same point is 9°. Find the horizontal and vertical distances of the point from the bottom of the tower.

9 From the top of a cliff 250 m high above low-water level the angle of depression of a floating buoy is 15° at low water and 14° 12' at high water. If the buoy rises and falls vertically with the tide, calculate (i) the horizontal distance of the buoy from the cliff, (ii) the difference in height between low and high water.

10 A man finds the angle of elevation of the top of a church spire to be 47°; after walking 100 m towards the spire he finds the angle of elevation to be 58°. Calculate the height of the spire. (If this is x m, then $x \tan 43° - \ldots = 100$.)

11 From the top of a cliff 250 m high the angles of depression of the top and bottom of a tower, whose foot is on the same level as the bottom of the cliff, are measured to be 26° and 55°. Find the height of the tower.

Ratios of some special angles The trigonometrical ratios of a few special angles can be calculated without using tables of sines, etc.

Angle 45° Draw an isosceles right-angled triangle ABC (see Fig. 243), in which CA = CB = 1, $\angle C = 90°$. Then $\angle B = 45°$.
Now $AB^2 = AC^2 + BC^2$ (Pythagoras' Theorem)
$\qquad = 1^2 + 1^2 = 2$.
$\therefore \quad AB = \sqrt{2}$.

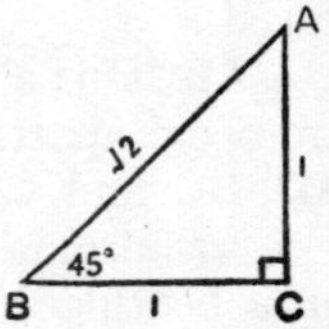

FIG. 243

$$\therefore \ \sin 45° = \frac{AC}{AB} = \frac{1}{\sqrt{2}},$$

$$\cos 45° = \frac{BC}{AB} = \frac{1}{\sqrt{2}},$$

$$\tan 45° = \frac{AC}{BC} = 1.$$

In order to calculate the numerical value of $\dfrac{1}{\sqrt{2}}$, given that $\sqrt{2} = 1\cdot4142$, we should say

$$\frac{1}{\sqrt{2}} = \frac{1 \times \sqrt{2}}{\sqrt{2} \times \sqrt{2}} = \frac{\sqrt{2}}{2} = \frac{1\cdot4142}{2} = 0\cdot7071.$$

Angles 30°, 60° Draw an equilateral triangle ABC (see Fig. 244), and let AD be an altitude.   Let AB = BC = CA = 2. Then BD = 1.

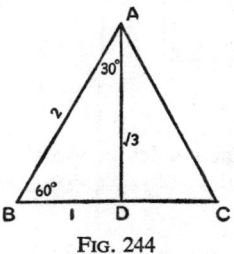

Fig. 244

Also $\angle ABD = 60°, \ \angle BAD = 30°.$

Now $AD^2 = AB^2 - BD^2$ (Pythagoras' Theorem)
$\qquad\qquad = 2^2 - 1^2 = 3.$

$\therefore \quad AD = \sqrt{3}.$

$$\therefore \ \sin 30° = \frac{BD}{AB} = \frac{1}{2}, \qquad \sin 60° = \frac{AD}{AB} = \frac{\sqrt{3}}{2},$$

$$\cos 30° = \frac{AD}{AB} = \frac{\sqrt{3}}{2}, \qquad \cos 60° = \frac{BD}{AB} = \frac{1}{2},$$

$$\tan 30° = \frac{BD}{AD} = \frac{1}{\sqrt{3}}, \qquad \tan 60° = \frac{AD}{BD} = \sqrt{3}.$$

Notice that, as 30° and 60° are complementary angles, sin 30° = cos 60° and cos 30° = sin 60°.

In order to calculate the numerical value of $\frac{1}{\sqrt{3}}$, given that $\sqrt{3} = 1.73205$, we should say

$$\frac{1}{\sqrt{3}} = \frac{1 \times \sqrt{3}}{\sqrt{3} \times \sqrt{3}} = \frac{\sqrt{3}}{3} = \frac{1.73205}{3} = 0.5774.$$

It is not necessary to learn all the foregoing results by heart, but you should remember the lengths of the sides of the two right-angled triangles in Fig. 245. All triangles with angles

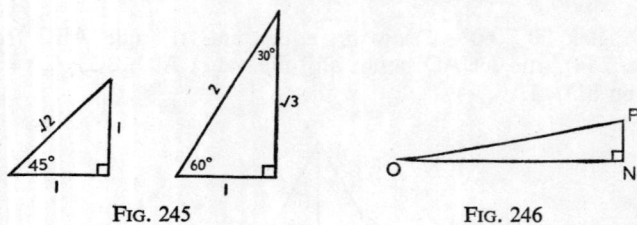

FIG. 245   FIG. 246

90°, 45°, 45° have their sides proportional to 1, 1, $\sqrt{2}$; and all triangles with angles 90°, 60°, 30° have their sides proportional to 1, 2, $\sqrt{3}$.

Angle 0°   In Fig. 246, suppose PON is a very small angle. PN is then very small, and the more nearly ∠PON approaches 0°, the more nearly PN approaches 0, and the points P and N become the same point. Hence, ON becomes the same as OP, and PN becomes 0.

$$\therefore \sin 0° = \frac{PN}{OP} = \frac{0}{OP} = 0,$$

$$\cos 0° = \frac{ON}{OP} = \frac{OP}{OP} = 1,$$

$$\tan 0° = \frac{PN}{ON} = \frac{0}{OP} = 0.$$

Angle 90°   In Fig. 247, suppose PON is a very large angle, almost 90°. ON is then very small, and the more nearly ∠PON approaches 90°, the more nearly ON approaches 0, and the points N and O become the same point. Hence, PN becomes the same as PO, and ON becomes 0.

$$\therefore \sin 90° = \frac{PN}{OP} = \frac{OP}{OP} = 1,$$

$$\cos 90° = \frac{ON}{OP} = \frac{0}{OP} = 0,$$

$$\tan 90° = \frac{PN}{ON} = \frac{OP}{0}.$$

Fig. 247

To see what happens to tan PON as the angle approaches 90°, suppose OP $=r$, and consider the quantities $\frac{r}{1}$, $\frac{r}{0\cdot1}$, $\frac{r}{0\cdot01}$, $\frac{r}{0\cdot001}$, and so on. The values of these fractions are r, $10r$, $100r$, $1000r$ . . . The smaller the denominator becomes (the numerator remaining constant), the bigger the fraction becomes. Hence tan PON increases more and more, without any limit being reached, the more nearly ∠PON approaches 90°. We write this: tan 90° $= \infty$ (read as 'infinity').

EXERCISE 94

Evaluate, without the use of tables:

1 $\dfrac{\sin 60°}{\cos 30°}$ **2** $\dfrac{\tan 60°}{\tan 30°}$ **3** $\dfrac{\sin 45°}{\cos 45°}$

4 $\sin 45° \cos 45°$ **5** $\sin 30° \cos 60° + \cos 30° \sin 60°$

6 $\tan^2 45° + 4 \cos^2 60°$ **7** $\sin^2 45° + \cos^2 45°$

8 $\sin^2 30° + \cos^2 30°$ **9** $\sin^2 30° + \sin^2 45°$

10 The longest side of a 90–60–30 set square is 6 cm. Find the lengths of the other sides.

11 O is the centre of a circle, P is a point on the circumference, Q is a point on the tangent at P, and ∠POQ $=60°$; OQ cuts the circle at R. Prove that OR $=$ RQ.

12 Calculate the area of an equilateral triangle of side 10 cm.

13 A wooden protractor in the shape of a rectangle 6 cm by 2 cm is shown in Fig. 248.

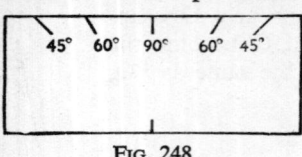

Show that the 45° mark is 1 cm from the top corner, and calculate the distance from the same corner of the 60° mark.

FIG. 248

33. THE QUADRATIC FUNCTION

THE graph of the function x^2 has already been drawn. (See p. 41, No. 5.) Notice that it is symmetrical about the y-axis, and lies entirely above the x-axis.

Now consider the graph of $2x^2$. In the table of values, all the values of y will be twice as great as they are in the table for the graph of x^2.

Next consider $y = \frac{1}{2}x^2$. All the values of y are one-half as great as they are in the table for x^2.

Fig. 249 shows the graphs of $y = x^2$, $y = 2x^2$, and $y = \frac{1}{2}x^2$, all

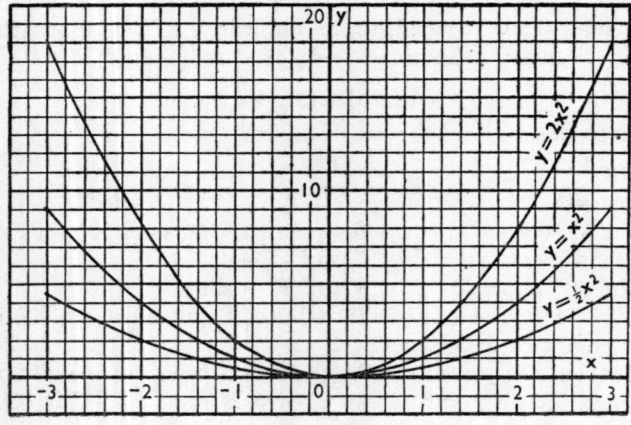

FIG. 249

drawn to the same scale. It will be noticed that they are all of the same type, but for any given value of x the graph of $2x^2$ is steeper than that of x^2, and the graph of x^2 is steeper than that of $\frac{1}{2}x^2$.

The graph of $y = -2x^2$ is the same shape as that of $y = 2x^2$, but turned over so as to lie entirely below the x-axis.

The graph of ax^2 is similar in type to that of x^2, whatever the value of a.

Now consider the graph of the function $x^2 + 3$. In the table of values, all the values of y will be 3 greater than those in the table of values for x^2. The effect is to raise the graph of $y = x^2$ through three units. Similarly, the graph of $x^2 - 3$ is like that of x^2, but lowered through three units. Both these graphs are shown in Fig. 250.

The graph of $ax^2 + c$ is the same as that of ax^2, but raised through c units.

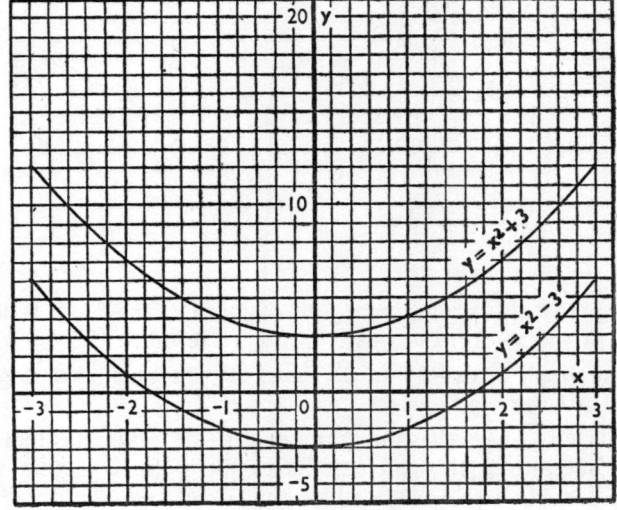

FIG. 250

Next we will consider the graph of $y = (x-2)^2$. The table of values is:

$x = -2$	-1	0	1	2	3	4
$x-2 = -4$	-3	-2	-1	0	1	2
$y = 16$	9	4	1	0	1	4

Fig. 251 shows the graph. It is like that of $y = x^2$, but moved through two units to the right.

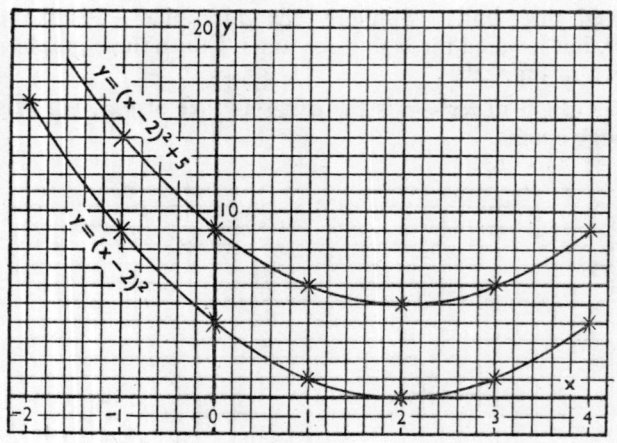

FIG. 251

Fig. 251 also shows the graph of $y = (x-2)^2 + 5$. It is like that of $y = (x-2)^2$, but raised through five units.

The graph of $(x-b)^2$ is the same as that of x^2, but moved through b units to the right.

It is easy to see that the graph of $a(x-b)^2$ resembles that of ax^2, but moved through b units to the right; and that the graph of $a(x-b)^2 + c$ resembles that of $a(x-b)^2$, but raised through c units. Hence we reach the conclusion:

The graph of the function $a(x-b)^2 + c$ is like that of ax^2, but moved through b units to the right and through c units upwards.

Thus we see that the graphs of the functions ax^2, $ax^2 + c$, $a(x-b)^2 + c$ are all alike in shape, differing only in their position with relation to the axes of co-ordinates. The curve in each case is called a **parabola.** A cricket ball, when thrown through the air, describes such a curve.

Now the function $a(x-b)^2 + c = a(x^2 - 2bx + b^2) + c$
$$= ax^2 - 2abx + (ab^2 + c),$$

which can be re-written

$$Ax^2 + Bx + C.$$

This is called the **general quadratic function.** Its graph is a parabola, the vertex or 'nose' being downwards if A is positive, upwards if A is negative. The terms Bx and C merely have the effect of moving the graph of Ax^2 to the right or left, up or down.

Quadratic function with factors If the quadratic function has factors, it is easy to sketch the graph. When an accurate graph is required, it is quicker to compile a table of values with the function in a factorised form than if the factors are multiplied out. The points at which the graph crosses the x-axis are given by the values of x which make either of the factors zero. For example, the graph of $y = (x-1)(x+3)$ crosses the x-axis at the points $(1, 0)$ and $(-3, 0)$.

Example 1 *Sketch the graph of the function $(x+2)(3-x)$.*
The values of x which make the value of the function zero are $-2, 3$.

∴ the graph crosses the x-axis at $(-2, 0)$, $(3, 0)$.

Since the coefficient of x^2 in the product $(x+2)(3-x)$ is -1, the graph resembles that of $y = -x^2$, which is a parabola with vertex upward.

If $x = 0$, $y = 6$. ∴ the curve passes through the point $(0, 6)$.

These facts enable us to sketch the graph, which is shown in Fig. 252 on the next page.

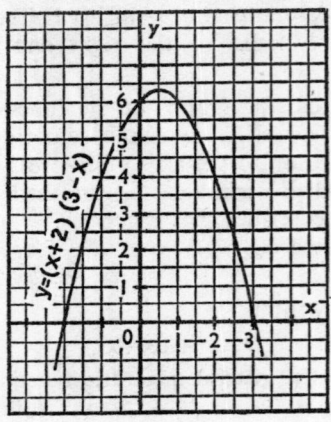

Fig. 252

EXERCISE 95

In the following exercise, do not plot any actual points unless you find they are necessary. A rough sketch of each graph is all that is needed.

Sketch the graphs of the following functions, using the same axes and scales for each group. Label each graph.

1 x^2, $x^2 - 1$, $x^2 + 2$

2 x^2, $3x^2$, $4x^2$, $\frac{1}{10}x^2$

3 x^2, $-x^2$, $-2x^2$

4 x^2, $(x-1)^2$, $(x+3)^2$

5 x^2, $(x-2)^2$, $(x-2)^2 + 3$

6 x^2, $(x-1)^2$, $3(x-1)^2$

7 $3(x+2)^2$, $3(x+2)^2 + 1$, $3(x+2)^2 - 2$

8 $x(x-4)$　　　　9 $(x-1)(2+x)$　　10 $x(3-x)$

11 $(2+x)(2x-1)$　12 $(x-1)(x-3)$

Example 2　*Draw the graph of the function $x^2 - 4x - 1$ from $x = -2$ to $x = 6$. State for what values of x the function has a value less than 4, and solve the equation $x^2 - 4x - 1 = 0$.*

The table of values is obtained by writing down the values of x from -2 to $+6$, and working in rows (not in columns), successive rows giving the values of x^2, $-4x$, -1 for different values of x. The sum of these values in each case gives the value of y.

$x =$	-2	-1	0	1	2	3	4	5	6
$x^2 =$	4	1	0	1	4	9	16	25	36
$-4x =$	8	4	0	-4	-8	-12	-16	-20	-24
$-1 =$	-1	-1	-1	-1	-1	-1	-1	-1	-1
$y =$	11	4	-1	-4	-5	-4	-1	4	11

The graph is shown in Fig. 253. Notice that it is symmetrical about the line $x = 2$, and has a minimum point, where y is least, at $(2, -5)$.

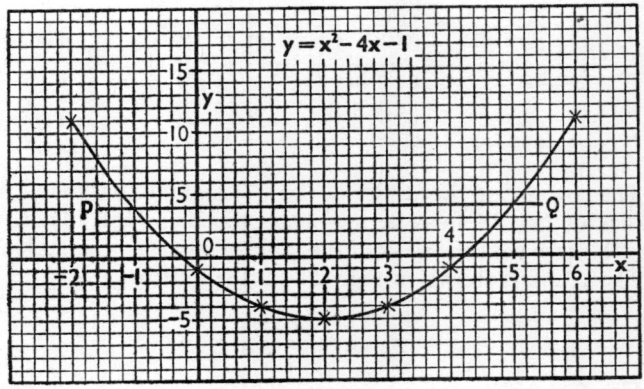

FIG. 253

The curve joins all the points whose x co-ordinate and y co-ordinate are connected by the equation $y = x^2 - 4x - 1$. It is, in fact, the locus of points on the graph-paper whose x co-ordinate and y co-ordinate satisfy this equation.

Now, if PQ is the line $y = 4$, for any point on the curve below the level of this line y has a value less than 4.   ∴ $x^2 - 4x - 1$ has a value less than 4 for all values of x between -1 and 5. This is called a **range of values,** the limits being $x = -1$ and $x = 5$.

In order to solve the equation $x^2 - 4x - 1 = 0$, we have to find where $y = 0$ on the graph.   This occurs at the two points where the curve crosses the x-axis, and the values of x at these points are 4·24 and $-0·24$.   These values are therefore the roots of the equation $x^2 - 4x - 1 = 0$.

Example 3   *Draw the graph of $y = 2x^2 - 5x - 3$ from $x = -2$ to $x = 4$.*

Since the expression $2x^2 - 5x - 3$ has factors $(2x + 1)(x - 3)$, it will be easier to compile the table of values from the factorised form:

$x = -2$	-1	0	1	2	3	4
$2x + 1 = -3$	-1	1	3	5	7	9
$x - 3 = -5$	-4	-3	-2	-1	0	1
$y = 15$	4	-3	-6	-5	0	9

The row giving the values of $(2x + 1)$ and the row giving the values of $(x - 3)$ must be *multiplied* together (not added, as was the case with the rows of the table of values in Example 2).

The graph is shown in Fig. 254 on the next page.

EXERCISE 96

Use Fig. 254 to answer the questions in Nos. 1–12, or draw your own graph on a larger scale.

1 What is the value of y when $x = 2·2$, 3·5, 0·2, $-1·2$?

2 What are the values of x when $y = 5$, -4, 0, 7, -1?

3 What is the least value of y, and for what value of x does it occur?

4 For what value of x is y equal to 12? Why can you find only one answer?

5 For what value of x is y equal to -10?

6 About what line is the curve symmetrical?

7 For what range of values of x is $2x^2 - 5x - 3$ negative?

8 Solve graphically the equation $2x^2 - 5x - 3 = 0$.

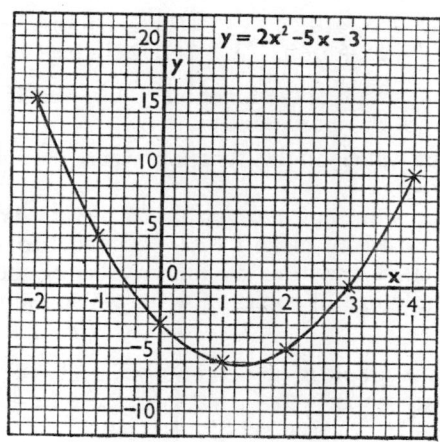

FIG. 254

9 Solve graphically $2x^2 - 5x = 0$. (First say, if $2x^2 - 5x = 0$, then $2x^2 - 5x - 3 = -3$. $\therefore y$ must have the value -3.)

10 Solve graphically $2x^2 - 5x + 2 = 0$. (First say, if $2x^2 - 5x + 2 = 0$, then $2x^2 - 5x = -2$. $\therefore 2x^2 - 5x - 3 = -5$.)

11 Solve graphically $2x^2 - 5x - 9 = 0$.

12 Solve graphically $2x^2 - 5x + 6 = 0$.

13. Draw the graph of the function $x^2 - 4x$ from $x = -2$ to $x = 5$. Find the minimum value of the function, and the value of x for which this occurs. For what range of values of x is the function negative? Use the graph to solve the equations: (i) $x^2 - 4x - 3 = 0$, (ii) $x^2 - 4x + 2 = 0$.

14 Draw the graph of $y = x^2 - 2x - 3$ from $x = -3$ to $x = 5$. State whether y has a maximum or minimum value, and what that value is. Use the graph to solve the equations:

(i) $x^2 - 2x - 3 = 0$,   (ii) $x^2 - 2x - 13 = 0$,
(iii) $x^2 - 2x - 1 = 0$,   (iv) $x^2 - 2x + 7 = 0$.

15 Draw the graph of the function $2x^2 + 5x$ from $x = -5$ to $x = 2$. Use the graph to solve the equations:

(i) $2x^2 + 5x = 10$,   (ii) $2x^2 + 5x - 5 = 0$,
(iii) $2x^2 + 5x + 6 = 0$,   (iv) $2x^2 + 5x + 1 = 0$.

16 Draw the graph of the function $1 + 3x - 2x^2$ from $x = -3$ to $x = 4$. From the graph, find:

(i) the value of the function when $x = 3 \cdot 4$, and the value when $x = -1 \cdot 4$,
(ii) the values of x which make $1 + 3x - 2x^2$ equal to -10, and those which make $1 + 3x - 2x^2$ equal to -6,
(iii) the maximum or minimum value of the function,
(iv) the range of values of x for which the function is positive.

17 Draw the graph of $y = 2x^2 + 9x - 3$, and use it to solve the equations: (i) $2x^2 + 9x - 3 = 0$,   (ii) $2x^2 + 9x - 9 = 0$, (iii) $2x^2 + 9x + 2 = 0$,   (iv) $2x^2 + 9x + 11 = 0$.

18 Draw the graph of $y = x^2 - 3x - 6$. Find from your graph:

(i) the values of x when $y = 1$,
(ii) the value of y when $x = 2 \cdot 6$,
(iii) the maximum or minimum value of y, and the value of x where it occurs,
(iv) the range of values of x for which $x^2 - 3x - 6$ is negative,
(v) the roots of the equation $x^2 - 3x - 2 = 0$.

19 With the same axes and scales, draw the graphs of $\frac{1}{2}(4 - 3x - x^2)$ and $\frac{1}{4}(5 - x)$ from $x = -4$ to 1. Find the range of values of x between -4 and 1 for which the first expression is greater than the second.

20 Draw the graph of $\frac{1}{2}(x-3)(x+1)$ from $x=-3$ to 5. Read off the two values of x which make $\frac{1}{2}(x-3)(x+1)$ equal to 1, and verify your answers by solving a quadratic equation.

21 Draw the graph of $y=2x^2+6x-1$ from $x=-4$ to 1. Estimate the least value of y, and find the values of x when $y=0$.

Quadratic inequations On page 278 we discussed linear inequations. Now consider the relation $x^2-3x+2>0$. This is an example of a **quadratic inequation,** since the left-hand side is of the second degree in x. We begin by factorising it.

$$(x-1)(x-2)>0.$$

The critical values of x, which make the left-hand side zero, are $x=1$ and $x=2$. We shall have to consider three regions, namely, when x is less than 1, when x is between 1 and 2, and when x is greater than 2.

If $x<1$, $(x-1)$ is negative and $(x-2)$ negative. Their product is therefore positive, and so $(x-1)(x-2)>0$.

If $1<x<2$, then $(x-1)$ is positive and $(x-2)$ is negative. Their product is therefore negative, and so $(x-1)(x-2)<0$.

If $x>2$, $(x-1)$ is positive and $(x-2)$ is positive. Their product is therefore positive, and so $(x-1)(x-2)>0$.

We conclude that $(x-1)(x-2)>0$ if $x<1$ or if $x>2$.

Fig. 255 shows a sketch graph of $y=x^2-3x+2$. The curve cuts the x-axis where $x=1$ and where $x=2$. It lies above the x-axis for values of x less than 1 or greater than 2. $\therefore$ $x^2-3x+2>0$ for these values of x. But $x^2-3x+2<0$ for values of x between 1 and 2.

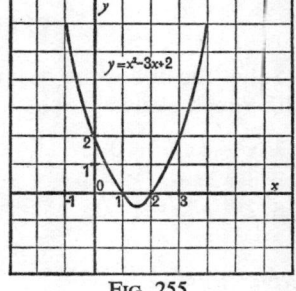

$y=x^2-3x+2$

FIG. 255

Example 4   *Solve the inequation* $6 + x - x^2 > 0$.

First factorise the left-hand side.   (Do *not* change the signs all through.)

$$(2 + x)(3 - x) > 0.$$

The critical values of x which make the left-hand side zero are $x = -2$ and $x = 3$.

Consider when $x < -2$. This makes $(2 + x)$ negative and $(3 - x)$ positive. The product is therefore negative, and $(2 + x)(3 - x) < 0$.

Consider next the case when $-2 < x < 3$. This makes $(2 + x)$ positive and $(3 - x)$ positive. The product is positive, and $(2 + x)(3 - x) > 0$.

Consider finally when $x > 3$. This makes $(2 + x)$ positive and $(3 - x)$ negative. The product is therefore negative, and $(2 + x)(3 - x) < 0$.

Hence, $(2 + x)(3 - x) > 0$ if $-2 < x < 3$.

The graph of $y = (2 + x)(3 - x)$ is shown in Fig. 252, page 302, where it will be seen that the curve lies above the x-axis only if x lies between -2 and 3.

Example 5   *Solve the inequation* $2x^2 - 5x - 3 \leqslant 0$.

The inequation is $(2x + 1)(x - 3) \leqslant 0$.

It is left as an exercise for the reader to see that the range of values of x for which the inequality is true is $-\frac{1}{2} \leqslant x \leqslant 3$.   The graph is Fig. 254, page 305.

EXERCISE 97

Solve the following inequations, illustrating your answers with rough sketch graphs:

1 $x^2 - 4x + 3 < 0$ **2** $x^2 - 2x - 3 > 0$

3 $3 - 2x - x^2 < 0$ **4** $x^2 > 9$

5 $2x^2 + 7x - 4 \leqslant 0$ **6** $3 + x > 2x^2$ (arrange the terms all on the left-hand side first)

7 $x^2 + x \leqslant 12$ **8** $12 - 11x + 2x^2 < 0$

The gradient of a quadratic function We defined the term 'gradient' in connection with a straight line graph, and found that the function $ax + b$ always has gradient a.   In the case of a curve, which is going up in one part of its course and coming down in another, and not always at the same rate, we must be clear what we mean by the term.

The gradient of a curve at a point is measured by the gradient of the tangent at that point.

Later on, you will learn a rule for finding the gradient of a function for a given value of x without even drawing an accurate graph; but, for the time being, the tangent at a point to a curve will have to be drawn with a ruler by eye.   By finding some convenient point through which this ruled line passes, we can calculate the gradient of the tangent, and hence the gradient of the function for that particular value of x.

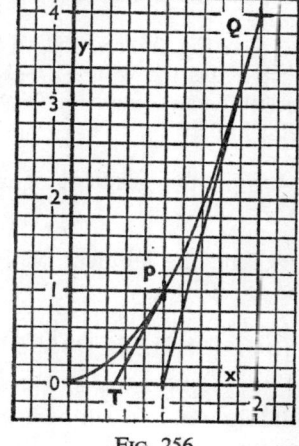

Fig. 256 shows a portion of the graph of $y = x^2$.   To find the gradient at the point P, which is the point (1, 1), the tangent at P is ruled.   This is found to pass through the point T ($\frac{1}{2}$, 0).

$\therefore$ the gradient of PT $= \dfrac{1}{\frac{1}{2}} = 2$.

$\therefore$ if x has the value 1, the gradient of the function x^2 is 2.

FIG. 256

Similarly, Q is the point (2, 4).   The tangent at Q is found to pass through the point (1, 0).   The gradient is $\frac{4}{1}$ or 4.

$\therefore$ if x has the value 2, the gradient of x^2 is 4.

Exercise In Fig. 254, page 305, place your ruler in the position of the tangent to the curve at the point (3, 0). You should find that the tangent passes through the point (4, 7). What value does this give for the gradient of $2x^2 - 5x - 3$ when $x = 3$?

EXERCISE 98

You should draw your own graphs for the following exercise, preferably on a larger scale than Figs. 249–254.

1 Find the gradients of $2x^2$ when $x = 2$ and when $x = -2$. (See Fig. 249, p. 298.)

2 Use Fig. 250, p. 299, to estimate the gradient of $x^2 + 3$ when $x = 2$. What is the gradient of $x^2 - 3$ when $x = 2$?

3 Use Fig. 251, p. 300, to estimate the gradient of $(x - 2)^2 + 5$ when x has the value (i) -1, (ii) 0, (iii) 1. What can you say about the gradients of $(x - 2)^2 + 5$ and $(x - 2)^2$ for the same values of x?

4 Find the gradient of $x^2 - 4x - 1$ when $x = 4$. (See Fig. 253, p. 303.)

5 Find the gradient of $2x^2 - 5x - 3$ when $x = 2$. (See Fig. 254, p. 305.)

34. THREE-DIMENSIONAL PROBLEMS

IN this section we shall solve various problems connected with solid figures. It will be useful to state a few facts about solid geometry, the truth of which you will probably have seen for yourself already.

Solid geometry (i) Two planes are either parallel or meet in a straight line. For example, two faces of a wooden block meet in an edge, unless they are opposite and parallel faces; two pages of an open book meet in the line of the binding.

(ii) If a line is perpendicular to two lines in a plane, it is perpendicular to every line in the plane, and is said to be perpendicular to the plane.

In order to see this, place two set squares, ABC and PQR, with the right-angled corners A and P together, as in Fig. 257,

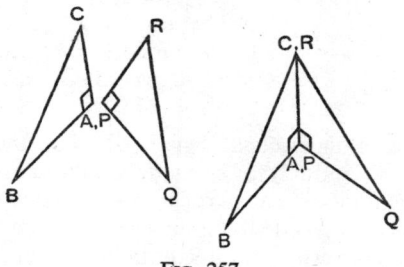

FIG. 257

and an edge of each, AB and PQ, lying on a horizontal table. Now rotate one set square about the line AB and the other about the line PQ, until the edges AC and PR come into contact. The common edge will in that position be perpendicular to the plane of the table.

Angle between two planes Take any convenient point on the line of intersection of the two planes. Through this point, draw in each plane a line perpendicular to the line of intersection. The angle between these lines is the angle between the planes. Thus, in Fig. 258, the planes meet in the line AB. Through the point P in that line we draw PX in one plane

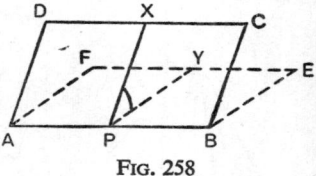

FIG. 258

and PY in the other, both perpendicular to AB. The angle XPY is called the **angle beween the planes** ABCD and ABEF. If the plane ABEF is horizontal, the line PX is called a **line of greatest slope of the plane** ABCD.

Angle between a line and a plane In Fig. 259, OP is a line meeting the plane ABCD at O; PN is drawn perpendicular to the plane, and ON is joined. On p. 292 we called this line the projection of OP on the plane. The angle PON, between the line OP and its projection, is the angle which OP makes with the plane ABCD.

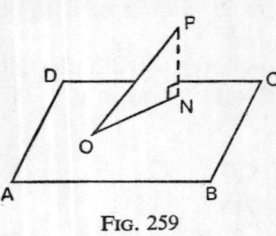

FIG. 259

Drawing three-dimensional figures Revise the hints given in Part I, pp. 41 and 67, for drawing a cuboid and a pyramid. Make parallel lines appear parallel in your drawing, instead of converging as they recede from the eye. Notice that a vertical line always looks vertical, and should be drawn parallel to the side edge of your paper; but horizontal lines do not always look horizontal, and should not always be drawn parallel to the bottom edge of your paper.

Sections of solids In a drawing of a three-dimensional solid, such as a cuboid, you will have noticed that many angles which are actually right angles do not appear as such. You will often find at first that it is useful to draw separate figures showing triangles and polygons as they really are. Such figures are called **sections**.

Example 1 *A right pyramid VABCD stands on a square base of side 4 cm. The slant edges are of length 8 cm. Find, by drawing and by calculation: (i) the height VO and the angle between a slant edge and the base, (ii) the angle between a sloping face and the base.*

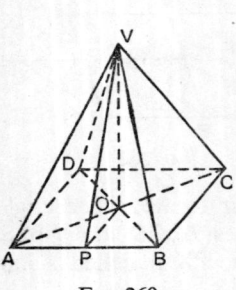

FIG. 260

In Fig. 260, V is the vertex, ABCD the square base whose diagonals cut at O.

(i) The height is VO, and the angle between a slant edge and the base is ∠VAO.

Draw the plan of the base, *abcd*, a square of side 4 cm. (See Fig. 261.) Let *ac* and *bd* cut at *o*, and produce *ob*. With centre *a* and radius 8 cm, make an arc to cut *ob* produced at *v*. Join *va*.

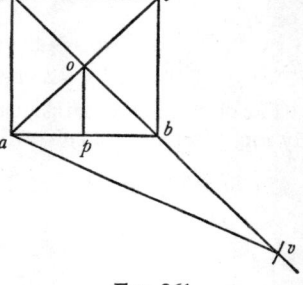

Now the diagonals of a square intersect at right angles.

$$\therefore \ \angle voa = 90°.$$

Hence, $\triangle voa$ is an accurate drawing of $\triangle VOA$ in Fig. 260; and VO and $\angle VAO$ are found by measuring *vo* and $\angle vao$.

FIG. 261

By measurement, $vo = 7 \cdot 5$ cm and $\angle vao = 69°$.

Calculation   Since $\angle abc = 90°$,
$$ac^2 = ab^2 + bc^2 \quad \text{(Pythagoras')}$$
$$= 16 + 16 = 32.$$
$$\therefore \ ac = \sqrt{32} = 4\sqrt{2} \text{ cm}.$$
$$\therefore \ ao = 2\sqrt{2} \text{ cm}.$$

Since
$$\angle voa = 90°,$$
$$vo^2 = va^2 - ao^2 \quad \text{(Pythagoras')}$$
$$= 64 - 8 = 56.$$
$$\therefore \ vo = \sqrt{56} = 7 \cdot 483 \text{ cm}.$$

Also
$$\cos \angle vao = \frac{ao}{va}$$
$$= \frac{2\sqrt{2}}{8} = \frac{1 \cdot 414}{4} = 0 \cdot 3535.$$
$$\therefore \ \angle vao = 69° \, 18'.$$

Hence the height of the pyramid is 7·48 cm and the angle between a slant edge and the base is 69° 18′.

(ii) If, in Fig. 260, P is the mid-point of AB, then PO is perpendicular to AB in the plane ABCD, and PV is perpendicular to AB in the plane VAB. The angle between the planes VAB and ABCD is therefore $\angle VPO$.

In order to draw $\triangle vpo$, obtain the length of vo from Fig. 261, and make $\angle vop$ a right angle.

From Fig. 261, $op = \frac{1}{2}cb$ (mid-point theorem)
$\qquad = 2$ cm.

The completed triangle vpo is shown in Fig. 262. By measurement, $\angle vpo = 75°$.

Calculation From Fig. 262, $\tan \angle vpo = \dfrac{vo}{op}$

$$= \frac{7\cdot483}{2} = 3\cdot742.$$

$$\therefore \ \angle vpo = 75° \, 2'.$$

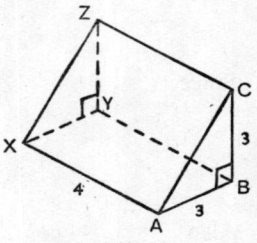

FIG. 262

EXERCISE 99

Name the angles between the lines and planes in Nos. 1–11, and find them either by accurate drawing or by calculation.

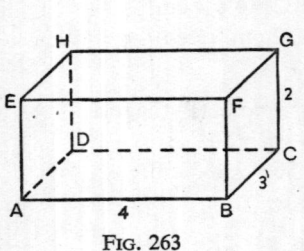

FIG. 263

FIG. 264

Nos. 1–7 refer to Fig. 263, which represents a cuboid 4 cm by 3 cm by 2 cm.

1 Planes ABGH and ABCD.
2 BH and the plane ABCD.
3 BH and the plane ADHE.
4 BH and the plane CDHG.
5 Planes BCHE and FGCB.
6 CE and the plane ABFE.
7 Planes ABH and EFBA.

Nos. 8–11 refer to Fig. 264, which represents a right prism; the ends ABC, XYZ are right-angled triangles, AB = BC = 3 cm, AX = BY = CZ = 4 cm.

8 BX and the plane ABC.
9 Planes ABYX and CZXA.
10 CX and the plane BAXY.
11 CY and the plane ABYX.

In drawing the following sections, all lengths must be obtained by construction.

12 For the cuboid in Fig. 263, draw the section HAC full-size. Measure ∠HAC.

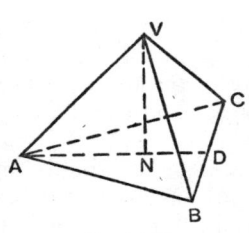

Fig. 265

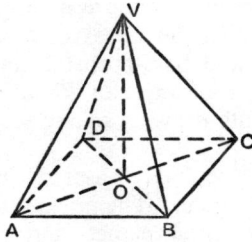

Fig. 266

13 Each edge of the tetrahedron in Fig. 265 is 8 cm long; D is the mid-point of BC. Draw the section VAD, and, by measuring the altitude VN of this triangle, find the height of the tetrahedron.

14 VABC is a regular tetrahedron, each edge of which is 8 cm long. A plane cuts VA at X, VB at Y, VC at Z; VX = 6 cm, VY = 4 cm, VZ = 2 cm. Find the lengths XY, YZ, ZX by making suitable drawings, and hence draw the section XYZ accurately.

15 The pyramid in Fig. 266 has a square base of side 4 cm, and each of the slant edges is 6 cm. Draw the section VAC, and hence find the height of the pyramid. Verify your result by calculation.

16 A pyramid has a vertex V and a square base ABCD of side 4 cm; each sloping face is an isosceles triangle with base angles 70°; P is the mid-point of AD, Q that of BC. Draw the section VPQ, and hence find the height of the pyramid.

17 A right pyramid has a vertex V and a square base ABCD of side 4 cm; VA = VB = VC = VD = 6 cm. Points, P, Q are taken on VA, VB, both 4 cm from V; points R, S are taken on VC, VD, both 2 cm from V. Make an accurate drawing of a face of the pyramid, find the lengths PQ, PR, RS, and hence draw the section PQRS.

18 OA, OB, OC are three edges of a cube which meet at a corner O. A section of the cube cuts OA, OB, OC at points which are 2 cm, 4 cm, 6 cm respectively from O. Draw the section and measure its angles.

19 V is the vertex of a solid right circular cone, of height 4 cm and base-radius 3 cm; AB is a chord of the base subtending an angle of 75° at the centre of the base. Make an accurate drawing of the section VAB, and measure the angle VAB.

20 The ends of a prism, 6 cm long, are equilateral triangles of side 4 cm. The prism rests with a rectangular face touching a horizontal plane. Draw a vertical section of the prism through a diagonal of a sloping rectangular face, and measure the angles of the section.

21 VABC is a regular tetrahedron, each edge 6 cm long; X, Y are points in the edges VA, VB respectively such that VX = 2 cm, VY = 4 cm. Draw a section by a plane which passes through XY and is parallel to VC.

Trigonometrical problems

Example 2 *A hill-side slopes at 15° to the horizon, and a path runs up the hill, making an angle of 32° with the line of greatest slope. Find the inclination of the path to the horizon.*

In Fig. 267, AB is the horizontal at

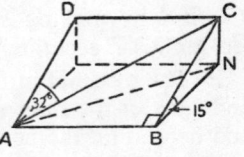

FIG. 267

the foot of the hill, BC and AD are lines of greatest slope, CD is a horizontal line on the hill; CN is perpendicular to the horizontal plane through A. Thus ∠CAN is the angle required.

Let AC = l. Then, from △ABC, BC = $l \cos 32°$.

From △BCN, CN = BC sin 15° = $l \cos 32° \sin 15°$.

From △CAN, $\sin CAN = \dfrac{CN}{AC}$

$$= \frac{l \cos 32° \sin 15°}{l} = \cos 32° \sin 15°.$$

cos 32°	$\bar{1}$·9284
sin 15°	$\bar{1}$·4130
sin 12° 41′	$\bar{1}$·3414

∴ the inclination of the path = 12° 41′.

Example 3 *A point* A *is* 200 *m due south of a tower. A point* B *is due east of the tower and on a bearing* 037° *from* A. *The angle of elevation of the top of the tower from* B *is* 18°. *Calculate the height of the tower, to the nearest metre.*

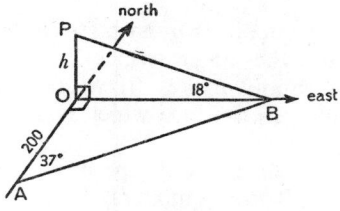

FIG. 268

In Fig. 268, PO represents the tower; OA runs south, OB runs east.

From △OAB, OB = OA tan 37° = 200 tan 37°.

From △POB, PO = OB tan 18° = 200 tan 37° tan 18°.

200	2·3010
tan 37°	$\bar{1}$·8771
tan 18°	$\bar{1}$·5118
48·97	1·6899

∴   PO = 48·97.

∴ the height of the tower = 49 m (to the nearest metre).

EXERCISE 100

(If Exercise 99, Nos. 1–11 were done by drawing, they should now be done by calculation.)

1 A flagstaff stands at the corner A of a square courtyard ABCD, each side of which is 50 m long. The elevation of the top of the flagstaff from B is 16°. Calculate (i) the height of the flagstaff, (ii) the angle of elevation of its top as seen from C.

2 VABCD is a right pyramid with a square base of side 10 cm. The height VN is 16 cm. Calculate (i) the length of VA, (ii) the angle between VA and the plane ABCD, (iii) the angle between the face VAB and the plane ABCD, (iv) the angle AVC.

3 The base of a cuboid is 6 cm by 8 cm, and the height is 5 cm. Calculate the angle which a diagonal of the cuboid makes (i) with the base, and (ii) with the face which is 8 cm by 5 cm.

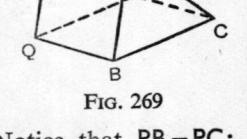

4 Fig. 269 represents a right prism; the ends ABC, PQR are equilateral triangles of side 4 cm and AP = 3 cm. Calculate the angle PBC and the angle

Fig. 269

between the planes ABC and PBC. (Notice that PB = PC; join the mid-point of BC to P and A.)

5 A blackboard is 1·2 m by 0·9 m. It stands on an easel, sloping at 70° with the horizontal and with the long edges horizontal. Calculate the inclination of a diagonal of the blackboard to the horizontal.

6 A hill-side slopes at 25° to the horizontal. A path runs up the hill, making an angle of 40° with the line of greatest slope. Calculate the inclination of the path to the horizontal.

7 The angle of elevation of the top of a tower from a point A due north of it is 26°, and that from a point B due east of it is 15°. If AB = 50 m, calculate the height of the tower.

8 A right pyramid VABC has a base ABC, which is an equilateral triangle of side 4 cm. The height of the pyramid is 6 cm. Calculate (i) the angle between the face VAB and the base ABC, (ii) the angle between VA and the plane ABC.

9 An aeroplane is flying due east at a constant height of 1000 m above the ground. When first seen, it is due south of an observer, and its angle of elevation is 50°. It is next seen to be south-east of the same observer. Calculate how far the aeroplane has travelled, and what is its new angle of elevation as seen by the observer.

10 A man sees a church spire due east of him, and observes the angle of elevation of its top to be 20°. He walks along a road which has a bearing 031°, and presently finds the spire to be due south of him. Find the angle of elevation of the top of the spire in the second position.

EXERCISE 101
(*Miscellaneous three-dimensional problems*)

1 Calculate the diagonal of a cube whose edge is 10 cm.

2 A room is 6·4 m long, 5·6 m wide and 3·6 m high. Calculate the distance from a corner of the floor to the opposite corner of the ceiling.

3 ABCD is a rectangle in which AB = 5 cm and BC = 3 cm, and the diagonals intersect at O; V is a point on the line through O drawn perpendicular to the plane of ABCD, and VA = 6 cm. Calculate the length of VO.

4 ABCD is a rectangle whose diagonals intersect at O; VO is perpendicular to the plane ABCD. Prove that △s VOA, VOB are congruent, and deduce that VA = VB = VC = VD.

5 V is the vertex and ABC is the triangular base of a pyramid. The triangle ABC is equilateral, and O is its circumcentre. If VO is perpendicular to the plane of ABC, prove that the triangles VOA, VOB are congruent, and deduce that VA = VB = VC.

6 The height of a right pyramid on a square base is equal to half the diagonal of the base. Prove that the faces are equilateral triangles.

7 ABCDEFGH is a cube (see Fig. 263, p. 314, for the way in which it is lettered). Prove that $\angle ACH = 60°$.

8 ABCDEFGH is a cuboid. What sort of quadrilateral is ABGH? Use a property of the diagonals of such a figure to prove that the diagonals of the cuboid meet at a point.

9 ABCD is the square base of a pyramid and V is the vertex. (The pyramid is not necessarily a right one.) P, Q, R, S are the mid-points of the edges VA, VB, VC, VD. Prove that PQRS is a square.

10 A right pyramid of height 4 m stands on a square base whose side is 6 m. Calculate the area of each sloping face.

11 Calculate the radius of the sphere which passes through all the eight vertices of a cuboid 2 cm by 3 cm by 6 cm. (Hint: the centre of the sphere is the mid-point of a diagonal.)

12 A sphere of radius 2 cm rests inside a hollow, inverted cone. If the slant height of the cone is equal to the diameter of its circular base, find the distance of the centre of the sphere from the vertex of the cone.

Plan and elevation; rabatment The method of sections is useful when we have to draw a plan and elevation in which lengths cannot be taken directly from the given dimensions of the figure.

Example 4 *Draw the plan, front elevation, and side elevation of a pyramid VABCD which has a square base of side 4 cm, slant edges each 6 cm long, the pyramid standing on the H.P., with AB inclined at 30° to the XY line.*

We begin with the plan, a square *abcd* of side 4 cm (see Fig. 270).

In order to draw the elevation, we require the height VO. This is obtained by drawing △VOA, imagining it to be hinged along OA and to be folded over until it lies in the H.P.   As

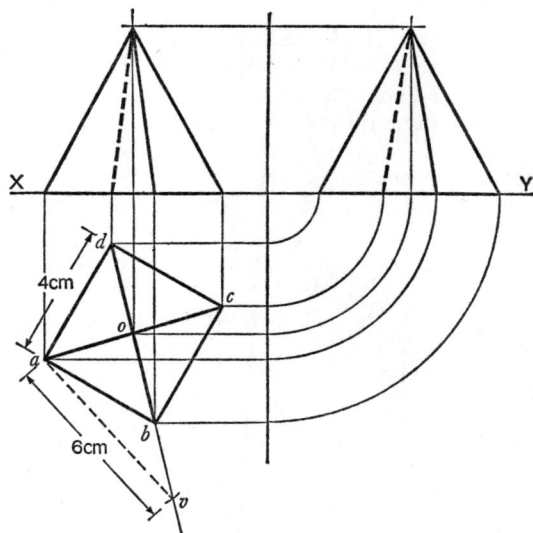

Fig. 270

∠VOA is a right angle, the point V will fall on *ob* produced. The position of *v* is found by drawing an arc, centre *a* and radius 6 cm (the length of VA), to cut *ob* produced.   The side *ov* of this triangle *aov* is the true height of the pyramid.   Draw a projection from *o* to the XY line, and produce it above the XY line a distance equal to *ov*.   Complete the elevations as shown in Fig. 270.

The process of rotating the plane containing △VOA about the line OA until it lies in the H.P. is called **rabatment**.

Example 5   *Draw the plan and front elevation of a regular tetrahedron whose edge is 3 cm, one edge of the face resting on the H.P. being inclined at 45° to the XY line.*

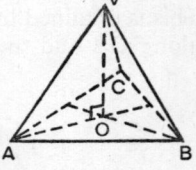

Fig. 271 is a drawing of the tetrahedron; O is the centre of the base ABC, and VO is the height.

Draw the plan *abc*, an equilateral triangle of side 3 cm.   Find the centre *o* by drawing two medians (or bisecting two angles).   Draw a line through *o* perpendicular to *ao*, and with centre *a*, radius *ab* (which is the same length as VA), make an arc to cut this perpendicular at *v*.   Then △*voa* is a rabatment

FIG. 271

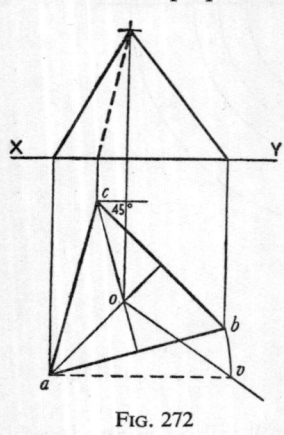

of △VOA in the H.P.   Draw a projection from *o* to the XY line, and produce it above the XY line a distance equal to *ov*.   Complete the elevation as shown in Fig. 272.

FIG. 272

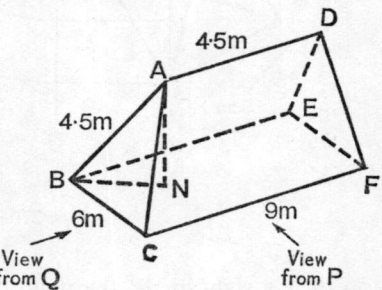

FIG. 273

Example 6   *Fig. 273 shows the roof of a house; the ridge AD is centrally placed with respect to the rectangle BCFE. Using a scale of 1 cm to represent 1 m, draw a plan of the roof, the front elevation (view from P), and side elevation (view from Q).*

The plan consists of a rectangle 9 cm by 6 cm, and a central line whose ends are 2·25 cm from the sides of the rectangle.

If N is the foot of the perpendicular from A to the plane BCFE, we require the length of AN in order to draw the elevation. The method is to rabat △ANB into the H.P. The plan and elevations are shown in Fig. 274.

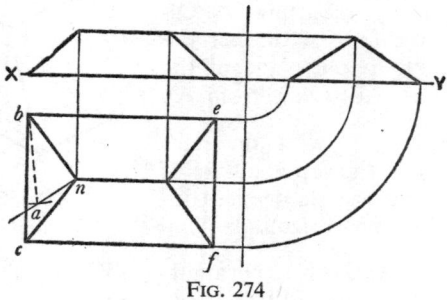

FIG. 274

EXERCISE 102

1 A pyramid VABCD has a square base ABCD of side 3 cm. Each slant edge is of length 5 cm. The pyramid stands on the H.P. with AB inclined at 30° to the XY line. Draw the plan, F.E. and S.E.

2 VABCD is a right pyramid on a rectangular base ABCD; AB = 4 cm, BC = 2 cm, VA = VB = VC = VD = 3·5 cm. The pyramid stands on the H.P. with AB inclined to the XY line at 15°. Draw the plan, F.E. and S.E.

3 A regular tetrahedron of edge 3 cm stands with one face on the H.P. and an edge of that face perpendicular to the XY line. Draw the plan, F.E. and S.E.

4 Draw the plan, F.E. and S.E. of a triangular prism, of edge 4 cm and 7 cm long, lying on a rectangular face with a long edge of that face inclined at 30° with the XY line.

5 A pyramid has a rectangular base 8 cm by 4 cm and the slant edges are 6 cm long. Find by drawing the height of the pyramid and the angle which a slant edge makes with the base.

6 Fig. 275 shows a block in which the base is a horizontal rectangle 42 cm by 30 cm and the top (also horizontal) is a square of side 18 cm. Each of the four slant edges is 24 cm long. Using a scale of 1 cm to represent 5 cm, draw a plan, and, by rabatting △PQR (where R is the foot of the perpendicular from P to the plane of the base) draw the F.E. (view from A).

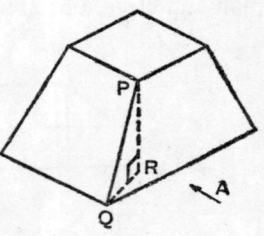

Fig. 275

7 Repeat No. 6, with the base 42 cm by 30 cm, the top a square of side 18 cm, and the slant edges inclined at 50° to the horizontal.

8 The base ABC of a pyramid VABC is an equilateral triangle, and the pyramid stands on a horizontal table; AB is equal to the side of a certain square, and VA, VB, VC are all equal to the half-diagonal of the same square. Find by drawing (i) the inclination of VA to the table, (ii) the inclination of the face VAB to the table.

9 The vertex of a pyramid is V, and the base ABC is an equilateral triangle of side 6 cm; VA = VB = VC = 4 cm, and N is the foot of the perpendicular from V to the plane ABC. Find AN and VN by drawing.

10 Find the height of a regular tetrahedron whose edge is 4 cm by plan and elevation methods.

11 The base ABCD of a pyramid is a square of side 3 cm. The faces VAB, VBC, VCD, VDA are isosceles triangles all of height 2·5 cm. Calculate (i) the height of the pyramid, (ii) the total surface area, (iii) the volume.

12 A cubical box of side 8 cm, open at the top, is placed on a horizontal table. A sphere of radius 5 cm rests on the box, in contact with all the four top edges. Find the height of the centre of the sphere above the bottom of the box.

13 A vertical equilateral triangle stands with one edge on horizontal ground in an east–west plane. When the sun is due south, at an elevation of 75°, the shadow of the triangle on the ground is an isosceles triangle. Calculate the vertical angle of this triangle.

14 A right pyramid, on a square base of side 10 cm, is 12 cm in height. Calculate (i) the length of a slant edge, (ii) the volume, (iii) the total surface area, (iv) the inclination of a sloping face to the base.

35. TRIGONOMETRY OF OBTUSE ANGLES: THE SINE RULE

Obtuse angles Hitherto we have dealt only with the trigonometrical ratios of acute angles. Such an angle is considered as one angle of a right-angled triangle. This is not possible when we have to deal with an obtuse angle, and we shall have to say what we mean by the sine, cosine and tangent of such an angle. The new definitions which we adopt must obviously be equivalent to the former definitions in the case of an acute angle, but must also give us a meaning for the trigonometrical ratios in the case of an obtuse angle.

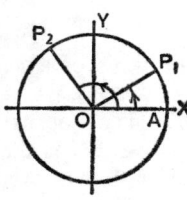

FIG. 276

Fig. 276 shows two axes OX, OY perpendicular to one another, like the axes we use for drawing graphs, and a circle, centre O and radius 1 unit. Suppose a radius starts from the position OA and rotates in a counterclockwise direction, i.e. from the x-axis towards the y-axis. When the radius reaches the position OP_1, it has swept out an angle P_1OX; when it reaches OP_2, it has swept out an angle P_2OX, and so on.

Definitions When the rotating radius reaches a position OP, let (x, y) be the co-ordinates of the point P, with the same conventions as to the signs of x and y as are used in graphical work. We make the following definitions:

$$\cos \text{POX} = \text{the } x \text{ co-ordinate of P,}$$
$$\sin \text{POX} = \text{the } y \text{ co-ordinate of P,}$$
$$\tan \text{POX} = \frac{\text{the } y \text{ co-ordinate of P}}{\text{the } x \text{ co-ordinate of P}}.$$

Consider first the application of these definitions to an acute angle. In Fig. 277, POX is an acute angle, OP = 1 unit, ON is the x co-ordinate of P, PN is the y co-ordinate of P, and both ON and PN are positive. The definition above says that $\cos \text{POX} = \text{ON}$, $\sin \text{POX} = \text{PN}$, and $\tan \text{POX} = \dfrac{\text{PN}}{\text{ON}}$. These

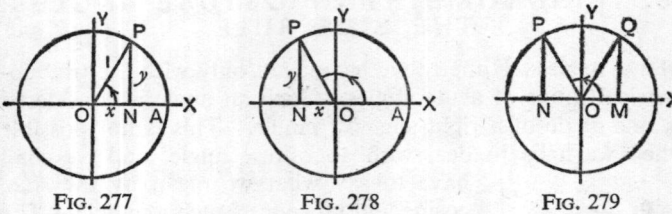

FIG. 277   FIG. 278   FIG. 279

are, of course, the same as our previous definitions of sine, cosine and tangent.

Now take an obtuse angle. In Fig. 278, POX is an obtuse angle, ON is the x co-ordinate of P and is negative, PN is the y co-ordinate of P and is positive. By the definition above, $\cos \text{POX} = \text{ON}$, which is negative; $\sin \text{POX} = \text{PN}$, which is positive.

As an illustration, let us take an angle of 120°. In Fig. 279, the radius of the circle is 1 unit, $\angle \text{POX} = 120°$, and $\angle \text{QOX} = 180° - 120° = 60°$; PN, QM are perpendicular to the x-axis. By definition,

$$\cos 120° = \text{ON},$$
$$\sin 120° = \text{PN},$$
$$\tan 120° = \text{PN/ON}.$$

But in $\triangle$s PNO, QMO,

$$\angle PNO = \angle QMO \quad \text{(rt. } \angle \text{s),}$$
$$\angle PON = \angle QOM \quad (60°),$$
$$OP = OQ \quad \text{(both 1 unit).}$$

$\therefore \triangle$s $\dfrac{PNO}{QMO}$ are congruent (AA corr. S).

$\therefore$ ON = OM and PN = QM, numerically.

But $\quad \dfrac{OM}{OQ} = \cos 60°. \quad \therefore$ OM = OQ $\cos 60° = \cos 60°.$

$\quad \dfrac{QM}{OQ} = \sin 60°. \quad \therefore$ QM = OQ $\sin 60° = \sin 60°.$

Since ON, PN are numerically equal to OM, QM, but ON is negative and PN positive, we find that

$$ON = -\cos 60°, \ PN = \sin 60°.$$
$$\therefore \cos 120° = ON = -\cos 60°,$$
$$\sin 120° = PN = \sin 60°,$$
$$\tan 120° = \frac{PN}{ON} = \frac{QM}{-OM} = \frac{-QM}{OM}$$
$$= -\tan QOM = -\tan 60°.$$

We have thus linked up the sine, cosine and tangent of an obtuse angle with those of the *supplement* of that obtuse angle; and since the supplement of an obtuse angle is necessarily acute, the tables can be used to give the actual numerical value, the plus or minus sign to be prefixed being given by the following rule:

The sine of an obtuse angle equals the sine of its supplement.

The cosine of an obtuse angle equals minus the cosine of its supplement.

The tangent of an obtuse angle equals minus the tangent of its supplement.

Examples $\quad \sin 142° = \quad \sin 38° = \quad 0·6157,$
$\qquad\qquad\ \cos 142° = -\cos 38° = -0·7880,$
$\qquad\qquad\ \tan 142° = -\tan 38° = -0·7813.$

EXERCISE 103

1 Use the tables to find the sine, cosine and tangent of the following angles: 162°, 137°, 170°, 129° 30′, 98° 26′.

2 Without using tables, write down (in terms of $\sqrt 2$ and $\sqrt 3$, where these occur) the sine, cosine and tangent of the following angles: 135°, 120°, 150°, 180°.

3 Find two values of x if $\sin x° = 0.848$.

4 Find y if $\cos y° = -0.809$.

5 Find from the tables the sine, cosine and tangent of the following angles: 140°, 165°, 110°, 180°.

Generalised formulae   The important fact about the definitions of the trigonometrical ratios of an obtuse angle which have now been adopted is that formulae which can be proved for acute angles also apply for obtuse angles.

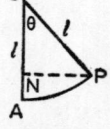

Fig. 280

Consider, for example, a rod OA of length l cm, pivoted at the end O, and hanging at rest in a vertical position. Suppose the rod is made to swing through an angle θ to the position OP. Draw PN perpendicular to OA.

In Fig. 280, θ is an acute angle.
The distance of P to the right of A

$$= PN = l \sin \theta. \quad . \quad . \quad . \quad (1)$$

The height of P above A

$$= AN = AO - NO = l - l \cos \theta . \quad . \quad . \quad (2)$$

In Fig. 281, θ is an obtuse angle.
The distance of P to the right of A $= PN = l \sin PON$.

Now $\angle PON$ and θ are supplementary angles;

$$\therefore \sin \theta = \sin PON.$$

$\therefore$ the distance of P to the right of A $= l \sin \theta$, which agrees with (1).

The height of P above A $= AN = AO + ON = l + l \cos$ PON.

But, since $\angle$ PON and θ are supplementary angles, $\cos \theta = -\cos$ PON.

$\therefore$ the height of P above A $= l - l \cos \theta$, which agrees with (2).

We are thus able to make the general statement, true for obtuse as well as for acute angles, that, when the rod has swung through an angle θ in a counter-clockwise direction from OA, the distance of P to the right of A is $l \sin \theta$, and the height of P above A is $l - l \cos \theta$.

Area of a triangle In Fig. 282, ABC is a triangle in which the lengths of the sides BC, CA, AB are denoted by a, b, c, and the sizes of the angles by A, B, C. Notice that a is opposite A, b opposite B, and c opposite C. This notation is standard in all future work on the triangle.

Draw CN perpendicular to AB.

FIG. 281

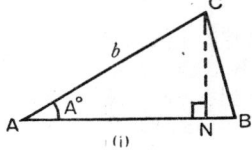
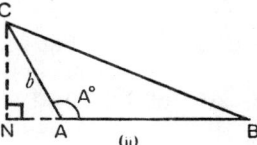

FIG. 282

In Fig. 282 (i), $\dfrac{CN}{CA} = \sin A.$

In Fig. 282 (ii), $\dfrac{CN}{CA} = \sin CAN = \sin (180° - A) = \sin A.$

$\therefore$ in both figures, $\dfrac{CN}{b} = \sin A$,   or $CN = b \sin A.$

The area of $\triangle$ABC $= \frac{1}{2}$ base $\times$ height $= \frac{1}{2}$AB . CN
$= \frac{1}{2}c \times b \sin A$ $= \frac{1}{2}bc \sin A.$

The Greek capital letter Δ (pronounced 'delta') is generally used to denote the area of $\triangle ABC$. The formula may therefore be written:

$$\Delta = \tfrac{1}{2}bc \sin A.$$

Similarly, by drawing the altitudes from A and B, we can prove that $\Delta = \tfrac{1}{2}ab \sin C$ or $\tfrac{1}{2}ca \sin B$; or, in words:

The area of a triangle is equal to half the product of two sides and the sine of the angle included between them.

Area of a parallelogram   Suppose that ABCD is a parallelogram in which $AB = x$, $BC = y$ and $\angle ABC = \theta$ (see Fig. 283). Draw CN perpendicular to AB.

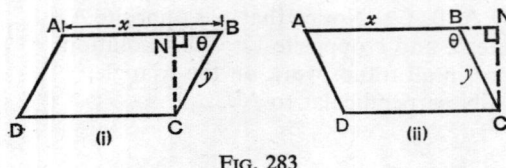

Fig. 283

CN = CB sin ABC in Fig. 283 (i), or CB sin CBN in Fig. 283 (ii).

$\therefore$ CN = $y \sin \theta$ in both figures.

The area of ABCD = base $\times$ height = AB . CN
$$= xy \sin \theta.$$

EXERCISE 104

Calculate the area of $\triangle ABC$ in Nos. 1–4.

1 $a = 7$ cm, $b = 8$ cm, $C = 30°$.

2 $b = 6{\cdot}7$ cm, $c = 4{\cdot}3$ cm, $A = 47° \, 25'$.

3 $a = 10$ cm, $c = 6$ cm, $B = 150°$.

4 $c = 3{\cdot}45$ cm, $a = 2{\cdot}85$ cm, $B = 103° \, 33'$.

5 Calculate the area of a parallelogram ABCD in which AB = 6 cm, BC = 9 cm, ∠ABC = 41° 27′.

6 Calculate the acute angle of a rhombus, if the area is 81 cm² and each side is 10 cm long.

7 Find the area of a parallelogram whose diagonals are 2·6 cm and 4 cm long, if the angle between the diagonals is 68°.

8 Calculate the area of a regular hexagon of side 6 cm.

The Sine Rule   Denote the radius of the circumcircle of △ABC by R. In Fig. 284 (i), A is acute; in Fig. 284 (ii), A is obtuse.

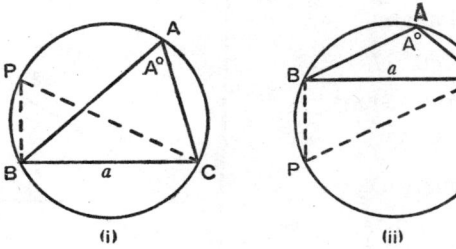

Fig. 284

Draw the diameter CP and join BP. Then CP = 2R, and ∠CBP = 90° (angle in semicircle).

In Fig. 284 (i), ∠P = ∠CAB = A (same seg.).

$$\therefore \frac{BC}{CP} = \sin P = \sin A.$$

In Fig. 284 (ii), ∠P = 180° − A (opp. ∠s of cyclic quad.).

$$\therefore \frac{BC}{CP} = \sin P = \sin (180° - A) = \sin A.$$

$\therefore$ in both figures, $\dfrac{a}{2R} = \sin A.$

$$\therefore \quad a = 2R \sin A.$$

$$\therefore \frac{a}{\sin A} = 2R.$$

Similarly, $\quad \dfrac{b}{\sin B} = 2R \quad$ and $\quad \dfrac{c}{\sin C} = 2R.$

We therefore have the following result, true for all triangles:

$$\frac{a}{\sin A} = \frac{b}{\sin B} = \frac{c}{\sin C} = 2R.$$

This is known as the **Sine Rule**.

Example   *In* △ABC *in which* $a = 2.76$ *cm*, $B = 32° 13'$, $C = 108° 14'$, *find the length of b.*

Begin with a rough freehand sketch, Fig. 285, marking the given side and angles.

$$B + C = 140° 27'.$$

$$\therefore A = 180° - 140° 27'$$

$$= 39° 33'.$$

From the Sine Rule,

$$\frac{b}{\sin 32° 13'} = \frac{2.76}{\sin 39° 33'}.$$

$$\therefore b = \frac{2.76 \sin 32° 13'}{\sin 39° 33'}.$$

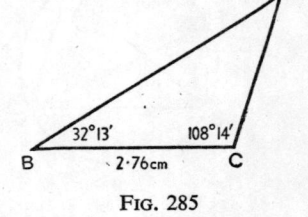

Fig. 285

No.	Log.
2·76	0·4409
sin 32° 13′	$\bar{1}$·7268
sin 39° 33′	0·1677 $\bar{1}$·8040
2·311	0·3637

$$\therefore b = 2.31 \text{ cm (approx.).}$$

Note Do not use the Sine Rule if the triangle is right-angled.   In Fig. 286, if B = 90°, the Sine Rule gives

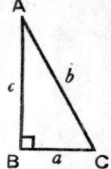

$$\frac{a}{\sin A} = \frac{b}{\sin 90°} = \frac{b}{1}.$$

∴ $a = b \sin A.$

But this could have been written down at once, without wasting time with the Sine Rule.

FIG. 286

An isosceles triangle should be solved by drawing the perpendicular from the vertex to the base, and not by applying the Sine Rule.

EXERCISE 105

Solve △ABC in Nos. 1–11.

1 $a = 7·8$ cm, B = 55°, C = 47°.

2 $b = 3·8$ cm, B = 71°, C = 58°.

3 $a = 4·7$ cm, B = 22° 16′, C = 30° 50′.

4 $a = 2·9$ cm, B = 41° 20′, A = 37° 9′.

5 $c = 14·2$ cm, A = 33°, B = 118°

6 $b = 10·1$ cm, B = 34° 22′, C = 64° 34′.

7 $c = 5·9$ cm, B = 54° 18′, C = 26° 13′.

8 $a = 7·8$ cm, C = 47° 14′, A = 104° 20′.

9 $b = 11·3$ cm, C = 44° 12′, A = 58° 46′.

10 $c = 17·9$ cm, A = 22° 45′, C = 118° 6′.

11 $a = 2·2$ cm, C = 49° 25′, B = 32° 10′.

12 A and B are two points 400 m apart on the same bank of a straight river, and C is a tree on the other bank, between A and B.   The angles CAB, CBA are found to be 63° 20′ and 74° 30′ respectively.   Calculate AC, and hence find the width of the river.

13 Calculate the longest side of △ABC if $a = 13·6$ cm, $B = 66° 19'$, $C = 54° 17'$.

14 Calculate the shortest side of △ABC if $c = 12$ cm, $A = 35°$, $B = 64°$.

15 In Fig. 287, AD bisects ∠BAC, and ∠ADC = θ. By applying the Sine Rule

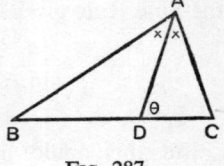

Fig. 287

to △ADB, prove that $BD = \dfrac{AB \sin \frac{1}{2}A}{\sin \theta}$

By applying the Sine Rule also to △ADC, prove that

$$\frac{BD}{DC} = \frac{AB}{AC}.$$

(This is a trigonometrical proof of Theorem 28, p. 259.)

16 AD is an altitude of △ABC. Express AD in two ways, using the right-angled triangles ADC, ADB, and hence prove that $\dfrac{b}{\sin B} = \dfrac{c}{\sin C}$. Consider the case (i) when B and C are both acute; (ii) when one of these angles is obtuse.

Deduce that, for any triangle,

$$\frac{a}{\sin A} = \frac{b}{\sin B} = \frac{c}{\sin C}.$$

(This is an alternative method of proving the Sine Rule. It does not show, however, that each ratio = 2R.)

17 A man on a ship observes a lighthouse to lie in a direction S. 38° E. After the ship has steamed a distance of 9 km in a direction N. 44° E., the lighthouse is observed to lie in a direction S. 11° W. Find how far from the lighthouse the ship then is.

18 An aeroplane is between two points which are 800 m apart on level ground, and directly above the line joining them. The angles of elevation of the aeroplane from the two points are 29° 41' and 36° 34'. Find the height of the aeroplane.

36. FURTHER PERCENTAGES (II)

Successive percentage increases Suppose a number is increased by 5%, and the new number is also increased by 5%. The total increase is not 10%. For, supposing that the original number is 100, the first increase brings it to 105.

The multiplying factor for the second increase is $\dfrac{105}{100}$.

$$\therefore \text{ the number becomes } \overset{21}{\cancel{105}} \times \frac{\overset{21}{\cancel{105}}}{\underset{20}{\cancel{100}}}_{4}$$

$$= \frac{441}{4} = 110\tfrac{1}{4}.$$

Thus the total increase per cent $= 10\tfrac{1}{4}\%$.

Notice that $5\% + 5\% = 10\%$ only if all the percentages refer to the same thing.

The next three worked examples show how to deal with successive increases or profits.

Example 1 *A buys an article for £40, and sells it to B at a profit of 60%; B sells it to C at a profit of 20%. Find how much C gave for the article.*

$$\text{B's cost price} = £40 \times \frac{160}{100}.$$

$$\text{C's cost price} = £\cancel{40} \times \frac{16\cancel{0}}{1\cancel{00}} \times \frac{12\cancel{0}}{10\cancel{0}}$$

$$= £\frac{384}{5}$$

$$= £76 \cdot 80.$$

Example 2 *The population of a certain town, taken every ten years, was found first to have increased by 10%, then to have increased by 5%, and lastly to have decreased by 5%, each increase or decrease being reckoned as a percentage of the number at the previous census. Find the percentage increase over the whole time.*

Suppose that the original population is represented by 100.
After the first increase of 10%, the number = 110.
After the second increase of 5%, the number

$$= 110 \times \frac{105}{100}.$$

After the decrease of 5%, the number

$$= 110 \times \frac{\overset{21}{\cancel{105}}}{\underset{20}{\cancel{100}}} \times \frac{\overset{19}{\cancel{95}}}{\underset{20}{\cancel{100}}}$$

$$= \frac{4389}{40}$$

$$= 109 \cdot 725.$$

∴ the increase over the whole period

$$= 9 \cdot 725 \text{ in } 100.$$

∴ the increase $\quad = 9 \cdot 725\%.$

Note The answer is not $10 + 5 - 5$, or 10%; for the percentage changes are percentages of different numbers.

Example 3 *The price of a house rose by* 20%, *then by* 5%, *and finally by* 25%. *If the final price was* £1890, *find the original price.*

Let £x be the original price.

The multiplying factors corresponding to the various increases are $\dfrac{120}{100}, \dfrac{105}{100}, \dfrac{125}{100}.$

$$\therefore \quad £x \times \frac{120}{100} \times \frac{105}{100} \times \frac{125}{100} = £1890.$$

$$\therefore \quad x \times \frac{6}{\cancel{5}} \times \frac{21}{20} \times \frac{\cancel{5}}{4} = 1890.$$

$$\therefore \quad x = \frac{\overset{270}{\cancel{1890}} \times 20 \times \overset{2}{\cancel{4}}}{\underset{3}{\cancel{6}} \times \underset{3}{\cancel{21}}}$$

$$= 1200.$$

∴ the original price was £1200.

EXERCISE 106

1 There are three substances A, B, C. The density of A exceeds that of B by 10%; that of C exceeds that of A by 20%. By how much per cent does the density of C exceed that of B?

2 A buys a car for £300, and sells it to B at a profit of 16%. B sells it at a profit of 20% to C, who sells it to D at a loss of 25%. Find how much D paid for it.

3 A builder sold a house at a profit of 40%. The purchaser sold it to another man at a profit of 20%, and he eventually sold it at a loss of 25% for £2205. Find how much the house cost the builder.

4 A school of 500 increases its numbers in one year by 20%, and in the next year by 10%. The following year the numbers fell by $16\frac{2}{3}$%. Find the new total in the school.

5 A car decreases in value every year by 20% of its value at the beginning of that year. Find the percentage decrease in value after 3 years.

6 A car is bought for £600. It decreases in value by 20% during the first year, and during each subsequent year it decreases in value by 10% of its value at the beginning of the year. Find its value at the end of 3 years.

7 The price of tobacco goes up by 25%. By what percentage must a man reduce the quantity of tobacco he smokes in order that it may cost the same as before?

8 A manufacturer's catalogue prices are 60% above his cost of manufacture, but he allows a trade discount of 15% from the catalogue price. What percentage profit does he actually make?

9 A is greater than B by 20%; B is less than C by 10%. Find by how much per cent A exceeds C.

10 The number of boys in a school who play games is $87\frac{1}{2}$% of the total. Of these, 80% play rugger and the remaining 20% play hockey. What percentage of the whole school play rugger, and what percentage play hockey?

11 A man's salary is £2500. He receives an increase of 10%, and subsequently another increase of 10%. Find his final salary, and find also what single percentage rise would have produced that salary.

12 The population of a city has increased by 4% in one year. If the present population is 1 872 000, find what it was a year ago.

Assuming that the population goes on increasing at the same rate, find what it will be (i) in 1 year's time, and (ii) in 2 years' time (to the nearest whole number).

13 If a car depreciates by 20% of its value at the beginning of the year, and at the end of two years the value is £336, find the original value of the car.

Profit and loss Part I, p. 228, Ex. 98 contained easy questions on profit and loss per cent. We shall now deal with some harder problems.

Example 4 *A man gains 25% by selling an article for £1·50. At what price must he sell it to gain 40%?*

$$\begin{array}{ccc} \text{C.P.} & \text{1st S.P.} & \text{2nd S.P.} \\ 100 & 125 & 140 \end{array}$$

$$\therefore \text{2nd S.P.} = \frac{140}{125} \text{ of 1st S.P.}$$

$$= \frac{\overset{28}{\cancel{140}}}{\underset{25}{\cancel{125}}} \times 1 \cdot \overset{0 \cdot 06}{\cancel{50}} = £1 \cdot 68.$$

Example 5 *If a man sold an article for £81 he would make 8% profit. Find his percentage profit or loss if he sold it for £70·50.*

$$\frac{\text{2nd S.P.}}{\text{1st S.P.}} = \frac{70\frac{1}{2}}{81} = \frac{141}{162} = \frac{47}{54}.$$

Suppose the C.P. = £100. Then the 1st S.P. = £108.

$$\therefore \text{2nd S.P.} = \frac{47}{54} \times £108 = £94.$$

$$\therefore \text{ the loss would be } 6\%.$$

EXERCISE 107

1 By selling an article for £1·62 a shopkeeper makes 35% profit. Find the selling price at which he would make 20% profit.

2 If a man sold an article for £336, he would gain 12%. Find his gain per cent if he sold it for £357.

3 By selling a car for £273 a man gains 56%. For how much must he sell it if he wishes to make 40% profit?

4 A shopkeeper gains 40% by selling an article for £5·88. At what price should he sell it to gain 45%?

5 A man sold an article for £30·24 at a profit of 12%. Find his gain per cent if he sold it for £33·75.

6 By selling eggs at 7 for 18p a man calculates that he makes $28\frac{4}{7}$% profit. Find his percentage profit if he sold them (i) at 8 for 18p; (ii) at 3p each.

7 A greengrocer gained 40% on his cost price by selling potatoes at 28p for 10 kg. He reduced his selling price so as to make 20% profit. Find the new price for 10 kg.

8 A sells a car to B at a profit of 10%. B sells it to C at a loss of 12% on his own outlay. If C pays £532·40 for it, find for how much A originally bought the car.

9 A wholesale dealer A made a profit of 40% on his outlay by selling goods to a retailer B. The retailer then sold the same goods to a customer, and the customer's payment to B was 75% greater than A's outlay. Find what percentage profit B made on his own outlay.

10 A man gains 4% on his outlay by selling articles at 96p each. Find what his gain or loss per cent would be if he sold them at 88p each.

11 A manufacturer sells an article to a retailer at a profit of 50%. The retailer sells it to a customer for £2·25, thereby making 20% profit on his cost price. Find what the article cost the manufacturer.

12 An article for sale has a marked price of £2·40. The shopkeeper allows a discount of 12½% of the marked price, and still makes a profit of 20% on his own cost price. Find the cost price to the shopkeeper and the profit per cent if the article is sold at the marked price.

13 A manufacturer sells goods to a shopkeeper at a profit of 10% on his outlay. The shopkeeper sells so as to make 15% profit on his own outlay. Find to the nearest penny the cost of manufacturing an article which is sold in the shop for £2·30.

14 A tradesman makes a profit of 20% by selling an article for 36p. When he has sold five-eighths of his stock at this price, he sells the remainder at 24p each. Find what percentage profit he makes on the whole stock.

15 A sells an article to B at a profit of 10%; B sells it to C at a gain of 5%; C sells it to D at a gain of 2½%, each person reckoning his gain per cent on his own cost price. If A had sold the article direct to D at the same price that D actually paid, find to the nearest whole number what would have been A's profit per cent.

16 A firm's expenses consist of overheads, labour, materials in the ratios 3:4:8. If overheads increase by 5%, cost of labour by 12½% and cost of materials by 10%, find the increase per cent in the total expenses. If the total expenses increase to £329 000, what were they before?

17 A wholesaler made 20% profit on his cost price by selling an article to a shopkeeper. The latter sold the article for £42, thereby making 40% profit on what he paid the wholesaler. Find how much the article cost the wholesaler.

18 A bought a house and sold it to B at a profit of 10% on his cost price. Subsequently B sold it back to A, making 10% on his own cost price. A found that he had lost £945 as a result of the whole deal. Find how much A originally gave for the house.

19 A shopkeeper makes a profit of 20% on his cost price by selling an article for 75p. He sells four-fifths of his stock at this price, and reduces the price of the remaining fifth to 50p. Find what percentage profit he makes on the whole stock.

20 A tradesman marks goods in the shop at 40% above what they cost him, but he allows a discount of 10% of the marked price in a sale. Find what profit per cent he actually makes on goods purchased during the sale, and the amount of profit he makes on an article which is sold in the sale for £25·83.

21 The population of a town was 328 020 in the 1931 census. This was an increase of 10% on the 1921 census, and the 1921 census figures showed an increase of $6\frac{1}{2}$% on the 1911 census. Find the population in 1911, and by how much per cent the population increased between 1911 and 1931.

22 A car is timed over a measured distance, and the speed is calculated to be 59·5 km/h. If there is a possible error of 4% in the time taken, and of 2% in the measured distance, find the greatest and least possible average speeds of the car.

37. TRANSFORMATION OF FORMULAE

Change of subject If the base of a triangle is b cm and the height h cm, we know that the formula for the area $\triangle$ square centimetres is

$$\triangle = \tfrac{1}{2}bh.$$

This is a sentence of which $\triangle$ is the subject and the 'equals' sign is the verb.

Now suppose that we want to find the base of a triangle of given height and area. Let us find a formula for b in terms of h and $\triangle$.

$$\tfrac{1}{2}bh = \triangle.$$

Multiply both sides by 2, $bh = 2\triangle.$

Divide both sides by h, $\qquad b = \dfrac{2\triangle}{h}.$

From this formula, if we substitute the values of $\triangle$ and h, we can calculate the value of b. The process of taking a formula such as $\triangle = \tfrac{1}{2}bh$, and transforming it so that another letter, such as b, appears *by itself* on one side, is called **changing the subject of the formula** from $\triangle$ to b.

To take another illustration, if S right angles is the angle-sum of a polygon of n sides, we proved in Theorem 2 (p. 21) that

$$S = 2n - 4.$$

This formula has S as the subject. Suppose we require to make n the subject.

Add 4 to both sides, $\quad S + 4 = 2n.$

Divide both sides by 2; $\dfrac{S + 4}{2} = n,$

or $\qquad\qquad\qquad n = \dfrac{S + 4}{2}.$

Notice that the methods used (adding the same quantity to both sides, multiplying both sides by the same quantity, and so on) are the same as in solving equations.

The ability to change the subject of a formula saves a good deal of memory work in mathematics. Most formulae are remembered in some standard form, and if, for the purpose of some special problem, it is necessary to have a different letter as the subject, we do not memorise a new formula. We merely change the subject of the old one, thus making one formula do the work of several.

For example, the formula

$$I = \frac{PRT}{100}$$

gives the simple interest on £P for T years at R% per annum. But if we want a formula for T in terms of I, P and R, we proceed as follows:

Multiply both sides by 100; $PRT = 100\,I.$

Divide both sides by PR; $\quad T = \dfrac{100\,I}{PR}.$

This is a formula which will tell us in what time a certain principal £P will earn a certain interest £I at R% p.a. Such a formula need not be learned by heart, as it is so quickly obtained from the familiar

$$I = \frac{PRT}{100}.$$

EXERCISE 108 (Oral)

1 $y = mx + c$.   Make (i) c, (ii) m, (iii) x the subject.

2 $C = 2\pi r$.   Make r the subject.

3 $I = \dfrac{PRT}{100}$.   Make (i) P, (ii) R the subject.

4 $P = 2l + 2b$.   Make b the subject.

5 $S = 2\pi rh$.   Make h the subject.

6 $V = \frac{1}{3}\pi r^2 h$.   Make h the subject.

7 $v = u + at$.   Make (i) u, (ii) a, (iii) t the subject.

8 $A = lb$.   Make l the subject.

9 $V = lbh$.   Make h the subject.

10 $S = 2\pi r^2 + 2\pi rh$.   Make h the subject.

Example 1   *The area* A *cm²* *of a circle of radius* r *cm is given by the formula* $A = \pi r^2$.   *Make* r *the subject of the formula.*

$$\pi r^2 = A.$$

Divide both sides by π: $r^2 = \dfrac{A}{\pi}.$

Take the square root of both sides;

$$r = \sqrt{\frac{A}{\pi}}.$$

Note   It would be wrong to divide both sides of the equation $r^2 = \dfrac{A}{\pi}$ by r, giving $r = \dfrac{A}{\pi r}$; for the right-hand side of this also contains r, and the formula would not enable us to find the value of r if we knew that of A.

Example 2 *Make l the subject of the formula* $T = 2\pi\sqrt{\dfrac{l}{g}}$.

$$2\pi\sqrt{\frac{l}{g}} = T.$$

Square both sides; $\qquad 4\pi^2\dfrac{l}{g} = T^2.$

Multiply both sides by g; $\quad 4\pi^2 l = gT^2.$

Divide both sides by $4\pi^2$; $\qquad l = \dfrac{gT^2}{4\pi^2}.$

The last example indicates that the steps in transforming a formula are:

(1) Remove any root signs and fractions (by squaring both sides or multiplying both sides by some quantity).

(2) Put all the terms containing the letter required on one side of the equation (whichever side is the more convenient in order to avoid a lot of negative signs), and all the terms not containing that letter on the other side.

(3) Factorise the terms containing the letter required, by taking that letter outside a bracket as a common factor.

(4) Make the required letter the subject.

Some of these steps may, in a particular problem, be unnecessary.

Example 3 *Make h the subject of the formula* $a = b\dfrac{1+2h}{1-h}$.

(1) *Clear of fractions and brackets.*
Multiply both sides by $(1-h)$; $a(1-h) = b(1+2h)$.
Remove brackets; $\qquad\qquad a - ah = b + 2bh$.

(2) *Isolate on one side (in this case the right) the terms containing h.*
Subtract b from both sides, and add ah,
$$a - b = ah + 2bh.$$

(3) *Factorise the right-hand side as h*(. . . .).
$$a - b = h(a + 2b).$$

(4) *Make h the subject.*

Divide both sides by $(a+2b)$; $\quad \dfrac{a-b}{a+2b}=h,$

or $\qquad\qquad\qquad\qquad\qquad h=\dfrac{a-b}{a+2b}.$

EXERCISE 109

1 $\dfrac{ax+b}{cx+d}=\dfrac{5}{7}.$ Make x the subject.

2 $y=\dfrac{1\cdot37\text{P}}{x^2t}.$ Make x the subject.

3 $i=\dfrac{n\text{V}}{\text{R}+nr}.$ Make n the subject.

4 $\dfrac{a}{bx+c}=\dfrac{d}{ex-f}.$ Make x the subject.

5 $x=\dfrac{ay}{3a-2y}.$ Make y the subject.

6 $\dfrac{3x+a}{2x+b}=\dfrac{p}{q}.$ Make x the subject.

7 $x=\dfrac{5-2y}{6y-3}.$ Make y the subject.

8 $\text{E}=\dfrac{\text{W}(a-b)}{2a\text{P}}.$ Make a the subject.

9 $cx=\tfrac{3}{4}(12a+c-b).$ Make c the subject.

10 $x=\dfrac{7-3y}{4y-2}.$ Make y the subject.

11 $p=\dfrac{\text{W}}{\pi(\text{R}^2-r^2)}.$ Make R the subject.

12 $\text{P}=\tfrac{9}{10}(5\text{R}^2\text{Q}-\text{T}).$ Make Q the subject.

13 $p=q-\sqrt{q^2+r^2}.$ Make r the subject.

14 $\text{V}=0\cdot2716d^2h.$ Make d the subject.

15 $\text{V}=\pi l\{\text{R}^2-(\text{R}-t)^2\}.$ Make R the subject.

EXERCISE 110

In the calculations, use logarithms wherever convenient, and give answers correct to three significant figures. Take log π as 0·4971.

1 The distance s centimetres through which a stone falls in t seconds from the instant at which it is dropped is given by the formula $s = \frac{1}{2}gt^2$, where g is approximately 981. Find a formula for t in terms of s and g, and calculate the time required for the stone to fall 31 metres.

2 If $C°$ and $F°$ are corresponding readings on the Celsius and Fahrenheit thermometers, it is known that $F = 32 + \frac{9C}{5}$. Make C the subject of the formula, and find what Celsius readings correspond to 32° F and 212° F.

3 The surface area, A cm², of a sphere of radius r cm (see p. 232) is given by the formula $A = 4\pi r^2$. Make r the subject, and calculate the radius of a sphere whose surface area is 50 cm².

4 If A cm² is the area of a trapezium with parallel sides a cm and b cm at a distance h cm apart, then $A = \frac{1}{2}(a+b)h$. Make (i) h, (ii) a the subject.

Find the length of one of the parallel sides of a trapezium of area 44·5 cm², if the other parallel side is 4·2 cm and the height of the trapezium is 5 cm.

5 Make sin B the subject of the sine rule $\frac{a}{\sin A} = \frac{b}{\sin B}$.

Find two values of B if $a = 2$, $b = 3$ and $A = 35°$.

6 Make T the subject of the formula $A = P + \frac{PRT}{100}$.

Find in how many years £95 amounts to £108·30 at $3\frac{1}{2}$% p.a. simple interest.

7 If $s = \frac{1}{2}(u+v)t$, make (i) t, (ii) u, (iii) v the subject.

8 From a point h metres above sea-level, it is possible to see D kilometres, where $D = \sqrt{\dfrac{Rh}{500}}$, R km being the radius of the earth. Make h the subject of this formula, and find h if D = 15, R = 6370.

9 If V cm³ is the volume of a sphere of radius r cm, then $V = \frac{4}{3}\pi r^3$. Make r the subject, and calculate the radius of a sphere whose volume is 3270 cm³.

10 Make (i) h, (ii) r the subject of the formula $V = \pi r^2 h$. Find the radius of a cylinder whose volume is 90 cm³ and height 6 cm.

11 A formula for rating the power of motors is $H = \frac{2}{5}nd^2$. Make (i) n, (ii) d the subject.

12 Hooke's Law states that the tension T kg wt in a piece of elastic of unstretched length a cm when stretched to a length x cm is given by the formula $T = \dfrac{\lambda}{a}(x-a)$, where λ is some constant number. Make (i) x, (ii) a the subject.

13 The Cosine Rule (see p. 369) states that, for a triangle ABC, $a^2 = b^2 + c^2 - 2bc \cos A$. Make $\cos A$ the subject.
Find A if $a = 8$, $b = 7$, $c = 6$.

14 In the formula $T = 2\pi\sqrt{\dfrac{I}{MH}}$, T seconds is the time of one complete oscillation of a suspended magnet, M is the magnetic moment of the magnet, H is the strength of the earth's magnetic field, and I is the moment of inertia of the magnet. Make M the subject of the formula; and calculate the moment of a magnet which takes 12·9 s for one complete oscillation when suspended, the strength of the earth's magnetic field being 0·176 units and the moment of inertia of the magnet being 380 units.

15 Make (i) u, (ii) a the subject of the formula $s = ut + \frac{1}{2}at^2$.

16 Make g the subject of the formula $T = 2\pi\sqrt{\dfrac{l}{g}}$, which gives the time of swing T seconds of a pendulum of length l cm.

Find the value of g from the fact that a pendulum of length 99·4 cm takes 2 seconds for a swing.

17 Make x the subject of the formula $A = xy\sin\theta$.

18 Make (i) sin A, (ii) b the subject of the formula $\triangle = \frac{1}{2}bc\sin A$.

19 If a wire x cm long is stretched between two points on the same level l cm apart, the sag d cm is given by the formula $d = \sqrt{\dfrac{3l(x-l)}{8}}$. Make x the subject of this formula.

Calculate the length of wire necessary to join two points 60 cm apart, allowing for a maximum sag of 2 cm.

20 Make (i) s, (ii) u the subject of the formula $v^2 = u^2 + 2as$.

21 If a force of P grammes wt is applied to a body of weight W grammes and moves it through x cm, so increasing its speed from u cm/s to v cm/s, then it is known that $Px = \dfrac{W}{2g}(v^2 - u^2)$, where g is approximately 981. Make (i) x, (ii) W, (iii) v, (iv) u the subject of this formula. (Do not substitute for g.)

22 A formula connected with a spherical mirror is $\dfrac{1}{u} + \dfrac{1}{v} = \dfrac{1}{f}$. Change the subject to (i) f, (ii) v, and calculate the value of v when $f = 6\cdot3$, $u = 4\cdot9$. (Reciprocal tables are helpful.)

23 If V cm³ of water are poured into a spherical bowl of radius r cm, and the greatest depth of the water is h cm, it can be shown that $V = \pi h^2(r - \frac{1}{3}h)$. Find a formula for V in terms of r if $h = \frac{1}{2}r$, and make r the subject of the formula you obtain.

24 If the area of a circular running track is A square metres, the inner radius r metres, and the width of the track d metres, show that $A = \pi\{(r + d)^2 - r^2\}$. Make r the subject of the formula.

25 Using the formula $A = 2\pi rh + 2\pi r^2$ for the total surface area of a cylinder, make h the subject of the formula.

26 Make b the subject of the formula $t = \dfrac{2br - c}{b + 2a}$.

27 A formula in connection with a lens is

$$\frac{1}{f} = (u - 1)\left(\frac{1}{r} - \frac{1}{s}\right).$$

Make (i) u, (ii) f, (iii) r the subject.

28 Make a the subject of the formula $S = \dfrac{n}{2}\{2a + (n-1)d\}$, and find the value of a if $S = 564$, $n = 12$ and $d = 6$.

Solution of simultaneous equations by the method of substitution   The method of solving simple simultaneous equations by addition or subtraction, after equalising coefficients of one of the two unknowns, was explained in § 2.   This is usually the best method when both equations are of the first degree, but the method which is now to be explained is applicable when one equation is of the first degree and the other is of higher degree.   In the method of **substitution,** we make x or y (whichever is easier) the subject of one of the equations, and substitute this expression in the other equation, thus obtaining an equation in one unknown only.

Example 4   *Solve the simultaneous equations*

$$3x - 5y = 21, \quad . \quad . \quad . \quad . \quad . \quad (1)$$
$$4x + y = 5. \quad . \quad . \quad . \quad . \quad . \quad (2)$$

Make y the subject of (2);

$$y = 5 - 4x \quad . \quad . \quad . \quad . \quad (3)$$

Substitute this expression for y in (1):

$$3x - 5(5 - 4x) = 21.$$
$$\therefore \quad 3x - 25 + 20x = 21.$$
$$\therefore \qquad\qquad 23x = 46.$$
$$\therefore \qquad\qquad\quad x = 2.$$

Replace x in (2) by the value 2:

$$8+y=5, \quad \therefore \ y=-3.$$
$$\therefore \text{ the solution is } x=2, \ y=-3.$$

Check. If $x=2$, $y=-3$, the left-hand side of (1) is $6+15$, or 21.

If $x=2$, $y=-3$, the left-hand side of (2) is $8-3$, or 5.

In this example, we have eliminated y by substitution, because y was easily made the subject of the equation (2). If we made x the subject, we should obtain $x=\dfrac{21+5y}{3}$ from (1), or $x=\dfrac{5-y}{4}$ from (2), both of which involve fractions. In the next example, fractions are unavoidable, whichever unknown letter is eliminated.

Example 5   *Solve the simultaneous equations*

$$5x-6y=27, \quad \cdot \quad \cdot \quad \cdot \quad \cdot \quad (1)$$
$$4x+9y=-6. \quad \cdot \quad \cdot \quad \cdot \quad \cdot \quad (2)$$

Make x the subject of (1):

$$5x=27+6y.$$
$$\therefore \ x=\frac{27+6y}{5}. \quad \cdot \quad \cdot \quad \cdot \quad (3)$$

Substitute this expression for x in (2):

$$\frac{4(27+6y)}{5}+9y=-6.$$

$$\therefore \ 108+24y+45y=-30.$$
$$\therefore \quad\quad\quad\quad 69y=-138.$$
$$\therefore \quad\quad\quad\quad\quad\quad y=-2.$$

Replace y by -2 in (1): $5x+12=27$.

$$5x=15, \quad \therefore \ x=3.$$

$\therefore$ the solution is $x=3$, $y=-2$.

Check   If $x = 3$, $y = -2$, the left-hand side of (1) is $15 + 12$, or 27.

If $x = 3$, $y = -2$, the left-hand side of (2) is $12 - 18$, or -6.

EXERCISE 111

Solve the following simultaneous equations by the method of substitution, first considering carefully which letter is the easier to eliminate.

1 $x + 3y = 15$,
$3x + 2y = 17$

2 $3x + 4y = 22$,
$y - 5x = 17$

3 $2x + y = 9$,
$x - 3y = 8$

4 $5y - 3x = 36$,
$y = 10 + 2x$

5 $x = 4y + 7$,
$y = 3x - 21$

6 $6x - 4y = 2$,
$5x + 7y = 43$

7 $3x = y - 19$,
$5x = 2y - 34$

8 $5x + 2y = -5$,
$3x + 4y = -17$

9 $2x - y = 21$,
$x - 5y = 9$

10 $4l + 5m = 13$,
$26l + 3m + 4 = 0$

11 $5a - 3b = 1$,
$3a = 5 + b$

12 $x - 2y = 24$,
$2x + 5y = 12$

38. LOCI (II)

IN § 19, p. 161, we stated four important loci, confining our attention to points in one plane, e.g. the plane of the paper. We shall now extend these results to points in space, or, as we say, to *three dimensions*. It will first be useful to explain why we speak of space as three-dimensional.

You are already familiar with the method of representing the position of a point P in the plane of your paper by means of two co-ordinates, x and y, referred to axes OX, OY drawn on the paper (see Fig. 288). P is called the point (x, y).

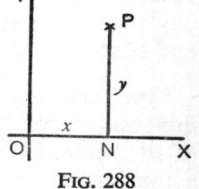

FIG. 288

To represent a point in space, make a drawing of the corner of a room, as in Fig. 289. OX and OY are two edges of the

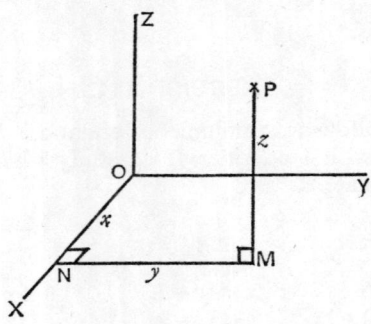

FIG. 289

floor, OZ is vertical. Suppose that a point M is fixed in the plane of the floor by two co-ordinates x and y referred to the axes OX, OY. Then ON $= x$, NM $= y$. Imagine a vertical stick MP, of length z, with the end M resting on the floor. The point P is called the point (x, y, z), and the three numbers x, y, z are called its **three co-ordinates,** referred to the axes OX, OY, OZ. In order to arrive at P, the point (x, y, z), you start from the origin O, measure a length x units along OX, to N. Then measure a length y units, parallel to OY, to the point M. Finally, measure a length z units, parallel to OZ, to the point P. Just as any point in a plane can be represented by two co-ordinates, and a plane is said to be two-dimensional, so any point in space can be represented by three co-ordinates, and space is said to be **three-dimensional.**

Lines and planes as loci In co-ordinate geometry of two dimensions, we found that $x = 2$ is the equation of the locus of all points in the plane which are 2 units from the y-axis, i.e. a line parallel to the y-axis and 2 units away.

In three-dimensional space, $x = 2$ represents the locus of all points which are 2 units from the plane YOZ, i.e. a plane parallel to the plane YOZ and 2 units away. Similarly, $y = 3$ is the equation of the plane parallel to the plane ZOX and 3 units away; and $z = 1$ is the equation of the plane parallel to the plane XOY and 1 unit away.

Four important loci in three dimensions We shall now take the four loci stated on p. 161 and extend them to three dimensions:

I. The locus of points at a given distance from a given point O is a sphere with O as centre and the given distance as radius.

II. The locus of points at a given distance from a given straight line AB is the surface of a circular cylinder whose axis is AB and whose radius is the given distance.

III. The locus of points equidistant from two given points A and B is the plane bisecting AB at right angles.

IV. The locus of points equidistant from two given intersecting straight lines AOB, COD is the pair of planes, perpendicular to the plane containing the fixed lines and passing through the bisectors of the angles between them.

EXERCISE 112

1 Suppose that Fig. 289 represents a corner of a room 5 m by 4 m, and 3 m high, and OX lies along the length of the room. Taking 1 m as the unit, state the equations of (i) the long walls, (ii) the short walls, (iii) the floor, (iv) the ceiling.

2 Give the equation of the locus of points at a distance of 2 units from the plane XOY and above it.

What is the equation if the points are 2 units from the plane XOY and below it?

State the locus in space of the following (Nos. 3–11), all lines and planes being considered as of indefinite extent.

3 Points equidistant from two given intersecting planes.

4 Points equidistant from the planes $y=2$ and $y=4$.

5 The mid-point of a straight rod whose ends slide on the inside of a hollow sphere.

6 The centre of a sphere which rolls on a plane.

7 Points 3 cm from a fixed line AB.

8 Points which are 3 m from the floor of a room and 1 m from a given wall.

9 Points which are 2 m from the floor of a room and 1 m from a vertical stick standing with one end on the floor.

10 Points 1 m from a wall of a room, and 2 m from an adjacent wall. How many points in this locus are also 3 m from the floor?

11 (i) Points which are 3 cm from a fixed point O, (ii) points which are 3 cm from a fixed point O and lying in a plane which is less than 3 cm from O.

12 A and B are two points 2 cm apart. What is the locus in space of points which are 3 cm from A and from B?

13 A and B are two points 2 cm apart. What is the locus in space of points which are $2\frac{1}{2}$ cm from A and 3 cm from B?

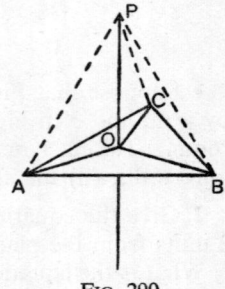

14 In Fig. 290, O is the circumcentre of △ABC; P is any point on the line through O perpendicular to the plane ABC. Prove by congruence that PA = PB = PC.

Use this fact to enable you to state the locus in space of a point equidistant from three fixed points A, B, C which do not lie in a straight line.

FIG. 290

Plotting a locus In Exercise 91 of Part I (p. 215), loci were obtained by plotting various positions of a point which moved according to a given law. Some examples from that Exercise might be revised at this stage before harder problems on this work are begun. Most loci which occur in elementary mathematics are straight lines and circles, but Exercise 113 contains one or two illustrations to show that this is not always the case.

Example 1 *Mark two points* A *and* B, 2·5 *cm apart. Plot the locus of a point* P *such that* PA : PB = 3 : 2.

The point which divides AB internally in the ratio 3 : 2 is 1·5 cm from A and 1 cm from B. The point which divides AB externally in the ratio 3 : 2 is 7·5 cm from A and 5 cm from B. We therefore need values of PB from 1 to 5 cm, and the corresponding values of PA, which equals $\frac{3}{2}$PB, are shown in the following table:

PB	1·0	1·5	2·0	2·5	3·0	3·5	4·0	4·5	5·0
PA	1·5	2·25	3·0	3·75	4·5	5·25	6·0	6·75	7·5

With centre B and radii 1·0, 1·5, 2·0 . . . 5·0 cm, draw a series of circles. With centre A and radii 1·5, 2·25 . . . 7·5 cm, draw arcs to cut these circles, thus plotting the locus shown in Fig. 291. It is a circle of radius 3 cm with its centre on AB produced. This is a particular case of a locus known as the **circle of Apollonius**:

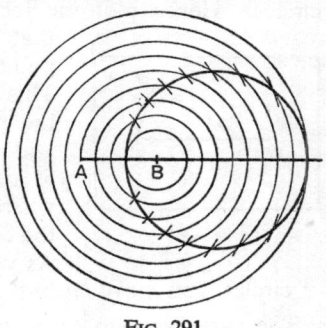

If A **and** B **are fixed points, the locus of a point** P **which is such that** PA : PB **is constant is a circle.**

See page 262, No. 12, where the proof is indicated.

Fig. 291

EXERCISE 113

1 Mark a sheet of centimetre graph paper as in Fig. 292; AB is the lowest thick line, S is 4 cm from AB, O is the mid-point of the perpendicular from S to AB. With centre S, radii $2\frac{1}{2}$, 3, 4, 5 ... 12 cm, draw arcs of circles to cut the lines which are $2\frac{1}{2}$, 3, 4, 5 ... 12 cm respectively from AB. Hence draw the locus of a point P whose distance from the line AB is equal to its distance from S. (O is obviously one possible position of P. Include positions of P on both sides of OS.)

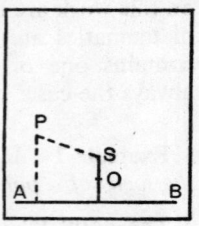

FIG. 292

2 On the same paper as in No. 1, taking O as origin, the parallel to AB through O as x-axis, OS produced as y-axis, and 1 cm as the unit on both axes, draw the graph of $y = \frac{1}{8}x^2$, plotting the points for which $x = 0, 1, 2, 3 \ldots 9$.

You should find that this is the same curve as that plotted in No. 1 as the locus of P, thus showing that the locus is a **parabola**. See p. 298, Fig. 249. S is called the **focus** of the parabola.

3 Draw a straight line SOS' on a sheet of squared paper, as in Fig. 293; SO = OS' = 3 cm. With centres S and S' in turn, and radii 1, $1\frac{1}{2}$, 2, 3, 4, 5, 6, $6\frac{1}{2}$, 7 cm, draw a series of circles. Hence plot the locus of a point P which is such that PS + PS' = 8 cm. (Begin with the point A, 1 cm from S and 7 cm from S'. This is one position of P. Then take the points where the circle, centre S and radius $1\frac{1}{2}$ cm cuts the circle, centre S' and radius $6\frac{1}{2}$ cm; next the points where the S circle of radius 2 cm cuts the S' circle of radius 6 cm, and so on. As you move *outwards* on the S series of circles, you move *inwards* on the S' series.)

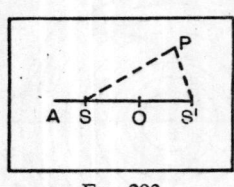

FIG. 293

The curve you obtain is called an **ellipse**; S and S' are its

foci (plural of *focus*). It is the curve you see when a circle is looked at from the side. The earth and the planets move in ellipses round the sun as a focus.

The same curve can be drawn more quickly by putting two drawing-pins in the paper at S and S', placing a loop of string 14 cm long round the pins, and keeping the string taut by means of a pencil.

4 Mark two points, A and B, 6 cm apart. Plot the locus of a point P which is such that $PA = \frac{1}{2}PB$. (Take values of PB from 4 cm to 12 cm.)

Construction of circles, using intersecting loci In order to construct a circle satisfying certain conditions, the method is to draw two loci on which the centre of the required circle must lie. The point or points of intersection of these loci determine the required centre.

Example 2 A *is a point on the circumference of a circle, centre* O *and radius* 2 *cm.* B *is a point* 4 *cm from* O *and* 2·6 *cm from* A. *Construct a circle to touch the given circle at* A *and to pass through* B.

The required circle has to satisfy the following conditions: (i) it is to touch the given circle at A, (ii) it is to pass through A and B.

The locus of the centre of a circle which satisfies (i) is the radius OA (produced in both directions).

The locus of the centre of a circle which satisfies (ii) is the perpendicular bisector of the line AB.

In Fig. 294, these loci are shown by dotted lines. Their

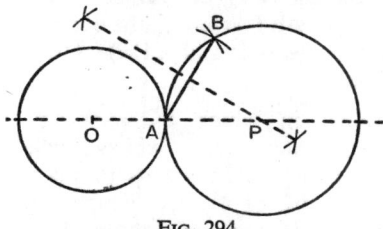

Fig. 294

intersection P is the centre of the required circle, PA is the radius.

Part I, pages 218–220, on the intersection of loci should be revised before starting the next Exercise.

EXERCISE 114

State the locus of the centre of a circle which satisfies the following conditions, and illustrate in each case with a free-hand sketch showing several such circles:

1 Passing through two given points A and B.

2 Touching two given intersecting lines AOB, COD.

3 Touching two given parallel lines AB, CD.

4 Touching a given line at a given point in the line.

5 Touching a given circle at a given point on the circle.

6 Of given radius, passing through a given point A.

7 Of given radius, touching a given line PQ.

8 Of radius 1 cm, touching externally a given circle of radius 3 cm.

9 Of radius 1 cm, touching internally a given circle of radius 3 cm.

10 Of radius 2 cm, touching internally a given circle of radius 1 cm.

11 Draw two lines AB, CD intersecting at an angle of 60°, and construct a circle of radius 2 cm to touch the two lines. (Hint: what is the locus of the centre of a circle of radius 2 cm which touches AB? What is the locus of the centre of a circle which touches AB and CD?) How many possible solutions are there?

12 Draw △ABC in which BC = 4·0 cm, CA = 2·4 cm, AB = 3·6 cm. Construct a circle which touches BC at B and also passes through A. Measure its radius. (Hint: what is the locus of the centre of a circle which touches BC at B? What is the locus of the centre of a circle which passes through A and B?)

13 Draw a straight line AB and mark a point P distant 2 cm from AB. Construct a circle of radius 3 cm which touches AB and passes through P. How many solutions are there?

14 Draw two straight lines AOB, COD such that $\angle$AOC = 75°, and mark a point P in OA such that OP = 2 cm. Construct a circle which touches AB at P and also touches CD. Measure its radius. How many solutions are there?

15 Draw a circle of radius 3 cm and mark a point P 5 cm from its centre. Construct a circle of radius 4 cm which touches the first circle externally and also passes through P. (There are two solutions.)

16 Draw a circle of radius 3 cm and mark a point P on its circumference. Construct a circle of radius 2 cm to touch the first circle (i) externally, (ii) internally, at P.

17 Draw a circle of radius 6·0 cm, and mark a point P 4·8 cm from the centre. Construct two circles of radius 3·6 cm which touch the first circle internally and pass through P.

18 Mark a point O distant 6 cm from a straight line XY, and with centre O, radius 3·6 cm, draw a circle. Construct a circle of radius 2·4 cm to touch XY and to touch the first circle externally. (There are two solutions.)

19 AB is a chord of a circle of radius 6 cm, and the length of the perpendicular from the centre of the circle to AB is 2·5 cm. Construct as many circles as possible of radius 1·5 cm which touch both AB and the given circle.

20 O is the centre of a circle of radius 6 cm; OA, OB are two radii inclined at an angle of 50°. Construct a circle which touches OA, OB and the arc AB internally. Measure its radius. (Hint: draw the tangent to the given circle at the mid-point of the arc AB. The required circle is the incircle of the triangle formed by this tangent, OA produced and OB produced.)

39. PYTHAGORAS' THEOREM: THE COSINE RULE

Pythagoras' Theorem was stated in Part I of this book and has often been used in numerical problems. (See p. 142.) It has usually been regarded as giving an equation connecting the lengths of the sides of a right-angled triangle, namely, $a^2 = b^2 + c^2$, where a cm is the length of the hypotenuse and b cm, c cm are the lengths of the other two sides. It is in this form that the theorem is most used in examples. In the first method of proof now given, however, the theorem gives a result connecting the areas of certain squares. The area of the square on a line AB is AB × AB, usually written AB^2. Similarly, the area of the rectangle ABCD is AB × BC, usually written AB.BC. Brackets such as $(AB + AC)^2$ are dealt with in just the same way as $(a+b)^2$. Thus,

$$(AB + AC)^2 = AB^2 + 2\,AB.AC + AC^2.$$

THEOREM 29 (Pythagoras' Theorem)

In a right-angled triangle the area of the square on the hypotenuse is equal to the sum of the areas of the squares on the other two sides.

Method 1

Given a △ABC with a right angle at A and squares BCDE, CAFG, ABHK drawn on the sides.

To prove that BCDE = CAFG + ABHK.

Construction Draw a line through A parallel to BE to cut BC at X and ED at Y. Join AE, HC.

Proof ∠s BAC and BAK are right angles.

∴   ∠BAC + ∠BAK = 2 rt. ∠s.

∴ CAK is a straight line   (adj. ∠s supp.).

∴   △HBC = ½ sq. ABHK   (same base HB, same ‖s HB, KC).

Also   △ABE = ½ rect. BXYE   (same base BE, same ‖s BE, AY).

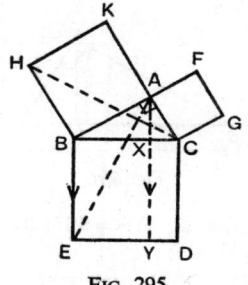

FIG. 295

In the △s HBC, ABE,

$$HB = AB \qquad \text{(sides of square),}$$
$$BC = BE \qquad (\;\; ,, \quad ,, \quad ,, \;),$$
$$\angle HBC = \angle ABE \qquad \text{(each angle } 90° + \angle ABC).$$

∴ △s$_{ABE}^{HBC}$ are congruent (SAS).

∴ area HBC = area ABE.

But △HBC = ½ sq. ABHK, △ABE = ½ rect. BXYE (proved).

∴ ABHK = BXYE.

Similarly, CAFG = CXYD.

∴ CAFG + ABHK = CXYD + BXYE
$$= BCDE.$$

Reference $\angle BAC = 90°,$

∴ $BC^2 = AB^2 + AC^2$ (*Pythagoras'*).

This is called the Euclidean proof, as it is the one given by Euclid. He lived in the third century B.C., and wrote a geometry text-book still known as *Euclid's Elements*.

The proof which follows is a trigonometrical proof. It is shorter than the Euclidean proof, but not so elegant.

Method 2

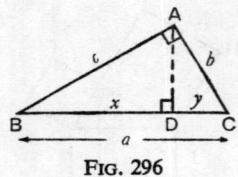

Fig. 296

Given a $\triangle ABC$ in which $\triangle A = 90°$; $BC = a$, $CA = b$, $AB = c$.
To prove that $a^2 = b^2 + c^2$.
Construction Draw AD perpendicular to BC. Let $BD = x$, $DC = y$.

Proof From $\triangle BAC$, $\cos B = \dfrac{c}{a}$.

From $\triangle BDA$, $\cos B = \dfrac{x}{c}$.

$$\therefore \quad \frac{c}{a} = \frac{x}{c}.$$

$$\therefore \quad c^2 = ax.$$

Similarly, $\qquad\qquad\qquad b^2 = ay.$

$$\therefore \; b^2 + c^2 = ay + ax$$
$$= a(y + x)$$
$$= a \,.\, a = a^2.$$

The converse of the theorem We shall assume the truth of the converse without proof:

If the square on one side of a triangle is equal to the sum of the squares on the other two sides, then these sides contain a right angle.

EXERCISE 115

1 Remove brackets from the following:

$$(BC + BD)^2, \quad (XY - XZ)^2, \quad (AB + AC)(AB - AC).$$

2 Factorise:

$PQ^2 + 2PQ.PR$, $XY.XA - 3XA^2$, $AP^2 - 9AQ^2$.

3 Simplify: (i) the square of 2AB,   (ii) the square of 3PQ, (iii) the square of $(AB + \frac{1}{2}AD)$.

4 In Fig. 295, prove in full that CAFG = CXYD.

5 In Fig. 296, prove in full that $b^2 = ay$.

6 ABCD is a quadrilateral in which $\angle A = \angle C = 90°$. Prove that $AB^2 + AD^2 = CB^2 + CD^2$.

7 AD is an altitude of $\triangle ABC$.   Prove that
$$AB^2 - BD^2 = AC^2 - CD^2.$$

8 The diagonals of the quadrilateral ABCD cut at right angles.   Prove that $AB^2 + CD^2 = AD^2 + BC^2$.

9 AD, BE are altitudes of $\triangle ABC$.   Prove that
$$AE^2 + BE^2 = AD^2 + BD^2.$$

10 P is a point inside a rectangle ABCD; the lengths of the perpendiculars from P to AB, BC, CD, DA are a, b, c, d units respectively.   Prove that $PA^2 = a^2 + d^2$, and, by writing down three similar results, deduce that
$$PA^2 + PC^2 = PB^2 + PD^2.$$

Is the same result true if P is *outside* ABCD?

11 ABCD is a rhombus.   Prove that $AC^2 + BD^2 = 4AB^2$.

12 ABC is an equilateral triangle, P is a point in BC such that $BP = \frac{1}{3}BC$.   Prove that $AP^2 = \frac{7}{9}AB^2$.   (Hint: draw the altitude AD, and let each side of $\triangle ABC$ be $6a$ units.)

13 In the quadrilateral ABCD, $\angle BAD = 90°$.   If $AB^2 + AD^2 = CB^2 + CD^2$, prove that $\angle C = 90°$.

14 Prove that a triangle whose sides are of lengths $x^2 + y^2$, $x^2 - y^2$, $2xy$ units is right-angled.

Distance between two points

(i) *Two dimensions*

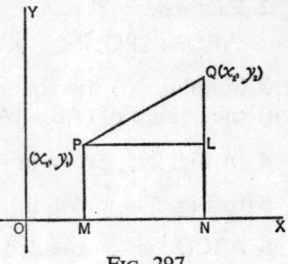

FIG. 297

In Fig. 297, let P be the point (x_1, y_1), Q the point (x_2, y_2). Draw PM, QN perpendicular to OX and draw PL perpendicular to QN.

Then
$$OM = x_1, \quad ON = x_2;$$
$$PM = y_1, \quad QN = y_2.$$
$$\therefore PL = MN = ON - OM = (x_2 - x_1).$$
$$QL = QN - LN = QN - PM = (y_2 - y_1).$$

Since
$$\angle PLQ = 90°,$$
$$PQ^2 = PL^2 + QL^2 \quad \text{(Pythagoras')}$$
$$= (x_2 - x_1)^2 + (y_2 - y_1)^2.$$

$\therefore$ the distance between (x_1, y_1) and (x_2, y_2) is
$$\sqrt{\{(x_2 - x_1)^2 + (y_2 - y_1)^2\}}.$$

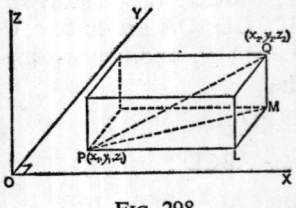

FIG. 298

(ii) *Three dimensions*

In Fig. 298 the axes OX, OY are at right angles to one another in a horizontal plane, and OZ is vertical. P is (x_1, y_1, z_1), Q is (x_2, y_2, z_2). Think of PQ as the diagonal of a rectangular block, held with its length PL parallel to OX, breadth LM parallel to OY, height MQ parallel to OZ.

$$PL = x \text{ co-ordinate of } Q - x \text{ co-ordinate of } P$$
$$= (x_2 - x_1).$$

Similarly, $LM = (y_2 - y_1)$ and $MQ = (z_2 - z_1)$.

Now $\angle QMP = 90°$.
$$\therefore PQ^2 = PM^2 + MQ^2 \quad \text{(Pythagoras')}.$$

Also, by Pythagoras' Theorem, since $\angle PLM = 90°$,
$$PM^2 = PL^2 + LM^2.$$

$$\therefore PQ^2 = PL^2 + LM^2 + MQ^2$$
$$= (x_2 - x_1)^2 + (y_2 - y_1)^2 + (z_2 - z_1)^2.$$

$\therefore$ the distance between (x_1, y_1, z_1) and (x_2, y_2, z_2) is

$$\sqrt{\{(x_2 - x_1)^2 + (y_2 - y_1)^2 + (z_2 - z_1)^2\}}.$$

Notice, in both these formulae for the distance between two points, that it does not matter which way round we take the difference of the co-ordinates, since $(x_1 - x_2)^2$ is the same as $(x_2 - x_1)^2$. Similarly for $(y_1 - y_2)$ and $(z_1 - z_2)$.

Trigonometrical form of Pythagoras' Theorem

If we take a circle, centre O and radius 1 unit, and two perpendicular axes OX, OY as in Fig. 299, we have already explained how an angle POX is regarded as being produced by a radius rotating counter-clockwise from the position OA to some position OP. Suppose that $\angle POX = \theta$. The cosine and sine of the angle θ were defined on page 326, whatever the size of the angle, as follows:

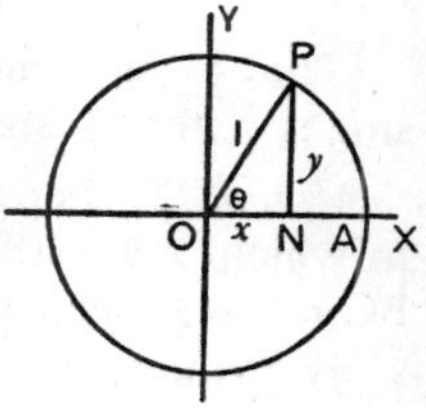

cos θ = the x co-ordinate of P = ON,
sin θ = the y co-ordinate of P = PN.

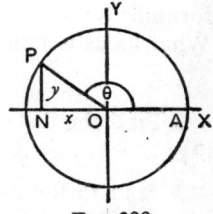

FIG. 299

Now, since $\angle PNO = 90°$,

$$PN^2 + ON^2 = OP^2 \quad \text{(Pythagoras')}.$$
$$\therefore (\sin \theta)^2 + (\cos \theta)^2 = 1.$$

The expressions $(\sin \theta)^2$ and $(\cos \theta)^2$ are always written as $\sin^2 \theta$, $\cos^2 \theta$. Thus

$$\sin^2 \theta + \cos^2 \theta = 1.$$

The proof is general, and does not depend upon the size of θ. Fig. 300 shows the case where θ is an obtuse angle, and x is consequently negative, but it is still true that $x^2 + y^2 = 1$.

It is important to remember that Pythagoras' Theorem cannot be proved by using the identity $\sin^2 \theta + \cos^2 \theta = 1$. This fact is merely the translation of

FIG. 300

Pythagoras' Theorem into terms of trigonometry. In the worked example which follows, the first method uses the trigonometrical identity, while the second method uses Pythagoras' Theorem. The two methods are really equivalent.

Example 1 *If* $\sin \theta = \frac{3}{5}$, *find the value of* $\cos \theta$, *without using tables.*

Method 1

$$\sin^2 \theta + \cos^2 \theta = 1.$$

$$\therefore \quad \tfrac{9}{25} + \cos^2 \theta = 1.$$

$$\therefore \qquad \cos^2 \theta = 1 - \tfrac{9}{25} = \tfrac{16}{25}.$$

$$\therefore \qquad \cos \theta = \pm \tfrac{4}{5}.$$

(The $+$ sign should be taken if θ is the *acute* angle whose sine is $\frac{3}{5}$, the $-$ sign if θ is the *obtuse* angle.)

Method 2 Let θ be the angle A of a right-angled $\triangle$ABC, in which $\angle$B$=90°$. (See Fig. 301.) Take BC to be 3; then AC$=5$, since $\sin \theta = \frac{3}{5}$.
By Pythagoras' Theorem, AB$=4$.

$$\therefore \cos \theta = \frac{\text{AB}}{\text{AC}} = \tfrac{4}{5}.$$

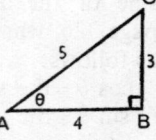

Fig. 301

This gives the numerical value of $\cos \theta$.
Since θ may be acute or obtuse, $\cos \theta = \pm \frac{4}{5}$.

EXERCISE 116

1 By making x_2 and y_2 zero in the formula for the distance between two points in two dimensions on p. 364, obtain a formula for the distance of the point (x, y) from the origin. What locus is represented by the equation

$$x^2 + y^2 = 9?$$

2 Find the distance between the points (i) $(2, 3)$ and $(5, 7)$, (ii) $(1, -4)$ and $(6, 8)$, (iii) $(-2, 12)$ and $(5, -12)$.

3 Find to the nearest tenth of a unit the distance between (i) $(-1, 3)$ and $(5, 6)$, (ii) $(4, -6)$ and $(-2, 3)$.

4 Find a formula for the distance of the point (x, y, z) from the origin. Use your result to say what locus is represented by the equation

$$x^2 + y^2 + z^2 = 25.$$

5 Find the distance between the points (i) $(4, 1, 0)$ and $(6, 4, 6)$, (ii) $(-4, -1, -4)$ and $(-7, -5, 8)$.

6 Find to the nearest tenth of a unit the distance between the points (i) $(1, 2, 3)$ and $(2, 3, 4)$, (ii) $(-3, 5, 7)$ and $(2, -4, 6)$.

7 A rectangular room is l metres long, b metres broad, h metres high. Prove that the length of a diagonal is $\sqrt{l^2 + b^2 + h^2}$ metres.

8 If $\sin \theta = \frac{12}{13}$, find $\cos \theta$ without using tables.

9 If $\cos \theta = \frac{7}{25}$, find $\sin \theta$ without using tables.

10 Simplify: (i) $a^2 - a^2 \sin^2 \theta$, (ii) $\sqrt{a^2 - a^2 \cos^2 \theta}$.

11 If $\sin \theta = s$, express $3 - 2\cos^2 \theta - 3\sin \theta$ in terms of s. Factorise your answer, and hence find the values of θ between $0°$ and $180°$ for which $3 - 2\cos^2 \theta - 3\sin \theta = 0$.

12 Express $\cos^2 \alpha - \sin^2 \alpha$, (i) in terms of $\cos \alpha$ only, (ii) in terms of $\sin \alpha$ only.

13 If $P \cos \alpha = 11$ and $P \sin \alpha = 60$, calculate the value of P. (Square the two equations and add them together.)

The Cosine Rule Pythagoras' Theorem tells us the square on the side of a triangle opposite a right angle; in Fig. 302 (i), $a^2 = b^2 + c^2$. If, now, the angle A is made less than a right angle, the sides AB and AC remaining unchanged in length, as in Fig. 302 (ii), it is obvious that the new value of a^2 will be *less* than $b^2 + c^2$.

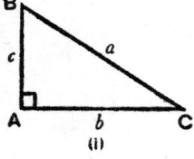 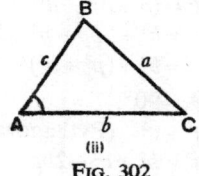 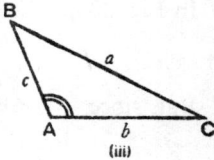

FIG. 302

If, on the other hand, the angle A is made greater than a right angle, as in Fig. 302 (iii), then the new value of a^2 will be *greater* than $b^2 + c^2$.

The object of the Cosine Rule is to answer the question: how much less or greater in each case? and to find a formula for a^2 in terms of b, c and angle A, whatever may be the size of that angle.

Let ABC be a triangle in which $\angle A$ is acute in Fig. 303, obtuse in Fig. 304.

Draw BN perpendicular to AC. Let $BN = h$, $AN = p$, so that $CN = b - p$ in Fig. 303, or $b + p$ in Fig. 304.

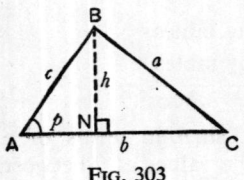

FIG. 303

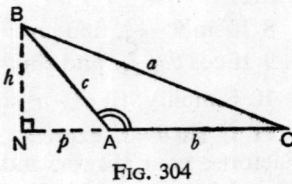

FIG. 304

Since $\qquad \angle BNC = 90°$,
$$a^2 = CN^2 + BN^2 \quad \text{(Pythagoras')}.$$

In Fig. 303, $\qquad a^2 = (b-p)^2 + h^2$
$$= b^2 - 2bp + p^2 + h^2$$
$$= b^2 + (p^2 + h^2) - 2bp.$$

But, since $\qquad \angle BNA = 90°$,
$$p^2 + h^2 = c^2 \quad \text{(Pythagoras')}.$$
$$\therefore \qquad a^2 = b^2 + c^2 - 2bp.$$

Now in the right-angled $\triangle BNA$, $p = c \cos A$.
$$\therefore \qquad a^2 = b^2 + c^2 - 2bc \cos A.$$

In Fig. 304, $\qquad a^2 = (b+p)^2 + h^2$
$$= b^2 + 2bp + p^2 + h^2$$
$$= b^2 + (p^2 + h^2) + 2bp.$$

But, since $\qquad \angle BNA = 90°$,
$$p^2 + h^2 = c^2 \quad \text{(Pythagoras')}.$$
$$\therefore \qquad a^2 = b^2 + c^2 + 2bp.$$

Now in the right-angled $\triangle$BNA,

$$p = c \cos \text{BAN}$$
$$= c \cos (180° - \text{A}) = -c \cos \text{A}.$$
$$\therefore \ a^2 = b^2 + c^2 - 2bc \cos \text{A}.$$

Thus, whether A is acute or obtuse,

$$a^2 = b^2 + c^2 - 2bc \ cos \ \text{A}.$$

This is the **Cosine Rule.** In a similar way it can be proved that

$$b^2 = c^2 + a^2 - 2ca \cos \text{B},$$
and $$c^2 = a^2 + b^2 - 2ab \cos \text{C}.$$

The Cosine Rule is true also for a right-angled triangle; for if A = 90°, cos 90° = 0, and the formula becomes $a^2 = b^2 + c^2$.

Notice that when we are writing down the expression for the square on the side of $\triangle$ABC opposite $\angle$A, the first two terms on the right are exactly the same as they would be if $\angle$A were a right angle. We then proceed to take away $2bc \cos$ A. If $\angle$A is acute, we are subtracting a positive quantity; but if $\angle$A is obtuse, its cosine is negative, and we are subtracting a negative quantity, i.e. in fact, *adding* something. This agrees with what was said about Fig. 302 (ii) and (iii). Thus the one formula $a^2 = b^2 + c^2 - 2bc \cos$ A gives the square on the side of a triangle in terms of the other two sides and the angle they include, whether that angle is acute, obtuse, or a right angle.

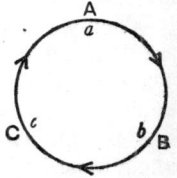

FIG. 305

Notice also that every term in the Cosine Rule is of the second degree (for cos A is a *ratio* and has no dimensions).

The other forms of the Cosine Rule can be deduced from the formula $a^2 = b^2 + c^2 - 2bc \cos$ A by changing the letters in what is called **cyclic order,** i.e. a becomes b, b becomes c, c becomes a, and similarly for capital letters. (See Fig. 305.) This gives $b^2 = c^2 + a^2 - 2ca \cos$ B. A similar change in this result produces $c^2 = a^2 + b^2 - 2ab \cos$ C.

Since $\qquad a^2 = b^2 + c^2 - 2bc \cos A,$

$\qquad \therefore 2bc \cos A = b^2 + c^2 - a^2.$

Thus, making $\cos A$ the subject of the Cosine Rule, we obtain

$$\cos A = \frac{b^2 + c^2 - a^2}{2bc},$$

which is a useful formula for finding the angle A when the three sides are known.   Similarly,

$$\cos B = \frac{c^2 + a^2 - b^2}{2ca},$$

$$\cos C = \frac{a^2 + b^2 - c^2}{2ab}.$$

Use of the Cosine Rule   On account of the unsuitability of the Cosine Rule for logarithmic calculation, use tables of squares and square roots to shorten the work.   Even then the calculation is apt to be tedious unless the lengths of the sides are easy numbers.

When solving a triangle in which two sides and the included angle are given, first find the third side by the Cosine Rule. Then use the Sine Rule to find the smaller of the two unknown angles.   This avoids any doubt as to whether the angle whose sine is obtained should be acute or obtuse, for the smaller angle must be acute.

When solving a triangle in which the three sides are given, find the largest angle by the Cosine Rule.   Then find a second angle by the Sine Rule.   In this way you avoid the need to decide whether the angle found by the Sine Rule is acute or obtuse.

It is never necessary to use the Cosine Rule more than once in solving a triangle.

Example 2   *Solve* $\triangle ABC$ *in which* $b = 15 \cdot 7$, $c = 7 \cdot 69$, $A = 27° 8'$.

$\qquad a^2 = b^2 + c^2 - 2bc \cos A$

$\qquad\quad = 15 \cdot 7^2 + 7 \cdot 69^2 - 2 \times 15 \cdot 7 \times 7 \cdot 69 \cos 27° 8'.$

THE COSINE RULE 371

$$\therefore a^2 = 246 \cdot 5 + 59 \cdot 14 - 214 \cdot 9$$

No.	Log.
2	0·3010
15·7	1·1959
7·69	0·8859
cos 27° 8′	$\bar{1}$·9494
214·9	2·3322

$$= 305 \cdot 6 - 214 \cdot 9$$

$$= 90 \cdot 7.$$

$$\therefore a = 9 \cdot 525.$$

Since c is less than b, C must be less than B, and must therefore be acute. By the Sine Rule,

$$\frac{\sin C}{c} = \frac{\sin A}{a}.$$

No.	Log.
7·69	0·8859
sin 27° 8′	$\bar{1}$·6590
	0·5449
9·525	0·9788
sin 21° 36′	$\bar{1}$·5661

$$\therefore \sin C = \frac{c \sin A}{a}$$

$$= \frac{7 \cdot 69 \sin 27° 8'}{9 \cdot 525}.$$

$$\therefore \quad C = 21° 36'.$$

$$\therefore \quad B = 180° - (27° 8' + 21° 36')$$

$$= 180° - 48° 44'$$

$$= 131° 16'.$$

The fourth figures throughout are unreliable, but should be retained in the working. The answers should then be corrected to three significant figures:

$$a = 9 \cdot 52, \quad C = 21° 36', \quad B = 131° 16' \text{ (approx.)}.$$

Example 3 *Solve* △ABC *in which* $a = 3 \cdot 67$, $b = 8 \cdot 16$, $c = 5 \cdot 21$.

We begin by finding the largest angle, B (opposite the biggest side).

$$\cos B = \frac{c^2 + a^2 - b^2}{2ca}$$

$$= \frac{5 \cdot 21^2 + 3 \cdot 67^2 - 8 \cdot 16^2}{2 \times 5 \cdot 21 \times 3 \cdot 67}$$

$$= \frac{27 \cdot 14 + 13 \cdot 47 - 66 \cdot 59}{2 \times 5 \cdot 21 \times 3 \cdot 67}$$

$$= \frac{40 \cdot 61 - 66 \cdot 59}{2 \times 5 \cdot 21 \times 3 \cdot 67}$$

$$= -\frac{25 \cdot 98}{2 \times 5 \cdot 21 \times 3 \cdot 67}.$$

No.	Log.
25·98	1·4147
2	0·3010
5·21	0·7168
3·67	0·5647
Den.	1·5825
cos 47° 12′	$\bar{1}$·8322

$$\therefore B = 180° - 47° 12'$$
$$= 132° 48' \text{ (approx.)}.$$

We next find A. By the Sine Rule,

$$\frac{\sin A}{a} = \frac{\sin B}{b}.$$

$$\therefore \sin A = \frac{a \sin B}{b}$$

$$= \frac{3 \cdot 67 \sin 132° 48'}{8 \cdot 16}.$$

No.	Log.
3·67	0·5647
sin 47° 12′	$\bar{1}$·8655
Num.	0·4302
8·16	0·9117
sin 19° 16′	$\bar{1}$·5185

$\therefore$ A $= 19°$ 16′ (approx.).

$\therefore$ C $= 180° - (132°$ 48′ $+ 19°$ 16′$)$

$\qquad = 180° - 152°$ 4′

$\qquad = 27°$ 56′ (approx.).

EXERCISE 117

1 $b = 8$, $c = 5$, A $= 60°$; find a.

2 $a = 3$, $c = 4$, B $= 45°$; find b.

3 $a = 4$, $b = 5$, C $= 120°$; find c.

4 $a = 4$, $b = 5$, $c = 6$; find A and B.

5 $a = 10$, $b = 5$, $c = 8$; find C and B.

6 A $= 140°$, $b = 9$, $c = 11$; find a.

7 $a = 6·1$, $b = 7·8$, $c = 2·4$; find B.

8 $a = 51·2$, $b = 37·5$, $c = 15·0$; find A.

9 $a = 17$, $b = 8$, $c = 10$; find the smallest angle.

10 $b = 15$, $c = 11$, A $= 108°$; find a.

Solve the following triangles:

11 $b = 11·2$, $c = 12·9$, A $= 56°$.

12 $a = 36·9$, $b = 51·7$, C $= 19°$.

13 B $= 114°$, $a = 22$, $c = 19·5$.

14 $a = 10·9$, $b = 5·8$, $c = 6·2$.

15 $a = 41·7$, $b = 56·3$, $c = 76·8$.

16 $a = 2·53$, $c = 3·26$, B $= 41°$ 36′.

17 $b = 20·6$, $c = 36·5$, A $= 113°$ 22′.

18 $a = 133$, $b = 468$, $c = 372$.

The following problems contain applications of the Sine and Cosine Rules.

19 A and B are two ports 8 km apart on a straight piece of coast, B being due E. of A. A ship leaves A at noon, and steams at 16 km/h on a bearing 030°. Calculate to the nearest minute the time at which the ship is north-west of B.

20 P and Q are two stations 6 km apart, and S is a ship at sea. It is found that $\angle SPQ = 65°$ and $\angle SQP = 78°$. Find SP, SQ, and the perpendicular distance of S from the line PQ.

21 AB and BC are two straight roads; AB = 430 m, BC = 560 m and $\angle ABC = 152°$. Find to the nearest metre how much shorter it is to go from A to C in a straight line across the fields instead of going by road.

22 Two searchlights A and B, 4 km apart, are both turned on an aeroplane which is vertically above the line AB. The angle of elevation of the beam from A is 73°, while that from B is 49°. Find the height of the aeroplane in metres.

23 Two sides of a parallelogram are 8 and 11 cm long, and one angle is 50°. Find the lengths of the diagonals.

24 Two sides of a parallelogram are 2 cm and 3 cm, and one of the diagonals is 4·1 cm long. Find the angles of the parallelogram.

25 Two ships leave a port at the same time; one steams at 10 km/h on a bearing 115°, the other steams at 16 km/h on a bearing 345°. Find their distance apart after 2 hours.

26 Two ships are observed from a lighthouse. One is found to be 4 km away in a direction N. 31° E., the other 5 km away in a direction N. 15° W. Find the distance apart of the two ships, and also the bearing of the first ship from the second.

27 ABCD is a kite in which AB = AD = 90 cm, CB = CD = 180 cm and AC = 240 cm. Find the length of BD.

28 A and B are two observers, A being 5000 m due W. of B. They both take the bearings of a position P; A finds it to be on a bearing 056°, while B finds it to be on a bearing 017°. Find the distance of P from A.

29 A ship is steaming due E. At a certain moment, it is observed from a shore station to be 4 km distant on a bearing 020°. Ten minutes later the ship is observed from the same station to be on a bearing 035°. Calculate the speed of the ship.

30 Find by calculation whether the triangles whose sides are (i) 8, 15, 17 cm, (ii) 9, 15, 18 cm have their largest angle acute, right, or obtuse.

31 A triangle ABC is marked out on horizontal ground; AB = 8 m, BC = 15 m, CA = 20 m. A vertical pole AP, 15 m long, is erected at A. Calculate the angle BPC.

32 Find without drawing whether the greatest angle in each of the following triangles is acute, right, or obtuse: (i) sides 15, 12, 7 cm, (ii) sides 15, 12, 10 cm, (iii) sides 50, 48, 14 cm.

33 In the rectangle ABCD, AB = 9 cm and BC = 4 cm; P is a point in the side AB, and AP = 6 cm. Find without drawing whether $\angle$CPD is acute, right, or obtuse.

34 A and B are two boats at sea, 500 m apart, in line with the foot of a cliff, A being the nearer boat. The angles of depression of A and B from the top of the cliff are 41° and 25°. Calculate the distance in a straight line from A to the top of the cliff, and hence find the height of the cliff.

35 In $\triangle$ABC, B = 120°, a = 6·4 cm, c = 4 cm. Calculate b and the angles A and C.

36 In $\triangle$ABC, AC = 21 cm, AB = 15 cm, BC = 9 cm. Prove that $\angle$ABC = 120°, and find $\angle$ACB.

37 In the quadrilateral ABCD, AB = 3 cm, BC = 3 cm, CD = 5 cm, DA = 8 cm and BD = 7 cm. Prove that the quadrilateral is cyclic. (*Hint*. Find cos A and cos C.)

38 A and B are two points on a hillside, and PQ is a tower at the top of the hill; A, B and the foot Q of the tower are in the same line, and AB = 60 m. The angle of elevation of P from A is 52° 51′, and from B it is 72° 35′; AB makes an angle of 18° with the horizontal. Calculate AP and the height of P above A.

THEOREM 30 (Apollonius' Theorem)

The sum of the squares on two sides of a triangle is equal to twice the square on half the third side plus twice the square on the median which bisects the third side.

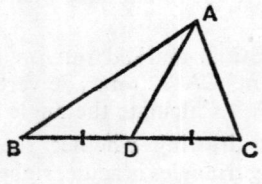

FIG. 306

Given a $\triangle$ABC, in which D is the mid-point of BC.

To prove that
$$AB^2 + AC^2 = 2BD^2 + 2AD^2.$$

Proof

In $\triangle$BDA, $AB^2 = BD^2 + AD^2 - 2BD \cdot AD \cos ADB$
                                            (Cosine Rule).

In $\triangle$CDA, $AC^2 = DC^2 + AD^2 - 2DC \cdot AD \cos ADC$
                                            (Cosine Rule).

But $BD = DC$ (given).

           $\therefore BD^2 = DC^2$.

Also $\angle ADB = 180° - \angle ADC$.

           $\therefore \cos ADB = -\cos ADC$.

Hence, $AB^2 = BD^2 + AD^2 + 2BD \cdot AD \cos ADC$,

and $AC^2 = BD^2 + AD^2 - 2BD \cdot AD \cos ADC$.

Adding, $AB^2 + AC^2 = 2BD^2 + 2AD^2$.

Reference AD is a median,

          $\therefore AB^2 + AC^2 = 2BD^2 + 2AD^2$ (*Apollonius'*).

Example 4 ABCD *is a parallelogram in which* AB = 11 *cm,* BC = 12 *cm and the diagonal* BD = 13 *cm. Calculate the length of the diagonal* AC.

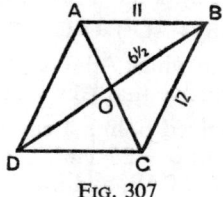

Fɪɢ. 307

Let BD and AC cut at O. Then BO = $6\frac{1}{2}$ cm.

In △BAC, BO is a median (diags. of parm. bisect one another).

$$\therefore \quad BA^2 + BC^2 = 2AO^2 + 2BO^2 \quad \text{(Apollonius')}$$
$$\therefore \quad 121 + 144 = 2AO^2 + 2 \times \tfrac{169}{4}.$$
$$\therefore \quad 265 = 2AO^2 + 84\tfrac{1}{2}.$$
$$\therefore \quad 2AO^2 = 180\tfrac{1}{2} = \tfrac{361}{2}.$$
$$\therefore \quad AO^2 = \tfrac{361}{4}.$$
$$\therefore \quad AO = \tfrac{19}{2}.$$
$$\therefore \quad AC = 2AO = 19 \text{ cm.}$$

EXERCISE 118

1 In △ABC, AB = 14 cm, BC = 18 cm, CA = 8 cm. Calculate the length of the median from A.

2 Calculate to the nearest mm the lengths of the three medians of a triangle whose sides are 4, 5, 6 cm long.

3 In △ABC, AB = 13 cm, AC = 29 cm and the median AD = 12 cm. Calculate the length of BC.

4 The sides of a parallelogram are 9 cm and 13 cm and one diagonal is 10 cm long. Calculate the length of the other diagonal.

5 ABCD is a rectangle, and P is any point in the plane ABCD. The diagonals of ABCD intersect at O, and PO is joined. By applying Apollonius' Theorem to △s PBD and PAC, prove that $PA^2 + PC^2 = PB^2 + PD^2$.

Is the same result true if P is *outside* the plane ABCD?

6 ABCD is a parallelogram. Prove that

$$2(AB^2 + AD^2) = AC^2 + BD^2.$$

7 ABC is a triangle in which $AB = AC$; BC is produced to D, such that $BC = CD$. Prove that $AD^2 = 2BC^2 + AB^2$.

8 A and B are two fixed points 4 cm apart; P is a variable point such that $PA^2 + PB^2 = 26$ cm². Find the locus of P. (Join P to the mid-point of AB, and use Apollonius' Theorem.)

9 The side BC of △ABC is trisected at P and Q, so that $BP = PQ = QC$. By applying Apollonius' Theorem to △s ABQ, APC, prove that $AB^2 + AC^2 = AP^2 + AQ^2 + 4PQ^2$.

10 AD, BE, CF are the medians of △ABC. Prove that:

(i) $2AB^2 + 2AC^2 = 4AD^2 + BC^2$;

(ii) $4AD^2 + 4BE^2 + 4CF^2 = 3AB^2 + 3BC^2 + 3CA^2$.

40. THE ALTERNATE SEGMENT PROPERTY OF THE CIRCLE

IN Fig. 308, XAY is a tangent to the circle at A, and AB is any chord drawn through the point of contact A. The two angles formed between the chord and the tangent are $\angle BAY$ and $\angle BAX$.

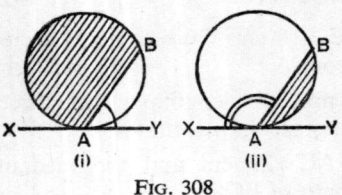

FIG. 308

In Fig. 308 (i), the shaded segment is said to be **alternate** to $\angle BAY$; in Fig. 308 (ii), the shaded segment is alternate to $\angle BAX$.

In Exercise 65, p. 202, Nos. 32 and 33, it was proved that $\angle BAY$ in Fig. 308 (i) equals any angle subtended by AB in the shaded major segment; and that $\angle BAX$ in Fig. 308 (ii) equals any angle subtended by AB in the shaded minor segment. The formal proof of this theorem now follows.

THEOREM 31

If a straight line touches a circle and, from the point of contact, a chord is drawn, the angles between the chord and the tangent are equal to the angles in the alternate segments.

Given a straight line XAY touching a circle at A, and a chord AB. In Fig. 309 (i), $\angle$BPA is an angle in the segment alternate to $\angle$BAY; in Fig. 309 (ii), $\angle$BQA is an angle in the segment alternate to $\angle$BAX.

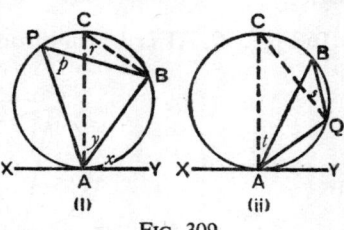

To prove that
(i) $\angle$BAY = $\angle$BPA,
(ii) $\angle$BAX = $\angle$BQA.

FIG. 309

Construction Draw the diameter AC. Join CB in Fig. (i), CQ in Fig. (ii).

Proof (i) In Fig. (i), let $\angle$BAY $=x$, $\angle$BAC$=y$, $\angle$BPA$=p$, $\angle$BCA$=r$.

$$\angle ABC = 90° \quad (\angle \text{ in semicircle}),$$

and $\quad y+r+ \angle ABC = 180° \quad$ (angle-sum of $\triangle$).

$$\therefore \; y+r=90°.$$

But $\quad\quad\quad\quad y+x=90° \quad$ (tan. perp. radius).

$$\therefore \quad x=r.$$

Also $\quad\quad\quad\quad\quad r=p \quad$ (same seg.).

$$\therefore \quad x=p.$$

(ii) In Fig. (ii), let $\angle$BQC $=s$, $\angle$BAC$=t$.

$$\angle CQA = 90° \quad (\angle \text{ in semicircle}),$$

and $\quad\quad\quad \angle CAX = 90° \quad$ (tan. perp. radius).

$$\therefore \quad \angle BAX = 90°+t$$

and $\quad\quad\quad \angle BQA = 90°+s.$

But $\quad\quad\quad\quad\quad t=s \quad$ (same seg.),

$$\therefore \quad \angle BAX = \angle BQA.$$

Reference $\quad\quad \angle$BAY $= \angle$BPA $\quad$ (*alt. seg.*),

$\quad\quad\quad\quad\quad\quad \angle$BAX $= \angle$BQA $\quad$ (*alt. seg.*).

The Converse of the Alternate Segment Theorem, which we shall assume without proof, states:

If a straight line is drawn through one end of a chord of a circle making with the chord an angle equal to the angle in the alternate segment, then the straight line is a tangent to the circle.

In Fig. 310, AT is drawn through the end A of the chord AB.

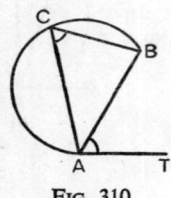

Fig. 310

If ∠BAT = ∠BCA, then AT will be the tangent at A to the circle ABC.

EXERCISE 119

1 In Fig. 311, if ∠BAT = 30° and ∠BAC = 70°, calculate ∠s ATB, ABC.

2 In Fig. 311, if ∠CAT = 130° and ∠ATB = 20°, calculate ∠s ABC, BAT, BCA.

3 In Fig. 311, if ∠ABC = 66° and ∠ATB = 33°, prove that △ACT is isosceles.

4 In Fig. 311, if ∠BAT = 26° and ∠CAS = 49°, calculate the angles of △ABC.

5 In Fig. 312, if ∠BAY = 43°, calculate ∠s BPA, BQA.

6 In Fig. 312, if ∠BPA = 38° and ∠PAX = 54°, calculate ∠s BAY, PAB and PBA.

7 In Fig. 312, if ∠QAX = 155°, calculate ∠ABQ.

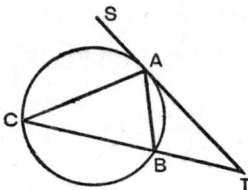

TAS is the tangent at A;
TBC is a straight line

FIG. 311

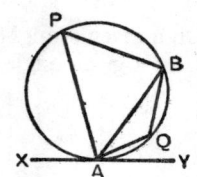

XAY is the tangent at A

FIG. 312

8 In Fig. 312, if $\angle PAX = 50°$ and $\angle BQA = 120°$, calculate the angles of $\triangle PAB$.

9 In Fig. 312, if $\angle QAY = 30°$ and $\angle BPQ = 20°$, calculate $\angle$s BQA, BPA.

10 In Fig. 313, if $\angle YXZ = 70°$ and $\angle XYZ = 44°$, calculate $\angle$s A and B.

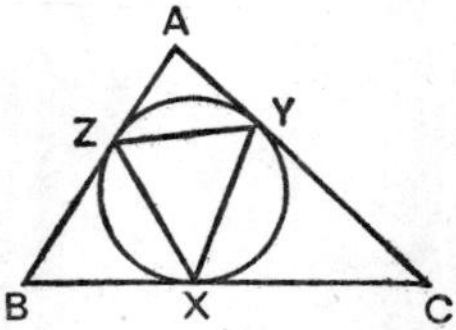

X,Y,Z are the points of contact of the inscribed circle

FIG. 313

11 In Fig. 313, if $\angle ZBX = 70°$, calculate $\angle ZYX$.

12 In Fig. 313, if $\angle B = 54°$ and $\angle C = 28°$, calculate the angles of $\triangle XYZ$.

13 In Fig. 311, draw the bisector of $\angle BAC$ to meet BC at D. If $\angle BAC = 64°$ and $\angle ACB = 31°$, calculate $\angle$s TAD, TDA, and deduce that the triangle TAD is isosceles.

14 In the triangle ABC, $\angle ABC = 44°$ and $\angle ACB = 62°$. D is a point in the side BC such that $\angle BAD = 30°$. Prove that CA is the tangent at A to the circle through the points A, B, D.

15 ABCD is a cyclic quadrilateral, and the diagonals AC, BD are joined. The parallel through D to AB meets AC at X. If the angle $ABD = 24°$, calculate the angles BDX, DCX. To what circle is DB the tangent at D?

CONSTRUCTION 8

On a given straight line, to construct a segment of a circle to contain a given angle.

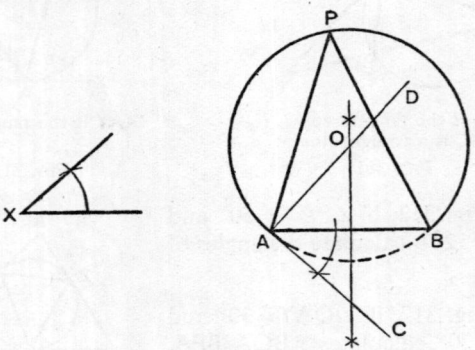

FIG. 314

Given a straight line AB and an angle X.

To construct a segment of a circle on AB to contain an angle equal to ∠X.

Construction   Construct at A an angle BAC equal to ∠X.
Draw AD perpendicular to AC.
Draw the perpendicular bisector of AB, and let it cut AD at O.
With centre O, radius OA, draw a circle.
Then the segment of this circle which is alternate to ∠BAC is the required segment.

Proof   Let APB be any angle in this segment.
Since O lies on the perpendicular bisector of AB (constr.),

$$OA = OB.$$

∴ the circle passes through B.
Since OA is a radius and ∠OAC = 90° (constr.),
AC is a tangent to the circle (tan. perp. radius).

∴	∠BAC = ∠APB	(alt. seg.).
But	∠BAC = ∠X	(constr.),
∴	∠APB = ∠X.	

EXERCISE 120

(*Numerical*)

1 In Fig. 315, if ∠QAT = 16° and ∠QBT = 37°, calculate ∠s APB, AQB, AOB, ATB.

2 In Fig. 315, if ∠ATB = 48° and ∠QBT = 42°, calculate ∠s AOB, APB, QAT.

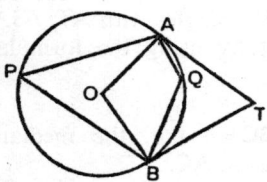

TA, TB are tangents to the circle, centre O

FIG. 315

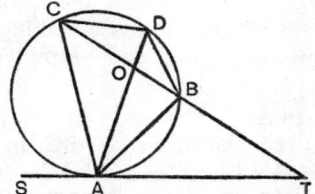

SAT is the tangent at A; TBC is a straight line

FIG. 316

3 In Fig. 315, if ∠ATB = 54° and ∠OAQ = 75°, calculate ∠s APB, QBT.

4 In Fig. 316, if ∠ATB = 35°, ∠ACB = 40° and ∠BCD = 26°, calculate ∠s ABC, AOC.

5 In Fig. 316, if ∠COD = 72° and ∠CBD = 31°, calculate ∠BAT.

6 In Fig. 316, if ∠BAT = 53° and ∠BTA = 46°, calculate ∠CAS.

7 In Fig. 313, if ∠XYZ = 51° and ∠XYC = 67°, calculate the angles of △ABC.

8 A and B are the points of contact of the tangents from a point T to a circle, and AC is a chord of the circle parallel to TB. If ∠ATB = 68°, calculate the angles of △ABC.

9 In Fig. 316, if ∠BTA = ∠BAT = 38° and TO = TA, calculate ∠s OAT, CDA, CAD.

10 In Fig. 316, if ∠BAT = 53° and ∠BTA = 23°, and P is the mid-point of the minor arc AC, calculate ∠s CPA, PCB, CDB.

Constructions

11 On a straight line 6 cm long, construct a segment of a circle to contain an angle of 67°. Measure the radius.

12 On a straight line 5 cm long, construct a segment of a circle to contain an angle of 130°. Measure the radius.

13 Draw a circle of radius 4 cm, and mark a point A on it. Inscribe in the circle a triangle ABC such that $\angle B = 57°$, $\angle C = 48°$. (Draw the tangent TAS at A, and draw chords AB, AC of the circle making appropriate angles with AT, AS.) Measure BC, and verify your result by using the formula $\dfrac{a}{\sin A} = 2R$.

14 Construct $\triangle ABC$ in which BC = 4 cm, the median AD = 4·6 cm and $\angle BAC = 40°$. Measure AC.

15 Construct $\triangle ABC$ in which AB = 6·8 cm, the altitude CN = 2 cm and $\angle ACB = 105°$. Measure AC.

16 Construct a quadrilateral ABCD in which AB = 5·6 cm, AD = 4·5 cm, BD = 8 cm, DC = 5 cm and $\angle BCD = 80°$. Measure AC.

17 In Fig. 317, A and B are two landmarks on the coast, 4 km apart, and S is a ship at sea. The navigation chart says that, if $\angle ASB$ is greater than 104°, there is danger from

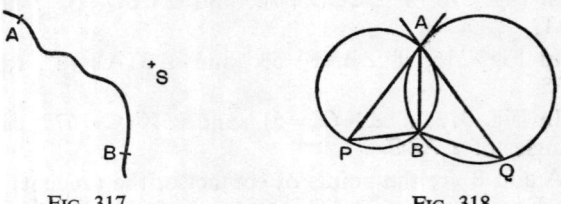

Fig. 317   Fig. 318

hidden rocks. Draw an accurate diagram to the scale of 2 cm to the kilometre and shade the part of the sea which is dangerous.

(Riders)

18 In Fig. 318, AP and AQ are the tangents at A to the circles. Prove that $\angle ABP = \angle ABQ$.

19 In Fig. 311, p. 381, prove that $\angle ABT = \angle CAT$.

20 In Fig. 319, prove that $\angle ABC = \angle ATB$.

21 In Fig. 320, prove that $\angle TAE = \angle ETC$.

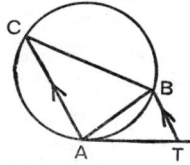

AT is the tangent at A

FIG. 319

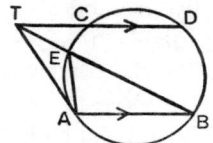

TA is the tangent at A;
TCD, TEB are straight lines

FIG. 320

22 In Fig. 311, if the bisector of $\angle BAC$ meets BC at D, prove that $TA = TD$.

23 The bisector of $\angle A$ of $\triangle ABC$ meets BC at D. A circle is drawn touching BC at D and passing through A, and this circle cuts AB at P, AC at Q. Prove that $\angle PDB = \angle QDC$.

24 XAY is the tangent at A to a circle, and AB is a chord. If P, Q are the mid-points of the two arcs into which the chord divides the circle, prove that AP, AQ are the bisectors of the angles between the chord AB and the tangent at A.

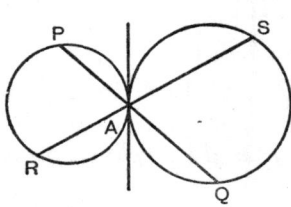

FIG. 321

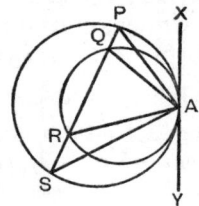

FIG. 322

25 In Fig. 321, the circles touch externally at A; PAQ, RAS are straight lines. Prove that RP is parallel to QS.

26 In Fig. 322, the circles touch internally at A, and PQRS is a straight line; XAY is the common tangent at A. If $\angle PAX = x°$ and $\angle QAX = y°$, express $\angle$s QRA, RSA, PAQ in terms of x and y, and deduce that $\angle PAQ = \angle RAS$.

27 In Fig. 312, assume that $\angle BAY = \angle BPA$, and prove that $\angle BAX = \angle BQA$. (Use the fact that $\angle$s BPA, BQA are opposite angles of the cyclic quadrilateral APBQ.) This is an alternative method of proving part (ii) of Theorem 31.

28 In Fig. 323, prove that $\angle ACX = \angle CDX$. Hence prove that AC is the tangent at C to the circumcircle of $\triangle DXC$.

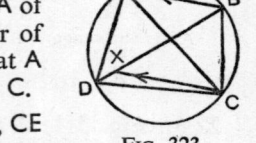

29 The internal bisector of the angle A of $\triangle ABC$ meets the perpendicular bisector of AC at P. Prove that AB is the tangent at A to the circle which passes through A, P, C.

30 ABCDE is a regular pentagon; BD, CE intersect at X. Prove that BC is a tangent to the circumcircle of $\triangle BXE$.

Fig. 323

31 ABCD is a cyclic quadrilateral in which $AB = BC$; the diagonals AC, BD intersect at X. Prove that BC is a tangent to the circle CXD.

41. GRAPHS AND GRAPHICAL SOLUTIONS

The cubic function in x has terms up to the third degree, and can be written, in its most general form, as

$$Ax^3 + Bx^2 + Cx + D.$$

We shall begin with the simplest cubic function, namely x^3.

Example 1 *Draw the graph of the function x^3 for values of x from -3 to $+3$, and find from the graph:* (i) *the cube of* $2 \cdot 6$, (ii) *the cube root of* 10.

The table of values is:

$x=$	-3	$-2\frac{1}{2}$	-2	$-1\frac{1}{2}$	-1	$-\frac{1}{2}$	0	$\frac{1}{2}$	1
$y=$	-27	$-15 \cdot 6$	-8	$-3 \cdot 4$	-1	$-0 \cdot 1$	0	0.1	1

$x=$	$1\frac{1}{2}$	2	$2\frac{1}{2}$	3
$y=$	$3 \cdot 4$	8	$15 \cdot 6$	27

Take 2 cm as the unit on the x-axis, 0·2 cm as the unit on the y-axis.   The graph is shown in Fig. 324.

When $x = 2·6$, $y = 17·6$. $\therefore$ $(2·6)^3 = 17·6$ (approx.).

When $y = 10$, $x = 2·2$. $\therefore$ $\sqrt[3]{10} = 2·2$ (approx.).

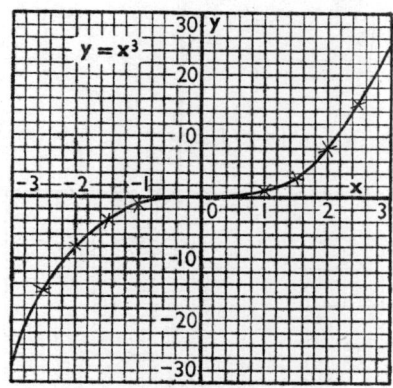

FIG. 324

Notice the following features of the graph:

(i) It occupies the first and third quadrants, and the two portions are similar.

(ii) It touches the x-axis at the origin.

(iii) The part in the first quadrant resembles part of the graph of $y = x^2$, but it is flatter near the origin and later rises more steeply.

(iv) It is symmetrical about the origin.   If (a, b) lies on the graph, so does $(-a, -b)$.

The student should draw his own graph of $y = x^3$ accurately, and then sketch in the same figure the graphs (i) $y = -x^3$, (ii) $y = \frac{1}{2}x^3$.

Example 2 *Draw the graph of the function* $x^3 - 3x + 1$ *from* $x = -3$ *to* $x = +3$.

The table of values is:

$x =$	-3	-2	-1	0	1	2	3
$x^3 =$	-27	-8	-1	0	1	8	27
$-3x =$	9	6	3	0	-3	-6	-9
1	1	1	1	1	1	1	1
$y =$	-17	-1	3	1	-1	3	19

The graph is shown in Fig. 325.

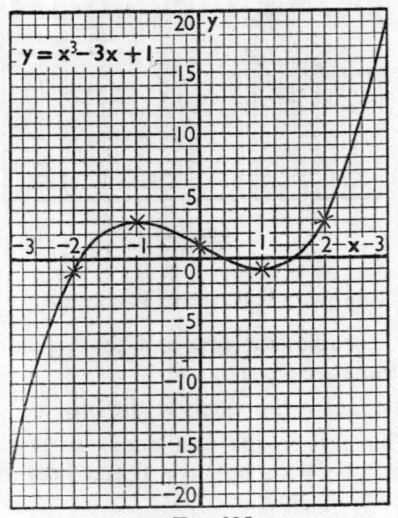

Fig. 325

Cubic function consisting of factors The function $(2x - 1)(x + 1)(x + 3)$ is a cubic function, for, upon multiplication of the factors, the highest power of x which occurs is the third power.

Example 3   *Sketch the graph of $y = (2x-1)(x+1)(x+3)$.*

The values of x for which $y = 0$ are $\frac{1}{2}$, -1, -3. These give the points marked A, B, C in Fig. 326. When $x = 0$, $y = -3$. This gives the point D. If x is large and positive, y is large and positive; but if x is large and negative, y is large and negative. When $x = -2$, $y = 5$. This gives the point E. The sketch of the graph is shown in Fig. 326.

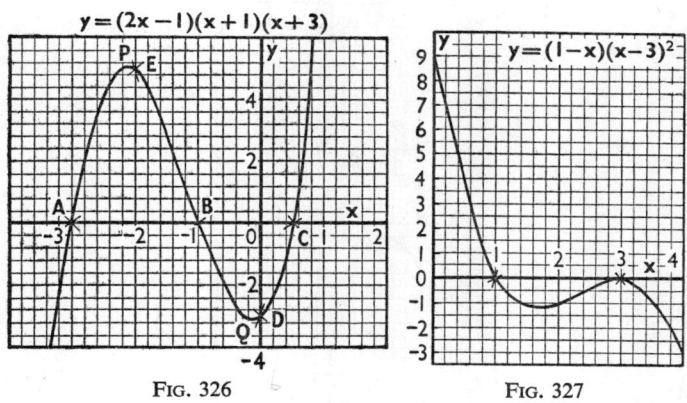

FIG. 326   FIG. 327

This is the typical cubic graph. It has two bends, whereas the quadratic graph has only one bend; in both cases, one less than the degree of the curve. A straight line cannot cut the cubic graph in more than three points. At the two points marked P and Q, the tangent is parallel to the x-axis, i.e., the gradient is 0. P is called a **maximum** point, Q a **minimum** point.

Cubic function with two factors equal

Example 4   *Sketch the graph of $y = (1-x)(x-3)^2$.*

The values of x which make y zero are 1, 3, 3. Two of the three points where the graph cuts the x-axis have now become one point, and the curve *touches* the x-axis at the point (3, 0). If $x = 0$, $y = 9$. If x is large and positive, y is large and negative;

but if x is large and negative, y is large and positive. The graph is sketched in Fig. 327.

Cubic function with three factors equal

Example 5 *Sketch the graph of $y = (x-2)^3$.*

The only value of x for which $y = 0$ is $x = 2$. All the three points where the graph crosses the x-axis have become one

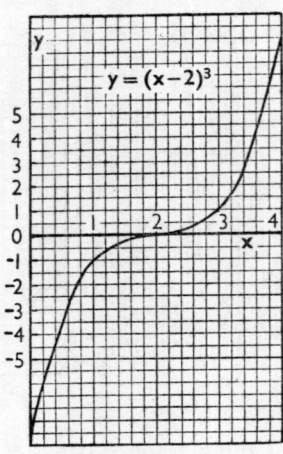

FIG. 328

point, and the graph touches the x-axis at $(2, 0)$. It crosses its own tangent at this point. If $x = 0$, $y = -8$.

The graph is sketched in Fig. 328. It resembles that of $y = x^3$, but is moved two units to the right.

EXERCISE 121

Plotting only a few necessary points, sketch the graphs of the following functions (Nos. 1–10):

1 $(x+1)(x-1)(x-3)$ **2** $(x+1)(1-x)(x-3)$

3 $x(x^2-9)$ **4** $x(4-x^2)$

5 $(x-1)(x+3)^2$ **6** $(2x-1)(x+1)(3x+2)$

7 $x^2(x-3)$ **8** $(x+2)^3$

9 $(3-x)(x+2)^2$ **10** $x(x+2)^2$

11 Draw accurately the graph of $y=\frac{1}{10}x(x^2-9)$ from $x=-4$ to $+4$, and use it to answer the following:

    (i) For what positive value of x has the function $x(x^2-9)$ a minimum value?

    (ii) For what negative value of x has the function a maximum value?

    (iii) For what values of x has the function $\frac{1}{10}x(x^2-9)$ the value $\frac{1}{2}$?

    (iv) Solve the equation $\frac{1}{10}x(x^2-9)=\frac{1}{5}$.

    (v) By drawing a tangent, estimate the gradient of the curve at the point where $x=3$.

12 Draw accurately the graph of $y=\frac{1}{5}x(x-2)(x+4)$ from $x=-4$ to $x=3$, and use it to answer the following:

    (i) For what value of x has the function $x(x-2)(x+4)$ a maximum value?

    (ii) For what value of x has the function a minimum value?

    (iii) For what value of x has the function $x(x-2)(x+4)$ the value 5?

    (iv) Solve the equation $x(x-2)(x+4)=12$.

    (v) By drawing tangents, estimate the gradients at the points where $x=2,\ -1,\ -3$.

13 Sketch the graphs of (i) $y=x^4$, (ii) $y=x^4+3$.

14 Draw an accurate graph of the function x^3 from $x=-3$ to $+3$, and, by drawing tangents, find the gradients of the function when x has the values: (i) 1, (ii) $1\frac{1}{2}$, (iii) -2, (iv) $2\frac{1}{2}$.

Graphical solution of equations One of the uses of graphs is the solution of equations which can be solved only with considerable labour, if at all, by other means. In order to explain the method, we shall commence with some simultaneous linear equations and easy quadratic equations which are more quickly solved by methods which the student knows already.

Example 6 *Solve graphically the simultaneous equations*

$$2y - 3x = 1,$$
$$y + 3x = 5.$$

Since these equations are of the first degree, their graphs are straight lines. Three points only need be plotted on each line (the third point as a check).

For the graph of $2y - 3x = 1$, take $x = -1,$ 0,   3.
                                   $y = -1,$ $\frac{1}{2},$ 5.
For the graph of $y + 3x = 5$, take $x =$ 0,   1,   2.
                                     $y =$ 5,   2, $-1.$

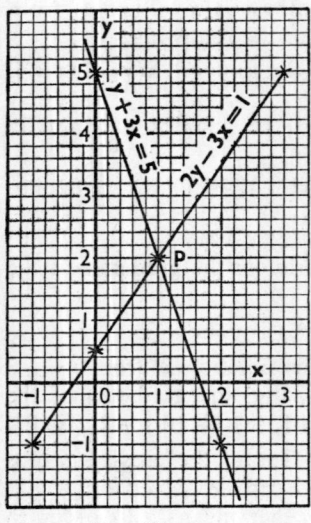

The graphs are shown in Fig. 329. The co-ordinates of the point of intersection P must satisfy *both* equations $2y - 3x = 1,$ $y + 3x = 5,$ for one line joins up all the points whose co-ordinates satisfy the first equation, and the other line joins up all the points whose co-ordinates satisfy the second equation, and P lies on both graphs. Now the co-ordinates of P are $x = 1, y = 2.$

∴ the solution of the simultaneous equations is $x = 1, y = 2.$

It is clear that the above method is quite general, and can be used for graphs which are not straight lines.

To solve a pair of simultaneous equations in x and y graphically, draw the graphs corresponding to the two equations, with the same axes and scales. The co-ordinates of the point (or points) of intersection of the graphs are the solutions of the simultaneous equations.

Fig. 329

Graphical solution of a quadratic

Example 7 *Solve graphically the equations:*

$$\text{(i) } x^2 - 4x - 1 = 0, \quad \text{(ii) } x^2 - 4x - 3 = 0.$$

(i) The graph of the function $x^2 - 4x - 1$ was drawn in Fig. 253, p. 303, and the equation $x^2 - 4x - 1 = 0$ was there solved by reading off the x co-ordinates of the points where the graph crosses the x-axis. This is equivalent to finding the intersections of the graphs of $y = x^2 - 4x - 1$ and $y = 0$. The roots are found to be 4·24, −0·24.

(ii) To solve the equation $x^2 - 4x - 3 = 0$,

$$\text{we say} \qquad x^2 - 4x \quad = 3.$$
$$\therefore \ x^2 - 4x - 1 = 2.$$

The solutions of the equation are the x co-ordinates of the points on the graph where the function has the value 2, i.e. where $y = 2$.

The roots are found to be 4·65, −0·65.

It is obvious that any equation of the type $x^2 - 4x - c = 0$ which has roots can be solved by the method just explained, using only the one graph, $y = x^2 - 4x - 1$.

Now consider the equation $x^2 - 2x - 4 = 0$. Instead of drawing a new graph, that of the function $x^2 - 2x - 4$, we can make use of the graph we have already (Fig. 253, p. 303) as follows:

$$x^2 - 2x - 4 = 0.$$
$$\therefore \ x^2 \qquad = 2x + 4.$$
$$\therefore \ x^2 - 4x - 1 = 2x + 4 - 4x - 1.$$
$$\therefore \ x^2 - 4x - 1 = -2x + 3,$$

thus making the left-hand side the same as the function whose graph we already possess.

The roots of the required quadratic are the x co-ordinates of the points of intersection of the graphs of $y = x^2 - 4x - 1$ and $y = -2x + 3$.

The graph of the first of these is Fig. 253. The graph of $y = -2x + 3$ is a straight line, which can easily be drawn. If a ruler is placed across Fig. 253 in the position of a straight line joining $(0, 3)$ and $(3, -3)$, the roots will be found to be $3 \cdot 24$, $-1 \cdot 24$.

Another method of solving graphically the equation $x^2 - 2x - 4 = 0$ (without using the graph of $y = x^2 - 4x - 1$) is to find the x co-ordinates of the points of intersection of the graphs of $y = x^2$ and $y = 2x + 4$. This is the method used in the next example.

Example 8 *Solve graphically the equation $x^2 - 2x - 4 = 0$.*
This is the same equation as $x^2 = 2x + 4$.
The graphs of $y = x^2$ and $y = 2x + 4$ are shown in Fig. 330

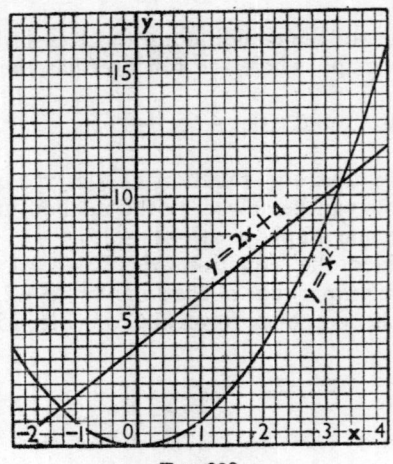

FIG. 330

The x co-ordinates of the points of intersection are $3 \cdot 24$, $-1 \cdot 24$. These are therefore the roots of the quadratic $x^2 - 2x - 4 = 0$.

The method just explained has the advantage that, once the

graph of $y = x^2$ has been carefully drawn, any quadratic equation can be solved (if it has roots) by drawing a line in pencil across the graph, or merely placing a ruler in the required position, and reading off the x co-ordinates of the points of intersection of the parabola and the straight line. If the line does not cut the parabola, the explanation is that the quadratic we are trying to solve has no roots.

A more difficult quadratic equation, such as $4x^2 - 7x - 9 = 0$, is dealt with as follows:

$$4x^2 - 7x - 9 = 0.$$
$$\therefore \qquad 4x^2 = 7x + 9.$$
$$\therefore \qquad x^2 = \frac{7x + 9}{4}.$$

The roots of the equation are therefore the x co-ordinates of the points of intersection of the straight line $y = \dfrac{7x + 9}{4}$ with the graph of $y = x^2$.

EXERCISE 122

Solve graphically the following simultaneous equations:

1 $y = 3x - 1,$
$y = 2 - x$

2 $y = 1 + 2x,$
$2y + x = 6$

3 $y - x = 3,$
$3y + x = 3$

4 $4x + 3y = 4,$
$3y - 4x = 8$

5 $3x + y = 3,$
$x - 3y = 4$

Solve graphically the equations in Nos. 6–12 by drawing the graph of $y = x^2$ from $x = -3$ to $+3$, using a scale of 2 cm on the x-axis and 1 cm on the y-axis, and drawing a suitable line in pencil across the graph.

6 $x^2 + x - 4 = 0$

7 $x^2 - 2x - 2 = 0$

8 $x^2 + 3x + 1 = 0$

9 $x^2 - x - 3 = 0$

10 $2x^2 + x - 8 = 0.$ (Rearrange as $x^2 = 4 - \frac{1}{2}x$.)

11 $3x^2 - 4x - 9 = 0.$ (Rearrange as $x^2 = \frac{4}{3}x + 3$.)

12 $5x^2 - 4x - 15 = 0$

Graphical solution of a cubic equation

A similar method in the case of a cubic equation is to find the intersection of a straight line with the graph of $y = x^3$, as in the next example.

Example 9   *Solve graphically the equation $x^3 - 4x + 2 = 0$.*

The equation is $x^3 = 4x - 2$. $\therefore$ the roots are the x co-ordinates of the points of intersection of the graphs of $y = x^3$ and $y = 4x - 2$. These graphs are shown in Fig. 331. The solutions are $x = -2\cdot21$, $0\cdot54$ or $1\cdot67$.

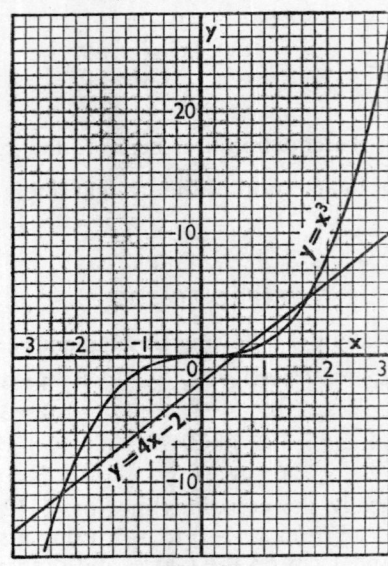

Fig. 331

EXERCISE 122 (*continued*)

Solve graphically the equations in Nos. 13–18 by drawing the graph of $y = x^3$ from $x = -3$ to $+3$, and drawing a suitable line in pencil across the graph.

13 $x^3 + 5x + 10 = 0$ **14** $x^3 - 7x - 4 = 0$.

15 $3x^3 - 8x - 15 = 0$. $\left(\text{Rearrange as } x^3 = \dfrac{8x + 15}{3}. \right)$

16 $2x^3 + 5x - 30 = 0$ **17** $5x^3 - 36x - 15 = 0$

18 $4x^3 - 27x + 27 = 0$

Solve graphically the equation $x^3 - 4x - 2 = 0$ by the methods indicated in Nos. 19–21, and compare your answers.

19 Draw the graph of $y = x^3 - 4x - 2$ from $x = -2$ to $+3$ and read off the values of x for which $y = 0$.

20 Draw the graph of $y = x(x-2)(x+2)$ from $x = -2$ to $+2\frac{1}{2}$ and read off the values of x for which $y = 2$.

21 Draw the graph of $y = x^3$ and a suitable straight line.

The inverse proportion graph In Fig. 62, p. 44, the time in hours to travel 120 km is plotted against the speed in km per hour. It is the graph of $\dfrac{120}{x}$. This is the typical inverse proportion graph. Its equation is $y = \dfrac{120}{x}$, or, as it is sometimes written, $xy = 120$, and it is of the second degree. As the value of x becomes larger and larger, that of y becomes smaller and smaller, and the graph approaches nearer and nearer to the x-axis. Similarly, as the value of y becomes larger and larger, that of x, or $\dfrac{120}{y}$, becomes smaller and smaller, and the graph approaches nearer and nearer to the y-axis. The graph shown on page 44 is drawn only for positive values of x and y. If x is negative, y is also negative; hence the graph occurs only in the first and third quadrants. The complete graph is shown in Fig. 332, on the next page. It must be regarded as a single graph, not as two graphs, and the two parts of the graph cannot be joined. There is no value of y corresponding to $x = 0$; for a journey of 120 km would never be completed if the speed were 0. Near $x = 0$, the function $\dfrac{120}{x}$ becomes greater and greater beyond measure.

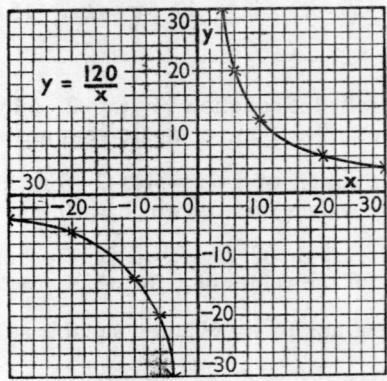

Fig. 332

When y is inversely proportional to x, then y is *directly* proportional to $\dfrac{1}{x}$, and the graph of y plotted against $\dfrac{1}{x}$ $\Bigl($ or x plotted against $\dfrac{1}{y}\Bigr)$ is a straight line. Such a graph is more useful, from a practical point of view, than that of $xy = k$.

The graph of $y = \dfrac{1}{x}$, or of $y = \dfrac{A}{x}$, where A is any number, will resemble Fig. 332. The graphs of the functions $\dfrac{120}{x}, \dfrac{120}{x-1}$, and $\dfrac{120}{x+3}$ differ only in their position relative to the axes. Graphs such as these are called **hyperbolic graphs**.

If a function does not exist for a certain value a of x, we call the line which consists of all the points $x = a$ an **asymptote**. The x-axis and the y-axis are the asymptotes of the curve $y = \dfrac{A}{x}$.

EXERCISE 123

When two graphs are to be drawn in the same question, the same axes and scales are to be used.

1 Copy and complete the following table of values for the graph of $y = \dfrac{x-3}{x-2}$.

$x=$	-4	-3	-2	-1	0	1	$1\frac{1}{2}$	$2\frac{1}{2}$	3	4	$4\frac{1}{2}$	5
$x-3=$	-7	-6					$-1\frac{1}{2}$	$-\frac{1}{2}$			$1\frac{1}{2}$	
$x-2=$	-6	-5					$-\frac{1}{2}$	$\frac{1}{2}$			$2\frac{1}{2}$	
$y=$	$1\frac{1}{6}$	$1\frac{1}{5}$					3	-1			$\frac{3}{5}$	

Plot the points, taking 1 cm as the unit for x and 2 cm as the unit for y.

Join up with a smooth curve the first 7 points plotted, and join up with another smooth curve the last 5 points. Do not try to plot a value for $x=2$ or to connect the two curves you have drawn. The function $\dfrac{x-3}{x-2}$ does not exist when $x=2$, and there is a break in the graph there.

2 Copy and complete the following table of values of the function $\dfrac{2x}{3+x}$ from $x=-6$ to $x=-3\frac{1}{2}$, and from $x=-2\frac{1}{2}$ to $x=4$.

$x=$	-6	-5	-4	$-3\frac{1}{2}$	$-2\frac{1}{2}$	-2	-1	0	1	2	3	4
$2x=$	-12	-10										
$3+x=$	-3	-2										
$y=$	4	5		14	-10	-4						

Draw the graph of the function from $x=-6$ to $-3\frac{1}{2}$ and from $x=-2\frac{1}{2}$ to 4. Do not attempt to plot a value for $x=-3$, or to join the two curves you have obtained.

3 Draw the graph of $y=x+\dfrac{6}{x}$ for values of x from -5 to $+5$ (excluding $x=0$). Find the least value of y when x is positive.

4 Draw the graph of $y = x - \dfrac{3}{x}$ from $x = -4$ to $+4$, excluding $x = 0$.

5 Draw on the same axes and scale the graphs of the functions $\dfrac{3x-1}{x+4}$ and $\dfrac{3x-5}{2}$, from $x = -3$ to $x = 3$. For what range of values of x is the first function greater than the second?

6 Draw the graph of $y = \dfrac{2-x}{1+x}$ from $x = -\frac{1}{2}$ to 4. Find from your graph a value of x within this range for which $y = 2x$. Check your solution by solving a certain equation.

7 Draw the graphs of the functions $\frac{1}{2}(x+1)(4-x)$ and $\dfrac{4}{x+3}$ from $x = -2$ to 3. Hence find two roots of the equation $(x+1)(4-x)(x+3) = 8$.

8 Draw the graph of $y = (x-1)(x+2)$ from $x = -3$ to 2. Draw also the graph of $y = \dfrac{4}{x+6}$, and use the graphs to find two roots of the equation $(x+6)(x-1)(x+2) = 4$.

42. SIMILAR FIGURES AND SOLIDS (II)

Similar figures were defined in § 10 as figures which are equiangular and have their corresponding sides proportional (see p. 79); that is, the larger figure is a magnification of the smaller. In the same way, two solids are said to be similar if all corresponding angles are equal and the ratio of corresponding lengths is constant.

Thus, two rectangles which have lengths 12 cm and 8 cm, breadths 9 cm and 6 cm, are similar; for they are equiangular (all the angles being right angles), and $\frac{12}{8} = \frac{9}{6} (= \frac{3}{2})$. Notice also that the ratio of *any* two corresponding lengths, e.g. the diagonals or perimeters, is $3 : 2$. The magnification is $\frac{3}{2}$.

Two right circular cones with heights 15 cm and 9 cm, base-radii 10 cm and 6 cm, are similar; for corresponding angles are equal (e.g. the angles between the axes and the planes of the bases, or between the axes and the slant heights), and $\frac{15}{9} = \frac{10}{6} (= \frac{5}{3})$. The ratio of the slant heights, or of the diameters of the bases, or of the circumferences of the bases, is $5 : 3$. The magnification is $\frac{5}{3}$.

Similar triangles It was pointed out in § 10 that polygons can be equiangular but not similar (for example, a square and a rectangle), and that polygons can have their corresponding sides proportional but not be similar (for example, a square and a rhombus). But this is not possible in the case of triangles. Exercise 22 showed that triangles which are equiangular to one another necessarily have their corresponding sides proportional, and are in fact similar; and also that triangles which have their corresponding sides proportional have their corresponding angles equal, and are in fact similar. The tests for similarity of triangles justify us in making the assumptions which follow:

ASSUMPTION 12 **If two triangles are equiangular, their corresponding sides are proportional.**

Thus, if $\triangle$s ABC, PQR are such that $\angle A = \angle P$, $\angle B = \angle Q$, and $\angle C = \angle R$, then $\triangle$s $\begin{smallmatrix}\text{ABC}\\\text{PQR}\end{smallmatrix}$ are similar, and $\dfrac{AB}{PQ} = \dfrac{BC}{QR} = \dfrac{CA}{RP}$.

ASSUMPTION 13 **If the three sides of one triangle are proportional to the three sides of another triangle, then the triangles are equiangular and therefore similar.**

Thus, if $\triangle$s ABC, PQR are such that $\dfrac{AB}{PQ} = \dfrac{BC}{QR} = \dfrac{CA}{RP}$, then

$\triangle$s $\begin{smallmatrix}\text{ABC}\\\text{PQR}\end{smallmatrix}$ are similar, and $\angle P = \angle A$, $\angle Q = \angle B$, $\angle R = \angle C$.

Exercise Draw $\triangle$ABC in which $\angle A = 43°$, $AB = 6$ cm and $AC = 9$ cm. Draw also $\triangle$PQR in which $\angle P = 43°$, $PQ = 4$ cm and $PR = 6$ cm. Measure BC and QR, and also $\angle$s B and Q.

The two triangles ABC, PQR which you have drawn are such that $\angle A = \angle P$, and PQ, PR are two-thirds of AB, AC. You should have found that the triangles are equiangular, and that QR is two-thirds of BC. We now have a further test for the similarity of two triangles:

ASSUMPTION 14 If two triangles have an angle of one equal to an angle of the other, and the sides about these equal angles proportional, the triangles are equiangular and similar.

Thus, if $\triangle$s ABC, PQR are such that $\angle A = \angle P$ and $\dfrac{AB}{PQ} = \dfrac{AC}{PR}$, then $\triangle$s $\dfrac{ABC}{PQR}$ are similar, and $\angle B = \angle Q$, $\angle C = \angle R$.

Hints for riders

(i) When you have proved that two triangles ABC, PQR are similar, take the ratio of each side of $\triangle$ABC to the corresponding side of $\triangle$PQR, i.e.

$$\frac{AB}{PQ} = \frac{BC}{QR} = \frac{CA}{RP},$$

and then delete the ratio which is not required. This is better than to write $\dfrac{AB}{BC} = \dfrac{PQ}{QR}$ and $\dfrac{BC}{CA} = \dfrac{QR}{RP}$. See the paragraph on page 83 on two ways of comparing ratios of sides.

(ii) If you are told to prove a result in rectangle form, such as $BD \cdot BC = BA^2$, change it first into ratio form, e.g. $\dfrac{BD}{BA} = \dfrac{BA}{BC}$.

EXERCISE 124

State whether the figures and solids in Nos. 1–12 are similar; and if they are, state the magnification.

1 Two rectangles, lengths 3·5 cm and 2·5 cm, breadths 2·8 cm and 2 cm.

2 Two circles, radii 3 cm and 5 cm.

3 Two squares, sides $1\frac{1}{2}$ cm and 2 cm.

4 A triangle ABC in which $\angle A = 60°$, AB = 8 cm, AC = 4 cm, and a triangle XYZ in which $\angle Y = 60°$, XY = 11 cm, YZ = 5·5 cm.

5 Two parallelograms ABCD, PQRS, in which AB = 9 cm, BC = 6 cm, $\angle ABC = 54°$, PQ = 24 cm, QR = 16 cm, $\angle SPQ = 126°$.

6 $\triangle$ABC in which $\angle$B$=51°$, AB$=12$ cm, BC$=4$ cm, and $\triangle$XYZ in which $\angle$X$=51°$, YZ$=9$ cm, XZ$=3$ cm.

7 A rhombus with sides 4 cm and another rhombus with sides 8 cm.

8 A trapezium ABCD in which the parallel sides AB, DC are 8 cm and 12 cm, $\angle$C$=\angle$D$=61°$, and a trapezium PQRS in which the parallel sides PQ, SR are 14 cm and 21 cm, and $\angle$P$=\angle$Q$=119°$.

9 Two right circular cones, with heights 9 cm, 12 cm, and base-radii 2 cm, 3 cm.

10 Two spheres, radii 8 cm, 10 cm.

11 Two circular cylinders, radii 4 cm, 7 cm, and lengths 6 cm, $10\frac{1}{2}$ cm.

12 A pyramid, height 10 cm, on a square base of side $2\frac{1}{2}$ cm, and a pyramid, height 18 cm, on a square base of side $4\frac{1}{2}$ cm.

(*Riders*)

13 ABC is a triangle, and a straight line parallel to BC meets AB at X and AC at Y. Prove that the $\triangle$s AXY, ABC are similar, and write down two ratios equal to AY : AC.

14 P is a point in the side AB of $\triangle$ABC, Q is a point in the side AC, and PQCB is a cyclic quadrilateral. Prove that $\triangle$s APQ, ACB are similar, and write down two ratios equal to $\dfrac{PQ}{CB}$.

15 The diagonals AC, BD of a trapezium ABCD, in which AB is parallel to DC, intersect at O. Prove that

$$\frac{OA}{OC}=\frac{OB}{OD}=\frac{AB}{CD}.$$

16 In $\triangle$ABC, $\angle$A$=90°$ and AD is an altitude.

(i) Prove that $\triangle$s ADB, CAB are similar, and complete the relation $\dfrac{BD}{BA}=\dfrac{AB}{—}$;

(ii) prove that $\dfrac{CD}{CA}=\dfrac{CA}{CB}$; and that $\dfrac{DA}{DC}=\dfrac{DB}{DA}$.

17 The altitudes AD, BE of △ABC meet at H. (i) Prove that △s BEC, ADC are similar, and write down two ratios equal to $\dfrac{AD}{BE}$. (ii) Prove that △s AHE, BHD are similar, and complete the relation $\dfrac{BD}{DH} = \dfrac{}{EH}$.

18 ABCD is a parallelogram; a straight line through C meets AB at P and DA produced at Q. Prove that $\dfrac{BC}{DQ} = \dfrac{BP}{DC}$. (Take △s BPC, DCQ.)

19 Two triangles ABC, PRS are such that $\dfrac{BA}{PS} = \dfrac{CB}{PR} = \dfrac{AC}{RS}$. Name the triangles in corresponding order of letters.

20 In the quadrilateral ABCD, ∠A = ∠C and $\dfrac{AB}{AD} = \dfrac{CD}{CB}$. Prove two triangles similar, and deduce that AB is parallel to DC, and AD is parallel to BC.

21 ABCD is a quadrilateral in which BD bisects ∠ABC, and $\dfrac{AB}{BD} = \dfrac{BD}{BC}$. Prove that △s ABD, DBC are similar, and find an angle equal to ∠ADB.

22 In Fig. 333, prove the following pairs of triangles similar: (i) APB, DPC, (ii) BCQ, DAQ, (iii) ACQ, DBQ.

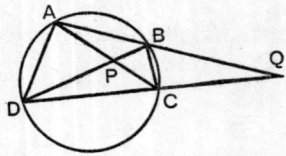

AC, BD meet at P; AB, DC produced meet at Q

FIG. 333

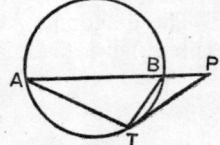

ABP is a straight line, PT is a tangent

FIG. 334

23 In Fig. 334, prove that △s PTB, PAT are similar, and complete the relation $\dfrac{PT}{PB} = \dfrac{PA}{}$.

24 AB is a diameter of a circle, and any point C on the circumference is joined to A and B; P is a point on AC, and N is the foot of the perpendicular from P to AB. Prove that
$$\frac{AP}{AN} = \frac{AB}{AC}.$$

25 In Fig. 335, prove that $BP \cdot BQ = BA^2$.

26 ABC is a triangle inscribed in a circle; AD is an altitude of the triangle, and AK is a diameter of the circle. Prove that $\triangle s$ ABK, ADC are similar, and deduce that
$$AB \cdot AC = AD \cdot AK$$

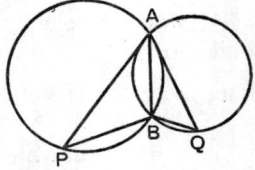

27 AB is a diameter of a circle, and P is any point on the circumference; N is the foot of the perpendicular from P to the tangent at A. Prove that
$$PN \cdot AB = AP^2.$$

AP, AQ are tangents at A

FIG. 335

Ratio of the areas of similar figures Consider two rectangles, one 12 cm by 9 cm, and the other 8 cm by 6 cm. These are similar, with a magnification $\frac{12}{8}$ or $\frac{3}{2}$.

The ratio of the areas of the rectangles $= \dfrac{12 \times 9}{8 \times 6}$

$$= \frac{12}{8} \times \frac{9}{6} = \left(\frac{3}{2}\right)^2,$$

which is the square of the magnification.

Again, consider two circles of radii 7 cm, 6 cm. These (like all circles) are similar figures, and the magnification is $\frac{7}{6}$.

The ratio of the areas of the circles $\quad = \dfrac{\pi \times 7^2}{\pi \times 6^2} = \left(\dfrac{7}{6}\right)^2,$

which is the square of the magnification.

From examples such as these, we see that

If any two plane figures are similar, the ratio of the area of the larger to that of the smaller is equal to the square of the magnification.

Corresponding surfaces, plane or curved, of similar solids are similar figures. It follows that

If any two solids are similar, the ratio of the areas of corresponding surfaces is equal to the ratio of the squares of corresponding lengths.

Ratio of the volumes of similar solids Now consider two similar rectangular blocks, one 15 cm by 10 cm by 5 cm, the other 24 cm by 16 cm by 8 cm. The magnification is $\dfrac{8}{5}$.

$$\text{The ratio of the volumes} = \frac{24 \times 16 \times 8}{15 \times 10 \times 5}$$

$$= \frac{24}{15} \times \frac{16}{10} \times \frac{8}{5} = \left(\frac{8}{5}\right)^3,$$

which is the cube of the magnification.

Again, consider two right circular cones, one of height 9 cm and base-radius 6 cm, the other of height 12 cm and base-radius 8 cm. These are similar solids, the ratio of corresponding lengths being $\dfrac{12}{9}$ or $\dfrac{4}{3}$.

$$\text{The ratio of the volumes} = \frac{\frac{1}{3}\pi \times 8^2 \times 12}{\frac{1}{3}\pi \times 6^2 \times 9}$$

$$= \left(\frac{8}{6}\right)^2 \times \frac{12}{9} = \left(\frac{4}{3}\right)^2 \times \frac{4}{3} = \left(\frac{4}{3}\right)^3,$$

which is the cube of the magnification. Thus we see that

If two solids are similar, the ratio of their volumes is equal to the ratio of the cubes of corresponding lengths.

The ratio of the areas of similar triangles There is a particular case of the general principle stated above which is of special interest in geometry. This is proved in Theorem 32.

THEOREM 32

The ratio of the areas of two similar triangles is equal to the ratio of the squares on corresponding sides.

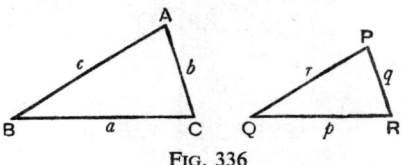

Fig. 336

Given two similar triangles ABC, PQR.

To prove that $\dfrac{\text{area of } \triangle ABC}{\text{area of } \triangle PQR} = \dfrac{BC^2}{QR^2}$

Proof   Denote the sides of $\triangle ABC$ by a, b, c, and those of $\triangle PQR$ by p, q, r.

$$\triangle ABC = \tfrac{1}{2}ab \sin C,$$
$$\triangle PQR = \tfrac{1}{2}pq \sin R.$$
$$\therefore \frac{\triangle ABC}{\triangle PQR} = \frac{\tfrac{1}{2}ab \sin C}{\tfrac{1}{2}pq \sin R}$$
$$= \frac{ab \sin C}{pq \sin R}.$$

Because the triangles are similar, they are equiangular.

$$\therefore \quad \angle C = \angle R.$$
$$\therefore \quad \sin C = \sin R.$$

Because the triangles are similar, their corresponding sides are proportional.

$$\therefore \quad \frac{a}{p} = \frac{b}{q}.$$
$$\therefore \quad \frac{\triangle ABC}{\triangle PQR} = \frac{a}{p} \times \frac{b}{q}$$
$$= \left(\frac{a}{p}\right)^2 = \frac{a^2}{p^2} = \frac{BC^2}{QR^2}.$$

Reference $\dfrac{\triangle ABC}{\triangle PQR} = \dfrac{BC^2}{QR^2}$ ($\triangle s$ *ABC*, *PQR similar*).

Corollary **If two triangles ABC, PQR are such that** $\angle C = \angle R$.

then $\dfrac{\triangle ABC}{\triangle PQR} = \dfrac{CA.CB}{RP.RQ}$.

EXERCISE 125

Find the ratio of (i) the areas of the surfaces, (ii) the volumes, of the following solids (Nos. 1–3):

1 Two similar cylinders, radii $1\frac{1}{2}$ cm, 2 cm.

2 Two spheres, radii 2 cm, $2\frac{1}{2}$ cm.

3 Two similar cones, heights 6 cm, 10 cm.

4 The weight of a rectangular block of length 6 cm is 200 g. Find in kilogrammes the weight of a similar rectangular block of the same material, if it is 30 cm long.

5 The weight of a solid metal sphere of radius 3 cm is 13·5 kg. Find the weight of a solid sphere of the same metal of radius 2 cm.

If it costs £5·40 to gild the first sphere, how much will it cost to gild the smaller one?

6 A plaster model of a statue is 30 cm high and weighs 14 kg. If the statue is 3·6 m high, and is made of stone which is three times as heavy as plaster, find the weight of the statue in tonnes.

7 The areas of two circles are 4·5 cm² and 8 cm². Find the ratio of their radii.

8 The volumes of two spheres are 54, 1024 cm³. Find the ratio of (i) their diameters, (ii) their surfaces.

9 The volumes of two similar cones are 24, 375 cm³. Find the ratio of (i) their heights, (ii) their curved surfaces, (iii) the circumferences of their bases, (iv) their slant heights.

10 On a certain map, an actual area of 1 km² is represented by 16 cm². Find the R.F. of the map.

11 On a certain map, 1 cm² represents 2500 km². Find the R.F. of the map.

12 If the area of a county, on a map whose R.F. is $\dfrac{1}{100\,000}$, is 6 cm², find its area on a map whose R.F. is $\dfrac{1}{250\,000}$.

13 The R.F. of a map is $\dfrac{1}{200\,000}$. What area on the map represents a county whose area is actually 2480 km². (Give the answer in square centimetres.)

14 V is the vertex of a pyramid, ABCD is the base (not necessarily rectangular). Points P, Q, R, S are marked on the edges VA, VB, VC, VD such that VP $=\frac{1}{3}$VA, VQ $=\frac{1}{3}$VB, VR $=\frac{1}{3}$VC, VS $=\frac{1}{3}$VD. If the area of ABCD is 45 cm², and the volume of VABCD is 540 cm³, find the area of PQRS and the volume of VPQRS.

15 In Fig. 337, if AP : AB $=2:5$, and the area of $\triangle$ABC $=$ 50 cm², calculate the area of $\triangle$APQ, and the ratio of $\triangle$APQ to the quadrilateral BPQC.

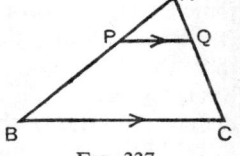

16 In Fig. 337, if BP : PA $=4:3$, what is the ratio of the areas of $\triangle$s APQ, ABC?

FIG. 337

17 The shortest side of a triangle is 6 cm and the area is 4 cm². Calculate the shortest side of a similar triangle of area 9 cm².

18 H, K are points on the sides AB, AC of $\triangle$ABC such that AH $=\frac{1}{3}$AB, AK $=\frac{3}{5}$AC. Find the ratio of the areas of $\triangle$s AHK and ABC. (Use the corollary of Theorem 32.)

19 Find the ratio of the areas of two similar triangles, if (i) two corresponding sides are 6 cm, 8 cm, (ii) their perimeters are 210 cm, 252 cm, (iii) two corresponding altitudes are 12 cm, 8 cm.

20 In Fig. 337, if $AP = \frac{1}{3}PB$, find the ratio of $\triangle APQ$ to the quadrilateral BPQC.

21 In Fig. 337, if $PQ = 3$ cm and $BC = 5$ cm, find the ratio of $\triangle APQ$ to the quadrilateral BPQC.

22 The sides of $\triangle ABC$ are 12 cm, 15 cm, 21 cm, and those of $\triangle XYZ$ are 8 cm, 10 cm, 14 cm.   Find the ratio of (i) their perimeters, (ii) their areas, (iii) the radii of their circumcircles.

23 In Fig. 337, if the area of $\triangle APQ = 16$ cm², that of the quadrilateral BPQC $= 33$ cm² and $BC = 10\cdot5$ cm, find PQ.

24 The sides of a triangle are $(a^2 - b^2)$, $2ab$, $(a^2 + b^2)$ centimetres.   Prove that the triangle is right-angled, and find the area.

Find the sides and area of a similar triangle whose perimeter is $(a^2 + ab)$ centimetres.

25 In Fig. 338, the sides of the triangle ABC are trisected as shown.   If the area of $\triangle ABC = 18$ cm², calculate the area of the figure PQRSTU.

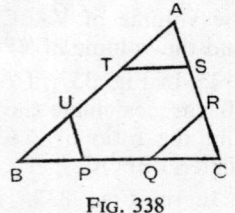
Fig. 338

26 A circle is inscribed in a regular hexagon, and the points of contact are joined to form a second regular hexagon. If r cm is the radius of the circle, prove that the lengths of the sides of the hexagons are $2r \tan 30°$ and r cm, and deduce the ratio of the areas of the two hexagons.

27 ABCD is a square, and equilateral triangles ABX, ACY are drawn on AB, AC.   Calculate the ratio of the area of $\triangle ABX$ to that of $\triangle ACY$.

28 The radius of a soap bubble increases by 2%.   Find the percentage increase in (i) the surface area, (ii) the volume, to three significant figures.

29 A rectangular table, 2·4 m long and 1·5 m wide and 90 cm high, stands on a level floor under a hanging lamp.   The shadow on the floor of the shorter side of the table is 2·4 m long.   Find the length of the shadow of the longer side and the height of the lamp above the table.

(*Riders on Theorem* 32)

30 Two chords AB, CD of a circle intersect at X. Prove that $\triangle AXC : \triangle DXB = AX^2 : DX^2$.

31 In $\triangle ABC$, P is a point in AB and Q is a point in AC such that $\angle AQP = \angle ABC$. Prove that

$$\triangle APQ : \triangle ABC = AP^2 : AC^2.$$

32 In Fig. 337, if BQ and CP intersect at O, prove that $\triangle POQ : \triangle COB = AP^2 : AB^2$.

33 The bisector of the angle A of $\triangle ABC$ meets BC at D; AD is produced to meet at E the parallel through C to AB. Prove that $\triangle ABD : \triangle ECD = AB^2 : AC^2$.

34 AB is a diameter of a circle whose centre is O, and C is any point on the circumference. If the tangents at A and C meet at T, prove that $\triangle ATC : \triangle BOC = AT^2 : OB^2$.

35 ABCD is a parallelogram; P, Q are the mid-points of BC, CD. Prove that $\triangle APQ$ is three-eighths of the area of the parallelogram ABCD. (Hint: find what fraction $\triangle PQC$ is of $\triangle BDC$.)

36 In Fig. 334, p. 404, prove that

$$\triangle PAT : \triangle PTB = TA^2 : TB^2.$$

By regarding PA and PB as the bases of the $\triangle$s PAT, PTB, show that $PA : PB = TA^2 : TB^2$.

37 ABCD is a square; the bisector of $\angle BAC$ meets BD at X and BC at Y. Prove that the area of $\triangle ABX$ is one-half of the area of $\triangle ACY$.

38 P is one of the two points of intersection of two circles. Straight lines APX, BPY, CPZ cut one circle at A, B, C and cut the other circle at X, Y, Z. Prove that

$$\triangle ABC : \triangle XYZ = AB^2 : XY^2.$$

43. RECTANGLE PROPERTY OF THE CIRCLE

Segments of a line   Suppose that AB is any straight line, and that P is any point, either on AB or on AB produced in either direction, as in Fig. 339 (i) and (ii).

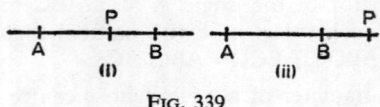

Fig. 339

PA and PB are called the **segments** into which P divides the line AB.   Each segment is measured from the point P which divides the line internally or externally.   A rectangle, of which one side is equal to PA and the adjacent side equal to PB, is said to be **contained by the segments** PA, PB.   Its area is PA.PB.

It is important not to confuse PA.PB with PA : PB, or $\frac{PA}{PB}$.

In Fig. 341 (i), p. 413, XA and XB are the segments of the chord AB, XC and XD are the segments of the chord CD. In Fig. 341 (ii), XA and XB, both measured from X, are the segments of the chord AB.

The rectangle property of the circle, proved in Theorem 33, concerns the area of the rectangle contained by these segments. No actual rectangles, however, are drawn either in the course of the proof or in the application of the result, just as no actual geometrical squares appear in the proof of Pythagoras' Theorem by Method 2, p. 362.

A **secant** is a straight line which cuts a circle at two distinct points, as in Fig. 340.

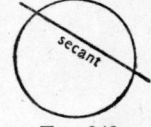

Fig. 340

THEOREM 33

If two chords of a circle, produced if necessary, cut one another, the rectangle contained by the segments of the one chord is equal to the rectangle contained by the segments of the other.

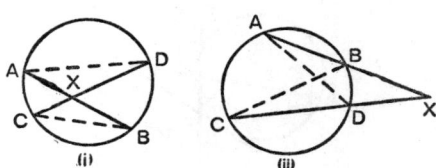

FIG. 341

Given two chords AB, CD of a circle, cutting at X; the point X lies inside the circle in Fig. 341 (i), outside the circle in Fig. 341 (ii).

To prove that XA . XB = XC . XD.

Construction Join AD, CB.

Proof In the △s AXD, CXB,

$$\angle A = \angle C \quad \text{(same seg.)},$$

$$\angle AXD = \angle CXB \quad \text{(vert. opp. in Fig. (i), same } \angle \text{ in Fig. (ii))};$$

∴ the third angles ADX, CBX are equal.

∴ △s $\begin{smallmatrix} AXD \\ CXB \end{smallmatrix}$ are similar.

∴ $\quad\quad \dfrac{XA}{XC} = \dfrac{XD}{XB} \quad$ (corr. sides proportional).

∴ $\quad\quad XA . XB = XC . XD.$

Reference XA . XB = XC . XD (*rect. prop. of circle*).

THEOREM 34

If, from any point outside a circle, a secant and a tangent are drawn, the rectangle contained by the whole secant and the part of it outside the circle is equal to the square on the tangent.

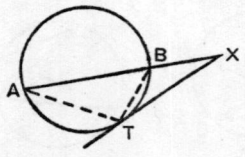

FIG. 342

Given a secant XBA, cutting a circle at B, A, and a tangent XT touching the circle at T.

To prove that $XA . XB = XT^2$.

Construction   Join TA, TB.

Proof   In the $\triangle$s XTB, XAT,

$$\angle TXB = \angle AXT \quad \text{(same } \angle\text{),}$$
$$\angle XTB = \angle XAT \quad \text{(alt. seg.).}$$

$\therefore$ the third angles TBX, ATX are equal.

$\therefore$ $\triangle$s $\begin{matrix} XTB \\ XAT \end{matrix}$ are similar.

$\therefore$ $\qquad\qquad \dfrac{XB}{XT} = \dfrac{XT}{XA} \quad$ (corr. sides proportional).

$\therefore$ $\qquad XA . XB = XT^2$.

Reference $XA . XB = XT^2$ (*rect. prop. of circle*).

Summary of Theorems 33 and 34 Whether the chords AB, CD cut at X inside or outside the circle,

$$XA \cdot XB = XC \cdot XD = XT^2,$$

where T is the point of contact of the tangent from X, and XT^2 is included only if XT can be drawn, i.e. if X is outside the circle.

Distance of the visible horizon In Fig. 343, AOB repre-

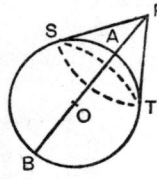

Fig. 343

sents a diameter of the earth, and P is a point vertically above A. The points of contact of the tangents from P to the earth lie on a circle ST. This circle is called the **visible horizon**.

Let $PA = h$ kilometres, $AO = R$ kilometres.
$PT^2 = PA \cdot PB$ (rect. prop. of circle)
$= h(2R + h) = 2Rh + h^2.$

Now h is always very small compared with R, and therefore we can ignore h^2 compared with $2Rh$.

∴ $PT^2 = 2Rh$ (approx.).

∴ the distance of the horizon $= PT = \sqrt{2Rh}$ km (approx.).

Usually it is more convenient to measure the height above sea-level in metres instead of kilometres. In that case we must replace h by $\dfrac{h}{1000}$. Taking the radius of the earth as 6370 kilometres, the distance of the horizon from a point h metres above sea-level is thus approximately

$$\sqrt{2 \times 6370 \times \frac{h}{1000}} \text{ km}$$

$$= \sqrt{12 \cdot 74h} \text{ km} = 3 \cdot 57 \sqrt{h} \text{ km}.$$

For example, from the top of Snowdon (1085 m), the distance of the visible horizon

$= 3 \cdot 57 \times \sqrt{1085}$ km
$= 3 \cdot 57 \times 32 \cdot 94 = 118$ km (to the nearest kilometre).

CONSTRUCTION 9

To construct a square equal in area to a given rectangle.

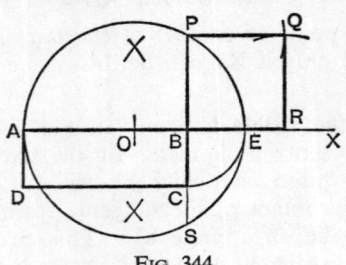

FIG. 344

Given a rectangle ABCD.

To construct a square equal in area to ABCD.

Construction Produce AB to X.

Along BX, mark off BE equal to BC.

Bisect AE at O.

With centre O, radius OA, draw a circle, and let this circle meet CB produced at P.

On BP, construct a square BPQR.

Then BPQR is the required square.

Proof Produce BC to meet the circle at S.

Since $\angle ABC$ is a right angle ($\angle$ of rectangle), PS is a chord perpendicular to the diameter AE.

$$\therefore \qquad\qquad BP = BS.$$

But $\qquad\qquad BP \cdot BS = BA \cdot BE$ (rect. prop. of circle),

and $\qquad\qquad BE = BC$ (constr.).

$$\therefore \qquad\qquad BP^2 = BA \cdot BC.$$

$\therefore$ square BPQR = rect. ABCD.

Note If $a : x = x : b$, the number x is called the **mean proportional** of a and b. Since $\dfrac{a}{x} = \dfrac{x}{b}$, $\therefore x^2 = ab$ and $x = \sqrt{ab}$.

Thus, the length BP in Construction 9 is the mean proportional of BA and BC, for $BP^2 = BA \cdot BC$.

EXERCISE 126

1 In Fig. 341 (i), p. 413, if AX $=4\frac{1}{2}$ cm, BX $=8$ cm and CX $=3$ cm, calculate DX.

2 In Fig. 341 (i), if AB $=12$ cm, CX $=4$ cm and X is the mid-point of AB, calculate CD.

3 In Fig. 341 (i), if AX $=4$ cm, AB $=13$ cm, CX $=3$ cm, calculate CD.

4 In Fig. 341 (ii), if AB $=3$ cm, XB $=5$ cm, XD $=4$ cm, calculate CD.

5 In Fig. 341 (ii), if CD $=7$ cm, DX $=3$ cm, XB $=5$ cm, calculate AB.

6 In Fig. 342, p. 414, if XB $=9$ cm, AB $=7$ cm, calculate XT.

7 In Fig. 342, if XB $=4$ cm, AB $=2\cdot25$ cm, calculate XT.

8 AB is a diameter of a circle whose centre is O and radius 9 cm. C is a point on OB such that OC $=5$ cm. A chord PQ passes through C, and CP $=8$ cm. Calculate CQ.

9 In Fig. 342, if XT $=6$ cm, XB $=4$ cm, calculate AB.

10 In Fig. 342, if XT $=4$ cm and AB $=6$ cm, calculate XB. (Hint: denote XB by x, and form an equation to find x.)

11 The roadway of a bridge is in the form of an arc ACB of a circle; A and B are on the same level, and the highest point C of the roadway is 1·2 m above AB. If AB $=7\cdot2$ m, calculate the radius of the circle of which the arc forms part. (Draw the diameter through C.)

12 Water stands to a depth of 6 cm in a hemispherical bowl whose radius is 10 cm. Calculate (i) the radius of the circle formed by the water surface, (ii) the area of this circle, taking π to be $\frac{22}{7}$.

13 Two perpendicular chords AB, CD of a circle intersect at X; AX $=4$ cm, XB $=12$ cm, CX $=3$ cm. Calculate XD, and the radius of the circle, correct to the nearest millimetre. (Hint: draw perpendiculars from the centre of the circle to the chords.)

14 Find the distance of the visible horizon from the following places: (i) Flamborough Head, 54 m, (ii) Snaefell, 620 m, (iii) Ben Nevis, 1343 m.

15 Draw a rectangle with sides 4·8 cm and 2·6 cm, and construct a square equal in area to it. Measure the side of the square.

16 Draw a parallelogram with sides 4·2 cm and 2·8 cm, and an angle of 50°. Construct: (i) a rectangle equal in area to the parallelogram, (ii) a square equal in area to the rectangle you have drawn. Measure the side of the square.

17 Find by construction the mean proportional between two lines of lengths 3·2 cm and 4·4 cm.

18 Find √6 by constructing the mean proportional of 2 and 3.

(Riders)

19 Two circles intersect at A and B; P is a point on AB produced; two straight lines PCD, PEF are drawn through P, cutting one circle at C, D and the other circle at E, F. Prove that PC . PD = PE . PF.

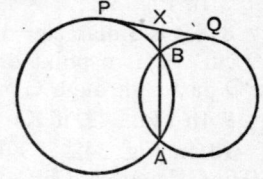

20 In Fig. 345, two circles intersect at A and B; PQ is the common tangent, touching the circles at P, Q; AB produced meets PQ at X. Prove that PX = XQ.

FIG. 345

21 Two circles intersect at A and B; P is any point on AB produced. Prove that the tangents from P to the circles are equal.

22 The altitudes BE, CF of △ABC intersect at H. Prove that

　　　　(i) HB . HE = HC . HF,
　　　　(ii) AF . AB = AE . AC,
　　　　(iii) BH . BE = BF . BA.

23 ABC is a triangle inscribed in a circle; a straight line parallel to the tangent at A cuts AB at X and AC at Y. Prove that AX . AB = AY . AC. (Hint: first prove that BXYC is cyclic.)

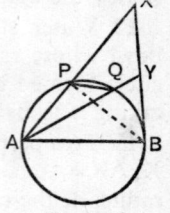

24 In Fig. 346, AB is a diameter of the circle; the tangent at B meets AP produced at X and AQ pro-

FIG. 346

duced at Y. Prove that (i) ∠PQA = ∠PXY,
　　　　　　　　　　　　(ii) AP . AX = AQ . AY.

44. TESTS FOR CONCYCLIC POINTS

Angle tests for concyclic points

The converses of Theorems 7–9 provide us with tests for determining whether points are concyclic.

Converse of Theorem 7   If the straight line joining two points subtends equal angles at two other points on the same side of it, then the four points are concyclic.

Reference   (See Fig. 347.)

$$\angle APB = \angle AQB,$$

∴ A, P, Q, B are concyclic.

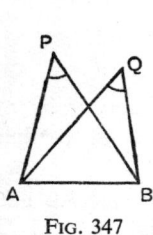

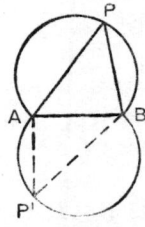

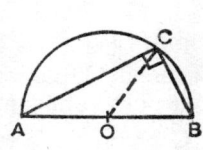

Fig. 347   Fig. 348   Fig. 349

A corollary of this fact is the **constant-angle locus**:

The locus of points at which a fixed straight line AB subtends a constant angle is two equal arcs of equal circles on opposite sides of AB.

The complete locus is shown in Fig. 348, where AB subtends an angle APB, or AP′B, of constant size. The method of drawing the arc was explained in Construction 8, page 382.

Converse of Theorem 8   The circle described on the hypotenuse of a right-angled triangle as diameter passes through the opposite vertex.

Thus, in Fig. 349, the circle on AB as diameter passes through C.

Corollary 1   The locus of points at which a fixed straight line AB subtends a right angle is the circle on AB as diameter.

Corollary 2 The line joining the mid-point of the hypotenuse of a right-angled triangle to the opposite vertex is equal to half the hypotenuse.

In Fig. 349, OA = OB = OC.

Converse of Theorem 9

(1) If a pair of opposite angles of a quadrilateral are supplementary, the quadrilateral is cyclic.

(2) If, when a side of a quadrilateral is produced, the exterior angle so formed is equal to the interior opposite angle, the quadrilateral is cyclic.

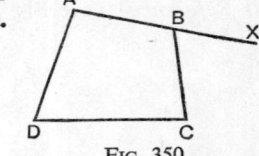

References (See Fig. 350.)

(i) $\angle ABC + \angle ADC = 180°$,
    ∴ ABCD is cyclic.

(ii) $\angle CBX = \angle ADC$,
    ∴ ABCD is cyclic (*ext. ∠ = int. opp. ∠*).

FIG. 350

Rectangle tests for concyclic points The converses of Theorems 33 and 34 provide further tests for seeing whether four points are concyclic.

Converse of Theorem 33 (i) If two straight lines AB and CD cut at X so that XA.XB = XC.XD, the points A, B, C, D are concyclic. (See Fig. 351.)

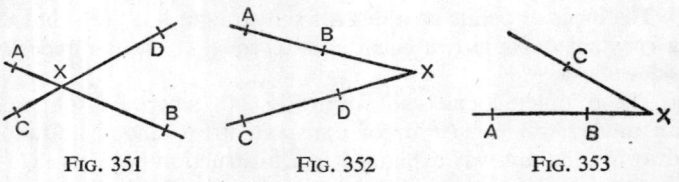

FIG. 351   FIG. 352   FIG. 353

Converse of Theorem 33 (ii) If two straight lines AB and CD, both produced, cut at X so that XA.XB = XC.XD, the points A, B, C, D are concyclic. (See Fig. 352.)

Converse of Theorem 34 If X is a point on the straight line AB produced, and C is a point (not on AB) such that XA.XB = XC², the circle through A, B, C touches XC at C. (See Fig. 353.)

EXERCISE 127

1 ABCD is a quadrilateral in which $\angle ABC = 64°$, $\angle ACB = 44°$ and $\angle BDC = 72°$. Prove that the quadrilateral is cyclic, and find $\angle ADB$.

2 ABCD is a quadrilateral whose diagonals AC, BD intersect at X. $\angle BXC = 118°$, $\angle BAC = 43°$, $\angle ACD = 75°$, $\angle CAD = 51°$. Prove that ABCD is cyclic, and calculate $\angle DBC$.

3 In the quadrilateral ABCD, $\angle ABC = 81°$, $\angle ACD = 44°$, $\angle CAD = 37°$. Prove that the quadrilateral is cyclic, and calculate $\angle ABD$.

4 In the quadrilateral ABCD, $\angle CAD = 56°$, $\angle BAC = 48°$, $\angle CBD = 56°$. Calculate $\angle BCD$.

5 ABC is a triangle in which AB = AC and $\angle BAC = 36°$. The parallel through C to BA is drawn, and this meets the bisector of $\angle ABC$ at D. Show that A, B, C, D are concyclic, and calculate $\angle ADB$.

6 ABC is an equilateral triangle. The line through C perpendicular to BC is drawn, and this meets the bisector of $\angle ABC$ at D. Prove that A, B, C, D are concyclic.

7 In Fig. 354, the exterior angles of the quadrilateral ABCD are bisected, thus forming the quadrilateral PQRS. If $\angle ABC = 106°$, $\angle BCD = 120°$ and $\angle ADC = 48°$, calculate $\angle DAB$, $\angle APB$ and $\angle CRD$, and prove that the quadrilateral PQRS is cyclic.

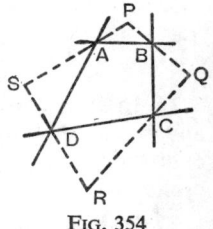

Fig. 354

8 Draw a straight line AB 5 cm long. Construct an arc of a circle in which AB subtends an angle of 65°.

9 In Fig. 351, if AX = 4 cm, AB = 16 cm, CX = 3 cm, CD = 19 cm, prove that ACBD is cyclic.

10 In Fig. 352, if AB = 4 cm, BX = 8 cm, CD = 10 cm, DX = 6 cm, prove that A, B, C, D are concyclic.

11 In Fig. 353, if AB = 7·8 cm, BX = 5 cm, CX = 8 cm, prove that XC touches the circle ABC.

(Theoretical)

12 In Fig. 355, prove that B, F, E, C lie on a circle. Where is the centre of this circle?

13 In Fig. 355, prove that AEHF is a cyclic quadrilateral, and that ∠AHE = ∠AFE.

14 Two straight lines meet at O; L and M are the feet of the perpendiculars from any point P to the lines. Prove that O, L, P, M are concyclic.

15 AB, AC are the equal sides of an isosceles triangle ABC, and N is the mid-point of BC. Prove that the circle on AB as diameter passes through N.

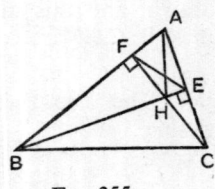

Fig. 355

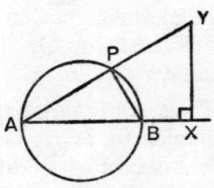

Fig. 356

16 In Fig. 356, the diameter AB is produced to X; Y is any point on the perpendicular through X to AX, and AY cuts the circle at P. Prove that the quadrilateral PYXB is cyclic.

17 In Fig. 355, prove that

  (i) ∠AEF = ∠ABC,   (ii) ∠EFC = ∠EBC,
  (iii) ∠CFE = ∠HAE,   (iv) ∠EHC = ∠BAC.

18 The diagonals of a rhombus ABCD intersect at O. Prove that the circles on AB, BC, CD and DA as diameters all pass through O.

19 Given two fixed points A and B, state the locus of points P which are such that ∠APB = 90°.

20 In Fig. 357, ABCD is a parallelogram. Any circle through A and D cuts AB at P and DC at Q. Prove that PBCQ is cyclic.

21 In Fig. 358, the bisectors of the interior and exterior angles at B and C are drawn. Prove that BICJ is a cyclic quadrilateral.

22 In Fig. 355, if X is the mid-point of BC, prove that XE = XF, and that ∠FXE = 2∠ABE = 180° − 2∠BAC.

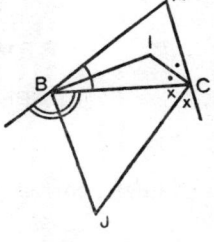

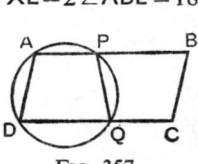

Fig. 357

Fig. 358

23 In Fig. 359, ABC is a triangle with any points X, Y, Z marked on the sides. The circumcircles of triangles BXZ, CXY cut at O. Prove that the quadrilateral AYOZ is cyclic. (Hint: use Theorem 9 and its converse.)

24 In Fig. 354, the exterior angles of the quadrilateral ABCD are bisected, thus forming the quadrilateral PQRS.

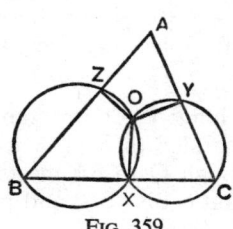

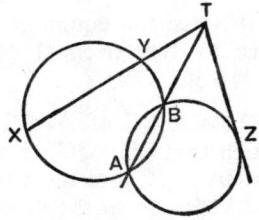

Fig. 359

Fig. 360

If ∠DAB = a°, ∠ABC = b°, ∠BCD = c° and ∠CDA = d°, prove that the number of degrees in ∠APB = $\frac{1}{2}(a + b)$. State the number of degrees in ∠CRD, and prove that the quadrilateral PQRS is cyclic.

25 In Fig. 360, XY and AB produced meet at T, and TZ is a tangent at Z. Prove that TZ is a tangent to the circle XYZ.

26 D, E are the mid-points of the sides BC, CA of $\triangle$ABC; a circle, touching CA at E and passing through D, meets BC again at X. Prove that A, E, X, B are concyclic.

REVISION PAPERS

PAPERS 24–28 (§ 24–30)

Paper 24

1 Evaluate, correct to three significant figures,

$$\frac{243 \times (0{\cdot}0526)^3}{\sqrt[3]{2{\cdot}28}}.$$

2 Find, correct to three significant figures, the radius of the base of a circular cone whose height is 5 cm and volume 12 cm^3.

3 AB, CD are two vertical poles whose tops, A and C, are joined by a rod. If AB $= 2$ m and CD $= 5$ m, find the height above the ground of the mid-point of AC.

4 (i) Solve the equation $3x^2 - 10x - 3 = 0$, giving the roots correct to two decimal places. (ii) Solve the inequation $5(x+1) > 3(x+2)$.

5 The side BC of $\triangle$ABC is 5 cm long; P, Q are points in BC such that BP $=$ QC $= 2$ cm; the parallel through P to CA meets BA at X, and the parallel through Q to BA meets CA at Y. Write down the value of the ratio BX : BA, and prove that XY is parallel to BC.

6 Draw the graph of the function $1 - 4\frac{1}{2}x$, and find (i) when the function has the value 0, (ii) for what range of values of x

$$1 - 4\tfrac{1}{2}x > 4.$$

Paper 25

1 Evaluate, to three significant figures,
$$\frac{0 \cdot 8164 \times 0 \cdot 0417 \times 874}{11 \cdot 63 \times 0 \cdot 5423}.$$

2 The base of a right pyramid is a square of side 4 cm and the height of the pyramid is 6 cm. Find (i) the volume, (ii) the area of each of the sloping faces in square centimetres, correct to three significant figures.

3 ABCD is a parallelogram, and P is the mid-point of CD; a line drawn through C, parallel to PA, meets DA produced at Q. Prove that AQ = BC, and that CQ bisects AB.

4 (i) Solve the inequation $7(x-4) \leqslant 12(x-2)$. (ii) Find the roots of the equation $2x^2 - 7x + 1 = 0$, correct to two places of decimals.

5 An empty flask weighs 20 g. When full of water, it weighs 58g, and when full of oil it weighs 56·1 g. Find the density of oil.

6 A straight line drawn through the origin O meets the line AB, whose equation is $y = 6 - 2x$, at the point P, where $x = 1$. Find the value of y at P, and state the gradients of the lines OP, AB.

Paper 26

1 Find, correct to three significant figures, the circumference of a circle of area 20 cm².

2 The base-radius of a cone is 60 cm and the height is 90 cm. Find, correct to three significant figures, (i) the volume in cubic metres, (ii) the area of the curved surface in square metres.

3 Solve the equation $x + \dfrac{1}{x} = 3 \cdot 5$, giving the roots correct to two places of decimals.

4 The diagonals of a quadrilateral ABCD intersect at X. If AX = 1·5 cm, BX = 2·5 cm, CX = 1·2 cm, DX = 2 cm, prove that AB is parallel to DC.

5 The density of air is $1 \cdot 3 \, \text{kg m}^{-3}$. Calculate in kilogrammes, to the nearest whole number, the weight of air in a building 14 m long, 8 m wide, 3 m high.

6 A linear function of the form $a + bx$ has the value -7 when $x = 2$, and the value -12 when $x = 3$. Find the function, and state for what value of x its value is 0.

Paper 27

1 Evaluate, to three significant figures, $\sqrt{\dfrac{0 \cdot 471 \times 863}{26 \cdot 84 \times 3 \cdot 018}}$.

2 A cylindrical tank has a diameter 75 cm and height $1 \cdot 8$ m. Find its capacity in litres, to three significant figures.

3 ABC is a triangle, and D is the mid-point of BC; a straight line through B parallel to DA meets CA produced at P, and a straight line through C parallel to DA meets BA produced at Q. Prove that (i) BP = CQ, (ii) PQ is equal and parallel to BC.

4 △ABC is right-angled at A; AB = 4 cm, AC = 3 cm; the bisector of ∠C meets AB at X. Calculate AX.

5 The density of iron is 7600 kg m^{-3}, and a square metre of sheet iron weighs 15 kg. Find the thickness of the sheet iron in millimetres, to two significant figures.

6 Find what linear function of x has the value 1 if $x = 1$, and the value 13 if $x = 4$. For what value of x is the value of the function 23? What is the gradient of the function?

Paper 28

1 From the formula $G = 19 \cdot 7 \times \sqrt{\dfrac{HD^5}{L}}$, calculate, to three significant figures, the value of G when H = 34, L = 160, D = $0 \cdot 687$.

2 Find, correct to three significant figures, the radius of a sphere whose volume is 25 cm^3.

3 Draw a straight line AB $6 \cdot 4$ cm long, and divide it geometrically into five equal parts. Construct also the point X which divides AB externally in the ratio 7 : 3, and measure BX.

4 Solve the equation $x^2 + 2x = 7$, giving the roots correct to three significant figures.

5 P is the point dividing the side AB of $\triangle$ABC in the ratio $2:5$. PX is drawn parallel to BC to meet AC at X, PY is drawn parallel to AC to meet BC at Y; PX $= 1 \cdot 8$ cm, PY $= 3 \cdot 5$ cm. Calculate AC and BC.

6 A metal pipe has an internal radius of $3\frac{1}{2}$ cm, and the metal is $\frac{1}{2}$ cm thick. Find in kilogrammes the weight of a metre length, if the density of the metal is 7200 kg m^{-3}.

PAPER 29–33 (§ 31–37)

Paper 29

1 Evaluate without using tables (i) $(0 \cdot 3)^3$, (ii) $(0 \cdot 25)^{-\frac{1}{2}}$, (iii) $81^{\frac{1}{4}}$.

2 In $\triangle$ABC, $\angle$B $= 63°$ and $\angle$C $= 48°$; the altitude from A to BC is 6 cm. Find the lengths of the sides of the triangle.

3 (i) Sketch the graph of $y = (x + 1)(3 - x)$, plotting only a few necessary points. (ii) Solve the inequality $3 + 2x > x^2$.

4 ABCD is a face of a cuboid; AE, BF, CG, DH are edges; AB $= 6$ cm, BC $= 5$ cm, BF $= 4$ cm. A point P in FG, such that FP $= 3$ cm, is joined to A and B. Draw accurately the section APB, and calculate the angle which this plane makes with the plane ABCD.

5 Solve $\triangle$ABC in which A $= 42°$, B $= 58°$, $c = 12 \cdot 8$.

6 After reducing the sale price of an article by 35%, the price is £29·25. Find the cost of the article before the reduction.

Paper 30

1 The base of a right pyramid is a square of side 5 cm and the slant edges are each 8 cm long. Find, correct to three significant figures (i) the height in centimetres, (ii) the volume in cubic centimetres.

2 Simplify: (i) $3^a \times 3^{-a}$, (ii) $\sqrt{1\frac{11}{25}x^{-2}}$, (iii) $\sqrt[3]{8x^{-6}}$.

3 Find the values of x and y if:

(i) $\cos x° = \sin 51°$, (ii) $\cos y° = \sin (y° + 20°)$.

4 (i) Draw the graph of $y = 2x^2 - 3x$ from $x = -2$ to $x = 2$. By drawing a tangent, find the gradient of the curve at the origin. (ii) Solve the inequation $2x^2 - 3x \leqslant 2$.

5 A cuboid is 8 cm long, 7 cm wide, 5 cm high. Find the angle which a diagonal of the cuboid makes with the base.

6 A sells an article to B at a profit of 20%. B sells it to C at a profit of 15% on his cost price. If C pays £248·40 for it, find how much A paid for it.

Paper 31

1 Simplify: (i) $\sqrt{8} \times \sqrt{\frac{1}{8}}$, (ii) $(\sqrt{2} + \sqrt{3})^2$, (iii) $\sqrt{125} \div \sqrt{5}$.

2 In an isosceles triangle, the base is 6·2 cm and each of the base angles is 54° 26'. Find the lengths of the equal sides, and the area of the triangle.

3 Draw the graph of the function $x^2 - 3x$ from $x = -1$ to 4. Use your graph to solve the equation $x^2 - 3x - 2 = 0$.

4 A right pyramid stands on a rectangular base ABCD, and V is the vertex; AB = 4 cm, BC = 3 cm, and the height of the pyramid is 5 cm. Find the angles between the following: (i) the planes VAB and ABCD, (ii) the planes VBC and ABCD, (iii) the edge VA and the plane ABCD.

5 If A is an obtuse angle whose sine is $\frac{12}{13}$, find, without using tables, the values of cos A and tan A.

6 Make (i) f, (ii) v the subject of the formula $\dfrac{1}{u} + \dfrac{1}{v} = \dfrac{1}{f}$.

Paper 32

1 Given that $\sqrt{5} = 2·2361$, find the values of (i) $\dfrac{1}{\sqrt{5}}$, (ii) $\sqrt{45}$, to four decimal places.

2 In Fig. 361, AB, BC, CD are three rods hinged at their ends; AD is horizontal, AB makes an angle of 55°, BC makes 20°, CD makes 60°, all with the horizontal; AB = 40 cm, BC = 50 cm. Calculate the depth of C below AD, and the distance AD.

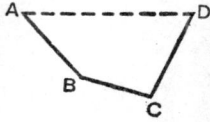

Fig. 361

3 V is the vertex of a solid right circular cone of height 5 cm and base-radius 4 cm; AB is a chord of the base, distant 2 cm from the centre. Make an accurate drawing of the section VAB, measure ∠VAB, and verify your result by calculation.

4 In △ABC, if A = 130°, B = 31° 25′, a = 36·2, find b and c.

5 By selling an article for £63, a man gains 12½% on his cost price. Find his gain or loss per cent if he sells it for £51·80.

6 If $P = \dfrac{W}{10} + 3·5$, and $E = \dfrac{W}{6P}$, express E in terms of P.

Paper 33

1 A ship steams 4·6 km on a bearing 049° and then 7·6 km on a bearing 032°. Find the total distance it has steamed (i) in the direction north, (ii) in the direction east.

2 Draw the graph of the function $5x - x^2$. For what values of x is the function positive? What is the maximum value of the function? Solve the inequation $5x - x^2 > 6$.

3 VABC is a right pyramid with vertex V, the base ABC being an equilateral triangle of side 6 cm. The height of the pyramid is 5 cm. Find the angles (i) between VA and the plane ABC, (ii) between the planes VAB and ABC.

4 Find from the tables the values of:
(i) cos 98° 26′, (ii) tan 120°, (iii) sin 140°, (iv) cos 160° 32′.

5 The price of certain goods in a trade catalogue is £450, but this is subject to a deduction of 20%, then a deduction of 10% from the reduced price, and finally a deduction of 2½%

from the last price. Find the actual cost of the goods to a purchaser.

6 (i) Make a the subject of the formula

$$S = \frac{n}{2}\{2a + (n-1)d\}.$$

(ii) Solve the inequality $3x^2 - 7x < 4(1 + x)$.

PAPERS 34–38 (§ 38–44)

Paper 34

1 State the locus in space of points which are 2 m from the floor of a room and 1 m from a vertical stick with one end on the floor.

2 ABC is an equilateral triangle with side 4 cm, and D is the mid-point of BC; P is the point in AB produced, such that BP = 3·4 cm. Calculate ∠BPD.

3 A and B are the points of contact of the tangents PA, PB to a circle. A chord AC is drawn, parallel to PB. If ∠APB = 56°, calculate the angles of △ABC.

4 Draw the graph of $y = \frac{1}{10}x(4 - x^2)$ from $x = -4$ to $+4$. For what positive values of x has the function $x(4 - x^2)$ a maximum value, and for what negative value of x has the function a minimum value? Solve the equation $x(4 - x^2) = 1$.

5 ABC is a triangle inscribed in a circle, and AK is a diameter of the circle; AD is an altitude of the triangle. Prove by similar triangles that AB . AC = AK . AD.

6 Water stands to a depth of 5 cm in a hemispherical bowl and the water surface is a circle of radius 8 cm. Calculate the diameter of the sphere of which the bowl forms part.

Paper 35

1 Calculate to the nearest mm the length of the longest median of a triangle with sides 5, 7, 8 cm.

2 ABC is a triangle in which ∠A = 38° and ∠B = 64°; BC is produced to a point D, such that ∠CAD = 40°. Prove that AB is a tangent to the circle ACD.

3 AB is a diameter of a circle, P is a point on the circumference, and N is the foot of the perpendicular from P to AB. If AN = 5 cm, NB = 12·8 cm, calculate PN.

4 The areas of two similar triangles are 18, 50 cm². If the longest side of the larger one is 13 cm, find the longest side of the smaller one.

5 AB is a diameter of a circle, centre O; P and Q are points on the circumference, on the same side of AB, and AP = PQ. Prove that △s APQ, POB are similar, and deduce that AP . PB = AQ . OP.

6 The base BC of △ABC is fixed, and ∠BAC is constant in size. What is the locus of A?

If the altitudes BE, CF of the triangle intersect at H, state and prove the locus of H for different positions of A.

Paper 36

1 Draw a triangle ABC in which AB = 5·8 cm, BC = 5·2 cm, CA = 3·4 cm. Find by construction a point P which is equidistant from AB and AC, and is also equidistant from B and C, and measure PA.

Construct also the circumcircle of △ABC, and measure the radius.

2 A town A is 15 km from O in a direction N. 57° E., and a town B is 24 km from O in a direction N. 48° W. Calculate the distance and direction of A from B.

3 Sketch the graphs of (i) $(x+1)(x-2)^2$, (ii) $(x-1)^3$, plotting only a few necessary points.

4 The top of a table is a rectangle 3 m by 2½ m, and the height is 1·2 m. A light is situated 2·7 m above the floor. Find the area of the shadow on the floor of the table top.

5 ABC is a triangle, and D is a point on the bisector of ∠A such that $AD^2 = AB . AC$. Prove that △s ABD, ADC are similar.

Deduce that BD is a tangent to the circle ADC.

6 ABCD is a rectangle; the perpendicular through C to AC meets AB produced at P and AD produced at Q. Prove that $\angle ADB = \angle BPC$, and deduce that the quadrilateral PBDQ is cyclic.

Paper 37

1 In $\triangle ABC$, find $\angle A$ if $a = 9.2$, $b = 4.9$, $c = 5.3$.

2 A is a fixed point, and a variable line AP, of fixed length, passes through A and meets a fixed plane at P. The point Q lies anywhere on the variable line AP. State the locus in space of P, and that of Q.

3 ABC is an isosceles triangle in which AB = AC; a circle is drawn to touch BC at B and also to pass through A, and this circle cuts AC again at D. Prove that BC = BD.

4 Draw the graphs of $y = x^2$ and $y = 2 + 3x$ on the same axes and scale. What quadratic equation is solved from the intersections of the graphs? Solve this equation.

5 The bisector of $\angle A$ of $\triangle ABC$ meets BC at D; the circle, centre C, radius CD, cuts AD (produced if necessary) at E. Prove that $\triangle$s ABD, ACE are similar. Use this result to give an alternative proof of Theorem 28 (page 259).

6 AB is a diameter of a circle, centre O, and PQ is a chord perpendicular to AB; X is any point on AB, and QX produced meets the circle at Y. Prove that (i) $\angle PXY = 2\angle PQY$, (ii) $\angle PXY = \angle POY$, (iii) O, P, Y, X are concyclic.

Paper 38

1 (i) A, B are two points 5 cm apart. A point P moves so that $PA = \frac{1}{2}PB$. Constuct the locus of P.

(ii) Find the distance between the points (5, 2, 5) and (2, -2, -7).

2 In $\triangle ABC$, AB = 15 cm, BC = 21 cm, CA = 27 cm. Prove that $\angle B$ is obtuse, and calculate the lengths of the segments into which CA is divided by the perpendicular from B.

3 Construct $\triangle PQR$ in which QR = 5 cm, $\angle QPR = 50°$, and the length of the median from P to the mid-point of QR is 4 cm. Measure PR.

4 Draw the graph of $y = \dfrac{x^2}{x+2}$ from $x = -1$ to 5. Draw also the graph of $y = 3x - 1$ on the same scale and axes, and obtain, in its simplest form, the equation of which one root is found from the intersection of the graphs. What is this root?

5 From a point X outside a circle, a tangent XT is drawn to touch the circle at T, and a secant XAB is drawn cutting the circle at A and B. If XB = 2XT, prove that XT = 2XA and that AB = 3AX.

6 In Fig. 362, where ABC is any right-angled triangle, prove that the sum of the areas of the semicircles on AB and AC equals the area of the semicircle on BC.

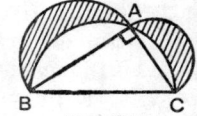

FIG. 362

Deduce that the sum of the two shaded portions equals the triangle ABC.

PAPERS 39–43 (§ 24–44)

Paper 39

1 Evaluate, to three significant figures:

(i) $\left(\dfrac{36 \cdot 84}{71 \cdot 44}\right)^{\frac{3}{5}}$,   (ii) $10^{\bar{2} \cdot 6177}$.

2 Solve the equation $x^2 + 5x - 3 = 0$, giving the roots correct to two decimal places.

3 Sketch the graphs of: (i) $y = 3x - 6$, (ii) $y = 3 - 6x$, (iii) $3y = 2x - 1$, and indicate by shading the region defined by $y \geqslant 3x - 6$, $y + 6x \geqslant 3$, $3y \leqslant 2x - 1$.

4 A lighthouse lies on a bearing 024° from a ship, from which it is 8 km distant. The ship sails due west until the lighthouse bears 051° from the ship. Find the distance through which the ship has sailed.

5 Make (i) v, (ii) T_1 the subject of the formula $H = \dfrac{v(T_1 - T_2)}{550}$.

6 P is any point on the major arc AB, and Q is any point on the minor arc AB, of a circle. The tangents at A and B meet at T. Prove that $\angle QAT + \angle QBT = \angle APB$. By joining TQ and producing it, show that $\angle AQB = \angle ATB + \angle APB$.

Paper 40

1 The area of the surface of a sphere is 16 m². Find, correct to three significant figures (i) the radius in metres, (ii) the volume in cubic metres.

2 Simplify: (i) $\sqrt{36a^{-4}}$; (ii) $(8x^3)^{-\frac{2}{3}}$; (iii) $(0.4)^{-2}$.

3 Draw the graph of $y = (1-x)(2x+1)$ from $x = -2$ to 3. What is the maximum value of y, and for what range of values of x is the function $(1-x)(2x+1)$ positive? Verify the last result by calculation.

4 Draw the plan, front elevation and side elevation of a right pyramid VABC which has an equilateral triangle of side 4 cm as base, the slant edges each 6 cm long, the pyramid standing on the H.P. with AB inclined at 45° to the XY line.

5 If an article is sold for £41·40, the gain is 15%. Find the selling price if the loss is $3\frac{3}{4}\%$.

6 Mark two points S and S′ which are 6 cm apart. Plot carefully the locus of a point P which moves so that PS + PS′ = 8 cm.

Paper 41

1 Solve the equation $2x^2 - 9x - 2 = 0$, giving the roots correct to two decimal places.

2 In Fig. 363, calculate x and y.

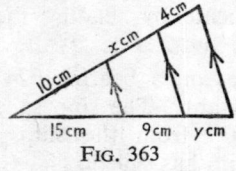

Fig. 363

3 The effort P kg wt necessary to raise a load W kg by means of a certain machine is given by the following table:

W = 10	14	16	24	26
P = 6·6	8·2	9	12·2	13

Plot a graph, show that these results fit a formula of the type $P = a + bW$, and find a and b.

4 A is 8 km due south of a port O, and B is 2 km due east of A. A ship leaves O, and steams at 20 km/h in a straight line to B. It then steams S. 41° W. Calculate the distance of the ship from O an hour after leaving O.

5 The cost of a car increases by 25%. Subsequently, the price again rises by 25% of the increased price. As a result, the price of the car is £90 more than before the first increase. Find the final price.

6 In $\triangle ABC$, $\angle A = 90°$. The perpendicular bisector of BC meets AB at P. Prove by similar triangles that $BP = \dfrac{BC^2}{2BA}$ and calculate BP if BA = 5 cm and AC = 3 cm.

Paper 42

1 Evaluate, to three significant figures, $\dfrac{\sqrt{7\cdot214} + \sqrt{0\cdot7214}}{(4\cdot661)^2}$.

2 A circular cylinder is 50 cm high and holds 140 litres. Find in centimetres, to the nearest centimetre, the internal radius.

3 ABCD is a parallelogram; P, Q are the mid-points of AB, CD. Prove that (i) PC, AQ are parallel, (ii) if PC and AQ cut BD at X, Y, then BX = XY = YD.

4 The vertices of $\triangle ABC$ are (1, 1), (13, 6) and (8, 18). Calculate the lengths of the sides, and show that ABC is an isosceles right-angled triangle.

5 A and B are two ports 14 km apart, and B is due south-east of A. A ship leaves A and steams on a course S. 75° E. After one hour the ship is due north of B. Find the speed of the ship in km per hour.

6 Solve graphically the equation $x^3 - x - 3 = 0$.

Paper 43

1 Make l the subject of the formula

$$H = \frac{v^2}{2g}\left(a + \frac{4fl}{d}\right).$$

2 Find which of the following points does not lie on the line $3y + 4x = 22$: A(-2, 10), B(4, -2), C(-5, 14), D(1, 6). Find also the equation of the straight line through B, parallel to the line $3y = 2x$, the length of AC, and the length of CD.

3 Two ships sail from a port at the same moment, one in a direction N. 18° E. at 20 km/h and the other in a direction N. 74° E. at 16 km/h. Find their distance apart (i) in a northerly direction, (ii) in an easterly direction, after half an hour's sailing.

4 ABCD is a regular tetrahedron, each edge 6 cm long; P is a point in AD 2 cm from A, Q is a point in BD 2 cm from B, and R is the mid-point of CD. Make an accurate drawing of the section PQR.

5 On the same axes, sketch the graphs of the functions x^2, $(x-1)^2$, $(x-1)^2 + 3$ and $(x-1)^2 - 2$. What are the equations of the axes of symmetry of the last three graphs?

6 The jib of a crane is 4·7 m long. It is inclined at an angle of 65° to the horizontal, and its highest point is connected by a tie to a point 3·2 m vertically above the foot of the jib. Find the length of the tie.

PAPERS 44–58 (§ 1–44)

Paper 44

1 A sold a house to B at a profit of 10% on his cost price. Later, B sold it back to A, making a profit of 10% on his own cost price, and A had to give £315 more than he gave originally. Find for how much B bought the house from A.

2 Factorise: (i) $4a^2 - 25b^2$, (ii) $x^2 - 9x + 18$, (iii) $2x^3y^2z - 6x^2y^4 + 2xy^3z^2$, and solve the equation (iv) $2x^2 + 11x - 21 = 0$.

3 (i) Find a linear function of x which has the value $1\frac{1}{2}$ when $x = 1$, and the value $12\frac{1}{2}$ when $x = 3$. For what value of x has the function the value 0?

(ii) Solve the inequation $3 - 2x < 7$.

4 AB is a diameter, and O is the centre, of a circle of radius 5 cm. A circle whose centre is P, radius r cm, touches the first circle internally, and also touches AB at C; AC = 7 cm. Write down the lengths of the sides of △OCP, and hence find r.

5 Draw a triangle in which AB = 6 cm, BC = 8 cm, CA = 9 cm. Construct the circumcircle, and measure its radius.

6 ABC is a triangle, the bisectors of ∠s ABC, ACB meet at I, and the bisectors of the exterior angles at B and C, formed by producing AB and AC, meet at I_1. Prove that $BICI_1$ is a cyclic quadrilateral, and that A, I, I_1 are in a straight line.

Paper 45

1 Use tables to evaluate the following, correct to three significant figures: (i) $\sqrt{365\cdot7}$, (ii) $\dfrac{1}{32\cdot96}$, (iii) $(0\cdot273)^2$.

2 Solve the equations:

(i) $\dfrac{x+1}{x+2} + \dfrac{x-1}{x-2} = 2\frac{1}{3}$,

(ii) $\dfrac{1}{t+1} + \dfrac{1}{t+2} + \dfrac{1}{t+3} = 0$, correct to two decimal places.

3 (i) ABCDE is a regular pentagon, and a square ABXY is drawn on AB, inside the pentagon. Calculate ∠s CBX, XBD, BXC.

(ii) Calculate the interior angle of a regular polygon of 15 sides.

4 ABCD is a parallelogram; points P, Q, R, S are taken on AB, BC, CD, DA respectively such that AP = CR, BQ = DS. Prove that the quadrilateral formed by joining AR, BS, CP, DQ is a parallelogram.

5 ABC is an equilateral triangle inscribed in a circle; P, Q are the mid-points of the minor arcs AB, AC; PQ intersects AB at X and AC at Y. Calculate ∠s PAX, APX, and deduce that △AXY is equilateral.

6 In the quadrilateral ABCD, ∠B = ∠C = 90°, BC = 18 cm; ∠ADB = 76°, ∠BDC = 53°. Calculate the area of the quadrilateral, to the nearest square centimetre.

Paper 46

1 The base of a pyramid is a triangle with sides 5 cm, 6 cm, 8 cm, and the height of the pyramid is 4 cm. Find the volume in cubic centimetres, correct to three significant figures.

2 Simplify: (i) $\dfrac{2}{x+2} + \dfrac{3x+4}{x^2-4}$, (ii) $\dfrac{2}{x+3} + \dfrac{1}{2(x+3)} - \dfrac{2}{3(x+3)}$,

(iii) $\left(\dfrac{3}{x-1} - \dfrac{1}{x-2}\right) \div \left(\dfrac{2}{x-1} - \dfrac{1}{x-3}\right)$.

3 ABC is an equilateral triangle, and P is a point in the side BC such that ∠APC = 75°. The perpendicular through P to BC meets AB at Q. Prove that AQ = QP.

4 ABCD is a square; P is a point in DC and Q is a point in AD, such that AP = BQ; AP and BQ intersect at X. Prove that (i) ∠AXB = 90°, (ii) DQXP is cyclic.

5 AB is a diameter of a circle, CD is any chord; M, N are the feet of the perpendiculars from A, B to CD, produced if necessary. Prove that MC = DN. (Draw the perpendicular from the centre of the circle to CD.)

6 ABC is the equilateral base of a pyramid, and the vertex V is 6 cm vertically above the centre of the base; AB = 4 cm. Calculate the angle between VA and the base ABC.

A plane cuts VA at P, VB at Q, VC at R, and VP = 4 cm, VQ = 2 cm, VR = 3 cm. Make an accurate drawing of the section PQR.

Paper 47

1 Use logarithms to evaluate, correct to three significant figures, $(26 \cdot 38 \times 0 \cdot 417) + \sqrt{0 \cdot 5818}$.

2 Solve the equations:

(i) $0 \cdot 3(x - 0 \cdot 2) = 0 \cdot 2(x - 0 \cdot 1)$,

(ii) $x(x - 2) - 3(2x - 1) = (2 + x)(3 - x) - 7$.

3 O is any point inside a triangle ABC. The parallelograms OAEC, OCDB, OBFA are drawn. Prove that (i) BF is equal and parallel to CE, (ii) EF = BC, (iii) △s ABC, DEF are congruent.

4 Construct a quadrilateral ABCD in which AB = 2·1 cm, BC = 2·9 cm, CD = 5·1 cm, DA = 4 cm and the diagonal BD = 5·1 cm. Find by construction a point P in AB produced such that △ADP is equal in area to the quadrilateral ABCD. Draw a perpendicular from P to DA, and calculate the area of ABCD.

5 ABC is a triangle, D is the mid-point of BC, and X is the mid-point of AD; the parallel to BA through D meets AC at P, and the parallel to BA through X meets AC at Q. Prove that (i) $AQ = \frac{1}{4}AC$, (ii) $QX = \frac{1}{4}AB$.

6 ABCD is a quadrilateral in which AB = AD = 9·3 cm, CB = CD, ∠BAD = 52° and ∠BCD = 94°. Calculate the lengths of AC and BD.

Paper 48

1 Simplify, without the use of tables:

(i) $\sqrt{12} \times \sqrt{18} \times \sqrt{98} \times \sqrt{75}$,

(ii) $\left(\sqrt{2} + \dfrac{1}{\sqrt{2}} \right)^2$, (iii) $\dfrac{\sqrt{20}}{\sqrt{5}} + \dfrac{\sqrt{28}}{\sqrt{7}}$.

2 Solve the equations: $\dfrac{x-1}{5} - \dfrac{y-2}{4} = 2\frac{3}{4}$,

$$\frac{2-x}{4} - \frac{y+3}{5} + \frac{3}{5} = 0.$$

3 Make (i) H, (ii) A the subject of the formula

$$W = w\left(\frac{wH}{5AP} - 1 \right).$$

4 ABC is a triangle; P is any point on AC produced, F is the mid-point of AB; FP cuts BC at Q, and the parallel through C to AB meets FP at X. Use similar triangles to obtain ratios equal to BQ : QC and AP : CP, and hence prove that these ratios are equal.

5 Any point O inside $\triangle$ABC is joined to the vertices of the triangle; through any point X on OA, a parallel is drawn to AB, meeting OB at Y, and a parallel is drawn to AC, meeting OC at Z. Prove that YZ is parallel to BC.

6 Two men, stationed at A and B, 100 m apart, take observations of a point C. They find that $\angle$ABC $= 48° 16'$ and $\angle$BAC $= 61° 50'$. Calculate the distance of C from B.

7 Draw a sketch and leave unshaded the region consisting of points satisfying the inequalities $2y - 3x \leqslant 6$, $x + 2y \geqslant 4$.

Paper 49

1 Use tables to evaluate, correct to three significant figures:

(i) $\sqrt{22 \cdot 7^2 + 31 \cdot 9^2}$, (ii) $\dfrac{1}{3 \cdot 147} + \dfrac{1}{2 \cdot 862}$, (iii) $(10^{2 \cdot 112})^2$.

2 (i) Expand $(1 - x)(1 + x + x^2)$; (ii) find the coefficient of x^3 in the product of

$$(2 - x + 3x^2 + 2x^3 - x^4) \quad \text{and} \quad (1 + 3x + 4x^2 - x^3 + 3x^4).$$

3 (i) Draw the graph of the function $x^2 - 5x + 1$ from $x = 0$ to 5. Use the graph to solve the equation $x^2 - 5x + 2 = 0$.
(ii) Solve the inequation $x^2 - 5x > 6$.

4 Explain why a median of a triangle divides the triangle into two triangles of equal area.

CF is a median of $\triangle$ABC, and X is the mid-point of CF; AX produced meets BC at Y, and FY is joined. Prove that the triangles BFY, AFY, ACY are equal in area.

5 AB is a diameter of a circle, centre O, and AC is any chord through A; N is the foot of the perpendicular from O to AC. Prove that ON $= \frac{1}{2}$BC.

6 ABC is an equilateral triangle of side 5 cm; P is a point in AB, Q is a point in AC, and AP = 3 cm, AQ = 2 cm. Calculate the area of $\triangle$APQ, and express this area as a fraction of the area of $\triangle$ABC.

Paper 50

1 Use logarithms to evaluate, correct to three significant figures:

$$\frac{0 \cdot 1832 \times (4 \cdot 118)^2}{6 \cdot 172 \times \sqrt[3]{28 \cdot 41}}.$$

2 Factorise: (i) $x^2 - xy + 3x - 3y$, (ii) $a^2 - 4ab - 21b^2$, (iii) $2p^2 - 8q^2$.

3 Simplify:

(i) $\dfrac{9^{x+y} \times 4^y}{6^{2y}}$, (ii) $\left(\dfrac{x^{-1}}{4y^2}\right)^{-2}$, (iii) $\sqrt{2} \times \sqrt[3]{2} \times \sqrt[9]{2}$.

4 Two circles intersect at A, B; straight lines PAQ, RAS cut one circle at P, R and the other at Q, S. Prove that $\triangle$s BPR, BQS are similar, and deduce that BP : BR = BQ : BS.

5 The bisector of $\angle$BAC of $\triangle$ABC meets BC at D; H and K are points on BA, CA respectively such that BH = BD, CK = CD. Prove that HK is parallel to BC.

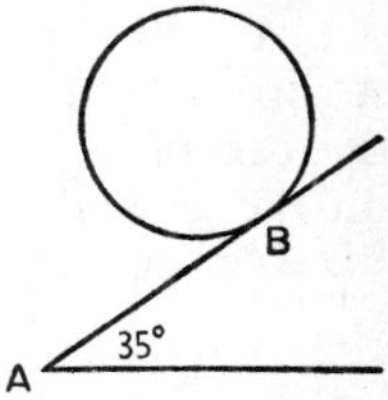

6 Fig. 364 represents a wheel of radius 60 cm rolling up an incline of 35°. Find the height of the highest point of the wheel above the level of A, when the point of contact B is at a distance 3 m from A.

Fig. 364

Paper 51

1 The price of petrol is reduced by 10%, and a motorist then uses 10% more. Find how much per cent he saves.

2 Solve the equations:

$$\frac{x-1}{4} - \frac{7-3y}{2} = 1\tfrac{3}{4},$$

$$\frac{x+5}{3} + \frac{3y-2}{2} = 6.$$

3 A spiral spring is suspended from one end, and different loads are hung from the other end. The readings of the load w grammes and the length l cm are given in the following table:

w . . .	100	300	500	600	700
l . . .	43·4	44·6	45·8	46·4	47

Plot these readings, show that they obey a law of the type $l = a + bw$, and find the values of a and b. Find also the length of the spring when there is no load, and the load which will stretch the spring to a length 44·2 cm.

4 From a point T outside a circle a tangent TA, touching the circle at A, and a secant, TBC, cutting the circle at B, C, are drawn. By considering the ratio of the areas of $\triangle$s ABT, ACT in two ways, prove that $BT : CT = BA^2 : AC^2$.

5 ABCD is a rhombus. Prove that $AC^2 + BD^2 = 4AB^2$, and that the area of the rhombus is $\frac{1}{2}AC.BD$.

6 A vertical pole AB is 6 m high and stands on level ground. A rope 8·7 m long joins the top A to a point C on the ground due east of B. A second rope 7·5 m long joins A to a point D on the ground due south of B. Show that $BC = 6.3$ m and $BD = 4.5$ m, and calculate $\angle CAD$.

Paper 52

1 A piece of work can be done by 30 men in 6 days. They work for 2 days, after which 6 of the men are taken off and put on to another job. How many days will it take for the remaining 24 men to finish?

2 Simplify: (i) $\dfrac{x^2 - 9x + 20}{x^2 - 4x + 3} \times \dfrac{x^2 - 2x - 3}{x^2 - 2x - 8} \div \dfrac{x^2 - 4x - 5}{x^2 - 4}$,

(ii) $\dfrac{x}{3(x-1)} + \dfrac{2x}{5x - 5} + \dfrac{3x}{1 - x}$.

3 ABC is a triangle; BA is produced to P, making $BA = AP$, and CA is produced to Q, making $CA = AQ$. Prove that CP and BQ are parallel.

4 ABCD is a quadrilateral; the inscribed circles of △s ABD, CBD touch BD at the same point. Prove that AB + CD = AD + BC.

5 Draw a circle of radius 4 cm, and construct a triangle, inscribed in the circle, with angles 74°, 57° and 49°. Measure the longest side of the triangle. (Begin by drawing a tangent at any point, and make an angle of 74° at the point of contact.)

6 AOB, COD are two perpendicular diameters of a circle; P is any point on OA, Q is any point on OB; CP produced and CQ produced meet the circle at X, Y respectively. Prove that (i) ∠CPO = ∠ODX, (ii) CP.CX = CO.CD, (iii) PQYX is cyclic.

7 Solve the inequality $4x + 1 < 5x^2$.

Paper 53

1 The simple interest on £450 for 5 years is £78·75. Find the rate per cent per annum.

2 Use logarithms to evaluate, correct to three significant figures:

$$\frac{\sqrt[3]{0·08714} \times 61·4}{(0·522)^2}.$$

3 Draw the graph of the function $(x-1)(x-2)(x-3)$ from $x = 0$ to $x = 4$. By drawing tangents, verify that the function has the same gradient when $x = 1$ as when $x = 3$, and find that gradient. Find also the greatest positive value of m, if the equation $(x-1)(x-2)(x-3) = mx$ has three distinct roots.

4 A is a fixed point outside a sphere, and P is the point of contact of any tangent from A to the sphere. State what is the locus of P, and what kind of surface AP traces out as P describes this locus.

5 Two circles intersect at A, B; P is any point on one circle, and PA, PB (produced if necessary) cut the other circle at R, S. Prove that RS is parallel to the tangent at P.

6 A man walks 38 m due north from a tree to a point A; he then walks 71 m from A, on a bearing 074°, to a point B. Find the bearing and distance of the tree from B.

Paper 54

1 A rectangular block of metal 36 cm by 25 cm by 12·5 cm is drawn into wire of radius 0·125 cm. Find the length of wire in kilometres, correct to three significant figures.

2 Solve the equations:

$$\text{(i)}\ \frac{2x-3}{5}=2+\frac{1-3x}{6},\quad \text{(ii)}\ t^2=2(5t-12).$$

3 AB, AC are equal chords of a circle; the bisector of $\angle ABC$ meets the circle at D, and AD produced meets BC produced at E. If $\angle ABC=2x°$, write down the numbers of degrees in the angles CAD, ACB, AEC, and deduce that CA = CE.

4 Draw a circle, radius 2·5 cm, and mark a point P distant 6 cm from its centre. Construct a chord of the circle which is 3 cm long and which, when produced, passes through P. (Begin with the locus of the mid-points of chords which are 3 cm long.)

5 (i) In $\triangle$ABC, AB = 7 cm, BC = 9 cm, CA = 4 cm. Calculate the length of the median from A to the mid-point of BC.

(ii) Find the distance between the points $(2, 5, -6)$ and $(-2, -1, 6)$.

6 Without using tables, find the numerical values of:

(i) $2 \tan^2 60° + 4 \cos^2 45° + \dfrac{3}{\cos^2 30°}$

(ii) $\cos 60° + \tan 45° + \tan^2 30° - \sin^2 60°$.

Paper 55

1 A shopkeeper sells a piece of furniture for £68·25, thus making 5% profit on his cost price. Find his gain or loss per cent if he had sold it for £62·40.

2 Factorise:

(i) $3ax - 3a^2 - 2x + 2a$,   (ii) $(x+2)^2 - (x+2)(2x-1)$,
(iii) $(a+b)^2 - 16$,   (iv) $\frac{1}{3}\pi r^2 h + \frac{4}{3}\pi r^3$.

3 Two circles, centres X, Y, intersect at A, B; a line PBQ meets one circle at P and the other at Q. Prove that $\angle AXB + \angle AYB = 360° - 2\angle PAQ$.

Deduce that, if the four points A, X, B, Y are concyclic, $\angle PAQ = 90°$.

4 P is the point in the side AB of $\triangle ABC$ such that $AP = \frac{2}{3}AB$; Q is the point in AC such that $AQ = \frac{3}{4}AC$. Express the area of each of triangles BPC, CPQ, APQ as fractions of the area of $\triangle ABC$.

5 Two perpendicular chords AB, CD of a circle intersect at X, inside the circle. If AX = 5 cm, XB = 15 cm and AC = 13 cm, calculate CX and XD.

If O is the centre of the circle, calculate OX. (Draw perpendiculars from O to AB, CD.)

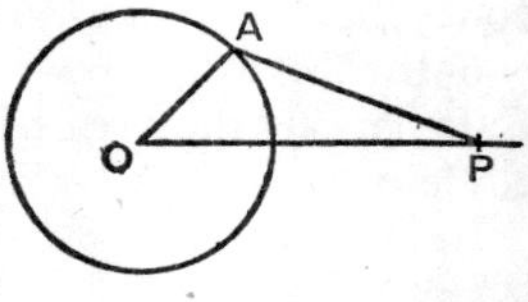

Fig. 365

6 The crank OA, 30 cm long, turns in a vertical circle about the end O (see Fig. 365); AP is a connecting-rod, 1·2 m long, hinged at A, and the end P is forced to move along a horizontal straight line through O. Find the distance OP when (i) $\angle AOP = 33°$, (ii) $\angle AOP = 150°$.

Paper 56

1 (i) Find the surface of a cube whose edge is 2·8 cm.
   (ii) Find the surface of a sphere whose diameter is 2·8 cm.
     (Take π to be $\frac{22}{7}$.)

2 Simplify:

$$\text{(i)} \quad \frac{x}{1-x} - \frac{x}{1+x} + \frac{2x}{1-x^2},$$

$$\text{(ii)} \quad \frac{a^2 - 2ab - 15b^2}{a^2 + ab - 30b^2};$$

and solve the equation $2x^2 - 17x - 9 = 0$.

3 The volume of metal in a tube is given by the formula $V = \pi l\{R^2 - (R - t)^2\}$, where l is the length, R the external radius, t the thickness of the metal. Make R the subject of the formula, and find the value of R when $V = 200$, $l = 8$, $t = 3$. (Take π as 3·142.)

4 A regular tetrahedron, of edge 3 cm, stands on the H.P. with an edge of its base parallel to the XY line. Draw the plan, front elevation and side elevation.

5 Draw $\triangle ABC$ in which $AB = 4 \cdot 5$ cm, $BC = 4 \cdot 0$ cm, $CA = 3 \cdot 0$ cm, and mark D, the mid-point of BC. Construct a circle to touch BA at A and to pass through D, and measure the radius of this circle.

If the circle cuts BC produced at X, and BA is produced to a point Y such that $BA = AY$, prove without any measurement that: (i) $BC \cdot BX = 2BA^2$, (ii) the four points A, C, X, Y are concyclic.

6 In $\triangle ABC$, $AB = 3$ cm, $BC = 5$ cm and $\angle ABC = 116°$. Calculate (i) the area of $\triangle ABC$, (ii) the radius of the circumcircle of $\triangle ABC$.

Paper 57

1 The ages of four boys are as follows: 14 years 6 months, 14 years 10 months, 15 years 3 months, 14 years 1 month. Find their average age.

They are joined by a fifth boy, and his arrival makes the average age of the group 14 years 9 months. Find the age of the fifth boy.

2 Simplify: (i) $(1 + 3x)(2 - x - x^2)$, (ii) $(1 - x)^2 + (2 - 3x)^2$; solve the inequation

(iii) $2x - 3 < 4x - 9$,

and solve the equation

(iv) $\frac{1}{2}(2x - 3) - \frac{2}{7}(x + 6) = 5$.

3 Draw the graphs of $y = x(3 - x)$ and $y = \dfrac{2}{x}$ on the same scale and axes. Hence solve the equation $x^3 - 3x^2 + 2 = 0$.

4 A sphere of radius 2 cm rests inside a hollow inverted cone whose vertical angle is 60°. Find the distance of the centre of the sphere from the vertex of the cone, and prove that the volume of water which must be poured into the cone so as just to cover the sphere is $\dfrac{40\pi}{3}$ cubic centimetres.

5 A square PQRS, of area 52 cm², is placed in a square ABCD, of area 100 cm², with its vertices P, Q, R, S on AB, BC, CD, DA respectively. Calculate the lengths of the segments into which the sides of ABCD are divided.

6 Draw the plan, front elevation and side elevation of a pyramid standing on the H.P., its square base having a side 3 cm, the slant edges each 5 cm long, and one edge of the base inclined at an angle of 20° to the XY line.

7 Find the distance between the points (13, 9) and (−11, 2).

Paper 58

1 A, B, C, D are four consecutive vertices of a regular nine-sided figure inscribed in a circle. Calculate the angles of △ABD.

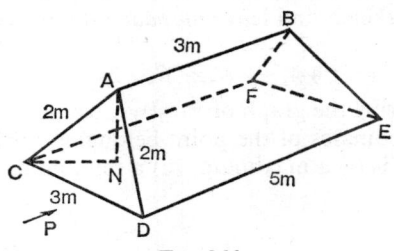

Fig. 366

2 Fig. 366 represents a roof. CDEF is a rectangle; AC, AD, BE, BF are all 2 m long and AB = 3 m; CD = 3 m, DE = 5 m; N is the foot of the perpendicular from A to the plane CDEF. Draw △ANC to the scale of 2 cm to 1 m, and hence draw a plan and side elevation (view from P).

Find also, by drawing or calculation, the angle made with the plane CDEF by (i) the line AC, (ii) the end ACD.

3 A man sold an article for £9·20 at a profit of 15% on his own cost price. Find what the selling price would have to be if he wanted to make a profit of 25%.

4 (i) Simplify, without the use of tables:

$$(0{\cdot}01)^{\frac{1}{2}}, \quad (0{\cdot}027)^{-\frac{1}{3}}, \quad \left(\frac{125}{64}\right)^{\frac{2}{3}}.$$

(ii) Find x if $9^x = 27$.

(iii) Solve the inequality

$$2x^2 - 3x > 12 + 2x.$$

5 Draw the graphs of the functions x^3 and $5x + 3$ for values of x from -3 to $+3$. Hence solve the equation $x^3 - 5x - 3 = 0$. By drawing another straight line, find a root of the equation $x^3 - 5x - 8 = 0$.

6 ABCD is a rectangular courtyard; AB = 24 m, BC = 18 m. A vertical flagstaff stands at A. A boy, whose eye is $1\frac{1}{2}$ m from the ground, finds that the angle of elevation of the top of the flagstaff from D is 42°. Find the height of the flagstaff, and the angle of elevation for the same boy at C.

7 Draw a sketch and leave *unshaded* the region represented by

$$y \leqslant x + 4, \quad y + 2x \leqslant 7, \quad 2y + x \geqslant 5.$$

By considering the graph of $x + y = c$, where c is any number, find the co-ordinates of the point belonging to this region for which $(x + y)$ is (i) a maximum, (ii) a minimum.

INDEX

See also Table of Contents

i

TABLES

LOGARITHMS

	0	1	2	3	4	5	6	7	8	9	1	2	3	4	5	6	7	8	9
10	·0000	0043	0086	0128	0170	0212	0253	0294	0334	0374	4	8	12	17	21	25	29	33	37
11	·0414	0453	0492	0531	0569	0607	0645	0682	0719	0755	4	8	11	15	19	23	26	30	34
12	·0792	0828	0864	0899	0934	0969	1004	1038	1072	1106	3	7	10	14	17	21	24	28	31
13	·1139	1173	1206	1239	1271	1303	1335	1367	1399	1430	3	6	10	13	16	19	23	26	29
14	·1461	1492	1523	1553	1584	1614	1644	1673	1703	1732	3	6	9	12	15	18	21	24	27
15	·1761	1790	1818	1847	1875	1903	1931	1959	1987	2014	3	6	8	11	14	17	20	22	25
16	·2041	2068	2095	2122	2148	2175	2201	2227	2253	2279	3	5	8	11	13	16	18	21	24
17	·2304	2330	2355	2380	2405	2430	2455	2480	2504	2529	2	5	7	10	12	15	17	20	22
18	·2553	2577	2601	2625	2648	2672	2695	2718	2742	2765	2	5	7	9	12	14	16	19	21
19	·2788	2810	2833	2856	2878	2900	2923	2945	2967	2989	2	4	7	9	11	13	16	18	20
20	·3010	3032	3054	3075	3096	3118	3139	3160	3181	3201	2	4	6	8	11	13	15	17	19
21	·3222	3243	3263	3284	3304	3324	3345	3365	3385	3404	2	4	6	8	10	12	14	16	18
22	·3424	3444	3464	3483	3502	3522	3541	3560	3579	3598	2	4	6	8	10	12	14	15	17
23	·3617	3636	3655	3674	3692	3711	3729	3747	3766	3784	2	4	6	7	9	11	13	15	17
24	·3802	3820	3838	3856	3874	3892	3909	3927	3945	3962	2	4	5	7	9	11	12	14	16
25	·3979	3997	4014	4031	4048	4065	4082	4099	4116	4133	2	3	5	7	9	10	12	14	15
26	·4150	4166	4183	4200	4216	4232	4249	4265	4281	4298	2	3	5	7	8	10	11	13	15
27	·4314	4330	4346	4362	4378	4393	4409	4425	4440	4456	2	3	5	6	8	9	11	13	14
28	·4472	4487	4502	4518	4533	4548	4564	4579	4594	4609	2	3	5	6	8	9	11	12	14
29	·4624	4639	4654	4669	4683	4698	4713	4728	4742	4757	1	3	4	6	7	9	10	12	13
30	·4771	4786	4800	4814	4829	4843	4857	4871	4886	4900	1	3	4	6	7	9	10	11	13
31	·4914	4928	4942	4955	4969	4983	4997	5011	5024	5038	1	3	4	6	7	8	10	11	12
32	·5051	5065	5079	5092	5105	5119	5132	5145	5159	5172	1	3	4	5	7	8	9	11	12
33	·5185	5198	5211	5224	5237	5250	5263	5276	5289	5302	1	3	4	5	6	8	9	10	12
34	·5315	5328	5340	5353	5366	5378	5391	5403	5416	5428	1	3	4	5	6	8	9	10	11
35	·5441	5453	5465	5478	5490	5502	5514	5527	5539	5551	1	2	4	5	6	7	9	10	11
36	·5563	5575	5587	5599	5611	5623	5635	5647	5658	5670	1	2	4	5	6	7	8	10	11
37	·5682	5694	5705	5717	5729	5740	5752	5763	5775	5786	1	2	3	5	6	7	8	9	10
38	·5798	5809	5821	5832	5843	5855	5866	5877	5888	5899	1	2	3	5	6	7	8	9	10
39	·5911	5922	5933	5944	5955	5966	5977	5988	5999	6010	1	2	3	4	5	7	8	9	10
40	·6021	6031	6042	6053	6064	6075	6085	6096	6107	6117	1	2	3	4	5	6	8	9	10
41	·6128	6138	6149	6160	6170	6180	6191	6201	6212	6222	1	2	3	4	5	6	7	8	9
42	·6232	6243	6253	6263	6274	6284	6294	6304	6314	6325	1	2	3	4	5	6	7	8	9
43	·6335	6345	6355	6365	6375	6385	6395	6405	6415	6425	1	2	3	4	5	6	7	8	9
44	·6435	6444	6454	6464	6474	6484	6493	6503	6513	6522	1	2	3	4	5	6	7	8	9
45	·6532	6542	6551	6561	6571	6580	6590	6599	6609	6618	1	2	3	4	5	6	7	8	9
46	·6628	6637	6646	6656	6665	6675	6684	6693	6702	6712	1	2	3	4	5	6	7	7	8
47	·6721	6730	6739	6749	6758	6767	6776	6785	6794	6803	1	2	3	4	5	5	6	7	8
48	·6812	6821	6830	6839	6848	6857	6866	6875	6884	6893	1	2	3	4	4	5	6	7	8
49	·6902	6911	6920	6928	6937	6946	6955	6964	6972	6981	1	2	3	4	4	5	6	7	8
50	·6990	6998	7007	7016	7024	7033	7042	7050	7059	7067	1	2	3	3	4	5	6	7	8
51	·7076	7084	7093	7101	7110	7118	7126	7135	7143	7152	1	2	3	3	4	5	6	7	8
52	·7160	7168	7177	7185	7193	7202	7210	7218	7226	7235	1	2	2	3	4	5	6	7	7
53	·7243	7251	7259	7267	7275	7284	7292	7300	7308	7316	1	2	2	3	4	5	6	6	7
54	·7324	7332	7340	7348	7356	7364	7372	7380	7388	7396	1	2	2	3	4	5	6	6	7

	0	**1**	**2**	**3**	**4**	**5**	**6**	**7**	**8**	**9**	**1**	**2**	**3**	**4**	**5**	**6**	**7**	**8**	**9**
55	·7404	7412	7419	7427	7435	7443	7451	7459	7466	7474	1	2	2	3	4	5	5	6	7
56	·7482	7490	7497	7505	7513	7520	7528	7536	7543	7551	1	2	2	3	4	5	5	6	7
57	·7559	7566	7574	7582	7589	7597	7604	7612	7619	7627	1	2	2	3	4	5	5	6	7
58	·7634	7642	7649	7657	7664	7672	7679	7686	7694	7701	1	1	2	3	4	4	5	6	7
59	·7709	7716	7723	7731	7738	7745	7752	7760	7767	7774	1	1	2	3	4	4	5	6	7
60	·7782	7789	7796	7803	7810	7818	7825	7832	7839	7846	1	1	2	3	4	4	5	6	6
61	·7853	7860	7868	7875	7882	7889	7896	7903	7910	7917	1	1	2	3	4	4	5	6	6
62	·7924	7931	7938	7945	7952	7959	7966	7973	7980	7987	1	1	2	3	3	4	5	6	6
63	·7993	8000	8007	8014	8021	8028	8035	8041	8048	8055	1	1	2	3	3	4	5	5	6
64	·8062	8069	8075	8082	8089	8096	8102	8109	8116	8122	1	1	2	3	3	4	5	5	6
65	·8129	8136	8142	8149	8156	8162	8169	8176	8182	8189	1	1	2	3	3	4	5	5	6
66	·8195	8202	8209	8215	8222	8228	8235	8241	8248	8254	1	1	2	3	3	4	5	5	6
67	·8261	8267	8274	8280	8287	8293	8299	8306	8312	8319	1	1	2	3	3	4	5	5	6
68	·8325	8331	8338	8344	8351	8357	8363	8370	8376	8382	1	1	2	3	3	4	4	5	6
69	·8388	8395	8401	8407	8414	8420	8426	8432	8439	8445	1	1	2	2	3	4	4	5	6
70	·8451	8457	8463	8470	8476	8482	8488	8494	8500	8506	1	1	2	2	3	4	4	5	6
71	·8513	8519	8525	8531	8537	8543	8549	8555	8561	8567	1	1	2	2	3	4	4	5	5
72	·8573	8579	8585	8591	8597	8603	8609	8615	8621	8627	1	1	2	2	3	4	4	5	5
73	·8633	8639	8645	8651	8657	8663	8669	8675	8681	8686	1	1	2	2	3	4	4	5	5
74	·8692	8698	8704	8710	8716	8722	8727	8733	8739	8745	1	1	2	2	3	4	4	5	5
75	·8751	8756	8762	8768	8774	8779	8785	8791	8797	8802	1	1	2	2	3	3	4	5	5
76	·8808	8814	8820	8825	8831	8837	8842	8848	8854	8859	1	1	2	2	3	3	4	5	5
77	·8865	8871	8876	8882	8887	8893	8899	8904	8910	8915	1	1	2	2	3	3	4	4	5
78	·8921	8927	8932	8938	8943	8949	8954	8960	8965	8971	1	1	2	2	3	3	4	4	5
79	·8976	8982	8987	8993	8998	9004	9009	9015	9020	9025	1	1	2	2	3	3	4	4	5
80	·9031	9036	9042	9047	9053	9058	9063	9069	9074	9079	1	1	2	2	3	3	4	4	5
81	·9085	9090	9096	9101	9106	9112	9117	9122	9128	9133	1	1	2	2	3	3	4	4	5
82	·9138	9143	9149	9154	9159	9165	9170	9175	9180	9186	1	1	2	2	3	3	4	4	5
83	·9191	9196	9201	9206	9212	9217	9222	9227	9232	9238	1	1	2	2	3	3	4	4	5
84	·9243	9248	9253	9258	9263	9269	9274	9279	9284	9289	1	1	2	2	3	3	4	4	5
85	·9294	9299	9304	9309	9315	9320	9325	9330	9335	9340	1	1	2	2	3	3	4	4	5
86	·9345	9350	9355	9360	9365	9370	9375	9380	9385	9390	1	1	2	2	3	3	4	4	5
87	·9395	9400	9405	9410	9415	9420	9425	9430	9435	9440	0	1	1	2	2	3	3	4	4
88	·9445	9450	9455	9460	9465	9469	9474	9479	9484	9489	0	1	1	2	2	3	3	4	4
89	·9494	9499	9504	9509	9513	9518	9523	9528	9533	9538	0	1	1	2	2	3	3	4	4
90	·9542	9547	9552	9557	9562	9566	9571	9576	9581	9586	0	1	1	2	2	3	3	4	4
91	·9590	9595	9600	9605	9609	9614	9619	9624	9628	9633	0	1	1	2	2	3	3	4	4
92	·9638	9643	9647	9652	9657	9661	9666	9671	9675	9680	0	1	1	2	2	3	3	4	4
93	·9685	9689	9694	9699	9703	9708	9713	9717	9722	9727	0	1	1	2	2	3	3	4	4
94	·9731	9736	9741	9745	9750	9754	9759	9763	9768	9773	0	1	1	2	2	3	3	4	4
95	·9777	9782	9786	9791	9795	9800	9805	9809	9814	9818	0	1	1	2	2	3	3	4	4
96	·9823	9827	9832	9836	9841	9845	9850	9854	9859	9863	0	1	1	2	2	3	3	4	4
97	·9868	9872	9877	9881	9886	9890	9894	9899	9903	9908	0	1	1	2	2	3	3	4	4
98	·9912	9917	9921	9926	9930	9934	9939	9943	9948	9952	0	1	1	2	2	3	3	4	4
99	·9956	9961	9965	9969	9974	9978	9983	9987	9991	9996	0	1	1	2	2	3	3	3	4

ANTI-LOGARITHMS

	0	1	2	3	4	5	6	7	8	9	1	2	3	4	5	6	7	8	9
·00	1000	1002	1005	1007	1009	1012	1014	1016	1019	1021	0	0	1	1	1	1	2	2	2
·01	1023	1026	1028	1030	1033	1035	1038	1040	1042	1045	0	0	1	1	1	1	2	2	2
·02	1047	1050	1052	1054	1057	1059	1062	1064	1067	1069	0	0	1	1	1	1	2	2	2
·03	1072	1074	1076	1079	1081	1084	1086	1089	1091	1094	0	0	1	1	1	1	2	2	2
·04	1096	1099	1102	1104	1107	1109	1112	1114	1117	1119	0	1	1	1	1	2	2	2	2
·05	1122	1125	1127	1130	1132	1135	1138	1140	1143	1146	0	1	1	1	1	2	2	2	2
·06	1148	1151	1153	1156	1159	1161	1164	1167	1169	1172	0	1	1	1	1	2	2	2	2
·07	1175	1178	1180	1183	1186	1189	1191	1194	1197	1199	0	1	1	1	1	2	2	2	2
·08	1202	1205	1208	1211	1213	1216	1219	1222	1225	1227	0	1	1	1	1	2	2	2	3
·09	1230	1233	1236	1239	1242	1245	1247	1250	1253	1256	0	1	1	1	1	2	2	2	3
·10	1259	1262	1265	1268	1271	1274	1276	1279	1282	1285	0	1	1	1	1	2	2	2	3
·11	1288	1291	1294	1297	1300	1303	1306	1309	1312	1315	0	1	1	1	2	2	2	2	3
·12	1318	1321	1324	1327	1330	1334	1337	1340	1343	1346	0	1	1	1	2	2	2	3	3
·13	1349	1352	1355	1358	1361	1365	1368	1371	1374	1377	0	1	1	1	2	2	2	3	3
·14	1380	1384	1387	1390	1393	1396	1400	1403	1406	1409	0	1	1	1	2	2	2	3	3
·15	1413	1416	1419	1422	1426	1429	1432	1435	1439	1442	0	1	1	1	2	2	2	3	3
·16	1445	1449	1452	1455	1459	1462	1466	1469	1472	1476	0	1	1	1	2	2	2	3	3
·17	1479	1483	1486	1489	1493	1496	1500	1503	1507	1510	0	1	1	1	2	2	2	3	3
·18	1514	1517	1521	1524	1528	1531	1535	1538	1542	1545	0	1	1	1	2	2	2	3	3
·19	1549	1552	1556	1560	1563	1567	1570	1574	1578	1581	0	1	1	1	2	2	3	3	3
·20	1585	1589	1592	1596	1600	1603	1607	1611	1614	1618	0	1	1	1	2	2	3	3	3
·21	1622	1626	1629	1633	1637	1641	1644	1648	1652	1656	0	1	1	2	2	2	3	3	3
·22	1660	1663	1667	1671	1675	1679	1683	1687	1690	1694	0	1	1	2	2	2	3	3	3
·23	1698	1702	1706	1710	1714	1718	1722	1726	1730	1734	0	1	1	2	2	2	3	3	4
·24	1738	1742	1746	1750	1754	1758	1762	1766	1770	1774	0	1	1	2	2	2	3	3	4
·25	1778	1782	1786	1791	1795	1799	1803	1807	1811	1816	0	1	1	2	2	2	3	3	4
·26	1820	1824	1828	1832	1837	1841	1845	1849	1854	1858	0	1	1	2	2	3	3	3	4
·27	1862	1866	1871	1875	1879	1884	1888	1892	1897	1901	0	1	1	2	2	3	3	3	4
·28	1905	1910	1914	1919	1923	1928	1932	1936	1941	1945	0	1	1	2	2	3	3	4	4
·29	1950	1954	1959	1963	1968	1972	1977	1982	1986	1991	0	1	1	2	2	3	3	4	4
·30	1995	2000	2004	2009	2014	2018	2023	2028	2032	2037	0	1	1	2	2	3	3	4	4
·31	2042	2046	2051	2056	2061	2065	2070	2075	2080	2084	0	1	1	2	2	3	3	4	4
·32	2089	2094	2099	2104	2109	2113	2118	2123	2128	2133	0	1	1	2	2	3	3	4	4
·33	2138	2143	2148	2153	2158	2163	2168	2173	2178	2183	0	1	1	2	2	3	3	4	4
·34	2188	2193	2198	2203	2208	2213	2218	2223	2228	2234	1	1	2	2	3	3	4	4	5
·35	2239	2244	2249	2254	2259	2265	2270	2275	2280	2286	1	1	2	2	3	3	4	4	5
·36	2291	2296	2301	2307	2312	2317	2323	2328	2333	2339	1	1	2	2	3	3	4	4	5
·37	2344	2350	2355	2360	2366	2371	2377	2382	2388	2393	1	1	2	2	3	3	4	4	5
·38	2399	2404	2410	2415	2421	2427	2432	2438	2443	2449	1	1	2	2	3	3	4	4	5
·39	2455	2460	2466	2472	2477	2483	2489	2495	2500	2506	1	1	2	2	3	3	4	5	5
·40	2512	2518	2523	2529	2535	2541	2547	2553	2559	2564	1	1	2	2	3	4	4	5	5
·41	2570	2576	2582	2588	2594	2600	2606	2612	2618	2624	1	1	2	2	3	4	4	5	5
·42	2630	2636	2642	2649	2655	2661	2667	2673	2679	2685	1	1	2	2	3	4	4	5	6
·43	2692	2698	2704	2710	2716	2723	2729	2735	2742	2748	1	1	2	3	3	4	4	5	6
·44	2754	2761	2767	2773	2780	2786	2793	2799	2805	2812	1	1	2	3	3	4	4	5	6
·45	2818	2825	2831	2838	2844	2851	2858	2864	2871	2877	1	1	2	3	3	4	5	5	6
·46	2884	2891	2897	2904	2911	2917	2924	2931	2938	2944	1	1	2	3	3	4	5	5	6
·47	2951	2958	2965	2972	2979	2985	2992	2999	3006	3013	1	1	2	3	3	4	5	5	6
·48	3020	3027	3034	3041	3048	3055	3062	3069	3076	3083	1	1	2	3	4	4	5	6	6
·49	3090	3097	3105	3112	3119	3126	3133	3141	3148	3155	1	1	2	3	4	4	5	6	6

	0	1	2	3	4	5	6	7	8	9	1	2	3	4	5	6	7	8	9
·50	3162	3170	3177	3184	3192	3199	3206	3214	3221	3228	1	1	2	3	4	4	5	6	7
·51	3236	3243	3251	3258	3266	3273	3281	3289	3296	3304	1	2	2	3	4	5	5	6	7
·52	3311	3319	3327	3334	3342	3350	3357	3365	3373	3381	1	2	2	3	4	5	5	6	7
·53	3388	3396	3404	3412	3420	3428	3436	3443	3451	3459	1	2	2	3	4	5	6	6	7
·54	3467	3475	3483	3491	3499	3508	3516	3524	3532	3540	1	2	2	3	4	5	6	6	7
·55	3548	3556	3565	3573	3581	3589	3597	3606	3614	3622	1	2	2	3	4	5	6	7	7
·56	3631	3639	3648	3656	3664	3673	3681	3690	3698	3707	1	2	3	3	4	5	6	7	8
·57	3715	3724	3733	3741	3750	3758	3767	3776	3784	3793	1	2	3	3	4	5	6	7	8
·58	3802	3811	3819	3828	3837	3846	3855	3864	3873	3882	1	2	3	4	4	5	6	7	8
·59	3890	3899	3908	3917	3926	3936	3945	3954	3963	3972	1	2	3	4	5	5	6	7	8
·60	3981	3990	3999	4009	4018	4027	4036	4046	4055	4064	1	2	3	4	5	6	6	7	8
·61	4074	4083	4093	4102	4111	4121	4130	4140	4150	4159	1	2	3	4	5	6	7	8	9
·62	4169	4178	4188	4198	4207	4217	4227	4236	4246	4256	1	2	3	4	5	6	7	8	9
·63	4266	4276	4285	4295	4305	4315	4325	4335	4345	4355	1	2	3	4	5	6	7	8	9
·64	4365	4375	4385	4395	4406	4416	4426	4436	4446	4457	1	2	3	4	5	6	7	8	9
·65	4467	4477	4487	4498	4508	4519	4529	4539	4550	4560	1	2	3	4	5	6	7	8	9
·66	4571	4581	4592	4603	4613	4624	4634	4645	4656	4667	1	2	3	4	5	6	7	9	10
·67	4677	4688	4699	4710	4721	4732	4742	4753	4764	4775	1	2	3	4	5	7	8	9	10
·68	4786	4797	4808	4819	4831	4842	4853	4864	4875	4887	1	2	3	4	6	7	8	9	10
·69	4898	4909	4920	4932	4943	4955	4966	4977	4989	5000	1	2	3	5	6	7	8	9	10
·70	5012	5023	5035	5047	5058	5070	5082	5093	5105	5117	1	2	4	5	6	7	8	9	11
·71	5129	5140	5152	5164	5176	5188	5200	5212	5224	5236	1	2	4	5	6	7	8	10	11
·72	5248	5260	5272	5284	5297	5309	5321	5333	5346	5358	1	2	4	5	6	7	9	10	11
·73	5370	5383	5395	5408	5420	5433	5445	5458	5470	5483	1	3	4	5	6	8	9	10	11
·74	5495	5508	5521	5534	5546	5559	5572	5585	5598	5610	1	3	4	5	6	8	9	10	12
·75	5623	5636	5649	5662	5675	5689	5702	5715	5728	5741	1	3	4	5	7	8	9	10	12
·76	5754	5768	5781	5794	5808	5821	5834	5848	5861	5875	1	3	4	5	7	8	9	11	12
·77	5888	5902	5916	5929	5943	5957	5970	5984	5998	6012	1	3	4	5	7	8	10	11	12
·78	6026	6039	6053	6067	6081	6095	6109	6124	6138	6152	1	3	4	6	7	8	10	11	13
·79	6166	6180	6194	6209	6223	6237	6252	6266	6281	6295	1	3	4	6	7	9	10	11	13
·80	6310	6324	6339	6353	6368	6383	6397	6412	6427	6442	1	3	4	6	7	9	10	12	13
·81	6457	6471	6486	6501	6516	6531	6546	6561	6577	6592	2	3	5	6	8	9	11	12	14
·82	6607	6622	6637	6653	6668	6683	6699	6714	6730	6745	2	3	5	6	8	9	11	12	14
·83	6761	6776	6792	6808	6823	6839	6855	6871	6887	6902	2	3	5	6	8	9	11	13	14
·84	6918	6934	6950	6966	6982	6998	7015	7031	7047	7063	2	3	5	6	8	10	11	13	15
·85	7079	7096	7112	7129	7145	7161	7178	7194	7211	7228	2	3	5	7	8	10	12	13	15
·86	7244	7261	7278	7295	7311	7328	7345	7362	7379	7396	2	3	5	7	8	10	12	13	15
·87	7413	7430	7447	7464	7482	7499	7516	7534	7551	7568	2	3	5	7	9	10	12	14	16
·88	7586	7603	7621	7638	7656	7674	7691	7709	7727	7745	2	4	5	7	9	11	12	14	16
·89	7762	7780	7798	7816	7834	7852	7870	7889	7907	7925	2	4	5	7	9	11	13	14	16
·90	7943	7962	7980	7998	8017	8035	8054	8072	8091	8110	2	4	6	7	9	11	13	15	17
·91	8128	8147	8166	8185	8204	8222	8241	8260	8279	8299	2	4	6	8	9	11	13	15	17
·92	8318	8337	8356	8375	8395	8414	8433	8453	8472	8492	2	4	6	8	10	12	14	15	17
·93	8511	8531	8551	8570	8590	8610	8630	8650	8670	8690	2	4	6	8	10	12	14	16	18
·94	8710	8730	8750	8770	8790	8810	8831	8851	8872	8892	2	4	6	8	10	12	14	16	18
·95	8913	8933	8954	8974	8995	9016	9036	9057	9078	9099	2	4	6	8	10	12	15	17	19
·96	9120	9141	9162	9183	9204	9226	9247	9268	9290	9311	2	4	6	8	11	13	15	17	19
·97	9333	9354	9376	9397	9419	9441	9462	9484	9506	9528	2	4	7	9	11	13	15	17	20
·98	9550	9572	9594	9616	9638	9661	9683	9705	9727	9750	2	4	7	9	11	13	16	18	20
·99	9772	9795	9817	9840	9863	9886	9908	9931	9954	9977	2	5	7	9	11	14	16	18	20

	0'	6'	12'	18'	24'	30'	36'	42'	48'	54'	1 to 11	13 to 23	25 to 35	37 to 47	49 to 59
0°	−∞	3̄·242	3̄·543	3̄·719	3̄·844	3̄·941	2̄·020	2̄·087	2̄·145	2̄·196					
1	2̄·2419	2832	3210	3558	3880	4179	4459	4723	4971	5206					
2	2̄·5428	5640	5842	6035	6220	6397	6567	6731	6889	7041	35	32	29	27	25
3	2̄·7188	7330	7468	7602	7731	7857	7979	8098	8213	8326	23	22	21	20	19
4	2̄·8436	8543	8647	8749	8849	8946	9042	9135	9226	9315	18	17	16	15	15
5	2̄·9403	9489	9573	9655	9736	9816	9894	9970	*0046*	*0120*	14	14	13	13	12
6	1̄·0192	0264	0334	0403	0472	0539	0605	0670	0734	0797	12	11	11	11	10
											1'	2'	3'	4'	5'
7	1̄·0859	0920	0981	1040	1099	1157	1214	1271	1326	1381	10	19	29	38	48
8	1̄·1436	1489	1542	1594	1646	1697	1747	1797	1847	1895	8	17	25	34	42
9	1̄·1943	1991	2038	2085	2131	2176	2221	2266	2310	2353	8	15	23	30	38
10	1̄·2397	2439	2482	2524	2565	2606	2647	2687	2727	2767	7	14	20	27	34
11	1̄·2806	2845	2883	2921	2959	2997	3034	3070	3107	3143	6	12	19	25	31
12	1̄·3179	3214	3250	3284	3319	3353	3387	3421	3455	3488	6	11	17	23	28
13	1̄·3521	3554	3586	3618	3650	3682	3713	3745	3775	3806	5	11	16	21	26
14	1̄·3837	3867	3897	3927	3957	3986	4015	4044	4073	4102	5	10	15	20	24
15	1̄·4130	4158	4186	4214	4242	4269	4296	4323	4350	4377	5	9	14	18	23
16	1̄·4403	4430	4456	4482	4508	4533	4559	4584	4609	4634	4	9	13	17	21
17	1̄·4659	4684	4709	4733	4757	4781	4805	4829	4853	4876	4	8	12	16	20
18	1̄·4900	4923	4946	4969	4992	5015	5037	5060	5082	5104	4	8	11	15	19
19	1̄·5126	5148	5170	5192	5213	5235	5256	5278	5299	5320	4	7	11	14	18
20	1̄·5341	5361	5382	5402	5423	5443	5463	5484	5504	5523	3	7	10	14	17
21	1̄·5543	5563	5583	5602	5621	5641	5660	5679	5698	5717	3	6	10	13	16
22	1̄·5736	5754	5773	5792	5810	5828	5847	5865	5883	5901	3	6	9	12	15
23	1̄·5919	5937	5954	5972	5990	6007	6024	6042	6059	6076	3	6	9	12	15
24	1̄·6093	6110	6127	6144	6161	6177	6194	6210	6227	6243	3	6	8	11	14
25	1̄·6259	6276	6292	6308	6324	6340	6356	6371	6387	6403	3	5	8	11	13
26	1̄·6418	6434	6449	6465	6480	6495	6510	6526	6541	6556	3	5	8	10	13
27	1̄·6570	6585	6600	6615	6629	6644	6659	6673	6687	6702	2	5	7	10	12
28	1̄·6716	6730	6744	6759	6773	6787	6801	6814	6828	6842	2	5	7	9	12
29	1̄·6856	6869	6883	6896	6910	6923	6937	6950	6963	6977	2	4	7	9	11
30	1̄·6990	7003	7016	7029	7042	7055	7068	7080	7093	7106	2	4	6	9	11
31	1̄·7118	7131	7144	7156	7168	7181	7193	7205	7218	7230	2	4	6	9	11
32	1̄·7242	7254	7266	7278	7290	7302	7314	7326	7338	7349	2	4	6	8	10
33	1̄·7361	7373	7384	7396	7407	7419	7430	7442	7453	7464	2	4	6	8	10
34	1̄·7476	7487	7498	7509	7520	7531	7542	7553	7564	7575	2	4	6	7	9
35	1̄·7586	7597	7607	7618	7629	7640	7650	7661	7671	7682	2	4	5	7	9
36	1̄·7692	7703	7713	7723	7734	7744	7754	7764	7774	7785	2	3	5	7	9
37	1̄·7795	7805	7815	7825	7835	7844	7854	7864	7874	7884	2	3	5	7	8
38	1̄·7893	7903	7913	7922	7932	7941	7951	7960	7970	7979	2	3	5	7	8
39	1̄·7989	7998	8007	8017	8026	8035	8044	8053	8063	8072	2	3	5	6	8
40	1̄·8081	8090	8099	8108	8117	8125	8134	8143	8152	8161	1	3	4	6	7
41	1̄·8169	8178	8187	8195	8204	8213	8221	8230	8238	8247	1	3	4	6	7

Where the integer changes, the numbers are italicised.

	0′	6′	12′	18′	24′	30′	36′	42′	48′	54′	1′	2′	3′	4′	5′
42°	$\bar{1}$·8255	8264	8272	8280	8289	8297	8305	8313	8322	8330	1	3	4	6	7
43	$\bar{1}$·8333	8346	8354	8362	8370	8378	8386	8394	8402	8410	1	3	4	5	7
44	$\bar{1}$·8418	8426	8433	8441	8449	8457	8464	8472	8480	8487	1	3	4	5	6
45	$\bar{1}$·8495	8502	8510	8517	8525	8532	8540	8547	8555	8562	1	2	4	5	6
46	$\bar{1}$·8569	8577	8584	8591	8598	8606	8613	8620	8627	8634	1	2	4	5	6
47	$\bar{1}$·8641	8648	8655	8662	8669	8676	8683	8690	8697	8704	1	2	3	5	6
48	$\bar{1}$·8711	8718	8724	8731	8738	8745	8751	8758	8765	8771	1	2	3	4	6
49	$\bar{1}$·8778	8784	8791	8797	8804	8810	8817	8823	8830	8836	1	2	3	4	5
50	$\bar{1}$·8843	8849	8855	8862	8868	8874	8880	8887	8893	8899	1	2	3	4	5
51	$\bar{1}$·8905	8911	8917	8923	8929	8935	8941	8947	8953	8959	1	2	3	4	5
52	$\bar{1}$·8965	8971	8977	8983	8989	8995	9000	9006	9012	9018	1	2	3	4	5
53	$\bar{1}$·9023	9029	9035	9041	9046	9052	9057	9063	9069	9074	1	2	3	4	5
54	$\bar{1}$·9080	9085	9091	9096	9101	9107	9112	9118	9123	9128	1	2	3	4	5
55	$\bar{1}$·9134	9139	9144	9149	9155	9160	9165	9170	9175	9181	1	2	3	3	4
56	$\bar{1}$·9186	9191	9196	9201	9206	9211	9216	9221	9226	9231	1	2	3	3	4
57	$\bar{1}$·9236	9241	9246	9251	9255	9260	9265	9270	9275	9279	1	2	2	3	4
58	$\bar{1}$·9284	9289	9294	9298	9303	9308	9312	9317	9322	9326	1	2	2	3	4
59	$\bar{1}$·9331	9335	9340	9344	9349	9353	9358	9362	9367	9371	1	1	2	3	4
60	$\bar{1}$·9375	9380	9384	9388	9393	9397	9401	9406	9410	9414	1	1	2	3	4
61	$\bar{1}$·9418	9422	9427	9431	9435	9439	9443	9447	9451	9455	1	1	2	3	3
62	$\bar{1}$·9459	9463	9467	9471	9475	9479	9483	9487	9491	9495	1	1	2	3	3
63	$\bar{1}$·9499	9503	9506	9510	9514	9518	9522	9525	9529	9533	1	1	2	3	3
64	$\bar{1}$·9537	9540	9544	9548	9551	9555	9558	9562	9566	9569	1	1	2	2	3
65	$\bar{1}$·9573	9576	9580	9583	9587	9590	9594	9597	9601	9604	1	1	2	2	3
66	$\bar{1}$·9607	9611	9614	9617	9621	9624	9627	9631	9634	9637	1	1	2	2	3
67	$\bar{1}$·9640	9643	9647	9650	9653	9656	9659	9662	9666	9669	1	1	2	2	3
68	$\bar{1}$·9672	9675	9678	9681	9684	9687	9690	9693	9696	9699	0	1	1	2	2
69	$\bar{1}$·9702	9704	9707	9710	9713	9716	9719	9722	9724	9727	0	1	1	2	2
70	$\bar{1}$·9730	9733	9735	9738	9741	9743	9746	9749	9751	9754	0	1	1	2	2
71	$\bar{1}$·9757	9759	9762	9764	9767	9770	9772	9775	9777	9780	0	1	1	2	2
72	$\bar{1}$·9782	9785	9787	9789	9792	9794	9797	9799	9801	9804	0	1	1	2	2
73	$\bar{1}$·9806	9808	9811	9813	9815	9817	9820	9822	9824	9826	0	1	1	1	2
74	$\bar{1}$·9828	9831	9833	9835	9837	9839	9841	9843	9845	9847	0	1	1	1	2
75	$\bar{1}$·9849	9851	9853	9855	9857	9859	9861	9863	9865	9867	0	1	1	1	2
76	$\bar{1}$·9869	9871	9873	9875	9876	9878	9880	9882	9884	9885					
77	$\bar{1}$·9887	9889	9891	9892	9894	9896	9897	9899	9901	9902					
78	$\bar{1}$·9904	9906	9907	9909	9910	9912	9913	9915	9916	9918					
79	$\bar{1}$·9919	9921	9922	9924	9925	9927	9928	9929	9931	9932					
80	$\bar{1}$·9934	9935	9936	9937	9939	9940	9941	9943	9944	9945					
81	$\bar{1}$·9946	9947	9949	9950	9951	9952	9953	9954	9955	9956					
82	$\bar{1}$·9958	9959	9960	9961	9962	9963	9964	9965	9966	9967			Use Interpolation		
83	$\bar{1}$·9968	9968	9969	9970	9971	9972	9973	9974	9975	9975					
84	$\bar{1}$·9976	9977	9978	9978	9979	9980	9981	9981	9982	9983					
85	$\bar{1}$·9983	9984	9985	9985	9986	9987	9987	9988	9988	9989					
86	$\bar{1}$·9989	9990	9990	9991	9991	9992	9992	9993	9993	9994					
87	$\bar{1}$·9994	9994	9995	9995	9996	9996	9996	9996	9997	9997					
88	$\bar{1}$·9997	9998	9998	9998	9998	9999	9999	9999	9999	9999					
89	$\bar{1}$·9999	9999	0·000	0·000	0·000	0·000	0·000	0·000	0·000	0·000					

SUBTRACT

	0'	6'	12'	18'	24'	30'	36'	42'	48'	54'	1'	2'	3'	4'	5'
0°	0·0000	0000	0000	0000	0000	0000	0000	0000	0000	1̄·9999					
1	1̄·9999	9999	9999	9999	9999	9998	9998	9998	9998	9998					
2	1̄·9997	9997	9997	9997	9996	9996	9996	9995	9995	9994					
3	1̄·9994	9994	9993	9993	9992	9992	9991	9991	9990	9990					
4	1̄·9989	9989	9988	9988	9987	9987	9986	9985	9985	9984					
5	1̄·9983	9983	9982	9981	9981	9980	9979	9978	9978	9977		Use Interpolation			
6	1̄·9976	9975	9975	9974	9973	9972	9971	9970	9969	9968					
7	1̄·9968	9967	9966	9965	9964	9963	9962	9961	9960	9959					
8	1̄·9958	9956	9955	9954	9953	9952	9951	9950	9949	9947					
9	1̄·9946	9945	9944	9943	9941	9940	9939	9937	9936	9935					
10	1̄·9934	9932	9931	9929	9928	9927	9925	9924	9922	9921					
11	1̄·9919	9918	9916	9915	9913	9912	9910	9909	9907	9906					
12	1̄·9904	9902	9901	9899	9897	9896	9894	9892	9891	9889					
13	1̄·9887	9885	9884	9882	9880	9878	9876	9875	9873	9871					
14	1̄·9869	9867	9865	9863	9861	9859	9857	9855	9853	9851	0	1	1	1	2
15	1̄·9849	9847	9845	9843	9841	9839	9837	9835	9833	9831	0	1	1	1	2
16	1̄·9828	9826	9824	9822	9820	9817	9815	9813	9811	9808	0	1	1	1	2
17	1̄·9806	9804	9801	9799	9797	9794	9792	9789	9787	9785	0	1	1	2	2
18	1̄·9782	9780	9777	9775	9772	9770	9767	9764	9762	9759	0	1	1	2	2
19	1̄·9757	9754	9751	9749	9746	9743	9741	9738	9735	9733	0	1	1	2	2
20	1̄·9730	9727	9724	9722	9719	9716	9713	9710	9707	9704	0	1	1	2	2
21	1̄·9702	9699	9696	9693	9690	9687	9684	9681	9678	9675	0	1	1	2	2
22	1̄·9672	9669	9666	9662	9659	9656	9653	9650	9647	9643	1	1	2	2	3
23	1̄·9640	9637	9634	9631	9627	9624	9621	9617	9614	9611	1	1	2	2	3
24	1̄·9607	9604	9601	9597	9594	9590	9587	9583	9580	9576	1	1	2	2	3
25	1̄·9573	9569	9566	9562	9558	9555	9551	9548	9544	9540	1	1	2	3	3
26	1̄·9537	9533	9529	9525	9522	9518	9514	9510	9506	9503	1	1	2	3	3
27	1̄·9499	9495	9491	9487	9483	9479	9475	9471	9467	9463	1	1	2	3	3
28	1̄·9459	9455	9451	9447	9443	9439	9435	9431	9427	9422	1	1	2	3	3
29	1̄·9418	9414	9410	9406	9401	9397	9393	9388	9384	9380	1	1	2	3	4
30	1̄·9375	9371	9367	9362	9358	9353	9349	9344	9340	9335	1	1	2	3	4
31	1̄·9331	9326	9322	9317	9312	9308	9303	9298	9294	9289	1	2	2	3	4
32	1̄·9284	9279	9275	9270	9265	9260	9255	9251	9246	9241	1	2	2	3	4
33	1̄·9236	9231	9226	9221	9216	9211	9206	9201	9196	9191	1	2	2	3	4
34	1̄·9186	9181	9175	9170	9165	9160	9155	9149	9144	9139	1	2	3	3	4
35	1̄·9134	9128	9123	9118	9112	9107	9101	9096	9091	9085	1	2	3	4	5
36	1̄·9080	9074	9069	9063	9057	9052	9046	9041	9035	9029	1	2	3	4	5
37	1̄·9023	9018	9012	9006	9000	8995	8989	8983	8977	8971	1	2	3	4	5
38	1̄·8965	8959	8953	8947	8941	8935	8929	8923	8917	8911	1	2	3	4	5
39	1̄·8905	8899	8893	8887	8880	8874	8868	8862	8855	8849	1	2	3	4	5
40	1̄·8843	8836	8830	8823	8817	8810	8804	8797	8791	8784	1	2	3	4	5
41	1̄·8778	8771	8765	8758	8751	8745	8738	8731	8724	8718	1	2	3	4	6
42	1̄·8711	8704	8697	8690	8683	8676	8669	8662	8655	8648	1	2	3	5	6
43	1̄·8641	8634	8627	8620	8613	8606	8598	8591	8584	8577	1	2	4	5	6
44	1̄·8569	8562	8555	8547	8540	8532	8525	8517	8510	8502	1	2	4	5	6

SUBTRACT

SUBTRACT

	0′	6′	12′	18′	24′	30′	36′	42′	48′	54′	1′	2′	3′	4′	5′
45°	1̄·8495	8487	8480	8472	8464	8457	8449	8441	8433	8426	1	3	4	5	6
46	1̄·8418	8410	8402	8394	8386	8378	8370	8362	8354	8346	1	3	4	5	7
47	1̄·8338	8330	8322	8313	8305	8297	8289	8280	8272	8264	1	3	4	6	7
48	1̄·8255	8247	8238	8230	8221	8213	8204	8195	8187	8178	1	3	4	6	7
49	1̄·8169	8161	8152	8143	8134	8125	8117	8108	8099	8090	1	3	4	6	7
50	1̄·8081	8072	8063	8053	8044	8035	8026	8017	8007	7998	2	3	5	6	8
51	1̄·7989	7979	7970	7960	7951	7941	7932	7922	7913	7903	2	3	5	6	8
52	1̄·7893	7884	7874	7864	7854	7844	7835	7825	7815	7805	2	3	5	7	8
53	1̄·7795	7785	7774	7764	7754	7744	7734	7723	7713	7703	2	3	5	7	8
54	1̄·7692	7682	7671	7661	7650	7640	7629	7618	7607	7597	2	4	5	7	9
55	1̄·7586	7575	7564	7553	7542	7531	7520	7509	7498	7487	2	4	6	7	9
56	1̄·7476	7464	7453	7442	7430	7419	7407	7396	7384	7373	2	4	6	8	10
57	1̄·7361	7349	7338	7326	7314	7302	7290	7278	7266	7254	2	4	6	8	10
58	1̄·7242	7230	7218	7205	7193	7181	7168	7156	7144	7131	2	4	6	8	10
59	1̄·7118	7106	7093	7080	7068	7055	7042	7029	7016	7003	2	4	6	9	11
60	1̄·6990	6977	6963	6950	6937	6923	6910	6896	6883	6869	2	4	7	9	11
61	1̄·6856	6842	6828	6814	6801	6787	6773	6759	6744	6730	2	5	7	9	12
62	1̄·6716	6702	6687	6673	6659	6644	6629	6615	6600	6585	2	5	7	10	12
63	1̄·6570	6556	6541	6526	6510	6495	6480	6465	6449	6434	3	5	8	10	13
64	1̄·6418	6403	6387	6371	6356	6340	6324	6308	6292	6276	3	5	8	11	13
65	1̄·6259	6243	6227	6210	6194	6177	6161	6144	6127	6110	3	6	8	11	14
66	1̄·6093	6076	6059	6042	6024	6007	5990	5972	5954	5937	3	6	9	12	15
67	1̄·5919	5901	5883	5865	5847	5828	5810	5792	5773	5754	3	6	9	12	15
68	1̄·5736	5717	5698	5679	5660	5641	5621	5602	5583	5563	3	6	10	13	16
69	1̄·5543	5523	5504	5484	5463	5443	5423	5402	5382	5361	3	7	10	14	17
70	1̄·5341	5320	5299	5278	5256	5235	5213	5192	5170	5148	4	7	11	14	18
71	1̄·5126	5104	5082	5060	5037	5015	4992	4969	4946	4923	4	8	11	15	19
72	1̄·4900	4876	4853	4829	4805	4781	4757	4733	4709	4684	4	8	12	16	20
73	1̄·4659	4634	4609	4584	4559	4533	4508	4482	4456	4430	4	9	13	17	21
74	1̄·4403	4377	4350	4323	4296	4269	4242	4214	4186	4158	5	9	14	18	23
75	1̄·4130	4102	4073	4044	4015	3986	3957	3927	3897	3867	5	10	15	20	24
76	1̄·3837	3806	3775	3745	3713	3682	3650	3618	3586	3554	5	11	16	21	26
77	1̄·3521	3488	3455	3421	3387	3353	3319	3284	3250	3214	6	11	17	23	28
78	1̄·3179	3143	3107	3070	3034	2997	2959	2921	2883	2845	6	12	19	25	31
79	1̄·2806	2767	2727	2687	2647	2606	2565	2524	2482	2439	7	14	20	27	34
80	1̄·2397	2353	2310	2266	2221	2176	2131	2085	2038	1991	8	15	23	30	38
81	1̄·1943	1895	1847	1797	1747	1697	1646	1594	1542	1489	8	17	25	34	42
82	1̄·1436	1381	1326	1271	1214	1157	1099	1040	0981	0920	10	19	29	38	48

Difference for 1′				
1 to 11	13 to 23	25 to 35	37 to 47	49 to 59

	0′	6′	12′	18′	24′	30′	36′	42′	48′	54′	1 to 11	13 to 23	25 to 35	37 to 47	49 to 59
83	1̄·0859	0797	0734	0670	0605	0539	0472	0403	0334	0264	10	11	11	11	12
84	1̄·0192	0120	0046	9970	9894	9816	9736	9655	9573	9489	12	13	13	14	14
85	2̄·9403	9315	9226	9135	9042	8946	8849	8749	8647	8543	15	15	16	17	18
86	2̄·8436	8326	8213	8098	7979	7857	7731	7602	7468	7330	19	20	21	22	23
87	2̄·7188	7041	6889	6731	6567	6397	6220	6035	5842	5640	25	27	29	32	35
88	2̄·5428	5206	4971	4723	4459	4179	3880	3558	3210	2832					
89	2̄·242	2·196	2·145	2·087	2·020	3·941	3·844	3·719	3·543	3·242					

SUBTRACT

Where the integer changes, the numbers are italicised.

LOG. TANGENTS

	0'	6'	12'	18'	24'	30'	36'	42'	48'	54'	1 to 11	13 to 23	25 to 35	37 to 47	49 to 59
											Difference for 1'				
0°	—∞	$\bar{3}$·242	$\bar{3}$·543	$\bar{3}$·719	$\bar{3}$·844	$\bar{3}$·941	$\bar{2}$·020	$\bar{2}$·087	$\bar{2}$·145	$\bar{2}$·196					
1	$\bar{2}$·2419	2833	3211	3559	3881	4181	4461	4725	4973	5208					
2	$\bar{2}$·5431	5643	5845	6038	6223	6401	6571	6736	6894	7046	35	32	29	27	25
3	$\bar{2}$·7194	7337	7475	7609	7739	7865	7988	8107	8223	8336	23	22	21	20	19
4	$\bar{2}$·8446	8554	8659	8762	8862	8960	9056	9150	9241	9331	18	17	16	15	15
5	$\bar{2}$·9420	9506	9591	9674	9756	9836	9915	9992	*0068*	*0143*	14	14	13	13	12
6	$\bar{1}$·0216	0289	0360	0430	0499	0567	0633	0699	0764	0828	12	12	11	11	11

	0'	6'	12'	18'	24'	30'	36'	42'	48'	54'	1'	2'	3'	4'	5'
7	$\bar{1}$·0891	0954	1015	1076	1135	1194	1252	1310	1367	1423	10	20	29	39	49
8	$\bar{1}$·1478	1533	1587	1640	1693	1745	1797	1848	1898	1948	9	17	26	35	43
9	$\bar{1}$·1997	2046	2094	2142	2189	2236	2282	2328	2374	2419	8	16	23	31	39
10	$\bar{1}$·2463	2507	2551	2594	2637	2680	2722	2764	2805	2846	7	14	21	28	35
11	$\bar{1}$·2887	2927	2967	3006	3046	3085	3123	3162	3200	3237	6	13	19	26	32
12	$\bar{1}$·3275	3312	3349	3385	3422	3458	3493	3529	3564	3599	6	12	18	24	30
13	$\bar{1}$·3634	3668	3702	3736	3770	3804	3837	3870	3903	3935	6	11	17	22	28
14	$\bar{1}$·3968	4000	4032	4064	4095	4127	4158	4189	4220	4250	5	10	16	21	26
15	$\bar{1}$·4281	4311	4341	4371	4400	4430	4459	4488	4517	4546	5	10	15	20	25
16	$\bar{1}$·4575	4603	4632	4660	4688	4716	4744	4771	4799	4826	5	9	14	19	23
17	$\bar{1}$·4853	4880	4907	4934	4961	4987	5014	5040	5066	5092	4	9	13	18	22
18	$\bar{1}$·5118	5143	5169	5195	5220	5245	5270	5295	5320	5345	4	8	13	17	21
19	$\bar{1}$·5370	5394	5419	5443	5467	5491	5516	5539	5563	5587	4	8	12	16	20
20	$\bar{1}$·5611	5634	5658	5681	5704	5727	5750	5773	5796	5819	4	8	12	15	19
21	$\bar{1}$·5842	5864	5887	5909	5932	5954	5976	5998	6020	6042	4	7	11	15	19
22	$\bar{1}$·6064	6086	6108	6129	6151	6172	6194	6215	6236	6257	4	7	11	14	18
23	$\bar{1}$·6279	6300	6321	6341	6362	6383	6404	6424	6445	6465	3	7	10	14	17
24	$\bar{1}$·6486	6506	6527	6547	6567	6587	6607	6627	6647	6667	3	7	10	13	17
25	$\bar{1}$·6687	6706	6726	6746	6765	6785	6804	6824	6843	6863	3	7	10	13	16
26	$\bar{1}$·6882	6901	6920	6939	6958	6977	6996	7015	7034	7053	3	6	9	13	16
27	$\bar{1}$·7072	7090	7109	7128	7146	7165	7183	7202	7220	7238	3	6	9	12	15
28	$\bar{1}$·7257	7275	7293	7311	7330	7348	7366	7384	7402	7420	3	6	9	12	15
29	$\bar{1}$·7438	7455	7473	7491	7509	7526	7544	7562	7579	7597	3	6	9	12	15
30	$\bar{1}$·7614	7632	7649	7667	7684	7701	7719	7736	7753	7771	3	6	9	12	14
31	$\bar{1}$·7788	7805	7822	7839	7856	7873	7890	7907	7924	7941	3	6	9	11	14
32	$\bar{1}$·7958	7975	7992	8008	8025	8042	8059	8075	8092	8109	3	6	8	11	14
33	$\bar{1}$·8125	8142	8158	8175	8191	8208	8224	8241	8257	8274	3	5	8	11	14
34	$\bar{1}$·8290	8306	8323	8339	8355	8371	8388	8404	8420	8436	3	5	8	11	14
35	$\bar{1}$·8452	8468	8484	8501	8517	8533	8549	8565	8581	8597	3	5	8	11	13
36	$\bar{1}$·8613	8629	8644	8660	8676	8692	8708	8724	8740	8755	3	5	8	11	13
37	$\bar{1}$·8771	8787	8803	8818	8834	8850	8865	8881	8897	8912	3	5	8	10	13
38	$\bar{1}$·8928	8944	8959	8975	8990	9006	9022	9037	9053	9068	3	5	8	10	13
39	$\bar{1}$·9084	9099	9115	9130	9146	9161	9176	9192	9207	9223	3	5	8	10	13
40	$\bar{1}$·9238	9254	9269	9284	9300	9315	9330	9346	9361	9376	3	5	8	10	13
41	$\bar{1}$·9392	9407	9422	9438	9453	9468	9483	9499	9514	9529	3	5	8	10	13
42	$\bar{1}$·9544	9560	9575	9590	9605	9621	9636	9651	9666	9681	3	5	8	10	13
43	$\bar{1}$·9697	9712	9727	9742	9757	9772	9788	9803	9818	9833	3	5	8	10	13
44	$\bar{1}$·9848	9864	9879	9894	9909	9924	9939	9955	9970	9985	3	5	8	10	13

Where the integer changes, the numbers are italicised.

LOG. TANGENTS

	0′	6′	12′	18′	24′	30′	36′	42′	48′	54′	1′	2′	3′	4′	5′
45°	0·0000	0015	0030	0045	0061	0076	0091	0106	0121	0136	3	5	8	10	13
46	0·0152	0167	0182	0197	0212	0228	0243	0258	0273	0288	3	5	8	10	13
47	0·0303	0319	0334	0349	0364	0379	0395	0410	0425	0440	3	5	8	10	13
48	0·0456	0471	0486	0501	0517	0532	0547	0562	0578	0593	3	5	8	10	13
49	0·0608	0624	0639	0654	0670	0685	0700	0716	0731	0746	3	5	8	10	13
50	0·0762	0777	0793	0808	0824	0839	0854	0870	0885	0901	3	5	8	10	13
51	0·0916	0932	0947	0963	0978	0994	1010	1025	1041	1056	3	5	8	10	13
52	0·1072	1088	1103	1119	1135	1150	1166	1182	1197	1213	3	5	8	10	13
53	0·1229	1245	1260	1276	1292	1308	1324	1340	1356	1371	3	5	8	11	13
54	0·1387	1403	1419	1435	1451	1467	1483	1499	1516	1532	3	5	8	11	13
55	0·1548	1564	1580	1596	1612	1629	1645	1661	1677	1694	3	5	8	11	14
56	0·1710	1726	1743	1759	1776	1792	1809	1825	1842	1858	3	5	8	11	14
57	0·1875	1891	1908	1925	1941	1958	1975	1992	2008	2025	3	6	8	11	14
58	0·2042	2059	2076	2093	2110	2127	2144	2161	2178	2195	3	6	9	11	14
59	0·2212	2229	2247	2264	2281	2299	2316	2333	2351	2368	3	6	9	12	14
60	0·2386	2403	2421	2438	2456	2474	2491	2509	2527	2545	3	6	9	12	15
61	0·2562	2580	2598	2616	2634	2652	2670	2689	2707	2725	3	6	9	12	15
62	0·2743	2762	2780	2798	2817	2835	2854	2872	2891	2910	3	6	9	12	15
63	0·2928	2947	2966	2985	3004	3023	3042	3061	3080	3099	3	6	9	13	16
64	0·3118	3137	3157	3176	3196	3215	3235	3254	3274	3294	3	7	10	13	16
65	0·3313	3333	3353	3373	3393	3413	3433	3453	3473	3494	3	7	10	13	17
66	0·3514	3535	3555	3576	3596	3617	3638	3659	3679	3700	3	7	10	14	17
67	0·3721	3743	3764	3785	3806	3828	3849	3871	3892	3914	4	7	11	14	18
68	0·3936	3958	3980	4002	4024	4046	4068	4091	4113	4136	4	7	11	15	19
69	0·4158	4181	4204	4227	4250	4273	4296	4319	4342	4366	4	8	12	15	19
70	0·4389	4413	4437	4461	4484	4509	4533	4557	4581	4606	4	8	12	16	20
71	0·4630	4655	4680	4705	4730	4755	4780	4805	4831	4857	4	8	13	17	21
72	0·4882	4908	4934	4960	4986	5013	5039	5066	5093	5120	4	9	13	18	22
73	0·5147	5174	5201	5229	5256	5284	5312	5340	5368	5397	5	9	14	19	23
74	0·5425	5454	5483	5512	5541	5570	5600	5629	5659	5689	5	10	15	20	25
75	0·5719	5750	5780	5811	5842	5873	5905	5936	5968	6000	5	10	16	21	26
76	0·6032	6065	6097	6130	6163	6196	6230	6264	6298	6332	6	11	17	22	28
77	0·6366	6401	6436	6471	6507	6542	6578	6615	6651	6688	6	12	18	24	30
78	0·6725	6763	6800	6838	6877	6915	6954	6994	7033	7073	6	13	19	26	32
79	0·7113	7154	7195	7236	7278	7320	7363	7406	7449	7493	7	14	21	28	35
80	0·7537	7581	7626	7672	7718	7764	7811	7858	7906	7954	8	16	23	31	39
81	0·8003	8052	8102	8152	8203	8255	8307	8360	8413	8467	9	17	26	35	43
82	0·8522	8577	8633	8690	8748	8806	8865	8924	8985	9046	10	20	29	39	49

Difference for 1′

	1 to 11	13 to 23	25 to 35	37 to 47	49 to 59

	0′	6′	12′	18′	24′	30′	36′	42′	48′	54′	1 to 11	13 to 23	25 to 35	37 to 47	49 to 59
83	0·9109	9172	9236	9301	9367	9433	9501	9570	9640	9711	11	11	11	12	12
84	0·9784	9857	9932	*0008*	*0085*	*0164*	*0244*	*0326*	*0409*	*0494*	12	13	13	14	14
85	1·0580	0669	0759	0850	0944	1040	1138	1238	1341	1446	15	15	16	17	18
86	1·1554	1664	1777	1893	2012	2135	2261	2391	2525	2663	19	20	21	22	23
87	1·2806	2954	3106	3264	3429	3599	3777	3962	4155	4357	25	27	29	32	35
88	1·4569	4792	5027	5275	5539	5819	6119	6441	6789	7167					
89	1·758	1·804	1·855	1·913	1·980	2·059	2·156	2·281	2·457	2·758					

Where the integer changes, the numbers are italicised.

NATURAL SINES

	0'	6'	12'	18'	24'	30'	36'	42'	48'	54'	1'	2'	3'	4'	5'
0°	·0000	0017	0035	0052	0070	0087	0105	0122	0140	0157	3	6	9	12	15
1	·0175	0192	0209	0227	0244	0262	0279	0297	0314	0332	3	6	9	12	15
2	·0349	0366	0384	0401	0419	0436	0454	0471	0488	0506	3	6	9	12	15
3	·0523	0541	0558	0576	0593	0610	0628	0645	0663	0680	3	6	9	12	15
4	·0698	0715	0732	0750	0767	0785	0802	0819	0837	0854	3	6	9	12	14
5	·0872	0889	0906	0924	0941	0958	0976	0993	1011	1028	3	6	9	12	14
6	·1045	1063	1080	1097	1115	1132	1149	1167	1184	1201	3	6	9	12	14
7	·1219	1236	1253	1271	1288	1305	1323	1340	1357	1374	3	6	9	12	14
8	·1392	1409	1426	1444	1461	1478	1495	1513	1530	1547	3	6	9	12	14
9	·1564	1582	1599	1616	1633	1650	1668	1685	1702	1719	3	6	9	11	14
10	·1736	1754	1771	1788	1805	1822	1840	1857	1874	1891	3	6	9	11	14
11	·1908	1925	1942	1959	1977	1994	2011	2028	2045	2062	3	6	9	11	14
12	·2079	2096	2113	2130	2147	2164	2181	2198	2215	2233	3	6	9	11	14
13	·2250	2267	2284	2300	2317	2334	2351	2368	2385	2402	3	6	8	11	14
14	·2419	2436	2453	2470	2487	2504	2521	2538	2554	2571	3	6	8	11	14
15	·2588	2605	2622	2639	2656	2672	2689	2706	2723	2740	3	6	8	11	14
16	·2756	2773	2790	2807	2823	2840	2857	2874	2890	2907	3	6	8	11	14
17	·2924	2940	2957	2974	2990	3007	3024	3040	3057	3074	3	6	8	11	14
18	·3090	3107	3123	3140	3156	3173	3190	3206	3223	3239	3	6	8	11	14
19	·3256	3272	3289	3305	3322	3338	3355	3371	3387	3404	3	5	8	11	14
20	·3420	3437	3453	3469	3486	3502	3518	3535	3551	3567	3	5	8	11	14
21	·3584	3600	3616	3633	3649	3665	3681	3697	3714	3730	3	5	8	11	14
22	·3746	3762	3778	3795	3811	3827	3843	3859	3875	3891	3	5	8	11	13
23	·3907	3923	3939	3955	3971	3987	4003	4019	4035	4051	3	5	8	11	13
24	·4067	4083	4099	4115	4131	4147	4163	4179	4195	4210	3	5	8	11	13
25	·4226	4242	4258	4274	4289	4305	4321	4337	4352	4368	3	5	8	11	13
26	·4384	4399	4415	4431	4446	4462	4478	4493	4509	4524	3	5	8	10	13
27	·4540	4555	4571	4586	4602	4617	4633	4648	4664	4679	3	5	8	10	13
28	·4695	4710	4726	4741	4756	4772	4787	4802	4818	4833	3	5	8	10	13
29	·4848	4863	4879	4894	4909	4924	4939	4955	4970	4985	3	5	8	10	13
30	·5000	5015	5030	5045	5060	5075	5090	5105	5120	5135	3	5	8	10	13
31	·5150	5165	5180	5195	5210	5225	5240	5255	5270	5284	2	5	7	10	12
32	·5299	5314	5329	5344	5358	5373	5388	5402	5417	5432	2	5	7	10	12
33	·5446	5461	5476	5490	5505	5519	5534	5548	5563	5577	2	5	7	10	12
34	·5592	5606	5621	5635	5650	5664	5678	5693	5707	5721	2	5	7	10	12
35	·5736	5750	5764	5779	5793	5807	5821	5835	5850	5864	2	5	7	9	12
36	·5878	5892	5906	5920	5934	5948	5962	5976	5990	6004	2	5	7	9	12
37	·6018	6032	6046	6060	6074	6088	6101	6115	6129	6143	2	5	7	9	12
38	·6157	6170	6184	6198	6211	6225	6239	6252	6266	6280	2	5	7	9	11
39	·6293	6307	6320	6334	6347	6361	6374	6388	6401	6414	2	4	7	9	11
40	·6428	6441	6455	6468	6481	6494	6508	6521	6534	6547	2	4	7	9	11
41	·6561	6574	6587	6600	6613	6626	6639	6652	6665	6678	2	4	7	9	11
42	·6691	6704	6717	6730	6743	6756	6769	6782	6794	6807	2	4	6	9	11
43	·6820	6833	6845	6858	6871	6884	6896	6909	6921	6934	2	4	6	8	11
44	·6947	6959	6972	6984	6997	7009	7022	7034	7046	7059	2	4	6	8	10

	0′	6′	12′	18′	24′	30′	36′	42′	48′	54′	1′	2′	3′	4′	5′
45°	·7071	7083	7096	7108	7120	7133	7145	7157	7169	7181	2	4	6	8	10
46	·7193	7206	7218	7230	7242	7254	7266	7278	7290	7302	2	4	6	8	10
47	·7314	7325	7337	7349	7361	7373	7385	7396	7408	7420	2	4	6	8	10
48	·7431	7443	7455	7466	7478	7490	7501	7513	7524	7536	2	4	6	8	10
49	·7547	7559	7570	7581	7593	7604	7615	7627	7638	7649	2	4	6	8	9
50	·7660	7672	7683	7694	7705	7716	7727	7738	7749	7760	2	4	6	7	9
51	·7771	7782	7793	7804	7815	7826	7837	7848	7859	7869	2	4	5	7	9
52	·7880	7891	7902	7912	7923	7934	7944	7955	7965	7976	2	4	5	7	9
53	·7986	7997	8007	8018	8028	8039	8049	8059	8070	8080	2	3	5	7	9
54	·8090	8100	8111	8121	8131	8141	8151	8161	8171	8181	2	3	5	7	8
55	·8192	8202	8211	8221	8231	8241	8251	8261	8271	8281	2	3	5	7	8
56	·8290	8300	8310	8320	8329	8339	8348	8358	8368	8377	2	3	5	6	8
57	·8387	8396	8406	8415	8425	8434	8443	8453	8462	8471	2	3	5	6	8
58	·8480	8490	8499	8508	8517	8526	8536	8545	8554	8563	2	3	5	6	8
59	·8572	8581	8590	8599	8607	8616	8625	8634	8643	8652	1	3	4	6	7
60	·8660	8669	8678	8686	8695	8704	8712	8721	8729	8738	1	3	4	6	7
61	·8746	8755	8763	8771	8780	8788	8796	8805	8813	8821	1	3	4	6	7
62	·8829	8838	8846	8854	8862	8870	8878	8886	8894	8902	1	3	4	5	7
63	·8910	8918	8926	8934	8942	8949	8957	8965	8973	8980	1	3	4	5	6
64	·8988	8996	9003	9011	9018	9026	9033	9041	9048	9056	1	3	4	5	6
65	·9063	9070	9078	9085	9092	9100	9107	9114	9121	9128	1	2	4	5	6
66	·9135	9143	9150	9157	9164	9171	9178	9184	9191	9198	1	2	3	5	6
67	·9205	9212	9219	9225	9232	9239	9245	9252	9259	9265	1	2	3	4	6
68	·9272	9278	9285	9291	9298	9304	9311	9317	9323	9330	1	2	3	4	5
69	·9336	9342	9348	9354	9361	9367	9373	9379	9385	9391	1	2	3	4	5
70	·9397	9403	9409	9415	9421	9426	9432	9438	9444	9449	1	2	3	4	5
71	·9455	9461	9466	9472	9478	9483	9489	9494	9500	9505	1	2	3	4	5
72	·9511	9516	9521	9527	9532	9537	9542	9548	9553	9558	1	2	3	3	4
73	·9563	9568	9573	9578	9583	9588	9593	9598	9603	9608	1	2	2	3	4
74	·9613	9617	9622	9627	9632	9636	9641	9646	9650	9655	1	2	2	3	4
75	·9659	9664	9668	9673	9677	9681	9686	9690	9694	9699	1	1	2	3	4
76	·9703	9707	9711	9715	9720	9724	9728	9732	9736	9740	1	1	2	3	3
77	·9744	9748	9751	9755	9759	9763	9767	9770	9774	9778	1	1	2	3	3
78	·9781	9785	9789	9792	9796	9799	9803	9806	9810	9813	1	1	2	2	3
79	·9816	9820	9823	9826	9829	9833	9836	9839	9842	9845	1	1	2	2	3
80	·9848	9851	9854	9857	9860	9863	9866	9869	9871	9874	0	1	1	2	2
81	·9877	9880	9882	9885	9888	9890	9893	9895	9898	9900	0	1	1	2	2
82	·9903	9905	9907	9910	9912	9914	9917	9919	9921	9923	0	1	1	2	2
83	·9925	9928	9930	9932	9934	9936	9938	9940	9942	9943	0	1	1	1	2
84	·9945	9947	9949	9951	9952	9954	9956	9957	9959	9960					
85	·9962	9963	9965	9966	9968	9969	9971	9972	9973	9974					
86	·9976	9977	9978	9979	9980	9981	9982	9983	9984	9985					
87	·9986	9987	9988	9989	9990	9990	9991	9992	9993	9993	Use Interpolation.				
88	·9994	9995	9995	9996	9996	9997	9997	9997	9998	9998					
89	·9998	9999	9999	9999	9999	1·000	1·000	1·000	1·000	1·000					

NATURAL COSINES

SUBTRACT

	0′	6′	12′	18′	24′	30′	36′	42′	48′	54′	1′	2′	3′	4′	5′
0°	1·0000	1·000	1·000	1·000	1·000	1·000	9999	9999	9999	9999	Use Interpolation.				
1	·9998	9998	9998	9997	9997	9997	9996	9996	9995	9995					
2	·9994	9993	9993	9992	9991	9990	9990	9989	9988	9987					
3	·9986	9985	9984	9983	9982	9981	9980	9979	9978	9977					
4	·9976	9974	9973	9972	9971	9969	9968	9966	9965	9963	—				
5	·9962	9960	9959	9957	9956	9954	9952	9951	9949	9947					
6	·9945	9943	9942	9940	9938	9936	9934	9932	9930	9928	0	1	1	1	2
7	·9925	9923	9921	9919	9917	9914	9912	9910	9907	9905	0	1	1	2	2
8	·9903	9900	9898	9895	9893	9890	9888	9885	9882	9880	0	1	1	2	2
9	·9877	9874	9871	9869	9866	9863	9860	9857	9854	9851	0	1	1	2	2
10	·9848	9845	9842	9839	9836	9833	9829	9826	9823	9820	1	1	2	2	3
11	·9816	9813	9810	9806	9803	9799	9796	9792	9789	9785	1	1	2	2	3
12	·9781	9778	9774	9770	9767	9763	9759	9755	9751	9748	1	1	2	3	3
13	·9744	9740	9736	9732	9728	9724	9720	9715	9711	9707	1	1	2	3	3
14	·9703	9699	9694	9690	9686	9681	9677	9673	9668	9664	1	1	2	3	4
15	·9659	9655	9650	9646	9641	9636	9632	9627	9622	9617	1	2	2	3	4
16	·9613	9608	9603	9598	9593	9588	9583	9578	9573	9568	1	2	2	3	4
17	·9563	9558	9553	9548	9542	9537	9532	9527	9521	9516	1	2	3	3	4
18	·9511	9505	9500	9494	9489	9483	9478	9472	9466	9461	1	2	3	4	5
19	·9455	9449	9444	9438	9432	9426	9421	9415	9409	9403	1	2	3	4	5
20	·9397	9391	9385	9379	9373	9367	9361	9354	9348	9342	1	2	3	4	5
21	·9336	9330	9323	9317	9311	9304	9298	9291	9285	9278	1	2	3	4	5
22	·9272	9265	9259	9252	9245	9239	9232	9225	9219	9212	1	2	3	4	6
23	·9205	9198	9191	9184	9178	9171	9164	9157	9150	9143	1	2	3	5	6
24	·9135	9128	9121	9114	9107	9100	9092	9085	9078	9070	1	2	4	5	6
25	·9063	9056	9048	9041	9033	9026	9018	9011	9003	8996	1	3	4	5	6
26	·8988	8980	8973	8965	8957	8949	8942	8934	8926	8918	1	3	4	5	6
27	·8910	8902	8894	8886	8878	8870	8862	8854	8846	8838	1	3	4	5	7
28	·8829	8821	8813	8805	8796	8788	8780	8771	8763	8755	1	3	4	6	7
29	·8746	8738	8729	8721	8712	8704	8695	8686	8678	8669	1	3	4	6	7
30	·8660	8652	8643	8634	8625	8616	8607	8599	8590	8581	1	3	4	6	7
31	·8572	8563	8554	8545	8536	8526	8517	8508	8499	8490	2	3	5	6	8
32	·8480	8471	8462	8453	8443	8434	8425	8415	8406	8396	2	3	5	6	8
33	·8387	8377	8368	8358	8348	8339	8329	8320	8310	8300	2	3	5	6	8
34	·8290	8281	8271	8261	8251	8241	8231	8221	8211	8202	2	3	5	7	8
35	·8192	8181	8171	8161	8151	8141	8131	8121	8111	8100	2	3	5	7	8
36	·8090	8080	8070	8059	8049	8039	8028	8018	8007	7997	2	3	5	7	9
37	·7986	7976	7965	7955	7944	7934	7923	7912	7902	7891	2	4	5	7	9
38	·7880	7869	7859	7848	7837	7826	7815	7804	7793	7782	2	4	5	7	9
39	·7771	7760	7749	7738	7727	7716	7705	7694	7683	7672	2	4	6	7	9
40	·7660	7649	7638	7627	7615	7604	7593	7581	7570	7559	2	4	6	8	9
41	·7547	7536	7524	7513	7501	7490	7478	7466	7455	7443	2	4	6	8	10
42	·7431	7420	7408	7396	7385	7373	7361	7349	7337	7325	2	4	6	8	10
43	·7314	7302	7290	7278	7266	7254	7242	7230	7218	7206	2	4	6	8	10
44	·7193	7181	7169	7157	7145	7133	7120	7108	7096	7083	2	4	6	8	10

SUBTRACT

Where the integer changes, the numbers are italicised.

SUBTRACT

	0'	6'	12'	18'	24'	30'	36'	42'	48'	54'	1'	2'	3'	4'	5'
45°	·7071	7059	7046	7034	7022	7009	6997	6984	6972	6959	2	4	6	8	10
46	·6947	6934	6921	6909	6896	6884	6871	6858	6845	6833	2	4	6	8	11
47	·6820	6807	6794	6782	6769	6756	6743	6730	6717	6704	2	4	6	9	11
48	·6691	6678	6665	6652	6639	6626	6613	6600	6587	6574	2	4	7	9	11
49	·6561	6547	6534	6521	6508	6494	6481	6468	6455	6441	2	4	7	9	11
50	·6428	6414	6401	6388	6374	6361	6347	6334	6320	6307	2	4	7	9	11
51	·6293	6280	6266	6252	6239	6225	6211	6198	6184	6170	2	5	7	9	11
52	·6157	6143	6129	6115	6101	6088	6074	6060	6046	6032	2	5	7	9	12
53	·6018	6004	5990	5976	5962	5948	5934	5920	5906	5892	2	5	7	9	12
54	·5878	5864	5850	5835	5821	5807	5793	5779	5764	5750	2	5	7	9	12
55	·5736	5721	5707	5693	5678	5664	5650	5635	5621	5606	2	5	7	10	12
56	·5592	5577	5563	5548	5534	5519	5505	5490	5476	5461	2	5	7	10	12
57	·5446	5432	5417	5402	5388	5373	5358	5344	5329	5314	2	5	7	10	12
58	·5299	5284	5270	5255	5240	5225	5210	5195	5180	5165	2	5	7	10	12
59	·5150	5135	5120	5105	5090	5075	5060	5045	5030	5015	3	5	8	10	13
60	·5000	4985	4970	4955	4939	4924	4909	4894	4879	4863	3	5	8	10	13
61	·4848	4833	4818	4802	4787	4772	4756	4741	4726	4710	3	5	8	10	13
62	·4695	4679	4664	4648	4633	4617	4602	4586	4571	4555	3	5	8	10	13
63	·4540	4524	4509	4493	4478	4462	4446	4431	4415	4399	3	5	8	10	13
64	·4384	4368	4352	4337	4321	4305	4289	4274	4258	4242	3	5	8	11	13
65	·4226	4210	4195	4179	4163	4147	4131	4115	4099	4083	3	5	8	11	13
66	·4067	4051	4035	4019	4003	3987	3971	3955	3939	3923	3	5	8	11	13
67	·3907	3891	3875	3859	3843	3827	3811	3795	3778	3762	3	5	8	11	13
68	·3746	3730	3714	3697	3681	3665	3649	3633	3616	3600	3	5	8	11	14
69	·3584	3567	3551	3535	3518	3502	3486	3469	3453	3437	3	5	8	11	14
70	·3420	3404	3387	3371	3355	3338	3322	3305	3289	3272	3	5	8	11	14
71	·3256	3239	3223	3206	3190	3173	3156	3140	3123	3107	3	6	8	11	14
72	·3090	3074	3057	3040	3024	3007	2990	2974	2957	2940	3	6	8	11	14
73	·2924	2907	2890	2874	2857	2840	2823	2807	2790	2773	3	6	8	11	14
74	·2756	2740	2723	2706	2689	2672	2656	2639	2622	2605	3	6	8	11	14
75	·2588	2571	2554	2538	2521	2504	2487	2470	2453	2436	3	6	8	11	14
76	·2419	2402	2385	2368	2351	2334	2317	2300	2284	2267	3	6	8	11	14
77	·2250	2233	2215	2198	2181	2164	2147	2130	2113	2096	3	6	9	11	14
78	·2079	2062	2045	2028	2011	1994	1977	1959	1942	1925	3	6	9	11	14
79	·1908	1891	1874	1857	1840	1822	1805	1788	1771	1754	3	6	9	11	14
80	·1736	1719	1702	1685	1668	1650	1633	1616	1599	1582	3	6	9	11	14
81	·1564	1547	1530	1513	1495	1478	1461	1444	1426	1409	3	6	9	12	14
82	·1392	1374	1357	1340	1323	1305	1288	1271	1253	1236	3	6	9	12	14
83	·1219	1201	1184	1167	1149	1132	1115	1097	1080	1063	3	6	9	12	14
84	·1045	1028	1011	0993	0976	0958	0941	0924	0906	0889	3	6	9	12	14
85	·0872	0854	0837	0819	0802	0785	0767	0750	0732	0715	3	6	9	12	14
86	·0698	0680	0663	0645	0628	0610	0593	0576	0558	0541	3	6	9	12	15
87	·0523	0506	0488	0471	0454	0436	0419	0401	0384	0366	3	6	9	12	15
88	·0349	0332	0314	0297	0279	0262	0244	0227	0209	0192	3	6	9	12	15
89	·0175	0157	0140	0122	0105	0087	0070	0052	0035	0017	3	6	9	12	15

SUBTRACT

NATURAL TANGENTS

	0′	6′	12′	18′	24′	30′	36′	42′	48′	54′	1′	2′	3′	4′	5′
0°	0·0000	0017	0035	0052	0070	0087	0105	0122	0140	0157	3	6	9	12	15
1	0·0175	0192	0209	0227	0244	0262	0279	0297	0314	0332	3	6	9	12	15
2	0·0349	0367	0384	0402	0419	0437	0454	0472	0489	0507	3	6	9	12	15
3	0·0524	0542	0559	0577	0594	0612	0629	0647	0664	0682	3	6	9	12	15
4	0·0699	0717	0734	0752	0769	0787	0805	0822	0840	0857	3	6	9	12	15
5	0·0875	0892	0910	0928	0945	0963	0981	0998	1016	1033	3	6	9	12	15
6	0·1051	1069	1086	1104	1122	1139	1157	1175	1192	1210	3	6	9	12	15
7	0·1228	1246	1263	1281	1299	1317	1334	1352	1370	1388	3	6	9	12	15
8	0·1405	1423	1441	1459	1477	1495	1512	1530	1548	1566	3	6	9	12	15
9	0·1584	1602	1620	1638	1655	1673	1691	1709	1727	1745	3	6	9	12	15
10	0·1763	1781	1799	1817	1835	1853	1871	1890	1908	1926	3	6	9	12	15
11	0·1944	1962	1980	1998	2016	2035	2053	2071	2089	2107	3	6	9	12	15
12	0·2126	2144	2162	2180	2199	2217	2235	2254	2272	2290	3	6	9	12	15
13	0·2309	2327	2345	2364	2382	2401	2419	2438	2456	2475	3	6	9	12	15
14	0·2493	2512	2530	2549	2568	2586	2605	2623	2642	2661	3	6	9	13	16
15	0·2679	2698	2717	2736	2754	2773	2792	2811	2830	2849	3	6	9	13	16
16	0·2867	2886	2905	2924	2943	2962	2981	3000	3019	3038	3	6	9	13	16
17	0·3057	3076	3096	3115	3134	3153	3172	3191	3211	3230	3	6	10	13	16
18	0·3249	3269	3288	3307	3327	3346	3365	3385	3404	3424	3	6	10	13	16
19	0·3443	3463	3482	3502	3522	3541	3561	3581	3600	3620	3	7	10	13	16
20	0·3640	3659	3679	3699	3719	3739	3759	3779	3799	3819	3	7	10	13	17
21	0·3839	3859	3879	3899	3919	3939	3959	3979	4000	4020	3	7	10	13	17
22	0·4040	4061	4081	4101	4122	4142	4163	4183	4204	4224	3	7	10	14	17
23	0·4245	4265	4286	4307	4327	4348	4369	4390	4411	4431	3	7	10	14	17
24	0·4452	4473	4494	4515	4536	4557	4578	4599	4621	4642	4	7	11	14	18
25	0·4663	4684	4706	4727	4748	4770	4791	4813	4834	4856	4	7	11	14	18
26	0·4877	4899	4921	4942	4964	4986	5008	5029	5051	5073	4	7	11	15	18
27	0·5095	5117	5139	5161	5184	5206	5228	5250	5272	5295	4	7	11	15	18
28	0·5317	5340	5362	5384	5407	5430	5452	5475	5498	5520	4	8	11	15	19
29	0·5543	5566	5589	5612	5635	5658	5681	5704	5727	5750	4	8	12	15	19
30	0·5774	5797	5820	5844	5867	5890	5914	5938	5961	5985	4	8	12	16	20
31	0·6009	6032	6056	6080	6104	6128	6152	6176	6200	6224	4	8	12	16	20
32	0·6249	6273	6297	6322	6346	6371	6395	6420	6445	6469	4	8	12	16	20
33	0·6494	6519	6544	6569	6594	6619	6644	6669	6694	6720	4	8	13	17	21
34	0·6745	6771	6796	6822	6847	6873	6899	6924	6950	6976	4	9	13	17	21
35	0·7002	7028	7054	7080	7107	7133	7159	7186	7212	7239	4	9	13	18	22
36	0·7265	7292	7319	7346	7373	7400	7427	7454	7481	7508	5	9	14	18	23
37	0·7536	7563	7590	7618	7646	7673	7701	7729	7757	7785	5	9	14	18	23
38	0·7813	7841	7869	7898	7926	7954	7983	8012	8040	8069	5	9	14	19	24
39	0·8098	8127	8156	8185	8214	8243	8273	8302	8332	8361	5	10	15	20	24
40	0·8391	8421	8451	8481	8511	8541	8571	8601	8632	8662	5	10	15	20	25
41	0·8693	8724	8754	8785	8816	8847	8878	8910	8941	8972	5	10	16	21	26
42	0·9004	9036	9067	9099	9131	9163	9195	9228	9260	9293	5	11	16	21	27
43	0·9325	9358	9391	9424	9457	9490	9523	9556	9590	9623	6	11	17	22	28
44	0·9657	9691	9725	9759	9793	9827	9861	9896	9930	9965	6	11	17	23	29
45	1·0000	0035	0070	0105	0141	0176	0212	0247	0283	0319	6	12	18	24	30
46	1·0355	0392	0428	0464	0501	0538	0575	0612	0649	0686	6	12	18	25	31
47	1·0724	0761	0799	0837	0875	0913	0951	0990	1028	1067	6	13	19	25	32

	0'	6'	12'	18'	24'	30'	36'	42'	48'	54'	1'	2'	3'	4'	5'
48°	1·1106	1145	1184	1224	1263	1303	1343	1383	1423	1463	7	13	20	27	33
49	1·1504	1544	1585	1626	1667	1708	1750	1792	1833	1875	7	14	21	28	34
50	1·1918	1960	2002	2045	2088	2131	2174	2218	2261	2305	7	14	22	29	36
51	1·2349	2393	2437	2482	2527	2572	2617	2662	2708	2753	8	15	23	30	38
52	1·2799	2846	2892	2938	2985	3032	3079	3127	3175	3222	8	16	24	31	39
53	1·3270	3319	3367	3416	3465	3514	3564	3613	3663	3713	8	16	25	33	41
54	1·3764	3814	3865	3916	3968	4019	4071	4124	4176	4229	9	17	26	35	43
55	1·4281	4335	4388	4442	4496	4550	4605	4659	4715	4770	9	18	27	36	45
56	1·4826	4882	4938	4994	5051	5108	5166	5224	5282	5340	10	19	29	38	48
57	1·5399	5458	5517	5577	5637	5697	5757	5818	5880	5941	10	20	30	40	50
58	1·6003	6066	6128	6191	6255	6319	6383	6447	6512	6577	11	21	32	43	53
59	1·6643	6709	6775	6842	6909	6977	7045	7113	7182	7251	11	23	34	45	56
60	1·7321	7391	7461	7532	7603	7675	7747	7820	7893	7966	12	24	36	48	60
61	1·8040	8115	8190	8265	8341	8418	8495	8572	8650	8728	13	26	38	51	64
62	1·8807	8887	8967	9047	9128	9210	9292	9375	9458	9542	14	27	41	55	68
63	1·9626	9711	9797	9883	9970	0057	0145	0233	0323	0413	15	29	44	58	73
64	2·0503	0594	0686	0778	0872	0965	1060	1155	1251	1348	16	31	47	63	78
65	2·1445	1543	1642	1742	1842	1943	2045	2148	2251	2355	17	34	51	68	85
66	2·2460	2566	2673	2781	2889	2998	3109	3220	3332	3445	18	37	55	73	92
67	2·3559	3673	3789	3906	4023	4142	4262	4383	4504	4627	20	40	60	79	99

											Difference for 1'				
											1 to 11	13 to 23	25 to 35	37 to 47	49 to 59
68	2·4751	4876	5002	5129	5257	5386	5517	5649	5782	5916	21	21	22	22	22
69	2·6051	6187	6325	6464	6605	6746	6889	7034	7179	7326	23	23	24	24	25
70	2·7475	7625	7776	7929	8083	8239	8397	8556	8716	8878	25	26	26	27	27
71	2·9042	9208	9375	9544	9714	9887	0061	0237	0415	0595	28	28	29	30	30
72	3·0777	0961	1146	1334	1524	1716	1910	2106	2305	2506	31	31	32	33	34
73	3·2709	2914	3122	3332	3544	3759	3977	4197	4420	4646	34	35	36	37	38
74	3·4874	5105	5339	5576	5816	6059	6305	6554	6806	7062	39	40	41	42	43
75	3·7321	7583	7848	8118	8391	8667	8947	9232	9520	9812	44	45	46	48	49
76	4·0108	0408	0713	1022	1335	1653	1976	2303	2635	2972	50	52	53	55	57
77	4·3315	3662	4015	4373	4737	5107	5483	5864	6252	6646	58	60	62	64	66
78	4·7046	7453	7867	8288	8716	9152	9594	0045	0504	0970	68	71	73	76	78
79	5·1446	1929	2422	2924	3435	3955	4486	5026	5578	6140	81	84	88	91	95
80	5·671	5·730	5·789	5·850	5·912	5·976	6·041	6·107	6·174	6·243	10	10	11	11	12
81	6·314	6·386	6·460	6·535	6·612	6·691	6·772	6·855	6·940	7·026	12	13	13	14	15
82	7·115	7·207	7·300	7·396	7·495	7·596	7·700	7·806	7·916	8·028	15	16	17	18	19
83	8·144	8·264	8·386	8·513	8·643	8·777	8·915	9·058	9·205	9·357	20	21	23	24	26
84	9·51	9·68	9·84	10·02	10·20	10·39	10·58	10·78	10·99	11·20	3	3	3	3	4
85	11·43	11·66	11·91	12·16	12·43	12·71	13·00	13·30	13·62	13·95	4	4	5	5	6
86	14·30	14·67	15·06	15·46	15·89	16·35	16·83	17·34	17·89	18·46	6	7	8	9	10
87	19·08	19·74	20·45	21·20	22·02	22·90	23·86	24·90	26·03	27·27	11	13	15	18	22
88	28·64	30·14	31·82	33·69	35·80	38·19	40·92	44·07	47·74	52·08					
89	57·29	63·66	71·62	81·85	95·49	114·6	143·2	191·0	286·5	573·0					

Where the integer changes, the numbers are italicised.

RECIPROCALS

	0	1	2	3	4	5	6	7	8	9	1	2	3	4	5	6	7	8	9
10	10000	9901	9804	9709	9615	9524	9434	9346	9259	9174	9	18	28	37	46	55	64	73	83
11	9091	9009	8929	8850	8772	8696	8621	8547	8475	8403	8	15	23	31	38	46	54	61	69
12	8333	8264	8197	8130	8065	8000	7937	7874	7813	7752	6	13	19	26	32	39	45	52	58
13	7692	7634	7576	7519	7463	7407	7353	7299	7246	7194	5	11	17	22	28	33	39	44	50
14	7143	7092	7042	6993	6944	6897	6849	6803	6757	6711	5	10	14	19	24	29	34	38	43
15	6667	6623	6579	6536	6494	6452	6410	6369	6329	6289	4	8	13	17	21	25	29	34	38
16	6250	6211	6173	6135	6098	6061	6024	5988	5952	5917	4	7	11	15	18	22	26	29	33
17	5882	5848	5814	5780	5747	5714	5682	5650	5618	5587	3	7	10	13	16	20	23	26	29
18	5556	5525	5495	5464	5435	5405	5376	5348	5319	5291	3	6	9	12	15	18	20	23	26
19	5263	5236	5208	5181	5155	5128	5102	5076	5051	5025	3	5	8	11	13	16	18	21	24
20	5000	4975	4950	4926	4902	4878	4854	4831	4808	4785	2	5	7	10	12	14	17	19	21
21	4762	4739	4717	4695	4673	4651	4630	4608	4587	4566	2	4	7	9	11	13	15	17	19
22	4545	4525	4505	4484	4464	4444	4425	4405	4386	4367	2	4	6	8	10	12	14	16	18
23	4348	4329	4310	4292	4274	4255	4237	4219	4202	4184	2	4	5	7	9	11	13	15	16
24	4167	4149	4132	4115	4098	4082	4065	4049	4032	4016	2	3	5	7	8	10	12	13	15
25	4000	3984	3968	3953	3937	3922	3906	3891	3876	3861	2	3	5	6	8	9	11	12	14
26	3846	3831	3817	3802	3783	3774	3759	3745	3731	3717	1	3	4	6	7	9	10	11	13
27	3704	3690	3676	3663	3650	3636	3623	3610	3597	3584	1	3	4	5	7	8	9	11	12
28	3571	3559	3546	3534	3521	3509	3497	3484	3472	3460	1	2	4	5	6	7	9	10	11
29	3448	3436	3425	3413	3401	3390	3378	3367	3356	3344	1	2	3	5	6	7	8	9	10
30	3333	3322	3311	3300	3289	3279	3268	3257	3247	3236	1	2	3	4	5	6	8	9	10
31	3226	3215	3205	3195	3185	3175	3165	3155	3145	3135	1	2	3	4	5	6	7	8	9
32	3125	3115	3106	3096	3086	3077	3067	3058	3049	3040	1	2	3	4	5	6	7	8	9
33	3030	3021	3012	3003	2994	2985	2976	2967	2959	2950	1	2	3	4	4	5	6	7	8
34	2941	2933	2924	2915	2907	2899	2890	2882	2874	2865	1	2	3	3	4	5	6	7	8
35	2857	2849	2841	2833	2825	2817	2809	2801	2793	2786	1	2	2	3	4	5	6	6	7
36	2778	2770	2762	2755	2747	2740	2732	2725	2717	2710	1	2	2	3	4	5	5	6	7
37	2703	2695	2688	2681	2674	2667	2660	2653	2646	2639	1	1	2	3	4	5	5	6	6
38	2632	2625	2618	2611	2604	2597	2591	2584	2577	2571	1	1	2	3	3	4	5	5	6
39	2564	2558	2551	2545	2538	2532	2525	2519	2513	2506	1	1	2	3	3	4	4	5	6
40	2500	2494	2488	2481	2475	2469	2463	2457	2451	2445	1	1	2	2	3	4	4	5	5
41	2439	2433	2427	2421	2415	2410	2404	2398	2392	2387	1	1	2	2	3	3	4	5	5
42	2381	2375	2370	2364	2358	2353	2347	2342	2336	2331	1	1	2	2	3	3	4	4	5
43	2326	2320	2315	2309	2304	2299	2294	2288	2283	2278	1	1	2	2	3	3	4	4	5
44	2273	2268	2262	2257	2252	2247	2242	2237	2232	2227	1	1	2	2	3	3	4	4	5
45	2222	2217	2212	2208	2203	2198	2193	2188	2183	2179	0	1	1	2	2	3	3	4	4
46	2174	2169	2165	2160	2155	2151	2146	2141	2137	2132	0	1	1	2	2	3	3	4	4
47	2128	2123	2119	2114	2110	2105	2101	2096	2092	2088	0	1	1	2	2	3	3	4	4
48	2083	2079	2075	2070	2066	2062	2058	2053	2049	2045	0	1	1	2	2	3	3	3	4
49	2041	2037	2033	2028	2024	2020	2016	2012	2008	2004	0	1	1	2	2	2	3	3	4
50	2000	1996	1992	1988	1984	1980	1976	1972	1969	1965	0	1	1	2	2	2	3	3	4
51	1961	1957	1953	1949	1946	1942	1938	1934	1931	1927	0	1	1	2	2	2	3	3	3
52	1923	1919	1916	1912	1908	1905	1901	1898	1894	1890	0	1	1	1	2	2	3	3	3
53	1887	1883	1880	1876	1873	1869	1866	1862	1859	1855	0	1	1	1	2	2	2	3	3
54	1852	1848	1845	1842	1838	1835	1832	1828	1825	1821	0	1	1	1	2	2	2	3	3

Find the position of the decimal point by inspection.

SUBTRACT

	0	1	2	3	4	5	6	7	8	9	1	2	3	4	5	6	7	8	9
55	1818	1815	1812	1808	1805	1802	1799	1795	1792	1789	0	1	1	1	2	2	2	3	3
56	1786	1783	1779	1776	1773	1770	1767	1764	1761	1757	0	1	1	1	2	2	2	3	3
57	1754	1751	1748	1745	1742	1739	1736	1733	1730	1727	0	1	1	1	2	2	2	2	3
58	1724	1721	1718	1715	1712	1709	1706	1704	1701	1698	0	1	1	1	1	2	2	2	3
59	1695	1692	1689	1686	1684	1681	1678	1675	1672	1669	0	1	1	1	1	2	2	2	3
60	1667	1664	1661	1658	1656	1653	1650	1647	1645	1642	0	1	1	1	1	2	2	2	2
61	1639	1637	1634	1631	1629	1626	1623	1621	1618	1616	0	1	1	1	1	2	2	2	2
62	1613	1610	1608	1605	1603	1600	1597	1595	1592	1590	0	1	1	1	1	2	2	2	2
63	1587	1585	1582	1580	1577	1575	1572	1570	1567	1565	0	0	1	1	1	1	2	2	2
64	1563	1560	1558	1555	1553	1550	1548	1546	1543	1541	0	0	1	1	1	1	2	2	2
65	1538	1536	1534	1531	1529	1527	1524	1522	1520	1517	0	0	1	1	1	1	2	2	2
66	1515	1513	1511	1508	1506	1504	1502	1499	1497	1495	0	0	1	1	1	1	2	2	2
67	1493	1490	1488	1486	1484	1481	1479	1477	1475	1473	0	0	1	1	1	1	2	2	2
68	1471	1468	1466	1464	1462	1460	1458	1456	1453	1451	0	0	1	1	1	1	1	2	2
69	1449	1447	1445	1443	1441	1439	1437	1435	1433	1431	0	0	1	1	1	1	1	2	2
70	1429	1427	1425	1422	1420	1418	1416	1414	1412	1410	0	0	1	1	1	1	1	2	2
71	1408	1406	1404	1403	1401	1399	1397	1395	1393	1391	0	0	1	1	1	1	1	2	2
72	1389	1387	1385	1383	1381	1379	1377	1376	1374	1372	0	0	1	1	1	1	1	2	2
73	1370	1368	1366	1364	1362	1361	1359	1357	1355	1353	0	0	1	1	1	1	1	2	2
74	1351	1350	1348	1346	1344	1342	1340	1339	1337	1335	0	0	1	1	1	1	1	1	2
75	1333	1332	1330	1328	1326	1325	1323	1321	1319	1318	0	0	1	1	1	1	1	1	2
76	1316	1314	1312	1311	1309	1307	1305	1304	1302	1300	0	0	1	1	1	1	1	1	2
77	1299	1297	1295	1294	1292	1290	1289	1287	1285	1284	0	0	0	1	1	1	1	1	1
78	1282	1280	1279	1277	1276	1274	1272	1271	1269	1267	0	0	0	1	1	1	1	1	1
79	1266	1264	1263	1261	1259	1258	1256	1255	1253	1252	0	0	0	1	1	1	1	1	1
80	1250	1248	1247	1245	1244	1242	1241	1239	1238	1236	0	0	0	1	1	1	1	1	1
81	1235	1233	1232	1230	1229	1227	1225	1224	1222	1221	0	0	0	1	1	1	1	1	1
82	1220	1218	1217	1215	1214	1212	1211	1209	1208	1206	0	0	0	1	1	1	1	1	1
83	1205	1203	1202	1200	1199	1198	1196	1195	1193	1192	0	0	0	1	1	1	1	1	1
84	1190	1189	1188	1186	1185	1183	1182	1181	1179	1178	0	0	0	1	1	1	1	1	1
85	1176	1175	1174	1172	1171	1170	1168	1167	1166	1164	0	0	0	1	1	1	1	1	1
86	1163	1161	1160	1159	1157	1156	1155	1153	1152	1151	0	0	0	1	1	1	1	1	1
87	1149	1148	1147	1145	1144	1143	1142	1140	1139	1138	0	0	0	1	1	1	1	1	1
88	1136	1134	1133	1133	1131	1130	1129	1127	1126	1125	0	0	0	1	1	1	1	1	1
89	1124	1122	1121	1120	1119	1117	1116	1115	1114	1112	0	0	0	1	1	1	1	1	1
90	1111	1110	1109	1107	1106	1105	1104	1103	1101	1100	0	0	0	0	1	1	1	1	1
91	1099	1098	1096	1095	1094	1093	1092	1091	1089	1088	0	0	0	0	1	1	1	1	1
92	1087	1086	1085	1083	1082	1081	1080	1079	1078	1076	0	0	0	0	1	1	1	1	1
93	1075	1074	1073	1072	1071	1070	1068	1067	1066	1065	0	0	0	0	1	1	1	1	1
94	1064	1063	1062	1060	1059	1058	1057	1056	1055	1054	0	0	0	0	1	1	1	1	1
95	1053	1052	1050	1049	1048	1047	1046	1045	1044	1043	0	0	0	0	1	1	1	1	1
96	1042	1041	1040	1038	1037	1036	1035	1034	1033	1032	0	0	0	1	1	1	1	1	1
97	1031	1030	1029	1028	1027	1026	1025	1024	1022	1021	0	0	0	0	1	1	1	1	1
98	1020	1019	1018	1017	1016	1015	1014	1013	1012	1011	0	0	0	0	0	1	1	1	1
99	1010	1009	1008	1007	1006	1005	1004	1003	1002	1001	0	0	0	0	0	1	1	1	1

SUBTRACT

Find the position of the decimal point by inspection.

SQUARES

	0	1	2	3	4	5	6	7	8	9	1	2	3	4	5	6	7	8	9
10	1000	1020	1040	1061	1082	1103	1124	1145	1166	1188	2	4	6	8	10	13	15	17	19
11	1210	1232	1254	1277	1300	1323	1346	1369	1392	1416	2	5	7	9	11	14	16	18	21
12	1440	1464	1488	1513	1538	1563	1588	1613	1638	1664	2	5	7	10	12	15	17	20	22
13	1690	1716	1742	1769	1796	1823	1850	1877	1904	1932	3	5	8	11	13	16	19	22	24
14	1960	1988	2016	2045	2074	2103	2132	2161	2190	2220	3	6	9	12	14	17	20	23	26
15	2250	2280	2310	2341	2372	2403	2434	2465	2496	2528	3	6	9	12	15	19	22	25	28
16	2560	2592	2624	2657	2690	2723	2756	2789	2822	2856	3	7	10	13	16	20	23	26	30
17	2890	2924	2958	2993	3028	3063	3098	3133	3168	3204	3	7	10	14	17	21	24	28	31
18	3240	3276	3312	3349	3386	3423	3460	3497	3534	3572	4	7	11	15	18	22	26	30	33
19	3610	3648	3686	3725	3764	3803	3842	3881	3920	3960	4	8	12	16	19	23	27	31	35
20	4000	4040	4080	4121	4162	4203	4244	4285	4326	4368	4	8	12	16	20	25	29	33	37
21	4410	4452	4494	4537	4580	4623	4666	4709	4752	4796	4	9	13	17	21	26	30	34	39
22	4840	4884	4928	4973	5018	5063	5108	5153	5198	5244	4	9	13	18	22	27	31	36	40
23	5290	5336	5382	5429	5476	5523	5570	5617	5664	5712	5	9	14	19	23	28	33	38	42
24	5760	5808	5856	5905	5954	6003	6052	6101	6150	6200	5	10	15	20	24	29	34	39	44
25	6250	6300	6350	6401	6452	6503	6554	6605	6656	6708	5	10	15	20	25	31	36	41	46
26	6760	6812	6864	6917	6970	7023	7076	7129	7182	7236	5	11	16	21	26	32	37	42	48
27	7290	7344	7398	7453	7508	7563	7618	7673	7728	7784	5	11	16	22	27	33	38	44	49
28	7840	7896	7952	8009	8066	8123	8180	8237	8294	8352	6	11	17	23	28	34	40	46	51
29	8410	8468	8526	8585	8644	8703	8762	8821	8880	8940	6	12	18	24	29	35	41	47	53
30	9000	9060	9120	9181	9242	9303	9364	9425	9486	9548	6	12	18	24	30	37	43	49	55
31	9610	9672	9734	9797	9860	9923	9986				6	13	19	25	31	38	44	50	57
31								1005	1011	1018	1	1	2	3	3	4	5	5	6
32	1024	1030	1037	1043	1050	1056	1063	1069	1076	1082	1	1	2	3	3	4	5	5	6
33	1089	1096	1102	1109	1116	1122	1129	1136	1142	1149	1	1	2	3	3	4	5	5	6
34	1156	1163	1170	1176	1183	1190	1197	1204	1211	1218	1	1	2	3	3	4	5	6	6
35	1225	1232	1239	1246	1253	1260	1267	1274	1282	1289	1	1	2	3	4	4	5	6	6
36	1296	1303	1310	1318	1325	1332	1340	1347	1354	1362	1	1	2	3	4	4	5	6	7
37	1369	1376	1384	1391	1399	1406	1414	1421	1429	1436	1	2	2	3	4	5	5	6	7
38	1444	1452	1459	1467	1475	1482	1490	1498	1505	1513	1	2	2	3	4	5	5	6	7
39	1521	1529	1537	1544	1552	1560	1568	1576	1584	1592	1	2	2	3	4	5	6	6	7
40	1600	1608	1616	1624	1632	1640	1648	1656	1665	1673	1	2	2	3	4	5	6	6	7
41	1681	1689	1697	1706	1714	1722	1731	1739	1747	1756	1	2	2	3	4	5	6	7	7
42	1764	1772	1781	1789	1798	1806	1815	1823	1832	1840	1	2	3	3	4	5	6	7	8
43	1849	1858	1866	1875	1884	1892	1901	1910	1918	1927	1	2	3	3	4	5	6	7	8
44	1936	1945	1954	1962	1971	1980	1989	1998	2007	2016	1	2	3	4	4	5	6	7	8
45	2025	2034	2043	2052	2061	2070	2079	2088	2098	2107	1	2	3	4	5	5	6	7	8
46	2116	2125	2134	2144	2153	2162	2172	2181	2190	2200	1	2	3	4	5	6	7	7	8
47	2209	2218	2228	2237	2247	2256	2266	2275	2285	2294	1	2	3	4	5	6	7	8	9
48	2304	2314	2323	2333	2343	2352	2362	2372	2381	2391	1	2	3	4	5	6	7	8	9
49	2401	2411	2421	2430	2440	2450	2460	2470	2480	2490	1	2	3	4	5	6	7	8	9
50	2500	2510	2520	2530	2540	2550	2560	2570	2581	2591	1	2	3	4	5	6	7	8	9
51	2601	2611	2621	2632	2642	2652	2663	2673	2683	2694	1	2	3	4	5	6	7	8	9
52	2704	2714	2725	2735	2746	2756	2767	2777	2788	2798	1	2	3	4	5	6	7	8	9
53	2809	2820	2830	2841	2852	2862	2873	2884	2894	2905	1	2	3	4	5	6	7	9	10
54	2916	2927	2938	2948	2959	2970	2981	2992	3003	3014	1	2	3	4	5	7	8	9	10

Find the position of the decimal point by inspection.

	0	1	2	3	4	5	6	7	8	9	1	2	3	4	5	6	7	8	9
55	3025	3036	3047	3058	3069	3080	3091	3102	3114	3125	1	2	3	4	6	7	8	9	10
56	3136	3147	3158	3170	3181	3192	3204	3215	3226	3238	1	2	3	5	6	7	8	9	10
57	3249	3260	3272	3283	3295	3306	3318	3329	3341	3352	1	2	3	5	6	7	8	9	10
58	3364	3376	3387	3399	3411	3422	3434	3446	3457	3469	1	2	4	5	6	7	8	9	11
59	3481	3493	3505	3516	3528	3540	3552	3564	3576	3588	1	2	4	5	6	7	8	10	11
60	3600	3612	3624	3636	3648	3660	3672	3684	3697	3709	1	2	4	5	6	7	8	10	11
61	3721	3733	3745	3758	3770	3782	3795	3807	3819	3832	1	2	4	5	6	7	9	10	11
62	3844	3856	3869	3881	3894	3906	3919	3931	3944	3956	1	3	4	5	6	7	9	10	11
63	3969	3982	3994	4007	4020	4032	4045	4058	4070	4083	1	3	4	5	6	8	9	10	11
64	4096	4109	4122	4134	4147	4160	4173	4186	4199	4212	1	3	4	5	6	8	9	10	12
65	4225	4238	4251	4264	4277	4290	4303	4316	4330	4343	1	3	4	5	7	8	9	10	12
66	4356	4369	4382	4396	4409	4422	4436	4449	4462	4476	1	3	4	5	7	8	9	11	12
67	4489	4502	4516	4529	4543	4556	4570	4583	4597	4610	1	3	4	5	7	8	9	11	12
68	4624	4638	4651	4665	4679	4692	4706	4720	4733	4747	1	3	4	5	7	8	10	11	12
69	4761	4775	4789	4802	4816	4830	4844	4858	4872	4886	1	3	4	6	7	8	10	11	13
70	4900	4914	4928	4942	4956	4970	4984	4998	5013	5027	1	3	4	6	7	8	10	11	13
71	5041	5055	5069	5084	5098	5112	5127	5141	5155	5170	1	3	4	6	7	9	10	11	13
72	5184	5198	5213	5227	5242	5256	5271	5285	5300	5314	1	3	4	6	7	9	10	12	13
73	5329	5344	5358	5373	5388	5402	5417	5432	5446	5461	1	3	4	6	7	9	10	12	13
74	5476	5491	5506	5520	5535	5550	5565	5580	5595	5610	1	3	4	6	7	9	10	12	13
75	5625	5640	5655	5670	5685	5700	5715	5730	5746	5761	2	3	5	6	8	9	11	12	14
76	5776	5791	5806	5822	5837	5852	5868	5883	5898	5914	2	3	5	6	8	9	11	12	14
77	5929	5944	5960	5975	5991	6006	6022	6037	6053	6068	2	3	5	6	8	9	11	12	14
78	6084	6100	6115	6131	6147	6162	6178	6194	6209	6225	2	3	5	6	8	9	11	13	14
79	6241	6257	6273	6288	6304	6320	6336	6352	6368	6384	2	3	5	6	8	10	11	13	14
80	6400	6416	6432	6448	6464	6480	6496	6512	6529	6545	2	3	5	6	8	10	11	13	14
81	6561	6577	6593	6610	6626	6642	6659	6675	6691	6708	2	3	5	7	8	10	11	13	15
82	6724	6740	6757	6773	6790	6806	6823	6839	6856	6872	2	3	5	7	8	10	12	13	15
83	6889	6906	6922	6939	6956	6972	6989	7006	7022	7039	2	3	5	7	8	10	12	13	15
84	7056	7073	7090	7106	7123	7140	7157	7174	7191	7208	2	3	5	7	8	10	12	14	15
85	7225	7242	7259	7276	7293	7310	7327	7344	7362	7379	2	3	5	7	9	10	12	14	15
86	7396	7413	7430	7448	7465	7482	7500	7517	7534	7552	2	3	5	7	9	10	12	14	16
87	7569	7586	7604	7621	7639	7656	7674	7691	7709	7726	2	4	5	7	9	10	12	14	16
88	7744	7762	7779	7797	7815	7832	7850	7868	7885	7903	2	4	5	7	9	11	12	14	16
89	7921	7939	7957	7974	7992	8010	8028	8046	8064	8082	2	4	5	7	9	11	13	14	16
90	8100	8118	8136	8154	8172	8190	8208	8226	8245	8263	2	4	5	7	9	11	13	14	16
91	8281	8299	8317	8336	8354	8372	8391	8409	8427	8446	2	4	5	7	9	11	13	15	16
92	8464	8482	8501	8519	8538	8556	8575	8593	8612	8630	2	4	6	7	9	11	13	15	17
93	8649	8668	8686	8705	8724	8742	8761	8780	8798	8817	2	4	6	7	9	11	13	15	17
94	8836	8855	8874	8892	8911	8930	8949	8968	8987	9006	2	4	6	8	9	11	13	15	17
95	9025	9044	9063	9082	9101	9120	9139	9158	9178	9197	2	4	6	8	10	11	13	15	17
96	9216	9235	9254	9274	9293	9312	9332	9351	9370	9390	2	4	6	8	10	12	14	15	17
97	9409	9428	9448	9467	9487	9506	9526	9545	9565	9584	2	4	6	8	10	12	14	16	18
98	9604	9624	9643	9663	9683	9702	9722	9742	9761	9781	2	4	6	8	10	12	14	16	18
99	9801	9821	9841	9860	9880	9900	9920	9940	9960	9980	2	4	6	8	10	12	14	16	18

Find the position of the decimal point by inspection.

SQUARE ROOTS

	0	1	2	3	4	5	6	7	8	9	1 2 3	4 5 6	7 8 9
10	1000	1005	1010	1015	1020	1025	1030	1034	1039	1044	0 1 1	2 2 3	3 4 4
11	1049	1054	1058	1063	1068	1072	1077	1082	1086	1091	0 1 1	2 2 3	3 4 4
12	1095	1100	1105	1109	1114	1118	1122	1127	1131	1136	0 1 1	2 2 3	3 4 4
13	1140	1145	1149	1153	1158	1162	1166	1170	1175	1179	0 1 1	2 2 3	3 3 4
14	1183	1187	1192	1196	1200	1204	1208	1212	1217	1221	0 1 1	2 2 2	3 3 4
15	1225	1229	1233	1237	1241	1245	1249	1253	1257	1261	0 1 1	2 2 2	3 3 4
16	1265	1269	1273	1277	1281	1285	1288	1292	1296	1300	0 1 1	2 2 2	3 3 4
17	1304	1308	1311	1315	1319	1323	1327	1330	1334	1338	0 1 1	2 2 2	3 3 3
18	1342	1345	1349	1353	1356	1360	1364	1367	1371	1375	0 1 1	1 2 2	3 3 3
19	1378	1382	1386	1389	1393	1396	1400	1404	1407	1411	0 1 1	1 2 2	3 3 3
20	1414	1418	1421	1425	1428	1432	1435	1439	1442	1446	0 1 1	1 2 2	2 3 3
21	1449	1453	1456	1459	1463	1466	1470	1473	1476	1480	0 1 1	1 2 2	2 3 3
22	1483	1487	1490	1493	1497	1500	1503	1507	1510	1513	0 1 1	1 2 2	2 3 3
23	1517	1520	1523	1526	1530	1533	1536	1539	1543	1546	0 1 1	1 2 2	2 3 3
24	1549	1552	1556	1559	1562	1565	1568	1572	1575	1578	0 1 1	1 2 2	2 3 3
25	1581	1584	1587	1591	1594	1597	1600	1603	1606	1609	0 1 1	1 2 2	2 3 3
26	1612	1616	1619	1622	1625	1628	1631	1634	1637	1640	0 1 1	1 2 2	2 2 3
27	1643	1646	1649	1652	1655	1658	1661	1664	1667	1670	0 1 1	1 2 2	2 2 3
28	1673	1676	1679	1682	1685	1688	1691	1694	1697	1700	0 1 1	1 1 2	2 2 3
29	1703	1706	1709	1712	1715	1718	1720	1723	1726	1729	0 1 1	1 1 2	2 2 3
30	1732	1735	1738	1741	1744	1746	1749	1752	1755	1758	0 1 1	1 1 2	2 2 3
31	1761	1764	1766	1769	1772	1775	1778	1780	1783	1786	0 1 1	1 1 2	2 2 3
32	1789	1792	1794	1797	1800	1803	1806	1808	1811	1814	0 1 1	1 1 2	2 2 2
33	1817	1819	1822	1825	1828	1830	1833	1836	1838	1841	0 1 1	1 1 2	2 2 2
34	1844	1847	1849	1852	1855	1857	1860	1863	1865	1868	0 1 1	1 1 2	2 2 2
35	1871	1873	1876	1879	1881	1884	1887	1889	1892	1895	0 1 1	1 1 2	2 2 2
36	1897	1900	1903	1905	1908	1910	1913	1916	1918	1921	0 1 1	1 1 2	2 2 2
37	1924	1926	1929	1931	1934	1936	1939	1942	1944	1947	0 1 1	1 1 2	2 2 2
38	1949	1952	1954	1957	1960	1962	1965	1967	1970	1972	0 1 1	1 1 2	2 2 2
39	1975	1977	1980	1982	1985	1987	1990	1992	1995	1997	0 1 1	1 1 2	2 2 2
40	2000	2002	2005	2007	2010	2012	2015	2017	2020	2022	0 0 1	1 1 1	2 2 2
41	2025	2027	2030	2032	2035	2037	2040	2042	2045	2047	0 0 1	1 1 1	2 2 2
42	2049	2052	2054	2057	2059	2062	2064	2066	2069	2071	0 0 1	1 1 1	2 2 2
43	2074	2076	2078	2081	2083	2086	2088	2090	2093	2095	0 0 1	1 1 1	2 2 2
44	2098	2100	2102	2105	2107	2110	2112	2114	2117	2119	0 0 1	1 1 1	2 2 2
45	2121	2124	2126	2128	2131	2133	2135	2138	2140	2142	0 0 1	1 1 1	2 2 2
46	2145	2147	2149	2152	2154	2156	2159	2161	2163	2166	0 0 1	1 1 1	2 2 2
47	2168	2170	2173	2175	2177	2179	2182	2184	2186	2189	0 0 1	1 1 1	2 2 2
48	2191	2193	2195	2198	2200	2202	2205	2207	2209	2211	0 0 1	1 1 1	2 2 2
49	2214	2216	2218	2220	2223	2225	2227	2229	2232	2234	0 0 1	1 1 1	2 2 2
50	2236	2238	2241	2243	2245	2247	2249	2252	2254	2256	0 0 1	1 1 1	2 2 2
51	2258	2261	2263	2265	2267	2269	2272	2274	2276	2278	0 0 1	1 1 1	2 2 2
52	2280	2283	2285	2287	2289	2291	2293	2296	2298	2300	0 0 1	1 1 1	2 2 2
53	2302	2304	2307	2309	2311	2313	2315	2317	2319	2322	0 0 1	1 1 1	2 2 2
54	2324	2326	2328	2330	2332	2335	2337	2339	2341	2343	0 0 1	1 1 1	1 2 2

Find the first significant figure and the position of the decimal point by inspection.

	0	1	2	3	4	5	6	7	8	9	1 2 3	4 5 6	7 8 9
10	3162	3178	3194	3209	3225	3240	3256	3271	3286	3302	2 3 5	6 8 9	11 12 14
11	3317	3332	3347	3362	3376	3391	3406	3421	3435	3450	1 3 4	6 7 9	10 12 13
12	3464	3479	3493	3507	3521	3536	3550	3564	3578	3592	1 3 4	6 7 8	10 11 13
13	3606	3619	3633	3647	3661	3674	3688	3701	3715	3728	1 3 4	5 7 8	10 11 12
14	3742	3755	3768	3782	3795	3808	3821	3834	3847	3860	1 3 4	5 7 8	9 11 12
15	3873	3886	3899	3912	3924	3937	3950	3962	3975	3987	1 3 4	5 6 8	9 10 11
16	4000	4012	4025	4037	4050	4062	4074	4087	4099	4111	1 2 4	5 6 7	9 10 11
17	4123	4135	4147	4159	4171	4183	4195	4207	4219	4231	1 2 4	5 6 7	8 10 11
18	4243	4254	4266	4278	4290	4301	4313	4324	4336	4347	1 2 3	5 6 7	8 9 10
19	4359	4370	4382	4393	4405	4416	4427	4438	4450	4461	1 2 3	5 6 7	8 9 10
20	4472	4483	4494	4506	4517	4528	4539	4550	4561	4572	1 2 3	4 6 7	8 9 10
21	4583	4593	4604	4615	4626	4637	4648	4658	4669	4680	1 2 3	4 5 6	8 9 10
22	4690	4701	4712	4722	4733	4743	4754	4764	4775	4785	1 2 3	4 5 6	7 8 9
23	4796	4806	4817	4827	4837	4848	4858	4868	4879	4889	1 2 3	4 5 6	7 8 9
24	4899	4909	4919	4930	4940	4950	4960	4970	4980	4990	1 2 3	4 5 6	7 8 9
25	5000	5010	5020	5030	5040	5050	5060	5070	5079	5089	1 2 3	4 5 6	7 8 9
26	5099	5109	5119	5128	5138	5148	5158	5167	5177	5187	1 2 3	4 5 6	7 8 9
27	5196	5206	5215	5225	5235	5244	5254	5263	5273	5282	1 2 3	4 5 6	7 8 9
28	5292	5301	5310	5320	5329	5339	5348	5357	5367	5376	1 2 3	4 5 6	7 7 8
29	5385	5394	5404	5413	5422	5431	5441	5450	5459	5468	1 2 3	4 5 5	6 7 8
30	5477	5486	5495	5505	5514	5523	5532	5541	5550	5559	1 2 3	4 4 5	6 7 8
31	5568	5577	5586	5595	5604	5612	5621	5630	5639	5648	1 2 3	3 4 5	6 7 8
32	5657	5666	5675	5683	5692	5701	5710	5718	5727	5736	1 2 3	3 4 5	6 7 8
33	5745	5753	5762	5771	5779	5788	5797	5805	5814	5822	1 2 3	3 4 5	6 7 8
34	5831	5840	5848	5857	5865	5874	5882	5891	5899	5908	1 2 3	3 4 5	6 7 8
35	5916	5925	5933	5941	5950	5958	5967	5975	5983	5992	1 2 2	3 4 5	6 7 8
36	6000	6008	6017	6025	6033	6042	6050	6058	6066	6075	1 2 2	3 4 5	6 7 7
37	6083	6091	6099	6107	6116	6124	6132	6140	6148	6156	1 2 2	3 4 5	6 7 7
38	6164	6173	6181	6189	6197	6205	6213	6221	6229	6237	1 2 2	3 4 5	6 6 7
39	6245	6253	6261	6269	6277	6285	6293	6301	6309	6317	1 2 2	3 4 5	6 6 7
40	6325	6332	6340	6348	6356	6364	6372	6380	6387	6395	1 2 2	3 4 5	6 6 7
41	6403	6411	6419	6427	6434	6442	6450	6458	6465	6473	1 2 2	3 4 5	5 6 7
42	6481	6488	6496	6504	6512	6519	6527	6535	6542	6550	1 2 2	3 4 5	5 6 7
43	6557	6565	6573	6580	6588	6595	6603	6611	6618	6626	1 2 2	3 4 5	5 6 7
44	6633	6641	6648	6656	6663	6671	6678	6686	6693	6701	1 2 2	3 4 5	5 6 7
45	6708	6716	6723	6731	6738	6745	6753	6760	6768	6775	1 1 2	3 4 4	5 6 7
46	6782	6790	6797	6804	6812	6819	6826	6834	6841	6848	1 1 2	3 4 4	5 6 7
47	6856	6863	6870	6877	6885	6892	6899	6907	6914	6921	1 1 2	3 4 4	5 6 7
48	6928	6935	6943	6950	6957	6964	6971	6979	6986	6993	1 1 2	3 4 4	5 6 6
49	7000	7007	7014	7021	7029	7036	7043	7050	7057	7064	1 1 2	3 4 4	5 6 6
50	7071	7078	7085	7092	7099	7106	7113	7120	7127	7134	1 1 2	3 4 4	5 6 6
51	7141	7148	7155	7162	7169	7176	7183	7190	7197	7204	1 1 2	3 4 4	5 6 6
52	7211	7218	7225	7232	7239	7246	7253	7259	7266	7273	1 1 2	3 3 4	5 6 6
53	7280	7287	7294	7301	7308	7314	7321	7328	7335	7342	1 1 2	3 3 4	5 5 6
54	7348	7355	7362	7369	7376	7382	7389	7396	7403	7409	1 1 2	3 3 4	5 5 6

Find the first significant figure and the position of the decimal point by inspection.

SQUARE ROOTS

	0	1	2	3	4	5	6	7	8	9	1 2 3	4 5 6	7 8 9
55	2345	2347	2349	2352	2354	2356	2358	2360	2362	2364	0 0 1	1 1 1	1 2 2
56	2366	2369	2371	2373	2375	2377	2379	2381	2383	2385	0 0 1	1 1 1	1 2 2
57	2387	2390	2392	2394	2396	2398	2400	2402	2404	2406	0 0 1	1 1 1	1 2 2
58	2408	2410	2412	2415	2417	2419	2421	2423	2425	2427	0 0 1	1 1 1	1 2 2
59	2429	2431	2433	2435	2437	2439	2441	2443	2445	2447	0 0 1	1 1 1	1 2 2
60	2449	2452	2454	2456	2458	2460	2462	2464	2466	2468	0 0 1	1 1 1	1 2 2
61	2470	2472	2474	2476	2478	2480	2482	2484	2486	2488	0 0 1	1 1 1	1 2 2
62	2490	2492	2494	2496	2498	2500	2502	2504	2506	2508	0 0 1	1 1 1	1 2 2
63	2510	2512	2514	2516	2518	2520	2522	2524	2526	2528	0 0 1	1 1 1	1 2 2
64	2530	2532	2534	2536	2538	2540	2542	2544	2546	2548	0 0 1	1 1 1	1 2 2
65	2550	2551	2553	2555	2557	2559	2561	2563	2565	2567	0 0 1	1 1 1	1 2 2
66	2569	2571	2573	2575	2577	2579	2581	2583	2585	2587	0 0 1	1 1 1	1 2 2
67	2588	2590	2592	2594	2596	2598	2600	2602	2604	2606	0 0 1	1 1 1	1 2 2
68	2608	2610	2612	2613	2615	2617	2619	2621	2623	2625	0 0 1	1 1 1	1 2 2
69	2627	2629	2631	2632	2634	2636	2638	2640	2642	2644	0 0 1	1 1 1	1 2 2
70	2646	2648	2650	2651	2653	2655	2657	2659	2661	2663	0 0 1	1 1 1	1 2 2
71	2665	2666	2668	2670	2672	2674	2676	2678	2680	2681	0 0 1	1 1 1	1 1 2
72	2683	2685	2687	2689	2691	2693	2694	2696	2698	2700	0 0 1	1 1 1	1 1 2
73	2702	2704	2706	2707	2709	2711	2713	2715	2717	2718	0 0 1	1 1 1	1 1 2
74	2720	2722	2724	2726	2728	2729	2731	2733	2735	2737	0 0 1	1 1 1	1 1 2
75	2739	2740	2742	2744	2746	2748	2750	2751	2753	2755	0 0 1	1 1 1	1 1 2
76	2757	2759	2760	2762	2764	2766	2768	2769	2771	2773	0 0 1	1 1 1	1 1 2
77	2775	2777	2778	2780	2782	2784	2786	2787	2789	2791	0 0 1	1 1 1	1 1 2
78	2793	2795	2796	2798	2800	2802	2804	2805	2807	2809	0 0 1	1 1 1	1 1 2
79	2811	2812	2814	2816	2818	2820	2821	2823	2825	2827	0 0 1	1 1 1	1 1 2
80	2828	2830	2832	2834	2835	2837	2839	2841	2843	2844	0 0 1	1 1 1	1 1 2
81	2846	2848	2850	2851	2853	2855	2857	2858	2860	2862	0 0 1	1 1 1	1 1 2
82	2864	2865	2867	2869	2871	2872	2874	2876	2877	2879	0 0 1	1 1 1	1 1 2
83	2881	2883	2884	2886	2888	2890	2891	2893	2895	2897	0 0 1	1 1 1	1 1 2
84	2898	2900	2902	2903	2905	2907	2909	2910	2912	2914	0 0 1	1 1 1	1 1 2
85	2915	2917	2919	2921	2922	2924	2926	2927	2929	2931	0 0 1	1 1 1	1 1 2
86	2933	2934	2936	2938	2939	2941	2943	2944	2946	2948	0 0 1	1 1 1	1 1 2
87	2950	2951	2953	2955	2956	2958	2960	2961	2963	2965	0 0 1	1 1 1	1 1 2
88	2966	2968	2970	2972	2973	2975	2977	2978	2980	2982	0 0 1	1 1 1	1 1 2
89	2983	2985	2987	2988	2990	2992	2993	2995	2997	2998	0 0 1	1 1 1	1 1 2
90	3000	3002	3003	3005	3007	3008	3010	3012	3013	3015	0 0 0	1 1 1	1 1 1
91	3017	3018	3020	3022	3023	3025	3027	3028	3030	3032	0 0 0	1 1 1	1 1 1
92	3033	3035	3036	3038	3040	3041	3043	3045	3046	3048	0 0 0	1 1 1	1 1 1
93	3050	3051	3053	3055	3056	3058	3059	3061	3063	3064	0 0 0	1 1 1	1 1 1
94	3066	3068	3069	3071	3072	3074	3076	3077	3079	3081	0 0 0	1 1 1	1 1 1
95	3082	3084	3085	3087	3089	3090	3092	3094	3095	3097	0 0 0	1 1 1	1 1 1
96	3098	3100	3102	3103	3105	3106	3108	3110	3111	3113	0 0 0	1 1 1	1 1 1
97	3114	3116	3118	3119	3121	3122	3124	3126	3127	3129	0 0 0	1 1 1	1 1 1
98	3130	3132	3134	3135	3137	3138	3140	3142	3143	3145	0 0 0	1 1 1	1 1 1
99	3146	3148	3150	3151	3153	3154	3156	3158	3159	3161	0 0 0	1 1 1	1 1 1

Find the first significant figure and the position of the decimal point by inspection.

	0	1	2	3	4	5	6	7	8	9	1 2 3	4 5 6	7 8 9
55	7416	7423	7430	7436	7443	7450	7457	7463	7470	7477	1 1 2	3 3 4	5 5 6
56	7483	7490	7497	7503	7510	7517	7523	7530	7537	7543	1 1 2	3 3 4	5 5 6
57	7550	7556	7563	7570	7576	7583	7589	7596	7603	7609	1 1 2	3 3 4	5 5 6
58	7616	7622	7629	7635	7642	7649	7655	7662	7668	7675	1 1 2	3 3 4	5 5 6
59	7681	7688	7694	7701	7707	7714	7720	7727	7733	7740	1 1 2	3 3 4	5 5 6
60	7746	7752	7759	7765	7772	7778	7785	7791	7797	7804	1 1 2	3 3 4	4 5 6
61	7810	7817	7823	7829	7836	7842	7849	7855	7861	7868	1 1 2	3 3 4	4 5 6
62	7874	7880	7887	7893	7899	7906	7912	7918	7925	7931	1 1 2	3 3 4	4 5 6
63	7937	7944	7950	7956	7962	7969	7975	7981	7987	7994	1 1 2	3 3 4	4 5 6
64	8000	8006	8012	8019	8025	8031	8037	8044	8050	8056	1 1 2	2 3 4	4 5 6
65	8062	8068	8075	8081	8087	8093	8099	8106	8112	8118	1 1 2	2 3 4	4 5 5
66	8124	8130	8136	8142	8149	8155	8161	8167	8173	8179	1 1 2	2 3 4	4 5 5
67	8185	8191	8198	8204	8210	8216	8222	8228	8234	8240	1 1 2	2 3 4	4 5 5
68	8246	8252	8258	8264	8270	8276	8283	8289	8295	8301	1 1 2	2 3 4	4 5 5
69	8307	8313	8319	8325	8331	8337	8343	8349	8355	8361	1 1 2	2 3 4	4 5 5
70	8367	8373	8379	8385	8390	8396	8402	8408	8414	8420	1 1 2	2 3 4	4 5 5
71	8426	8432	8438	8444	8450	8456	8462	8468	8473	8479	1 1 2	2 3 4	4 5 5
72	8485	8491	8497	8503	8509	8515	8521	8526	8532	8538	1 1 2	2 3 3	4 5 5
73	8544	8550	8556	8562	8567	8573	8579	8585	8591	8597	1 1 2	2 3 3	4 5 5
74	8602	8608	8614	8620	8626	8631	8637	8643	8649	8654	1 1 2	2 3 3	4 5 5
75	8660	8666	8672	8678	8683	8689	8695	8701	8706	8712	1 1 2	2 3 3	4 5 5
76	8718	8724	8729	8735	8741	8746	8752	8758	8764	8769	1 1 2	2 3 3	4 5 5
77	8775	8781	8786	8792	8798	8803	8809	8815	8820	8826	1 1 2	2 3 3	4 4 5
78	8832	8837	8843	8849	8854	8860	8866	8871	8877	8883	1 1 2	2 3 3	4 4 5
79	8888	8894	8899	8905	8911	8916	8922	8927	8933	8939	1 1 2	2 3 3	4 4 5
80	8944	8950	8955	8961	8967	8972	8978	8983	8989	8994	1 1 2	2 3 3	4 4 5
81	9000	9006	9011	9017	9022	9028	9033	9039	9044	9050	1 1 2	2 3 3	4 4 5
82	9055	9061	9066	9072	9077	9083	9088	9094	9099	9105	1 1 2	2 3 3	4 4 5
83	9110	9116	9121	9127	9132	9138	9143	9149	9154	9160	1 1 2	2 3 3	4 4 5
84	9165	9171	9176	9182	9187	9192	9198	9203	9209	9214	1 1 2	2 3 3	4 4 5
85	9220	9225	9230	9236	9241	9247	9252	9257	9263	9268	1 1 2	2 3 3	4 4 5
86	9274	9279	9284	9290	9295	9301	9306	9311	9317	9322	1 1 2	2 3 3	4 4 5
87	9327	9333	9338	9343	9349	9354	9359	9365	9370	9375	1 1 2	2 3 3	4 4 5
88	9381	9386	9391	9397	9402	9407	9413	9418	9423	9429	1 1 2	2 3 3	4 4 5
89	9434	9439	9445	9450	9455	9460	9466	9471	9476	9482	1 1 2	2 3 3	4 4 5
90	9487	9492	9497	9503	9508	9513	9518	9524	9529	9534	1 1 2	2 3 3	4 4 5
91	9539	9545	9550	9555	9560	9566	9571	9576	9581	9586	1 1 2	2 3 3	4 4 5
92	9592	9597	9602	9607	9612	9618	9623	9628	9633	9638	1 1 2	2 3 3	4 4 5
93	9644	9649	9654	9659	9664	9670	9675	9680	9685	9690	1 1 2	2 3 3	4 4 5
94	9695	9701	9706	9711	9716	9721	9726	9731	9737	9742	1 1 2	2 3 3	4 4 5
95	9747	9752	9757	9762	9767	9772	9778	9783	9788	9793	1 1 2	2 3 3	4 4 5
96	9798	9803	9808	9813	9818	9823	9829	9834	9839	9844	1 1 2	2 3 3	4 4 5
97	9849	9854	9859	9864	9869	9874	9879	9884	9889	9894	1 1 2	2 3 3	4 4 5
98	9899	9905	9910	9915	9920	9925	9930	9935	9940	9945	0 1 1	2 2 3	3 4 4
99	9950	9955	9960	9965	9970	9975	9980	9985	9990	9995	0 1 1	2 2 3	3 4 4

Find the first significant figure and the position of the decimal point by inspection.

ANSWERS

SECTION A

Page 1   EXERCISE 1

1 $37\frac{1}{2}\%$, $33\frac{1}{3}\%$, 80%, 180%, $\frac{1}{5}\%$, 7%, 35%, $\frac{1}{10}\%$

2 $\frac{1}{8}$, $\frac{2}{3}$, $1\frac{1}{4}$, $\frac{1}{6}$, $\frac{1}{40}$, $1\frac{3}{4}$ **3** 8 cm   **4** £2·10   **5** $7\frac{1}{2}$p

6 33 g   **7** £41   **8** $133\frac{1}{3}\%$ **9** 60%

10 $33\frac{1}{3}\%$ **11** 24% **12** 150% **13** 300%

Page 2   EXERCISE 2

1 (i) $\dfrac{130}{100}$; (ii) $\dfrac{104}{100}$; (iii) $2\frac{1}{2}$; (iv) $\dfrac{103\frac{1}{2}}{100}$; (v) $\dfrac{100+p}{100}$

2 (i) 1·155; (ii) 3·5; (iii) 1·0425   **3** (i) 0·975; (ii) 0·92; (iii) 0.

4 (i) $33\frac{1}{3}\%$ decrease; (ii) $16\frac{2}{3}\%$ decrease; (iii) 100% increase;
  (iv) 25% increase

5 $\frac{65}{100}$, $\frac{100}{65}$ **6** $\frac{100}{113}$, 13   **7** $\frac{100}{107}$ **8** $\frac{93}{100}$

9 $\frac{213}{100}$ **10** 25%

Page 3   EXERCISE 3

1 10 : 11   **2** 2 : 7   **3** 3 : 4   **4** 8 : 7

5 324   **6** 70   **7** $x(100 + r)/100$ **8** 50

9 20   **10** $50-\frac{1}{2}x$ **11** 19   **12** 15

Page 3   EXERCISE 4

1 (i) $\frac{2}{5}$, $\frac{23}{25}$, $\frac{53}{50}$, $\frac{3}{8}$;   (ii) 0·4, 0·92, 1·06, 0·375

2 (i) $\frac{27}{20}$, $\frac{1}{16}$, $\frac{7}{40}$, $\frac{271}{400}$; (ii) 1·35, 0·0625, 0·175, 0·6775

3 $8\frac{1}{3}$, $113\frac{1}{3}$, $92\frac{1}{2}$, 175% **4** 16, $18\frac{3}{4}$, 44, $8\frac{1}{2}\%$

5 625   **6** £485   **7** £1·25   **8** 360

9 £6   **10** £400   **11** 25%, 20% **12** £2·32

13 £2·03   **14** £3·01   **15** 45% **16** £550

17 $48\cdot6\%$ **18** £2·52   **19** $32\frac{1}{4}$

xxx

Page 7   EXERCISE 5

1 12, 9	**2** 2, 1	**3** 3, 7	**4** 2, -1
5 1, -2	**6** 3, 4	**7** 4, -2	**8** 4, 2
9 5, -1	**10** 4, 1	**11** 9, 3	**12** 4, 5
13 -1, -1	**14** 6, -1	**15** 5, 1	**16** 1, -3
17 $\frac{5}{7}$, $\frac{1}{7}$	**18** $1\frac{8}{21}$, $-2\frac{1}{7}$	**19** 13, -12	**20** $\frac{1}{2}$, $\frac{2}{5}$
21 $-\frac{5}{23}$, $\frac{21}{23}$	**22** $1\frac{3}{4}$, $\frac{7}{12}$	**23** 2, 1	**24** $1\frac{1}{2}$, $-\frac{1}{6}$
25 $\frac{1}{2}$, $-\frac{1}{2}$	**26** 2, -1	**27** 3, -8	**28** -4, 3
29 2, 3	**30** $7\frac{4}{5}$, $-1\frac{2}{5}$	**31** $\frac{2}{5}$, $\frac{1}{5}$	**32** 17, -16
33 $-\frac{7}{8}$, $-\frac{1}{4}$	**34** $\frac{3}{5}$, $\frac{2}{3}$	**35** $\frac{1}{3}$, $2\frac{1}{3}$	**36** $1\frac{1}{5}$, $1\frac{3}{15}$
37 -2, 3	**38** 1, 5	**39** $7\frac{1}{4}$, $-2\frac{3}{4}$	**40** 2, 0
41 -3, 2	**42** $1\frac{1}{3}$, $3\frac{1}{2}$		

Page 9   EXERCISE 6

1 31, 11	**2** 8, 5	**3** 26, 8	**4** £25, £8
5 45	**6** 12, 8	**7** 11p	**8** 42p, 36p
9 40, 16	**10** 53, 25	**11** 48, 3	**12** 18, 15
13 £1·56, £1·80	**14** 50, 96	**15** 365	

Page 23   EXERCISE 9

1 9   **2** 7 rt. $\angle$s   **3** 10   **4** 36°
5 (i) 6; (iii) 9; (iv) 15; (v) 30

Page 35   EXERCISE 11

1 65°   **2** 97°   **3** 71°   **4** 73°
5 $2x + y = 360$ **6** 21°, 111°, 69°   **7** $90 - \frac{1}{2}x$
8 59°   **9** 98°   **10** 33°
11 $(180 - 2b - q)$ degrees   **12** 27°   **13** 89°
14 q, $(p + q)$, $(180° - p - q)$ degrees   **25** $2x$, $2y$, $x - y$

Page 40   EXERCISE 12

1 (3, 2), $(-2, -1)$, $(-1, 2)$, (1, 1), (2, -2), (2, 0), (0, 3)
6 -1, -3 **7** -7, -4, -1, 2, **5**

Page 46 EXERCISE 13

1 (i) 5·76, 8·64, −1·24; (ii) 2·58, −0·58; 3·24, −1·24; 4·16, −2·16; (iii) 9

3 2·2 **5** (ii) 1; (iii) 0 to 2 **8** (i) 2·43, −1·10; (ii) −2, 0; 0, 4

9 (i) 12·8 m, 16·8 m, 3·8m: (ii) 0·59, 3·41; (iii) 20 m, 2 s; (iv) 4 s; (v) 3·46

Page 56 EXERCISE 15

9 3·20 cm **10** 2·80, 4·85 cm **11** 5·12 cm

Page 66 EXERCISE 17

1 3·21, 2·14 cm; 7·70 cm² **2** 2·64 cm, 13·20 cm²

3 1·70, 3·18 cm; 5·09 cm² **4** 5·09, 2·52 cm; 30·4 cm²

5 7·92 cm² **6** 60 cm² **7** 24 cm² **8** 6 cm

9 18 cm², 4·5 cm **10** 10·5 cm² **11** 6 cm

12 22·5 cm², 7·5 cm **13** 12 cm², 3·2 cm

14 24 cm², 4·8 cm **15** 90 cm²

16 2 ab cm² **17** 50 cm² **18** 36 cm²

19 48 900 m² **20** 61 700 m²

Page 71 EXERCISE 18

1 8·91 cm **2** 6·91 cm **3** 8·17 cm **4** 4·01 cm

5 3·69 cm **6** 6·05 cm, 12·1 cm² **7** 10·3 cm²

8 4·90 cm **9** 3·45 cm **12** BCD **13** AXD

Page 75 EXERCISE 19

1 $x^2 + 2x$ **2** $3x - 15$ **3** $2a + a^2$ **4** $2b^2 - 6b$

5 $2t^3 + 2t^2$ **6** $a^2b + ab^2$ **7** $6y^2 + 2y$ **8** $8a^2 - 10a$

9 $b^2x - 2bx^2$ **10** $21x + 7x^2$ **11** $3x^2 + 12x^3 + 3x^4$

12 $3a^2 + 6ab - 3a$ **13** $6x^3 + 2x^2 - 8x$ **14** $3y^4 - 6y^3 + 9y^2$

15 $4a^3b + 4a^2b^2 - 4ab^3$ **16** $a^2 + 3a + 2$ **17** $x^2 + 6x + 8$

18 $2y^2 + 3y + 1$ **19** $2x^2 + 5x - 3$ **20** $x^2 - 9$

21 $6 - 5x + x^2$ **22** $ax - ay + bx - by$ **23** $x^2 + 2x + 1$

24 $a^2 + 6a + 9$ **25** $x^2 - 2x + 1$ **26** $3x^2 + 14x + 8$

27 $a^2 - 10a + 25$ **28** $b^2 + b - 12$ **29** $6x^2 + 5xa + a^2$

30 $y^2 - 4$ **31** $4p^2 + 12pq + 9q^2$ **32** $x^2 - 2xy - 3y^2$

33 $12 - 5a - 2a^2$ **34** $a^2 + 2ab + b^2$ **35** $a^2 - 2ab + b^2$
36 $a^2 - b^2$ **37** $4x^2 - 1$ **38** $10 - 19x - 2x^2$
39 $3x^2 + 5x - 28$ **40** $a^2 + az - ax - xz$ **41** $7y^2 - 2y - 5$
42 $12x^2 + 5x - 2$ **43** $2a^2 + 5a - 12$ **44** $2 - 11x + 15x^2$
45 $2y^2 - 13y + 15$ **46** $6 - x - 2x^2$ **47** $3b^2 - 2b - 96$
48 $8x^2 + 2x - 3$ **49** $8a^2 - 6ab - 9b^2$ **50** $6x^2 - xy - 15y^2$

Page 77   EXERCISE 20

1 $x^2 + 10x + 25$ **2** $y^2 + 2y + 1$ **3** $a^2 - 2a + 1$
4 $9x^2 + 6xy + y^2$ **5** $9a^2 + 12a + 4$ **6** $a^2 + 4ab + 4b^2$
7 $b^2 - 2ab + a^2$ **8** $16x^2 + 8xy + y^2$ **9** $25p^2 - 30pq + 9q^2$
10 $x^2 + x + \frac{1}{4}$ **11** $\frac{1}{4}x^2 + xy + y^2$ **12** $4b^2 - 4ba + a^2$
13 $9a^2 - 24ab + 16b^2$ **14** $4x^2 - 12xy + 9y^2$ **15** $4a^2 - \frac{4}{3}a + \frac{1}{9}$
16 $4a^2b^2 - 2ab + \frac{1}{4}$ **17** $9b^2 - 42b + 49$ **18** $4a^2c^2 - 4ac + 1$
19 $a^2 + 4abc + 4b^2c^2$ **20** $4 - 20x + 25x^2$ **21** $10\,404$
22 $998\,001; \ 996\,004$ **23** $2x^2$ **24** $x^2 - 13x$
25 $8 - 32x$ **26** $x - 5$ **27** $x^2 + 3x - 1$ **29** 0 **30** 3
31 -16 **32** $-1\frac{1}{2}$

Page 80   EXERCISE 21

1 6·6, 5·4 cm; 3·3, 2·7 cm   **2** 7·3, 3·3 cm; 4·8, 2·2 cm
3 56°, 83°, 41°   **4** $46\frac{1}{2}°$, $104\frac{1}{2}°$, 29°

Page 83   EXERCISE 22

1 $\angle A = \angle P = 99°$, PQ = $3\frac{1}{2}$ cm, PR = 3 cm
2 $\angle N = 46\frac{1}{2}°$, $\angle P = 104\frac{1}{2}°$, PQ = 2 cm, PR = 3 cm
3 $\angle C = 32°$, $\angle Z = 126°$, BC = 9 cm, XZ = $1\frac{1}{3}$ cm
4 $\angle P = \angle Y = 82\frac{1}{2}°$, $\angle X = 56°$, $\angle M = 41\frac{1}{2}°$
5 $\angle A = 38°$, $\angle D = 22°$, AB = 3 cm, CD = $10\frac{1}{2}$ cm
6 $\angle P = \angle S = 25°$, AQ = 0·9 cm, RS = 2·4 cm
7 $\angle P = \angle R = 37°$, $\angle A = 90°$, $\angle N = 53°$
8 $\angle Y = \angle Q = 35°$, $\angle P = 59°$, $\angle R = 86°$
10 12·25, 10·5 cm   **11** 4·5, 3·9 cm   **12** 4·2 0·5 cm
14 5 cm   **15** 9, 7·5 cm   **18** 40 m

Page 93   EXERCISE 23

1 0·3640, 0·5774, 1, 1·1918, 1·7321
2 11° 19′, 38° 40′, 50° 12′, 64° 32′
3 0·3269, 0·5418, 0·8967, 1·7735, 3·7629
4 26° 18′, 42° 30′, 63° 36′, 48° 44′, 35° 38′, 70° 20′
5 (i) BC/AB; (ii) RP/PQ; (iii) XZ : XY
6 (i) tan C, (ii) tan Z, (iii) tan R
7 9·81 cm   **8** 5·00 cm   **9** 4·80 cm   **10** 54° 28′
11 38° 40′   **12** 36° 52′   **13** 68° 23′   **14** 64° 41′
15 2·33 cm   **16** 2·70 cm   **17** 3·76 cm   **18** 18·7 m
19 56° 19′   **20** N. 39° 21′ E. **21** 173 m   **22** 3·93 cm
23 5 cm, 8·66 cm, 43·3 cm²   **24** 5·5 m   **25** 7·81 m
26 39° 48′, 50° 12′   **27** N. 60° 57′ E.   **28** 33° 41′
29 5·50 cm   **30** 79° 36′, 100° 24′   **31** 161 m, 39° 48′

Page 100   EXERCISE 24

1 0·3090, 0·9511, 0·5, 0·8660, 0·9397, 0·3420
2 (i) 48° 35′; (ii) 36° 52′; (iii) 28° 2′
3 (i) 60°; (ii) 49° 27′; (iii) 71° 20′
4 (i) 0·2588; (ii) 0·4540; (iii) 0·3107; (iv) 0·6739; (v) 0·9326;
  (vi) 0·4868; (vii) 0·3819; (viii) 0·6805; (ix) 0·5819; (x) 0·8762
5 (i) 0·9659; (ii) 0·8910; (iii) 0·9505; (iv) 0·7388; (v) 0·3608;
  (vi) 0·8735; (vii) 0·9242; (viii) 0·7327; (ix) 0·8133; (x) 0·4820
6 (i) 20° 12′; (ii) 59° 18′; (iii) 51° 31′; (iv) 34° 50′; (v) 31° 15′;
  (vi) 71° 3′; (vii) 45° 38′; (viii) 8° 1′; (ix) 44° 49′; (x) 20° 34′
7 (i) 24° 6′; (ii) 64° 36′; (iii) 48° 11′; (iv) 57° 44′; (v) 76° 17′;
  (vi) 36° 27′; (vii) 17° 4′; (viii) 80° 8′; (ix) 52° 45′; (x) 71° 27′
8 (i) BC/AC; (ii) PR/RQ; (iii) XY/YZ; (iv) PR/RQ; (v) XZ/YZ;
  (vi) AB/BC; (vii) BC/AC; (viii) XZ/XY; (ix) XY/YZ;
  (x) AB/AC
9 (i) sin C, cos A; (ii) tan Q; (iii) sin Y, cos Z; (iv) tan A;
  (v) sin R, cos Q; (vi) sin Z, cos Y; (vii) sin A, cos C;
  (viii) sin Q, cos R; (ix) tan Z; (x) tan C
10 8·99, 4·38 cm   **11** 2·87, 4·10 cm.   **12** 5·44, 2·54 cm
13 23° 35′   **14** 53° 8′   **15** 13·7, 8·24 cm **16** 77° 10′
17 64·7 m   **18** 6·43 cm   **19** 19° 28′   **20** 20·8 m
21 5·74, 8·19 cm

Page 102   EXERCISE 25

1 104 m   **2** 15° 58′   **3** 33·8 m   **4** 178 m
5 63·4, 136 m   **6** 59° 2′   **7** 48° 35′   **8** 6·64 cm
9 139 m   **10** 36·3 cm   **11** 3·53 cm   **12** 108 m
13 7 cm   **14** 6·55 cm   **15** 6·40 m   **16** 21·8 cm²
17 7·22 cm   **18** 3·90, 1·80 cm   **19** 4·13 cm, 39° 23′
20 5·88, 3·09, 0·955 cm   **21** 15·5, 29·9 cm   **22** 1·24, 1·90 cm
23 5·78 cm, 41° 49′   **24** 112 m, 10° 37′   **25** 30° 58′, 106° 16′
26 111° 54′, 8·29 cm   **27** 3·37, 8·16 cm

Page 104   EXERCISE 26

1 £42, £642   **2** £22·50, £272·50   **3** £3·75, £63·75
4 £27·65, £343·65   **5** £4·77, £84·27   **6** £0·93, £50·53
7 £1·97   **8** £78·05   **9** £4·11
10 £24·07

Page 107   EXERCISE 27

1 $3\frac{1}{2}$ **2** 6   **3** $4\frac{1}{2}$ **4** £720   **5** £1720
6 £1224   **7** $3\frac{3}{4}$ y   **8** 3 months   **9** $3\frac{1}{3}$ y   **10** £450
11 £124   **12** £86·40   **13** $11\frac{1}{4}$ y   **14** £126   **15** 5
16 $6\frac{2}{3}$ **17** 40   **18** £210   **19** £750   **20** £1440
21 £1200   **22** $3\frac{3}{4}$ **23** $3\frac{1}{2}$ **24** £36·63   **25** 73
26 $1\frac{2}{3}$ y

Page 113   EXERCISE 29

1 17 y 1 month   **2** $(328+31x)/(8+x)$, 12   **3** $176\frac{1}{2}$ cm
4 $\frac{5}{12}a$ h, 4·8 km/h   **5** $(6x+5y)$ km, $(6x+5y)/(x+y)$ km/h
6 £876   **7** 81   **8** $216x$ pence, 72p
9 $28x/(x+1)$
10 $(bx+gy)/(x+y)$ years
11 1308, 51·7
12 751 mm

Page 116   EXERCISE 30

1 $2\frac{2}{9}$ h   **2** $2\frac{1}{2}$ days   **3** 36 days   **4** $1\frac{1}{3}$ h
5 9 days   **6** 4   **7** 38   **8** 8
9 (i) 2·1; (ii) 21   **10** 3

Page 118 EXERCISE 31

1 $3(x+y)$ 2 $a(a+b)$ 3 $3(2a+y)$
4 $2x(3x+2)$ 5 $2a(2a-3b)$ 6 $2y(1-4x)$
7 $4ab(2+b)$ 8 $x(3x+2y+1)$ 9 $a^2(a-b)$
10 $6ab(a-3b)$ 11 None   12 $a(x+y+z)$
13 $3x^2(2x-a)$ 14 $5x(x+3y)$ 15 None
16 $P\left(1+\dfrac{RT}{100}\right)$ 17 $W(b-a)$ 18 $g(M+m)$
19 $\frac{1}{2}v^2(M+m)$ 20 $r(\pi+2)$ 21 $(W+w)u/g$
22 $3x(y-2z+1)$ 23 $xy(y-3x)$ 24 $4a(3a-4x)$
25 $ab(a+b+c)$ 26 $2(2+x^2)$ 27 $a(3a-b+c)$
28 $2x^2y(x-3y+5)$ 29 $2\pi r(r+h)$ 30 $\pi r^2(h+\frac{2}{3}r)$
31 $\frac{1}{2}m(2v+1)$ 32 $4xyz(2x+y+3z)$ 33 $2x(2x^2+3y^2)$
34 7900   35 9800   36 4600   37 400
38 13 000   39 44   40 2900   41 16 600
42 434·6   43 8637   44 172·48   45 1 586 000
46 £3   47 141·3   48 3080   49 $2\pi(R-r)$, 6·28 cm

Page 120 EXERCISE 32

1 $(x+y)(a-b)$ 2 None   3 $(x+y)(a+b)$
4 $(y-z)(3x-2)$ 5 $3a(x+y)(a-2b)$ 6 $(a-b)(a-b-2)$
7 $(x-1)(p+1)$ 8 $(x-y)(1-a)$ 9 None
10 $(y+1)(2x+d)$ 11 None   12 $(1-x)(4+a)$
13 $(a-b)(a-3)$ 14 $a(a-x)(2a+x)$ 15 $(x+2y)(a+b)$
16 $(x-y)(x^2-y)$ 17 $(2x+y)(3a+4b)$ 18 $(x+y)(a-c)$
19 $(a+b+c)(x-z)$ 20 $3(x-2y)(3a+b)$ 21 None
22 $(c+d)(a-b)$ 23 $(qr+st)(pq+rs)$ 24 $(b+2x)(a+2c)$
25 $(x-4y)(1+p)$ 26 None   27 $(x-y)(p-1)$
28 None   29 $(3-x)(2+y)$ 30 $(a-b)(a-b+3)$
31 $(x-1)(x-1-y)$ 32 $(x+2y)(x-y+3)$ 33 $(x-1)(x-y)$
34 $(1+x^2)(1+xy)$ 35 $(x+y)(a^2-bc)$ 36 None
37 $(x+3)(x+a)$ 38 $(p+q+r)(x+y)$ 39 $(x^2+1)(x-1)$
40 $(x-7)(3x+2)$ 41 $(a+b)(5+x)$ 42 None
43 $2(x^2-3x+1)(x^2+2)$ 44 $(x+2)(1-3y)$ 45 $(a+b)^2(x-3y)$

46 None   **47** $(x-y)(3x-3y+8a)$ **48** $(x+2)(x^2-2x-4)$

49 $(4x+2y-z)(p-2q-5r)$ **50** $(p-2q)(p-2q-1)$

51 $(x-2ay)(a+2b)$ **52** $(x+1)(y+x-1)$ **53** $(2a-3b)(x-2y)$

54 $(p-q)(p+q-2)$ **55** None   **56** $(x+y)(x+y-3)$

57 $(x-3)(4a-9)$ **58** $(x+3a)(y-4b)$ **59** None

60 $(a^2-bc)(b+c)$ **61** $(x-4)(a-b)$ **62** $(1+x)(1+x^2)$

63 $(1-x)(a-x)$ **64** $(7a-b)(p-q)$ **65** $(a-b)(2a+3)$

66 $(x+3)(ax^2+1)$ **67** $(x-4y)(xy+1)$ **68** $(xt-y)(1-3t)$

69 $(x^2+2)(3-5y)$

Page 125   EXERCISE 33

1 $(x+2)(x+5)$ **2** $(x+2)(x+3)$ **3** $(x+1)(x+4)$

4 $(2x+1)(x+2)$ **5** $(2x+1)(x+3)$ **6** $(y+3)(y+4)$

7 $(3t+2)(t+1)$ **8** $(2x+1)(x+5)$ **9** None

10 $(a+1)(a+7)$ **11** $(3+x)(6+x)$ **12** $(x+3)(4x+1)$

13 $(x+3)^2$ **14** $2(x-1)(x+5)$ **15** $(2x+5)(x-2)$

16 $(x-3)(x+2)$ **17** $(2x-1)(x+4)$ **18** None

19 $(a-2)(a-6)$ **20** $(3x-4)(x-2)$ **21** $(x-5)(x+2)$

22 None   **23** $(y-5)(y+10)$.   **24** $(3x-2)(2x+3)$

25 $(1+5x)(1-2x)$ **26** $(2a+3)(a-5)$ **27** None

28 $(1-5x)(1+4x)$ **29** $(2y-3)(3y-1)$ **30** $(2x-3)(x+4)$

31 $(2x-3)(x+2)$ **32** None   **33** $(2x+y)(3x-2y)$

34 None   **35** $(3x-y)(x-5y)$ **36** $(x+2)(4x-1)$

37 None   **38** $(5x+3a)(x-2a)$ **39** $(t-2)(4t-3)$

40 $(2a+1)(4a-3)$ **41** $(1+4x)^2$ **42** $(4-5x)(1-2x)$

43 $(3x+5)(x-4)$ **44** $(2x-3y)(x-4y)$ **45** $(1-2x)(2+3x)$

46 $(3x-5)(2x+3)$ **47** $(3y-5)(y-2)$ **48** $(7x-3y)(x+2y)$

49 $(3x-2)^2$ **50** $(3xy+1)(xy+1)$ **51** $(6+a)(2-3a)$

52 $(3x+2)(3x-7)$ **53** $(7x-5y)(x+2y)$ **54** $(3+2a)(1-2a)$

55 $(3x-2)(2x+3)$ **56** $(3t+2)(t-5)$ **57** $(7x+5y)(x-y)$

58 $(18+t)(4-t)$ **59** $(5x-2)(x-3)$ **60** $(4x-3)(x+4)$

61 $(3b-2)(2b+7)$ **62** $(7x-4)(2x+7)$ **63** $(7x-3)(x+4)$

64 $(3xy+5)(xy-1)$ **65** $2(x-3)(x+4)$ **66** $(6-y)(1+y)$

67 $3(a-6)(a+5)$ **68** $(8-x)(x-3)$ **69** None

70 $(5c-2)(2c+3)$ **71** $(4a-3)(3a+2)$ **72** $(2x+1)^2$

Page 127   EXERCISE 34

1 $(x+5)(x-5)$ **2** $(2a+b)(2a-b)$ **3** $(3+4xy)(3-4xy)$

4 $(5x+7a)(5x-7a)$ **5** None   **6** $(t+2)(t-2)$

7 $(3x+8)(3x-8)$ **8** $(a+3b)(a-3b)$ **9** $(1+7t)(1-7t)$

10 $(10x+1)(10x-1)$ **11** $(5+2x)(5-2x)$ **12** None

13 $(xy+4a)(xy-4a)$ **14** $(7+3y)(7-3y)$ **15** $(y+13)(y-13)$

16 $(11x+12y)(11x-12y)$ **17** $9(3p+2q)(3p-2q)$

18 None   **19** $2(2+x)(2-x)$.   **20** None

21 $3(x+8)(x-8)$.   **22** $(6ab+5x)(6ab-5x)$

23 $7(a+3b)(a-3b)$ **24** None   **25** $5(3+2a)(3-2a)$

26 $(abc+10)(abc-10)$ **27** $(5x+5y+1)(5x+5y-1)$

28 None   **29** $(a-b)(a+b)(a^2+b^2)$ **30** $3(a+2)(a-2)$

31 199   **32** 200   **33** 1078   **34** 10 200

35 9600   **36** 9400   **37** 180   **38** 6

39 1200   **40** 1·572   **41** 530 000   **42** 21 600

43 99   **44** 998 000   **45** 74   **46** 5800

47 2480   **48** 166 000   **49** 11   **50** 319

51 $\frac{1}{2}$ **52** $\pi(R^2-r^2)$; 17·6

Page 127   EXERCISE 35

1 $(x+y)(x+4)$ **2** $9(a+5)(a-5)$ **3** $(x-5)(x-7)$

4 $(a-2b)(4a-3b)$ **5** None   **6** None

7 $(x+4)(y-3)$ **8** $(5+4x)(5-4x)$ **9** $(2x+1)^2$

10 $3(3x+5y^2)(3x-5y^2)$.   **11** $(3x+2)(x-4)$ **12** $(1+x^2)(2+xy)$

13 $(4ab+1)(3ab-1)$ **14** $(a+5)(a-7)$ **15** $2(2x+3)(2x-3)$

16 $5(x+2a)(x-2a)$ **17** $(3x-5)(x+4)$ **18** $(x+6)(x-3)$

19 $(x-1)(4x+9)$ **20** $(a+6xy^2)(a-6xy^2)$ **21** None

22 $3(a+b)(p-2q)$ **23** $(1-3x)(1+5x)$ **24** $(x^2+5)(x^2-5)$

25 None   **26** $(x-y+2)(x-y-2)$ **27** $3(x-2)(x-6)$

28 $(x-6)(x-9)$ **29** $(x^2-3)(x+2)(x-2)$ **30** None

31 $(15x+1)(15x-1)$ **32** $(x+1)(x^2+1)$ **33** $(x-2)(x-y)$

34 $(b-c)(2a+1)$ **35** $(3-2x)(2+5x)$ **36** None

37 $(x+2)(4x-1)$ **38** None   **39** $(x+2y+3)(x+2y-3)$

40 $(2x-3)(x+5)$ **41** $(b-c)(a-d)$ **42** $(t+3)(4t+1)$

43 $n(n+4)$ **44** $(x-4)^2$ **45** $(2a-b)(a+3b)$

46 $(a+3)(a-10)$ **47** $a(x+y)(x-y)$ **48** $(4+t)(5-t)$

49 $3a(a+2b)(a-2b)$ **50** $(p-2a)(p+3b)$

51 $(x-b)(x+b+2a)$ **52** $(x-2a)(x+3b)$ **53** $(a-3)(a+3)(a-3)$

54 $(x-1)(x-2)(3x+2)$ **55** $2(1+6t)(1-6t)$

56 $(a+bx+c)(a+bx-c)$ **57** $(3x+4)^2$

58 $(4x-9)(3x+2)$ **59** $(5x+2y)(5x-2y+4)$

60 $(3t+2)(2t-5)$ **61** $(a+b)(a-b)(x-y)(x-y)$

62 $(p-2q)(2p+q-1)$ **63** $(5a+7b)(a+5b)$

64 $(2a+3)(6a-5)$ **65** $(a-b)(a+b-1)$

66 $4ab(a^2-3b)$ **67** $(2x-5)(4x^2-3)$

68 $(8y-3)(y+4)$ **69** $\pi h t(2r+t)$

70 $(3+x-y)(3-x+y)$ **71** $(4p-3q)(3p+2q)$

72 $(a+2b+5c)(a+2b-5c)$ **73** $2(2x+3y)(2x-3y)$

74 $\pi h(R+r)(2R+2r-h)$ **75** $(2x+1)^2$

76 $(a+2b)(a-2b+3)$ **77** $(x+2y-1)(x+2y-3)$

78 $(x-7y)(3x-y-4)$ **79** $(a-b-2c)(a-2b-4c)$

80 $(a-2)(x+5)$ **81** $(p-q)(p-q+1)$ **82** $(2y-x)(3y+z)$

83 $(1+a)^2(1-a)$ **84** $(a-bc)(c-ab)$

Page 130   **EXERCISE 36**

1 0 **2** No   **3** 0 **4** 0

5 $x=0$ if $a\neq b$ **6** $x\neq 0$ **7** No   **8** $y=3$

9 $y=7$ or -2 **10** $t=0$ or $2\frac{1}{2}$ **11** $(x-4)(x-5)=0$

12 $x(x+4)=0$ **13** $(x-1)(x-2)(x-3)=0$ **14** $x(2x-3)=0$

15 $(2x-1)(3x+1)=0$ **16** $1, 9$ **17** $3, -5$

18 $0, -1, -7$ **19** $2, 2$ **20** $0, 0$ **21** $0, -4$

22 $-3, 8$ **23** $1, 3, -2$ **24** $2, 5, 6$ **25** $0, -6$

26 $0, 0, 1$ **27** $0, 1, 1$ **28** $0, \frac{1}{2}, \frac{2}{3}$ **29** $-\frac{1}{4}, -4$

30 $3, 3$ **31** $0, 2\frac{1}{3}$

Page 132   **EXERCISE 37**

1 $1, 2$ **2** $-1, -2$ **3** $2, 3$ **4** $6, -1$

5 $0, 3$ **6** $4, -4$ **7** 1 **8** $1, -1$

9 $4, -3$ **10** $-5, 1$ **11** $2, -\frac{1}{2}$ **12** $\frac{1}{2}, \frac{1}{3}$

13 $2\frac{1}{2}, -2$ **14** $\frac{2}{3}, -1$ **15** $3, 7$ **16** $2, 1\frac{1}{2}$

17 $0, -1$ **18** $\frac{1}{2}$ **19** $0, 2$ **20** $4, 1\frac{1}{2}$

Page 132. EXERCISE 37—*continued.*

21 $-2, -\frac{2}{3}$ 22 $\frac{1}{2}, -3$ 23 $\frac{2}{3}, -1\frac{1}{2}$ 24 $6, -4$

25 $2, -7$ 26 $3, -3$ 27 $4, 7$ 28 $3\frac{1}{2}, -2\frac{1}{2}$

29 $7, -9$ 30 $2, 3$ 31 $10, -5$ 32 $\frac{2}{3}, -1$

33 $1, 1\frac{3}{4}$ 34 $-1\frac{1}{2}$ 35 $2\frac{1}{2}, -1$ 36 -3

37 $3, \frac{2}{5}$ 38 $-1, -2$ 39 $5, -5$ 40 $-1\frac{1}{2}, -2\frac{1}{2}$

41 $4, -3$ 42 $\frac{1}{3}, -2$ 43 $3, -1$ 44 $0, 1$

45 $\frac{2}{3}, -3\frac{1}{2}$ 46 $\frac{1}{4}, 1\frac{1}{2}$ 47 $0, 2$ 48 $0, -1$

49 $1, -1\frac{2}{3}$ 50 $3, \frac{1}{3}$ 51 $0, \frac{2}{3}$ 52 $2, -3$

53 $\frac{1}{2}, -4$ 54 $1\frac{3}{5}, -1$ 55 $1, -\frac{1}{4}$ 56 $2, -1\frac{1}{2}$

57 $3\frac{1}{2}, -4$ 58 $2\frac{2}{3}, -2\frac{2}{3}$ 59 $3, 4$ 60 $1\frac{2}{3}, -\frac{2}{3}$

61 $3, -7$ 62 $4, -\frac{1}{6}$ 63 $5, -\frac{1}{3}$ 64 $0, -1\frac{1}{3}$

65 $2, -1\frac{1}{4}$ 66 $\frac{1}{2}, -\frac{1}{5}$ 67 $-1, -\frac{1}{6}$ 68 $\frac{3}{4}, -1\frac{1}{3}$

69 $-1\frac{1}{2}, -1\frac{1}{3}$ 70 $0, 3, -3$ 71 $0, 2, -1$

72 $(5x+2)(2x-3)=0$ 73 $x(5x+4)=0$

74 $(2x-1)(3x-2)=0$ 75 $(7x-4)(4x-3)=0$

76 $(2x+3)(3x+7)=0$ 77 $(x-2)(x+2)=0$

78 $(4x-3)(4x+3)=0$ 79 $x(x-1)(x-3)=0$

80 $x(3x-2)(3x+2)=0$ 81 $(x-1)(x+1)(3x+1)=0$

Page 134   EXERCISE 38

1 9   2 8 m by 13 m   3 8 cm   4 $6\frac{1}{2}$, 4 m

5 3 m   6 3 m   7 10   8 $1\frac{1}{2}$ cm

9 12   10 8 cm   11 4   12 $7\frac{1}{2}$

13 10, 11, 12   14 12 m   15 4   16 6, 14

17 5, 4 m   18 8, 32 cm

Page 138   EXERCISE 39

These are four-figure answers.

1 27 230   2 23 200 000   3 583·2   4 0·02654

5 3 038 000   6 0·001005   7 1·917   8 5107

9 0·000001137   10 99 980 000   11 0·07377   12 61 520 000

13 0·8066   14 11 320   15 454·6   16 42·81

17 5069   18 0·2911   19 552·3   20 148 200

21 0·004583   22 772 600   23 18·65   24 17 710 000

25 1 450 000   26 0·0004080   27 20·90   28 0·4208

29 101·9   30 0·1006   31 322 400   32 0·00009742

Page 140   EXERCISE 40

These are four-figure answers.

1 2·168	**2** 6·856	**3** 21·75	**4** 0·6877
5 9·165	**6** 2·915	**7** 29·15	**8** 92·43
9 0·2923	**10** 2923	**11** 4·241	**12** 0·6580
13 31·62	**14** 0·02358	**15** 153·6	**16** 0·3162
17 0·7071	**18** 18·89	**19** 0·2530	**20** 0·8082
21 0·02449	**22** 2·711	**23** 3·174	**24** 96·53
25 9644	**26** 0·1981	**27** 30·82	**28** 29·56
29 0·4165	**30** 19·10	**31** 0·02236	**32** 0·8367

Page 141   EXERCISE 41

1 $\frac{3}{4}$	**2** $\frac{17}{20}$	**3** $\frac{7}{12}$	**4** $\frac{14}{15}$	**5** $\frac{9}{40}$
6 $2\frac{2}{3}$	**7** $4\frac{1}{2}$	**8** $1\frac{1}{4}$	**9** $2\frac{1}{6}$	**10** $2\frac{1}{4}$
11 $3\frac{1}{2}$	**12** $4\frac{1}{3}$	**13** $6\frac{2}{3}$	**14** $2\frac{3}{8}$	**15** $2\frac{1}{5}$

Page 142   EXERCISE 42

These are four-figure answers.

1 0·04105	**2** 1·310	**3** 0·1189	**4** 190·1
5 0·0003665	**6** 0·03398	**7** 0·00001473	**8** 4255
9 6·519	**10** 5·721	**11** 0·2737	**12** 0·02742
13 0·00003325	**14** 19·99	**15** 0·4888	**16** 0·2879
17 3·496	**18** 2·886	**19** 0·1827	**20** 2·122

Page 144   EXERCISE 43

1 10·5	**2** 19·7	**3** 6·09	**4** 19·6
5 18·6	**6** 7·88 cm	**7** 316 m	**8** 170 m
9 12·5 cm	**10** 5·7 cm	**11** 3·76 cm	**12** 5·5 cm
13 145	**14** (i) 6·73m, (ii) 7·58 m	**15** 10·3 cm	
16 6·93 cm	**17** 10·7, 5·4, 12·1 cm	**18** 5·47, 2·73, 7·09 cm	
19 7·55 cm	**20** 5·12 cm	**21** 3·05	**22** 84·4
23 $-31·1$	**24** 9·14 πt cm³; 3·02 cm		

Page 148 EXERCISE 44

1 $\dfrac{a}{x}$ **2** $\dfrac{y}{z}$ **3** $\dfrac{a}{d}$ **4** $-\dfrac{3x}{2a}$ **5** $\dfrac{x+y}{y}$

6 $\dfrac{3a}{4b}$ **7** $\dfrac{1}{2x^3}$ **8** $\dfrac{1+3x}{6x^2}$ **9** $7b$ **10** $-3x^2$

11 $1\frac{1}{5}$ **12** $2{\cdot}3$ **13** $\dfrac{3}{3x+1}$ **14** $\dfrac{a}{5a+1}$ **15** $\dfrac{x+1}{xy}$

16 $\dfrac{5x}{2}$ **17** $\dfrac{6a}{2a+c}$ **18** $\dfrac{1}{x-1}$ **19** $\dfrac{5a^2x}{3y^2}$ **20** $-\dfrac{2x^2y^2}{5}$

21 $\dfrac{1+3a}{1+9a}$ **22** $\dfrac{3a}{2b}$ **23** $\dfrac{2x}{b}$ **24** $-\dfrac{2a^2}{3b^2}$ **25** $\dfrac{a+2}{a+4}$

26 $\dfrac{a^2}{a^2-b^2}$ **27** $\dfrac{3a^2}{b^2x}$ **28** $-\dfrac{x^2+2x}{4}$

Page 149 EXERCISE 45

1 $\dfrac{x}{x+3}$ **2** $\dfrac{a}{3}$ **3** $\dfrac{2}{x-y}$ **4** $a+4$ **5** $\dfrac{x-1}{x-5}$

6 $\dfrac{x-3}{2x}$ **7** $\dfrac{x-2}{2}$ **8** $\dfrac{x+y}{x-y}$ **9** $\dfrac{x+4}{2x+3}$ **10** $\dfrac{x}{a}$

11 $\dfrac{x+y}{x-5y}$ **12** $\dfrac{2x-3}{2x}$ **13** $\dfrac{2x+1}{x-5}$ **14** $\dfrac{3x-y}{2}$ **15** $\dfrac{1}{4b(a-b)}$

16 $\dfrac{2a+1}{a-1}$ **17** No simpler form **18** No simpler form

19 $\dfrac{x+2}{2x-1}$ **20** $\dfrac{3}{3x+5}$ **21** $\dfrac{1-2x}{1-4x}$

Page 151 EXERCISE 46

1 $1\frac{3}{20}$ **2** $\dfrac{13x}{20}$ **3** $\dfrac{13}{20x}$ **4** $\dfrac{a}{24}$ **5** $\dfrac{11a}{24}$

6 $\dfrac{7}{2x}$ **7** $\dfrac{2x+7}{2x}$ **8** $\dfrac{1}{2x}$ **9** $\dfrac{13}{12x}$ **10** $\dfrac{1}{6a}$

11 $\dfrac{x}{30}$ **12** $\dfrac{a}{3b}$ **13** $\dfrac{x}{3y}$ **14** $\dfrac{4}{3a}$

15 $\dfrac{x^2+y^2+2xy}{xy}$ **16** $\dfrac{x+6}{3}$ **17** $\dfrac{4x}{7}$ **18** $\dfrac{2+a^2}{2a}$

19 $\dfrac{4}{9y}$ **20** $\dfrac{x+y+z}{xyz}$ **21** $\dfrac{2x^2+3x+4}{x^3}$ **22** $\dfrac{5a+b}{6}$

23 $\dfrac{x^2}{8}$ **24** $\dfrac{3x^2+4x+1}{6x}$ **25** $\dfrac{xy+x^2}{y^2}$ **26** $\dfrac{9x}{2a}$

27 $\dfrac{7x}{12y}$ **28** $\dfrac{19x+26y}{10}$ **29** $\dfrac{x-2}{6}$ **30** $\dfrac{y-x}{3x}$

31 $\dfrac{10x-y}{6x}$ **32** $\dfrac{y-x}{xy}$ **33** $\dfrac{x-5}{5}$ **34** $\dfrac{b-a}{a^2}$

35 $\dfrac{7ac-3bc-4ab}{6abc}$ **36** $\dfrac{3bx-2ax}{ab}$ **37** $\dfrac{x+11}{3}$

38 $\dfrac{3x-y}{20}$ **39** $\dfrac{11x-21}{20}$ **40** $\dfrac{4a-3}{18}$

Page 153 **EXERCISE 47**

1 $10(x+y)$ **2** $6(a+b)(a-b)$ **3** $6(x+1)(x-1)$
4 $ab(a+b)(a-b)$ **5** $(a-b)(a+b)^2$ **6** $(x-1)(x-2)(x-3)$
7 $8(x-y)$ **8** $3(x-2y)$ **9** $(x-1)(x-3)(x+3)$

10 $(x-y)(x-3y)(2x-y)$ **11** $\dfrac{2x}{(x-1)(x-1)}$

12 $\dfrac{2x+3}{(x+1)(x+2)}$ **13** $\dfrac{4}{(a+2)(a-2)}$ **14** $\dfrac{x^2+y^2}{(x+y)(x-y)}$

15 $-\dfrac{x+9}{(x+3)(x-3)}$ **16** $\dfrac{2x-y}{x(x-y)}$ **17** $\dfrac{1}{6(x-y)}$

18 $\dfrac{x^2+y^2}{xy(x+y)}$ **19** $\dfrac{2x-1}{3(x+2)}$ **20** $\dfrac{a^2+b^2}{a(a+b)^2}$

21 -1 **22** $\dfrac{2a+x}{2(2a-x)}$ **23** $\dfrac{1}{x-y}$

24 $\dfrac{x}{(x+y)(x-y)}$ **25** $\dfrac{x+5}{4(x-1)(x+1)}$ **26** $\dfrac{2x^2}{(x-2)(x-2)}$

27 $\dfrac{2x-2}{x(x-3)}$ **28** $\dfrac{3}{x(x+3)}$ **29** $\dfrac{x^2-x+2}{4(x-2)^2}$

Page 153. EXERCISE 47—*continued*.

30 $\dfrac{3a-4b}{a-b}$ **31** $\dfrac{2x^2+2}{(2x-1)(3x-1)}$ **32** $\dfrac{7-x}{(x-1)(x+2)}$

33 $\dfrac{2a+10}{(a-1)(a-4)}$ **34** $\dfrac{3}{(y+1)(y-2)}$ **35** $\dfrac{2x}{1-x}$

36 $\dfrac{2}{(1-t)(1+t)}$ **37** $\dfrac{10x}{(2x-1)(2x+1)}$

Page 154 EXERCISE 48

1 $2x$ **2** $\dfrac{xy}{2}$ **3** 1 **4** -1

5 $\dfrac{x}{y(x-2y)}$ **6** $\dfrac{3a}{2}$ **7** $\dfrac{x+1}{(x-1)(x+3)}$ **8** $\dfrac{x(x-1)}{x+3}$

9 $\dfrac{(x-1)(x+2)}{x+1}$ **10** $\dfrac{x+1}{x+2}$ **11** 4 **12** $\dfrac{4x}{3(x+3)}$

13 $\dfrac{x+y}{x-2y}$ **14** $\dfrac{a^2}{2(a-3)}$ **15** $\dfrac{x^2}{y^2}$ **16** $\dfrac{x+4}{x+1}$

Page 155 EXERCISE 49

1 4 **2** $7\frac{7}{15}$ **3** $\frac{6}{17}$ **4** 18 **5** $1\frac{3}{16}$

6 $\frac{26}{77}$ **7** $\frac{6}{7}$ **8** $2\frac{4}{5}$ **9** $\frac{1}{2}$ **10** $\frac{13}{30}$

11 $3\frac{21}{25}$ **12** $1\frac{4}{5}$ **13** $2 \cdot 12$ **14** $66 \cdot 25$ **15** $3 \cdot 8625$

16 400

Page 157 EXERCISE 50

1 2 **2** -1 **3** -3 **4** $-\frac{2}{3}$ **5** 4

6 $\frac{1}{3}$ **7** $-1\frac{1}{4}$ **8** -80 **9** -4 **10** $-\frac{3}{4}$

11 $-\frac{1}{2}$ **12** $\frac{1}{4}$ **13** $-2\frac{11}{16}$ **14** 4 **15** -5

16 $1\frac{2}{5}$ **17** $\frac{7}{9}$ **18** $-\frac{3}{4}$ **19** -16 **20** $-4\frac{1}{3}$

21 15 **22** $-17\frac{1}{2}$ **23** $\frac{25}{36}$ **24** 0 **25** 4

26 $23\frac{2}{3}$ **27** -8 **28** -3 **29** $1\frac{1}{4}$ **30** $10\frac{3}{4}$

31 $3, 1$ **32** $12, 8$ **33** $8, -6$ **34** $4, -\frac{1}{4}$ **35** $1, -3$

36 $-9, 10$ **37** $1\frac{1}{3}, -2$ **38** $4, -3$ **39** $-10, -2$ **40** $4, -5$

Page 159   EXERCISE 51
1 20   **2** 3 cm   **3** 3p   **4** 10 km/h
5 48 km   **6** 40 km/h   **7** 5 km   **8** 1 km
9 19   **10** 7, $7\frac{1}{2}$ km/h   **11** 12   **12** 12p
13 (180n–360)/n, 360/n; 10   **14** 20 km/h

Page 165   EXERCISE 52
2 2·53, 6·74 cm   **3** 3·6 cm   **4** 1·26 cm   **5** 6·34 cm
6 5·20 cm   **7** 6·97 cm   **8** 2·09, 3·40, 5·67, 8·88 cm

Page 166   EXERCISE 53
1 a^5 **2** b^7 **3** c^4 **4** x^6 **5** x^6
6 x^2 **7** a^9 **8** 1   **9** x^8 **10** y^5
11 a^6 **12** x^{10} **13** a^{10} **14** d^5 **15** a^7
16 x^{15} **17** x^{12} **18** a^9 **19** a^6 **20** a^2b^3

Page 169   EXERCISE 54
1 a^4, a^6, a^8, a, a^3 **2** $a^2, a^4, a^{\frac{1}{2}}, a^3$
3 a^6, a^9, a^{12}, a^2 **4** $a, a^2, a^{\frac{1}{3}}, a^{\frac{2}{3}}$
5 a^{12} **6** a^6 **7** $a^{\frac{3}{2}}$ **8** a^6 **9** a^{12}
10 $a^{\frac{3}{2}}$ **11** $a^{\frac{2}{3}}$ **12** a^3 **13** 5   **14** 0·01
15 0·1   **16** 3   **17** 6   **18** 10   **19** 1
20 $\frac{1}{8}$ **21** $\frac{1}{5}$ **22** 1   **23** $\frac{1}{3}$ **24** 2
25 0·001   **26** 0·001   **27** 4   **28** 4
29 (i) 1·414, (ii) 4·472, (iii) 1·732, (iv) 3·162   **30** 1·779

Page 171   EXERCISE 55
1 (i) 4; (ii) 1·6; (iii) 3·5; (iv) 8; (v) 2·9
2 (i) $10^{0·18}$; (ii) $10^{0·4}$; (iii) $10^{0·9}$; (iv) $10^{0·7}$; (v) $10^{0·81}$
3 2, 3·16; 6·32   **4** 0·34, 0·43; 6·6
6 8·25   **7** 6·25   **8** 8·9   **9** 0·9, 0·3; 4
11 1·9   **12** 1·8

Page 173   EXERCISE 56

The indices are:

1 0·5563	**2** 0·7993	**3** 0·9138	**4** 0·9031
5 0·4771	**6** 0·4409	**7** 0·5623	**8** 0·7559
9 0·4800	**10** 0·0334	**11** 0·7076	**12** 0·8281
13 0·9124	**14** 0·5228	**15** 0·6117	**16** 0·9991
17 0·4782	**18** 0·9399	**19** 0·3021	**20** 0·7775
21 0·9641	**22** 0·7375	**23** 0·0029	**24** 0·4477
25 0·6482	**26** 0·6263	**27** 0·8562	**28** 0·4842
29 0·3243	**30** 0·8237		

Page 174   EXERCISE 57

These are four-figure answers.

1 3·000	**2** 8·600	**3** 6·400	**4** 9·220	**5** 3·060
6 4·620	**7** 7·640	**8** 8·690	**9** 3·243	**10** 4·682
11 8·057	**12** 6·317	**13** 1·854	**14** 3·227	**15** 1·487
16 1·007	**17** 3·404	**18** 1·115	**19** 1·758	**20** 5·592
21 7·241	**22** 8·300	**23** 2·050	**24** 9·802	**25** 3·910
26 1·422	**27** 1·206	**28** 7·290	**29** 8·267	**30** 1·198
31 6·838	**32** 4·467			

Page 175   EXERCISE 58

1 5·529	**2** 8·364	**3** 8·650	**4** 7·625	**5** 9·016
6 6·607	**7** 3·058	**8** 1·566	**9** 5·260	**10** 3·218
11 2·005	**12** 1·414			

Page 177   EXERCISE 59

1 1·5051	**2** 3·6880	**3** 4·9227	**4** 1·8549
5 2·4781	**6** 0·7543	**7** 2·3359	**8** 6·5008
9 4	**10** 2·6088	**11** 5	**12** 5·7854
13 6·6990	**14** 0	**15** 1·8513	**16** 4·5926
17 3·4341	**18** 2	**19** 1·7161	**20** 4·6788
21 42·87	**22** 3000	**23** 780·5	**24** 55 600

25 486 100	**26** 2·042	**27** 1995	**28** 10 000
29 107·3	**30** 4140	**31** 3697	**32** 561·4
33 29·05	**34** 30 560	**35** 631·0	**36** 94·78
37 778 100	**38** 1·323	**39** 3291	**40** 121·1

Page 179   EXERCISE 60

These are four-figure answers.

1 1303	**2** 456·4	**3** 24 930	**4** 816·6	**5** 211·1
6 112·6	**7** 855·5	**8** 15 900	**9** 34·87	**10** 14 400
11 8·624	**12** 602·7	**13** 21·36	**14** 890 000	**15** 82·69
16 759·0	**17** 768 100	**18** 1275	**19** 29·61	**20** 19·74
21 1372	**22** 25 410	**23** 98·47	**24** 3·058	**25** 484 200
26 6·575	**27** 14·87			

Page 181   EXERCISE 61

1 $\bar{1}$·8286	**2** $\bar{3}$·5416	**3** $\bar{2}$·7545	**4** $\bar{1}$·9934	**5** $\bar{2}$·4886
6 $\bar{4}$·8451	**7** $\bar{1}$·0043	**8** $\bar{4}$·7782	**9** $\bar{3}$·7053	**10** $\bar{1}$·5021
11 0·8837	**12** $\bar{2}$·0170	**13** 1·0278	**14** $\bar{4}$·6561	**15** $\bar{1}$·9080
16 $\bar{3}$·3979	**17** $\bar{4}$	**18** 1·2896	**19** $\bar{1}$·2009	**20** 2·3189
21 $\bar{3}$·4886	**22** $\bar{1}$·6628	**23** $\bar{5}$·8177	**24** 4·7324	**25** $\bar{5}$·3522
26 0·4297	**27** 0·0005818	**28** 0·01175	**29** 0·00001191	
30 0·2402	**31** 0·007446	**32** 0·3000	**33** 0·0009954	
34 0·003142	**35** 45 090	**36** 0·03743	**37** 0·00005858	
38 0·5060	**39** 398·1	**40** 0·004613		

Page 183   EXERCISE 62

1 $\bar{5}$·7	**2** $\bar{4}$·4	**3** $\bar{2}$·2	**4** 0·2	**5** 2·0
6 4·1	**7** $\bar{7}$·3	**8** $\bar{5}$·7	**9** 0·8	**10** $\bar{2}$·5
11 $\bar{3}$·6	**12** 4·5	**13** 4·5	**14** $\bar{7}$·7	**15** 0·6
16 2·8	**17** $\bar{4}$·8	**18** $\bar{2}$·8	**19** $\bar{9}$·2	**20** $\bar{7}$·5
21 $\bar{1}$·2	**22** $\bar{2}$·7	**23** $\bar{2}$·9	**24** $\bar{1}$·8	**25** $\bar{3}$·1
26 $\bar{3}$·7	**27** $\bar{3}$·85	**28** $\bar{1}$·74	**29** $\bar{1}$·2	**30** $\bar{1}$·5851
31 $\bar{2}$·825	**32** $\bar{1}$·96			

Page 184   EXERCISE 63

These are four-figure answers.

1 2·038	**2** 0·1954	**3** 0·02437	**4** 0·005844
5 0·1127	**6** 151·6	**7** 398·7	**8** 0·1274
9 80·40	**10** 0·002370	**11** 6·623	**12** 2329
13 469·4	**14** 130·7	**15** 264·2	**16** 21·76
17 3·989	**18** 0·3022	**19** 0·4070	**20** 0·0001585
21 0·3716	**22** 0·000003388	**23** 0·8138	**24** 0·3851
25 0·9780	**26** 0·05991	**27** 0·1913	**28** 0·6044
29 0·000005121		**30** 0·5357	

Page 189   EXERCISE 64

1 4·47 cm	**2** 11·5 cm	**5** 3·7 cm	**6** 3·57 cm
7 3·46 cm	**8** 8·31 cm	**9** 8 cm	**10** 5·12 cm
12 5, 44 cm², 13·3 cm		**13** 3·6, 1·72 cm	
14 7·21 cm		**15** (i) 7·79 cm; (ii) 1·16 cm	
16 5 cm	**30** 1·54 cm	**32** 3·31 cm	**34** 8·94 cm
35 12·6 cm	**36** 7 cm		

Page 199   EXERCISE 65

1 7·4 cm   **2** 11·5 cm   **3** (i) 7 cm; (ii) 3 cm
4 7, 5, 8 cm   **5** 126°   **6** 4·87 cm   **7** 1·12 cm
8 142°   **9** 6·46 cm   **10** 55°, 61°, 64°
11 73°, 59°, 48°   **12** 91°, 101°, 89°, 79°   **14** 12 cm
15 5·25 cm   **25** $(a+b+c+d)$ cm   **29** $\frac{1}{2}ar, \frac{1}{2}br, \frac{1}{2}cr$ cm²

Page 205   EXERCISE 66

1 20°, 120°, 60°, $\frac{2}{9}, \frac{1}{9}, \frac{1}{3}, \frac{4}{9}$ **3** 4·9 cm
5 7·33 cm; (ii) 22 cm²   **6** 10·5 cm
7 (i) 6·28 cm; (ii) 15·7 cm²   **8** 126 cm², 25·1 cm
9 72°, 72°, 36°   **10** (i) 30°; (ii) 60°
11 15°; $7\frac{1}{2}°, 22\frac{1}{2}°$, 150°   **12** 105°, 30°, 45°
14 45°, $112\frac{1}{2}°, 22\frac{1}{2}°$; $67\frac{1}{2}°, 45°, 67\frac{1}{2}°$ **15** 102°, 102°

Page 207   PAPER 1

1 (i) 174 p (ii) 81p; (iii) £15·66   **2** 2, $\frac{1}{2}$
4 103°   **5** 4·24, −0·24   **6** 12, 21 cm²

Page 207   PAPER 2

1 £1750   **2** $\frac{3}{5}$, $\frac{2}{5}$ **4** 100°   **6** 5·48 cm; 11·0 cm²

Page 208   PAPER 3

1 (i) £433·50; (ii) £600   **2** 3, −2   **3** 135°
4 29°   **5** 1·22, 3·28

Page 209   PAPER 4

1 £13·37   **2** −2, $1\frac{1}{3}$ **4** 6 cm   **6** 10

Page 209   PAPER 5

1 12p   **2** $\frac{1}{2}$, $2\frac{1}{4}$ **4** 162°   **6** 3·68 cm, 3·92 cm²

Page 210   PAPER 6

1 (i) $10x^2 - 11xy - 6y^2$; (ii) $1 - 4a + 4a^2$; (iii) $x^2 + 2 + 1/x^2$
2 2·4, 3·6 cm   **3** 162 cm   **4** $4\frac{1}{2}\%$ **5** 64

Page 210   PAPER 7

1 (i) $12 + x - x^2$; $a^2 + 7ab + 10b^2$; (ii) $(2x+1)(x-4)$;
    $3(y+5)(y-5)$ **2** 18 cm   **3** 69°31′
4 6%   **6** 3 or 8

Page 211   PAPER 8

1 20, 7 cm   **2** 3·39, 2·12 cm   **3** £1225
5 60   **6** (i) $(b+2c)(a-3)$; (ii) $(2x-1)(3x-1)$;
    (iii) $(x+4t)(x-4t)$; $\frac{1}{3}$, −2

Page 211   PAPER 9

1 (i) $2ab - a^2 - b^2$; (ii) $25x^2 - \frac{1}{4}a^2$ **2** $37\frac{1}{2}$ m
3 5·20 cm, 15·6 cm²   **4** $4\frac{1}{2}$ y   **5** 10
6 (i) $(1+4x)(1-x)$; (ii) $6a^2(1-3a)$; −1, $-1\frac{1}{2}$

Page 212   **PAPER 10**

1 (i) $x^2-5x+20$; (ii) $4ab$; (iii) $t-1/t$ **2** 20, 27 cm
3 336 m   **4** £640
6 (i) $(x+5)(x-1)$; (ii) $\pi R(R+2h)$; (iii) $2(3a+2b)(3a-2b)$;
     $-\frac{1}{2}$, $-\frac{1}{4}$

Page 213   **PAPER 11**

1 41·9   **2** (i) $\dfrac{16x-30}{21(x-1)(x-2)}$; (ii) $\dfrac{3y-2x}{2y+3x}$

3 (i) 27·4; (ii) 0·444   **4** 3·07, 7·87 cm
5 60°   **6** 45°, 60°, 75°

Page 213   **PAPER 12**

1 (i) 9·42; (ii) 0·0750   **2** (i) $\dfrac{2x^2+x-3}{2x+1}$;
   (ii) $\dfrac{15}{(2x+3)(1-x)}$; $-\dfrac{15}{2x+1}$ **3** (i) 0·149; (ii) 0·189
4 1·56 cm   **5** 38°, 41°

Page 214   **PAPER 13**

1 (i) 6·00; (ii) 4·62   **2** (i) $\frac{1}{9}$; (ii) $\frac{13}{90}$
3 (i) 3·98; (ii) 365   **5** 98°, 88°, 82°, 92°
6 (i) 13 cm, (ii) 20 cm

Page 214   **PAPER 14**

1 (i) 68·0; (ii) 2140; (iii) 0·0216   **2** (i) $\frac{5}{16}$; (ii) 50000
3 (i) 11100; (ii) 0·000284   **4** 3·13 cm
5 (i) $1\frac{1}{2}$ cm; (ii) $5\frac{1}{2}$ cm

Page 215   **PAPER 15**

1 (i) 1·34; (ii) 0·206   **2** $\frac{7}{20}$
3 (i) 0·0395; (ii) 0·801   **4** 10 cm   **6** 4·13 cm

Page 216   **PAPER 16**

1 £91·77   **3** 1 cm
5 (i) $\dfrac{14x-5}{(2x-1)(3x-1)}$ (ii) $\dfrac{3x(x-1)}{x-2}$ **6** 19·5 cm

Page 216 PAPER 17

1 $\frac{1}{2}$, $-1\frac{1}{2}$ 3 (i) $(x-y)(a-b)$; (ii) $(x+\frac{1}{2}y)(x-\frac{1}{2}y)$;
(iii) $(x-2)(6x-1)$ 4 (i) 0·257; (ii) 85·6
5 1·29 cm 6 12·5 cm

Page 217 PAPER 18

1 £24, £9 2 $90+\frac{1}{2}x$ 3 20 cm, 90 cm²
5 (i) 0, -3, $-\frac{1}{2}$, (ii) 2, -4

Page 217 PAPER 19

2 $-1·29$ 3 18·1 cm² 4 29·4 6 4·57 cm²

Page 218 PAPER 20

1 1·64 2 $3\frac{2}{5}$ 3 (i) $(x-y)(ax+ay+b)$;
(ii) $a^4(1+a^2)(1+a)(1-a)$; (iii) $2ab(a-3b-4c)$
4 (i) -7; (ii) $\frac{1}{4}$, $-\frac{1}{3}$
5 (i) $12\frac{1}{7}$; (ii) $\dfrac{1+x}{x(x-2)}$ 6 2·70 cm

Page 219 PAPER 21

1 $(4a-7)(3a+7)$, $5(x+2y)(x-2y)$, $(a+2)(a-3b)$ 2 1·081
3 -4, $3\frac{1}{2}$ 4 (i) 4, (ii) $4(1+x)$ 5 300/x, 15

Page 219 PAPER 22

1 £4·20, 1·75p 2 $\dfrac{9x+33}{(x-1)(x+5)}$
3 $4xy(x^2-3y)$, $(a+2b)(a-2b+3)$, $(2x-3)(x+4)$
4 (i) 11·7; (ii) 0·839 5 4·04, 5·88 cm
6 3·16 cm, 19·0 cm²

Page 220 PAPER 23

1 4101, 1599 2 48/x, 6 3 $3\frac{7}{15}$ 4 (i) 3, (ii) $\frac{1}{3}$, (iii) 26
5 (i) 5·25, $-5·56$; (ii) 4·9, $-0·9$ 6 31°

SECTION B

EXERCISE 67

These are four-figure answers.

1 30520	**2** 0·1320	**3** 0·3695	**4** 20·21
5 0·1012	**6** 6·513	**7** 0·0005321	**8** 10·70
9 1·201	**10** 0·01213	**11** 1·661	**12** 2·005
13 52·78	**14** 303·4	**15** 0·04991	**16** 0·006531
17 4·900	**18** 0·001550	**19** 0·3077	**20** 0·0004038
21 0·3699	**22** 0·02364	**23** 0·1408	**24** 15·38
25 0·2353	**26** 0·02342	**27** 2·599	**28** 8·310
29 1·181	**30** 31·84	**31** 2·687	**32** 0·01494
33 0·5980	**34** 0·04422	**35** 0·2115	**36** 0·6159
37 4·873	**38** 0·1441	**39** 0·01385	**40** 0·3016
41 20·52	**42** 0·4439	**43** 0·5053	**44** 35·42
45 0·6877	**46** 6·527	**47** 0·7230	**48** 0·7823
49 0·2938	**50** 1·009		

Page 224 EXERCISE 68

These are four-figure answers.

1 25·33	**2** 0·02935	**3** 5·895	**4** 0·6866
5 6965	**6** 0·1159	**7** 131·9	**8** 5·794
9 807·1	**10** 1507	**11** 4220	**12** 0·2665 m²
13 475·1	**14** 1·930	**15** 0·004996	**16** $9·835 \times 10^{25}$
17 $9·506 \times 10^{9}$			

Page 227 EXERCISE 69

1 3910 cm²	**2** 86·9 cm	**3** 52·5 cm²
4 8·33 cm	**5** 11·1 cm²	**6** 5·18 cm²
7 7·29 cm²	**8** 3·52 cm	**9** 1·93 cm, 3·86 cm²
10 2·30 cm²	**11** 12 cm²	**12** 14·7 cm²
13 33·9 cm²	**14** 62·4 cm²	**15** 2·4 cm
16 260 cm²	**17** 4·42 cm²	**18** 3·63 cm, 21·8 cm²

Page 230   EXERCISE 70

1 72 cm³   **2** 24·3 m³   **3** 216 cm³
4 222 cm, 3940 cm² **5** 135 m, 1440 m²   **6** 155 cm²
7 228 cm³, 82·9 cm² **8** 1920 cm³, 2200 cm² **9** 87·5 cm³, 77·8 cm²
10 2160 cm²   **11** (i) 79 cm³, (ii) 628 cm³

Page 233   EXERCISE 71

1 32 cm³   **2** 72 cm³   **3** 16 cm³
4 13·9 cm³   **5** 39·7 cm³   **6** 400 cm³, 360 cm²
7 151 cm³   **8** 37·7 cm³   **9** 51·3 cm³
10 251 cm²   **11** 160 cm²   **12** 180 cm³, 154 cm²
13 2480 cm³, 887 cm² **14** 2·43 cm   **15** 905 cm³, 479 cm²
16 7270 cm³   **17** $\frac{2}{3}\pi r^3$, $\frac{4}{3}\pi r^3$, $2\pi r^3$

Page 235   EXERCISE 72

1 18·8 g   **2** 22·4 m²   **3** 11·8 cm²
4 75·0 cm   **5** 0·296 cm   **6** 0·025 cm
7 2517 g   **8** 11 cm   **9** 18·8, 12·9 cm; 114 cm²
10 3·8 cm   **11** 1·49 km   **12** 8·40 g
13 26000   **14** (i) 11500 (ii) 71875 **15** 1013 tons
16 1530   **17** 34·5 lb   **18** 24·9 in
19 140 yd²   **20** 0·203 ft³   **21** 534 in³
22 (i) 120 in³ (ii) 115 in²   **23** 127 in³, 27·8 lb
24 (i) $2\frac{2}{11}$ ac, (ii) 0·0033 in

Page 244   EXERCISE 74

1 5, −5   **2** 2, 3   **3** 2, −3   **4** 1, −1
5 3, −7   **6** 5, −1   **7** $2\frac{1}{2}$, −1   **8** 3, −$1\frac{1}{3}$
9 5, −3   **10** 6, −$2\frac{1}{2}$ **11** −$3\frac{2}{3}$ **12** 2, 5
13 4, $\frac{1}{2}$ **14** 2, −7   **15** −$5\frac{1}{2}$, 0

Page 245   EXERCISE 75

1 4, $(x+2)^2$ **2** 36, $(x+6)^2$ **3** $\frac{25}{9}$, $(x-\frac{5}{3})^2$
4 $\frac{25}{4}$, $(x+\frac{5}{2})^2$ **5** $\frac{1}{25}$, $(x-\frac{1}{5})^2$ **6** $\frac{1}{49}$, $(x+\frac{1}{7})^2$
7 $\frac{49}{324}$, $(x+\frac{7}{18})^2$ **8** $\frac{49}{36}$, $(x-\frac{7}{6})^2$ **9** $\frac{1}{4}$, $(x-\frac{1}{2})^2$

Page 247 EXERCISE 76

1 1, −7 **2** 7, −3 **3** 2, 0 **4** $-\frac{2}{3}$, $-1\frac{1}{3}$
5 $-\frac{1}{2}$, $-3\frac{1}{2}$ **6** $5\frac{1}{5}$, $2\frac{4}{5}$ **7** 8·681, −2·681
8 2·117, −6·117 **9** −5·768, −2·232 **10** 8·74, 3·26
11 9·472, −1·472 **12** −6·234, −3·766 **13** −1·59, −4·41
14 5·32, −1·32 **15** 0·47, −8·47 **16** 3·45, −1·45
17 0·29, −10·29 **18** 5·41, 2·59 **19** 5·30, 1·70
20 4·56, 0·44

Page 250 EXERCISE 77

1 −2·62, −0·38 **2** 0·62, −1·62 **3** 3·24, −1·24
4 1·71, 0·29 **5** 2·29, −0·29 **6** 1·87, −5·87
7 $\frac{1}{2}$, −2 **8** 0·54, −5·54 **9** 0·52, −3·19
10 3·14, −0·64 **11** 1·39, −0·72 **12** 3, 7
13 $1\frac{1}{2}$, $-2\frac{1}{2}$ **14** 2·78, 0·72 **15** −0·31, −1·29
16 No roots **17** −1·29, 9·29 **18** 1, $\frac{1}{2}$
19 3·65, −1·65 **20** 4·31, −0·31 **21** −2, $-\frac{1}{2}$
22 2·11, −7·11 **23** 2·79, −1·79 **24** $\frac{1}{4}$, −2
25 No roots **26** 5·08, −1·08 **27** 0·16, −6·16
28 $1\frac{1}{2}$, $\frac{1}{3}$ **29** 2·21, 6·79 **30** −0·56, −4·44
31 0·24, 1·19 **32** No roots **33** 0·57, 1·77
34 1·76, −0·76 **35** −1, $\frac{5}{6}$ **36** 0·17, 5·83
37 1, −4 **38** 5·24, 0·76 **39** 1·30, −2·30
40 2·79, −1·79 **41** 2, −13 **42** 1, 4
43 0·76, −5·26 **44** 1, 15 **45** 3·85, 0·65

Page 251 EXERCISE 78

1 8 **2** 8 m **3** 3 m **5** 6 cm
6 2 m **7** 11 **8** 10 m **9** 9·5
10 1·5 cm **11** 16·9, 18·9 cm **12** 2 cm **13** 8, 9, 10
14 24 **15** 7 cm **16** 4 **17** 2·07
18 60 **19** 30

Page 257 EXERCISE 79

1 12, $7\frac{1}{2}$ cm **2** 28, 14 cm **3** 2·8, 4·2 cm
4 3·5, 15·75 cm **5** 4, 27 cm **6** 7·2 cm
7 5·62 cm **8** 2·93 **9** 3·88

Page 261   EXERCISE 80

1 3·75, 15 cm   2 40 cm   3 18, 12 cm
4 $1\frac{1}{3}$ cm   5 $ca/(b+c)$, $ba/(b+c)$ 11 9·6 cm   12 90°

Page 263   EXERCISE 81

1 20·5 kg   2 6990 kg m^{-3} 3 1850 kg m^{-3}
4 411 kg   5 2·33 g   6 14·2 kg
7 10500 kg m^{-3} 8 264 g   9 6·88 kg

Page 265   EXERCISE 82

10 (i) yes, (ii) no, (iii) no   11 90, $\frac{1}{2}$; $y=6x$
12 $y=\frac{8}{3}x$; 12, $\frac{3}{4}$

Page 268   EXERCISE 83

1 3, -2; 7, -1
2 $1\frac{4}{5}$, 32, $-17\frac{7}{9}$; (i) 104, 131, 172·4° F; (ii) $36\frac{2}{3}$, $6\frac{5}{9}$, $-12\frac{2}{9}$°C
3 0·24, 2·2; 9·88 kg wt, 10·8 kg   4 0·35, 2·5; 2·5 cm, 15·4 g
6 $y=\frac{3}{2}x+30$ 10 (3, 7)   11 (0, 5)

Page 272   EXERCISE 84

1 (i) 6, (ii) 1, (iii) -3, (iv) $\frac{1}{3}$, (v) $-\frac{1}{4}$; $y=6x$, x, $-3x$, $\frac{1}{3}x$, $-\frac{1}{4}x$
2 $\frac{1}{3}$
3 (i) $y=2x+1$; (ii) $y=-x+2$; (iii) $y=-\frac{1}{2}x+3$; (iv) $y=\frac{3}{10}x$
4 $y=3x-1$ 5 (i) $y=-\frac{1}{3}x+2$; (ii) $y=3x+1$

Page 273   EXERCISE 85

1 1.37$\frac{1}{2}$ p.m., 26 km   2 1.45 p.m., 35 km
3 2.45 p.m., 38$\frac{1}{2}$ km   4 1.23 p.m., 9·7 km, 1.42 p.m.
5 1.14 p.m., 77 km

Page 277   EXERCISE 86

9 (i) $y\geqslant 1$, $y\geqslant x$; (ii) $-2\leqslant y\leqslant 1$
10 (i) $y\leqslant x+1$, $x+y\leqslant 2$; (ii) $y\geqslant x$, $y\leqslant 2x$

Page 280   EXERCISE 87

1 $x > \frac{1}{3}$ 2 $x < \frac{1}{2}$ 3 $x \geqslant -\frac{1}{3}$ 4 $x < -1$
5 $x \geqslant -5$ 6 $x < -2$ 7 $y \geqslant \frac{5}{2}$ 8 $x < -2$
9 $x > 1$ 10 all x 11 $x > 3$ 12 $x < 5$
13 $x < 2$ 14 $x \geqslant 6$ 15 $x > 2$ 16 $x < -\frac{7}{2}$
17 $x > -\frac{5}{2}$ 18 $x < \frac{2}{3}$ 19 $x \geqslant 2$ 20 $y > 1$
21 $x > -2$ 22 $y \geqslant \frac{1}{6}$ 23 $x > -\frac{1}{3}$ 24 all x

Page 281   EXERCISE 88

1 $\frac{1}{9}$ 2 1   3 3   4 9
5 4   6 0·2   7 $\frac{1}{10}$ 8 $\frac{1}{17}$
9 $\frac{81}{16}$ 10 10   11 0·09   12 1
13 $\frac{1}{5}$ 14 $\dfrac{1}{25x}$ 15 $4x^4$ 16 $\frac{4}{3}$

Page 282   EXERCISE 89

1 3×10^4 2 $1·2 \times 10^2$ 3 $6·67 \times 10^{25}$
4 $1·41 \times 10^{18}$ 5 $1·681 \times 10^{13}$, $1·681 \times 10^{-11}$
6 $1·35 \times 10^{-23}$

Page 285   EXERCISE 90

1 $4\sqrt{3}$ 2 $2\sqrt{15}$ 3 $2\sqrt{2}$ 4 $3\sqrt{3}$ 5 $3\sqrt{2}$
6 $2\sqrt{6}$ 7 $24\sqrt{3}$ 8 $6\sqrt{3}$ 9 $12\sqrt{2}$ 10 $5\sqrt{5}$
11 $12\sqrt{5}$ 12 $3\sqrt{10}$ 13 $\sqrt{45}$ 14 $\sqrt{192}$ 15 $\sqrt{80}$
16 $\sqrt{200}$ 17 $\sqrt{72}$ 18 $\sqrt{54}$ 19 $\sqrt{147}$ 20 $\sqrt{6}$
21 $5\sqrt{10}$ 22 $6\sqrt{6}$ 23 6   24 $6\sqrt{6}$ 25 4
26 $\sqrt{2}$ 27 1   28 $6\sqrt{5}$ 29 $4\sqrt{6}$ 30 $3 + 2\sqrt{2}$
31 $3 - 2\sqrt{2}$ 32 2   33 $\sqrt{2}$ 34 $5 - 2\sqrt{6}$ 35 1
36 0·577   37 2·121   38 4·472   39 0·141   40 2·309
41 1·767

Page 287   EXERCISE 91

1 $B = 39°$, $a = 6·94$, $b = 5·62$ 2 $A = 28° 30'$, $B = 61°30'$, $a = 6·30$
3 $A = 52° 8'$, $B = 37° 52'$, $c = 4·04$
4 $A = 28° 27'$, $B = 61° 33'$, $b = 8·63$
5 $B = 67°$, $a = 1·80$, $c = 4·61$.   6 $B = 54°$, $b = 7·86$, $c = 9·71$
7 $A = 23° 50'$, $a = 1·59$, $c = 3·95$
8 $A = 31° 35'$, $b = 3·69$, $c = 4·33$

Page 289

EXERCISE 92

1 8·66 cm, 15·2 cm²   **2** 68° 23′, 11·4 cm
3 77° 4′, 12·6 cm²   **4** (i) 88° 14′; (ii) 7·60 cm²
5 (i) 4·07 cm; (ii) 9·57 cm² **6** 4·85 cm, 10·2 cm²
7 (i) 73° 8′, (ii) 3·86 cm, (iii) 14·3 cm²   **8** 74° 30′
9 2·4 sin 57°, 3·12 cm²   **10** 16·4 cm²
11 4·82 cm   **12** 28·0 cm, 15·9 cm
13 5·43, 8·62 cm   **14** 6·25, 2·34 cm
15 10·8 cm, 70° 18′   **16** 172 cm²
17 260 cm²   **18** 7·49 cm, 25·3 cm²
19 11·7, 2·04, 4·89 cm   **20** 7·55 m, 63° 51′
21 4·3 m   **22** 2·76, 4·17 cm
23 2·90 cm   **24** 5·10 cm
25 36·8, 35·2 cm   **26** 7·77, 7·39 cm

Page 293

EXERCISE 93

1 650 831 m   **2** 052° 51′, 16·5 km
3 254 m, 17° 41′   **4** 5·61, 8·51, 1·4 cm
5 130 km, 044° 35′   **6** 192 m
7 840 m   **8** 276, 43·8 m
9 (i) 933 m; (ii) 13·9 m   **10** 325 m   **11** 165 m

Page 297

EXERCISE 94

1 1   **2** 3   **3** 1   **4** $\frac{1}{2}$ **5** 1
6 2   **7** 1   **8** 1   **9** $\frac{3}{4}$
10 3, 3 $\sqrt{3}$ cm   **12** 43·3 cm²   **13** 1·85 cm

Page 304

EXERCISE 96

These answers are more accurate than it is usually possible to obtain graphically.

1 −4·32, 4, −3·92, 5·88   **2** 3·61, −1·11; 2·28, 0·22; 3, $\frac{1}{2}$;
   3·81, −1·31; 2·85, −0·35   **3** −6·12, 1·25
4 −1·76   **5** None   **6** $x = 1·25$ **7** −$\frac{1}{2}$ to 3
8 3, −$\frac{1}{2}$ **9** 0, 2$\frac{1}{2}$ **10** 2, $\frac{1}{2}$ **11** 3·71, −1·21
12 No roots   **13** −4, 2; 0 to 4; (i) 4·65, −0·65; (ii) 3·41, 0·59

Page 304. EXERCISE 96—*continued*.

14 Minimum −4; (i) 3, −1; (ii) 4·74, −2·74; (iii) 2·41, −0·41; (iv) no roots

15 (i) 1·31, −3·81; (ii) 0·77, −3·27, (iii) no roots; (iv) −2·28, −0·22

16 (i) −11·92, −7·12; (ii) 3·21, −1·71; 2·77, −1·27; (iii) maximum 2·12; (iv) −0·28 to 1·78

17 (i) 0·31, −4·81; (ii) 0·84, −5·34; (iii) −0·23, −4·27; (iv) no roots

18 (i) 4·54, −1·54; (ii) −7·04; (iii) minimum −8·25, 1·5; (iv) −1·37 to 4·37; (v) 3·56, −0·56

19 −3 to ½   **20** 3·45, −1·45   **21** −5·5; 0·16, −3·16

Page 308   EXERCISE 97

1 $1 < x < 3$ **2** $x < -1$ or $x > 3$

3 $x < -3$ or $x > 1$ **4** $x < -3$ or $x > 3$

5 $-4 \leqslant x \leqslant \frac{1}{2}$ **6** $-1 < x < \frac{3}{2}$

7 $-4 \leqslant x \leqslant 3$ **8** $\frac{3}{2} < x < 4$

Page 310   EXERCISE 98

1 8, −8   **2** 4, 4   **3** (i) −6; (ii) −4; (iii) −2

4 4   **5** 3

Page 314   EXERCISE 99

1 33° 42′   **2** 21° 48′   **3** 47° 59′   **4** 33° 51′

5 63° 26′   **6** 33° 51′   **7** 56° 19′   **8** 53° 8′

9 45°   **10** 30° 58′   **11** 36° 52′   **12** 60°

13 6·53 cm   **14** 5·29, 3·46, 5·29 cm   **15** 5·29 cm

16 5·12 cm   **17** 2·67, 3·33, 1·33 cm

18 81° 52′, 60° 15′, 37° 52′   **19** 68° 34′

20 61° 17′, 90°, 28° 43′

Page 318   EXERCISE 100

1 (i) 14·3 m; (ii) 11° 28′

2 (i) 17·5 cm; (ii) 66° 9′; (iii) 72° 39′; (iv) 47° 42′

3 (i) 26° 34′; (ii) 32° 28′   **4** 66° 25′, 40° 53′

5 34° 19′   **6** 18° 54′   **7** 11·7 m

8 (i) 79° 6′; (ii) 68° 57′   **9** 840 m, 40° 7′   **10** 12° 20′

Page 319   EXERCISE 101

1 17·3 cm   **2** 9·23 m   **3** 5·24 cm
10 15 m²   **11** 3½ cm   **12** 4 cm

Page 323   EXERCISE 102

5 (i) 4 cm, (ii) 42°   **8** (i) 35°, (ii) 55°   **9** 3·46, 2·0 cm
10 3·27 cm   **11** (i) 2 cm, (ii) 24 cm², (iii) 6 cm³
12 11 cm   **13** 130° 12′
14 (i) 13·9 cm, (ii) 400 cm³, (iii) 360 cm², (iv) 67° 23′

Page 328   EXERCISE 103

1 0·3090, −0·9511, −0·3249; 0·6820, −0·7314, −0·9325;
  0·1736, −0·9848, −0·1763; 0·7716, −0·6361, −1·2131;
  0·9892, −0·1466, −6·743

2 $\dfrac{1}{\sqrt{2}}, -\dfrac{1}{\sqrt{2}}, -1; \dfrac{\sqrt{3}}{2}, -\dfrac{1}{2}, -\sqrt{3}; \dfrac{1}{2}, -\dfrac{\sqrt{3}}{2}, -\dfrac{1}{\sqrt{3}}; 0, -1, 0$

3 58, 122   **4** 144

5 0·6428, −0·7660, −0·8391; 0·2588, −0·9659, −0·2679;
  0·9397, −0·3420, −2·7475;   0,   −1,   0

Page 330   EXERCISE 104

1 14 cm²   **2** 10·6 cm²   **3** 15 cm²
4 4·78 cm²   **5** 35·7 cm²   **6** 54° 6′
7 4·82 cm²   **8** 93·5 cm²

Page 333   EXERCISE 105

1 $b = 6\cdot53$ cm, $c = 5\cdot83$ cm, $A = 78°$
2 $a = 3\cdot12$ cm, $c = 3\cdot41$ cm, $A = 51°$
3 $b = 2\cdot23$ cm, $c = 3\cdot01$ cm, $A = 126° 54′$
4 $b = 3\cdot17$ cm, $c = 4\cdot70$ cm, $C = 101° 31′$
5 $a = 15\cdot9$ cm, $b = 25\cdot9$ cm, $C = 29°$
6 $c = 16\cdot2$ cm, $a = 17\cdot7$ cm, $A = 81° 4′$
7 $a = 13\cdot2$ cm, $b = 10\cdot8$ cm, $A = 99° 29′$
8 $b = 3\cdot83$ cm, $c = 5\cdot91$ cm, $B = 28° 26′$
9 $a = 9\cdot91$ cm, $c = 8\cdot08$ cm, $B = 77° 2′$
10 $a = 7\cdot85$ cm, $b = 12\cdot8$ cm, $B = 39° 9′$
11 $b = 1\cdot18$ cm, $c = 1\cdot69$ cm, $A = 98° 25′$ **12** 574, 513 m
13 14·5 cm   **14** 6·97 cm   **17** 11·8 km   **18** 258 m

Page 337   EXERCISE 106

1 32%   **2** £313·20 **3** £1750   **4** 550   **5** 48⅘%
6 £388·80   **7** 20%   **8** 36%   **9** 8%   **10** 70, 17½%
11 £3025, 21% **12** 1 800 000; (i) 1 946 880, (ii) 2 024 755
13 £525

Page 339   EXERCISE 107

1 £1·44   **2** 19%   **3** £245   **4** £6·09
5 25%   **6** (i) 12½%, (ii) 50%   **7** 24p   **8** £550
9 25%   **10** 4⅔% loss   **11** £1·25   **12** £1·75, 37½%
13 £1·82   **14** 5%   **15** 18%   **16** 9⅔%, £300 000
17 £25   **18** £4500   **19** 12%   **20** 26%, £5·33
21 280 000; 17·15%   **22** 63·1, 56 km/h

Page 343   EXERCISE 108

1 (i) $c = y - mx$; (ii) $m = (y-c)/x$; (iii) $x = (y-c)/m$ **2** $r = C/2\pi$
3 (i) $P = 100I/RT$; (ii) $R = 100I/PT$ **4** $b = (P-2l)/2$
5 $h = S/2\pi r$ **6** $h = 3V/\pi r^2$
7 (i) $u = v - at$; (ii) $a = (v-u)/t$; (iii) $t = (v-u)/a$
8 $l = A/b$ **9** $h = V/lb$ **10** $h = (S - 2\pi r^2)/2\pi r$

Page 345   EXERCISE 109

1 $(7b - 5d)/(5c - 7a)$ **2** $1.17\sqrt{P/yt}$
3 $Ri/(V - ri)$ **4** $(af + cd)/(ae - bd)$
5 $3ax/(a + 2x)$ **6** $(aq - bp)/(2p - 3q)$
7 $(3x + 5)/(6x + 2)$ **8** $Wb/(W - 2PE)$
9 $(36a - 3b)/(4x - 3)$ **10** $(2x + 7)/(4x + 3)$
11 $\sqrt{(W + p\pi r^2)/p\pi}$ **12** $(10P + 9T)/45R^2$
13 $\sqrt{(p^2 - 2pq)}$ **14** $1.92\sqrt{V/h}$
15 $(V + \pi l t^2)/2\pi l t$

Page 346   EXERCISE 110

1 $t = \sqrt{(2s/g)}$; 2·51 s   **2** $C = (5F - 160)/9$; 0° C, 100° C
3 $r = \frac{1}{2}\sqrt{A/\pi}$; 1·99 cm
4 (i) $h = 2A/(a + b)$; (ii) $a = (2A - bh)/h$; 13·6 cm
5 $\sin B = b \sin A/a$; 59° 21′, 120° 39′

6 $T = 100(A - P)/PR$; 4

7 (i) $t = 2s/(u + v)$; (ii) $u = (2s - vt)/t$; (iii) $v = (2s - ut)/t$

8 $h = 500 \, D^2/R$, 17·7   9 $r = \sqrt[3]{3V/4\pi}$; 9·21 cm

10 (i) $h = V/\pi r^2$; (ii) $r = \sqrt{V/\pi h}$; 2·18 cm

11 (i) $n = 5H/2d^2$; (ii) $d = \sqrt{5H/2n}$

12 (i) $x = a(T + \lambda)/\lambda$; (ii) $a = \lambda x/(T + \lambda)$

13 $\cos A = (b^2 + c^2 - a^2)/2bc$; 75° 31′

14 $M = 4\pi^2 I/T^2 H$; 512

15 (i) $u = (2s - at^2)/2t$; $a = 2(s - ut)/t^2$

16 $g = 4\pi^2 l/T^2$; 981   17 $x = A/y \sin \theta$

18 (i) $\sin A = 2\Delta/bc$; (ii) $b = 2\Delta/c \sin A$

19 $x = (8d^2 + 3l^2)/3l$; 60·2 cm

20 (i) $s = (v^2 - u^2)/2a$; (ii) $u = \sqrt{v^2 - 2as}$

21 (i) $s = W(v^2 - u^2)/2Pg$; (ii) $W = 2Pgs/(v^2 - u^2)$;
 (iii) $v = \sqrt{(2gPs + Wu^2)/W}$; (iv) $u = \sqrt{(Wv^2 - 2gPs)/W}$

22 (i) $f = uv/(u + v)$; (ii) $v = uf/(u - f)$; −22·05

23 $V = 5\pi r^3/24$; $r = \sqrt[3]{24V/5\pi}$

24 $r = (A - \pi d^2)/2\pi d$

25 $h = (A - 2\pi r^2)/2\pi r$

26 $b = (2at + c)/(2r - t)$

27 (i) $u = (rs + fs - fr)/f(s - r)$; (ii) $f = rs/(u - 1)(s - r)$;
 (iii) $r = (fus - fs)/(s + fu - f)$

28 $a = (2S - n^2d + nd)/2n$; 14

Page 351   EXERCISE 111

1 3, 4	2 −2, 7	3 5, −1	4 −2, 6
5 7, 0	6 3, 4	7 −4, 7	8 1, −5
9 $10\frac{2}{3}, \frac{1}{3}$	10 $-\frac{1}{2}, 3$	11 $3\frac{1}{2}, 5\frac{1}{2}$	12 16, −4

Page 353   EXERCISE 112

1 (i) $y = 0$, $y = 4$; (ii) $x = 0$, $x = 5$; (iii) $z = 0$, (iv) $z = 3$

2 $z = 2$, $z = -2$ 4 $y = 3$

Page 358   EXERCISE 114

12 3·04 cm   14 1·53 or 2·61 cm   20 1·78 cm

Page 362 EXERCISE 115

1 $BC^2+2BC.BD+BD^2$, $XY^2-2XY.XZ+XZ^2$, AB^2-AC^2

2 $PQ(PQ+2PR)$, $XA(XY-3XA)$, $(AP+3AQ)(AP-3AQ)$

3 (i) $4AB^2$; (ii) $9PQ^2$; (iii) $AB^2+AB.AD+\frac{1}{4}AD^2$

Page 366 EXERCISE 116

1 $\sqrt{(x^2+y^2)}$; circle, centre O, radius 3

2 (i) 5, (ii) 13, (iii) 25   3 (i) 6·7, (ii) 10·8

4 $\sqrt{(x^2+y^2+z^2)}$; sphere, centre O, radius 5

5 (i) 7, (ii) 13   6 (i) 1·7, (ii) 10·3

8 $\pm\frac{5}{13}$ 9 $\frac{24}{25}$ 10 (i) $a^2\cos^2\theta$; (ii) $a\sin\theta$

11 $1-3s+2s^2$; $(1-s)(1-2s)$; 30°, 90°, 150°

12 (i) $2\cos^2\alpha-1$, (ii) $1-2\sin^2\alpha$ 13 61

Page 373 EXERCISE 117

1 7   2 2·83   3 7·81

4 41° 24′, 55° 46′   5 52° 24′, 29° 41′   6 18·8

7 127° 36′   8 151° 39′   9 17° 6′

10 21·2   11 $a=11·4$, B=54° 28′, C=69° 32′

12 $c=20·7$, A=35° 32′, B=125° 28′

13 $b=34·8$, A=35° 14′, C=30° 46′

14 A=130° 31′, B=23° 51′, C=25° 38′

15 A=32° 4′, B=45° 48′, C=102° 8′

16 $b=2·17$, A=50° 46′, C=87° 38′

17 $a=48·5$, B=22° 57′, C=43° 41′

18 A=12° 40′, B=129° 30′, C=37° 50′   19 12.22 p.m.

20 9·75, 9·04, 8·84 km   21 29 m   22 3400 m

23 8·47, 17·3 cm   24 71° 29′, 108° 31′   25 47·4 km

26 3·63 km, S. 67° 20′ E   27 115 cm

28 7600 m   29 7·58 km/b

30 (i) right, (ii) obtuse   31 35° 51·

32 (i) obtuse, (ii) acute, (iii) right   33 Obtuse

34 767, 503 m   35 9·09 cm, 37° 36′, 22° 24′

36 38° 13′   38 145, 115 m

Page 377   EXERCISE 118
  1 7 cm   **2** 3·4, 4·4, 5·1 cm   **3** 38 cm
  4 20 cm
  8 Circle, centre the mid-point of **AB**, radius 3 cm

Page 80   EXERCISE 119
  1 50°, 80°   **2** 50°, 30°, 30°   **4** 105°, 49°, 26°
  5 43°, 137°   **6** 38°, 88°, 54°   **7** 25°
  8 60°, 70°, 50°   **9** 130°, 50°   **10** 40°, 92°
 11 55°   **12** 41°, 63°, 76°   **13** 63°
 15 24°, CDX

Page 383   EXERCISE 120
  1 53°, 127°, 106°, 74°   **2** 132°, 66°, 24°
  3 63°, 48°   **4** 75°, 101°   **5** 41°   **6** 99°
  7 56°, 78°, 46°   **8** 56°, 68°, 56°   **9** 71°, 76°, 33°
 10 104°, 91°, 129°   **11** 3·26 cm   **12** 3·26 cm
 13 7·73 cm   **14** 3·72 or 6·03 cm **15** 2·45 or 5·74 cm
 16 7·53 cm   **26** $y°$, $x°$, $(y-x)°$

Page 390   EXERCISE 121
  These answers are more accurate than it is usually possible to
obtain graphically.
 11 (i) 1·73; (ii) −1·73; (iii) 3·25, −0·59, −2·66; (iv) 3·1,
        −0·2, −2·9; (v) 1·8
 12 (i) −2·43; (ii) 1·1; (iii) 2·34, −0·57, −3·77; (iv) 2·67,
        −1·36, −3·31; (v) 2·4, −1·8, 1·4
 14 (i) 3; (ii) 6·75; (iii) 12; (iv) 18·75

Page 395   EXERCISE 122
  1 0·75, 1·25   **2** 0·8, 2·6   **3** −1·5, 1·5
  4 −0·5, 2   **5** 1·3, −0·9   **6** 1·56, −2·56
  7 2·73, −0·73   **8** −0·38, −2·62   **9** 2·30, −1·30
 10 1·77, −2·27   **11** 2·52, −1·19   **12** 2·18, −1·38
 13 −1·43   **14** 2·90, −0·63, −2·27 **15** 2·21
 16 2·12   **17** 2·88, −0·43, −2·45 **18** 1·5, 1·5, −3
 19, 20, 21 2·21, −0·55, −1·66

Page 399 EXERCISE 123

3 4·9 **5** −2·62 to 2·29 **6** 0·5
7 −0·31, 3·75 **8** −2·33, 1·18

Page 402 EXERCISE 124

1 $\frac{7}{5}$ **2** $\frac{5}{3}$ **3** $\frac{4}{5}$ **4** $\frac{11}{8}$
5 $\frac{8}{3}$ **8** $\frac{7}{4}$ **10** $\frac{5}{4}$ **11** $\frac{7}{4}$
12 $\frac{9}{5}$ **13** AX : AB, XY : BC
14 AP : AC, AQ : AB **19** ABC, SPR **21** ∠DCB

Page 408 EXERCISE 125

1 (i) 9 : 16; (ii) 27 : 64 **2** (i) 16 : 25; (ii) 64 : 125
3 (i) 9 : 25; (ii) 27 : 125 **4** 25 kg **5** 4 kg, £2·40
6 72·6 tonnes **7** 3 : 4 **8** (i) 3 : 8; (ii) 9 : 64
9 (i) 2 : 5; (ii) 4 : 25; (iii) 2·5; (iv) 2 : 5 **10** 1 : 25000
11 1 : 5000000 **12** 0·96 cm² **13** 620 cm²
14 5 cm², 20 cm³ **15** 8 cm², 4 : 21
16 9 : 49 **17** 9 cm **18** 1 : 5
19 (i) 9 : 16; (ii) 25 : 36; (iii) 9 : 4 **20** 1 : 15
21 9 : 16 **22** (i) 3 : 2; (ii) 9 : 4; (iii) 3 : 2 **23** 6 cm
24 $ab(a^2-b^2)$ cm²; $\frac{1}{2}(a^2-b^2)$, ab, $\frac{1}{2}(a^2+b^2)$ cm, $\frac{1}{4}ab(a^2-b^2)$ cm²
25 12 cm² **26** 4 : 3 **27** 1 : 2
28 (i) 4·04%; (ii) 5·12% **29** 3·84, 1·5 m

Page 417 EXERCISE 126

1 12 cm **2** 13 cm **3** 15 cm **4** 6 cm
5 1 cm **6** 12 cm **7** 5 cm **8** 7 cm
9 5 cm **10** 2 cm **11** 6 m
12 (i) 9·16 cm; (ii) 264 cm² **13** 16, 10·3 cm
14 (i) 26·2 km, (ii) 88·9 km, (iii) 131 km **15** 3·53 cm
16 3·0 cm **17** 3·75 cm **18** 2·45

Page 421 EXERCISE 127

1 44° **2** 51° **3** 44° **4** 76°
5 72° **7** 86°, 96°, 84° **24** $\frac{1}{2}(c+d)$

Page 424   PAPER 24

1 0·0269   **2** 1·51 cm   **3** $3\frac{1}{2}$ m
4 (i) 3·61, $-0·28$; (ii) $x > \frac{1}{2}$ **5** 2 : 5
6 (i) 0·22; (ii) $x < -0·67$

Page 425   PAPER 25

1 4·72   **2** (i) 32 cm³; (ii) 12·6 cm²
4 (i) $x \geqslant -\frac{4}{5}$; (ii) 3·35, 0·15   **5** 950 kg m⁻³
6 4; 4, -2

Page 425   PAPER 26

1 15·8 cm   **2** (i) 0·339 m³; (ii) 2·04 m²
3 3·19, 0·31   **5** 437 kg   **6** $3 - 5x$; $\frac{3}{5}$

Page 426   PAPER 27

1 2·24   **2** 795 litres   **4** $1\frac{1}{2}$ cm
5 2·0 mm   **6** $4x - 3$; $6\frac{1}{2}$; 4

Page 426   PAPER 28

1 3·55   **2** 1·81 cm   **3** 4·8 cm
4 1·83, $-3·83$ **5** 4·9, 6·3 cm   **6** 8·48 kg

Page 427   PAPER 29

1 (i) 0·027; (ii) 2; (iii) 3   **2** 8·46, 8·07, 6·73 cm   **3** $-1 < x < 3$
4 53° 8′   **5** $a = 8·70$, $b = 11·0$, $C = 80°$ **6** £45

Page 427   PAPER 30

1 (i) 7·18 cm; (ii) 59·8 cm³   **2** (i) 1; (ii) $6/5x$; (iii) $2/x^2$
3 (i) 39; (ii) 35   **4** (i) -3; (ii) $-\frac{1}{2} \leqslant x \leqslant 2$
5 25° 12′   **6** £180

Page 428   PAPER 31

1 (i) 1; (ii) $5 + 2\sqrt{6}$; (iii) 5   **2** 5·33 cm, 13·4 cm²
3 3·56, $-0·56$ **4** (i) 73° 18′; (ii) 68° 12′; (iii) 63° 26′
5 $-\frac{5}{13}, -\frac{12}{5}$ **6** (i) $f = uv/(u + v)$; (ii) $v = uf/(u - f)$.

Page 428 PAPER 32

1 (i) 0·4472; (ii) 6·7083 **2** 49·9, 98·7 cm
3 57° 15′ **4** 24·6, 15·1 **5** $7\frac{1}{2}\%$ loss
6 $E = (10P - 35)/6P$

Page 429 PAPER 33

1 (i) 9·46 km; (ii) 7·50 km **2** 0 to 5; 6·25; $2 < x < 3$
3 (i) 55° 17′; (ii) 70° 54′
4 (i) $-0·1466$; (ii) $-1·7321$; (iii) 0·6428; (iv) $-0·9428$
5 £315·90 **6** (i) $a = (2S + nd - n^2d)/2n$; (ii) $-\frac{1}{3} < x < 4$

Page 430 PAPER 34

2 21° 29′ **3** 62°, 56°, 62°
4 1·15, $-1·15$; 0·25, 1·86, $-2·11$ **6** 17·8 cm

Page 430 PAPER 35

1 7·1 cm **3** 8 cm **4** 7·8 cm

Page 431 PAPER 36

1 5·38 cm, 2·93 cm **2** 31·4 km, S. 75° 27′ E.
4 24·3 m²

Page 432 PAPER 37

1 128° 48′ **4** $x^2 - 3x - 2 = 0$; 3·56, $-0·56$

Page 432 PAPER 38

1 (ii) 13 **2** 9·5, 17·5 cm **3** 2·44 or 6·21 cm
4 $2x^2 + 5x - 2 = 0$; 0·35

Page 433 PAPER 39

1 (i) 0·672; (ii) 0·0415 **2** 0·54, $-5·54$ **4** 5·78 km
5 (i) $v = 550H/(T_1 - T_2)$; (ii) $T_1 = (550H + vT_2)/v$

Page 434   PAPER 40

1 (i) 1·13 m; (ii) 6·02 m³   **2** (i) 6/a^2; (ii) 1/4x^2; (iii) 6¼
3 1·125; $-\frac{1}{2}$ to 1   **5** £34·65

Page 434   PAPER 41

1 4·71, -0·21   **2,** 6, 6   **3** 2·6, 0·4
4 17·8 km   **5** £250   **6** 3·4 cm

Page 435   PAPER 42

1 0·163   **2** 30 cm   **4** 13, 18·4, 13   **5** 10·2 km/h   **6** 1·68

Page 436   PAPER 43

1 $(2g\mathrm{H}d - v^2ad)/4fv^2$ **2** B; $3y = 2x - 14$; 5, 10
3 (i) 7·31 km, (ii) 4·60 km   **5** $x = 1$ **6** 2·25m

Page 436   PAPER 44

1 £1650   **2** (i) $(2a + 5b)(2a - 5b)$; (ii) $(x - 3)(x - 6)$;
    (iii) $2xy^2(x^2z - 3xy^2 + yz^2)$; (iv) 1½, -7
3 (i) $5\frac{1}{2}x - 4$; $\frac{8}{11}$ (ii) $x > -2$ **4** r, $5 - r$, 2 cm; 2·1 cm
5 4·59 cm

Page 437   PAPER 45

1 (i) 19·1; (ii) 0·0303; (iii) 0·0745   **2** (i) 4, -4
    (ii) -1·42, -2·58   **3** (i) 18°, 18°, 81°; (ii) 156°
5 30°, 30°   **6** 375 cm²

Page 438   PAPER 46

1 20·0 cm³   **2** (i)$\dfrac{5x}{x^2 - 4}$; (ii) $\dfrac{11}{6(x + 3)}$; (iii) $\dfrac{(2x - 5)(x - 3)}{(x - 2)(x - 5)}$
6 68° 57′

Page 439   PAPER 47

1 11·8   **2** (i) 0·4; (ii) 4, ½
4 11·0 cm²   **6** 12·2, 8·15 cm

Page 439 PAPER 48

1 (i) 1260; (ii) $4\frac{1}{2}$; (iii) 4   **2** 6, −5
3 (i) $H = 5AP(W + w)/w^2$; (ii) $A = w^2H/5P(W + w)$ **6** 93·9 m

Page 440 PAPER 49

1 (i) 39·2; (ii) 0·667; (iii) 16700   **2** $1 − x^3$; 5
3 (i) 4·56, 0·46; (ii) $x < −1$ or > 6 **6** 2·60 cm²; $\frac{6}{25}$

Page 441 PAPER 50

1 0·165   **2** (i) $(x + 3)(x − y)$; (ii) $(a − 7b)(a + 3b)$;
    (iii) $2(p + 2q)(p − 2q)$ **3** (i) 3^{2x}; (ii) $16y^4x^2$; (iii) 2
6 2·81 m

Page 441 PAPER 51

1 1%   **2** −2, 4
3 42·8, 0·006, 42·8 cm; 233 g   **6** 56° 31′

Page 442 PAPER 52

1 5   **2** (i) $(x − 2)/(x − 1)$; (ii) $34x/15(1 − x)$
5 7·69 cm   **7** $x < −\frac{1}{3}$ or $x > 1$

Page 443 PAPER 53

1 $3\frac{1}{2}$ **2** 99·9   **3** 2, $\frac{1}{3}$ **6** 229° 51′, 89·3 m

Page 444 PAPER 54

1 2·29 km   **2** (i) $3\frac{2}{27}$; (ii) 4, 6   **3** $x, 2x, x$
5 (i) 3·5 cm, (ii) 14   **6** (i) 12; (ii) $1\frac{1}{12}$

Page 444 PAPER 55

1 4% loss   **2** (i) $(3a − 2)(x − a)$; (ii) $(x + 2)(3 − x)$;
    (iii) $(a + b + 4)(a + b − 4)$; (iv) $\frac{1}{3}\pi r^2(h + 4r)$ **4** $\frac{1}{3}, \frac{1}{6}, \frac{1}{2}$
5 12, 6·25 cm; 5·77 cm   **6** (i) 144 cm; 93 cm

Page 445   PAPER 56

1 (i) 47·0 cm²; (ii) 24·6 cm²
2 (i) $2x/(1-x)$; (ii) $(a+3b)/(a+6b)$, (iii) 9, $-\frac{1}{2}$
3 $R = (V + \pi l t^2)/2\pi l t$; 2·83   **5** 4·06 cm
6 (i) 6·74 cm²; (ii) 3·82 cm

Page 446   PAPER 57

1 14 y 8 months; 15 y 1 month
2 (i) $2 + 5x - 4x^2 - 3x^3$; (ii) $5 - 14x + 10x^2$; (iii) $x > 3$; (iv) $11\frac{1}{2}$
3 1, 2·73, $-0·73$ **4** 4 cm
5 4, 6 cm   **7** 25

Page 447   PAPER 58

1 40°, 120°, 20°   **2** (i) 25° 38′; (ii) 40° 54′
3 £10   **4** (i) 0·1, $3\frac{1}{3}$, $1\frac{9}{16}$; (ii) $1\frac{1}{2}$; (iii) $x < -\frac{3}{2}$ or $x > 4$
5 2·49, $-0·67$, $-1·82$; 2·8   **6** 17·7m, 28° 23′
7 (i) (1, 5); (ii) $(-1, 3)$

ANSWERS